STATE OF
SIEGE

Renewal or Privatisation for Australian State Public Services?

STATE OF SIEGE

Renewal or Privatisation for Australian State Public Services?

EVATT RESEARCH CENTRE

A study initiated by the Australian Public Service Federation

First published in 1989 by Pluto Press Australia Limited,
PO Box 199, Leichhardt, NSW 2040
in association with the Evatt Foundation and
the Australian Public Service Federation

© Copyright Evatt Research Centre 1989

Typeset, printed and bound by Southwood Press,
80 Chapel Street, Marrickville, NSW 2204

Cover design by Trevor Hood
Index compiled by Neale Towart

Australian Library Cataloguing in Publication Data

State of siege: renewal or privatisation for Australian State
public services?

Bibliography
includes index
ISBN 0 949138 37 1.

1. Privatization – Australia. 2. Government business enterprises –
Australia. 3. State governments – Australia.
I. H. V. Evatt Research Centre. II. Australian Public Service
Federation. III. H. V. Evatt Foundation.

351.007'0094

CONTENTS

List of Tables, Graphs and Figures

Chapter 14

ABBREVIATIONS

ACA	Australian Consumers' Association
ACF	Australian Conservation Foundation
ACOSS	Australian Council of Social Services
ACTU	Australian Council of Trade Unions
AFSCME	American Federation of State, County and Municipal Employees
AIHP	Authority for Intellectually Handicapped Persons (WA)
AIPS	Australian Institute of Political Science
ALJR	Australian Law Journal Reports
ANL	Australian National Line
ANZAAS	Australian and New Zealand Association for the Advancement of Science
APSF	Australian Public Service Federation
ARU	Australian Railways Union
ASIC	Australian Standard Industry Classification
ASTEC	Australian Science and Technology Council
ASWU	Australian Social Welfare Union
ATEA	Australian Telecommunications Employees Union
AUSSAT	Australian Satellite
BACA	Business and Consumer Affairs
BAE	Bureau of Agricultural Economics
BIIC	Building Industries Investment Commission
CAD	Current Account Deficit
CCA	Current Cost Accounting
CEDA	Centre for Economic Development of Australia
CGC	Commonwealth Grants Commission
CIRRV	Committee of Inquiry into Revenue Raising in Victoria
CITEC	Centre for Information Technology and Commerce
CLIRS	Computerised Legal Information Retrieval System
CPI	Consumer Price Index
CPSIR	Commonwealth Public Sector Interest Rate
CREA	Centre for Regional Economic Analysis
CRES	Centre for Resource and Environmental Studies
CRF	Consolidated Revenue Fund
CSIRO	Commonwealth Scientific and Industrial Research Organisation
CSV	Community Services Victoria
CTS	Community Tenancy Schemes, (NSW)
DHI	Dairy Herd Improvement, (Tasmania)
DIR	Department of Industrial Relations
DIRD	Directorate of Industrial Relations Development
DITAC	Department of Industry, Technology and Commerce
DMB	Department of Management and Budget, (Victoria)
DMR	Department of Main Roads, (NSW)
DMT	Department of Motor Transport, (NSW)
DPI	Department of Primary Industry,
E & WS	Engineering and Water Supply Department, (S.A.)
EAP	Ethnic Affairs Policy
EGW	Electricity, Gas and Water

Elcom	Electricity Commission (of New South Wales)
EPAC	Economic Planning and Advisory Council
EPEA	Electrical Power Engineers' Association
ERC	Expenditure Review Committee, (Commonwealth)
ETSA	Electricity Trust of South Australia
ETU	Electrical Trades Union
ETUI	European Trade Union Institute
FACS	Family and Community Services
FBT	Fringe Benefits Tax
FEDFA	Federated Engine Drivers' and Firemens' Association
FID	Finance Industry Duty
FRC	Functional Review Committee
FIT	Fund Investment Trust
GBC	The Gold Bank Corporation, (W.A.)
GDP	Gross Domestic Product
GEB	Grain Elevators Board, (Vic)
GFCE	Gross Fixed Capital Expenditure
GG	General Government
GHA	Grain Handling Authority, (NSW)
GIO	Government Insurance Office (of NSW)
GSP	Gross State Product
GWI	Gross Weekly Income
HEAS	Home Energy Advisory Service, (Victoria)
HEC	Hydro-Electric Commission, (Tasmania)
HES	Household Expenses Survey
HREOC	Human Rights and Equal Opportunity Commission
IAC	Industries Assistance Commission
ILO	International Labour Organisation
IMF	International Monetary Fund
IPA	Institute for Policy Analysis
IPA	Institute of Public Affairs
IPD	Implicit Price Deflator
ISC	Inter-State Commission
ISO	Industrial Supplies Office, (all states)
LBS	Launceston Bank for Savings
LGFA	Local Government Finance Authority, (S.A.)
LIRU	Labour and Industry Research Unit
LRC-Melb	Labour Research Centre
LRC	Law Reform Commission
MAIB	Motor Accident Insurance Board
MFTU	Metal Trades Federation of Unions
MMBW	Melbourne and Metropolitan Board of Works
MSB	Maritime Services Board, (NSW)
MTIA	Metal Trades Industry Association
NBER	National Bureau of Economic Research Inc.
NCOSS	New South Wales Council of Social Services
NFF	National Farmers' Federation
NFGDP	Non-Farm Gross Domestic Product
NFGSP	Non-Farm Gross State Product
NIEIR	National Institute of Economic and Industrial Research
NPWS	National Parks and Wildlife Service

NSE	Net Subsidy Equivalents
NZ RCSP	New Zealand Royal Commission on Social Policy
OECD	Organisation for Economic Co-operation and Development
OPDS	Office of Psychiatric Disability Services
PAD	Public Authority Dividend
PAYE	Pay As You Earn
PEP	Project Employment Personnel
PFCE	Private Final Consumption Expenditure
PICL	Petrochemical Industries Company Limited (W.A.)
PIRC	Pensions and Investment Research Centre, (UK)
PSA of NSW	Public Service Association of New South Wales
PSB of NSW	Public Service Board of New South Wales
PSB of Vic.	Public Service Board of Victoria
PSBR	Public Sector Borrowing Requirement
PTA	Precision Tool Annexe, (Tasmania)
PUC	Public Utilities Commission, (USA)
QCOSS	Queensland Council of Social Services
QCOSS	Queensland Council of Social Services
QEC	Queensland Electoral Commission
QGDA	Queensland Government Development Authority
QGPO	Queensland Government Printing Office
QHC	Queensland Housing Commission
QTU	Queensland Teachers' Union
RBA	Reserve Bank of Australia
RCA	Road Construction Authority
RCHCLP	Royal Commission into Certain Housing Commission Land and Other Matters
REDB	Regional Economic Development Board
RFC	Rural Finance Corporation
ROR	Rate of Return
RRR	Required Rate of Return
RRT	Resource Rent Tax
RTA	Road Transport Authority, (NSW)
RWC	Rural Water Commission
SAFA	South Australian Financing Authority
SAFL	South Australian Finance Limited
SAFTL	South Australian Financing Trust Limited
SAGASCO	South Australian Oil and Gas Company Limited
SASFIT	South Australian Superannuation Fund Investment Trust
SAULT	South Australian Urban Land Trust
SBSA	State Bank of South Australia
SBT	Savings Bank of Tasmania
SCTCI	Standing Committee on Transport, Communications and Infrastructure, (House of Representatives)
SEC	State Electoral Commission
SECV	State Electricity Commission of Victoria
SEQEB	South East Queensland Electricity Board
SGDP	State Gross Domestic Product
SGIC	State Government Insurance Commission
SGSL	State Goods and Services Levy
SIO	State Insurance Office, (Victoria)
SRA	State Rail Authority, (NSW)

SWRC	Social Welfare Resource Centre
TAFE	Technical and Further Education
TASCORP	Tasmanian Public Finance Corporation
TDA	Tasmanian Development Authority
TDC	Trade Development Council
TDCS	Trade Development Council Secretariat
TDH	Twin-Deficits Hypothesis
TDIA	Tasmanian Dairy Industry Authority
TFC	Tasmanian Film Corporation
TGIO	Tasmanian Government Insurance Office
TGPS	Tasmanian Government Printing Service
THIO	Tasmanian Herd Improvement Organisation
TOT	Terms of Trade
TPSA	Tasmanian Public Service Association
TT	Transport Tasmania
TUC	Trade Union Congress, (UK)
TWA	Trans World Airlines
UTA	Urban Transit Authority, (NSW)
VCM	Victorian Chamber of Manufactures
VEDC	Victorian Economic Development Corporation
VGPS	Victorian Government Printing Service
VIC	Victorian Investment Corporation
VMOHC	Victorian Ministry of Housing and Construction
VSJU	Victorian Social Justice Unit
VTBA	Victorian Transport Borrowing Authority
VVCF	Victorian Venture Capital Fund
WAGH	Western Australian Government Holdings
WST	Wholesale Sales Tax

PREFACE

Australia's status as a 'first world' economy is under question. If we are to remove that doubt the public sector in general — and the State public sector in particular — must play a leading role in equitable and efficient structural adjustment.

Yet perversely, at a time of great need, the legitimacy of public economic and social functions is being attacked. These attacks are orchestrated by a logically flawed and self-seeking ideology of economic rationalism.

This is not to say the State public sector does not require modernisation. This book, developed through a research project sponsored by the Australian Public Service Federation, shows that much of what the State public sectors currently do can be improved; and that *to meet new challenges, new forms of organisation and operation must be developed. The book also makes it clear that without the active participation of public sector workers and their Unions, this 'renewal' process cannot be successful.* The book reinforces ACTU policies on privatisation and worker participation, and displays the willingness of the sponsoring Unions to participate in the renewal process.

For too long the organisation of the State public sectors has been 'hierarchical' in conception and operation. Pyramid structures and bureaucratic processes have limited the opportunity for constructive participation by the work force in decision-making about the types of services which the public sector could provide and the mode of their delivery.

The organisational changes to the public sector canvassed in this book complement the aims of award restructuring. Such restructuring is designed to enhance the workers' input by breaking down these pyramid structures and bureaucratic processes.

The research makes it clear that, at the most basic level, 'renewal' requires adequate resources. Given the position of the States established in the Australian Constitution, this study concludes that the Federal Government must be more rational in its funding of State

activities. Because of Federal cutbacks, the States have become increasingly reliant on a regime of taxes and charges (including payroll taxes, stamp duties, businesses franchises, fuel taxes, alcohol and tobacco excises, motor vehicle taxes and charges) which are simply not designed to be the major vehicles for raising public finance. In toto State taxes are narrowly based, regressive in their effect, and they exhibit all the worst qualities of a consumption tax regime, not least because of their lack of transparency.

One of the central proposals put forward in the book is a recommendation for rationalising, and taking the pressure off, the current narrow, ad hoc and regressive regime of State taxes and charges through the introduction of a States Goods and Services Levy (SGSL) collected by the Federal Government on behalf of the States. This proposal is beneficial for both the States and the Federal Government and is therefore capable of winning a mutually acceptable compact.

The State Goods and Services Levy would:

— completely replace some undesirable State taxes and charges;
— ensure that other State taxes, which have socially desirable effects, as well as revenue-raising capacity (such as gambling, alcohol and tobacco levies), are instruments of social good rather than tax regression;
— ensure that user charges for a wide range of socially important State services such as public transport are kept in perspective;
— provide a fairer, more efficient and effective revenue-raising capacity for the States; and
— compensate those people who are currently not compensated for a range of regressive State taxes and charges.

These revenue-raising strategies stand in marked contrast to the New Right's proposals which would result in shifting responsibility away from a progressive system of personal and corporate income tax toward a regressive broad based consumption tax. The trade union movement was correct in its opposition to oppose such a position at the 1985 Tax Summit, and remains opposed to any such proposal.

This book also argues that State public sectors must become more responsive to emerging community needs, which would necessarily involve greater participation by the users of public services in the decision-making which affects their lives. The required structural changes outlined can only be undertaken with a greater commitment by government to democratic principles and practices. The time is long past when tokenistic 'community consultation' will suffice for active 'community participation'.

The positive and constructive tone of the Report's proposals contrast with the destructive proposals for 'reform through privatisation' advanced by conservatives, which are currently being implemented in New South Wales and evident in other States. There are no sustainable theoretical or practical justifications for this onslaught on the public sector.

The so-called theoretical basis for the destruction of the public sector is intellectually shallow and politically motivated. The economic analysis on which the privatisers depend ignores the fundamental role the State public sectors play, and they rely on an idealised view of economic relations which ignores the complex nature of modern societies. The use of privatisation to overcome State budgetary problems, for example, is a short-term and short-sighted strategy to deal with fiscal problems which are deep-seated. The financing proposals made in this Report, dealing with State taxes and enterprises, offer the only long-term solution to these long-term problems.

The book and its conclusions arise out of a most comprehensive study of State public services. The study has no taint of the parochialism of most work done on, or on behalf of, the Australian States. It recognises the problems and challenges which collectively face the State public sectors, and puts forward a 'renewal agenda' which is not only practicable, but which would enhance the quality of life of all Australians. The result is an important document which deserves not only to be read but to be implemented.

The Australian Public Service Federation has already exhibited its willingness to confront the real issues facing the States. The agenda for reform outlined in this book will form a solid basis for its approach to State public sector reform for some time.

Lachlan Riches,
Federal Secretary,
Australian Public Service Federation.

Helen Twohill,
General Secretary,
Public Service Association of New South Wales
and
APSF ACTU Executive Member.

ACKNOWLEDGEMENTS

The State of Siege Project was initiated by the Australian Public Service Federation on the basis of a decision taken by its Executive in 1988 to support research into the contribution of the State public sector to Australia's economy and society. As Don Dunstan put it, when launching the project in December 1988:

> 'The Australian Public Service Federation . . . has undertaken something which the combined Premiers of all the States have never been able to undertake, that is, a qualitative and quantitative comparison of each of the State public sectors. This will be a first, and I believe that this undertaking will not only further the interests of the trade union movement, it will increase the overall awareness and understanding of an important part of Australia's economy and society'.

The project was directed and co-ordinated by the Evatt Research Centre, Sydney. The Evatt Research Centre is supported by the H.V. Evatt Foundation, who made this project possible by providing accommodation and other forms of assistance.

The management committee for the project consisted of Don Dunstan, Professor E.L. Wheelwright, David Richardson, Dr Kerry Schott, Dr Peter Botsman, Helen Twohill (Public Service Association of New South Wales), David Haynes (Australian Public Service Federation), Bill Higham (Queensland Professional Officers' Association) and Adrian Butterworth (Public Service Association of South Australia).

Peter Botsman was Research Director and Stephen Rix was National Co-ordinator for the project. Their co-ordination, editorial and research efforts have been critical to the completion of this project. Along with the director and national co-ordinator, Peter Ewer played an important role as editor of the final manuscript. Peter is research officer of the Amalgamated Metal Workers Union and we thank them and Peter Ewer for his efforts. The other core staff on the project were Prudence Anderson who co-ordinated project communications and provided invaluable editorial assistance, Justine Heath who prepared the final manuscript, and Ben Reilly who proof read the draft. We are indebted to all these people.

The researchers for the project were, in Tasmania Dr Bruce Felmingham and Bob Rutherford from the University of Tasmania and Ian Morris; in *New South Wales* Dr Tony Aspromourgos and Matthew Smith from the University of Sydney, and Adam Farrar from the New South Wales Council of Social Services; in *South Australia* Dr William Mitchell and Mike Evans from the Flinders University of South Australia; in *Western Australia* Shane Bushe-Jones, Dr Ray Petridis, Associate Professor Herb Thompson and Gavin Wood from Murdoch University; in *Victoria* Patrick Xavier, David Hayward, Terry Burke and Barry Graham from Swinburne Institute of Technology; and in *Queensland* the research was carried out through the *Labour and Industry Research Unit* and was based on an earlier publication, 'Society and Economy in Queensland: The Strategic Role of the Public Sector', which was sponsored by the Professional Officers Association, the State Service Union and the Queensland Teachers Union. The Queensland chapter was researched by Dr Paul Boreham, Dr Craig Littler, Randal Stewart and Geoff Dow. The Director and the National Co-ordinator were also actively involved in the research effort, particularly in the first nine chapters of the report. Dr. William Mitchell was the primary researcher for Part Four.

There are many who should be thanked, but in particular the Evatt Research Centre would also like to acknowledge the assistance of Lachlan Riches and David Haynes from the Australian Public Service Federation, Greg Withers from the Queensland Professional Officers' Association, Michael Coll (President), Jim Young (Secretary) and Pam Sandon from the Victorian Public Service Association, Jan Guersen and Alan Evans from the Tasmanian Public Service Association, Mark Smith (Secretary) and David Howlett from the Civil Service Association of Western Australia, and Chris Mathews, David Perkins, Martin Stott, Linda Carruthers, Anne Crowley, Robyn Fortseque, Les Carr, Jane Timbrell and Sue Ohanian from the New South Wales Public Service Association, Michael Wright from the New South Wales Public Service Professional Officers' Association, Kevin Crawshaw (Secretary) and Con O'Neill from the Public Service Association of South Australia.

John de Ridder provided valuable assistance on technical aspects of pricing policy and we would also like to acknowledge Professor Peter Groenewegen, Russell Mathews, Peter Moylan (ACTU), Michael Salvaris, David Richardson, Dr Kerry Schott and Professor E.L. Wheelwright who provided advice or read manuscripts at various stages of finality, though they of course bear no responsibility for the final form of the book. We also thank Pluto Press for their help.

Finally, the management committee and staff of the Evatt Research Centre would like to thank everyone involved in this project for the dedication, perseverance and good humour they have shown to complete this ground-breaking work in the relatively short period of seven months. It was a real team effort.

SUMMARY

Background

This book extends the union movement's analysis of public sector funding and reform to the State tier of government. It follows the work of the Labour Resource Centre (1987), which examined the role of the public sector in general, and the H.V. Evatt Research Centre (1988), which considered the capital funding needs of the Federal public trading enterprises (PTEs).

Although this current work therefore forms part of the union movement's on-going public sector research effort, it is in many senses the first work of its kind. Never before have the needs of the States, both as a whole and individually, been subjected to such an analysis. On its own, this claim points to some serious deficiencies in Federal-State decision-making processes, which form one of the central themes of this book.

Faced with the many pressures on State services, and a public debate over their fate which has not so far produced any long-term strategy to deal with them other than by abandoning vital social and economic functions, the Australian Public Service Federation (APSF) commissioned the H.V. Evatt Research Centre to develop a program of public sector renewal. The magnitude of this task is such that although *State of Siege* addresses the role and funding of the States as a whole, the case studies of government departments and State PTEs which accompany the chapters analysing the individual States must necessarily be selective. *State of Siege* therefore attempts to define the general principles on which a program of public sector renewal must be built – the application of these principles to particular public agencies requires further research and consultation.

As with the H.V. Evatt Research Centre's earlier work, *State of Siege* is the product of a number of academic research teams, with the Centre co-ordinating and editing their work. In this case, a research team was established in each State to conduct the analysis on the 'home' State.

The findings of this work show clearly that much needs to be done to improve public sector performance, and that organisational deficiencies do exist in public agencies. *State of Siege* does not seek to hide these problems. However, these problems are not *a priori* functions of public ownership, but in many cases relate to an unfavourable regime of operating and financing constraints. Readers are invited to compare these carefully researched arguments with those provided by the supporters of privatisation, which rely more on slogans than science.

Structure

State of Siege is organised into five Parts, which outline the historical role of the State public sectors, the macro-economic environment in which they currently operate, the task of micro-economic reform and the part the States can play in it, a financing package and finally the particular needs and role of each of the States.

Where possible, each of the State chapters is structured in a similar way, with an opening section detailing the demographic and economic characteristics of the State under investigation, followed by a description of the functions and structure of the relevant State public sector. This work is followed by an analysis of the State's finances, and completed by the case studies of particular organisations already mentioned. Although this structure is followed as much as possible, some differences emerge between the State chapters for reasons of emphasis.

Overview

Part One sets the current debate over State public sector functions in an historical and political context, by briefly outlining the traditional – and successful – role the Australian States have played in economic and social development, and the evolution of Federal – State financial arrangements. It also places the public sector debate within the framework of the labour movement's strategy of the 1980s, the

Accord, the tripartism of which should give greater recognition to public sector activities.

Part Two: The Macro-Economic Context establishes the current economic climate in which the debate over the future of the public sector in general is taking place. This climate is overwhelmingly conditioned by the consequences for domestic policy of Australia's balance of payments difficulties, a challenge for policy which has hitherto focussed on cutting back the relative size of the public sector, including those of the States. The analysis provided here suggests that the rationale for this strategy – the 'twin deficits hypothesis' – is an inadequate basis for policy formulation. This hypothesis, which traces Australia's current account deficit to the public sector borrowing requirement, misinterprets a simple accounting identity in a way which leaves the size of the public sector as a target for public policy, regardless of whether public functions are directed to investment or consumption.

The conclusion to this analysis suggests an alternative macro-economic strategy; which: frees self-financing PTEs (at both Federal and State levels) from Loan Council control over their borrowing; establishes a more selective expenditure strategy which attaches a high priority to public investment; and includes a more active industry policy. In this way the task of socially equitable structural adjustment, which should emphasise a diversion of resources into the tradeable goods sector, can not just be complemented but *stimulated*.

These findings form the macro-economic goals for the State public sector, and they must be complemented by a supporting micro-economic strategy. *Part Three: Micro-Economic Reform and State Public Services* is therefore divided between chapters which provide an outline of the demands on State functions and the competing programs for meeting them – public sector renewal and privatisation. State functions are broken into three categories – economic, social and administrative – and the importance of each to micro-economic reform is considered. From this research, it is clear that the State public services can and should play a leading role in micro reform, first by achieving greater public outputs from a given set of inputs, and second by lowering input costs to the private sector. Stimulating genuine micro-economic reform is a task which only a program of public sector renewal can tackle. This program involves a sustainable financial strategy for the States (see below), the articulation of discrete social and economic objectives against which public sector performance can be measured and a strategy of organisational reform based on a move away from hierarchical management structures. Moreover, a new and more substantial research base for the Premiers' Conference and Loan Council is required to establish a more timely and meaningful system of Federal-State decision-making. Accordingly, *State of Siege* proposes that a permanent Premiers' Conference Secretariat be established to place inter-governmental Priority-setting and decision-making on a more orderly footing.

The philosophical rival of public sector renewal – privatisation – ignores the positive role of the public sector in combatting social inequality and creating social and economic opportunities. To take just one example, the latest privatisation trend of competitive tendering for functions previously undertaken in the public sector is founded on a theory of contestable markets, which can only be found in a highly idealised world. In practice, the alleged benefits of competitive tendering evaporate in problems over costly tender preparation and evaluation, and the seeming cost benefits of contracting out are achieved through cuts in wages and conditions, an achievement which involves a transfer of income from workers to capital and not an improvement in economic efficiency.

Part Four: Financing the State Public Sector forms the heart of *State of Siege*, because a more orderly funding arrangement must be the foundation on which public sector renewal at the State level is built. The research in this area reveals the way in which, under pressure from cutbacks in funding from the Federal Government, the revenue base of the States has narrowed. To meet this challenge, some States have taken generally positive initiatives like the establishment of a Public Authorities Dividend, but more harmfully, the overall consequence has been greater reliance on a range of largely regressive State taxes and charges.

The scale of this problem was borne out in the space of eleven days in June 1989. On 8 June the Victorian Government announced that, due to declines in several State revenue items (including stamp duties on marketable securities, oil royalties, petroleum-franchise fees and Tattersalls duty) it would have to institute cuts in services (*AFR*, 9/6/89). On 19 June the Western Australian Government announced that it would be using proceeds from asset sales to overcome State revenue constraints which have resulted from falls in stamp duty revenues consequent on the contraction of the housing and building industries in the tight interest rate environment (*AFR*, 20/6/89).

Chapter Six reviews the various tax reform options available to the States, and considers the general equity and efficiency principles which should guide the tax reform process. Armed with this analysis, *Chapter Seven* proposes a *State Government Services Levy (SGSL)*. This levy would be collected by the Federal Government and would apply to goods and services where the States agree to a revenue-neutral abolition of regressive State taxes and charges. *The authors and sponsors of State of Siege hasten to distinguish this proposal from the broad-based consumption tax proposed in 1985!* The SGSL is not predicated on a move away from direct taxation to indirect taxation, and it simply involves a rationalisation of existing indirect taxation. Indeed, this process of rationalisation offers to significantly improve the equity of Australian taxation arrangements, by removing the most narrow and regressive Federal and State taxes and charges. The first task of the Premiers' Conference Secretariat described above would be to develop an equitable and revenue-neutral means of implementing the SGSL, through a *Compact on State Taxes and Charges*. The Compact would provide for the abolition of the Wholesale Sales Tax and State taxes such as payroll tax and stamp duties for first home buyers. In doing so, the Compact would formalise the equity considerations which have hitherto been absent in the financial arrangements of Australian federalism. The Compact would provide guidelines so that State taxes such as alcohol or tobacco excises are levied for specific social purposes and do not become a regressive substitute for

inadequacies in the general system of public finance such as tax avoidance and evasion. Similarly, the Compact would establish principles and standards on the rates at which fees and fines and other State charges should be levied.

Chapter Seven also recommends that an inquiry into the distribution of wealth be established. One of the few progressive taxes available to the States – death duties – fell victim to tax competition in the 1970s and early 1980s. On the grounds of equity alone, the re-introduction of some form of wealth tax at the Federal level is required (with part of the revenue so raised returned to the States), and the terms of reference of the wealth inquiry should include consideration of the most effective form of wealth tax.

The other chapters in *Part Four* address borrowing and revenues from State development activities. *Chapter Eight* confirms that the indebtedness of the States is entirely within manageable propoRtions, and the current constraints imposed through the Loan Council on self-financing borrowings are therefore an impediment to structural adjustment. Accordingly, Loan Council controls on the borrowing activites of public trading enterprises should be relaxed, although the Council should, in the interest of macro-economic stability, monitor and analyse the purposes for which these funds are raised.

Chapter Nine examines the efforts of several States to develop alternative sources of revenue from a variety of development agencies, trusts and venture capital corporations. To say the least, these efforts have not been blessed with success, a record which indicates the difficulty in finding a substitute for a stable tax regime. Moreover, it is crucial that the legitimate role of the States in economic development remains distinct from the imperatives of revenue-raising. This separation is necessary because industry policy involves activities which, although vital for the economy as a whole, may not offer a return to the public purse. Accordingly, *Chapter Nine* contains an outline of an alternative model of economic development, built upon *State Development Grants*. These would provide development and equity finance to enterprises with growth potential, who would be required to repay the grant if they (or the product involved) achieved commercial viability.

Part Five comprises six chapters, each devoted to an analysis of the functions and needs of the individual States. This general treatment is complemented by a number of case studies of government departments or public trading enterprises in each State.

What emerges from this research is the tremendously diverse contribution the State public sectors have made – and are continuing to make – towards Australian social and economic development. In some States, such as South Australia, public economic activity has overcome significant deficiencies in fundamental natural endowments. Given the successful tradition of public sector development in tasks of considerable size and complexity, it is clear that the States are capable of actively facilitating the current structural adjustment needs of the Australian economy. Privatisation, in denying this role, simply adds an historical deficiency to its many other weaknesses.

Chapter Ten deals with New South Wales, and it is of course informed by the privatisation push already underway in that State, a campaign justified by the work of the 'Commission of Audit', otherwise known as the Curran Report. This document is quite unashamed in its blind ideological preference for private, rather than public, social and economic activity.

In what will become a recurring theme to readers, the New South Wales public sector is increasing its reliance on a narrow band of taxes, fees and fines (primarily payroll and motor vehicle taxes, and stamp duties), which increased from 28.2% of total revenues in 1981/82 to 30.5% in 1986/87. Although the avowed aim of the current Liberal-National Government is to cut debt (despite the relative low level of debt to New South Wales Gross State Product [GSP]) and taxes, this will only be achieved by asset sales and expenditure cuts which damage the ability of the State public sector to fulfil its obligations to social equity and structural adjustment. On this latter point, the Curran Report has opened up infrastructure developments to private developers, partly through a campaign of disinformation

and alarm over the State's debt holdings. There is no economic evidence to suggest that the community – as distinct from private interests – will benefit by transferring these investment functions out of the public sector.

The case studies provided in *Chapter Ten* are the Department of Health, the Electricity Commission (Elcom) and the Government Insurance Office (GIO). The study of the Department of Health confirms the gradual erosion of public functions, which will ultimately result in higher health costs to the community. In contrast, a model of public sector renewal in the health portfolio would involve:

   – an overall expansion of public hospital capacity;
   – a restructuring of health care coverage to distribute services to regions of greatest need; and
   – an increase in the permanently-employed medical and nursing staff to increase utilisation of health care facilities.

Clearly, this study illustrates the way in which public sector renewal cannot proceed unless State finances are rationalised in a way which stabilises and, in time, improves the revenue base of the States.

The New South Wales Electricity Commission illustrates the need to include organisational reform in the public sector renewal model. Elcom's difficulties are profound – excess capacity and a sizeable debt burden. It is apparently only recently that Elcom adopted formal appraisal procedures, and it must remain an open question as to how senior management made the capital expenditure decisions which have contributed to the Commission's current difficulties. Nevertheless, it is not clear how the government's embryonic plans to permit the establishment of private generation capacity will improve this situation when the key factor influencing the power industry is over-supply.

On a brighter note, the GIO is a successful and profitable public trading enterprise which at the same time fills an important social and economic purpose. It exerts a stabilising influence on the premium rates of the insurance industry, and its investment activities play a role in State development. Again, the advocates of privatisation do not explain how the one-off sale of the GIO would compensate the long-term loss to State revenue of such a sale, nor how public regulation of an otherwise private industry would be a better instrument of competition policy than the presence of a public trading enterprise in the insurance industry.

Chapter Eleven examines the Victorian State public sector, the demands on which are partly conditioned by an ageing population and the infrastructure needs associated with the development of further urban corridors around Melbourne. Victoria is of course a leading manufacturing State, but during the late 1970s and early 1980s the State suffered a lower rate of economic growth than the rest of Australia.

The policies of the Cain Labor Government have, however, reversed this relationship, and Victoria has been one of the country's fastest growing States. This performance has been matched by annual average growth in private investment of 7.9% since 1982/83, a rate 3.4% better than Australia as a whole.

This re-capitalisation of the Victorian economy has in part been the consequence of the far-sighted and active role played by the public sector. The Victorian Government has articulated a key role for the public sector in the development of its Economic and Social Justice Strategies, and the weaknesses of these programs – such as the poor performance of the Victorian Economic Development Corporation (VEDC) – should be measured against the government's overall success. Victoria has also witnessed some innovative reforms of public sector management practices – such as the Public Authorities Dividend (PAD) – which (provided they do not obscure the distinctiveness of public sector activities) are worthwhile developments.

However, Victoria is now labouring under a declining revenue base. Real Commonwealth grants to Victoria fell by about 5% in real terms in 1988/89, and the State has only avoided a period of fiscal austerity through substantial increases in its own-source revenues. Should the Commonwealth cutbacks continue, and should economic growth and/or property values continue to decline, the State will be even harder pressed to meet the demands on its public sector.

The case study provided in *Chapter Eleven* examines the privatisation of the public housing stock by a conservative government in the 1950s and 1960s. This study is a seminal and cautionary tale of the pitfalls of privatisation. The virtues of this exercise are manifold, if rarely cited by the advocates of privatisation. By selling off the best housing at a discounted price, the then Victorian Government bequeathed to the State a dilapidated housing stock, with huge maintenance bills and a waiting list of 33,000 households. This maintenance requirement has in turn been handed on to private contractors, whose work is of poor quality but whose predilection for tax avoidance is high. The fact that this scandalous situation has yet to be rectified after seven years of Labor Government indicates the difficulties of resuscitating public functions once they have been abandoned.

The role of South Australia's public services is analysed in *Chapter Twelve*. South Australia has a stable, if below average, population growth, which suggests that marked increases in public services will not be demanded as a result of rapidly increasing population. On the other hand, these demographic trends mean that, together with the restricted size of the market and the consequent reluctance of business to locate in the State, South Australia's tax base will increase slowly.

South Australia is the second smallest State economy, although its manufacturing sector is relatively large. However, this manufacturing base is dominated by a small number of industries – food, beverages and tobacco, metal products, other machinery and equipment and transport equipment. Furthermore, the State suffers from a relatively weak labour market, where earnings are below the national average, but unemployment is significantly worse.

Clearly then, the State public sector must seek to maintain and improve living standards through social wage initiatives, and its economic strategy should endeavour to diversify the State's economic structure. In undertaking these tasks, the State public sector can build on a tradition of active public sector development, which has overcome some daunting natural obstacles. To take three examples, State public agencies have provided water, power generation and forestry resources where the conditions for such development were not favourable.

This tradition is continuing in the work of the Department of State Development and Technology, which adopts a targeted approach to industry policy. Its work includes administration of the South Australian Development Fund, which has directly contributed to the creation and retention of 2,700 jobs and almost $160m in capital expenditure. Government backing for the construction of the ship lift facility at the Port Adelaide submarine complex is one example of the economic benefits of a robust public sector involvement in economic development.

The nature of South Australia's public finances resemble those of the other States: recurrent payments are less than cash receipts and Federal Grants (ie. gross capital payments) are partly funded by recurrent payments; payroll tax revenue is the largest source of tax receipts, followed by stamp duties and franchise taxes; and more than 50% of recurrent payments go to education and health. Indeed, South Australia makes an above average provision of resources to the community services area.

Three case studies of public agencies are included in *Chapter Twelve*: the Department of Lands, the Electricity Trust of South Australia (ETSA) and the South Australian Financing Authority (SAFA).

The Department of Lands provides an example of efficient public sector reforms, including the introduction of corporate planning, business planning and marketing strategies. The Department has been able to reduce the net cost of its operations over recent years, but not as a result of cuts to wages and conditions. Marketing of the Department's expertise has also resulted in export revenues, and the whole reform process contrasts to the sale of land-dealing information to a private corporation by the Federal, Victorian and New South Wales Governments. Under this arrangement, information which is essentially public in nature is only accessible through payment of a fee to private interests.

Turning to ETSA, the Trust has managed to keep its price rises lower than the CPI over recent years, although scope may have existed for charges to be even lower. Overall, ETSA's accounting methods are inappropriate since they are intended to hide their pricing policy effects. Again, such a conclusion reinforces the point that a public sector renewal strategy must contain an element of organisational reform, accompanied by timely public scrutiny and debate.

SAFA was created in January 1983 as a central borrowing agency, with debt management, cash management and investment functions, and it has displayed dramatic growth rates in its net income. In its six-year history, SAFA has earned $771m in profit and its dividends now form a significant and growing trend to State Revenue. However, it may be that this performance has been achieved at the expense of the Federal tax base. SAFA may therefore be an innovative means around the relative fiscal austerity of recent years, a motive which a more orderly Federal funding arrangement might dampen.

Chapter Thirteen considers the case of Western Australia. The performance of the Western Australian economy has, in the last decade, led Australia as a whole. The strength of the Western Australian export base is an important cause of this superior performance, and this in turn reflects the strong overseas orientation of the State's primary industries. However, the comparatively more dynamic nature of the Western Australian economy, in combination with its industrial structure, means that expansion tends to be more volatile than that of the Australian economy.

There are early signs that the previously healthy external account position may be reversed in the future. While it is too early to reach firm conclusions, recent structural adjustments could contribute to an erosion of the overseas trade surplus. Since Western Australia has traditionally experienced a deficit on interstate trade, such a deterioration would act as a constraint on future growth.

Like the other States, Western Australia has suffered from a sharp drop in the relative share of Commonwealth funds in its total revenue. In attempting to overcome this constraint, the

Burke Labor Government embarked on a program of revenue-raising from the activities of a number of specially created development agencies. The failure of this strategy is of course spectacularly well-publicised.

In the process, the legitimate development functions of State Government have been tarnished. The key lesson of this experience is the need to separate revenue-raising issues from those of State development, which should be geared to the long-term and not be based on the need for, or expectation of, a quick profit. By failing to maintain this separation, the Western Australian Government lost sight of the need for industry policy to include activities — like the re-capitalisation of mature industries — which may not offer a return to the public purse but which accrue substantial benefits to the economy as a whole. The outcome of this saga is that the whole of the Western Australian public sector is bearing a considerable financial burden, and its functions are therefore under threat.

The Chapter includes three case studies: the disposal of the State Engineering Works (SEW), the contracting out of services in the Department of Community Services and the introduction of voluntarism to the Authority for Intellectually Handicapped Persons. The loss of the SEW is a sorry case of the avoidable loss of key industrial and human resource capabilities in the tradeable goods sector, at a time when public policy should aim to enhance such capabilities.

The Western Australian example of contracting out confirms the more theoretical and general fears of the practice mentioned earlier. In the case of the Department of Community Services, the quantitative benefits of contracting out are untested and the qualitative effects on working conditions appear at this stage to be detrimental. In the Authority for Intellectually Handicapped Persons, voluntarism has thrown a burden previously shared by the community onto individual families, and only a campaign by the Civil Service Association has brought some respite to the process. It is clear that the community, and women in particular, are being manipulated into providing important social services for free to solve a fiscal crisis.

Bearing in mind the particular circumstances of the Western Australian case, *Chapter Thirteen* concludes with a sketch of an alternative public sector strategy for the State. This outline is provided to offer an alternative vision for public sector activities to the current quagmire into which they have been driven.

Chapter Fourteen is devoted to an analysis of public sector activities in Queensland, which is one of Australia's most decentralised and fastest growing States. These demographic features, together with the State's narrow industrial structure and high level of foreign ownership, point to the need for an aggressive strategy of public sector development.

Unfortunately, Queensland's per capita expenditure on industrial development is less than half the national average, although the average annual real growth of government expenditure has been considerably stronger than Gross State Product (GSP) growth. Moreover, the State's record in the provision of social services is mixed. Although spending in this area has kept pace with the growth in overall expenditure in the 1980s, this achievement has come off a poor base in the 1970s. Queensland ranks as the lowest of all States in terms of health funding as a proportion of all current outlays, and by far the lowest spending State on housing and community capital projects as a proportion of total capital outlays. In contrast, it is distinguished by its very high rate of public capital investment in economic and industry services, much of it devoted to the primary industries and not to diversification. The failure to plan for industrial growth is reflected in one of the worst unemployment records in Australia.

The financial condition of the Queensland public sector is under threat, but not on this occasion primarily due to Federal austerity. Indeed, Queensland has always received above average revenue assistance per capita from the Commonwealth.

Queensland's difficulties then are of a more domestic nature, and in particular the National Party Government's revenue collection strategy based on resource activities, complicated by the numerous tax concessions on offer to business, is collapsing. The appropriate replacement for this strategy is to use the broadened base of revenue available from the SGSL as a means of financing programs that create employment and value added (and thereby open up new sources of revenue).

The Tasmanian public sector forms the subject for *Chapter Fifteen*. Policy formulation in Tasmania is bedeviled by the problems of a small, geographically isolated economy: the small market limits domestic consumption and production possibilities, and there is a heavy reliance on primary products as a source of export revenue.

Historically, Tasmanian Governments have attempted to overcome these and other problems − like a steady net interstate emigration − through a development strategy based on the competitive advantages of cheap hydro-electricity. This strategy has come undone − hydro power is no longer cheap or abundant, and 12 major industries consume 70% of the output from Tasmania's energy grid. The one-dimensional nature of the State's development strategy has also left a legacy on the political process, since the information supplied to Parliament on the activities of public agencies is extremely limited, a factor which circumscribes the sort of analytical project of *State of Siege*.

In this environment, the Tasmanian public sector has had little room to manoeuvre in recent years. Commonwealth grants (and approved borrowings) have fallen by 26% in real terms over the past 5 years, a rate of decline which no other State has endured. Faced with this pressure, the State has fallen back on a narrow and regressive regime of taxes and charges. Nevertheless, a widespread cutback in social wage provision has fortunately not occurred, although the Tasmanian social wage has been relatively under-developed.

The case studies in *Chapter Fifteen* involve the Precision Tool Annexe, the Tasmanian Film Corporation, the Tasmanian Herd Improvement Organisation (THIO), the Port Arthur Historic Site and the general move towards the contracting out of public functions. The saga of the sale of the THIO is a particularly good example of the pitfalls of privatisation. In this case, a public agency undertaking work of considerable importance to the State economy was broken up, the profitable activities of artificial breeding passing to private hands and the unprofitable (but necessary) agricultural services remaining in the public sector. This textbook privatisation outcome, however, entirely failed to grasp that the organisational strength of the THIO lay in the integration of all these services within one agency. This synergy has now been lost to the rural community of Tasmania.

Part One

INTRODUCTION

Chapter 1

REFORMING AND DEVELOPING STATE PUBLIC SERVICES

1.1 Introduction

This book assembles, for the first time, a comparative but selective survey of public services in each Australian State. As with the Evatt Research Centre's *The Capital Funding of Public Enterprises* (1988), which was the first survey of the finances and role of a range of Commonwealth trading enterprises, it is designed as a benchmark for public sector policy research, an information source for education about the public sector, and above all, a serious contribution to debates about the role of the public sector in Australian society. However most importantly, this book seeks to address the question of how to 'renew' State public services given the economic constraints of the 1980s. It therefore puts forward strategies through which State public services can be improved and can contribute to the solution to Australia's current social and economic problems.

1.2 The History and Importance of State Public Services

In one of the all-day seminars that were held for researchers involved in the compilation of this book, Don Dunstan provided some illuminating insights into State Government and the political perception of State services. As with other successful Premiers, Dunstan was often urged to step into the Federal arena. His reply was always 'Why? I am doing important work where I am'. It's only at the finale of a book such as *State of Siege: Renewal or Privatisation for Australia's State Public Services?* that one can fully appreciate Dunstan's sentiment.

Regardless of the principles of centralism or of federalism, the plain facts are that in the evolution of Australian Government it has fallen to the States to deliver many important economic, social and administrative services. The rational reform of these services is, therefore, crucial for Australia's future development.

The combined 1,141,000 State public servants run or administer the majority of Australia's 'people services', with over 60% of their work force employed in services such as health care, education or social welfare (ABS, Cat. No. 1201, June 88). State public services are responsible for law and order, public transport, and for most business, environmental and social regulations. In most States, essential utilities like electricity, gas and water provision are also the responsibility of the State Government.

Commensurate with their responsibilities, the States' account for approximately 60% of public investment activity including support for the mining, manufacturing and rural industries through the provision and maintenance of vital economic infrastructure such as road and rail links (LRC, 1988).

In total, State-based public services provide many of the social benefits which distinguish Australian society from other less fortunate societies. To a very large extent these services underscore our unique Australian quality of life.

Two important influences on State public sector development are first, the nature of Federal financial relations and second, the actual growth and development of public services at the State level. These provide an important background for understanding the significant contemporary issues and problems that must be resolved if our State public sectors are to make a continuing contribution to Australia's economic and social development.

1.2.1 Australian Federal Financial Relations

Perhaps the most remarkable feature of Australian Federal financial relations is the dependence of the States on the Federal Government for funding, and the history of this arrangement is revealed in the chronology provided in Appendix 1.1. Australian State Governments are responsible for a larger share of total public expenditure than are the State/provincial Governments in other comparable Federations such as Canada, West Germany, Switzerland and the US. However they raise a much smaller proportion of taxation revenue than any of their counterparts (Oakes, 1985, p. 63). This is an important reason for many of the financial problems of the States today.

The States' Financial Dependence on the Commonwealth

The background to this dependence is subject to debate.[1] However, perhaps the most fundamental fact, agreed upon by all commentators, is that the current Australian Federal system has diverged from the one envisaged by the founding fathers and current Federal/State financial arrangements are inefficient (cf. Wran in Birrell (ed.), 1987, p. 135). While there are some desirable aspects to the centralisation of finances, the primary problem is that the States have retained their Constitutional responsibility for many functions while losing their revenue-raising powers.

Following Federation, Alfred Deakin commented that the unresolved nature of some of the Constitutional preconditions for national development would leave the States, if not legally bound, then 'financially bound to the chariot wheels of the central government'. Added to this, the framers of the Constitution:

'. . . admitted that it was quite an impossible task for them to lay down the whole financial basis of the Commonwealth. They made provisional arrangements for temporary periods, and . . . left the rest almost entirely, if not quite entirely, to the discretion of Parliament' (Barton's speech, 1898, cited in Headford, 1954, p. 164).

The general view at the time of Federation was that the Federal Government would need little revenue to carry out its functions. Furthermore, the expectations of the Convention members when negotiating the terms of the Constitution were that the Federal Government would not become the major government authority within the Federation. However, it was not too long before the Federal Government's expenditure surpassed revenue from customs and excise duties; and not too long again before its revenue-raising exceeded expenditure responsibilities.

Thus, although the Constitution was designed largely as a 'States' rights' document, there were important provisions which later opened the way for the Federal Government to take a dominant role in its relations with the States (Mathews, 1980). The States maintained responsibility for most of the domestic functions of government including maintenance of law and order, regulation of commerce and industry within their borders, the development of natural resources, the provision and maintenance of essential services such as water supply, electricity, gas and roads, the provision of education, health and housing services and the control of Local Government, but effectively lost control of public finance.

Currently the States have access to only a small number of low-yielding and narrow-based taxes such as stamp duties of various descriptions, payroll tax, motor vehicle taxes, gambling taxes, and land taxes. The interpretations by the High Court over the years of Sections 90 and 92 of the Constitution have disallowed revenue measures introduced by the States on a number of occasions. In consequence, while the States' financial independence has diminished over time their public responsibilities and services have not. As Russell Mathews has written:

'. . . while financial powers thus reside mainly with the Commonwealth, the States have responsibility for most of the functions which involve heavy capital expenditures, such as transport, power, urban development, rural development, education and health services' (Mathews, 1967).

This lucid summary still remains true; indeed, the economic problems of the eighties and the continuing importance of State public services have thrown Mathews' pioneering analyses of Australian public finance into stark relief.

1.2.2 The Evolution of State Services

The evolution of State services can be divided into a number of phases such as colonial socialism (1850-1914), the rise of the public regulatory functions (1914-1945) and the slow emergence of an Australian welfare state from 1945 to the present. In the 1980s economic austerity, economic restructuring and new and profound social problems set the context for debate over State public sector provision.

Colonial Socialism
For most Australian States, nineteenth century economic development was dominated by pastoral expansion and immigration. Large public works programs were begun from the 1850s, especially in transport and communications. During that decade railway and telegraph lines were first established; sewerage, gas lighting and water supply programs were also undertaken. The earliest railway projects actually were begun as private enterprises (though with government subsidies or guarantees), but they quickly had to be taken over by government due to soaring costs, in turn associated with the gold rushes. From 1852 government loans were floated for railway construction. During the latter part of the nineteenth century the largest proportion of New South Wales' public debt (mainly foreign capital) was incurred for financing railway construction. Similarly, publicly funded tramways were established in the 1880s (Fitzpatrick, 1949).

Colonial socialism is the term which best characterises the period in the latter half of the nineteenth century, when:

'. . . private economic activity was supported by the public provision of physical infrastructure, especially in transport and communications, and by the public encouragement of population growth' (Pincus, 1987, p. 311).

State Governments, in these formative decades, used direct regulation, taxation, public enterprise and legal scrutiny to simultaneously enhance growth and equity, progress and security. A favourable (that is, stable) environment for general economic well being and social citizenship (the use of collective resources to guarantee individual rights) made Australia a 'social laboratory' where comparatively large government (13% of GDP in 1913) was able to reduce risk and uncertainty for a relatively affluent population (Pincus, 1987, pp. 299, 302; see also Castles, 1985, Ch. 1).

In the pre-Federation era State Governments secured half the total foreign capital inflow and approximately 40% of total domestic capital formation, primarily in transport and communication. By 1900, State Governments owned approximately half the total fixed capital (excluding land) and conducted the largest enterprises in the economy, particularly in transport and communications and water and sewerage. They employed about 5% of the total work force and generated about 6% of GDP. State Governments also subsidised the influx of some 350,000 migrants, compared with total net immigration of 750,000 and a total net population increase of 2,600,000 (Butlin *et al.*, 1982, p. 16).

State Economic Development and Public Investment
The era of colonial socialism ended in 1914 and for the following decades, public provision of marketed services became a less significant aspect of government in Australia. More concern was given to regulatory activity, albeit to supplement private decision-making (Butlin, 1983, p. 83). Public enterprises continued, but governments were gradually expected to respond to problems of development; the Federal level took over State debt; expansion prospects began to decline; and public priorities began to change. The slogan of 'protection all-round' reflected an increased awareness (however uneasy) of a symbiotic relationship between manufacturers, rural producers and wage earners, and a consciousness of the need for political accommodation of these groups (Butlin, *et al.*, 1982, p. 330; Butlin, 1983, p. 91).

The extension in Federal regulatory and allocative practices did not diminish the States' public investment responsibilities. State Governments maintained active roles in economic development and continued to borrow large amounts of foreign capital. Outlays of government were directed by major developments in industry, education, health and social welfare sectors. In South Australia, Australia's first public housing scheme was initiated by Premier John Gunn (1924-1926). The plan was intended to provide jobs and housing financed by low interest loans from the State Bank. In addition, Gunn commenced a program of re-afforestation of the State's south-east with radiata pine, forming the basis of a significant State commercial enterprise in timber.

In this era, large-scale assisted immigration was resumed and, in response to an expanding manufacturing sector, the States assumed greater responsibility for education and training for industrial employment.

In the history of the State public sector, the 1930s provide the highwater mark in the development of public enterprise and regulations. Fitzpatrick described a 'remarkable change' in which 'systems like supervision of labour relations in industry, and the institution of public financial and industrial undertakings, . . . the New Protection and public competition with private enterprise in production' took hold. It gave '. . . an impression that an experiment in State control or modification of capitalism was being pursued . . . Labor Governments in Queensland and New South Wales, with State mines and factories and stock stations and shops, even a system of family endowment, seemed to be going further towards a State-controlled capitalism' (Fitzpatrick, 1949, pp. 271-75; cf. Butlin *et al.*, 1982, Ch. 2).

The development of State public sectors and trading enterprises were closely connected with the emergence of the organized labour movement. The New South Wales parliamentary Labor leader William Holman was 'the first Australian Statesman to inaugurate a planned economy for the social and material advancement of a whole State'. This program included railway development, irrigation schemes, State brickworks, bakeries, quarries, sawmills, trawlers and the State Monier Pipe and Reinforced Concrete Works. Evatt indicates that State enterprise 'succeeded in considerably

reducing prices either to the government itself or to the consumers or to both'. Political opposition to the public sector was not lacking then either, and any extension of public enterprise 'encountered a stream of propaganda, always directed to proving that, since State undertakings must ultimately fail, the sooner they are closed the better' (Evatt, 1979, pp. 259, 298-99, 376-79).

The reality was somewhat less sublime. The persistent public undertakings, notably the railways, were for the service of private enterprise, 'primarily as means of development', a task at which private enterprise had failed, and which it could not profitably resume. Further, some Labor Governments misunderstood the accepted purpose (as understood by private capital) of public undertakings, and entered into competition with private enterprise, yet private enterprise at no time lost its control of the country's economic organisation and life. For example, New South Wales had shipyards, brickworks, metal quarries, pipe and reinforced concrete works, but eventually sold its profitable brickworks, metal quarries and pipe works in 1936. The supply of coal for the State railways, and of power, light and heat for industrial and domestic purposes, was by then almost the only productive activity which the State permitted itself.

Two aspects of this experience are worth highlighting. The first is that even as late as 1937-38 State trading enterprises returned as much as 45% of the aggregate of all State revenues (the 1937-38 figure for New South Wales was 49.3%). The second is that:

'in the field in which socialist politicians had deemed State ownership and control most called for — the field of heavy industry from which they found or permitted themselves to be excluded — vast profit had been made by private capitalists who were content to leave to the State the vital but necessarily unremunerative business of providing and working the railways by which the country should be opened to exploitation, and by which the products of private enterprise should be taken on their way to market.'

The inter-war period also saw a substantial

increase in the range of Commonwealth responsibilities:

> 'From the 1920s until the beginning of World War II, Commonwealth activity increased markedly, though by no means always at the expense of the States . . . There was still little attempt by the Commonwealth to use many of the legislative powers potentially available to it under the Constitution' (Butlin, 1983, p. 50).

Public capital investment at this time exceeded levels prior to 1914, particularly in urban regions. Expenditure on urban-related infrastructure (wharves, roads, buildings, power stations, urban rail and tram and water and sewerage) rose from approximately 40% of gross capital formation to almost 80% during the period 1900 to 1929 (Butlin, *et al.*, 1982, p. 93). All these factors put considerable pressure on the supply of public sector services, largely within the jurisdiction of the States.

The Post-War Era: Industrialisation and the Australian 'Welfare State'

Australia's industrial capacity was extended and developed during the War, and after 1945 the principles of Keynesian macro-economic counter-cyclical policy were accepted by key personnel and institutions including the Australian Treasury. This national commitment to sustained macro-management (with full employment as its major substantive goal) was also accompanied by acceptance in some parts of the bureaucracy of the need to develop welfare state mechanisms. These twin aims constituted a significant watershed in public sector-private sector relationships (Butlin, 1978, p. 18). By 1949, however, it was apparent that the development of permanent institutional commitments to underpin these goals would not transpire in Australia.

So, although the formal adaptation of Keynesianism was proclaimed, no actual public sector development commensurate to the task was forthcoming (Harcourt, 1977). Nevertheless great changes in economic and social policy, with important ramification for Federal and State public sectors, took place.

Developments in foreign trade, international investment flows, entry of foreign investment and foreign technology and post-war European upheavals all served to increase the ambit of Federal Government's influence (Butlin, *et al.*, 1982).

Social policy developments in the post-war period also reflected important advances in implementation of elements of 'the social wage'. Federal Governments introduced innovations with respect to pharmaceutical and medical benefits, health services, pensions, education, housing and immigration. However, as Butlin has noted:

> 'the extension of a Labor concept of a welfare state was less marked than in many other countries because of prior development of old age, invalid and maternity benefits and child endowment and unemployment relief. It was coherence rather than sharp increase in outlays, arising from these cash benefits, that marked post-war Australian welfare policies' (Butlin, 1978, p. 19).

The Premier who best characterises this period of State public sector development was Thomas Playford, who led the South Australian government for nearly 27 years (1938-1965). Playford oversaw the industrialisation of the State, beginning with the establishment of munitions factories in the Second World War. The State's war industries opened the way for the creation of large industrial complexes, work force training and the exploitation of the State's traditional industries based on motor body and coach building and domestic hardware. After the war, South Australia was equipped with a skilled work force and available factory space. General Motors and Chrysler bought out the local motor body and coach builders and established motor car manufacture and assembly plants in Adelaide. In addition, the shipbuilding and steel-making facilities of Whyalla were expanded.

At the end of the Playford era the South Australian economy had been transformed from a primarily rural one to a predominantly industrial economy. Almost 60% of total production was in secondary industries, which reversed the situation at the beginning of the Playford era when primary industries accounted for 59% of the total. However, of the total factory work force, 25% were involved in the production of consumer durables and 15% were employed by the two major employers, GMH and Chrysler. One legacy of the Playford reign was a narrow industrial base. This signalled an ongoing role for the States in economic and social development.

Between 1945 and 1970, for the first time in Australian history, direct taxes on personal and company incomes provided enough revenue to meet the total welfare spending of all governments. Further, Commonwealth income tax reimbursements to the States under the Uniform Tax Agreement, and the general grants that later took their place, were sufficient to meet total State welfare payments. Only in 1963 did the income tax revenues retained by the Commonwealth fail to cover its welfare spending. However, after 1970, States' welfare expenditure exceeded income tax revenues transferred to them by the Commonwealth (Butlin *et al.*, 1982, p. 195).

During the post-war era, State responsibilities in areas such as urban infrastructure, housing, health, education and community welfare grew in importance, but the development of these services failed to meet demand.

Labor returned to Federal Office in 1972 with a mandate to correct these deficiencies and from 1972-75, the Whitlam Government attempted to inject Federal funds into specific State and Local Government arenas. Whitlam pronounced his Government's long-term intentions to the State Premiers:

'From now on we will expect to be involved in the planning of the functions in which we are financially involved. We believe that it would be irresponsible for the national Government to content itself with simply providing funds without being involved in the process by which priorities are met, and by which expenditures are planned and by which standards are met' (Burns, 1977, p. 92).

In 1974 the Federal Government also assumed full financial responsibility for tertiary education with corresponding reductions in financial assistance payments to the States.

To its credit the Whitlam Government endeavoured to streamline decision-making and funding between the tiers of government so that pressing social and economic problems such as housing shortages, the lack of sewer services in urban areas and a variety of other problems could be alleviated. Nevertheless Whitlam's initiatives brought Federal/State relations to an all time low. It is ironic that problems of cities, pollution, housing, child care, ageing, drug abuse and re-training are again resurfacing as urgent public problems. Many of these problems belong to the jurisdiction of the States, but there is no strong reason to imagine that Federal rather than State Governments will be willing to take on the doubtless costly responsibility for these social issues in the way Labor did in the 1970s. Meanwhile, there is not, as Galligan has noted, a well informed or rational debate about the appropriate role of our public sectors in dealing with such problems (Galligan, 1988, p. 291).

As the Playford South Australian Government had characterised the traditional role of the States in economic development and public enterprise, the Dunstan South Australian Government's achievements in fostering the social fabric of the State were exemplary in the 1970s. The Dunstan era was characterised by legislative and administrative reforms, improved services in education, health and welfare; creative town-planning ; improved transport services and the expansion of housing finance. In other words, Dunstan developed and extended many key elements of what is now known as the social wage.

The finale of the 1970s was Prime Minister Fraser's financial deal for the States. Fraser's revenue sharing arrangements were ostensibly a new arrangement giving States greater financial control. They in fact amounted to a new procedure for determining the amount to be transferred unconditionally to the States (Bird, 1986, p. 116).

State Public Services in the '80s — Economic Austerity, Economic Restructuring and New Social Problems
State public services in the 80s are faced with

fiscal cutbacks, while at the same time they must maintain the quality of social, administrative and economic services and infrastructure and face new social demands and problems. *It is this problematical environment, coupled with the paradoxical qualities of Federal financial relations, which has culminated in the so-called 'state of siege' which is the theme of this book.*

Despite the distribution of tax-sharing grants to the States in 1985, the great characteristic of the 80s is the all-consuming pressure on State Governments to reduce their overall levels of expenditure. General purpose grants to the States were reduced by $550m at the 1989 Premiers' Conference — the latest in a continuing series of cutbacks. Total net payments to the States have also declined in real terms since 1982. Added to this, at the 1989 Premiers' Conference the Commonwealth reduced State and Commonwealth statutory authority borrowings by $2.2b, which followed a reduction of $519m to the State/Local global borrowing limit in 1988/89, in turn preceded by a cut of $1b the previous year. The net Public Sector Borrowing Requirement for the State sector has dramatically declined as a percentage of GDP since 1982/83.

The effects of these cutbacks are becoming apparent (cf. 'Cain Warns of 75% Budget Shortfall', AFR, June 9, 1989, 'WA to Sell Assets to Boost its Revenue', AFR, June 20, 1989). State Government outlays have fallen dramatically in areas such as capital works. This is of concern because the State/Local Government sector is responsible for 75% of public sector capital outlays and the two tiers of government account for the major forms of public infrastructure including roads, public transport, electricity, water, schools and hospitals. In all, capital expenditure for these areas has declined from 7.5% of GDP in the late 1960s to 5% in 1987/88.

Also, augmenting the general pressure on the States, the Commonwealth has transferred responsibility for a number of services from Federal to State jurisdiction. Special revenue assistance equal to the estimated expenditure for these programs has been allocated, yet there has been some dispute as to whether such payments are adequate.

Initially the Hawke Government's budgetary strategy, as a form of Federal public sector growth constraint, elicited the prediction that it may achieve what the Fraser Government did not achieve, that is: '. . . forcing the States into more revenue-raising through imposing income tax surcharges which 1978 Federal legislation permits them to do' (Groenewegen, 1989b, p. 17). However, the Treasurer has indicated in recent times that he would move to block any attempt by the States to utilise their powers to tax income.

This action gives further emphasis to the narrowness of State financing options. And while it is true that lower growth in the Commonwealth funding of State public services has been partly offset by a rise in State revenue from stamp duties, business franchise taxes and other State taxes and charges, these rises are exceptional and cannot be the basis for stable fiscal strategy. The tendency towards more reliance on such taxes is also undesirable. As Barry Rowe argued in 1988:

> 'State taxes are unsatisfactory in terms of equity, administrative simplicity and economic efficiency. They are narrowly based and generally regressive in their impact. And yet the Commonwealth is, by making decisions such as those made at the Premiers' Conference two weeks ago, pushing the States to put greater reliance on these already unsatisfactory taxes. In States like Victoria the revenue-raising capacity of existing State taxes is exhausted' (Rowe, 1988, p. 6).

Reductions in State revenue have also led to a general emphasis on dismantling much of the State public sector. However, this process has neither been rational nor has it been the subject of debate or analysis. While 'big ticket' privatisations such as those of Australian Airlines, Qantas or the Commonwealth Bank have rightly been the subject of popular, public debate, in the State sphere, home care for the aged and disadvantaged, child care services, education, road maintenance, water services, agricultural services, State financial institutions, public transport, housing services and many other services have been cut, threatened with privatisation or 'commercialised' with little public input or attention.

The irony is that State and Local Government services are more directly relevant to ordinary Australians and constitute a larger sphere of economic activity than do the 'big ticket' items. Unlike the debate over Commonwealth public enterprises, where only one form of privatisation – a partial or full stock exchange float – was being proposed, in the States a virtual maze of activities is underway. This has further concealed the magnitude of privatisation at a State level.

Apart from direct sales and contracting out, the two best-known forms of privatisation, the abrogation of responsibility for services and the increasing reliance on government voluntary agencies, represents the 'newest wave' of privatisation and possibly the least understood or analysed. If care for the aged, the disadvantaged and pre-school children is seen to be the sole responsibility of the family or a non-government agency or private, commercial agency on the grounds of 'fiscal restraint', this represents a return to a more archaic state in which government simply assumes a sovereign-like role.

As all this should suggest, there is a great need to critically analyse the hitherto uncommented upon tendencies leading towards privatisation in the States, and this study examines these in general terms in Chapter Five and, in more detail, in the chapters on individual State public services.

1.3 The Accord, Economic Restructuring and the Public Sector

The current political framework in which the debate over the Australian public sector is taking place is the Accord between the Federal Labor Government and the trade union movement. This agreement stands, in an international sense, alongside the successful 'consensus' politics of Austria and Scandinavia.

Internationally, there have been two general strategies involved in domestic economic restructuring and reform. The first involves economic restructuring through tripartite consultation over economic management and policy, while the second involves free market policies and privatisation.

While there have been difficulties and setbacks, the economic successes of the Hawke Labor Government in areas such as employment creation and industry restructuring are indisputable when compared with conservative strategies abroad and with the record of previous governments. As this book also shows, State Governments in Australia, particularly those of Cain and Bannon, have also successfully developed models of tripartite consultation and political consensus as a central part of State economic planning and development.

For the most part, 'consensus government' has resisted the privatisation of public services. In South and Western Australia, for example, Labor Governments won office largely on the basis of campaigns against privatisation. Despite this fact, at a Federal level the privatisation of Commonwealth public enterprises was considered in 1988 and State Governments have sold or rationalised public services in varying degrees of severity.

One of the great limitations of Australian tripartism lies in its failure to recognise that the public sector has an important role in the economic restructuring process. The conservative rubric that 'the only good public sector is a small public sector' has been too readily accepted, and most significantly, governments have lacked a definite plan for incorporating public sector reform and improvement into the general blueprint of economic development (cf. Langmore, 1988; Botsman, 1988).

This deficiency in the Accord has to some extent given privatisation an entry into the policy debates of the labour movement. In these debates, privatisation is at odds with advocates of public sector development, and the following two sections give a brief overview of these competing visions of public sector activity.

1.4 Privatisation

The claims of privatisation supporters are mostly predicated on assumptions about the ability of this process to deliver economic restructuring and micro-economic reform. In truth, privatisation is not concerned with these issues at all, nor does it concern itself directly with solving the major social and economic problems of the day. It simply involves transferring assets and functions from the public sector to the private sector. As the English authors Heald and Thomas argued in 1986, the promises of privatisation were more 'theological' than real: privatisation offered a visionary society, whose premises were more a matter of belief than substance, it sweepingly rejected notions of accountability which do not operate through market mechanisms and its advocates were often unwilling to consider options for improving the performance of public firms other than privatisation (Heald & Thomas, 1986, p. 52).

As a general economic strategy, privatisation has had its day. Support for more privatisation in Britain, for example, is waning. The controversial case of the flotation of the Water Authorities is probably the last straw for the British electorate. Studies show that while the purchase of shares of privatised companies may be attractive because of initial underpricing, flotation will not solve the long-term financing problems of capital intensive areas such as the water industry. Because of increased infrastructure investment and environmental standards it is estimated that the British Water Authorities will need to generate up to 8 billion pounds over the next ten years (PIRC, 1989). Privatisation provides no means of meeting these new demands, nor of financing them (cf. *Financial Times*, Editorial, July 21, 1988). The likely options for the Water Authorities are asset stripping supplemented by a massive increase in revenue yields from existing consumers. One study estimates that real-term price rises of over 60% must occur over the next decade. A significant downgrading of services is also likely to occur (PIRC, 1989).

The relevance of this example for Australian State public sectors is profound. As Chapter Three clearly shows, the States deliver a wide variety of services in which there will be real rise in demand and costs in the future, but privatisation is no solution to these problems. The Greiner Liberal Government in New South Wales has gone to the extent of hiring British experts on privatisation and other private consultants to aid in the sale of State

assets (cf. Curran, 1988, Addendum). However, as with the case of the British Water Authorities, the Greiner brand of privatisation does not attempt to deal with the long-term issues which the States currently face and, in many areas, it may even lead to more severe problems in the future. For example, as the Victorian chapter shows, during the 1960s and 70s the Bolte Government in Victoria privatised some 50,000 units of public housing; now in 1989, Victoria has the fastest rising and largest waiting list for public housing and the poorest quality public housing stock of all the States. Apparently undetered or ignorant of this, the Greiner Government is currently adopting exactly the same strategy as a means of solving its housing crisis! (cf. Raine, 1989).

The claims of privatisation and free market economics cannot therefore be sustained. For example, in the UK and the US the question of who bears the burden of economic restructuring has been largely determined by the private sector, and has predominantly fallen on those who lack the market power to protect themselves – young school-leavers, immigrants, the unskilled female, ethnic and older workers in declining industrial sectors or regions. These groups and their dependants, unemployed, homeless and uneducated, grow in numbers day by day (eg. see *NY Times*, Jan 26 1989, p. B1).

In a callous fashion, Thatcher and Reagan calculated that an 'underclass' of this sort lacked the means to challenge the social order and were electorally insignificant or powerless, and could therefore be thrown to the wolves (Hall, 1987, p. 283).

The privatisation of public enterprises and services further exacerbated the fate of the underclass through cutbacks in employment and social services. Yet the decline of the public sector poses problems for economic development as many markets depend on an ancillary network of social institutions, often generated and sustained by state action. In short, it has been found that the withdrawal of the state may impair national markets more than help them (Hall, 1987).

The findings of this book should be closely studied. For above all they show that the strategies which highlight privatisation and uncritical cutbacks to the public sector are politically and economically flawed. The focus on the public sector as the site of all economic ills represents an ideological blind spot. It overlooks a central endeavour of government which is to improve (and not remove) public services. The strategy of public sector renewal articulated in this book offers a firmer foundation for government reform and development of public services than does privatisation.

1.5 The Task of State Public Sector Renewal

If the public services which are delivered through the States in Australia are to be renewed rather than irrationally and needlessly dismantled, a rigorous debate regarding their funding, their social, political and economic functions and goals, their productivity and internal efficiency must be initiated. This book inaugurates that debate but it represents only a first step towards public sector renewal because it deals with necessarily general issues and has been written by researchers who, no matter how concerned, can barely appreciate the extent of the contemporary assault on Australian State public services. The real agenda for public sector renewal lies with public sector workers in the many different State Government enterprises, departments and authorities where the real action and analysis must begin.

In the current fervour for micro-economic reform, it is important to stress the tremendous contribution the public sector plays – and can increasingly play – in the task of structural adjustment. The micro-economic reform and development of State public sectors should be seen as a means to stimulate and complement private sector micro-economic reform. This positive approach ensures that reform is socially, economically and politically successful. Apart from crucial services delivered at a State level such as waterfront services, training for industry and railway infrastructure, this book articulates a much broader set of objectives for micro-reform at the State level. It argues that selective State public infrastructure investment must be undertaken if Australia is to solve its economic problems. Furthermore, revitalised State public services also provide a means of more closely integrating wages, taxation and social wage programs. The reform and

development of State public services also provides a vehicle for more closely integrating public and private sector unions in terms of industrial policy. Finally 'renewing' public services is more in tune with and responsive to 'user needs', and is therefore an important way of extending social democracy and social justice. This final point is crucial as public sector renewal constitutes a way of delivering real improvements in community living standards as well as ensuring that the community can participate in social decision-making processes.

Appendix 1.1
The Evolution of Federal Financial Relations

1901 Commonwealth Financial Powers The Commonwealth was conferred exclusive power to impose customs and excise duties (s90) and concurrent power (s51[ii]) over all other forms of taxation provided there was no discrimination between States (See Mathews, 1979, pp. 33-34). The Commonwealth was to return any surplus revenues. Sections 87, 89, 93 and 94 provided for repatriation of such surpluses but the most important of these provisions, s94, did not come into operation (Saunders, 1987, p. 36).

1901 Special Grants to the States Section 96 empowered the Federal Government to grant financial assistance to any State on such terms and conditions as its Parliament 'deems fit' (a provision which remains relevant). The s96 provision, initially included for the protection of the States, in fact placed the initiative for additional revenue transfers firmly with the Commonwealth (McMillan *et al.*, 1983, pp. 117-118).

1901-1910 State Role In the early years of Federation, State authorities dominated public decision-making. The Constitution provided for a variety of fiscal transfers, primarily intended to redress the anticipated vertical fiscal inequalities from the loss of the States' main revenue sources.

1903-05 State Fiscal Concerns The States began to express concern about Federal financial arrangements and unsuccessfully sought a perpetuation of s87 which limited the Federal Government's 'own use' of customs and excise revenues (May, 1971, p. 3).

1908 State Fiscal Inequality Demands made for the recognition of the special difficulties faced by the smaller States (May, 1971, Ch. 1). The States' halcyon days were over (McMillan *et al.*, 1983, p. 120). By the 1930s Special Payments to 'less advantaged' States were entrenched, but there was no consistent method for assessing the amount to be paid in any particular case.

1908 Surplus Revenue Act After the initial financial agreement was completed, the Federal Parliament passed the Surplus Revenue Act providing for per capita payments to the States in lieu of the s87 requirements for customs and excise receipts. These payments represented a significant reduction in transfers to the States, but most States compensated by increased taxation and enterprise returns. The agreement continued until 1927 (Mathews & Jay, 1972).

1908 Commonwealth Social Role A notable shift from the States' dominance in public decision-making was the Deakin Government's introduction of invalid and old-age pensions to be funded in part from the 'surplus' monies which would otherwise have been paid to the States (Commonwealth Grants Commission, 1983, Ch. 1).

1914-18 Increasing Federal Fiscal Strength/ Autonomy The Commonwealth's role in World War I increased dramatically the relative fiscal strength of central government. Federal revenue-raising was extended into new areas including estate and death duties and entertainment taxes (May, 1971, pp. 5-6).

1915 Federal Income Tax The Commonwealth's entry in 1915 into the income tax field produced demands for simplification or uniformity in the tax system (Murphy, 1928, p. 298; May, 1971, p. 6). However, while in 1909-10 Commonwealth payments to the States were more than double their receipts from taxation, the situation was almost reversed by 1918-1919 (see Mathews & Jay, 1972).

1923 Formation of the Loan Council Commonwealth suggests that a voluntary, in-

formal Loan Council be established to co-ordinate government borrowing, to reduce inter-governmental competition for loans and associated pressure on interest rates. This Loan Council had some success but the changing circumstances of the 1920s saw pressure for a formal agreement to co-ordinate and regulate public borrowing.

1927 Financial Agreement The Financial Agreement provided for the setting up of the formal Australian Loan Council. Under s105, the Commonwealth was empowered to take over the States' existing debts. A 1910 amendment approved an extension to pre-Federation debts (Scott, 1983).

1936 'The Gentleman's Agreement' The early 1930s saw pressure for greater public expenditure. Local and semi-governmental bodies were encouraged by State Governments to expand utilisation of their borrowing capacity (outside the Loan Council program). The addition to the Financial Agreement of an informal addendum (the so-called Gentlemen's Agreement) resulted, which brought local and semi-government borrowing under Loan Council supervision.

1933 Commonwealth Grants Commission In response to the States' dissatisfaction, the Commonwealth Grants Commission was established. This was intended to supersede the series of *ad hoc* Royal Commissions of the post-federation period. An independent quasi-judicial authority, it was given responsibility for the States' applications for special financial assistance from the Commonwealth, basing its recommendations on the principle of 'financial need'. The disbursement of monies was to be based on an examination of the States' public finances in relation to national standards.

1942 The Uniform Tax Agreement Until World War II the States and Commonwealth levied income taxes. The Uniform Tax Agreement empowered the Commonwealth to take over the State income tax offices and levy a uniform income tax. Under the Act, States which did not levy an income tax were to be entitled to an annual payment determined by the Grants Commission. Four of the States subsequently challenged in the High Court, but the Act's validity was upheld under the defence power for the war's duration and under s96 for peacetime. Though legally free to levy income taxes, the States have refrained from doing so as such taxes would have disqualified them from receiving reimbursement

1946-1959-1970 Federal Reimbursements and Assistance Grants Arrangements for Federal reimbursements that originated in 1942 were altered in 1946 to encourage States to apply, if necessary, directly to the Commonwealth for additional assistance; in 1959 to reduce the scope for special grants and to introduce a system of financial assistance grants (implying that reimbursements were not automatic); and in 1970 (to once again encourage States to apply for special grants as budgetary constraints began to be felt).

1949-1966 The Menzies Era increased Federal domination of Loans Council. Subsequent governments were responsible for substantial increases in special purpose payments (350% between 1959-1972 cf. general revenue increases of 200%) impinging on the States' control over certain responsibilities.

1971 Payroll Tax the Federal government agreed to transfer payroll taxation to the States in return for a reduction in financial assistance grants. While this trade off was based on the previous Federal payroll rate of 2.5%, the States progressively increase the payroll tax rate to 5.0% and more.

1972-75 The Whitlam Era The Whitlam Government had a modified platform of strong central government with decentralisation through Local Government. The major component of the platform was the use of specific purpose programs to intervene in areas of State responsibility. By 1975 Federal-State relations 'were at an all-time low'. The political impact of the issue of 'State rights' was evident in the Opposition's new Federalism policy (Mathews, 1977, p. 14). Despite its 'fiscal generosity', the Whitlam Government's priorities antagonised the States as they attempted to usurp States' control over aspects of health, education, urban transport and regionalism (Groenewegen, 1987, pp. 244-5).

1976-1982 Fraser's 'Cooperative Federalism' The Fraser Government promised a new system of so-called 'revenue sharing' for the States (Personal Income Tax Sharing Act, 1976) and allocated to the States 33.6% of personal income tax collected by the Commonwealth (based on the estimated proportion of financial assistance grants to income tax collection in 1975-76, and subject to review). Representing a significant retreat from Federal tax monopoly, provision was made, in 1978, for individual States to impose personal income tax surcharges (or rebates). This provision has never been invoked. Fraser's revenue-sharing arrangements were ostensibly a new arrangement giving States greater financial control, but they in fact amounted to a new procedure for determining the amount to be transferred unconditionally to the States (Bird, 1986, p. 116).

1983-6 Financial Deregulation and Borrowing In 1983 the Loan Council completely deregulated domestic borrowing of semi-government authorities. In 1984 it removed restrictions on their foreign borrowing, and limits on borrowing by smaller authorities, trialling a substitute global limit on public authority borrowing. Originally designed to be a co-operative Federalist institution, the Loan Council remains Federally dominated, though greater efficiency results from the larger freedom given the States in the allocation of their loan funds (Groenewegen, 1989).

1985-89 The Hawke Era At the May 1985 Premiers' Conference the Hawke Government restored the concept of financial-assistance grants growing at a specified rate. A need for financial stringency in 1985-86, saw aggregate financial-assistance held constant in real terms as measured by the CPI; in the two years up to 1987-88, a 2% real increase was provided. In the interest of stabilisation in 1987/88, Federal funding for the States was cut in other areas instead, and particularly in loan and capital funds. In 1988/89 cuts continued, while at the 1989 Premiers' Conference grants to the States were cut by $550m and borrowings were reduced by $2.2b.

Notes

1 Russell Mathews has described a 'fiscal club' whose
   members (State Governments, the High Court, the
   Treasury and Federal politicians) have engineered an
   alliance to save both tiers of government the dis-
   comfort of public accountability (Mathews, 1987, p.
   95). Others have argued that a 'constitutional misfit'
   (section 96) has been allowed to override the letter
   and spirit of federalism's founding document
   (Saunders, 1987, p. 18) while Else-Mitchell sees the
   States becoming little more than 'administrative
   agencies giving effect to Commonwealth laws and
   policies' (Else-Mitchell, 1983, p. 18). One wartime
   chairman of the Grants Commission saw Australian
   federalism as a stepping stone to unitary government
   (see Bird, 1986, p. 130). Still more provocatively, Peter
   Wilenski has suggested that the existing structure of
   federalism is inherently conservative, limiting not
   only Federal powers but the possibility of strong,
   progressive, reform-oriented government (Wilenski,
   1983, p. 84).

Part Two

THE MACRO-ECONOMIC CONTEXT

Chapter 2

MACRO-ECONOMIC POLICY AND STATE PUBLIC SERVICES

2.1 Introduction

Economic circumstances in Australia and abroad have made policy formulation a challenging task in the 1980s, with unemployment and inflation remaining at unacceptably high levels since 'stagflation' was first encountered in the 1970s. The international economic environment has become more uncertain with the widening trade imbalances between major capitalist economies, and the large and (apparently) insurmountable debt problems of developing countries heightening instability in world financial and commodity markets. The most important altered circumstance for Australia, however, has been the substantial decline in its international trading performance over the course of the decade which has increased the economy's vulnerability to such external exigencies. Successive current account deficits on the balance of payments over the years have led to a rapid accumulation of foreign debt to unsustainably high levels.

These developments have generated much debate over an appropriate economic strategy. In the context of the deteriorating external situation, economic debate has intensified about the traditional role of government in the Australian economy, and in particular, about the appropriate size of the public sector at the State and Federal levels. Faced with a dwindling revenue base, the States have been progressively forced to reduce their own expenditures, and in the process, cut back on public services. Indeed the great casualty of the Federal Government's macro-economic policy is the relative size of the Australian (Federal and State) public sector. This chapter seeks to explain this process, challenge the economic rationale for this macro-economic policy and provide an alternative policy approach in which a renewed Australian public sector plays a positive role in a strategy designed to reconstruct the Australian economy.

2.2 Macro-Economic Constraints and Policy

This section examines the key issues in macroeconomic policy pertaining to the role of Australia's public sector in present economic circumstances. There are a number of related matters which this section analyses. These include the nature and seriousness of Australia's current economic predicament; the constraint which this problem imposes upon macroeconomic policy options; and the Federal Government's policy response.

2.2.1 State of Play

Australia's growth performance since 1983 has been impressive compared to most other OECD countries. Annual real growth has averaged around 3% over the decade corresponding to an annual employment growth of around 2%. Although this growth performance has been successful in reducing unemployment levels, it has been accompanied by a sharp deterioration in Australia's external position. Strong domestic demand, mostly related to final consumption expenditure, generated high import demand, which along with a sharp decline in export prices, has induced a significant decline in the nation's trading performance. Successive large current account deficits on the balance of payments have caused foreign debt to rise to historically high levels.

Though foreign debt has stabilised in more recent years (see Table 2.1), reflecting at least a temporary improvement in trade performance, the external situation remains serious. It presently imposes a formidable constraint on the Australian economy in the sense that a continued expansion in domestic demand, and thereby output and employment, will continue to induce high import expenditures which, in the absence of a substantial rise in export income, will lead to a further unsustainable increase in foreign debt. This means that until the external position is reversed there is little scope for making further progress in lowering unemployment levels and improving living standards through high economic growth. The cuts in living standards that have been endured by the Australian workforce during the 1980s are principally due to the deterioration of the external account, the effect having been moderated to some extent by strong employment growth. It is therefore the main source of Australia's present economic difficulties which, as widely acknowledged, is unlikely to be reversed in the immediate future. This can be better appreciated by a more detailed examination of the external problem and the economic factors which have produced it.

Table 2.1

Australia's Foreign Debt (Gross and Net)

At end of June	Gross Debt $b	Foreign Assets $b	Net Debt $b	Gross Debt/ GDP Ratio (%)	Foreign Assets/ GDP Ratio (%)	Net Debt/ GDP Ratio (%)
1980	13.5	6.6	6.9	11.1	5.4	5.6
1981	15.2	6.7	8.5	10.9	4.8	6.1
1982	24.2	7.8	16.4	15.5	5.0	10.5
1983	35.5	12.5	23.0	20.9	7.4	13.5
1984	43.7	14.2	29.5	22.9	7.5	15.4
1985	66.9	16.6	50.3	31.6	7.8	23.8
1986	91.3	17.1	74.2	38.7	7.2	31.4
1987	104.5	22.5	82.0	40.1	8.6	31.5
1988	116.3	26.3	90.0	39.8	9.0	30.8

Source: Reserve Bank of Australia Bulletin, 1988, various issues.

The rapid pace of the deterioration in Australia's external position in the 1980s (particularly since the deregulation of the foreign exchange markets begun in December, 1983) is illustrated in Table 2.1. Net foreign debt was $7b in June 1980, representing 5.6% of GDP, but by June 1988 it had reached $90b, representing 30.8% of GDP. Foreign borrowing on this scale is only economically justifiable when it is used to finance investment-related imports which expand the productive capacity of the tradeables sector which will, in turn, lead to an improvement in the nation's trading performance, from which foreign debt can then be serviced. However it is clear that foreign borrowing has not been fully used to this effect; rather, much of it has been used to finance goods and services imports (in excess of export income) to satisfy domestic demand in the form of consumption and investment expenditure. This is reflected in Australia's worsening external debt-service capacity, with debt-servicing costs (interest and annual debt repayments) growing at a faster rate than export receipts. Debt servicing costs as a proportion of export receipts (the debt servicing ratio) and as a proportion of GDP have risen to levels that have markedly reduced the country's international credit worthiness. As illustrated in Table 2.2, the debt-servicing ratio has risen dramatically; from a respectable 13.4% in 1980/81 to in excess of 60% in 1987/88.

Table 2.2

Australia's Debt Servicing Capacity

	Interest & Principal Repayments ($b) (%)	Exports of Goods & Services ($b) (%)	Debt Service Ratio (%)	Interest & Principal Repayments/ %GDP Ratio (%)
1979/80	1.8	21.7	8.5	1.5
1980/81	3.0	22.2	13.4	2.1
1981/82	4.1	22.9	18.1	2.7
1982/83	6.5	24.7	26.5	3.9
1983/84	7.8	28.0	27.8	4.1
1984/85	11.6	34.1	34.1	5.5
1985/86	16.7	37.9	46.1	7.1
1986/87	27.2	42.2	64.5[a]	10.4
1987/88	30.8	48.8	63.2	10.5

Note: (a) The large increase in interest and principal repayments in 1986/87 is partly attributable to the inclusion of non-official repayments by the banks. Excluding this adjustment to the figures the debt-service ratio in 1986/87 would have been 56.3.
Source: RBA Bulletin, December 1988.

The real problem with a continuation of this trend is that foreign creditors who provide the funds necessary to cover Australia's current account deficits on the balance of payments become increasingly concerned about the ability of the country to meet its debt commitments and, accordingly, demand higher premiums to cover the risk of lending. This means that progressively higher domestic interest rates (relative to overseas rates) are required in order to finance the ongoing current account deficit. Monetary policy in recent years has been increasingly conditioned by this external requirement. Persistently high rates of interest together with the significant real exchange rate depreciation that occurred in the mid-1980s have been the main mechanisms by which the worsening external balance has, in a direct manner, depressed living standards in the Australian economy in recent years. This underlines the imperative of winding back Australia's high foreign debt.

Of particular relevance to Australia is the tendency for foreign debt to promote its own accumulation through the adverse impact of external debt-servicing on the current account on the balance of payments. The current account essentially consists of three parts: the merchandise trade balance (which covers trade

flows of goods); the net services item (which covers trade flows of services like insurance, shipping and financial services) and the net incomes component (which represents the balance of credits and debits on investment income such as interest payments and dividends). With large net foreign debt the interest payments on this net debt cause the net incomes balance to go into deficit and ceteris paribus, the current account runs a deficit (CAD). This in turn increases the need for higher foreign borrowings to cover the CAD and so on. This vicious circle can be exacerbated by high foreign rates of interest and currency depreciations which tend to increase debt-servicing payments for debtor countries such as Australia. The contribution to the CAD by the net incomes component has increased markedly over the 1980s. Whereas it accounted for only 34.4% of the CAD in 1981/82, by 1987/88 it accounted for nearly 90.0%. To improve the debt-servicing capacity of the economy and hence reverse foreign debt accumulation, it will be necessary to produce a sizeable and growing surplus on the merchandise trade (and/or services) account, which can more than offset the net incomes deficit, and hence reduce the CAD. Table 2.3 illustrates this point, indicating the need for a substantial and persistent improvement in the Balance of Trade just to wind back the CAD as a ratio of GDP.

The prospects for such a persistent trade adjustment are remote while Australia continues to rely predominantly on rural and mineral-based exports which are particularly sensitive to downturns in the international economy, and continues to import predominantly manufactured commodities which have a relatively high income elasticity of demand. This underlies the long-term structural nature of Australia's external problem. While export composition is weighted heavily towards low value-added primary commodities, income growth in industrial countries especially (which provide by far the largest source of world demand) has seen a progressive dominance in world trade of high value-added manufactures and services. This is directly connected to the long-term decline in Australia's Terms of Trade (TOT) — the prices received for our primary exports have for most of the post-war period not kept pace with the prices paid for our mostly manufactured imports. The TOT (which virtually mirrors the variation of manufactured prices to primary commodity prices for the world as a whole) has in fact been declining since the early post-war period. This trend has been masked, in part, by cyclical swings in our primary export prices.

Table 2.3

Current Account ($b)

	1983/84	1984/85	1985/86	1986/87	1987/88
Exports	23.7	29.2	32.2	35.4	40.6
Imports	-23.5	-30.1	-35.6	-37.1	-40.4
Bal. on Merchandise Trade	0.2	-0.9	-3.4	-1.7	0.2
Net Services	-3.0	-4.0	-4.1	-3.5	-3.2
Bal. on Goods and Services	-2.8	-4.9	-7.5	-5.2	-3.0
Net Income	-4.7	-6.5	-8.1	-9.3	-11.0
Unrequited Transfers	0.2	0.3	0.8	1.3	1.8
Bal. on Current Account	-7.3	-11.1	-14.8	-13.2	-12.2
Net Income and Transfers as a Percentage of Balance on Current Account	64.8	58.8	54.4	7 0.0	89.6
Balance on Current Account as a Percentage of GDP	-3.8	-5.2	-6.3	-5.1	-4.2

Source: ABS, Cat. No. 5303.0 and 5301.0, Balance of Payments.

The very sharp and unusually long cyclical downturn in the TOT in the early to mid 1980s, that precipitated the deterioration in the external account, revealed quite comprehensively the inadequate structural composition of Australia's trade flows. This has been reinforced by the increasing difficulties associated with expanding our export volumes; with agricultural commodities increasingly encountering trade barriers and facing severe price competition from subsidised agricultural products in world markets, and mineral exports also subject to greater competition mainly from less developed debtor countries desperate for foreign currency income. It is now widely recognised that sustained improvement in trade performance (which would also lessen exposure to TOT swings and their disruptive impact upon the economy) depends on medium to long-term restructuring of manufactured-related commodities, as well as improved performance in services, so lessening the reliance on traditional primary exports for foreign currency earnings.

The task of strengthening the tradeables sector will demand a fundamental restructuring of much of the economy's industry and infrastructure. This is because restructuring the 'tradeables sector' does not simply relate to export-producing and import-competing industries, but must also refer to potential exporters and import-competitors and, importantly, to all industries whose output enters directly and indirectly into the production of (potential) tradeable commodities (in technical terms this could be called the 'vertically integrated tradeables sector'). Structural adjustment will therefore encompass most areas of the Australian economy including, it should be noted, the public sector which is responsible for providing important infrastructure such as transport and communications, as well as other economic inputs such as education and health which are all indispensable for industry restructuring.

A crucial requirement for the restructuring of the industrial base is improved investment performance (both private and public). The proportion of Australia's GDP devoted to total investment is approximately 23%, considerably lower than for most OECD countries. Throughout the 1980s investment growth remained at disturbingly low levels. Only recently has there been a pick up in investment, mainly in the private sector in response to strong domestic demand. Low investment growth in the past has in fact led to a serious productive capacity constraint in recent years. This constraint implies a shortage of modern productive facilities including machinery and equipment, as well as skilled labour to operate them. Such superior inputs are necessary for the process of instituting improved techniques of production which, in turn, would improve the competitiveness (price and quality) of the tradeables sector. The National Institute for Economic and Industry Research (NIEIR) has estimated that investment as a proportion of GDP must rise to about 27% in order to overcome this capacity constraint and ensure a real economic growth rate of 4-5% (Brain & Manning, 1987).

There is need not only for a marked increase in the level of investment but also a change in the sectoral composition of investment for appropriate structural adjustment (Schott,

1988). Investment should be used to support an expansion of the tradeable goods sector. The restructuring process therefore requires an appropriate composition of investment directed primarily towards expanding the industrial base of the economy's tradeable goods sector. It must be directed toward upgrading education and skills training and research and development, and towards the installation of modern plant and equipment which overcomes the capacity constraint in a manner that will expand the 'tradeables sector' and ultimately improve Australia's trade performance. While there are some tentative signs that this is now occurring, there is doubt that it is occurring on a sufficiently large scale to bring about a sustained improvement in the economy's external account compatible with even a moderate rate of economic growth.

2.2.2 General Policy Implications

The above considerations indicate that current economic circumstances pose very real difficulties for macro-economic policy setting. The balance of payments constraint means that in the short-term, domestic demand, output and employment can only be permitted to grow at a rate consistent with an improvement in the external debt-servicing capacity of the economy. The parameters under which the economy is currently operating suggest that if the debt situation is to be stabilised in the short-term, growth in Australia needs to be moderated and certainly held below the growth of our trading partners. This implies the need for a moderately restrictive macro-economic policy aimed at containing domestic demand. *It should be emphasised, however, that such a restrictive policy cannot be regarded as a solution to the problem, but rather as an acquiescence to it.* The main focus of macro-economic policy should be on enhancing industry restructuring, thereby strengthening the tradeables sector, with the ultimate purpose of easing the external constraint. In the absence of appropriate structural adjustment to relieve the external constraint, the Australian economy will be locked into lower rates of growth, attendant higher levels of unemployment, lower living standards and 'stop-go' policies. Hence the success of structural adjustment policies will determine the degree to which macro-economic policy restraint is necessary.

The adoption of a tight macro-economic policy in order to restrain domestic demand in the short-run, while implementing medium to long-term structural adjustment strategies, provides something of a dilemma for policy making. Structural adjustment will involve an expansion in the productive capacity of the tradeables sector of the economy, an expansion which is likely to be inhibited by weaker aggregate demand resulting from austerity measures. This dilemma is further heightened by the need for infrastructure development, much of which is the province of the public sector, to accommodate industry restructuring. Reductions in public expenditure, particularly public investment which provides an important contribution to industry restructuring, would be counterproductive in this regard.

All this suggests that macro-economic policy should concentrate on altering the composition of public and private expenditure (both investment and consumption) in the economy. Consistent with the external constraint on aggregate demand growth, the required growth in net exports (and derivatively, net investment) requires some mix of restraint in the growth of public and private consumption demand. Furthermore, a wider than customary range of policy instruments to facilitate restructuring is desirable. This type of policy would involve a more planning-orientated approach in the pursuit of strategic economic objectives and a more proactive role by the public sector in achieving these objectives.

2.2.3 Policy Response of the Federal Government

The platform on which the Federal Government's economic strategy has been built is the Prices and Incomes Accord with the trade union movement. It has served as an important vehicle for ongoing consultation and cooperation through which common agreement could be reached as to the nature and extent of the economic problems facing the country and by which the government could formulate its policy response. Through the Accord the Federal Government has been able to strike wage agreements with the ACTU which have

significantly minimised the damage which could otherwise have been inflicted on the economy and living standards by the severe deterioration of Australia's TOT and external account. These agreements have mainly consisted of the trade union movement delivering wage restraint in return for government concessions in aspects of its policy. Policy concessions have mainly related to social wage provisions, industry restructuring, and tax relief. With regard to the social wage, the Federal Government, with the cooperation of the trade union movement, has made important progress in dealing with adverse social effects arising from the balance of payments problem. Nevertheless, there remains serious doubts about the appropriateness of the Federal Government's economic strategy in enhancing structural adjustment.

The Federal Government's policy response to the external problem has basically consisted of a three-pronged strategy. First, to improve international cost competitiveness by obtaining wage restraint and real wage reductions through negotiation with the ACTU under the Accord. This has been especially important in containing inflationary pressures in the economy. Wage restraint was vital in ensuring that the sharp depreciation of the exchange rate (measured by the Trade Weighted Index rather than comparing single currency values) translated into a sustainable improvement in the international competitiveness of the tradeables sector. Along with other structural measures discussed below, the government has placed considerable faith in the effectiveness of this currency depreciation to bring about a swift adjustment in the trade account. The second prong is a longer-term strategy to encourage structural adjustment. The strategy aims to bring greater flexibility to markets so as to strengthen the economy's ability to respond to changing economic conditions (especially external conditions). It has consisted of a variety of measures – mainly deregulatory measures – designed to increase market competitiveness so as to improve the economy's ability to efficiently utilise resources. The major deregulatory measures have been applied to the financial sector, including a progressive lifting of controls on interest rates, the licensing of sixteen new (foreign) banks and the floating of the exchange rate. There has also been a liberalisation of foreign investment policy and impending moves to deregulate the road transport, airline and shipping industries as well as the grain industry.

As far as industry policy goes the Federal Government has shown a distinct reluctance to adopt interventionist measures, relying instead on the operation of market forces. Nevertheless, industry plans have been formulated for heavy engineering, motor vehicle manufacturing, ship building, steel and the textile, clothing and footwear industries. These plans are directly related to various tripartite agreements between the industry unions, employers and government, usually entailing major changes to work-practices, an undertaking by employers to engage in an investment program to improve the competitiveness of the industry, a reduction in tariff protection and the provision of financial assistance by the government to retrain workers over the transition period. Under the Accord the union movement have also moved towards award restructuring within the centralised wage system. While these measures have represented an important step in the process of industry restructuring, they suffer to a great extent from a lack of

planned coordination between industries, especially with respect to investment.

Despite the considerable importance of the above measures for enhancing Australia's cost competitiveness, productivity growth in the economy has remained low and the deterioration of the balance of payments has not as yet been adequately corrected. This has caused the government to turn the focus of its strategy toward restraining domestic demand by the adoption of restrictive fiscal and monetary policies.

The government's fiscal austerity program has been directed toward reducing Federal expenditures in order to produce a budget surplus with the ultimate purpose of drastically cutting the Public Sector Borrowing Requirement (PSBR: the PSBR measures total public sector borrowings necessary to finance all public sector activities including the borrowings by fully commercial public enterprises). Table 2.4 shows the extent to which the government has successfully turned around the budget deficit and reduced the PSBR in recent years. Its obsession with cutting the PSBR seems to be based on the rather misguided notion that a twin-deficit relationship holds between the current account deficit and the public sector deficit (See Section 2.2.4 below).

Table 2.4

Federal Budget and the PSBR

	1983/84	1984/85	1985/86	1986/87	1987/88	1988/89[a]
Federal Outlay ($m)	56962	64319	70429	75491	78764	82013
% of GDP	29.8	30.4	29.8	29.0	26.9	n/a
Federal Revenues						
($m)	48976	57617	64792	72846	80806	87481
% of GDP	25.7	27.2	27.4	28.0	27.6	n/a
Budget Deficit/						
Surplus ($m)	-7986	-6702	-5637	-2645	2042	5468
% of GDP	-4.2	-3.2	-2.4	-1.0	-0.7	n/a
PSBR as a % of GDP	8.1	7.0	5.9	4.0	1.5	0.6

Note: (a) Budget estimates.
Source: Budget Statement, Statement No. 1, 1988/89.

In part the government's success in attaining a budget surplus has been due to fairly strong growth in Federal revenues attributable to the tax reform package introduced in 1985, which

widened the tax base, and the strong growth in national income. The reduction of Federal outlays has been considerable, consisting of reductions in its own-purpose expenditures and also

Federal financial assistance to the States. Large reductions have been imposed on financial assistance to the States aimed at procuring cutbacks in public expenditures by the State Governments (See Section 2.2.2 below). In addition to this fiscal austerity policy, the Federal Government has more recently adopted a high interest rate monetary policy in order to further dampen what it regards as stubbornly high domestic demand in the economy. The Federal Government's policy response to the external problem has been increasingly dominated by a strategy of macroeconomic austerity. Even the wage-tax trade-offs announced in the April 1989 economic package implies a continued policy of fiscal contraction that will ultimately lead to a relatively smaller Australian public sector.

2.2.4 The 'Twin-Deficits' Hypothesis — An Inadequate Basis for Policy Formulation

The argument most often used by policy makers for contractionary fiscal policy in the context of Australia's current economic circumstances is the twin deficits hypothesis (TDH). Essentially the TDH consists of the proposition that a fiscal deficit (and thereby higher public debt) in an open economy induces a corresponding one-for-one deficit on the current account on the balance of payments (and thereby higher foreign debt) as available domestic savings are utilised by the private sector. The policy conclusion which follows from an acceptance of this proposition is clear: an improvement in Australia's current account performance can only be achieved by a reduction in the government's fiscal deficit.

The TDH has been derived by its proponents from a simplistic National Accounting Identity which links the current account deficit (CAD) to the PSBR. This identity states that over any given time period the level of private investment (I) must, by definition, be identically equal to the level of saving drawn from private households (S), the public sector (PSBR) and overseas sources (CAD). Put another way, the current account deficit (which is itself identically equal to net capital inflow) is equal to the PSBR plus the excess of domestic saving over investment, expressed symbolically as:

$$(1) \; CAD = PSBR * (S - I)$$

On the basis of this identity it is argued that, all other things remaining constant, an increase in the PSBR arising from a fiscal deficit will bring about an accompanying identical increase in the CAD. According to the hypothesis an expansionary fiscal policy which reduces government saving will, other things remaining constant, reduce the flow of saving from which to finance private investment such that the shortfall will be met from overseas savings through a a widening CAD. It is evident from identity (1), however, that a close twin-deficits relationship is heavily dependent on the assumption that the level of saving net of investment remains constant. As Kearney (1988) has shown, such an assumption is far from realistic: saving and investment as a proportion of Australia's GDP vary considerably over time and in relation to the CAD and PSBR. This means that within the logic of identity (1) it is quite possible for the PSBR to move into surplus but for the CAD to simultaneously worsen because, for example, the level of private household savings has declined (consumption may have increased) or the level of private investment has increased. The problem is that the TDH fails to take full account of the behavioural relation between the economic variables involved. This undermines the whole argument of its proponents for a reduction in the PSBR (rise in public savings) in order to improve the CAD and reduce Australia's reliance on foreign savings (borrowings).

The PSBR will be determined by the excess of capital and recurrent outlays over recurrent revenues. It is possible to reduce the PSBR either by cutting recurrent outlays, cutting capital outlays, or by increasing recurrent revenues. The reduction of public capital outlays in order to generate public sector savings would make little economic sense. It would imply a reduction in the level of outlays on the construction and maintenance of public infrastructure such as roads, bridges, hospitals etc. A well-maintained and extensive public infrastructure is absolutely essential to private sector investment; roads and bridges, for example, lower the costs of producing and distributing private sector goods and services.

The deterioration of Australia's public infrastructure can only impede private sector capital formation. The reduction of public sector recurrent outlays as a means of reducing the PSBR may also be problematic. This is because a reduction in government outlays may produce a 'crowding in' effect, in which a decline in public sector consumption is matched (or even possibly exceeded) by an increase in private consumption; corresponding to a reduction in private savings that offsets the rise in public sector savings. Thus a reduction in public expenditures on, say, health and education may be matched or even exceeded by an increase in private consumption in the form of private education expenses and private health insurance. The CAD would therefore remain unchanged.

The above discussion illustrates the serious weakness of the TDH, or any other economic proposition for that matter, which is postulated in terms of a highly simplified national accounting framework. To have any validity such a proposition must be postulated by a cogent set of behavioural equations systematically linking the economic variables, which in the case of the TDH would need to establish a systematic causal relationship running from the PSBR to the CAD. This is precisely what has been missing in the arguments of those who have actively propagated the TDH. In an endeavour to give justification to a 'small government' ideology they have ignored economic facts and failed to apply satisfactory economic reasoning in pursuit of self-servicing propositions.

Within mainstream open-economy models (of the usual Fleming-Mundell type) it is possible to generate a twin deficits relationship, but only under extremely special assumptions. Properly articulated in this theoretical framework the TDH is really an extension of the financial crowding out doctrine (Evatt, 1988, pp. 90-93). To explain the TDH in this conventional framework we shall assume that international capital flows are highly mobile in a deregulated financial market integrated with world financial centres and that a flexible exchange rate is in operation. In Australia's case the assumptions are pertinent. Providing that the demand for money is negatively related to

the interest rate and that a neutral monetary policy is in place, a growing public sector deficit (combined Federal and State deficits which cause an expansion in the PSBR) will raise interest rates relative to rates prevailing overseas. After accounting for relative currency-designated asset risks and exchange rate expectations, this make overseas borrowing and foreign investment in Australian financial assets attractive. This induces large foreign borrowing (net capital inflows) which drives the exchange rate upwards. The resulting loss of competitiveness to the import competing and export sectors of the economy from the currency appreciation worsens the CAD. In this open-economy case of financial crowding out, a debt-financed fiscal expansion encourages the private sector to access relatively cheaper overseas sources of capital funding. The strong form TDH holds that the stimulatory effect of a fiscal expansion on output and employment will be completely transmitted abroad as the CAD 'twins' the PSBR. Such a close 'twin relationship', however, is dependent on a number of highly unrealistic assumptions; most particularly, that different currency-designated assets are perfectly substitutable, investment is highly sensitive to interest rates, international capital flows are highly insensitive to trade performance, that there is a high price elasticity (of demand and supply, ie, high responsiveness of exports and imports to exchange rate movements) of imports and exports and that there is full employment of resources in the economy. To paraphrase Argy (1979) since '. . . .none of these extreme assumptions is at all likely to hold . . .' it can be concluded that the TDH '. . . is of only academic interest' (also see Kearney, 1988, pp. 31-3). In summary even in conventional economics the TDH is no more than a remote special case (Genberg, 1989).

The fallacy of the TDH essentially lies in the underlying proposition about the determination of national income and saving. It entails the mistaken notion that public expenditures utilise a given amount of national savings (resources) at the expense of the private sector which must then resort to overseas savings. In other words, it is supposed that there is a shortage of domestic saving available to the private sector which hence must supplement it through foreign borrowings. This relation makes little economic sense. By definition the CAD (the net demand for foreign currency) must be equal (under a flexible exchange rate) to net capital inflows (the net supply of foreign currency); the latter broadly consisting of net foreign currency borrowings and foreign investment in Australian equity and other securities. (Whereas net capital inflows in the 1960s and 70s largely consisted of equity investments, following financial deregulation in the 1980s there was a considerable shift toward foreign borrowing.) While there are significant economic differences between these two forms of capital inflow, they nevertheless represent an augmentation to net foreign liabilities. To regard net capital inflows as net foreign saving is economically meaningless because it depends entirely on the level of CAD (which it necessarily finances) and can only be reduced with a reduction in the CAD.

In the standard Keynesian theory of income determination, domestic saving (given the propensity to save) is a function of national income. Domestic saving (public and private) can only be increased (other than by an autonomous change in the propensity to save by the community) by an increase in the level of national income. Should this be accompanied by higher import demand then it is likely to lead to increased foreign borrowing to finance the widening CAD. Contrary to the TDH, a widening CAD is quite compatible with an increase in national income and saving as well as consumption and investment. In fact, the only economic logic in advocating a reduction in the PSBR through public spending cuts, with the aim of reducing Australia's foreign debt reliance, is that it will contract the level of domestic demand and thereby import demand of the economy and so improve the CAD.

In as much as public sector expansion raises national income (and saving) it may conflict with external objectives. This is the balance of payments constraint outlined earlier, derived from a Keynesian causation in accordance with the principle of effective demand.

It is precisely because the TDH wrongly specifies the nature of the external constraint operating on the Australian economy (particularly with respect to the

public sector) that it cannot in any way form the basis for appropriate policy formulation. Some further comments on the TDH are warranted in this regard.

It is very likely that maintenance of high rates of interest relative to overseas rates could encourage large capital inflows with counterproductive effects on the external account. The TDH, however, supposes that a debt-financed fiscal expansion is the root cause of higher rates of interest. This is an empirical issue on which there is no firm conclusion (See Evatt, 1988, pp. 93-6 and 105-6). Studies carried out over a wide range of OECD countries have found no strong correlation between the size of public debt and interest rate levels (see Neville, 1983; Buiter, 1986; Dwyer, 1985). A more important determinant of interest rate levels is monetary policy which has a large impact on the ability of financial institutions to mediate between assets and liabilities in the absorption of newly issued government debt. With respect to Australia, Neville (as cited in Evatt, 1988, p. 87) has correctly concluded:

'While there are various channels through which large deficits can put upward pressure on interest rates my judgement is that in practical terms these are unimportant in Australia. This is certainly in accord with past experience. In the short run the major influence on interest rates in. Australia is monetary policy and the rate of growth in the money supply. In the longer run, unless there is a change in the long-term prospects for the Australian dollar exchange rate, changes in Australian interest rates are largely determined by changes in overseas rates, especially those in the USA . . .'

Given that no systematic connection can be made between rising public debt and high interest rates the TDH again loses much of its force. And yet, as the US experience of the early 1980s illustrates, a massive deficit-financed fiscal expansion which gives considerable impetus to domestic demand (and hence import demand) in combination with an unnecessarily tight monetary policy may induce large foreign capital inflows which causes external imbalance. The main causal factor in this case (which proponents of the TDH look upon as the classic example of its proposition in operation) was not a high level of public debt *per se* (when State surpluses are balanced against the massive Federal deficit, US public debt is more moderate than often perceived) but the adoption by the monetary authorities of a high interest rate policy which attracted large capital inflows (to a reserve currency) and so irresponsibly allowed the US dollar to soar to levels incompatible with the nation's fundamental trading strength (Bhaduri, 1986, pp. 150-166). This if anything was the lasting legacy of monetarism, US-style, put into practice. The adoption of such a restrictive monetary policy by the authorities of any country would conceivably produce this result even in the absence of public sector deficits of any significance.

The TDH ought to be rejected on economic logic. This is confirmed by empirical evidence indicating that there is at best only a weak correlation between fiscal deficits and current account deficits among OECD countries (Kearney and Fallick, 1987; *Economist*, 5th December, 1987). The point is that severe balance of payments problems are not systematically related to, and can not be explained by, the size of an economy's public debt. No robust causal relationship can be identified in this regard. Policy makers can therefore not use the TDH as a valid justification for reducing the size of Australia's public sector which, by OECD standards, is relatively small.

2.2.5 An Alternative Policy Approach
There is universal agreement that the imperative of macro-economic policy is to provide the economic environment in which large-scale industry restructuring can occur — so leading to a stronger tradeables sector and a sustained improvement in Australia's trade performance. It cannot be overemphasised that, without an alleviation of the external pressures now operating on the Australian economy, we are destined to experience a continuous decline in living standards and depressed employment growth. But an appropriate economic strategy can only be devised with a clear understanding of the constraints which the external imbalance places on macro-economic policy options.

In the first place, monetary policy tends to be locked into maintaining high interest rates (relative to overseas rates) to both dampen domestic demand, finance the ongoing CAD and (by attracting inflows of capital) to protect the exchange rate from excessive instability. Persistently high interest rates inhibit public debt growth because of the constraints which higher debt-servicing costs place on own-expenditure choices. This implies a greater shift toward recurrent revenues to finance public capital expenditures. And yet with economic circumstances pressing down on real incomes, it is difficult in practical terms to increase revenues via a higher tax burden. Second, there is a constraint on public expenditures that would adversely increase import expenditures via higher domestic demand. This means that public expenditures in areas which do not significantly contribute (directly or indirectly) to industry restructuring or the maintenance of the social wage ought to be given low priority.

Even in the context of these real limitations, the fiscal austerity policy that the Federal Government has engaged in over the past few years can not be regarded as anything other than an acquiescence to the external problem. The strategic emphasis on drastically reducing the PSBR via a contractionary fiscal policy is a negative policy approach to the macro-economic problems. *The notion that slashing the PSBR will encourage the higher investment needed for structural adjustment by making more resources (saving) available to the private sector has already been refuted. Nor is there any economic reasoning to justify a downgrading of the role of the public sector in the restructuring process. On the contrary, as Neville (1987) has argued with respect to the need for greater public capital formation, the public sector should play a more proactive role in any economic strategy for restructuring Australian industry.*

A more creative macro-economic policy is required. The main focus of fiscal policy should be turned to altering the composition of public expenditures to serve two complementary goals. The first and most important is to encourage an alteration in the pattern of economic demands, most particularly the sectoral composition of investment (public and private), which would enhance the necessary structural adjustment in the economy. In this regard, an indicative planning approach is required in order to coordinate investment so as to ensure that it flows into industries which strengthen the tradeables sector rather than lead to higher import demands. The greater involvement of the public sector in economic restructuring will entail a more interventionist industry policy to make 'market forces' work favourably in the achievement of the strategic objectives. The second is to ensure that the burden of income restraint is spread equitably throughout the economy.

The tripartism between the Federal Government, ACTU and employers under the Accord provides a model for the development of such a policy approach. The Accord, in fact, laid the groundwork for the tripartite economic strategy and its successes in bringing about fundamental changes in industry policy.

2.3 The Implications of Macro-Economic Policy for State Public Financing

The purpose of this Section is to examine the manner in, and extent to which, the Federal Government's macro-economic policy has influenced State public sector financing. A simple framework of analysis is presented to show the mechanisms through which fiscal austerity implemented by the Federal Government can constrain State finances (Sec. 2.3.1.), followed by an examination of the trend in Federal financial assistance to the States and borrowings by the States as constrained by the Federal Government through the Loan Council (Sec. 2.3.2.). The conclusion advances an alternative approach for the Commonwealth in its financial dealings with the States consistent with the kind of macro-economic difficulties outlined in Section 2.2.3.

2.3.1 Framework of Analysis: The Case of Fiscal Austerity

By way of approaching the financial implications for the States of macro-economic policy, we shall make use of some accounting identities which illustrate, in a simple way, the financial connection between the States and the Federal Government. The nature of this connection under Australia's Federal system (since 1942) is clearly one of State financial

dependence on the Federal Government. About 44% of the States' recurrent revenue depends on Federal Government financial assistance grants. It is mainly through its impact on the size of these assistance grants (or net payments to the States) that the Federal Government's fiscal policy affects the financial position of the States. Additionally, the Federal Government can significantly influence the borrowing capacity of the States through its quite considerable control over public authority borrowings via the Loan Council. These are the two main financial mechanisms by which the Federal Government can affect the States' budgetary position in Australian Fiscal Federalism.

Defining the budgetary time period as one year the Federal Government budget identity can be given as follows: recurrent revenues (CR) less total expenditures will be identically equal to the Federal budget balance (CB) which must in turn be financed by public debt borrowing (and/or money creation). Total Federal Government expenditures divide between own-purpose expenditures (CE) and net payments to the States (SP). It should be noted that Federal Government revenues will greatly exceed its own-purpose expenditures, that is, $CR > CE$. This identity can be given symbolic form as:

$$(1)\ CR - (CE + SP) = CB$$

and rearranging,

$$(2)\ CR - CB = CE + SP$$

where identity (2) indicates that Federal Government revenue, less the budget balance (deficit–/surplus +), must be equal to Federal Government own-purpose expenditures plus net payments to the States.

Consider the basic budgetary framework at the State level: total expenditures (SE) must be equal to recurrent revenues plus State borrowings (plus net asset sales) (SB); with recurrent revenues consisting of State net payments (SP) and internal sources of State tax and commercially related revenues (SR). This identity can be stated symbolically as:

$$(3)\ SE = (SP + SR) + SB$$

In identity (3), net payments to the States and State borrowings (strictly only borrowings of State authorities) are assumed to be determined exogenously – outside the State's budgetary decision-making framework. For the reasons discussed earlier, the size of net payments to the States depends on Federal Government budgetary policy. While net payments to the States appear as an expenditure component of the Federal Government budget as expressed in identities (1) and (2), it is a revenue source to the State's budget expressed as a parameter in identity (3). Similarly, State borrowings (ie net new money borrowings required to finance the State deficit) are subject to global limits which for all intents and purposes are determined by the Federal Government through the Loan Council.

This budgetary framework provides a simple conceptual basis for analysing the financial implications for the States of the adoption of fiscal austerity by the Federal Government, whose major objective is to reduce the size of the public sector borrowing requirement (PSBR). (See Section 2.2.3 above.)

Under Australian fiscal Federalism, to reduce the level of national public debt, the Federal Government could adopt two austerity measures. The first is to obtain an increased (decreased) Federal budget surplus (deficit) which requires that the Federal Government increase revenues net of expenditures. Because an austerity policy is designed to contain the size of the Federal budget this would be achieved by expenditure restraint in relation to revenue growth. This can be achieved by a mix of tax increases (as a proportion of GDP) and/or expenditure reduction (again, percentage of GDP). In fact, the burden is largely being borne by expenditure restraint. Expenditure reduction may entail reductions in both Federal Government own-purpose expenditures and net payments to the States. Given Federal Government revenues, achieving its fiscal objective of a Federal budget surplus (or a lower deficit), the government can determine how the expenditure reductions are to be proportionately distributed between its own-purpose expenditures and net payments to the States. For instance, the Federal Government could shift the greater part of the burden of austerity on to the States by obtaining greater proportional reductions in net payments to the States than in its

own-purpose expenditure, measured by the change in the relative proportions of net State payments and own-purpose expenditures to the level of Federal Government revenues. This decision obviously has an important bearing on the relative severity of the financial restraint imposed on the States. The second austerity measure consists of the Federal Government attaining a reduction in the level of new borrowings by the non-budget sectors at the Federal and State levels via a lowering of global limits under the authority of the Loan Council. In view of the fact that a large proportion of the PSBR consists of State public sector borrowings, this financial measure is necessary in order to achieve an effective reduction in the total size of the PSBR.

The simultaneous application of both of the above austerity measures by the Federal Government will clearly place significant constraints upon State finances. A reduction in the level of Federal grants assistance and the amount of borrowings which the State public authorities can undertake leaves the States with one of two options: either to raise their internal sources of recurrent revenues or apply a reduction in their own expenditures. Political factors and the practicalities of Australian Federalism present a considerable barrier to pursuing the first option which consists of raising State taxes and charges (and/or expanding the State tax bases and range of charges on State traded goods and services; though the conservative government in New South Wales has responded to Federal reductions in net payments to the States in just this manner) (See Part Four for a more detailed account). The adoption of an austerity program by the Federal Government as described will therefore inevitably lead to reductions in State expenditures; and in particular, the lowering of State borrowing capacity will have an adverse impact on capital expenditures and thereby State public sector capital formation.

A further Federal policy stance which can influence States' budgetary situation is monetary policy. Should the Federal Government accompany its tight fiscal stance with a tight monetary policy (in a period of deregulated financial controls) producing high rates of interest, then the latter can also constrain own-purpose expenditures, especially capital expenditures of the States as well as the Federal Government, because of the consequent increase in debt-servicing costs on outstanding debt. This monetary policy effect should not be underrated.

The scenario we have analysed is an accurate characterisation of the impact on State finances of the austerity program which the Federal Government has undertaken in the past few years as a key part of its strategy to tackle Australia's external imbalances. *There is no doubt that the financial imposition placed on the States by the Federal Government has been intended to restrain the expenditure capacity of the States and achieve the Federal Government's primary objective of reducing the size of the PSBR.*

2.3.2 Federal Financial Assistance

Financial assistance provided by the Federal Government to the States consists of general purpose grants (which currently represent 55% of total payments) and specific purpose grants. The latter are designed to financially assist States in the provision of specified services and are granted on conditional terms. No significant change has occurred in the composition of these two types of grants over recent years.

There has been a marked reduction in the growth of total Federal financial assistance to the States. Between 1983/84 and 1987/88 the annual growth in net payments to the States decelerated markedly in nominal terms from around 14% to 3%. Confirming the continuation of this trend, and as a result of decisions made by the Federal Government at the May 1988 Premiers' Conference, net payments to the States will be increased by only 1.1% in 1988/89, representing a significant reduction in real terms. This compares with the deceleration in the Federal Government's own-purpose expenditures from around 17% in 1983/84 to an estimated 5.7% in 1988/89.

In terms of the Federal Government's fiscal austerity program, this trend belies the greater burden of Federal Government expenditure reductions being borne by the States. Although the Federal Government has applied restraint to its own-purpose expenditures, reducing them as a proportion of GDP by over 9% between 1983/84 and 1987/88, net payments to the States as a proportion of GDP has declined by 18% during this period. This development is further supported by the fact that net payments to the States as a percentage of Federal Government revenues has declined from about

Table 2.5

Federal Budget
Outlays for Own-Purpose & Assistance to
the States & the Northern Territory

	1983/84	1984/85	1985/86	1986/87	1987/88	1988/89[a]
Federal Revenues ($m)	48976	57617	64792	72486	80806	87481
Annual % Change	9.4	17.6	12.5	11.9	11.5	8.3
Federal Own-purpose						
Expenditures ($m)	36197	41706	46390	50048	52564	55537
Annual % Change	16.9	15.2	11.2	7.9	5.0	5.7
Net Payments to the						
States & NT ($m)	19078	20757	22048	23369	24092	24352
Annual % Change	14.2	8.8	6.2	6.0	3.1	1.1
Net Payments to the						
States as a % of GDP	10.0	9.8	9.3	9.0	8.2	n.a
Net Payments to the						
States as a % of Federal						
Revenues	38.9	36.0	34.0	32.2	29.8	27.8

Note: (a) Budget Estimate.
Source: Budget Papers Nos. 1 & 4, 1988/89, Budget Paper No. 7, 1985/86.

39% in 1983/84 to about 28% in 1987/88; leaving a greater proportion of Federal Government revenues to finance its own-purpose expenditures. These trends, which are shown in Table 2.5, strongly suggest that the Federal Government has been able to successively lower the budget deficit and then procure a surplus over the past five years in large part through reductions in Federal financial assistance to the States.

General Purpose Grants
Since the May 1985 Premiers' Conference, when the Federal Government abandoned the general tax revenue sharing agreement which had been introduced in 1981 and returned to the system of financial assistance grants, there has been a marked slowdown in the growth of general purpose grants to the States. Between 1984/85 and 1987/88 the annual rate of growth

of general revenue grants in nominal terms decelerated markedly from 6% to a low 2.2%. Average growth over this period was well below the inflation rate. This included a considerable decrease in general purpose capital grants which were halved in nominal terms in 1987/88. At the May 1988 Premiers' Conference it was decided that under new funding arrangements, Federal financial provision for hospital and Medicare services was to be reclassified from general-purpose to specific-purpose grants assistance to the States. This explains the nominal decrease of 12.1% in 1988/89. After excluding these health grants from figures in both years, general purpose grants are estimated to increase in nominal terms in 1988/89 but to decline by 5.5% in real terms. These trends are clearly illustrated in Table 2.6.

Table 2.6

General Revenue Assistance to the States

	1984/85	*1985/86*	*1986/87*	*1987/88*	*1988/89*[a]
General Revenue Grants ($m)	10974	11914	13216	14248	12451
Annual % Change	5.9	8.6	10.9	7.8	-12.6
General Purpose Capital Grants ($m)	1702	1736	1336	621	621
Annual % Change	6.4	2.0	-23.0	-54.0	0
Total General Purpose Grants ($m)	12676	13649	14552	14869	13072
Annual % Change	6.0	7.7	6.6	2.2	-12.1

Note: (a) Federal Government Budget Estimate.
Source: Budget Paper No. 4, 1988/89.

Specific Purpose Grants. Table 2.7 below shows that specific purpose grants have mirrored the trend in general purpose grants over the past few years. Between 1984/85 and 1987/88 they grew at an annual average rate of 6.5%, representing a decline in real terms, with specific capital grants experiencing a severe real decline. Due to compensation for an elimination of general revenue assistance for hospital funding, specific purpose grants are estimated to rise markedly in 1988/89. When this hospital funding component is excluded from the 1988/89 figures, there is a significant reduction in real terms.

Loan Council Borrowing and State Deficit Financing
State Public Authority borrowing represents an important source of funding State capital expenditures in the provision of economic infrastructure. Over the past five years the Federal Government has exercised its considerable power over State (and Local) Government borrowing via the Loan Council to drastically reduce new borrowings (equivalent to State/Local sector gross PSBR) by public authorities. As a proportion of GDP, State/Local sector borrowings, as approved under the Loan Council global approach, has fallen

from 3.5% in 1983/84 to 1.9% in 1987/88; and is estimated to decline further to 1.5% in 1988/89.

A further aspect of the financial squeeze being placed on the States is that there has been a marked reduction in Federal Government net advances in the form of general-purpose and specific-purpose capital advances to effectively

meet the States' public sector deficit (basically consisting of net borrowing for capital expenditures). This reflects a dramatic reduction in the State Government Loan Council Borrowing Program over recent years. To emphasise this point, in 1987/88, net advances actually augmented the States' deficit.

Table 2.7
Specific Purpose Capital Grants

	1984/85	1985/86	1986/87	1987/88	1988/89[a]
Recurrent Grants ($m)	5447	5750	6027	6393	8560
Annual % Change	18.3	5.6	4.8	6.1	33.9
Capital Grants ($m)	2633	2649	2791	2830	2721
Annual % Change	3.0	0.6	5.4	1.4	-3.9
Specific Purpose Grants ($m)	8080	8399	8818	9223	11281
Annual % Change	12.8	3.9	5.0	4.6	22.3

Note: (a) Budget Estimate.
Source: Budget Paper No. 4, 1988/89.

As a result of these borrowing constraints imposed by the Federal Government, the States are coming under increasing pressure to reduce their budget deficits either through outright reductions in capital outlays or by increasingly financing them out of recurrent revenues. There is already evidence to suggest that States are cutting back on their capital programs; with State sector capital outlays as a proportion of GDP having declined from 6.1% in 1982/83 to 4.8% in 1987/88. Given that the States are responsible for over 60% of total public sector capital expenditures this trend portends a marked rundown in Australia's public capital formation. Table 2.8 illustrates the significant Federal Government-imposed reductions on State borrowings and the corresponding decline in State sector capital outlays.

2.4 Conclusion
The evidence of recent years strongly indicates that the fiscal austerity program undertaken by the Federal Government has placed a great financial burden on the States. Indeed, the Federal Government's ability to procure a Federal budget surplus and thereby drastically reduce the Federal Government sector PSBR has in large part come from reductions in revenue assistance to the States.

With the large reduction in Federal Govern-

ment revenue assistance, together with the severe restrictions imposed on its global borrowings by the Loan Council, the States are coming under increased pressure to develop new revenue sources in order to meet their usual expenditure commitments (See Part Four). In the absence of significant progress in expanding their own revenue base, the Federal Government's austerity program will ultimately force the States to considerably reduce their expenditures and thereby cut back on public services. *In view of the fact that the States are responsible for delivering the vast majority of public goods and service in Australia, and more importantly still, for generating over 60% of public capital formation, this scenario has significant adverse macro-economic implications not only in terms of domestic output growth but more specifically in terms of facilitating industry restructuring necessary to strengthen the economy's tradeables sector. This should serve as a warning to any Federal Government which too heavily places the burden of austerity onto the States.*

A further aspect of concern with the Federal Government's macro-economic policy is that it will lead to unnecessary budgetary restraint, by the States as well as the Federal Government, because of its strategic emphasis on reducing the PSBR. As noted above, the PSBR measures total public sector borrowings neces-

Table 2.8

State/Local Sector Deficit & its Financing ($m)

	1983/84	1984/85	1985/86	1986/87	1987/88	1987/88[(a)]
State Deficit	5104	4408	5459	5890	3224	n.a
Net Advances from the Federal Government	996	791	786	546	-44	n.a
Net PSBR	4108	3617	4673	5344	3268	n.a
Gross PSBR*	6603	7067	7041	6395	5522	4845
Gross PSBR as % of GDP	3.5	3.3	3.0	2.5	1.9	1.5
State Capital Outlays as % of GDP	6.1	5.6	5.7	5.5	4.8	n/a

Notes: (a) Federal Government Budget Estimates.

* Gross PSBR is equivalent to 'Global' New Money Borrowing approved by the Loan Council. The conceptual difference between the gross and net PSBR (for State/Local sector) is the treatment of changes in the holding of financial assets which are reflected in the net PSBR. This means that when gross PSBR exceeds net PSBR for any given year, the State authorities have undertaken more new borrowings than were required to finance their outstanding deficits, such that they have potential loan funds at their disposal in the form of financial assets for future utilisation. (See Budget Paper No. 1, 1988/89, pp. 395-7.)

Source: Budget Paper No. 4, 1988/89.

sary to finance all public sector activities including the borrowings by fully commercial public enterprises. Cutting the PSBR will therefore place considerable financial constraints on these Federal and State public enterprises, hampering their commercial operations and effectively reducing the budgetary revenues generated by these enterprises. As was pointed out in Evatt (1988), it is difficult to find a budgetary rationale for subjecting these self-financing enterprises to the borrowing constraints appropriate to debt management for general (non-commercial) government borrowing. The counterpart to this is the removal of Loan Council controls over the borrowings of public enterprises who can service their debt entirely through commercially generated income and therefore without any financial recourse to the general government budget. For the purposes of macro-economic policy the Federal Government has a legitimate need to control State sector debt that is serviced out of State budgetary expenditures. However, there is no logical reason why fully commercial State public enterprises (as well as commercial Federal public enterprises) such as the State Bank of Victoria and the New South Wales Government Insurance Office, which operate in close

competition with private sector firms and have clearly demonstrated their capacity to self-finance their debt should have their borrowings subject to Loan Council control any more than regulatory controls should be placed on private sector debt (See Part Four).

The Federal Government's policy of fiscal austerity is leading to a smaller Australian public sector which will ultimately be economically counter-productive. In Section 2.2 a more positive policy approach with respect to the role of the Australian public sector was suggested. *This macro-economic strategy, built on the existing co-operative arrangements with the Trade Union movement under the Accord, would involve the Federal Government developing a selective expenditure strategy, especially with respect to public investment, in order to assist the process of restructuring the Australian economy. In this regard, public expenditures which would materially facilitate industry restructuring ought to be given priority. They should certainly not be reduced.* Given that the States have primary responsibility in Australia for the development of economic infrastructure which could significantly assist this process, their role is very important. In its financial dealings with the States, the Federal Government would be better served by placing emphasis on influencing the composition of State expenditures instead of simply procuring expenditure restraint from the States. The need to coordinate State public capital expenditures, at least in an indicative way, is as strategically important for a macro-economic policy designed to enhance structural adjustment as that of private investment. There is nothing revolutionary about this notion. Indeed, *central governments in the most successful post-war industrial economies such as Japan, Sweden and West Germany have adopted a similar approach whereby public expenditures are used to support industry development designed to strengthen the tradeables sector of the economy.* In Australia this will require a close liaison between macro-economic policy, industry policy, and the composition of public expenditures by the Federal and State Governments. Under Australian fiscal federalism, the Federal Government could impose its expenditure priorities on the States through existing mechanisms — through the greater use of specific-purpose grants and through the rehabilitation of the State Government Loan Council Borrowing Program in order to coordinate State development projects. Notwithstanding the practical problems, largely associated with divergent political interests, a more cooperative arrangement between the Federal Government and the States along these lines would have the benefit of focussing the States' activities more on national economic objectives.

Part Three

MICRO-ECONOMIC REFORM AND STATE PUBLIC SERVICES: PRIVATISATION OR RENEWAL?

Introduction

In his last speech to the English House of Commons, Aneurin Bevan summed up the problem which has beset Western domestic politics and policy formulation for the past two decades:

'. . . the central problem falling upon representative government . . . is how to persuade the people to forgo immediate satisfactions in order to build up the economic resources of the country' (Wilson, 1971, p. 19).

Bevan's portrayal of restraint as central to the politics of domestic government does indeed characterise the 1980s.

It also neatly sums up the major political and economic headache for Australian State Governments. As Part Two has shown, State Governments have become the, most involuntary, purveyors of public financial restraint in Australia. Their access to loans or Federal Government grants has been severely restricted. This has in turn led to unprecedented reliance on State taxes and charges – the most narrow and regressive taxes in Autralia – as a source of revenue.

At the same time as the ability to 'sell restraint' has become a necessary attribute of the 1980s politician, the cry for more and better State public services has grown louder. The demand for quality public housing, child and aged care has far outstripped supply. In other areas of State responsibility, such as the environment and infrastructure, the call is invariably for increased and more efficient public action and services.

Micro-Economic Reform

It is in this context of public fiscal restraint and social and economic demands that strategies of micro-economic reform must be developed.

Chapter Two established that the overwhelming goal of macro-economic strategy in Australia is the direction of resources to the tradeable goods sector. The task of micro-economic reform is to ensure that these resources are utilised in an efficient manner.

In this endeavour the State public sector can make two vital and related contributions. First, increasing public sector outputs from a given set of inputs which is obviously a desirable goal in itself. Second, by making these improvements, the public sector will be able to lower the relative costs of inputs to the trade exposed sector and improve the quality of those inputs. State social services also have an important role in the overall process of socio-economic development through extending and improving the social wage.

In Australia, the States deliver many of the major social and economic public services of direct relevance to the micro-economic reform process and in this respect a number of key questions must be asked:

What are the future demands for State public services and how can they be satisfactorily met? Should funding For State public services be continually restrained across the board? What are the consequences of this? what are the alternatives?

In order to address these questions, Chapter Three outlines some of the general functions and services which are delivered at the State level, together with a selected series of likely future demographic, social and economic demands which will call on State resources. Having outlined these general functions and future demands, Chapter Four examines how State public sectors could be reformed according to a model of public sector renewal. Chapter Five then outlines the problems of privatisation.

Chapter 3

STATE PUBLIC SECTOR FUNCTIONS AND FUTURE DEMANDS

3.1 Introduction

This chapter summarises some of the functions currently undertaken by the State public sectors. This outline is not meant to be exhaustive but it does provide an idea of the relative size and importance of the services of the State public sector.[1] It may come as a surprise to many people just how large the States' role are, particularly in the area of economic services. Indeed, the sheer size and quality of the States' functions makes their continued development important for Australia's future.

This chapter also surveys some of the emerging demands which must be met through the State public sectors. Again, for those unfamiliar with the role of the States, this information may surprise. The States, for example, will have a role to play in meeting the serious infrastructure needs of the Australian economy, and in areas as prosaic as the protection of soil quality. In terms of basic human needs, the States will need to meet demands such as those for child care and the provision of Aboriginal services. Disabled people, too, are becoming more vocal in their demands for social and economic equality and the States will increasingly have a responsibility in this area. The new fields of consumer protection and occupational health and safety will also place greater and greater demands on the States.

For the purposes of analysis, State public functions have been divided into three general categories: economic services and infrastructure, social service functions and administrative services. Each of these is examined in turn.

3.2 State Economic Services and Infrastructure

As Table 3.1 indicates State Governments provide a range of economic services and infrastructure.

Table 3.1

State Economic Services and Infrastructure: A Select List
industry and regional development;
industry training;
electricity generation and distribution;
port development;
railway construction and operation;
road construction and maintenance;
public housing;
water and sewerage services;
professional education;
public buildings;
recreational facilities
agricultural extension services;
insurance;
conservation

Graphs 3.1 and 3.2 show the State and Federal Government expenditure on economic services as real dollar values per capita in every year from 1978/79 to 1986/87. They indicate that State expenditure on economic services exceeds Federal Government expenditure in this area. This underlines the importance of the role of the States as active participants in the process of economic restructuring now underway across the Australian economy. The States deliver the backbone infrastructure for Australia's economic activities.

Graph 3.1

States' Economic Services Expenditure
1979/80 − 1986/7

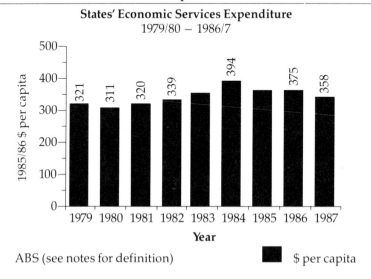

ABS (see notes for definition)　　　　　　　　 ■ $ per capita

Notes: All dollar values converted using 1985/86 Implicit Price Deflator for Non-farm GDP.
Economic services expenditure is defined as expenditure on Agriculture, Forestry, Fishing & Hunting; Mining Manufacturing & Construction; Other Economic Services and Transport & Communications.
Commonwealth and States' expenditure data includes expenditure on New Fixed Assets.
For States, population data does not include the ACT. States' data includes the Northern Territory.
Sources: ABS, State and Local Government Finance Australia, various issues, (ABS 5504.0); *Commonwealth Government Finance Australia,* various issues, (ABS, 5502).

To aid the process of economic restructuring the States must continue to invest in the infrastructure necessary to support industry. As the 1988 National Review of Australia's Infrastructure Expenditure maintained:

'Australia has no option but to look toward significant restructuring of its economy. This can be expected to require increased infrastructure investment, and desirable structural change in the Australian economy will generate a need for significant increases in private investment and a complementary need for public infrastructure investment' (SCTCI, 1987, p. xvii).

The report goes on to note that 'the shortfall in investment in potentially profitable public investment is a greater problem than any shortfall in efficiency' (SCTCI, 1987, p. xx). It further notes that the level of public investment in infrastructure appears to be largely determined by the amount of funds available after recurrent commitments have been met and a deficit target set.

3.2.1 National Priority Setting
National priority setting must play an increasingly important role in determining areas of public infrastructure investment. As for other social and administrative responsibilities,

'States rights' issues have too often thwarted rational national economic development and investment (cf. Wran in Birrell, 1987, p. 140). This report is not the first to note that the Premiers' Conference and Loan Council are inadequate as forums of intergovernmental decision-making in Australia. To remedy this situation the quality of input to both forums should be improved. There is a need for a national body capable of setting and adjudicating national infrastructure priorities. A recommendation for such a national secretariat as an adjunct to the Premiers' Conference and Loan Council is included in the following chapter.

Graph 3.2

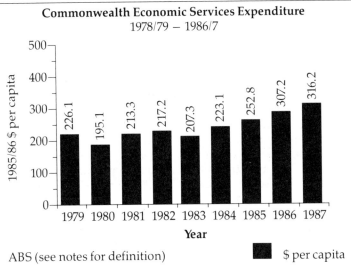

Commonwealth Economic Services Expenditure
1978/79 – 1986/7

ABS (see notes for definition)   ■ $ per capita

See Notes and Sources for Graph 3.1

Potential areas of State infrastructure investment in the future include *urban arterial roads, aspects of the rail network, rural communications, urban sewerage and water supply infrastructure.* These are all areas of State responsibility (APSF, 1987, p. 2). Economic restructuring of Australia's economy also requires changes in Australia's social infrastructure of which education and training services are one part.

The very nature of infrastructure is such that it should be managed and paid for on a long-term basis (SCTCI, 1987, p. 4). Australia's large area and small population makes the public sector the most appropriate developer of infrastructure. However, when these factors are combined with an inappropriate accounting system – one which considers public buildings as outputs rather than assets, for example – the difficulties of adequate planning are exacerbated (SCTCI, 1987, p. 22). The State public sectors should not only give greater attention to infrastructure development, but also to the management techniques utilised in the public sector which can be made more relevant to the task.

3.2.2 State Economic Development and Industry policy

Economic Development and Industry Policy at the State level is of crucial importance to the task of structural adjustment. The Economic Planning Advisory Council has documented the considerable array of industry development programs at the State level (EPAC, 1988, pp. 13-34).

It is widely acknowledged that public sectors also play an important strategic role through objectives such as economic development and securing State and national sovereignty. France has used its public sector to promote industrial development and structural adjustment by means of indicative planning and State entrepreneurship. Often a public sector economic role of this kind is based on the belief that there are key 'commanding heights' of the economy which warrant a domestic presence. For example, in the UK the (now defunct) National Enterprise Board financed and fostered the emergence, during the 1970s, of a domestically-based micro-electronics firm (INMOS), and Japan's MITI was prominent in sponsoring the rise of Japan's computer industry in the period from 1958-1982 (cf. Ouchi, 1987).

The Victorian Economic Development Strategy and the South Australian Financing Authority have also fostered industry initiatives. Public sector agencies often have a longer-term perspective than private enterprise. They can gain access to capital finance for important projects and in many instances public agencies can act as a catalyst for economic growth. While there have been some major setbacks in West Australia and Victoria when government has attempted to play a more direct role in financing industry initiatives, it is clear that the public sector will continue to be a key to the promotion of State economic development. This requires the development of clear guidelines for State strategic initiatives. (On this issue see Chapter Eight's recommendations.)

The States are the main providers of economic services, the key sources of industry training and skills acquisition and important stimulators of economic activity and employment. As Chapter Seven shows the Victorian Government has achieved a great deal in stimulating State manufacturing activity and employment. In the primary commodity-oriented Queensland and Tasmanian economies, the need for concerted industry development policies is paramount, for without them it is clear that industry will be unable to make the transition to a higher value-added production base.

The Victorian experience in the development of an industry development strategy assists in identifying what should be the key features of an industry development strategy. This includes, first, the clear identification of major industry sectors which require development in the economy. *This stands in marked contrast to the Queensland situation, where a report prepared by Stanford Institute (which has not been made public) has been paraphrased by a government intent on*

being seen to do something, but having no overall strategy or institutional framework for achieving anything.

The establishment by the States of Industrial Supplies Offices (ISOs), and their later national co-ordination, further demonstrates what can be achieved by the States in the area of economic restructuring. As they currently operate, the ISOs are designed to ensure that Australian producers of machinery and equipment are given full opportunity to supply to major investment projects. As of 30 September, 1988, six State offices in the ISO network had been successful in achieving 671 'wins' for Australian industry, valued at $238m: '. . . every $1m worth of imports replaced by local production reduced the national trade deficit by $1m, around 30-35 new jobs were generated, accompanied by an increase in consumer spending of around $260,000, a reduction in Commonwealth welfare payments of around $220,000 as well as increased taxation revenue of the order of $250,000' (ISO, Nov. 1988, p. 1).

The expansion of value-added production, however, does not solely depend on the origin and quality of capital utilised by industry. It also fundamentally depends on the quality and commitment of the workforce. One component of this is the provision of life-time skills and training. The States are responsible for skills training at TAFE Colleges, and it is clear that to meet the needs of industry and to complement the goals of award restructuring, reform of – and renewed investment in – the TAFE sector needs to occur (DITR, 1986, p. 49).

In the area of infrastructure development, in areas such as roads, rail, sewerage and water supply, the States play the dominant public sector role. Needed infrastructure investment includes the provision of such basic requirements as the conversion of the Victorian rail (V-Line) network to standard gauge which alone would facilitate economic activity in Eastern Australia (ARU, 1989).

In addition to these traditional areas of economic services expenditure, the emerging demands identified earlier in this chapter will also require considerable commitment from all levels of government. For example, a recent initiative taken under the land degradation program – the establishment of community-based soil conservation projects — has been allocated $45m (*AFR*, 21 April 1988). However, the pecuniary benefits which accrue from such government expenditure may not be identifiable in government revenue statistics, illustrating again the necessity for the selective application of some of the reform initiatives examined elsewhere in this report.

One modern characteristic of industry development involves advanced Research and Development (R&D). The public sector is a large purchaser and user of high technology products, a use which is not limited to Information Technology (IT). As a large user, the public sector should have a significant role in the Research and Development process itself.

For example, the New South Wales Department of Main Roads has licensed Amalgamated Wireless of Australasia Ltd (AWA) to market and install road traffic signalling equipment — developed by the Department of Main Roads — in the Peoples Republic of China. In addition, many New South Wales public enterprises provide assistance to Australian suppliers to develop their new products to a marketable stage, thus enhancing the opportunity for value-added exports.

The sheer cost of technological development makes such cooperation more and more attractive to both public and private users.

The process of micro-economic reform necessary to ensure successful economic restructuring includes skills training; capital modernisation; new forms of organisation, including more participative decision-making structures; the development of marketing expertise; and more responsive and effective management (DIR, MTFU, MTIA, 1988, p. 19). One initiative undertaken to assist in the achievement of these goals — and one where the States have potentially a large role to play — has been the establishment of Workplace Resource Centres by the Federal Government. In Victoria, the costs of the Centre's establishment is being shared equally by the Victorian Government.

These Workplace Resource Centres will provide a range of services (primarily of a consultant type) to enterprises where agreement has been reached between management, the workforce and their trade union representatives on the need for change. It has been decided that

priority will be given to enterprises planning to improve competitiveness and efficiency through the introduction of new awards and new forms of management and work organisation. They will operate as non-profit companies and are expected to be self-financing within three years. They will have tripartite management structures.

One of their more interesting roles will be to act as clearing-houses for information on both State and Federal Government programs covering industrial relations, the labour market, education and training and industry and technology. Centres have so far been established in Sydney, Melbourne and Adelaide, and the industries receiving particular attention are the retail industry; the textiles, clothing and footwear industries; and the motor vehicle industry (DIRD, 1989).

The Victorian Government's attitude and response to this initiative is indicative of the positive response necessary from all States if micro-economic reform is to proceed with employee and union involvement at the workplace level.

As Stretton has noted innovative economic polices are required if Australia is to maintain its currently good record on employment creation (Stretton, 1987, p. 101). Industry policies of the sort described above offer this potential, by ensuring that job creation can proceed in a way which enhances balance of payments stability.

3.2.3 The Environment
Environmental concerns constitute another reason for investment in infrastructure. Indeed, the theme embraces broad economic issues as well as Australia's natural heritage.

A major problem facing all Australian States is land degradation, which occurs through over-use and inappropriate irrigation practices (Russell & Isbell, 1986, p. 299 & p. 350). There are sound economic, as well as environmental reasons, for concern over the extent of the problem. The Federal Minister for Resources gave some indication of the scale of the losses in May 1988:

'. . . land degradation is costing this nation an amount approaching $600m annually just in lost production. To this we would have to add the very considerable, but as yet unquantified, off-site costs of water treatment, harbour dredging, road damage, and so on.

Furthermore the figure does not include the effects of the irreversible losses that have occurred to date or the lost capital, social and environmental values' (Cook, 1988, p. 4).

These monetary estimates to some extent obscure the real extent of the problem. Put in geographical terms, 45% of Australia's non-arid land (mainly agricultural) is sufficiently degraded to require remedial treatment, and 55% of arid land (mainly pastoral) is in the same condition (see Woods, 1984).

The States could play a large role in overcoming this serious economic and environmental problem by appropriate deployment of their departments, authorities and instrumentalities concerned with soil conservation, water resources, agriculture, environment, natural resources, mining, energy and development. In fact, the States are Constitutionally required to deal with such problems (Cook, 1988, p. 5).

Moreover there exists a real need for interstate cooperation, like the Murray-Darling Basin Agreement which, despite its faults, was a major step forward in dealing with the environmental concerns of the Murray-Darling. This was because it signalled '. . . a broadening of concern from simply dealing with water . . .' and represented '. . . an important step forward, certainly when compared with the previous River Murray Water Agreement. It accords with the *Water 2000* Report which identified the coordinated management and use of water and land resources as one of the eight major issues facing the water industry in Australia over the next two decades' (Crabb, 1988, p. 4).

The establishment of community advisory committees also marked a step forward because inhabitants of the Basin have a line of communication to the Ministerial Council – though the particular needs of Aboriginal people are not represented (Crabb, 1988 pp. 9-10).

The need for State public sector action on this problem has been confirmed by the 'National Land Management Program' produced by the Australian Conservation Foundation (ACF) and the National Farmer's Federation (NFF) and released in February 1989.

That Report identified necessary areas of State Government involvement in the long-term program both in determining the scope of action and ensuring its effectiveness. Three of the principles for the program of action are:

'. . . a major national integrated program which incorporates a local, cooperative, self-help approach, the development of individual property plans which are integrated into district plans, and increased assistance to State and Local Governments within an overall framework of Commonwealth policy guidance. There is a need for the development of a consistent legislative framework in all States. There is a substantial need for community education programs in both urban and regional areas' (ACF/NFF, 1989, p. 3).

Of the thirteen elements identified in the Report as being necessary to ensure the implementation of the program, ten require direct State involvement. They include the establishment of *Land Care Groups*, with the States identifying priority areas for their formation on a progressive basis; development of individual *property plans*, including the identification by the States of priority areas, and ensuring that the Property Plans are consistent with catchment/district guidelines set by the States; the provision of *technical support and advice* to the Land Care Groups, including training courses run by Agricultural Colleges and TAFEs to establish standards to be met by the plans; *direct government funding* for major district projects; *State support* and administrative services for all aspects of the Program, including the Land Care Groups; the development of *model State legislation* (the various legislative approaches already in existence need harmonisation); and the expansion of *conservation incentives*. These will require greater Federal support, and accordingly:

'The Commonwealth should introduce legislation to authorise payments to the

States to assist development of State programs aimed at conserving native vegetation' (ACF/NFF, 1989, p. 10).

The ACF and NFF were unable to quantify the cost to the States of such a Program, but have described them as 'significant' (ACF/NFF, 1989, p. 3).

A separate (though not altogether unrelated) issue, is that of forestry. It illustrates well the relationship between industrial/environmental concerns and State financing. In 1987, John Dargavel outlined the problems facing the forestry industry:

'Australia's mixed forest economy is beset with intractable problems. Over the last decade, public expenditure has overtaken revenue, the management of public forests has been severely criticised environmentally, private industries have been restructured, and the employment they provide has fallen. The emergent problems are those of State finances, unemployment, industrial concentration, regional decline, environment, and the legitimation and competence of the public service' (Dargavel, 1987, p. 31).

The problems related to State financing arose because:

. . . although the rates per cubic metre at which wood was sold generally kept pace with inflation, the rates themselves were low. Indeed the rates at which woodchips were sold were so low that they did not cover the full costs of regeneration work. On the revenue side . . . larger areas needed regeneration, and as environmental criticism mounted, the administrative costs of numerous inquiries rose, information and publicity sections were created within the forest services, many forest practices were modified, and new recreation facilities were built in the forests. Presumably, some costs to the forest services, though not to the public overall, were reduced through the transfer of forests to new National Parks' (Dargavel, 1987, p. 40).

Dargavel concludes that at least part of the State financing problem is due to poor financial and accounting systems in State authorities. Whatever the reason, it is clear that the demands placed on State forestry authorities are likely to increase as environmental, industrial, employment and financial issues require resolution.

Existing and emerging environmental problems will place great demands on State public sectors for many years to come and thus there is a clear need for further initiatives (cf. SMH, Feb 28, pp. 1, 8-9). As David Corbett has argued:

'. . . the same economic interests which promote pollution are also involved in restraining the State and rolling back its power. Only the State can restrict environmental destruction' (Corbett, 1988, p. 1).

3.3 State Social & Community Services

The States play a major role in the provision of services aimed at ensuring that the poor and other disadvantaged are provided with the resources and opportunities needed to ensure a reasonable standard of living. In addition, the States are also responsible for delivering a range of services which contribute to the living standards of all Australians. In short, the States are a major contributor to the 'social wage'.

As the following section demonstrates, the division of State services into economic, social and administrative is somewhat arbitrary. Many 'social wage' functions have a clear economic utility (for example, the provision of child care). Naturally in a democratic and equitable society the elements of the social wage are properly considered rights of citizenship. However, the social wage and its expansion can also be justified on the grounds of their contribution to micro-economic reform: by freeing up labour resources (child care) and by upgrading and maintaining these resources (health, education and training). It is therefore arguable that so-called micro-economic reform based on cutting the size of the public sector and the social wage is counter productive because it restricts the availability and quality of a key economic input.

Table 3.2 demonstrates that many components of the 'social wage' are delivered through the State public sector.

Table 3.2

State Social & Community Services: A Select List

legal aid;
custodial services;
social and community services (including
aged care, child care and care for the disabled);
child welfare and parole services;
adult education, including language training;
domestic utility services — water, electricity, gas,
sewerage (which involve community service
obligations such as subsidies to pensioners);
public and social welfare housing;
health services including all major urban and regional hospitals and clinics;
motor vehicle and accident insurance;
workers' compensation services including rehabilitation;
major State libraries, museums and art galleries;
waterway, riverbank and foreshore maintenance;
national parks and reserves;
primary and secondary education;
trade training and teacher training

Graphs 3.3 and 3.4 show just how significant the States are in the provision of social wage expenditure. In each year from 1978/79 to 1986/87 the States have contributed between one half and one third of total social wage expenditure used in Australia, even under the limited definition of social wage expenditure in *Australia* *Reconstructed*. If State expenditure on recreation and culture were included, the States' contribution is even greater. This alone illustrates the need for measures of the public sector's role in Australia to take into account the States and, also, Local Government.

Graph 3.3

States' Social Wage* Expenditure:
1978/79 − 1986/87

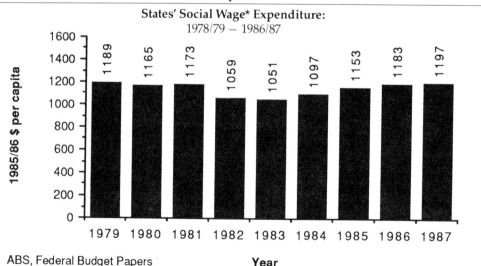

ABS, Federal Budget Papers
* Australia Reconstructed definition

Sources: Federal Budget Paper Number 7, *Payments to or for the States, the Northern Territory and Local Government Authorities* various issues: Australian Bureau of Statistics, *State and Local Government Finance Australia* various issues (ABS, Cat. No. 5504.0).
All dollar values converted using 1985/86 Implicit Price Deflator for Non-farm GDP.
Australia Reconstructed (AR) definition of expenditure on the Social Wage includes expenditure on Health; Education; Social Security & Welfare; and Housing & Community Amenities. The AR data on Federal Social Wage expenditure includes expenditure on Unemployment Benefits adjusted so as to exclude expenditure due to increased numbers receiving Unemployment Benefits (see AR pp. 52-53). AR also source of Commonwealth Social Wage graph.
States' Social Wage expenditure data 1982/82-1986/87 net of Federal Government Identified Health Grants for those years.
All States' expenditure data includes expenditure on New Fixed Assets.
States' population data does not include the ACT. States' data includes the Northern Territory.

Graph 3.4

Commonwealth Social Wage Expenditure
1979/80 − 1987/88

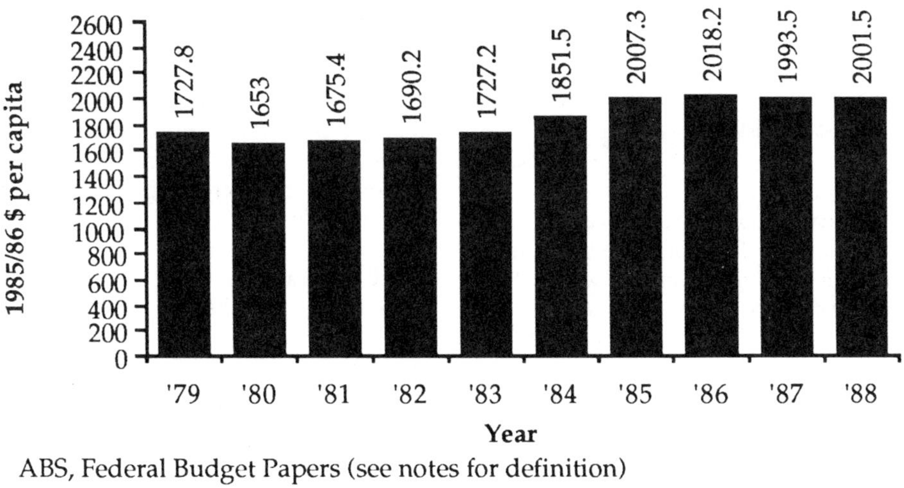

ABS, Federal Budget Papers (see notes for definition)

See Notes and Sources for Graph 3.1.

The importance of the social wage lies in its contribution to a stable and equitable incomes policy. For example, in some of the more successful industrial countries of Western Europe, wage expectations are assessed and negotiated in the broad context of general macro-economic policy settings, with regard to non-wage income and social expenditure by government. This has, of course, also been the broad framework for negotiations between the Australian union movement and the Hawke Labour Government.

Over the three years to 1985/86 the Hawke Government reversed the significant downward decline in real per capita social wage expenditure which had been the policy of the Fraser Government. Under the Accord, efforts were also made to target services, pensions and benefits to the more needy (Farrar, NCOSS, 1988).

These improvements played an important part in dampening wage pressures during this period. The 1986/87 Budget dramatically slowed down the improvement in the social wage at the same time as pressure was kept on wages. Indeed this was summed up in *Australia Reconstructed* as follows:

'The net result, however, is that Australia has not achieved anything like the degree of integration between wages policy and taxation and social wage programs that characterise the consensus economies of Europe and has not improved the social wage as much as it might have' (ACTU/TDC, 1987, p. 52).

Privatisation of education, health care and community services poses a considerable threat to the fair and equal distribution of the social wage. Increasingly a considerable proportion of tax-payers funds go to privately run institutions including private hospitals, schools and charities. Meanwhile, reduced expenditure can result in a deterioration of public services. In this context it is fundamental to reaffirm the importance of social services to national incomes and economic policy. The provision of social services should not be seen purely in terms of wage income. The essence of the formulation of the social wage is that it contributes to the standard of living by supplementing the industrial wage. It was in this context, that the concept of the standard of living was redefined to incorporate elements not before the object of trade union activity, for example, cultural life. However, there are many social, human and environmental benefits from social and community services which are intrinsically worthwhile and essential for a civilised society. These services underscore, and if developed, can further contribute to, the quality of social life in Australia. It is one of the travesties of public sector research that these intangible benefits tend often to be ignored.

3.3.1 Services for the Aged
Services for the aged are an important area for renewed State public sector investment. In common with much of the developed world, Australia's population is ageing. Consequently, the ratio of dependants to those in the workforce is increasing, and will continue to increase.

This has two major implications for the pub-

lic sector. Firstly, it has significant implications for the tax mix and the contribution of those in the workforce as against those who are not working. Secondly, it means that there will need to be an increasing proportion of social services devoted to the care of the aged (LRC, 1988).

The concentration of demand around aged services illustrates the need for flexibility and adaptability in State public service and infrastructure provision. The aged make the greatest use of medical services and with the number of persons aged 65 or more expected to double over the next 35 years we will see a rapid rise in demand for medical infrastructure. Such demands will require swift changes in public expenditure and resource allocation, which only a well developed public sector will be available to achieve (cf. EPAC, 1986).

At the same time, the aspirations of older people for humane treatment and human rights are becoming more clearly articulated. In this context, State public services must ensure that the standards in nursing homes and hostels can accommodate the needs and aspirations of the growing older population (Ronalds, 1989).

3.3.2 Child-care
Child-care is a further area in which State public sector investment is needed. Women continue to bear the major responsibility for raising children. This inequality is being exacerbated by current trends to privatise social service provision through the return of welfare and service provision to the family unit (Farrar, 1988, p. 16).

At the same time, an increasing proportion of women are entering the paid workforce. The participation rate for women increased from 44.9% in January 1982 to 51.3% in January 1989 (ABS, Cat. No. 6203.0; Mumford, 1986). The trend towards the greater participation of women in the paid workforce has not been isolated to Australia, and has resulted in similar child-care needs elsewhere (on the US case see Auerbach, 1975).

The impact of inadequate access to child-care (and other family support services) is the major reason for women's comparative labour market disadvantage:

'Individuals cannot compete equally in the marketplace until they are equally responsible for domestic work and child-care' (O'Donnell & Hall, 1988, p. 60).

The economic impact of this unequal access to paid employment is that the pool of available skills and expertise is reduced as women leave the workforce for long periods of time, and, as a result, skills and expertise may be lost or require upgrading. The situation in Australia compares unfavorably with the Swedish situation, which has a female labour force participation rate of 77.4% and where the expansion of child-care facilities was regarded as the most important family policy issue of the 1970s (O'Donnell & Hall, 1988, p. 62).

A combination of parental leave provisions (for both parents) and access to child care has obviously done much to contribute to the high Swedish female labour force participation rate.

Australian State Governments have a major role to play in the necessary expansion of child care services – the States are responsible for the licensing and regulation of services, the administration of Commonwealth funds and policy development and service planning. The direct provision of such services, particularly preschools, remains an important task.

As an example of what can be achieved by State Governments, the number of long day care centres in New South Wales increased from 32 in 1976 to 265 in 1986, and the number of preschools increased from 470 to 694 over the same period (O'Donnell & Hall, 1988, p. 68).

3.3.3 Youth Homelessness
Youth homelessness is an issue which came to national prominence in February 1989 with the release of 'Our Homeless Children', the Report of the National Inquiry into Homeless Children by the Human Rights and Equal Opportunity Commission. This Report estimated the number of homeless youth by age and by geographical area. The estimates based on age concluded that 'at the very least' there were 8,500 homeless 12-15 year olds over a 12 month period and 3,500 16 and 17 year olds at a given time:

'. . . a total of twelve thousand children and young people as a conservative minimum

figure. No State of Australia can claim that, for it, youth homelessness is not an issue' (HREOC, 1989, p. 6).

Australia is a party to the United Nations Declaration of the Rights of the Child, which established internationally agreed minimum standards for the protection of the rights of children. The Report notes that:

'As a relatively economically advanced society, and as a nation which prides itself on its human rights record and which takes an active part in promoting the international protection of human rights, Australia has a particular responsibility to meet these standards' (HREOC, 1989, p. 33).

The Report makes 77 recommendations and to implement many of them requires not only increased expenditure by the States, but also some change to the way in which existing State agencies operate. For example, the Report recommends that the States appoint youth tenancy officers to advise and assist young tenants (Recommendation 16.2); that State Governments urgently review the quality of care programs, to ensure that they adequately protect youth rights (Recommendation 20.6); and that each State establish (in the relevant Ministry) an office of Youth Affairs which would have an overall planning and coordination role within the State (Recommendation 24.5).

The general tenor of the Report is that the States have a major role to play in rectifying the problems of youth homelessness, but that to play that role the States will need to become more flexible and responsive in identifying and meeting the areas of need.

3.3.4 Community Services
The community services industry is a further area where increased State public sector activity will be needed in the future. Already 'the second largest sector in the economy, employing 17.7% of the workforce', forecasts indicate that more quality, professional community services will be needed in the years to come (NCOSS, 1988, p. 64). The role of the State public sector in supporting the expansion of

services and preserving standards will be critical.

Accordingly, the States need to address the fact that a large proportion of the paid labour in the industry does not have the protection afforded by industrial award coverage. Rates of pay and other conditions of employment are often arbitrarily set by the funding body or the community-based management committee, which feels compelled to limit the wages and conditions of the service providers in the face of a perceived community need and a limited budget (NCOSS, 1988, p. 11; O'Connor, 1989, p. 13).

In this respect, it has been noted that what virtually amounts to 'moral blackmail' can be imposed on the service providers, who are only too aware of the great need for the services provided.

The community services sector is also characterised by a particularly pernicious form of privatisation, in which the responsibility for particular services are abrogated, resulting in a return to (female) family members of functions previously recognised as a necessary area of public sector involvement. This includes activities such as care of the aged, disabled, those suffering from long-term illness and the young (Farrar, 1989, pp. 21-28). The problematical expectation here is that the services no longer provided in the public sector, or by publicly-supported community organisations, will nevertheless be provided in the home or through charitable institutions (NZ Royal Commission on Social Policy, 1988, vol. II, p. 213).

The vulnerability of the community services sector to cutbacks in public funding has also often placed an increased emphasis on the role of voluntary agencies such as the Brotherhood of St. Lawrence and St. Vincent de Paul. These agencies and more modern community organisations have always, and will always, play an important social welfare role. However, they cannot survive without public funds and are no substitute for public institutions in the spheres of health, education and social security (Farrar, 1989, pp. 59-62).

In recent years, under pressure from cutbacks in many areas of public service in the States (such as community-based service and

welfare programs), greater reliance has been placed on lowly-paid, voluntary workers. The forced reliance on voluntarism threatens much that has been achieved in recent years, and in particular the increased access to the paid community services work force obtained by professional community workers (for an earlier history of this problem cf. Adams, 1971; Kravetz, 1976; Tormey, 1976; Cantor, 1978; Cass, 1983). The constructive role of the volunteer is also threatened as the altruism and dedication of workers in the community sector is exploited further and as volunteers move from being 'para-community workers' to taking full responsibility for the maintenance and delivery of community services (Farrar, 1989, pp. 59-62).

Contracting out is another practice often used as a cost-cutting measure in the community services sector. For example, the New South Wales Department of Family and Community Services (previously Youth and Community Services) contracts social workers for adoption services; the New South Wales Department of Health is contracting personnel for health promotion campaigns; and as part of the Richmond community-based residential program for people with psychiatric disabilities, a commercial boarding house owner in Bowral is subsidised at the rate of $5 per day to provide accommodation.

As community services become more important it will not be satisfactory to allow public 'responsibility avoidance' to continue. The direction being pursued, once again most notably in New South Wales, of dismantling State services provides considerable potential for cooperation between welfare and public sector unions. Governments, and not just social planners, need to face up to their responsibilities to provide necessary services. The social cost of their failure to do so will be too high.

3.3.5 People with Disabilities

In common with many other minority groups in Australia, people with disabilities are now demanding the full human and civil rights which people without disabilities take for granted. F. Hall-Bentick, President of Disabled People International, expressed their demands in the following words:

'[Government and Society] must provide the freedom, funding, encouragement, education and training to enable all people regardless of their type of disability, to gain the skills they need to live, work, play and advocate the issues we determine are important' (Hall-Bentick, 1988).

To meet such demands will require – as it has in ensuring women's access to equal employment opportunities – State Government action. But it is also clear that governments will need to directly involve people with disabilities in the formulation and implementation of these policies, in the same way that women's advisory groups and other representative groups have been established. In terms of the public sector's own response, considerable action is still required to ensure disabled people's access to all services provided by State Governments, including outdoor services (Fraser, 1986).

3.3.6 The Needs of the Aboriginal Community

Aboriginal people are in desperate need of renewed and better coordinated State public services. Neville Wran acknowledged this when he wrote: 'There is no group of Australians who have learnt, to their cost, the meaning of States' rights, other than the Aboriginal people of Australia' (Wran in Birrell, ed., 1987, p. 140). Wran was referring to the inability of the Federal and State governments to develop joint action to aid the development of Aboriginal society. The result is that after 200 years of European settlement of Australia, Aboriginal people are still suffering; many are poor, unemployed, despairing and in ill-health (Daes, 1988, p. 38).

In her report, Daes notes that the following areas, among others, require urgent attention if the plight of Aboriginal people is to be improved: participation in Federal and State Governments; access to land and natural resources; improved education, health and housing; children's rights; and improved administration of justice (Daes, 1988, p. 12).

Notwithstanding the Constitutional Amendment of 1966, many of these problems need State Government action if they are to be resolved. For example, the States have found it necessary to institute many reforms to meet the recommendations of The Royal Commission into Aboriginal Deaths in Custody.

3.4 State Administrative Functions

In a world in which private industry plays an important role, adequate regulations and standards administered by an impartial public service are essential. State administrative functions play an important part in ensuring that safe, fair and equal standards are observed in the community. The regulation of industry and commerce, labour standards and other functions are important dimensions of a socially just society. These often unobserved and essential functions supplement the economic, social wage and social justice objectives of State and Federal Government.

Table 3.3

State Administrative Functions: A Select List
regulation of primary production; regulation of industry and commerce; (eg. consumer affairs, small claims tribunal; transport regulation, trading hours); regulation of labour standards (eg. workers' compensation, occupational health and safety, hours of work); supervision and maintenance of standards (eg. building standards, housing, food, fire safety; land valuation, liquor control, scaffolding; censorship, school education)

Graphs 3.5 and 3.6 show the real dollar per-capita expenditure by the States and the Federal Government on administrative services over the past eight years. Despite the important regulatory role played by the States they spend half of the amount spent by the Federal Government on administrative ser-

vices. In the context of growing demand for these services the fact that real per capita expenditure in 1986/7 was little higher than the level in 1978/79 indicates the increased level of expenditure required if these demands are to be met.

Graph 3.5

States' Administrative Services Expenditure: 1978/79 − 1986/87

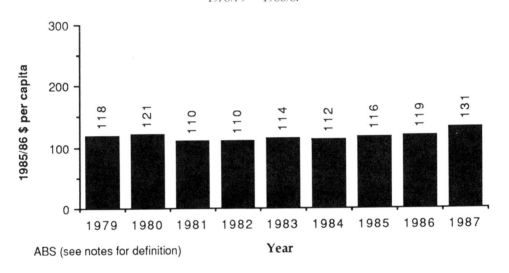

ABS (see notes for definition)

Administrative Services expenditure is defined as expenditure on General Public Services. See Notes and Sources for Graph 3.1.

Reforms to many State administrative services would lead to a better quality of life for many Australians. State administration of consumer protection, pollution control and health and safety standards at work already play a major role in ensuring that essential qualities and rights of social life are preserved; however; a more proactive approach by State agencies would ensure even greater efficiencies.

3.4.1 Occupational Health and Safety

In many different ways, State administrative structures can result in large savings to industry and society. Occupational health and safety legislation provides one example of this. In 1984/85, 223,000 workers made claims for workers' compensation in New South Wales. This represented 10% of the entire New South

Wales work force. Over half of the claims involved taking three or more days off work and 35,680 claims were not concluded within 25 weeks (McHarg, 1987, p. 5). A more vigorous health and safety inspectorate could play an important part in preventing this enormous cost of workplace accidents. As the costs of health care spiral upwards and demographic trends place increased pressure on our hospital systems, it is clear that emphasis on preventative regulations can yield big social dividends.

In general, Australia has a poor occupational health and safety record. In 1986 the then Federal Minister for Employment and Industrial Relations (Mr Willis) stated that:

'Compared to the standards of other Western industrialised nations, Australian workplaces are very unsafe places to be . . .' (CCH Australia, 1987, p. 102).

By 1988, the Labor Council of New South Wales was still able to say:

'. . . the annual rate of illness, injury, disability and death attributable to preventable occupational incidents and exposure remains unacceptably high in terms of human suffering and economic costs' (Labor Council of NSW, 1988 p. 134).

The latest available published workers' compensation statistics show that, for example, the cost of workers' compensation claims for occupation injury cases alone in New South Wales amounted to $443.8m in 1984/85, and in Victoria to $174.6m. The amount of time lost in each State amounted to 1.3 million weeks and 209,379 weeks respectively[2] (Worksafe Australia, 1989). To these costs have to be added the costs of Occupational Disease Cases.

The role of the States in alleviating the social and economic costs associated with such high rates of workplace injury and disease is a key one, through both their occupational health and safety legislation, their workers' compensation and other relevant legislation (eg. Factories, Shops and Industries; Construction Safety and Lifts and Cranes Acts).

Problems attached to occupational health and safety issues are often only expressed in dollar terms with much emphasis placed on reducing costs of workers' compensation. A more balanced view would incorporate accident prevention as the primary aim of any occupational health and safety legislation and practices, including the establishment of relevant workplace committees with the power to effect change in the workplace. At the same time, special attention needs to be given to particularly dangerous occupations such as the underground mining industry.

The problems associated with separate legislation in each State also need to be addressed: in common with differential rates of payroll tax (for example), different workers' compensation premium structures are also used to attract industry from State to State (New South Wales State Compensation Board, 1988).

The inadequacies of existing legislation also need to be overcome. For instance, in New South Wales:

'. . . public sector employers are disadvantaged by an occupational health and safety committee structure best suited to single worksites, where decision-making employer representatives can be realistically assessed and decisions implemented. This structure does not describe many public sector experiences. Further, government departments have knowingly and repeatedly breached statutory occupational health and safety requirements without prosecution or effective remedial action being taken' (Labour Council of New South Wales, 1988, p. 134).

3.4.2 Prices Surveillance

State administrative units also have a major role in monitoring prices, an essential part of any policy which involves income restraint. As the ACTU/TDC Report pointed out in Australia Reconstructed, there is room for reform in this area:

'The Commonwealth must liaise with the State Governments with a view towards implementing a common policy of price restraint' (ACTU/TDC, 1987, p. 56).

The seeming preference of Australian importers to maximise profits, rather than pass on potential price reductions available from exchange rate movements, is one indication of the need to reform and coordinate State activities in this area.

3.4.3 Consumer Protection

Consumer Protection is a further area which requires development in the State public sector. Over recent decades, the States have extended consumer rights, albeit unevenly, and usually backed them up with institutional support by the establishment of relevant Departments of Consumer Affairs and their inspectorates.

The Australian Consumers' Association (hereafter ACA) noted that:

'support from many Consumer Affairs Ministers over recent years has seen a new breed of legislation emerge, designed to redress the traditional imbalance of power between individual consumers and business interests. Every Australian has benefited from the review of old laws and outdated legal concepts' (ACA, September 1988, p. 9).

The advocates of deregulation, however, threaten to reverse this trend. The common argument of the deregulators is that self-regulation can take the place of government regulation. Moves in this direction pose a great danger to both the advances already made in consumer protection and to the necessary future expansion of such public sector activity. The following example illustrates how negative such deregulatory moves can be.

Credit Acts which can be used to protect victims from the lure of credit-based consumption '. . . were a great step forward for consumer protection' (ACA, September, 1988, p. 11). In 1988, the New South Wales Minister for Business and Consumer Affairs expressed his desire for the industry to return to self-regulation. If he had been successful, the industry would have remained 'free' from independent scrutiny by the public sector, which operates to protect relatively powerless individual consumers from more powerful corporate interests. Fortunately, the Minister was unsuccessful in meeting his objectives. This has been only one attempt by deregulators to turn the clock back. Others include similar efforts in the food and motor vehicle industries. The Consumers' Association is quite adamant in its support of government consumer bodies:

'Only the largest departments have sufficient funding – and legislative power – to take legal action to protect consumers and to force a trader to remedy a problem. Yet they are being squeezed hard. It is foolish to believe consumer affairs departments and bureaux can maintain their watchdog role with reduced funds . . .' (ACA, September 1988, p. 12).

Calls by consumers for regulation, initially rejected by industry but supported by public sector bodies, often became an economic necessity due to the key role of international trade in the Australian economy. A recent example is the case of hormone treatments for Australian beef, which were curtailed to meet overseas demand (ACA, December 1987, p. 9, see also ACA, 1989).

At the same time, State public authorities control large amounts of human and financial resources and are responsible for providing many of the basic services to the community. It is the ACA's view that the public accountability of such authorities is much broader than Ministerial accountability. Many public authorities (quite correctly) operate at some distance from direct, day-to-day Ministerial control. As such, the public has little opportunity to assess the effectiveness of the authorities in meeting their social goals. The ACA explains that:

'. . . every tenet of management and economic theory holds that bringing the consumer closer to the producer will only improve performance' (Smith & Marcus, 1988, p. 6).

Proposals developed by the ACA to bring consumers and authorities closer together include setting aside a separate section of the public authorities' annual reports to deal with specific policies and procedures employed by the agency to handle relations with consumers, including reference to any issues of concern or specific criticisms raised by consumers during the year under report; and the establishment of Consumer Councils consisting of equal numbers of domestic consumer representatives (from the organised consumer movement) and business consumer representatives.

In the administrative sphere, an expanded and developed public sector will be increasingly needed if industrial, social, urban and private rights are to be accessible, extendable and fairly distributed to all.

For example, the 'commodification of information' made possible by computers poses one of the most significant future challenges for the public sector and for social democracy. One of the major issues here is the tendency for the existing boundaries of public and private supply to change as a result of technology. With the coming of the computer-driven information revolution, specific areas of public information such as land titles are now potentially profitable commodities. The right to electronically collect and manipulate such information is keenly sought after by private entrepreneurs. Where such privatisation of public information takes place, there is not only an enormous loss of potential public revenue, but also a loss of public accountability over the uses of that information.

Comparing the strategies taken by the Department of Lands in New South Wales and its counterpart in South Australia gives some understanding of just how significant this issue is. The South Australian Department of Lands sees computerisation of land titles as a means of making the Department self-financing by 1990 (see Chapter Seven). In New South Wales the rights of computerisation in this area have been privatised. This means that in New South Wales, while the public sector bears the great burden of actually collecting information, it will be the private sector which reaps the rewards. In the process, taxpayers also lose an important source of public finance (Perkins, PSA of NSW, 1987).

The future computerisation of public information also gives rise to issues of access and democracy. Initiatives to ensure that public interests are safeguarded will be essential. Information and data which is collected through

public means should not be manipulated for profit or private purpose or by other public agencies. In Sweden a 'data police' have been established to check that, for example, employment, criminal or credit records cannot be manipulated for unlawful use (cf. Boyle *et al.*, 1988, pp. 186-88).

Conclusion

This chapter has provided considerable evidence to illustrate the role played by the States as major providers of services to the community. They also play a major role in providing the basic infrastructure needs of an advanced economy. In undertaking these functions, the States are capable of making a major contribution to micro-economic reform, but only if the privatisation campaign is halted and then reversed. Just as the States developed economic capacity and social services in the past, so now there is no reason to believe that market outcomes on their own will accomplish the structural adjustment Australia requires.

The conservative characterisation of public services as indolent and 'unworthy' cannot be sustained, either in terms of equity or economic rationality. Without the States' contribution, Australia will surely lapse into 'Third World' status.

Notes

1 More detail on these matters can be obtained from the individual State chapters in Part Five.
2 (Data not strictly comparable due to collection and compilation differences).

Graph 3.6

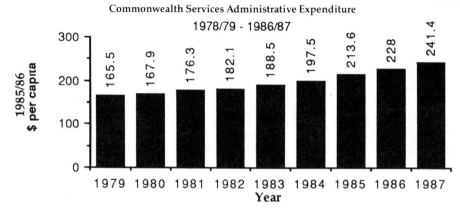

Commonwealth Services Administrative Expenditure
1978/79 - 1986/87

1985/86 $ per capita

165.5 167.9 176.3 182.1 188.5 197.5 213.6 228 241.4

Year: 1979 1980 1981 1982 1983 1984 1985 1986 1987

ABS (see notes for definition)

Chapter 4

PUBLIC SECTOR RENEWAL

4.1 Introduction

This chapter outlines a general framework through which public services can better meet social and economic goals. This involves developing a new model of reform which has the goal of *public sector renewal*. The word 'renewal' is meant to convey rejuvenation, new directions and a new willingness to solve the problems and challenges which we now face in Australia's economy and society.[1] Renewal, not privatisation, is the theme which will encourage rank and file public servants in every State to participate, as joint partners with government, management and the community, in creating public sector initiatives and new ways of working.

The strategy of renewal also signals the fact that change should build on the proud traditions of the State public sector, not destroy or deny them. As Chapter One has shown, the history of State public services can be divided into some clear periods. Australia owes much of its very birth and development to the endeavors of State governors and public servants.

In the 1980s and beyond a new spirit of public sector development is needed. Many public institutions were created in the early — to mid-twentieth century and require restructuring and new purpose. Restructuring should renew the public sector and enable public services and public sector workers to better fulfil their roles. The process of public renewal is a more positive alternative to the New Right's proposals because it offers a means of creating a more dynamic economy, a more responsive public sector and a more equitable and humane society. A spirit of cooperation between the different tiers of Australian Government, unions and the community will

be required if this positive reform is to be achieved.

4.2 A Model for Public Sector Reform and Development

The problem highlighted by Groenewegen in his critique of the New South Wales Curran Commission was that public service performance and productivity should not be measured by one yardstick of efficiency. This is a seminal point. If we are to adequately understand and plan for the respective roles of the private and public sectors, enhance the State public sector's ability to deal with social and economic problems, improve the efficiency, productivity and quality of public services and if we want to establish priorities for administrative effectiveness and policy making competence, then we have to develop a model for reform and development which is capable of defining and evaluating the qualitative goals of public services.

Swedish public sector unions, responding to this problem, have developed a model of public services which takes into account internal efficiency, productivity and politico-social utility (Tegle, 1988).

This union model was developed in response to a series of reports published by the Swedish Ministry of Finance which utilised and adapted concepts of efficiency and productivity to measure public service performance. The reports defined efficiency as the ratio between production value and production costs, that is, a kind of gross profit ratio where productivity was defined as cost productivity or the ratio between production volume and production costs. Because there were no market prices for many public sector operations, various yardsticks of production volume were developed and divided by the total costs of productivity. Examples of some of the approximations for output included for day care centres, the number of children involved; for old age homes, the number of beds; for employment offices, the number of job seekers; for hospitals, the number of patients treated, etc.

The Ministry of Finance reports were criticised for two major reasons. First, it was clear that the approximations of output did not measure what was actually produced. Second, they did not take into account any changes in the quality of service provision. These criticisms were greeted with some defensiveness by the Ministry of Finance, and resulted in attention being drawn to the important relation between the activities of the public sector and the impact these have on people. Unless this final qualitative element could be evaluated, then it was realised that the measures of productivity were virtually meaningless.

The debate also indirectly brought attention to the fact that the objectives of public sector operations were sometimes vague and that politicians, public sector managers and public sector unions and employees would benefit from having more concrete objectives. Tegle asked:

'Are day care centres primarily intended as a parking lot for small children, or are they supposed to have pedagogical/social welfare objectives?' (Tegle, 1988, p. 4).

The point is that depending on the objective, quite different evaluations of 'performance' apply. Tegle showed that in the Swedish Ministry of Finance's *quantitative evaluation*, it was 'the parking lot mentality' which prevailed because the evaluative framework could not take into account the *qualitative goals and functions* which are, in many cases, the *raison d'etre* of public service provision and operation.

In attempting to clarify these issues Tegle developed a triadic structure which distinguished between three relationships — internal efficiency, productivity and the socio-political effect or utility value of public service provision. This conceptualisation of public

sector performance requires an analysis of all three relationships.

Tegle's ideas have been adapted below to form an analytical framework for discussing some of the key elements of public sector renewal (Figure 4.1). We have added a fourth dimension to Tegle's original model — (financing strategy) — because the question of equitable and efficient public finance is a critical factor in many current critiques and analyses of public services. Establishing criteria for equitable and efficient public financing strategy is also one of the central contemporary issues for State Governments in Australia.

The relationships outlined in Figure 4.1, financing strategy, socio-political utility internal efficiency and productivity are the general themes around which the following discussion of public sector renewal below is structured.

4.3 Equitable and Efficient State Public Finances

'While the public sector grew steadily in size, except for brief periods it was forced to eschew much-needed public investment and to run down its capital stock. The poverty of public consumption in fields such as education, health, welfare services, public transport, essential services and environmental protection stood in marked contrast to the encouragement of trivial and titillating private consumption. . . . Concern for living standards, which shows up in discussion about wages and incomes as well as taxation policies, has invariably neglected the importance of publicly-provided goods and services in determining real living standards.

Along with the growth of the public sector has come an enormous increase in the level of taxation, associated with a shift in the distribution of tax burden from high-income to low-income tax payers and from companies and those who derive their income from property (profits, rents, interest, dividends) to wage and salary earners' (Russell Mathews, 'Is Business Income Measurable?', unpublished paper, 1989, p. 9).

Figure 4.1

The Elements of Public Sector Renewal

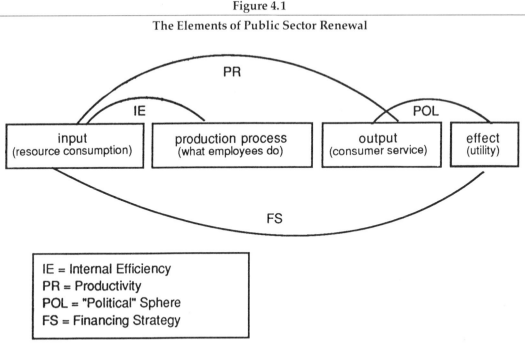

State public sector reform and development hinges on an equitable and efficient system of public finance. The socio-political goals of the public sector, organisational reform and strategies for improving productivity are not autonomous from questions of public finance (cf. Corbett, 1988; Considine, 1988). State public services are also affected by the actual ways in which public revenue is raised. If taxes, for example, are collected inequitably or narrowly then the social and political goals of public services may be undermined.

As Chapter One indicated, the most important characteristic of the Australian Federal system is the fact that the bulk of public revenue is raised and controlled by the Commonwealth Government. Over the past three years Commonwealth Government payments have comprised about 44% of total State Government funds.

Many public finance experts argue that the situation whereby one tier raises finance and another spends it makes for poor accountability and policy coordination. Nevertheless, despite the large body of scholarly literature on this subject, the problem has not been re-

solved. Chapter Five surveys the issues and provides a number of suggestions for co-ordinating Commonwealth/State financial relations.

Commonwealth fiscal policy in the 1980s has caused a series of problems for the States. Part Two has shown that the Commonwealth has achieved fiscal restraint in its total outlays, by restraining its own-purpose outlays and by cutting down the real level of net payments to the States. The Commonwealth has also not shared with the States the high growth in its own revenue, choosing to achieve a budget surplus in 1987/88 and 1988/89.

The Commonwealth fiscal cutbacks to the States have affected the ability of many different State public services to meet their key social, economic and political objectives and this has also adversely affected strategies of renewal whereby internal reforms and strategies for increased productivity could be achieved. Some would argue that public policy creativity in the 1980s has been devoted to either cutting expenditure or avoiding funding cuts!

State Governments have been faced with

three general alternatives. First, make up for the shortfalls and inadequacies of Commonwealth grants by relying more on the State system of taxes, charges, fees and fines. Part Four documents an ever increasing reliance by the States on State-based taxation and charges, involving, in some States, massive rises in their application. Tasmania, New South Wales and Queensland in particular have placed an increasing reliance on a narrow series of taxes and charges, with only Victoria pledging not to increase its taxes and charges in 1989/90. The problem with this is that State taxation and charges are narrowly based and are neither horizontally nor vertically equitable.

Second, there have been attempts to develop new means of raising public revenue at a State level. Victoria's equity trust, documented in the Victorian chapter, represents one example. However, perhaps the most spectacular case of State entrepreneurship was Brian Burke's WA Inc., which was developed explicitly to raise revenue by alternative routes for the State. The West Australian chapter outlines the major flaws in this strategy. Barring the activities of the South Australian Financing Authority (SAFA), which generated lucrative returns for the people of South Australia in 1987/88, attempts to generate funds through 'commercialisation' have not been successful.

The third response has been to cut public outlays by reducing the size of State public sectors. The difficulty with this strategy is that, as Chapter Three indicates, the States deliver key 'people services' in health, education and social welfare as well as key economic services and infrastructure vital to economic restructuring and micro-economic reform. Cuts to the States increasingly mean cuts in these areas. The contradiction of the April 1989 Economic Statement's social wage package, which involved indexing and increasing transfer payments to families, is that it was funded out of cuts to the States. This jeopardises the second stage of development of the social justice plan which is to be achieved through improving housing, employment and training – all services which are delivered through the States. A cash – and transfer – payment led social justice strategy will not replace these services (cf. Cass, 1989, pp. 11-15).

The general tendencies outlined above and detailed in each State chapter indicate that fiscal austerity does not necessarily produce a leaner and more rational system of State public services. It could even be argued that Commonwealth fiscal strategy has produced a situation in which inequitable and discriminatory taxes and charges are institutionalised, economic restructuring is hindered not promoted, risky commercial strategies are put forward and the capacity to deliver the social wage, economic services and infrastructure is reduced on an *ad hoc* basis (cf. Cain, Hunt, Jolly, Wran, Greiner in Birrell (ed.) 1988, pp. 1-18, 121-135, 135-144).

If these problems are to be avoided, a more stable package of financing options for the States must be developed. The principle underlying the financing package put forward below is that State finances should be collected more fairly and spent more efficiently. The strategy of renewing State public services through explicit social and political targeting, improved organisational structures and productivity depends on improved State financing strategy.

4.3.1 The Commonwealth and the States
The Federal Government should ensure the maintenance of real levels of State public sector capital formation in order to:

  – maintain and develop existing social and economic infrastructure;
  – directly aid in economic restructuring; and
  – allow special infrastructural needs to be met which would otherwise result in major inefficiencies and socio-economic problems in the future.

This recommendation should be contingent upon cooperation from the States in developing a better system of national, inter-governmental priority-setting.

Similarly, because of the States' key role as deliverers of the social wage, social services and infrastructure and administrative services, the Commonwealth should provide a level of recurrent funding to the States such that the fiscal constraint borne is no greater than that of the Federal Government's own-purpose out-lays. In this respect, it should be recognised that whereas the Commonwealth public sector is generally characterised by trading enter-prises and the delivery of transfer payments, services such as health, education and social welfare at a State level are highly capital-absorbing and labour-intensive and must be fairly funded through the general system of personal and corporate income taxation.

As many State services depend on the general taxation system for revenue, an equi-table and efficient Commonwealth system of taxation is in the interest of all State Govern-ments. Here it is important to counter three myths about Australian taxation. The first is the belief that Australia is a high taxing coun-try. This is not the case: Australia ranked 14th out of 23 OECD countries in terms of the level of personal income taxes relative to GDP, 15th for taxes on goods and services and 4th for property taxes, in 1982. The second myth is that the general system of personal income tax raises a far higher proportion of total taxes than in other countries. Again this view must be tempered by the facts: Australia ranked 9th in 1982 amongst the OECD countries in relation to the level of personal income taxes to total tax-ation revenue. A third argument frequently put forward in the context of tax reform is that Aus-tralia does not rely very heavily on taxes on goods and services. Against this, OECD data reveals that Australia ranks 8th for the share of total taxes raised from goods and services (Warren, 1987, p. 6).

The real criteria for judging and reforming our tax system should be equity, efficiency and simplicity of administration. That is, we should focus upon how equitably the tax burden is distributed between different individuals in the community, how simple the tax system is to administer and how taxes impact on the efficiency of the economy (Warren, 1987, pp. 6-7).

One of the problems of the Commonwealth tax system is that there has been a tendency for low and middle income tax payers to increas-ingly carry the burden of taxation in Australia. Warren gives the following figures: since 1954/55 Australian taxpayers on average pay had to face mean and marginal rates of 10 and

19%, in 1987/88 the corresponding rates were 25 and 46%. In 1954-55 only 1% of the full-time employed paid a tax rate of 46%, in 1987/88 more than 39% do. In 1954/55 the top marginal tax rate applied to those who earned 18 times average weekly earnings, however, in 1987/88 the rate is applied to those who earned 1.6 times average weekly earnings. All this has occurred in a period when the contribution of the upper income group to tax collection has fallen. In 1954/55 those earning more than 1.6 times average earnings paid 54% of tax, while in 1987 the figure was 21% (Warren, 1987, p. 7).

In line with this position, the tax cuts to low and middle income earners in the April 1989 Economic Statement were certainly overdue and justifiable. The problem is that they were not funded through improving the equity and efficiency of the tax system (though the Federal Government's efforts in this area are acknowl-edged). As the Federal Treasurer openly stated, the tax cuts were funded by cutting back the size of the public sector (Keating, 1989).

Parts Two and Four of this book focus specifi-cally on this issue and show the extent of cut-backs across the respective State public services. In particular, it is disturbing that State Governments which deliver most social and community services have cut back in social wage areas at a time when Bishop Peter Hollingworth has estimated that 1% of Aus-tralia's population controls 20 to 25% of its pri-vate wealth, 5% control 40 to 50% of Australia's wealth and 10% control 50 to 60%. This increas-ing polarisation between the rich and the poor combined with cuts in spending on social ser-vices and infrastructure has been accompanied by the formation of an Australian 'underclass' (Disney, 1989).

The social and economic objectives of public policy should be complementary. However the effect of 'razor gang' cuts means the traditional problem of playing off social service funding against funding for economic services and in-frastructure has been exacerbated for the States.

One initiative which should be taken by the Commonwealth to complement and solidify the tax/wage policy of April 1989 is an inquiry into the fairness and efficiency of the tax sys-tem and the distribution of wealth in Australia.

The focus of the inquiry should be to improve the equity and efficiency of State and Federal taxation. There are a number of recommendations on this topic put forward in Chapter Five which should be examined. Topics of inquiry should also include the possibility of levying a uniform estate and inheritance duty as well as measures to stop corporate tax evasion and avoidance.

Another point of attention could be the recent initiatives to broaden the tax base through the introduction of capital gains to fringe benefits taxation, the removal of the accelerated depreciation allowance and the reduction of some business tax concessions. ACOSS maintains that these changes have made the remaining loopholes in the income tax system more significant. It has pointed to continuing deficiencies in the capital gains tax, distortions in the treatment of real interest and debt, the use of tax havens and the evasion of non-PAYE income tax (Disney, 1989).

One final area of public finance which directly concerns Federal/State financial relations is borrowing. As the analysis in Parts Two and Four will suggest, while there are very real constraints and controls which must be acknowledged in this area, borrowing and debt financing are often the most equitable and efficient means of financing some public sector projects (Groenewegen, 1988).

4.3.2 State Taxation and Financing Strategies

Part Four has the specific purpose of developing more equitable and efficient State revenue raising strategies so only a broad set of principles will be covered here.

Two preliminary points should be made. First, as the Collins Report on the New South Wales State Tax system emphasises, '. . . after more than eight decades of unstructured and uncoordinated developments in Australia's Federal system of government', taxation and charges at the State level have not been the subject of enough analysis or monitoring (Collins, 1988, p. 1). Serious consideration of the system of State taxes and charges was, for example, most noticeably absent from the 1985 Tax Summit (Cain, 1988, p. 6) and, because of the lack of research and analysis in this area, there are no permanent and systematic means of determin-

ing which social groups are worst hit by the imposition of State tax and charge increases (cf. Collins, 1988, Chapter Four). Second, it is important to reiterate that the problems with the Australian taxation system are not that it taxes too much, nor that it is overbalanced towards personal income tax and nor are taxes on goods and services under-utilised in Australia. The problem of the Australian taxation system lies in *how it taxes*. The survey of State taxes and charges undertaken in this book reveals that on grounds of equity, efficiency and administrative simplicity: 'what is needed most in Australia is a rationalisation of what already exists', not more 'cogs' in an already complex machine (Warren, 1987, p. 2).

Two developments in particular crystalise this principle so far as the States' system of taxation and charges is concerned. First, cutbacks in Commonwealth grants to the States and Loans Council restrictions on State borrowings have increased the importance of State taxation and charges as a revenue base. Part Four shows that the States' system of taxation and charges is out of control. Thus New South Wales has radically increased taxes such as petroleum surcharges, motor registration fees, and a variety of user charges. Tasmania has increased its business franchises by 239% in three years. Queensland is reliant on fees and fines and there is increasing pressure on other States to follow suit. In this respect, the general effect of Commonwealth fiscal restraint has been to stimulate the development of a *de facto* consumption tax at State level which is uncoordinated, involves no compensation to low and middle income earners (who it hits harder) and is counterproductive to the national economic strategy (cf. Keating, *SMH*, 20/4/89).

The second factor which is important in evaluating State taxes and charges is competition to reduce taxes and charges between the States. Part Four shows that this has severely affected the stability of the State taxation base. For example, Queensland, famous for its abolition of estate and inheritance duties in 1977, now has the narrowest public revenue base of all the States and Premier Ahern plans to reduce the Governments call on payroll taxes (*Quality Queensland*, 1988). The net effect will be to make traffic offenders in Queensland increasingly responsible for public revenue and Queensland police increasingly responsible for the collection of enough 'taxes'. This is, of course, completely contrary to the principle of equity, efficiency and simplicity which define a good system of public revenue; it also indirectly undermines public support for State services.

These findings reinforce the views of Warren (1987) and others who have agreed that while Australia raises an amount comparable to that of OECD countries from taxes on goods and services, it is how these taxes are raised that is important. Most studies have focused only on Commonwealth indirect taxation, but this book surveys the total system of State taxation – put together, the results of Federal and State studies overwhelmingly endorse the case for rationalising the base of indirect taxation in Australia.

The need for this rationalisation is paramount because strategies of commercialisation have only limited potential to meet the financial needs of the States. The spectacular rise and fall of WA Inc. which is evaluated in Chapter Thirteen shows the pitfalls of this strategy. And from another perspective, the strategies advocated by the Curran Commission of Audit in New South Wales illustrate the problems of applying user-pays to all State services. The principles on commercialisation and user-pays advocated in this book are articulated on the basis of the type of public service organisation concerned. The most important guiding principle in these matters is the fact that the States should provide free and subsidised goods and services to users where they generate systematic externalities, and advance social equity. This principle applies to a large range of services within health, education, social welfare and transport. However, it is also clear that there are a range of public sector activities for which user charges can legitimately be charged. In these areas strategies for increased self financing activity and improved commercial performance are desirable and may include the application of full and partial user charges and competitive pricing consistent with principles of social justice.

In conclusion, while the criteria for an efficient and equitable public finance strategy should always be the subject of evaluation and argument, we believe that the broad proposals put forward in Part Four for a more equitable and efficient system of Federal corporate and personal income taxation, a rationalisation of indirect taxation to increase the fairness and stability of State taxes and charges, centralised State financing and industry cost recovery measures are the key ingredients for effective State public finances in the current social and political environment.

4.4 The Socio-political Objectives of State Public Services

'Many public sector companies have objectives other than maximising profits. Public sector operations often have . . . redistributive goals, such as providing the citizenry with good medical care. In these cases, we must relate efficiency to these goals. This means taking a stand on 'the political relationship' . . . The fact that this is difficult or that there may be different perceptions as to what the effects of an operation should be, for example among political parties, is no excuse for believing that privatisation solves all problems' (Tegle, 1988, p. 8).

The second important set of elements for a strategy of public sector renewal concerns the social and economic objectives and utility of public services.

An important distinction between the public and private sector is the fact that whereas the majority of public services and organisations have broad social and economic objectives, (even where they have a commercial role), the majority of private enterprises would define their primary task as profit maximisation. Accordingly, (and accepting the fact that there are some methods of operation common to both sectors), different concepts of productivity and performance should apply; however, it is frequently the case that the social and political utility of the public sector is not taken into account in assessments of its role and performance. For this reason one of the first goals of a strategy of public sector renewal is to ensure that the social and political objectives of public services are made more explicit and are capable of being monitored.

The obstacles to achieving a constructive framework for reforming and developing State public services were well illustrated at the 1988 Canberra Conference titled 'Making Public Enterprise More Enterprising.' Many speakers could only equate 'more enterprising' with privatisation. For others the key difference between the public and private sectors was that the private sector's whole endeavor was simple: to maximise returns (outputs over inputs). Compared with this, public sector managers were 'dogged' by their Ministers always getting in the way, by social obligations and by economic and accounting objectives set by external departments such as Finance and Treasury. In short, it was 'more difficult to do anything in the public sector' (Centre for Continuing Education, ANU, 1988).

However, the desire for the apparently simple world of the private sector is misguided. There are many tasks performed by the public sector which the private sector cannot or will not undertake either because they are too complex (eg. flight navigation, town planning), too unrewarding (eg. dam construction and maintenance), or too capital intensive (eg. hydro-electricity, airports). However, as Hugh Stretton's case study of the South Australia Housing Trust shows, the State public sector can creatively combine commercial and socio-economic obligations:

'. . . good housing can be very productive. It can increase national output and widen people's economic choices. It can help human relations and self-expression and cooperation . . . And good housing can help to make us more equal; it can do that in effective and popular ways without over-governing or over-taxing us' (Stretton, 1974, p. 58).

However, whereas determining the appropriate rate of return target may be all important for a private firm, the process of setting and determining social and economic objectives is crucial for public sector efficiency and productivity. This can be a complex task. For example, the question of class sizes in secondary schools may be judged from the perspective of a simple cost/benefit ratio which establishes the number of students to teachers. On the other hand, it may be that effective learning is a priority in which case smaller group teaching and student benefits may be a benchmark of productivity. In both cases, the criteria for determining efficiency and productivity depend on the agreed social and economic objectives of the service under evaluation.

One of the obstacles to setting an agenda for micro-economic reform in the public sector is that:

'most measures of productivity in public services . . . have been based on the producer perspective. This can be contrasted with the fact that measurements of the productivity of public services must be based on society's evaluation of the results. In other words, in the latter case the perspective is that of consumers' (Tegle, 1988, p. 2).

The fact is that any measure of productivity which does not take into account the objectives and needs of the users of public services fails to adequately measure public service productivity. Some first steps towards determining and developing State public service goals and making them more politically explicit and accountable are put forward below. All of the elements which this theme encompasses cannot be covered here, but three key areas are: intergovernmental cooperation and priority setting, the role of the States in restructuring Australian industry and the role of the States in the area of social justice. It is also argued that the most important means of ensuring the social and political accountability of public services is to extend more power in decision-making forums to public service consumers.

4.4.1 Inter-Governmental Priority Setting and Decision Making

'The path, which I believe we should avoid, is the narrow and barren path of so-called 'State rights'. It is a doctrine unsound in principle and unproductive in practice. . . . no great issue basic to the welfare of all

Australians, wherever they live, has ever been advanced a single step by a narrow insistence on state rights'.
Neville Wran, 'A Challenge of Three Great Reforms', in Birrell, ed., *The Australian States: Towards a Renaissance*, 1987, p. 140.

From a national perspective, State Governments lack policy coordination, focus, continuity and purpose. The *State of Siege* project confirms this across a range of different areas including public finance, government administration, economic restructuring, infrastructure investment and social justice. The only worthwhile organisation capable of undertaking studies of the States, the Inter-State Commission (ISC) has been little used (and some would argue, ill-used) in Australian constitutional history. In fact prior to the establishment of the ISC to examine matters relating to the waterfront (1986), which was a commendable initiative, the ISC has only effectively been in existence for eight years (1912-20). Australia can no longer afford to neglect research which focuses upon the social and economic role of the States and it must carefully examine the initiatives taken in countries such as Norway which has implemented long-term national plans in all areas of government responsibility (cf Royal Norwegian Ministry of Finance, 1984/85).

The epitomy of the lack of coordination and consultation at the top level of inter-governmental decision-making is the Premiers' Conference. As Corbett maintains:

'Each year Premiers go to Canberra for the annual meetings of the Loan Council and Premiers' Conference. In the build-up to these gatherings, Treasury officers of the States study their statistics and prepare their pleadings. The Premiers go as Oliver Twists, bowls outstretched, and return with little more than Fagin was prepared to give them in the first place, their pride gone, their prestige with their local State communities needlessly wasted' (Corbett, 1988, p. 9).

Premier Cain, for one, has argued that inter-governmental decision making needs to be improved (Cain, 1987, p. 7). Cain puts forward an example of the difficulties in this area which is most pertinent to the proposed scheme for a fairer indirect taxation system outlined in Chapter Six. Citing the case of Tax Reform and the 1985 Tax Summit he argues:

'The States' interest in the Commonwealth taxation system is almost equal to that of the Commonwealth itself, both because of the relationships between Commonwealth and State tax systems and because, under the present financial arrangements, the States necessarily share Commonwealth taxation revenues.'

However, at the tax summit, Cain goes on to say, no discussions took place between the Commonwealth and the States: 'The tax reform process, in fact, was confined to important, selected taxes at the Commonwealth level . . . Issues of State taxation were not addressed.' Cain concludes:

'And what is the result? After all that talk, after all the submissions and evaluations and calculations, one of the most widely criticised taxes of all, payroll tax, is left completely untouched. And with the best will in the world we are unable to do anything about it' (Cain, 1987, p. 7).

One means of encouraging better decision making and policy coordination would be to strengthen the Premiers' Conference and Loans Council as national policy forums. This should be achieved through the establishment of a secretariat, funded and staffed by State and Commonwealth Governments, which would provide background information and proposals for reforms in Federal financial relations and would encourage the development of joint State and Federal Government policy initiatives.

While there are many Commonwealth and State forums on infrastructure and social welfare matters, these are frequently hampered by ideological and political differences. In order to establish a more constructive basis for intergovernmental decision-making, a central and permanent national priority setting forum is needed. The coordination of national infrastructure provision would be an important issue to which a Premiers' Conference Secretariat could usefully contribute. Similarly, the coordination of spending on national social justice objectives such as the eradication of child poverty could be bolstered by submissions from the States to a secretariat capable of critically and objectively assessing and analysing national priorities. Above all, the aim of a National Secretariat would be to help take the Premiers' Conference and Loans Council out of the nineteenth century environment of Oliver Twist and into the twentieth century world of rational socio-economic planning and decision-making.

4.4.2 Defining Socio-Economic and Political Objectives

There are many broad social and political goals which the public sector provides or guarantees which should be taken into account when evaluating the performance of public organisations. However, it is important to establish a clear framework of social and economic objectives through which public sector productivity and performance can be judged. To facilitate this at the general political level, Premiers and Ministers should be required to establish the social and economic objectives that will be achieved over their three-or four-year period in office. Criteria for evaluating the performance of public organisations in meeting the targets which are assigned to them should also be established. The more specific the set of objectives, the more effective they are likely to be. As such, the Prime Minister's recent promise to eliminate child poverty in Australia by 1990 is one political pledge which should be emulated across all the domains of government.

Economic Restructuring and Development
In establishing economic objectives for the State public sectors, the key yardstick for measuring their success must be, for the foreseeable future, their relative contribution to overcoming the balance of payments constraint. Here, the clear enunciation of indicative economic goals in the Victorian Economic Strategy is a model worthy of replication.

State economic and industrial strategy should, as a priority, develop initiatives which will improve the competitiveness of the trade exposed sector in each State. As the summary of Victoria's economic strategy in Chapter Eleven further articulates, the first initial step towards this strategy is to develop an audit of development. This involves developing an analysis of:

– the natural and economic factors of production, such as the availability of labour and capital, which are specific to each State;
– the relative costs of gaining access to and developing these factors of production in each State; and
– the entrepreneurial skills, innovation and design, technology and marketing, which must be deployed or developed to produce and sell targeted State goods and services.

The competitiveness of State economies revolves around combining these '. . . factors of production at a cost and in a manner to compete successfully in meeting actual demand in trade-exposed areas' (*The Next Step*, 1984, pp. 1-5).

There are two levels of policy action which can be taken by State Governments in relation to this general objective. The first involves taking action to improve the economic environment in a way which will make State firms more competitive. Under this undertaking we recommend that State Governments:

– pursue a counter-cyclical macro-economy policy directed at expanding the economy in times of recession and restraining inflationary processes when growth accelerates;
– take steps to reduce irrational State costs and charges which are simply passed on to the general public through either reduced wages or higher prices;
– take action, in consultation with State Trades and Labour Councils, to improve the system of State industrial relations;
– examine and improve State business regulations;
– in consultation with public sector unions, develop a long-term program for improving the productivity and performance of the State public sector; and
– develop mechanisms for ensuring business and industry opportunities in desir-

able regional centres which would not be supported by the market.

The second sphere of action involves isolating the strategic areas of industry in each State in which there are potential or existing competitive advantages and involves developing policies which will enhance competitive strength and economic growth in these areas. Each State Government's role here is to concentrate its resources on strengthening those key areas of economic growth identified in the development audit, which are most likely to provide sources of competitive economic activity for the future (*The Next Step*, 1984, pp. 1-5).

The development of a State industry policy and economic strategy is more coherent and capable of measurement than the market driven State development strategy adopted by the Unsworth Labour Government. It is also a much more precise policy philosophy than the untargetted decentralisation incentives available under the current New South Wales and Queensland Governments which make no claim to easing the balance of payments constraint, and are not tied to performance undertakings from the corporate recipients.

As the key deliverer of economic services, the States have an important role to play ensuring Australian industry's future international competitiveness. The States must also deal with emerging social, economic and environmental demands, some of which are necessary to make economic restructuring possible while at the same time delivering equity and social justice goals.

Graphs 3.1 and 3.2 in Chapter Three show the relative readily-identifiable financial contributions the Federal and State Governments make to Australia's economic life. They clearly illustrate that the aggregate contribution by the States exceeds the contribution by the Federal Government. It is important to note, moreover, that these data do not show the contributions by the two levels of government to individual categories: for example, much of the Federal Government's economic services expenditure is accounted for by its expenditure in Transport and Communications. In other words, the two government sectors have different economic roles.

This brief outline of the role of the States in economic restructuring is not, of course, exhaustive. It does, however, indicate the broad range of demands to be met; an indication of the reform necessary to meet these demands; and the obvious requirement for sustainable revenue-generation at the State level. At the same time, the demands of economic restructuring need to be viewed in the context of the model of the public sector outlined above. This model provides the means by which conflicting demands can be mediated in a rational way.

The Social Wage and Social Justice

A better, more efficient, public sector means a secure 'social wage' for all Australians through the provision of reliable, high quality services in health, education, public infrastructure and leisure. State public services deliver major elements of the social wage, but it should be noted that Australia has not achieved anything like the degree of integration between wages policy and taxation and social wage programs that characterise the consensus economies of Europe, and has not improved the social wage as much as it should have. As *Australia Reconstructed* argued, there is room for major reform in this sphere.

One of the most important ways of enhancing the social wage is through realising social justice objectives and combatting social inequality in our society. To be successful, social justice strategies should have general targets and plans which can be realised through all the organs of government including the community service obligations of State trading enterprises and the general policy priorities of all State Government agencies. In this respect, the recently established National Social Justice Secretariat must play a more active role in encouraging State governments to form social justice strategy units and targets.

The Victorian 'social justice' strategy is the most advanced of all the States. Its general aims are to: *reduce the inequality caused by unequal access to economic resources and power, increase access to essential goods and services according to need, expand the opportunities for genuine social participation and protect and extend legal, industrial and political rights*. However, if these objectives are to mean anything concrete, an appropriate infrastructure for implementing them must be developed. A 'social justice budget' has a habit of financing a plethora of worthwhile but piecemeal activities. The next step towards an effective social justice strategy should involve entrenching social justice objectives in the day-to-day activities of the State public service. The task of building up 'social performance indicators' for public agencies is discussed in Section 4.5.3.

According to Michael Salvaris, the key principles of a social justice strategy should include:

— the development of long-term priority plans with intensive four year planning periods;
— comprehensive community involvement and clear public communications;
— a policy focus which attacks key social justice problems across all levels of the public sector and concentrates on the redistribution of resources and the long-term causes of inequality;
— building social justice into government at all critical decision points, especially coordination, planning and research, agency management, staff development, and above all, budget and resource allocation;
— an emphasis on clear definitions and objectives and the setting of concrete, achievable targets which are monitored annually,
— integration of social and economic policy; and
— the development of social indicators and a social research program to improve targeting which constitutes the basis of a long-term strategy (Salvaris, 1988, p. 1).

Finally, one of the reasons why social problems such as homelessness and child poverty persist in Australia is because there is a lack of policy coordination *and concerted action* between the appropriate Commonwealth and State Government instrumentalities and at State levels there is an inability to ensure that policy objectives and action are implemented both within public service organisations and also within other community service organisations. For this reason, social justice secretariats with cross portfolio expertise should be

formed and located in the executive departments of each State. Their primary task should be to implement, in an optimal time frame, social justice objectives across each level of the State public sector.

Some necessary areas for reform include the budget process: simplification of reporting systems, development of long-term budgeting procedures, better accounting and accountability in social agencies. The development of social priority and performance indicators including better processes for redeploying resources towards priority social goals, social impact evaluation of major policy proposals and the development of a public budget policy should also be undertaken according to a strict time-schedule.

State social justice secretariats should also develop plans for comprehensively integrating economic and social policy. To this end there should be close cooperation between policy development structures through socio-economic indicators and the identification of cooperative social/economic projects in key areas such as employment. Finally, to ensure effectiveness of the general objectives of each State social justice strategy, there should be regular policy reviews to assess the equity impact of programs and spending in each public service agency and department. In this respect, measures to ensure better targeting, better information and more effective measurement of inequality should be implemented by State Governments as a matter of priority. Salvaris has suggested that the primary step towards defining social and political goals at a State and regional level should involve: the development of specific social policy targets in areas such as poverty, youth employment, equality for women, the frail, the aged and the disabled; the development of State social indicators and the annual identification of State Government social justice targets; and the establishment of uniform public service social indicators (Salvaris, 1988, p. 69).

Extending Democracy and Enhancing Accountability
The most common and least demanding type of democratic participation is to vote in elections. However, the lives and concerns of

ordinary people are directly affected by the functioning of State public agencies whether through education or the provision of electricity, gas or sewerage facilities. As such, in the public sector of the future there must be renewed emphasis on real community participation and representation in decision-making. Without such action the signs are that there will be a severe loss of public confidence in many spheres of the public sector. Community participation in public sector decision-making is also an important means of ensuring action to ensure social justice objectives are met. In particular the government should establish a community/government social justice task force, enact a constitutional bill of citizens rights, develop a long-term community consultation process, develop a poverty action program to promote self-help amongst low income groups, develop an intensive review of consultation processes and guidelines, establish a network of locally-based, government information offices and set up a regional consultation network which enhances the role of peak community groups (Salvaris, 1988, p. 5).

As well as involving public service users in decision making forums, regular surveys of user needs should be undertaken in all areas of the public service. The initiation of programs based directly on user needs strengthens the community's willingness to defend and extend State public services; it also leads to greater efficiency in service provision and planning.

Accurately assessing user needs is not easy and various methods will probably need to be considered. Some basic requirements are:

— information must be obtained from the community directly. It will be important that such information-gathering be non-intrusive and that the methodology be refined as experience is obtained;
— regional, ethnic, gender and age differences will need to be recognised and respected. The era of 'shotgunning' social needs has long since passed;
— users of community services should become increasingly involved in administrative and policy decisions.

For any such strategy to be effective, public sector unions are key participants. The expertise and knowledge which they have already amassed is a significant community resource.

4.5 Productivity and Performance

The final elements of a strategy for public sector renewal is internal efficiency: in short, 'the productive process'. The broad initiatives put forward below are not meant as the final word on this subject, but they do provide a constructive general framework for improving productivity, responsiveness and flexibility in State public services.

One of the major shortcomings of privatisation is that it rarely achieves anything more than short-term efficiency gains which are derived from either cuts to labour costs or through asset sales. As the European Trade Union Institute has found:

'The privatisation of public undertakings which has recently taken place in a number of Western European countries has not altered market structures and has equally failed to improve the extent to which the needs of consumers or customers are met. It is also apparent that the privatisation of public services has not led to an improved level of services for users. In the majority of cases and more particularly where privatisation takes the place of contracting out to private firms, the quality of service deteriorates and the workers concerned receive lower wages and suffer poorer working conditions as a result of the change' (ETUI, 1988).

The focus of privatisation is usually on the relationship between quantified inputs and outputs (Wilenski, 1988). It has been argued above that this perspective is flawed because it fails to take into account the qualitative social and political objectives which most public enterprises must adhere to; as a narrower measure of productivity and performance, a strict focus on the input/production ratio is inadequate. This is because it can result in an over-emphasis by management on short-term measures such as personnel cuts, asset sales and the rationalisation of areas of production — all the hallmarks of the privatisation strategy.

The issue here is that '. . . lower costs are not automatically the same as higher productivity or even higher company profits' (Tegle, 1988, p. 8). And even when this is the case, a rise in productivity or an improvement in profit must be sustainable. There is nothing easier than cutting production costs in an operation if you ignore its impact on future productivity or profit making capacity.

The lesson of contemporary manufacturing industry is that the traditionally narrow concept of internal efficiency (defined on the basis of labour productivity) can lead to poor managerial decisions and ultimately inferior productivity. Wickham Skinner has argued that:

'the harder companies work to improve (labour) productivity, the less they sharpen the competitive edge that should be improved by better productivity. Elusive gains and vanishing market share point not to a lack of effort but to a central flaw in how that effort is conceived. The very way managers define productivity improvement and the tools they use to achieve it pushes their goals further out of reach' (Skinner, 1988, pp. 55-6).

Managers all too frequently concentrate on short-term efficiency and only try to cut labour costs, while ignoring ways of increasing long-term productivity such as changes in production and service quality, organisational structures, flexible production or service capacity and training systems for employees (Ford, 1982, pp. 443-453, Ford, 1984, pp. 54-65). In fact the appeal of privatisation is largely premised upon this kind of short-term thinking, yet, public sector managers should concentrate on the harder, but more rewarding prospects for increased productivity which arise through areas such as organisational change and workplace reform.

4.5.1 Improving Public Sector Organisational Structures and Working Environments

One of the important means of improving the efficiency and responsiveness of State public services is through reform to public sector organisational structures and working environ-

ments. However, just as there is mistrust between employees and management in the private sector in the initial and continuing phases of economic restructuring, so too there is distrust between management and employees in State public services. This distrust must be understood and resolved before significant micro-economic reform can take place.

Sewn over many years distrust between management and staff in many State public services results largely from the increased emphasis on short-term cost-cutting exercises which has accompanied State budget cut-backs (Corbett, 1988). Increased productivity is too often associated with reducing labour costs, while attempts to improve services to the public are ignored. The irony is that on many occasions the people who actually *deliver* public services can suggest a myriad of ways for improving service quality, productivity and performance, but this wellspring of innovation and ideas is rarely tapped (Watson, 1988).

The imperatives behind the quick-fix solutions and reforms to State public sector reform is well documented. As David Corbett maintains:

'In Australia's case it was not prosperity which promoted administrative innovation, it was rather the economic downturn of the latter half of the 1970s which caused State Governments to fear that they could not continue the public services they had undertaken or promised. In their anxiety they turned to new cost-cutting methods and mechanisms for administrative control' (Corbett, 1988, p.3).

Mark Considine has also raised this point but from a slightly different perspective. He argues that future historians of the public sector will characterise the current period of public sector development as one of profound change:

'From Local Government through to national bureaucracy . . . every important organisational relationship including budgeting, personnel and program administration is feeling the impact of the new order.'

Considine goes on to say that the change involves the public sector moving away from its traditional bureaucratic methodologies towards a structure and method of operation resembling the private sector:

'In the simple language of the corporate management textbooks this emerges as a change from a system which is most concerned about inputs to one which values outputs' (Considine, 1988, pp. 4-7).

According to Considine the problem with the new forms of coordination and control (in which traditional bureaucratic methods involving rules, specifications and procedures are substituted for 'output contracts negotiated with managers') is that these techniques have been used primarily to tighten cabinet control of the budget, cut expenditure and reduce ministerial and bureaucratic independence. As such, corporate management:

'risks reducing the capacity of many organisations to create workable solutions to social and economic problems because it squeezes and disciplines some of the groups most likely to articulate and support reforms' (Considine, 1988, pp. 16-17).

The new drive towards corporate management ideals has sometimes stymied industrial democracy initiatives within the public sector (Yeatman, 1987). Too often industrial democracy committees, new technology groups and equal opportunity groups are set up remote from key corporate decision making forums in government departments and enterprises. Rather than being a way of communicating with and participating in management, such committees are simply by-passed and become a waste of time for all concerned.

In this context for many public sector workers administrative changes are so familiar they breed contempt. As Corbett has argued, administrative changes within the State public sector are often *ad hoc*, directly political in motivation and inspired by fear of short-term economic or social problems (Corbett, 1988, pp. 5-14).

The main lesson from this is that politicians and management should have clear objectives for change and not just keep changing organisations. A coherent strategy should involve a stable infrastructure for innovation within the public sector organisation. This infrastructure for innovation involving management, unions, employees and public service users is necessary for three reasons. First, to be successful, workplace and organisational change should connect with the positive traditions of the work environment and organisation. Second, the reasons for organisational reform and development should be clearly understood and supported at all levels, from top management to rank and file workers. Third, one of the major means through which greater efficiencies and more effective ways of working can evolve is through engaging and allowing input from those with most expertise at the point of production or service delivery.

4.5.2 A Constructive Agenda for Change

In 1986, Peter Wilenski, then Chairman of the Commonwealth Government Public Service Board, noted that most public sector bodies grow incrementally resulting in pyramidal structures of responsibility. These structures often have an effect which is counter-productive to the essential aims of public organisations, that is, to provide *public* services.

Wilenski's view, which is also of relevance to the State Public sector, was that hierarchical public organisations have a number of undesirable effects:

'a) information is lost or distorted as it moves up or down the hierarchy;
b) there are too many points at which new ideas can be vetoed;
c) staff at the lower levels feel powerless and isolated from decision-making;
d) too many middle managers have no real responsibility and indulge in make-work activities overloading those above them and frustrating those below by over-supervision' (Wilenski, 1986, p. 11).

A further problem from a workplace point-of-view is the tendency for a blinkered work perspective to result if the overall objectives of the public organisation become clouded by supervisory hurdles and unproductive regulations (Wilenski, 1986, p. 11).

In order to solve these problems Wilenski proposed to 'flatten' the hierarchy, to remove unnecessary vertical lines of control and encourage the development of decision-making authority 'closer to the coal face'. Wilenski argued that this organisational structure would have a number of advantages including a more rational management structure, clearer and more rapid communication, job enrichment and greater individual control over worklife and improvements in productivity (Wilenski, 1986). Wilenski's concerns are particularly important for large bureaucracies. However, in the private sector, the 'Taylorist' model of industrial organisation '. . . in which the actual definition of jobs, as of acceptable standards of performance, rested on 'lowest common denominator' assumptions about workers' skill and motivation' is similarly under challenge. Under the Taylorist model '. . . management organised its own responsibilities into a hierarchy of specialised roles buttressed by a top-down allocation of authority and by status symbols attached to positions in the hierarchy' (Walton, 1985).

Challenges to the Taylorist form of work management or organisation have a great deal of relevance to the problems which Wilenski has identified in the public sector. The challenge of the future for both the public and private sector is to develop more flexible and responsive organisations. As Bjorn Gustavsen sees it:

> 'Public organisations of the future will consist of a conglomerate of changing organisational patterns. The concept of organisation will cease to be associated with uniformity and stability and will become more fluid and less definable, the whole workforce will take over many of the traditional responsibilities of top management and actively create and control work patterns. The actual form of organisation will lose much of its traditional significance, what will matter more is how the organisational patterns and responses are *created*' (Gustavsen, 1986, p. 374).

Transforming existing public services requires thorough going industrial democracy (ie. discussion, participation and cooperation in decision making between all levels of the workforce). In order to achieve change Gustavsen has developed a model for democratic dialogue in which the entire workforce of an organisation has an opportunity to participate in a two way flow of ideas and arguments leading to a platform for practical action. Through this process a more flexible organisational structure evolves and is supported because the entire workforce has played a part in developing it (Gustavsen, 1985).

Some of the organisational objectives which can be achieved through democratic dialogue directly complement Wilenski's ideas and include:

> — an integration of functions at point of service delivery;
> — a drastic reduction in the control and supervisory tasks of managers;
> — a halt to — and increasingly a reversal of
> — the proliferation of new levels of authority;
> — a shift from supervision to support in the tasks of the people remaining at the intermediate levels;
> — a more collective top management level;
> — a strengthening of worker representation and participation; and
> — decisions on important questions of organisational policy through direct dialogue between management and workers (Gustavsen, 1986, p. 375).

Rather than a pyramid, the structure of organisations which undergo this sort of democratic restructuring resembles the 'clothes-hanger' depicted in Figure 4.2 (Mintzberg, 1983). The top of the organisation expands and the middle levels are slimmed down, division of work is reduced and all operative functions tend to be brought together at a one-level point of production or service delivery.

The 'clothes-hanger' structure is a suitable organisational form for many service oriented State organisations. However, for State public service organisations to achieve the objective of flexibility through democratic dialogue, it is important to create *'an infrastructure for change'*. The role of public service unions is important here. As Gustavsen has argued:

> 'For direct democracy to be possible in an enterprise there must be a structure which links the rank-and-file workers with each other. Democratic dialogue is not only a discussion between those who exercise power and those who do not, it is also a discussion between the rank-and-file. The existence of a union therefore tends to reinforce a democratic structure' (Gustavsen, 1986, p. 376).

Organisations will also have to create their own consultative infrastructure for change which will be required to:

Figure 4.2

The 'Clothes-Hanger' Structure

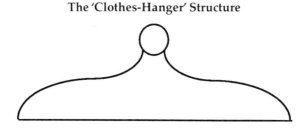

– monitor new forms of working life and develop positive examples which may be implemented in the enterprise or department concerned;
– organise meetings to bring people together to discuss the possibilities of change;
– initiate and support experimental projects;
– create training opportunities for new work processes and organisations;
– develop a system of communication upon which a process of democratic dialogue can develop; and
– develop policies for renewal including the selection of key areas for project development (Gustavsen, 1986, p. 379).

There are already infrastructures for organisational change in the State public sector which have achieved some promising results. The Civil Service Association (CSA) of Western Australia has been involved in 'broad banding' salaries and classifications since the late 1970s. (For another W.A. example, see JUAC, 1988) The CSA was instrumental in reducing some 250 classifications and 128 salary points to 9 classifications and 43 salary points (Howlett, 1986). In the process it has been something of a pioneer in experiencing the problems as well

as the triumphs of award restructuring (cf. 'Many Keyboard Classifications are Unfair', *CSA Journal*, Feb, 1987, p. 8). In the era of award restructuring, the CSA's role in this area needs to be more widely appreciated and supported by those who argue that the public sector is not responsive to change.

Another notable project has been undertaken in Victoria's State Insurance Office (SIO). While it is still premature to hail the SIO experience, it has provided a model for showing how the award restructuring process, industrial democracy and employee participation procedures can lead to greater efficiency and a more flexible workplace (Watson, 1988). The SIO's products – insurance packages – are subject to consistently changing forms and competitive pressures. In order to stay in front of the field the essential ingredient is a highly skilled and adaptable work force. The international trend in banking and insurance is away from the 'back room' production towards front-office functions including customer assistance, sales and product development. This requires a general up-skilling of the workforce, a significant commitment to training and a decentralisation of functions and decision-making. Increasingly, it is the quality of human resouces that determines the rate at which these changes can take place (OECD, 1988). In a unique experiment, SIO management, unions and workers began a 'search process' to link the vision of the organisation including its business goals, its customer goals and its people goals. They then formulated an action plan which embraced technological change, award restructuring, customer service, training and existing industrial democracy committees to achieve these goals. With the motto of 'earning for the people of Victoria a long-term rate of return that will protect and expand their investment' it may be that the SIO can turn the community service obligations – which, as a public enterprise, it is obliged to fulfill to a positive trading advantage. The process continues, and with the active participation of the VPSA it is certain that a lot can be achieved.

One further series of State initiatives has been undertaken in the hospital system. The Royal Australian Nurses Federation (RANF) in Victoria have, through consultative practices, improved rostering, shiftwork, ward budgets and management, patient dependency, admission and discharge policies in a variety of workplaces. (RANF, 1988) These are significant achievements, especially when the most authoritative surveys reveal that, as in the insurance industry, it is the investment in human resources and improved equipment which is the key to future productivity and performance in the health industry (Australian Institute of Health, 1989).

4.5.3 Improving the Performance of State Public Services and Enterprises

In order to develop adequate procedures for improving the performance of State public services and enterprises, it is important to acknowledge the different functions and kinds of organisations which operate in the States. Generally the whole idea of corporate plans and performance evaluation is appropriate to all forms of State organisations, not just State trading enterprises. However, as Xavier has argued, unless performance indicators and accountability structures are developed in full consultation with the management, workforce and unions of specific enterprises, then there is an inevitable tendency towards ineffectiveness and adversarial, rather than cooperative and instructive, managerial relations (Xavier, 1989).

The process of organisational reform described above provides a paradigm for developing effective performance targets and measurements for public organisations.

Well designed performance indicators can illustrate how well a particular public body is meeting its objectives, and they can also be used to enhance its financial performance. However, if they over-value this criteria, there are also many occasions where they are inappropriate. Performance indicators need to be developed which recognise the many objectives set for public bodies, which are more numerous and complex than those set for private sector bodies. Also the underlying principle of a good regime of performance indicators is that it should enhance managerial flexibility and autonomy as well as quality of service.

Excessive control of and interference with the operational decisions of the managers of State trading enterprises (in investment, product mix and pricing) can suffocate initiative and result in a loss of accountability and costly operational inefficiencies. It is only in a context where the role and responsibilities of government (ownership role), the board of directors (strategic role) and the management of the enterprise (operational role) are clearly defined that performance indicators can be useful (Ayub & Hegstad, 1987, pp. 26-29). In non-commercial public organisations, such as universities and other social agencies, it should be recognised that there are many qualitative factors which cannot easily be taken into account in the development of performance indicators. For example, the so-called 'publish or perish' mentality which has arisen in some university departments is a side-effect of poorly developed performance indicators. However, with these reservations, some general guidelines can be put forward as follows.

State Public Trading Enterprises

For State public trading enterprises which are self-sufficient monopolies, self sufficient semi-competitive bodies or self-sufficient fully competitive bodies, a range of commercial and socio-economic indicators should be required. As Patrick Xavier has argued in a paper on Australia's postal services:

'performance evaluation needs to extend beyond financial criteria and should encompass (at least) the following components of performance: *Economy, Economic Efficiency, Equity and Effectiveness*' (Xavier, 1989, emphasis added).

Each of these categories may involve different strategies and forms of analysis, and some of the key issues are canvassed below.

First, under the category of financial management, it is essential to have long and medium-term financial objectives, it must be possible to monitor progress towards them and managers must be responsible for the outcomes. For this reason, *corporate planning* is becoming a key feature of many State trading enterprises. Corporate plans should involve:

— objectives (such as rate-of-return targets, broad pricing guidelines, payment of dividends, use of surplus/funding of deficits, capital repayments to government, borrowing limits, service expansion and social objectives);
— environmental analysis (including an analysis of macro-trends, industry structure and product growth rate and portfolio);
— internal position analysis (the internal strengths and weaknesses of the organisation including an evaluation of personnel, information, processes and finance);
— strategies (detailed plans for achieving each objective);
— resource gaps (any gaps in personnel, expertise etc. that need to be filled);
— actions to acquire resources or amend strategies;
— development plans (by function and area with performance standards, control and evaluation measures); and finally
— budgets (to ensure that the strategies of the organisation are achieved by placing monetary targets into the planning process).

Second, the main measures of *financial performance* are return on assets or capital used, return on equity, dividend pay out ratios, debt-to-equity ratio and specified levels of internal financing on large investment projects. The Commonwealth Department of Finance and

several State Governments have introduced, or are considering, the introduction of various forms of rate-of-return reporting (Department of Finance, 1987; Department of Management and Budget, 1986; Department of Treasury, South Australia, 1987; Curran, 1988). In essence, the approach requires public sector trading entities to achieve a target rate-of-return using a prescribed method of calculation.

Some economists have argued that 'the extent to which the accounting rate-of-return on assets (as commonly calculated) is a useful indicator of economic performance is very much in question' and Heald has also maintained that the distinction between financial profitability and economic efficiency is especially relevant to public utilities (Xavier, 1989, p. 10; Harcourt, 1965; Fisher & McGowan, 1983; Byatt, 1986; Heald, 1988). In this respect, rate-of-return reporting has substantial political and management consequences for price justifications, negotiations on public dividend requirements and performance evaluations (See Chapter Seven). The important aim here should be to balance questions of efficiency and commercial performance with the capital needs and long-term productive growth of the enterprise.

Hugh Stretton has argued that:

'to treat public enterprise capital as equity, share-owned by the Australian people through an appropriate branch of their government, as it already is in Qantas and other publicly owned companies, is the most promising arrangement.'

However, the problem is that:

'. . . as governments face the regular agonies of annual budgets and periodical election campaigns they must not be tempted — which means they must not be able to — plunder their business enterprises for revenue or starve them of necessary capital for short-term or partisan political purposes. The government should acknowledge that when politicians come under the pressures characteristic of their profession, the corporate resources need to be protected by some equivalent of the time-locks which prevent unscheduled access to bank safes' (Stretton, 1988, pp. 32-33).

The management and workforce of viable public enterprises should be allowed to decide how to use their surpluses, once an agreed dividend payment has been made to the government as the major shareholder. Managers and workers who have made the profits are normally better placed to decide upon their productive use than others more remote from the enterprise. Also, in view of the strong demand for investment capital faced by many public enterprises, it may be that, unless carefully monitored, dividend policy could deplete internal funding capacity and result in increased dependence on borrowing, resulting in increased debt repayments and servicing charges and consequently price increases.[2] These problems underline the need for organisational evaluations to take into account more than just rate of return reporting.

It would be remiss not to mention the push towards 'accrual accounting' under the topic of financial performance. For although many public trading enterprises have routinely used forms of accrual accounting, there is now an increased demand to use these practices as a means of assessing the general performance of many different public organisations (Tierney 1979; Plater, 1988). Accrual accounting characterises a form of accounting close to that used by commercial enterprises in the private sector. It involves:

'recording financial transactions in the accounts as the transactions occur – as goods and services are purchased or used or as revenues are earned – even though cash may be received or paid at other dates' (Tierney, 1979).

This can be contrasted with 'cash accounting' which records cash receipts and payments. Accrual accounting is also usually accompanied by other changes such as program budgeting and the preparation of asset registers (Taylor, 1988). Program budgeting (arranging financial data so that transactions and operations can be analysed outside the traditional financial framework of simple receipts and payments on a line-item basis) has also been widely supported.

Two of the primary advantages of the application of accrual principles to public sector accounting are *accuracy* and *accountability*. The New South Wales Auditor-General argues that accrual accounting:

'. . . provides a means of listing the true annual costs of services. It aids in the preparation of an annual surplus/deficit that reflects the results of bringing to account all items as they are either earned or consumed. Finally, it indicates the full extent of assets and liabilities' (New South Wales Auditor-General, 1986-87).

Some argue that accrual accounting is applicable throughout the public sector. However this ignores some difficulties in application (Robson, 1988, pp. 1-20, Walker 1988, pp. 20-32). First, while there are obvious advantages of the accrual approach for public trading enterprises, there are also differences between private and public enterprises. We have already noted the distinction between the social and commercial goals of the public sector. The question inevitably rises as to whether accounting criteria developed for private, commercial enterprises can adequately account for the inevitable array of non-commercial obligations and objectives. Second, there are a large number of public sector institutions which in no way resemble the corporate structures of the private sector. The Secretary of the New South Wales Treasury has noted, for instance, that many Departments do not have an income and that therefore their performance cannot be measured on an income and expenditure basis (Allan, 1988). Third, the differences between the public and private sector may create conceptual difficulties for accounting purposes. Walker, for instance, has questioned whether the treatment of real estate as an asset in the private sector ('because it's subject to some legal claims, and is expected to produce some benefit either in use or on sale') is appropriate for public 'assets' such as national parks, schools and court houses. (Walker, 1988)

In conclusion, the differences which exist between the public and private sectors necessarily limits the applicability of a methodology designed to meet the objectives of profit-oriented commercial enterprises. For these reasons, accrual accounting techniques should be initially limited to clearly identifiable commercial enterprises and only selectively applied to other public sector spheres.

Economic efficiency in public trading enterprises should be gauged by analysing 'price efficiency' and the quantity and quality of goods and services which are produced, the technical efficiency of the enterprise and the dynamic efficiency or level of innovation which is evident in its operations and activities.

In terms of 'price efficiency', the States should continue to provide free and subsidised goods and services to users where they generate systematic externalities, advance social equity and assist people experiencing life crises. This principle applies to a large range of services within the areas of health, education, social welfare and public transport. However, there are a range of public sector activities for which user charges can legitimately be charged. *In these areas public enterprises should develop strategies for increased self-financing and commercial performance through extending full and partial user charges and competitive pricing policies which are consistent with the principles of social justice.*

In many different spheres such as electricity supply, postal services and telecommunications, public enterprises provide a universal service to each citizen regardless of the different costs involved. In recent times this strategy has come under challenge in both Commonwealth and State arenas. Some economists have called for competitive cost pricing for all services or a rationalisation of those services which do not provide a satisfactory commercial return. It is argued that it would be more cost efficient to provide direct cash subsidies to those who would be disadvantaged. However, the real issue does not concern the question of whether public enterprises should cross-subsidise particular kinds of users through their pricing policy. It is well accepted that either for geographical, social, economic or humane reasons certain groups of users should be cross-subsidised. The real issue concerns the form, extent and efficiency of the cross-subsidy. Public enterprises should be required to provide more information about the nature, direction and extent of cross subsidies and of joint and common costs and their recovery. Economists working within Australia Post, Telecom and other public enterprises are making efforts to develop effective means of accounting for and efficiently managing commercial and non-commercial objectives within public trading enterprises. (Xavier, 1989, p. 22; also see de Ridder, 1989.)

The evaluation of the *quality and effectiveness* of public services and organisations requires the establishment of both internal and external evaluative processes. The role of consumer and user groups is paramount. State Governments should provide financial support to enable such groups to actively survey and evaluate the priorities of public enterprises and departments such as water, electricity and gas authorities. Also, public enterprises should be encouraged to set service targets which can be monitored by independent reviews. The initiation of programs based directly on the assessment of user needs strengthens the community's willingness to defend and extend State public services and leads to greater efficiency in service provision and planning.

In order to attain maximum credibility, governments should consult with public sector unions and community representatives to develop a long-term and bipartisan strategy directed to assessing the community's requirements of public services as the first step in developing programs designed to meet these needs.

In terms of *technical efficiency* we have argued above that too often managers become preoccupied with minimising labour and capital costs as the sole guide towards increasing efficiency. Xavier has also argued that:

> 'calculating and publicising productivity on the basis of labour productivity also is far too simplistic and can be misleading' (Xavier, 1989, p. 28).

Resource management in public organisations can certainly gain nothing from such a narrow perspective.

State trading enterprises must also satisfy *social equity objectives* such as meeting community service obligations. As the Victorian Social Justice Strategy Unit has pointed out, it is not only the traditional 'social policy' Departments which affect people's access to resources but also those which are often thought as 'non-social sector' departments (Social Justice Strategy Unit, 1988). The problem here lies not in the fulfillment of these obligations, but in the fact that multiple objectives, with no clear priorities, can thwart good performance and accountability. (Ayub & Hegstad, 1987) Where public enterprises are expected to achieve social objectives it should be necessary for their goals to be clear and unambiguous so that precise measures of accountability can be developed. In this respect the separate identification and detailed costing of community service obligations is a necessary process because it allows an assessment of non-commercial objectives and the cost of the obligations to be taken into account when either monitoring commercial performance or regulating prices. And while there are a number of issues to be decided in relation to the appropriate methodology for determining the costs of community service obligations, there should be planned corporate targets in both social and commercial spheres of operation. As the above discussion indicates, targeting social equity, equality, access and participation is desirable and can be developed in tandem with the public trading enterprises' financial targets (cf. Lansdowne, 1989).

Social Performance Indicators

'If, as a society, we value as ends in themselves public participation in decision-making, freedom of information, or the rights of citizens in their interactions with the State to a fair hearing and a fair deal, and if we decide to pursue them as integral parts of our democratic system, it is conceptually muddled thinking to argue that they interfere with the 'efficiency' of public sector activities. They may well cost more, and in some cases affect the economy with which

activities are carried out (though in others they will improve the quality of decision-making and reduce implementation costs), but in nearly every case they may well improve efficiency (and input/output measure) as they are amongst the very outputs we are seeking to achieve. They are however not quantifiable' (Peter Wilenski, 'Social Change as a Source of Competing Values' in AJAPA, Vol. XLVII, No. 3, 1988).

It is harder, but by no means impossible to define concrete and quantifiable targets for more abstract social justice goals such as participation and democracy. The Swedish national five-year research study of power and democracy, the Norwegian long-term program report and the 1989 Swedish Inequality Study are all examples of analyses of power and participation which aim to develop practical reforms and provide concrete indicators (Royal Ministry of Finance, 1985, Petersson, 1987).

Social, as well as economic performance, should be subject to measures of accountability. To aid in this, State Governments should define two different kinds of goals. The first we have outlined above in Section 4.4.2, that is, the broad social and political goals of government. Under this category, for example, comes the Victorian Government's social justice objectives of reducing disadvantage, increasing access, expanding opportunities for participation and extending legal, industrial and political rights (Social Justice Strategy Unit, 1987). We have argued above that there are various measures which can be taken to ensure these objectives are meaningful, worthwhile and achievable and the ultimate performance sanction is through the electoral process. The second set of social goals pertains to the actual implementation of detailed components of each strategy through public services and organisations. It is this second area which is discussed in this section.

Aside from ensuring the maintenance of general rights, such as those outlined by Wilenski above, State Governments should define goals to be achieved through particular agencies, with carefully planned budgets, in specific areas of need, within a particular time frame. This will often involve targeting resources and a package of measures which can be implemented through a number of different public agencies. A State program targeting children in poverty, for example, might involve:

— cash payments for low-income families, such as Victoria's Education Maintenance Allowance, to help offset the costs associated with schooling and to encourage participation;
— special school-based programs for children who require extra coaching or assistance;
— action programs involving non-government organisations which are aimed to alleviate the distress of poverty as well as to combat the vicious cycle of self perpetuating poverty;
— special child-care programs for single parent families to enable the guardian to obtain work;
— *concerted* Commonwealth and State action in relation to housing for low-income families; and
— training and job creation programs for long-term unemployed people. The important aspect in this is that the package of measures must be coordinated and evaluated across each State agency and department.

The task of overall coordination should be the task of the State Social Justice Secretariat recommended earlier. These Secretariats could in turn work with the Premiers' Conference Secretariat we have recommended. Such an arrangement would help coordinate the States' social justice activities at a national level.

So far as ensuring that the actual day-to-day targets of social justice strategies are met, social performance indicators should be devised as part of the monitoring process overseen by departmental management and reviewed by the State Social Justice Secretariat. Agencies and departments should be required to develop their own indicators which show the qualitative and quantitative dimensions of their work. As the foregoing discussion on workplace change and State trading enterprises indicates, this process needs to be tailored to the particular goals and functions of the agency involved and may involve devising indicators for different purposes such as overall budgetary and resource considerations for funding agencies; targets, priorities and plans for corporate managers and day to day priorities for service providers.

Victoria's Department of Management and Budget and the Public Service Board of New South Wales have published a number of papers on how to develop performance indicators, and the general process of devising indicators should involve wedding social justice strategy goals to the particular functions and achievements of public organisations (DMB, 1987; PSB, 1986a, 1986b).

One general model for developing agency level social performance indicators has been outlined by Victoria's Social Justice Strategy Unit. Using Victoria's Home Energy Advisory Service (HEAS) and the TAFE Work Preparation and Occupational Skills Program, the VSJU outlines a number of steps in devising and implementing social performance indicators. The first step involves identifying the objectives of a department or unit and showing how they address general social justice objectives and other specific social priority areas. The second step involves identifying target groups within the ambit of social justice policy and which are also targetted by the specific agency for service delivery. The third step involves identifying the resource and non-resource inputs which are required to meet the needs of the target groups and to provide services. The fourth step involves specifying the activities through which the resource and non-resource inputs are turned into services or outputs. The fifth step involves specifying output results including the number of clients, types of clients and quantities of service produced. The sixth step involves assessing the net effect of the activities on the target population including showing 'the impact on the original problems, who receives assistance and the impact of the program on people's well being'. The seventh step involves devising indicators which are capable of assessing efficiency ('program delivery and administration in terms of input/output relationships'), productivity ('the amount of work performed by or expected of each unit of staff at a given time'), effectiveness ('including equity, utilisation, client satisfaction, accessibility and timeliness') and the cost effectiveness ('the total cost of achieving a given outcome') of the program. The eighth step involves checking that the indicators are valid for the organisation and evaluative process, and finally, the ninth step involves proscribing the use and meaning of the indicators. As the VSJU argue:

'The most constructive approach in using performance indicators is to acknowledge their imperfections where they occur and to qualify information accordingly' (VSJU, 1988, pp. 11-18).

The task of establishing social performance indicators will be enhanced by industrial democracy and the work organisation plans which are sketched above, however, in many different areas the development process is just beginning. In some cases social performance indicators have not been successful and have constituted an added administrative burden for already over-strapped service providers. However, in the 1980s era of economic rationalism in which the statistical idolisation of dollar values prevails, it will be increasingly necessary to provide sound and effective indicators of social performance. There is no doubt that if this task can be undertaken effectively the future of public services in many different areas will be assured; social performance continues to be a point of profound ignorance for 'the privatisers'.

Notes

1 The meaning of the word 'renewal' in this context is obviously different to that of the Scott Report (NSW) 1989.
2 Exemplifying this Mr J.R. Smith Chief General Manager of the SECV maintained in 1986 that: 'In the past eight years the SEC has paid $458m in dividends to governments. It has had to borrow that much more because of those dividends. Obviously electricity customers have to pay the interest bill on that extra debt.' *The Age.*

Chapter 5

THE PROBLEMS OF PRIVATISATION

5.1 Introduction

A great deal has been written about privatisation, and yet much of the cumbersome research and scholarship in the area is removed from the consideration of real social and economic policy contexts. In contrast, this chapter considers what the strategies of privatisation can offer in relation to the real issues and problems of Australian society as they relate to State public sectors. *How will privatisation solve the problems of the State public sector? Can privatisation be a vehicle for public sector reform? How effective has privatisation been in practice?*

As the UK and the US experiences show, one of the primary aims of a strategy of privatisation is to cut back the size of the public sector. This is justified by an argument that high taxation and government expenditure have been the fundamental cause of the rising unemployment and inflation associated with the 'stagflation' of the 1970s and 80s. The idea is to cut back government expenditures by selling off unnecessary assets and unproductive public enterprises to the private sector as a precondition for tax cuts (cf. Greiner, 1988).

The rationale for this position is that high income taxes have led to a decline in the supply of labour, allegedly because *high and rising taxation and increased social security benefits have reduced the rewards and incentive to work. Further taxes on capital[1] have resulted in decreased profits, inducing an out-flow of capital to lower taxed jurisdictions and sectors of the economy.* In short, high and spiraling government expenditure levels reputedly gnaw away inexorably at national income and savings, thereby restraining productivity and output growth.

Without going into unnecessary detail, these arguments have been rebutted in the H.V. Evatt Research Centre's *The Capital Funding of Public Enterprises* (Evatt, 1988, pp. 76-106). Privatisation arguments about the effects of taxation and social welfare collapse in a detailed comparison with other countries. In the taxation sphere, for example, Australia is rated 19th out of 23 OECD countries in terms of total tax burden and the Australian corporate sector contributes less to government revenue than their counterparts in a range of comparable OECD countries (LRC, 1988). Moreover, if public enterprises are sold to the private sector, any borrowings which such enterprises require in the future are merely reclassified as private. This does nothing to alleviate the pressure for funds in capital markets. Finally, rather than 'gnawing away at national savings', investment in many parts of the public sector results in ongoing social and economic returns. On the other hand, and as shown in *The Capital Funding of Public Enterprises* (Evatt Research Centre, 1988, p. 94), the sale of assets and enterprises produces only a one-off financial return. Also, as is argued below, the micro-economic claims of privatisation are not justifiable because there is no provision for concrete structural reforms or mechanisms for achieving increased productivity; it is simply assumed that a change from public to private ownership will result in greater efficiency. The case studies cited in Part Five indicate that this position cannot be sustained.

Another ideological cornerstone of privatisation is the view that greater individual freedom will result from a reduced government role in economic and social activity. New South Wales Premier Greiner, the best known advocate of privatisation in the State sphere, argues for privatisation as a means of increasing political freedom, liberty and enterprise.

At the heart of this view is the concept that

individual ownership of the bulk of property and assets is a necessary condition for political freedoms (Hayek, 1944). Whereas, it is alleged, State ownership allegedly encroaches upon freedom, liberty and enterprise by appropriating the rights of use and transfer over assets and property, subordinating individual interests to the 'dead hand of the State', privatisation returns assets to the individual and endows individuals with the freedom to choose when and how to utilise and dispose of their wealth. In contrast with this philosophy other connotations of the word 'freedom' are important. The freedom of taxpayers to spend their own income should be contrasted with the social goal of freedom from want and deprivation. Being free to participate in mainstream Australian society would be out of the question if the sick were priced out of the health market or if the old and infirm were priced out of the community service market. Basic government services; income support, health, education and other services do free people from deprivation and need which would otherwise severely limit their ability to participate in society.

The problem here, as the section on public sector renewal demonstrates, is that privatisation *throws the best parts and endeavors of the public sector out with the bath water.* Clearly there is great merit in ensuring the most effective use of public revenue, questioning the strategy of some public sector endeavors and in suggesting reforms which will result in increased efficiencies. This point gets lost, however, in the narrow and exclusive reference point provided by a theoretical model of the market place. The philosophy of privatisation ignores the positive role and methods of the public sector in combatting social inequality and creating otherwise lost economic and social opportunities. Due to this oversight, action taken to privatise the public sector has not secured freedom, liberty and enterprise for the majority. In reality the rhetoric of privatisation often functions as a blunt ideological instrument wielded by those not fully versed in the subtleties and complexities of government.

For example, Premier Greiner's quest to reduce public expenditure has resulted in severe cutbacks to the State's budget for schools and hospitals. A strategy to improve the cost efficiency of public expenditure would be more acceptable if a detailed survey was undertaken of where greater cost efficiency could be achieved. However, in New South Wales there has often been an assumption that public expenditure is bad *per se*. The result has been a disaster for social and economic justice. The positive benefits that result from small class teaching in secondary schools, school sports programs, language classes, classes for disabled children, regional welfare workers, regional hospitals and community service offices have simply not been registered or understood (*SMH*, 26/4/89).

Perhaps the most famous example of privatisation touted as a means of ensuring 'a property owning democracy' was the UK Government's sale of public assets and equity in nationalised industries. The idea was to revive a 'spirit of enterprise' where individuals become self-reliant rather than dependant upon State provision. Thus, through the sale of British Telecom, for example, the Thatcher Government induced purchases by individuals who would not otherwise have had the opportunity to purchase share capital and property. Other examples included the sale of assets to employees (as in the case of the National Freight Consortium) or public housing to tenants on favorable terms. As Chapter Eleven shows, this last example was pioneered in Victoria from the 1950s to the mid 1970s.

These moves have political appeal. However, as one leading member of the British Labour Party's National Executive Committee correctly observed;

> 'the term "property-owning democracy" has been cleverly used by the Prime Minister and reinterpreted as the "democracy based on property" . . . the reversal of the process achieved over the last 100 years is presented as the popular cause to free people from bureaucracy, government "interference"; and the "dead hand" of the State' (Blunkett, 1985, p. 67).

In effect the British Government merely substituted 'the dead hand of the State' for 'the cold shoulder of the private sector', for nationalised industries were sold with their monopoly powers intact. Contrary to the rhetoric of enhanced competitiveness and consumer choice, the de-nationalisation program primarily engineered a massive transfer of income generating assets from the British public to shareholders. Share issues at a discount have proved understandably popular and shareholdership has increased markedly to 20% of British households (British Treasury, 1987). There is, however, a noticeable tendency for individual shareholdings in de-nationalised concerns to be sold for quick profit soon after purchase (Thompson, 1988; Shackleton, 1984).

The success of the privatisation experiment has been further put into doubt through instances of asset-stripping after the sale of public enterprises.[2] In such instances a significant lump sum transfer occurs which benefits private shareholders to the detriment of the British taxpaying public.

5.2 Forms of Privatisation

Figure 5.1 outlines the various forms of privatisation evident in the State public sector and includes examples identified in the State chapters of this book. Neither the figure nor the case studies are exhaustive, but they do indicate how widespread privatisation is at the State level.

5.2.1 Direct Sale

Privatisation commonly refers to the sale or transfer of public sector assets or functions to the private sector. The most well known form of privatisation involves the direct and outright sale of ownership rights in a public asset. This can occur through:

- the grant or sale of shares to management;
- the sale of equity through a stock exchange flotation;
- the direct sale of an enterprise or asset to private firms; or
- through the direct sale of assets followed by their lease back on a rental basis.

5.2.2 Competitive Tendering

Privatisation also encompasses other policy programs which are designed to replace existing public sector activities with those of the private sector. For example, 'competitive tendering' involves the contracting out of work from the public sector to private firms. This is a practice which in recent times has become the single biggest, and most effective form of privatisation within the Commonwealth, State and local Government sectors.[3]

Traditionally, all tiers of government have regularly put out to tender the right to supply certain goods and services, in much the same way as we invariably collect three or four quotations from removal companies when moving to another house (*The Guardian*, Nov. 6th, 1988; Waterson, 1988). However, in the current era, competitive tendering practices have fundamentally changed, fuelled particularly by the theory of contestable markets (see below). Competitive tendering is seen as a way of improving the efficiency of traditional areas of public sector activity. Economists see it as a viable means of substituting private contract labour and organisations for public enterprises and services (see Domberger, 1988).

With continual cutbacks to public expenditure, competitive tendering has also become widespread in new arenas such as social and community services (Farrar, 1989, pp. 73-75). However, as contract labour becomes the norm significant problems of accountability, quality of service, motivation of staff and the loss of externalities which accompany traditional forms of public service provision arise.

5.2.3 Liberalisation and Deregulation

Two further strategies associated with privatisation are *liberalisation and deregulation*. Liberalisation refers to the removal of restraints on entry into markets formerly the statutory province of a publicly or privately owned monopoly (cf. the case of Australian Telecommunications, IAC, 1988). Deregulation involves the removal of those regulations governing the activity of incumbent finances in an industry. Such regulation can encompass safety, pricing, rates of return, borrowing limits and quality standards.

While frequently overlapping in practice, these two measures are conceptually distinct in that liberalisation can proceed without any

Table 5.1

The Privatisation of State Public Services

Organisations: enterprises or departments involved in the production of saleable goods.	**Assets:** public property equipment, physical resources and infrastructure.	**Functions:** public activities which provide goods and/or services.

Direct Sale: the sale of an enterprise or an asset, normally through a tendering process or through a 'management buy-out', the sale of equity through public listing or the sale or grant of shares to employees which may precede a stock exchange float.

Contracting Out: the acceptance of private contracts to undertake functions on behalf of the public sector. A traditional practice for the public sector now being used more commonly and indiscriminately to cut short-term costs.

Public Service Abrogation/ Voluntarism: the abrogation of responsibility for services by the State, leading to an over-reliance on charitable institutions and unpaid voluntary work.

Examples: NSW Lands information; health services via private hospitals; Investment Corp. (management buyout); State Brickworks & Abattoirs – closure and sale of all assets & land; Elcom – power stations; SRA (sections) – proposed; **Vic.** Public housing;: **SA** Amdel, an advanced R & D establishment partially privatised after conversion to company; **WA** State Engineering Works foundry, equipment and land; **Qld** Port of Brisbane Authority pilotage service; Borallon Prison (proposed lease); Government Garage (failed); **Tas.** Precision Tool Annexe; Tasmanian Film Corporation; Tasmanian Herd Improvement Organisation (failed); Passenger bus services (Hobart).

Examples: NSW Road construction; Elcom maintenance; Public Housing; Public health; **Vic.** Housing design, construction and maintenance; up-grading and maintenance of gas and electricity services; **SA & WA** some functions in State Electricity Commission and Water Authority, Employment and Training Support Program; Employment services for disabled persons (includes elements of voluntarism); Legal Aid and Crown Law Department contracting private practitioners; **Qld** Mines stratigraphic drilling services; TAFE course delivery; road construction; operation of Brisbane Gateway Bridge (franchise); adoption service consultants; **Tas.** Road construction; housing construction, Auditor-General's function; Herd Improvement Program.

Examples: NSW Hospitals' health services closed; one quarter FACS* District Centres close includes services such as disaster welfare work, Aboriginal and migrant community workers, child welfare services (eg. child/sexual abuse workers), emergency income maintenance transferred to charities, abolition of ethnic policy adviser and Ethnic Consumers' Unit (BACA), abolition of employment assistance Schemes, withdrawal of funding for Independent Tenancy Advice Services, abolition of Women's Unit; Ethnic Services, Disabilities Unit Department of Housing, school assistants positions abolished; **Vic.** Un-resourced deinstitutionalisation of mental health care; **SA** Country fire services; NPWS volunteers, in public hospitals; (clerical work and cleaning; unresourced psychiatric hospital deinstitutionalisation; school assistants, 85% of all ambulance personnel; **WA** employment services for disabled people; school assistant positions abolished; ambulance services; **Qld** Warilda Child Protection Facility transferred to voluntary agency; **Tas.** under 16 year olds not being made wards of the State, forced to shelter accommodation; young psychiatric sufferers under-resourced services, including those liable to sexual or physical abuse.

Note: * Family and Community Services.

relaxation of regulation (cf. Waterson, 1988, pp. 122-123; Vickers & Yarrow, 1986).

Liberalisation and deregulation programs have been particularly important in the US, with the policy receiving a considerable amount of attention in the case of the US airlines and telecommunications industry. The US and British experience suggests the following general patterns emerging as a consequence of liberalisation and de-regulation.

Firstly, prices in liberalised markets do fall in response to potential and actual competition (cf. Bailey *et al.*, 1985; Morrison & Winston, 1986); though this impact is by no means universal (e.g. airline fares between smaller U.S. cities have risen). Secondly, the benefits of price competition may have to be offset against the potential dangers of a more lax regulatory regime on such matters as safety.[4] Thirdly, in the longer-term, there is evidence that liberalised industries tend to restructure themselves in response to the vigorous competition unleashed by the policy. Mergers and strategic pricing behaviour designed to block entry or drive out small competitors is a common feature of such re-structuring. This longer-term tendency suggests that monopolisation tendencies in industries chosen for liberalisation are stronger than originally envisaged by policy makers. They may herald a new era of much less vigorous competition, if not tacit cartel behaviour.[5]

5.2.4 Public Service Abrogation

Another form of privatisation, 'public service abrogation' is particularly important in relation to Australian State public services because, as later sections demonstrate, it directly compromises State justice and equity objectives. 'Public service abrogation' is a withdrawal of responsibility for services by the State or a refusal to take responsibility for areas which, if left to private sector financial support, would result in social injustice and inequality.

Public sector abrogation can occur through shifting the onus of responsibility for community care of the elderly, handicapped, sick, etc, from the State to the family or through 'voluntarism'. Similar to the issue of 'contracting out', there is an increasing dependency by State Governments on voluntarism as a means

of combatting social injustice and inequality. In Western Australia, for example, Employment and Training support programs are being offered to non-government agencies, and in welfare services non-government agencies will get $23.3m (up 20%) of the $101.4m allocated to the Department for Community Services for the financial year 1988/89 (Budget Papers, Western Australia, 1988). In New South Wales, the Greiner Government has rationalised many planning staff in the Department of Family and Community Services, while at the same time, Virginia Chadwick, the responsible Minister, has pledged greater use of voluntary labour for social services (Chadwick, Speech, 17/6/88).

5.2.5 'User Pays'

As with competitive tendering and voluntarism, the 'users pays' principle has been radicalised by the philosophy of privatisation. There are, of course, many services where State public services should charge users and can implement more effective charging policies. Examples include scientific testing for business in government labouratories, provision of public infrastructure or services for business and use of water resources (cf. Paterson, 1987, p. 188; IAC, 1988).

However, the user pays principle has been used indiscriminately. The Curran report commissioned by the Greiner Government in New South Wales, for example, insists that 'opportunities exist to increase passenger fare scales beyond the recent increases' for the Urban Transport Authority (Curran, 1988, p. A.2). Ordinary bus fares were raised by up to 100% in the first few months of the Greiner Government's term of office and rises have continued a pace (cf. 'Income Tax Down, State fees Up', *SMH*, July 1, 1989, p. 6). Such increases are premised on the idea that if such authorities are forced to rely more on direct charges increased economic efficiency will result.

The fallacy of this logic, which models public enterprises on the principle of private profit maximisation, is that it ignores the largely regressive effect of increased charges (equity) and the consequences of raising bus charges to comparability with the costs of private transport (externalities). The positive externalities resulting from lower fares are, of course, obvious. However, proponents of the increased user charges route to economic efficiency fail to register these positive externalities (ie fewer traffic jams, lower pollution, reduced road maintenance, more efficient energy use, safety etc) of a reliable and cheap public transport system (Beed & Moriarty, 1988, pp. 57-68).

The efficiency of the Greiner Government's moves to increase fares on buses and trains can also be queried on the grounds that the price elasticity is such that such increases will reduce the use of public transport. The immediate impact is less revenue but, at the same time, there are hidden costs on the community as commuters.

5.3 Privatisation Versus State Public Service Objectives

Aside from the general ideology that the public sector is too big and must be cut back it is important to consider exactly how privatisation would specifically address or change the acknowledged objectives of the public sector. Privatisation simply does not address the need for public service provision nor does it solve problems which the State public sectors are currently faced with.

Three important reasons commonly invoked to justify government intervention are market failure, equity objectives and strategic considerations. Each of these is examined alongside strategies to minimise the involvement of the public sector. Though by no means a comprehensive survey, this enables a broad understanding of key issues arising from privatisation.

5.3.1 Market Failure

Market failure refers to those factors which cause markets to produce economically inefficient outcomes. Market failure has a number of possible sources including the case of natural monopolies. A natural monopoly occurs in an industry where the technical conditions of production and market size are such that it is undesirable to have more than one incumbent firm, as fewer resources are used than would be the case if a number of operators competed for both resources and markets (cf. Waterson, 1988).

Public Ownership or Regulation

There are two common public sector responses to the existence of natural monopoly. First there is 'regulation through public ownership' (cf. Domberger, 1988). In the Australian States, for example, the public sector has retained ownership of electricity generation and distribution, water supply and most public transport. The second response involves government regulation of a private monopoly. This practice, common in the US, usually involves a regulatory framework administered by a government agency. In New South Wales, the Australian Gas Light Company is a natural monopoly which operates under State legislation but which is also partly owned by the State Government.

The key advantages of public ownership over regulation of a private or semi-private natural monopoly are that the often considerable profits of the public enterprise are paid directly into general State revenue, and the government has a direct means of regulating industry and monitoring the enterprise's behaviour should it take undue advantage of its monopoly position. On the other hand, critics of public ownership argue that public enterprises are inefficient, can be a drain on the public purse and should be free to manage without government interference. As such privatisation and the regulatory role is favoured.

In the UK where the privatisation of nationalised industries has been rapid, evidence shows that the inefficiency of public enterprises is mythical when compared with the performance of the new private monopolies (eg. see The Economist, Dec 87; Thompson, 1988, pp. 35-9). Also in most cases, the government which sells an enterprise must forgo a regular return to general revenue (Thompson, 1988, p. 36).

There are also significant problems in regulating private monopolies (Thompson, 1988, pp. 31-4). For example, adequately determining and regulating fair prices is a major problem because regulators have no absolute means of determining correct cost levels. Apparently objective evaluations can also lead to problems. As an example, rate of return regulation encourages excessive investment in capital and equipment (Thompson, 1988, pp.

31-2; Domberger, 1988; Averch & Johnson, 1962). A second problem is the capture of regulatory agencies by powerful interest groups. A third involves the regulatory agency pursuing its own discretionary goals, resulting in inefficiencies or problems for the industry (Thompson, 1988, p. 32); and the fourth is the inefficiencies which can result from 'shadow management' by the public sector. (cf. EPEA, 1986).

Contestable Markets?

The theory of perfectly contestable markets developed by a group of American economists (Baumol *et al.*, 1982) has also brought into question the traditional role of the public sector in situations of natural monopoly, by suggesting that competition or contestability for markets can prove an effective discipline on monopoly behaviour.

The problem with the theory of contestable markets is that before it offers any advantages a set of very strict theoretical conditions must be followed. A monopoly must be confronted by a rival firm which can exactly replicate the existing output/price under identical cost and demand conditions. The monopoly must be compelled not to underprice its potential competitor upon entry and the competitor must be able to exit the market having lost nothing, that is, it must be able to retrieve the cost of all fixed assets (net of depreciation) by selling those assets in second-hand markets. If all these things apply, the theory is that the monopoly will be compelled not to raise prices over costs (cf. Gittens, *SMH*, 14/12/88).

Competitive Tendering

It is upon this foundation that competitive tendering has developed. The idea is that perfect contestability can be reached through the offer of recurrent short-term contracts which allow control over price/output. Where control over output is secondary, and as long as market conditions approximate those of perfect contestability, liberalisation is a key means of nullifying monopoly power.

There are a number of problems with this thesis. Perfect contestability requires that there be freedom of entry into the market and that, equally importantly, exit is costless.[6] In other words, the implication is that the public must ensure that the burden of sunk costs should be minimised by ensuring or supplying access to sunk facilities. Second, legislative impediments to entry and exit from markets would have to be relaxed.[7]

To use the perfect contestability thesis in practical policy entails high risks, as Yarrow (1986) amongst others has argued. There are a number of significant problems with the contestability hypothesis which render it of limited usefulness for practical policy use. It relies exclusively on particular cost structures and models which very rarely occur.

Despite this, competitive tendering has been popularised through the concept of contestable markets.[8] However, there are a number of problems with the contracting out process which contradict this purpose and these need to be noted.

In the first instance there are problems with the tendering process itself. It would seem sensible to elicit a large number of bids. However eliciting quotations is not 'free' in that there are the costs of arranging appointments, discussing requirements and evaluating tenders. In addition, producing tenders does cost money and the larger the number of bidders the greater the likelihood of tender failure and propensity to capitalise tender preparation costs into bids. Hence, a large number of bids may be counter-productive in terms of raising the bid which is on average realised (Forsyth, 1988). This is of course predicated on the absence of collusion amongst bidders which would 'rig' the tender process.

Second, the question of evaluating bids is problematical. In the case of readily specified, easily evaluated services or goods the size of the bid becomes the sole criterion. But what of products or services where quality criteria are central to tender evaluation? Problems are particularly evident when dealing with expensive goods/services whose technical complexity may render monitoring contractor performance a hazardous exercise. This can be aggravated by asymmetric information between evaluator and contractor concerning the technical conditions of production.

Thirdly, there is the problem of enforcing a contract. The emergence of unforeseen circumstances which cannot be identified as either outside or within the contractor's control may render the original quotation price unprofitable (AFCSME, 1988). This is most likely when manifold uncertainties surround the original specification (Williamson, 1986). If the original quotation is no longer profitable, alternative contractors will be unwilling to step in at that price. Arrangements to secure continuity of supply can be a problem and act to cement the original contractors and evaluator's relationship.

A fourth issue concerns contract type and length. In cases of granting an operating franchise, the auction framework mimics the perfectly contestable market where sunk costs are zero and the potential entrant is on an equal footing with the incumbent. But the incumbent has no incentive to foster use of assets in an economic way. Similarly with complete short-term contracts, incentive problems once again emerge in that the short-time horizon deters investment, and the government must deal with asset transfer and removal problems. Long-term contracts ameliorate some of these difficulties, but uncertainties about market and technical developments substantially increase. It is not possible to specify a precise price schedule for the entire length of contract, and promises on quality of service delivery must necessarily be vague. Furthermore, contract enforcement is weakened by risks of litigation, the deterrent effects of sequestration of long-lived assets and the understandable unwillingness of government officials to admit mistakes.

A fifth issue identified in the economic theory is the phenomenon of winners curse. The concept of winners' curse applies in the case of an auction where the bidders have the task of estimating the value of a resource or property right. A bidder who correctly estimates the value of the resource on average is likely to 'win' the auction when a mistake is made in the direction of over-estimating the value of a resource or property right in a particular case. There is evidence that this phenomenon is important in practice (cf. Grauvogl, 1988) The winners' curse phenomenon would suggest, especially in new areas where the private sector has little experience, that contractors will find they have over-estimated the value of the contract. In order to cover costs they may well be fored to reduce the quality of the service, try to reduce wages, or simply walk away from their obligations. This could well explain the high failure rate observed among private contractors.

On top of these problems, the evidence emerging from early experience with competitive tendering is that where significant cost savings are realised they are largely a result of forcing down wages and worsening working conditions in already low wage arenas of the economy. For example, in service areas such as bus transport (Teal et al., 1984), refuse collection and hospital domestic services (Domberger, 1988), substantial cost savings have been documented. Domberger, interpreting evidence on refuse collection and hospital domestic services in Britain, claims large savings of 20% and 25% p.a. respectively. Caution is warranted here because even in Domberger's study there are a significant number of instances where results have been mixed, with some contracts being rescinded at short notice (TUC, 1984; Waterson, 1988) and most importantly, one has to distinguish between cost savings whose source is improvement in factor productivities, and those which are attributable to deterioration in working conditions and wages. The latter example simply involves a transfer of income rather than an improvement in economic efficiency (Thompson, 1988, p. 39).

Further challenging the neatness of the new concept of competitive tendering is the fact that even given legitimate improvements in productivity, the causative factors of the improvement are independent of the actual process of competitive tendering and could just as easily be instituted in publicly run services and enterprises. This is a key issue that is addressed under the heading of public sector renewal.

Externalities
One of the most frequent cases of 'market failure' is where disadvantages arise from a commercial activity which either prohibit the activity or result in unacceptable social costs. There is a considerable economic literature on different examples of these 'externalities' including the case of common property

measures (Gordon, 1954), jointness in consumption and production activities and public goods (Boudway & Bruce, 1984).

The most significant thing to observe about externalities is that they are often central to the role and activities of the public sector. The State public sector has, for example, played a major role in undertaking those activities where there are extensive and lasting external public benefits but little financial return. Goods or services which are responsible for positive externalities ('merit goods': Cullis & Jones, 1987), are frequently provided by the State on a universal basis. Examples are health, education and housing.

Other examples include the creation and maintenance of national parks and roads. These fit into the category of 'public goods' which, in their theoretical form according to orthodox neo-classical economics, have the characteristics of being unaffected by their number of users and, once created, the service cost to an extra user is zero (cf. Boudway and Bruce, 1984, p. 118).

In fact, many 'public goods' such as national parks and roads are affected by the number of users (eg. trucks and campers) and maintenance costs are regular and considerable. In Chapter Three it was made clear that the cost of adequately maintaining Australia's social and economic infrastructure is a matter of national urgency especially if the process of economic restructuring is to proceed a pace (cf. SCTCI, 1988).

Despite the fact that 'congestion costs' are well recognised in the literature on public sector development, advocates of privatisation often fail to adequately take into account use and maintenance factors. One of the common mistakes to arise is the idea that many 'public goods' provided through the public sector are unaffected by extent of use and require little no or 'financial renewal' after an initial investment. This, in turn, results in a significant misunderstanding of the purposes of public revenue generation, an equally problematical assumption about the optimal size of public expenditure and finally, an underestimation of the need for well tuned problem solving, maintenance and service departments (H.V. Evatt, 1988, pp. 74-106).

'Negative externalities' are also of concern to the State public sector. Here such issues as land degradation, pollution and general safety standards are necessarily the subject of often costly, interventionist action by State and Commonwealth departments and authorities.

Taxes and statutory regulations which dissuade or prohibit the relevant activities can be enforced. It is frequently the case, however, that governments must deal with after-effects of either unforeseen or unregulated social or commercial events. For this reason, there is a growing body of opinion that maintains State action should be proactive rather than reactive. In areas such as occupational health and safety this approach requires investment, as well as experimentation and re-organisation of State institutions. This is most frequently opposed by the supporters of privatisation who argue for a minimal, thus reactive, role for the States (cf. the case of Victoria's Workcare, New South Wales' Workcover).

Another necessary, but less effective, route for dealing with 'negative externalities' which is guaranteed by various State statutory authorities involves measures designed to facilitate injured parties' access to litigation procedures (eg. Workers' Compensation tribunals, small claims tribunal, court system etc.).

Another form of market failure, which directly concerns those State public services which ensure legal rights and consumer protection, results from the fact that economically efficient choices in consumption and decision-making in production can only be secured with complete information. In the real world this can, of course, never be achieved and uncertainty must always be a factor of social and commercial decision-making. As a result, the public sector must often play an important mediatory role to prevent unfair trading advantages through administrative and regulatory action.

Consumer property resource problems inevitably require government intervention and involve the State in assigning property rights by such means as the allocation of licences or quotas. Market failure often results where information parity is not present between contracting parties. The insurance market is commonly cited here, but other consumer markets can be similarly troublesome. In such cases, consumer rights legislation is necessary to combat the problems which emerge due to the exploitation of information advantages by opportunistic traders (Williamson, 1975).

5.3.2 Equity and Justice Versus the Care-less Society?

Equity and justice are also widely accepted reasons for the establishment of public services, and are of particular significance to State public sectors, which deliver the majority of Australia's 'people services'. Proponents of privatisation often argue that consumption of welfare benefits *merely absorb an ever increasing share of GDP and waste scarce resources which would otherwise be productively employed in the private sector.* This, of course, ignores the fact that there is social inequality in our society which needs to be combated. As David Heald has pointed out, even in a perfect market which generates economically efficient outcomes, these outcomes may not be regarded as fair or just. For example:

'. . . the interaction of unequal starting positions and the process of market exchange, may quite unjustly limit the life chances of certain individuals and classes' (Heald, 1983, p. 120).

State public services deploy a number of mechanisms in pursuit of equity and justice. The major focus of State activity is to generate greater equality of opportunity through education, housing and health services, while the majority of Federal programs are aimed at providing greater equality of outcomes through income maintenance and social security programs which seek to modify the outcomes of the market mechanism. As an ageing population and higher levels of unemployment are continuing problems in almost all developed nations, the cash-transfer based equality of outcome programs have been growing fastest in recent times. However, it is clear that services promoting equality of opportunity will provide the most proactive means of combatting future social inequality in Australian society.

Further repudiating the proponents of privatisation is the fact that while welfare expenditure does not directly increase output there are considerable secondary benefits (externalities) for society and the economy as a whole. For example, health and education spending increase labour productivity, reduce production costs as well as improve the quality of social life. Welfare expenditure also helps to spread consumption evenly over an individual's life cycle. Furthermore, beneficiaries in the current period have usually contributed to government revenue and society in the past, or will do so in the future. Government spending thus serves to stimulate aggregate demand and employment in times of recession. All of these arguments are ignored by the proponents of privatisation.

Of even more significance for the purposes of this study are the consequences of ignoring problems such as youth poverty, homelessness, inequality and under-spending on social infrastructure and welfare services which are the logical outcome of privatisation and the other doctrines of economic rationalism.

Social inequality in Australia will increase significantly unless strategies are devised to make the public sector more responsive to community needs. If this does not occur Australia will undoubtedly move further down the path towards gross social inequity and the 'care-less' society.

The NZ Royal Commission on Social Policy has clearly defined the concept of 'Minimal State' involvement as:

'where the family is regarded as solely responsible for the care of dependants. In practice, this means the responsibility rests largely on women working without a wage within the household' (NZ RCSP, 1988, Vol II, p. 213).

In the light of this definition it should be noted here that one of the first actions of the Greiner Government in NSW was to rename the Department of Youth and Community Services, Family and Community Services. The following table indicates the differences between the 'minimal' State and the 'supportive' State approach.

Table 5.2

The State and Caring Work — Two Models	
The Minimal State	**The Supportive State**
Who benefits from care?	
Family care is a private good which benefits individual family members.	Family care is both a private and a social good because it benefits society as well as family members.
Who is responsible?	
The family is responsible for its dependent members.	Caring for dependants is a social responsibility shared by families and the State.
The State's main responsibility is not to interfere with family care.	The State's main responsibility is to support families in providing care.
What are the costs?	
Family care costs taxpayers nothing, whereas State care incurs costs which must be met from taxes.	All forms of care incur costs, including the caregiver's forgone earnings and labour market productivity.
Taxpayers' money can be saved by a policy of minimum assistance, targeted to only the most needy.	Over time, flexible, needs-based schemes assistance designed to support families is likely to give the best care at the lowest overall cost.
Who should be assisted, and how?	
State assistance is a substitute for family care. It should be provided only as a last resort.	State assistance provides essential support to families. Family care should be integrated into a continuum of services and programs.
The State must be careful not to encourage carers to evade their responsibilities.	The supportive State provides appropriate alternatives so that the family does not have to struggle to the point of breakdown.
Only the dependent should be eligible for assistance, when stand-alone family care has clearly broken down.	Dependents and caregivers form a unit and both require assistance. Supportive help ensures that families do not break down and are able to provide as much care as the can.

5.4 Privatisation and Public Sector Efficiency

The case for reducing the role of the public sector is sometimes expressed in terms of 'efficiency'. However, 'privatisors' invariably fail to acknowledge or conceptualise all the dimensions of economic efficiency, they simply focus on those measures which best suit their case. It is sometimes even argued that the private sector is inherently more efficient than the public sector. The Evatt Research Centre's *The Capital Funding of Public Enterprises* refuted this argument in some detail (Evatt, 1988, pp. 47-74).

However, it is important to reiterate and extend that Report's conclusions.

5.4.1 Allocative Efficiency

Perhaps the most used concept of efficiency in current debates about privatisation is that of *allocative efficiency*. To be allocatively efficient the existing resources of an economy cannot be re-allocated without making somebody worse off. The achievement of Pareto optimality (as it is known) is accomplished when the market operates under the assumptions necessary for neo-classical economics:

'. . . profit maximisation on the part of producers, prices equal at costs (marginal or minimum average) and consumer freedom (sovereignty) to maximise want satisfaction (utility)' (Groenewegen, 1988, p. 9).

In its survey of New South Wales State public services, the the Curran Report, almost exclusively used the concept of allocative efficiency. As a result it reached conclusions which included:

'. . . the widest possible application of "the user pay principle", replacing public by private provision of goods and services wherever possible, using vouchers for public services to increase consumer choice to the highest possible level and, for the same reason, to substitute cash subsidies for subsidies in kind' (Groenewegen, 1988, p. 9).

Groenewegen has shown how this type of analysis breaks down when it has to deal with real public sector issues and obligations such as:

'(a) externalities or interdependencies in want satisfaction and production where consumption/output patterns of one set of consumers/producers influence that of another;
(b) public good characteristics in which consumption is non-rival and it is either impossible or impractical to exclude persons from its benefits if they are not willing to contribute to the costs;
(c) goods or services which enhance aggregate social welfare (in terms of satisfaction) if provided free rather than charged for (toll free bridges or roads, for example; perhaps fare free public transport);
(d) merit wants provision where individual preferences are said to need correction for a variety of reasons by the higher authority of the State' (Groenewegen, 1988, p. 9).

Finally, the Curran Commission also ignored the efficiency consequences of distributing resources over time (inter-temporal efficiency) in the case of investment; and the costs of adjustment relative to the long-term gains which are expected to be made from a particular structural change or resource allocation (dynamic efficiency). The use of such a limited definition of efficiency ignores the fact that better means of assessing public sector performance are available (see Chapter Four). When these alternatives are utilised, the so-called efficiency reasons for privatisation are shown to be intellectually shallow and politically motivated.

5.4.2 The Profit Motive

In its findings the Commission also took up some well known ideological positions associated with privatisation. The Commission found that public enterprises will not perform as well as private organisations due to three factors: firstly, because public organisations lack a clear-cut profit objective, the assumed over-riding goal of private enterprise; secondly, public enterprises are assumed to follow a number of different and sometimes contradictory objectives amongst which cost minimisation has low priority and thirdly, the incentives confronting public sector management are not compatible with the pursuit of efficiency in production since neither their earnings nor tenure are directly related to any measure of performance such as profitability (See Curran, 1988, p. 72). These ideas echo well known dogma that the public sector is inefficient though lack of market discipline; that public sector managerial slackness is due to the fact that salaries and decision-making are not dictated by the discipline of performance based on profits and losses, that the public sector has no incentive to satisfy the preferences of customers and clients; the consequence is rigid bureaucratic managerial procedures which lack entrepreneurial and innovative flair (Reekie, 1984). It is also asserted that because of the security of the public sector, trade unions can negotiate higher wage increases than would otherwise be the case; monopoly positions allow the passing on of such cost increases in the form of higher prices or taxes (See Buchanon, 1975; Stigler, 1975; Posner, 1974; Mueller, 1979).

Clearly where and if these problems of

wastage or inefficiency exist in the public sector they should be remedied; however privatisation strategies provide no suggested method for reform other than to assert that *things are more efficient in the private sector and that the public sector should be turned over to the private sector.* As we have seen above this is not only unlikely in many areas, it is also undesirable (Wiltshire, 1988, p. 13). David Corbett has argued this model of efficiency:

'. . . can lead not only to an often misplaced preference for people with private sector experience; it can lead also to damaging cuts, simplistic corporate planning, inappropriate commercialisation and wrong application of the user pays principle and finally to privatisation at the expense of the community's genuine needs. All of these can so change the shape of the public sector and the motivations of its personnel as to vitiate the traditional public service values of service, guardianship, trusteeship of the community's common fabric, its property and heritage and its continuing policies' (Corbett, 1987, pp. 6-7).

It is all to easy to denigrate managers and employees in the public sector, as if 'professionalism' and dedication were the sole preserve of the private sector, but, this is clearly not the case. As Hugh Stretton has argued:

'. . . as the democratic world requires private enterprise to act with more and more social and environmental responsibility, private management will have to imitate more and more of the considerate, responsible character of the best of public management' (Stretton, 1987, p. 155).

A number of related points should also be made regarding personnel productivity and efficiency. Many conservative economists ignore the fact that the non-market sector of the economy, from schools to public transport, can and does define goals, incentives and penalties which are as effective as the profit motive in the private sector. Critics of the public sector do not, for instance, take into account the external discipline imposed by the managerial labour

market (Fama, 1980). If public servants wish to succeed in their career then it is better to be efficient and pursue the public interest as set down by government. Clearly improved performance can also arise from a pride taken in 'professionalism'. These issues are overlooked in much of the literature on so-called 'governmental and regulatory failure'.

As for wage increases in the public sector, all indicators show that in Australia over the past five years public servants have made only average gains in wage rises and benefits.

Finally, the evidence on productive efficiency in natural monopoly circumstances indicates that whether ownership is vested in public or private hands is largely irrelevant (Hogan, 1988; Domberger, 1988). Table 5.3 summarises the results of ten studies culled from reviews of such work. Examination of this list clearly demonstrates the absence of any systematic pattern to the results. As the 1988 H.V. Evatt Research Centre report on Commonwealth public enterprises noted, the conclusion to be drawn from this is that:

'. . . comparing the performance of public and private enterprise is difficult. Efficiency measures and criteria suitable for private enterprise may not be suitable for public enterprise. The intellectually honest conclusion is that neither pro-nor anti-public service advocates can post a clear victory on the basis of empirical studies of efficiency' (H.V. Evatt, 1988, p. 47).

5.5 Summary and Conclusion

Privatisation identifies many problems with the public sector including inefficiency, lack of choice, freedom and enterprise. Yet the proponents of such views rarely acknowledge the positive contribution of the public sector to problems such as market failure, the pursuit of social equity and justice and strategic public interest and economic objectives. The fact that privatisation consistently under-rates the importance of social welfare functions is of particular concern when considering State public sectors, which are responsible for the administration of many of Australia's 'people services'. As the NZ Royal Commission on Social Policy has maintained:

Table 5.3

Comparative Efficiency of Public and Private Enterprise in Natural Monopoly Settings			
AUTHORS	**COUNTRY**	**INDUSTRY**	**COMMENTS**
Wallis (1985)	Australia (Sydney)	Bus	Private bus operators have considerably lower unit costs in providing equivalent level of route service.
Freeman et al. (1985)	Canada	Railways	Productivity levels very close with public and private railway operator showing higher productivity in various years.
Pucher et al. (1983)	US	Bus Operators	Public ownership associated with significantly higher costs, but smaller fare increases & greater service expansion.
Mann & Mikesell (1978)	US	Water Utilities	Private ownership associated with higher operating costs. However, excessive capital investment by publicly owned utilities.
Lindsay (1984)	US	Water Utilities	Privately owned utilities result in per unit costs that are higher relative to publicly owned utilities.
Boland (1983)	US	Water Utilities	Operating costs 9% lower in private undertakings, but consumer charges considerably higher than in public undertakings.
Pascatrice Trapani (1980)	US	Electricity Supply	All other things equal, & costs if anything lower in publicly owned firms.
Foreman-Pack & Waterson (1988)	UK	Electricity Supply	Publicly owned firms were on average less efficient but the larger ones equally efficient as equivalent size private firms.
Millward & Ward (1987)	UK	Town Gas Supply	Weak evidence in favour of public firms being more efficient.
Caves & Christensen (1980)	Canada	Railways	Weak evidence in favour of public firms being more efficient.

Source: Hensher, 1987; Peterson, 1987; Waterson, 1988.

'. . . infrastructural decay such as closure of services like schools, hospitals, communication and transport links can make redevelopment prohibitively costly even where the activity would otherwise be economically efficient' (RCSP, 1988, Vol II, p. 372).

The consequences of replacing assets, enterprises or services also give added credence to the argument that the current 'tax revolt' spearheaded by the New Right is the product of a lack of understanding by Australian taxpayers of the extent to which they are taxed and the benefits they receive from the government in return (H.V. Evatt, 1988, p. 81).[9] Privatisation's proposed solutions to the problems of the public sector often result in the creation of new and worse ones. Put simply privatisation's claims to micro-economic reform are too general, too negative and are based on a series of false premises about the superiority of private sector initiatives in dealing with complex social and economic problems.

Notes

1 e.g. Corporation, profit and non-domestic property taxes.

2 For example, the sale to British Aerospace (BAE) of Royal Ordinance Factories (armaments) for 190 million sterling pounds, is to be investigated by the Auditor-General following the revelation that the denationalised factories owned development land worth up to 500 million sterling pounds. BAE is in the process of closing some of the factories, and after selling off the sites will be left with a substantial capital gain, as well as a viable armaments concern which is soon expected to generate 50 million pounds sterling to 60 million pounds sterling profits a year for BAE (The Guardian, 6 November, 1988, p. 12)

3 There are three different methods for operating competitive tenders. First, the *contracting-out* method. This involves the complete transfer of a state function (inclusive of provision of capital assets), to that contractor who in competitive tender has offered to execute the function on the most attractive terms (eg. lowest price). An example is the New South Wales Department of Main Roads construction work which is placed out to competitive tender. Second, the *operating franchise* or management contract method (Forsyth, 1988). In this case the management of state-owned assets and functions are offered to competitive tender (cf. J.G. Larson, 1980), and the British Government is experimenting along the same lines but with respect to public housing management. Finally, rights auctions. Here production rights are sold to the highest bidder who is then free to set the price at which the good or service is sold. This method is most commonly deployed to assign across rights to common property resources (eg. oil an gas exploration in the UK), but has also been advocated as a response to the natural monopoly problem (Demsetz, 1974).

4 In the context of the US deregulation of airlines, for example, the intensification of the 'hub and spoke' network concept has led to concerns about safety as traffic density on routes has increased and crews work much longer hours (Waterson, 1988).

5 Illustrative in this regard is the US airlines industry. In the period 1985-86, 'United bought Pan Am's Pacific network, Northwest Orient bought Republic, TWA was substantially restructured, Texas Air bought Eastern, People Express and Frontier' (Waterson, 1988, p. 142). In late 1986 the significant fare increase introduced by United was passively followed by the other airlines (Waterson, 1988, p. 143). The dominance of a small number of airlines is once again being established. In Britain, with respect to liberalisation of the Private Branch exchanges segment in Telecommunications, the dominant incumbent (British Telecom) has actually increased its market share between 1981 and 1984 from 65% to 74% (Gist and Meadowcroft, 1986). Also in Britain, the dominant incumbent in the Express Coaching Industry (National Express) has increased its market share following a period of vigorous competition consequent upon liberalisation in 1980 (Domberger, 1988).

6 The latter condition, which is usually referred to as zero sunk costs, is satisfied when tangible and intangible assets can be sold at their net of depreciation values or costlessly transferred to alternative uses. Not all assets can be so readily switched, and second-hand markets for fixed assets can lack depth.

7 Minimising the burden of sunk costs may be best achieved through public ownership, however it is hard to imagine an appropriate cost and market structure in which perfect contestability between the public and private sector was possible.

8 As noted above there has been a long history in 'contract' dealings between the public and private sector. This is because it is not feasible for governments to produce all their requirements 'in-house'. In addition, competitive tendering has been at one time or another a favoured policy instrument of both the left and right wing of the political spectrum. Nevertheless competitive tendering is often problematic and is an extremely unreliable means of enforcing progressive industrial policy which is better promoted through government policy in relation to its own permanent work force.

9 The case of the Los Angeles bus and train system which was sold to the private sector, was run-down, and is now too expensive to re-create reinforces this perspective. Not many could foresee the most nightmarish traffic jams and pollution in the world.

Part Four

FINANCING THE PUBLIC SECTOR

Introduction

Part Four develops recommendations for financing public sector renewal. It puts forward options for a more equitable, efficient and administratively coherent system of financing the Australian State public sector which complements the macro and micro-economic goals of economic restructuring and the principles of a socially just society.

To provide public services, governments at all levels must have the means to purchase the necessary resources and/or products. Revenue is also required to finance transfer payments between the public and the private sector.

Funds have traditionally been raised in three main ways:
- taxation;
- borrowing; and
- charges

Chapters Six, Seven & Eight provide an analysis of these areas of State finance and put forward recommendations for State revenue-raising. Chapter Nine outlines a range of new fund-raising mechanisms which have recently been developed (such as equity trusts).

In order to understand the current position of the States two important features of the Australian Federal System need to be reiterated. First, the dependence of the States on the Federal Government for finance. Second, the currently problematical financial position of the States in relation to their economic, social and administrative functions and responsibilities. Any program of public sector renewal must consider the consequences of this environment for public social and economic activities. Accordingly, these two issues are key targets for the following analysis.

Chapter 6

STATE TAXATION

6.1 The State Tax Base

One of the key reasons why there is a significant imbalance between the expenditure responsibilities held by the States and their revenue-raising capacities is the fact that taxing powers are dominated by the Federal Government. R.L. Mathews (1988, p. 261) explains that after World War II, the States':

'expenditure needs burgeoned as demographic, social and economic pressures made it necessary for them to *commit more and more resources to education, health, housing, transport, urban and manufacturing industries.* On the other hand, they were subjected to a three-pronged attack on their fiscal autonomy, as a result of their loss of access to income tax under the uniform taxation arrangements which the Commonwealth introduced during World War II, the Commonwealth's domination of the Loan Council (achieved through its supremacy in taxation and monetary policy) and its consequent control over State borrowing programs, and the High Court's refusal to permit the States to impose the more important taxes on the sales of goods which are available to States in other federations' (emphasis added).

Of the four main tax bases used in Australia (income, employers' payrolls, wealth [or property] and goods and services), the income tax base was given exclusively to the Federal Government in 1942, and has become increasingly more significant in relative terms over the last 25 years (around 35% of total Federal Government tax revenue in 1960, climbing to over 56% in 1985-86). Payroll Taxes were also an exclusive Federal Government tax, but were transferred to the States in 1971, and have become their most important source of own-revenue.

Current constitutional interpretation prevents the States from imposing taxes on the production or sale of goods and services in their own right. The States tax gambling, insurance, motor vehicles and also charge for business franchises. The latter source of revenue have become a way around the inability to impose excises. The States enact legislation which requires a licence to be obtained to sell a product from a particular outlet. The charge for the licence (the franchise) is scaled according to the turnover at the outlet in the last accounting period. This 'back-dating' of taxable revenue has been the basis upon which State franchises have been deemed legally separate from sales taxes which levy current revenue (cf. Dennis Hotels Pty. Ltd. v. Victoria, [1960], 104, CLR).

While legally distinct, business franchise taxes are similar in incidence and impact to a retail sales tax. Certainly, if the State Governments broadened the range of products that required licences, the franchise taxes would effectively become a broad-based retail sales tax.

In terms of the four bases identified above, the Commonwealth gains about 60% of its revenue from the income base, and about 30% from goods and services; whereas the States collected around 55% of their revenue from property and payroll taxes, and the rest from goods and services.

The sharing of tax responsibilities between the units of government that define the federal structure is an important aspect of the financing problem facing the State Governments. Table 6.1 provides a broad description of tax responsibilities among the levels of government and indicates some of the recent changes. It shows a real growth in Federal Government tax revenue of 18.4% between 1981/2 and 1986/7; a growth in State tax revenue by 22.6%; growth in Local Government tax revenue of 12.5% and an increase in total tax revenue of 18.7%.

These figures indicate a number of key political and economic developments. First, corporate tax has declined in real terms by 9.8% through both cuts in the company tax rates and persistent tax minimisation and avoidance (cf. Martin, 1989, pp. 72-77). Second, the growth in indirect taxation at both Federal and State levels amounts to the introduction of a consumption tax by stealth. Federal wholesale sales tax increased by 51% between 1981/2 and 1986/7. This increase represents a de facto movement from direct to indirect taxation since the overall contribution of the wholesale sales tax to total revenue rose from 7.5% to 9.6%. At the State level between 1980/81 and 86/87 the revenue raised through business franchise taxes (which ultimately fall on the consumer) have increased by 93.9%, and furthermore, entirely new indirect taxes like the Financial Institutions Duty were introduced.

Table 6.1

Real Tax Revenue by Governmental Units
1981-82 to 1986-87
$m at 1981-82 prices

| | 1981-82 | | | | 1986-87 | | | |
	Federal	State	Local	Total	Federal	State	Local	Total
Income Tax								
Individual	21205.0			1205.0	25842.6			25842.6
Company	4903.1			4903.1	4420.9			4420.9
Other	354.6			354.6	552.1			552.1
Excise Tax*	6226.4	138.4		6364.8	6638.5	222.6		6861.1
Sales Tax	2854.			2854.2	4310.2			4310.2
Customs	2059.7			2059.7	2197.7			2197.7
Payroll Tax	15.5	2434.0		2449.5	23.0	2500.5		2523.5
Stamp Duties	8.6	1123.7		1132.3	26.9	1502.9		1529.8
FIT1					179.7	240.6		420.3
Motor Taxes	10.6	996.8		1007.4	17.2	1154		1171.4
Property Tax	20.9	369.9	1720.9	2111.7	25.1	540.4	1932.5	2498.0
FBT					363.4			363.4
Other**	283.7	2165.9	96.0	2545.6	308.3	2088.9	112.4	2509.6
Total	37942.3	7228.7	1816.9	46987.9	44905.6	8250.1	2044.9	55200.6

Notes: * For the States this comprises levies in statutory corporations.
     ** For the States this includes *Taxes on Gambling* (1981/82 $718.8m 1986/87 $845.5m, an increase of 17.6%); *Taxes on Insurance* (1981/82 $435.5m 1986/87 $482.7m, an increase of 10.8%); and *Franchise Taxes* (1981/82 $499.8m, 1986/87 $969.6m, an increase of 93.9%).

State revenue from stamp duties increased by 33.7% and from property taxes by 46%. However, these increases were largely obtained by the States from the property boom. The essentially windfall nature of these recent revenue benefits is not a sound foundation on which to base the future of public sector activity, as the Victorian and Western Australian Premiers have recently made clear (cf *AFR*, 8th June, 1989).

Unfortunately one of the few progressive and broad based taxes available to the States has become a casualty of tax competition and administrative difficulties. In the 1970s, most

Australian States imposed death duties which were variously imperfect and subject to inestimable evasion by the wealthy. Small estates were heavily taxed, and fluctuations in the amount and timing of real tax burdens (as inflation rose) created uncertainty. The Queensland Government, sensitive to the liquidity burdens of the tax on small farmers and businesses, abolished the tax in 1977. The abolition proceeded despite the more obvious solution of indexing brackets and varying thresholds. The other States, principally New South Wales and Victoria, feared that their tax bases would be eroded through migration to Queensland, and accordingly began to abolish their own death duties, with Victoria finally abandoning the tax in 1983.

6.1.1 The Current Tax Position of the States

In this section the relative contributions of the various taxes and charges imposed by State Governments in Australia to their respective total taxation revenue is further developed and the differences between the States in terms of the distribution of tax revenue across the various taxes are analysed.

The States reacted to the developments in federalism in the latter half of the 1970s in two contradictory ways:

— they appeared to rely increasingly on Federal grants; and
— they sought ways of increasing the contribution of taxes under their control, particularly business taxes, gambling taxes and motor vehicle taxes (see Mathews, 1988, p. 264).

They did not embrace the income tax opportunities restored by the 'new federalism', preferring to pressure the Federal Government to improve the grants system, which had become the exemplar of Federal domination (or the anathema of fiscal independence).

To facilitate comparative analysis, all the data presented in this section is drawn from the ABS Taxation Revenue in Australia 1985/86 Cat. No. 5506.0, although similar but less uniform information can be found in the individual Budget Papers of each State.

While the States are excluded from imposing any substantial broad-based tax, in sum, they employ a large number of narrowly-based taxes (29 in all, according to the ABS classification, although each individual State only imposes a subset of the total range of taxes). In this section a more aggregated classification (9 categories) is used to simplify analysis and presentation (New South Wales Tax Task Force, 1988, Review of the State Tax System, p. 19; hereafter referred to as the Collins Report).

Tables 6.2 and 6.3 present the relative contribution of the nine categories of taxes to the total revenue raised in each State. It should be noted that similar tables appear in the Collins Report (1988, pp. 20-21). However, the figures presented in this chapter are different to those in the Collins Report due to classification errors in the latter. The authors of that Report fail to consistently decompose the State and the Local Government sectors, and therefore, overstate certain categories of State tax revenue.

From Table 6.2, it is clear that payroll taxes are the largest source of taxation revenue for all the States (ranging from 24.6 to 28.4%). The Federal Government agreed to transfer payroll taxation to the States in return for a reduction in financial assistance grants in 1971. While this trade-off was based on the previous Federal payroll rate of 2.5%, the States progressively increased the payroll tax rate to 5.0% and more. Payroll taxation is a strong growth tax, but is inferior to more broad-based taxes on the use of goods and services because it directly discriminates against labour.

The payroll tax contributions vary across States due to variations in rates of taxation and to differences in thresholds. Both South Australia and Western Australia receive a lower contribution from their respective payroll taxes. South Australia has no surcharge over the basic rate of 5%, whereas Western Australia introduces its tax at the lower rate of 3.75% (although it does impose a progressive tax rate).

Queensland has a similar structure to South Australia but receives a larger contribution from its payroll tax because its total taxation receipts are relatively lower than the other States. The per capita figures (See Table 6.3) confirm the lower tax impact in Queensland ($569.57 per person compared to the average for all States of $753.93 per person), and also show the per capita similarity between South Australia and Tasmania.

Taxes on property are divided between Taxes on immovable property (ABS Categories 311-319) which are shared between State (land taxes, metropolitan improvement rates, contributions to fire brigades, and other taxes) and Local Government (municipal rates); and Taxes on financial and capital transactions like stamp duties and Financial Institutions Tax (FID). In the past, States also raised revenue by imposing the Estate Inheritance and Gift Duties and any revenue from this category reflected past liabilities only (the question of death duties is dealt with in a later section of this chapter).

Table 6.2

Relative Contribution of Individual Taxes to States' Tax Revenue
1986-87

	NSW $m	Vic. $m	Qld $m	SA $m	WA $m	Tas. $m
Payroll Taxes	1489.2	1108.4	423.0	223.6	310.5	81.2
%	28.4	28.8	28.0	24.6	26.7	27.7
Taxes on Property						
Imov. Property	349.3	227.4	96.3	46.2	67.9	12.6
%	6.6	5.9	6.4	5.1	5.8	4.3
Fin. & Capital	1024.4	819.1	292.9	154.8	219.9	40
%	9.6	21.3	19.4	17	18.9	13.
Taxes on Provision of Goods and Services						
Stat. Corp. Levies	32.5	217.9	7.1	31.1	31	8.4
%	0.6	5.7	0.5	3.4	2.7	2.9
Gambling	571.9	353.2	150.3	80	65.8	22.6
%	10.9	9.2	9.9	8.8	5.7	7.7
Insurance	286.2	208.2	63.7	81.3	60	11.6
%	5.5	5.5	4.2	8.9	5.2	3.9
Taxes on Use of Goods and Services						
Motor Vehicles	683.1	394.4	280.4	133.4	160.6	39.3
%	13	10.3	18.6	14.7	13.8	13.4
Franchises	539.8	430.7	69.8	127.7	203.2	65.8
%	10.3	11.2	4.6	14.1	17.5	22.4
Fees and Fines		260.5	86.0	126.1 11.9	30.1	42.9
	4.9	2.2	8.4	3.3	3.7	4.1
Total	5236.9	3845.3	1509.6	908.2	1161.8	293.4

Source: ABS Taxation Revenue Australia 1986/87, Cat. No. 5506.0, p. 17.

Land taxes are the most important contributor in this general category. Interstate variations in this contribution (varying between 6.6% in New South Wales to 4.3% in Queensland) can be attributed to the rates imposed, the growth in the relative land values, and the amount of taxable land. Tasmania has lower land values and a small amount of land, whereas New South Wales with a lower relative tax rate (to other States) has experienced rapid growth in land value.

The other major contributor to total revenue (with Tasmania being an exception) is the financial and capital transactions taxes, with stamp duties being the most significant in this category. There is a plethora of stamp duties imposed across the States which makes a comparative analysis difficult. New South Wales has experienced rapid growth in stamp duties reflecting the land value escalation and its progressive rate structure. The other States have received a fairly stable contribution from stamp duties.

The revenue capacity derived from the FID clearly depends upon the strength of the financial sector in the State concerned. Again, States like Victoria and New South Wales, which account for a significant proportion of the financial transactions in Australia, gain more from this tax (from lower rate scales), than the smaller States like Tasmania (despite the higher rate in Tasmania). The per capita figures confirm this relative advantage. Queensland does not impose a FID, but capital revenue still accounts for a large proportion of total tax revenue due to the burgeoning Gold Coast property market and the stamp duties derived from this.

The States are prevented by constitutional fiat (and later High Court interpretations) from imposing broader-based retail sales taxes, more excises or customs duties. The States do receive revenue from Taxes on the provision of goods and services by imposing:

— excises in the form of levies on statutory corporations (ABS category 42);
— taxes on gambling (ABS categories 441-449); and
— taxes on insurance (ABS categories 451-459).

Victoria gains an appreciable amount from its statutory corporations levy (5.7% of total tax receipts) because it bases its rate on the accumulated public equity held in the public authorities. The other States receive much more modest contributions because their coverage is more narrow than in Victoria, and they levy on revenue rather than accumulated equity. This levy is a recent source of revenue for the States.

Gambling taxes are imposed on government agencies (TABs and State lotteries) and on private activities (bookmakers, clubs, casinos, lotteries etc). They are tantamount to a consumption tax. However, these taxes have a socially useful purpose and there is widespread community support for taxes on windfalls. Revenue potential is high because gambling tends to increase as per capita incomes grow.

Table 6.3

Per Capita Contribution of Individual Taxes to Total States' Tax Revenue						
1986-87						
$s per person						
	NSW	*Vic.*	*Qld*	*SA*	*WA*	*Tas.*
Payroll Taxes	267.29	264.90	159.60	161.06	209.83	181.49
Taxes on Property						
Immovable Property	62.70	54.35	36.33	33.88	45.88	28.16
Financial and						
Capital	183.87	195.76	110.51	111.50	148.60	89.41
Taxes on the Provision of Goods and Services						
Levies on Stat Corps	5.83	52.08	2.68	22.40	20.95	18.78
Gambling	102.65	84.41	56.71	57.62	44.47	50.51
Insurance	51.37	49.76	24.03	58.56	40.55	25.93
Taxes on the Use of Goods and Services						
Motor vehicles	122.61	94.26	105.80	96.09	108.53	87.84
Franchises	96.89	102.93	26.34	91.98	137.32	147.07
Fees and Fines	46.76	20.55	47.58	21.68	28.99	26.57
Total	939.96	919.00	569.57	654.18	785.11	655.20

Source: ABS Taxation Revenue Australia 1986/87, (Cat. No. 5506.0). Population figures are the estimated mean resident population for the financial year as published by the ABS Australian Demographic Statistics (Cat. No. 3101.0).

The relatively large contribution of gambling taxes to total revenue in New South Wales arises because it is the only State which levies a poker machine tax. Western Australia languishes behind the other States in gambling tax receipts because its lottery is poorly subscribed and the range of gambling taxed is relatively narrow.

Insurance tax receipts vary as a consequence of the relative rate structures on third-party insurance, the size of the tax base (Tasmania has fewer motor vehicles), and the size of the contribution of the private insurance companies (low in Tasmania and high in Victoria). South Australia relies most heavily on insurance tax (raising $58.56 per person compared to the average for all States of $41.70 per person). A large stamp duty on insurance component (based on annual premiums rather than the sum insured as in other States), contributes significantly to the total South Australian insurance tax receipts.

Taxes on the use of goods and the performance of activities (ABS category 5) are divided between Motor Vehicle taxes (ABS categories 511-514), Franchise taxes (ABS categories 521-524), and other taxes (ABS category 53). *Queensland places considerable reliance on motor vehicle taxes (18.6% of total receipts compared to around 11-15% elsewhere).*

Franchise taxes include taxes on gas, petroleum products, tobacco and liquor franchises. Their contribution in real terms to total State revenue (all States) has nearly doubled since 1981-2, and in 1986-87 accounted for around 43% of taxes raised under this category (taxes on the use of goods and the performance of activities), whereas in 1981-82 this share was only 30%.

Queensland gains a very small amount of revenue from this source because it has not levied gas, petrol, or tobacco franchises until recently. Although three States levy gas franchise taxes (New South Wales, Victoria and South Australia) their contribution is small. Tasmania offsets its size disadvantage by imposing significantly higher tobacco and petrol levies and as a result it raises in per capita terms the highest franchise revenue.

The final category is Fees and Fines (ABS category 91-93, and 94). Both State and Local Governments gain revenue from taxes and charges in these tax categories. Table 6.4 shows the share of each tier of government.

Table 6.4

Share of State and Local Government in Fees and Fines
1986-87
%

	NSW	Vic.	Qld	SA	WA	Tas.
Fees from Regulatory Services						
State	170.2	36.2	88.9	16.5	22.9	9.4
Local	41.1	33.8	31.1	6.2	2.8	2.0
Fines						
State	90.3	49.8	37.2	13.6	20.0	2.5
Local	2.6	27.9	5.0	5.8	4.9	1.6
Total Fees and Fines	304.2	147.7	162.2	42.1	50.6	15.5

Source: ABS Taxation Revenue Australia 1986/87 (Cat. No. 5506.0).

The notable feature is the relative emphasis that the Queensland State Government places on Fees and Fines as a source of revenue. While this category contributed less than 5% of total revenue in all the other States (New South Wales receiving 4.9% and Victoria 2.2%),

Queensland received 8.4% of its total tax revenue from this source. It has been noted that Queensland's total tax burden is lower than other States, but the per capita contribution of fees and fines shows that its relatively large percentage contribution is not a consequence of the small total revenue raised.

6.1.2 The Changing Pattern of State Taxation

Table 6.2 shows the share of taxation at the various levels of government in real terms between 1981-82 and 1986-87. While the static picture (as at 1986-87) of the distribution of the total State revenue across the various States according to the range of taxes imposed is useful, it is also important to discuss how the picture changes over time.

Three aspects of this changing picture can be considered:

– the changing percentage contributions of the individual taxes across the States;
– the changing percentage distribution in real terms; and

– the changing concentration of the tax base measured by the changing contribution of the largest three categories in each State.

Table 6.5 augments the earlier information adding data for 1977-78. This allows for a comparison over the decade in terms of the changes in percentage contribution of the individual taxes. Note that a similar Table appears in the Collin's Report (Table 2.5, p. 27) comparing 1976-77 to 1986-87. The data for both periods in that Table appears to be subject to arithmetic errors, arising in part from the previous failure of that Report to decompose the Local and State sectors correctly. Table 6.5 in this section compares the 1977-78 figures with the most recent available (1986-87) because the 1976-77 data was not published in the same format, using the ABS categories currently employed. In addition, Table 6.5 separates the estate inheritance and gift duties component of property taxes from the taxes on immovable property.

Table 6.5

Percentage Contribution of Taxes to Total State's Tax Revenue
1976-77 to 1986-87
%

	NSW	Vic.	Qld	SA	WA	Tas
			Financial Year Ending			
	1978/1987	1978/1987	1978/1987	1978/1987	1978/1987	1978/1987
Payroll Taxes	35.9/28.4	30.8/31.7	39.5/28.8	38.5/24.6	38.9/26.7	37.0/27.3
Taxes on Provision of Goods and Services						
Property	6.8/6.6	5.6/5.9	2.8/6.4	5.4/5.1	4.8/5.8	4.0/4.3
Estate/gifts*	5.4/0.0	6.8/0.0	3.1/0.0	4.9/0.0	4.1/0.0	14.3/0.0
Capital	13.2/19.6	17.9/21.3	18.6/19.4	16.0/17.0	15.1/18.9	14.3/13.6
Taxes on Provision of Goods and Services						
Levies	0.0/0.6	1.8/5.7	0.8/0.5	0.0/3.4	1.9/2.7	0.0/2.9
Gambling	12.0/10.9	10.7/9.21	5.9/9.9	5.3/8.8	5.5/5.7	7.2/7.7
Insurance	1.8/5.5	2.2/5.4	4.3/4.2	2.7/8.9	4.3/5.21	4.0/3.9
Taxes on Use of Goods and Services						
Vehicles	14.4/13.0	16.3/10.3	15.6/18.6	17.7/14.7	17.0/13.8	19.9/13.4
Franchises	5.1/10.3	4.5/11.2	4.5/4.6	5.3/14.1	5.8/17.5	3.9/22.4
Fees and Fines	5.4/4.9	2.3/2.2	3.4/8.4	2.2/3.3	2.7/3.7	3.8/4.1

Note: * Outstanding Estate inheritance and gift duties in 1986-88 for New South Wales were $1.9m which represented 0.03% of total revenue in that year; in Victoria $1.8m and 0.04%.
Source: ABS Taxation Revenue Australia 1982/83 and 1986/87 (Cat. No. 5506.0).

Table 6.5 indicates that significant changes in the relative contributions to the total tax revenue for each State have occurred, despite the contributions of some taxes remaining roughly constant. So, as some taxes have declined, old taxes have been made more potent and/or new taxes have been introduced.

Reading from the top, all the States (except Victoria) have experienced significant declines in the revenue derived from their most important tax, employers' payroll taxes. Victoria has experienced a modest increase in its relative receipts from payroll taxes.

In all cases (except Queensland), taxes on immovable property have remained relatively constant. The decline in contribution (as a result of abolition) in estate inheritance and gift duties is striking. It is ironic that Queensland, which led the way in the abolition of estate duties, has always received the lowest contribution from this source, but is the only State to have bolstered the relative contribution of immovable property taxes. This relative growth probably reflects the boom in Gold Coast real estate and low tax levels in Queensland.

Tasmania has lost a significant amount from the abolition of estate duties, and has not replaced the revenue with growth in the relative contribution of the other property taxes. Victoria, South Australia and Western Australia have developed the revenue contribution of the financial and capital taxes, partially compensating for the loss of estate duties. New South Wales has expanded the revenue capacity from this source by almost 50%.

The growth in the relative importance of levies on statutory corporations has been uniformly modest, with the exception of Victoria for reasons noted previously. Gambling taxes have been a modest growth area for the States which have opened casinos (South Australia, Western Australia and Tasmania), with small relative declines in New South Wales and Victoria. The contribution of insurance has been static in Queensland and Tasmania but has been a growing source of revenue for New South Wales (threefold growth), Victoria (250% growth), South Australia (330% growth) and Western Australia (23% growth).

For all States except Queensland, franchise taxes have significantly increased in their relative contribution to total revenue. New South Wales has *doubled the contribution of franchise taxes, while the increase in the other States is even more striking: Victoria (11.2% from 4.5%), South Australia (14.1% from 5.3%), Western Australia (17.5% from 5.8%) and Tasmania (22.4% from 3.9%). It is clear from these large changes that the franchise taxes represent the largest relative source of revenue growth in the States mentioned.*

Vehicle taxes have generally declined in relative importance, although Queensland is the notable exception, choosing to expand the contribution of these taxes while engaging in inter-State competitive actions on other taxes. Fees and fines have been approximately constant in their contribution for all States.

Table 6.6 reports the percentage changes on the real tax revenue received by each State for the period 1977-78 to 1986-87. In terms of total real revenue growth, Western Australia experienced the largest real increase (39.8%) over the period, followed by Tasmania (31.8%), New South Wales and Victoria (around 28%), Queensland (23.4%), with South Australia an emphatic last on 4.7%. The trends in the mix of the States' taxes are clearly shown.

There has been growth in business taxes like franchises, capital taxes and insurance. However, the pattern is not uniform across all States. Queensland is the notable exception, where the growth taxes have been property (179.2% compared to the average of the other States of 33.5%); gambling (108.1% compared to the average 37.8%); and fees and fines (205.5% compared to an average of 46.9%). Payroll taxes grew in Victoria (19.8%) and New South Wales (1.5%), but declined in all other States. Motor Vehicle taxation also declined in Victoria, South Australia and Tasmania.

Table 6.6 shows the general trends over the past decade. These developments reflect the development of new taxes in the early 1980s.

Another dimension of the trends in taxes is the per capita level and growth in real taxation. Table 6.7 displays these figures in terms of total real taxation for each State for the period 1977-78, and the two sub-periods 1977-78 to 1981-82, and 1981-82 to 1986-87. The per capita measure corrects for population growth, and allows the distinction to be made between the growth in total taxation revenue (shown in Table 6.1) and the growth in the burden of taxation (per capita real taxes).

Table 6.6

Percentage Changes in Real Taxes
(1980-81 prices)
1977-78 to 1986-87
%

	NSW	Vic.	Qld	SA	WA	Tas.
Payroll Taxes	1.5	19.8	-12.5	-33.	-4.	-1.8
Taxes on Property						
Property	24.1	33.4	179.2	-1.7	70.6	40.0
Capital	90.0	52.0	28.7	11.7	75.2	5.5
Taxes on Provision of Goods and Services						
Levies	—	304.0	-31.3	—	101.1	—
Gambling	16.9	10.1	108.1	75.7	44.6	41.8
Insurance	297.0	111.2	21.0	252.1	70.0	29.1
Taxes on Use of Goods and Services						
Vehicles	15.3	-20.0	34.8	-22.3	14.8	-13.6
Franchises	159.3	214.2	25.4	180.4	320.5	664.2
Fees and Fines	18.9	23.3	205.5	59.5	92.7	40.3
Total	28.1	27.8	23.4	4.7	39.8	31.9

Source: ABS Taxation Revenue Australia 1986/87 (Cat. No. 5506.0).

Table 6.7

Real Per Capita Taxation
(1980-81 prices)

	$			% Changes		
	77-78	81-82	86-87	77-78/81-82	81-82/86-87	77-78/86-87
NSW	499.9	495.2	578.1	-0.9	16.7	15.6
Vic.	480.2	490.4	565.2	2.1	15.3	17.7
Qld	349.8	363.8	350.3	4.0	-3.7	0.1
SA	412.8	333.8	402.3	-19.1	20.5	2.5
WA	419.8	462.2	482.8	10.1	4.5	14.9
Tas.	328.7	342.5	403.2	4.2	17.7	22.7

From Table 6.7, real per capita tax obligations have risen in all States except South Australia over the period 1977-78 to 1986-87. Queensland has marginally increased its receipts, although the level of taxes per person in Queensland is much lower than the rest of the States. New South Wales and Victoria tax their respective populations at much higher levels (per person) than the other States.

It is also evident that all the States bar Western Australia faced financial stringency in the first period (1977-78 to 1981-82), and the improved per capita revenue-raising in the second period (1981-82 to 1986-87) reflected a change in attitude. *Specifically, the States sought and developed new tax bases like franchises and financial taxes.*

Table 6.8 disaggregates the information in Table 6.7 and displays for the period 1977-78 to 1986-87 the percentage growth in the individual taxes imposed. The changing tax mix in real terms is once again evident.

Table 6.8

Changes in Per Capita Real Taxes (1980-81 Prices)
1977-78 to 1986-87
%

	NSW	Vic.	Qld	SA	WA	Tas.
Payroll Taxes	-8.4	10.3	-28.9	-37.7	-31.1	-8.6
Taxes on Property						
Property	12.0	22.8	126.7	-8.6	40.3	30.3
Capital	71.5	39.9	4.5	4.0	44.0	16.8
Taxes on Provision of Goods and Services						
Levies	–	271.6	-44.2	–	65.4	–
Gambling	5.6	1.4	68.9	63.5	19.0	32.0
Insurance	258.6	94.5	-1.8	227.6	39.9	20.2
Taxes on Use of Goods and Services						
Vehicles	4.1	-26.0	9.4	-27.8	-6.5	-19.5
Franchises	134.1	189.3	1.8	160.9	245.9	611.4
Fees and Fines	7.3	13.5	147.9	48.4	58.5	30.7
Total	15.7	17.7	0.1	-2.6	14.9	22.7

Source: ABS Taxation Revenue Australia 1986/87 (Cat. No. 5506.0).

6.1.3 Measuring the Narrowness of the States' Tax Bases

It has been emphasised that a significant imbalance exists in the Australian Federal system which is, in part, due to the extreme narrowness of the States' tax bases. A narrowly based tax structure means that tax revenue is raised from a small number of taxes. The preceding analysis shows that in all States, a large percentage of the tax revenue is raised from payroll, motor vehicle, and financial and capital taxes. It is also apparent that in recent years, the franchise taxes have become a significant contributor in all the States except for Queensland.

The Committee of Inquiry into Revenue Raising in Victoria Report (1983) proposed a measure of the narrowness of the tax base which draws on the concept of concentration in the literature on industry economics. Two measures of concentration are shown in Table 6.9. The first calculates the cumulative percentage share in total tax revenue raised by the three most important contributors for 1977-78 and 1986-87. To account for the increased emphasis on franchise taxes, the second measure

of concentration uses the top four contributors to total taxation. The addition of the franchise taxes is important because without it the top three measure is somewhat misleading.

Based on the top three measure, all the States experienced decreased concentration over the period shown, which means that new sources of revenue were found and/or an increased contribution from previously imposed taxes occurred. In 1977-78, New South Wales and Victoria had the least concentrated tax bases, whereas the remaining States had noticeably higher levels of concentration.

Over the period shown, both New South Wales and Victoria experienced modest declines in their respective degrees of tax-base concentration. The striking changes occurred in South Australia, Western Australia and Tasmania which experienced large reductions in their tax base concentration. These changes placed these States below New South Wales and Victoria. While Queensland also experienced a large reduction it remained the most concentrated of all the States.

Table 6.9

Measures of Concentration in States' Tax Bases
1977-78 and 1986-87
% of Total Tax Revenue

	Top Three Taxes*		Top Four Taxes**	
	1977-78	1986-87	1977-78	1986-87
NSW	63.5	61.0	68.6	71.3
Vic.	65.0	63.3	9.5	74.5
Qld	73.7	66.8	77.2	71.4
SA	72.2	56.3	77.5	60.4
WA	71.0	59.4	76.8	76.9
Tas.	71.2	54.3	75.1	76.7

Notes: * Top three taxes are Payroll, Financial and Capital, and Motor Vehicles.
Notes: ** Top four taxes add franchise taxes to the top three.

These relative changes are partly a consequence of the significant increase in the contribution from the franchise taxes in all States, bar Queensland. In Victoria, Western Australia and Tasmania the top three taxes in 1986-87 would include franchises taxes, and exclude motor vehicles. South Australia receives an almost equal contribution from franchise taxes (5.3% in 1977-78 and 14.1% in 1986-87) and motor vehicle charges (17.7% in 1977-78 and 14.7% in 1986-87).

The top four measure of concentration incorporates these important trends in States' taxation. The rankings are the same for 1977-78 using both measures (except that South Australia and Queensland swap positions at the top). This reflects the uniform insignificance of franchise taxes in this earlier period. Comparing this ranking with that in 1986-87 for the top four measure, significant differences are noted relative to the same comparison for the top three measure.

On the top four measure, all States except for South Australia and Queensland have increased their concentration. This is partly explained by the rising prominence of the franchise taxes, and a less-than-proportionate decline in the other three taxes included in the measure. More relevant is the fact that the States (Tasmania excepted) have tried to broaden their tax bases by introducing the Financial Institutions Duty (FID). The introduction of the FID does not reduce either concentration measure because it is included in the capital tax category. This aggregation problem demonstrates the care that should be

taken in interpreting concentration measures. In other words, as the aggregated categories include more than one specific tax, the tax base could be broadening, while the concentration measure, which is insensitive to these disaggregated changes, will indicate the opposite.

The declining contribution of the payroll tax, and the rising importance of franchise taxes, have changed South Australia from the most concentrated to the least concentrated. Queensland's concentration decline can be attributed almost exclusively to the fall off in the payroll tax contribution.

Although the tax mix of each State differs to some degree the more general difficulties of State revenue raising are clearly apparent. The State tax base is extremely narrow and, even though attempts have been made in recent years to introduce new forms of taxation, these have been largely regressive. Taxes such as FID and business franchises are new and piecemeal additions to the State tax base and the overall regime of indirect taxation in Australia, while more progressive taxes like death duties have fallen victim to tax competition among the States. Other increases in State revenue have been obtained in areas like stamp duties, but these windfall gains over the last few years are not a sound basis for stable budgetary planning, much less a program of public sector renewal.

6.2 Federal-State Tax Arrangements: Collection and Distribution of Revenue
The development of a stable fiscal base for

public services is an urgent priority. Resolving the imbalance in Federal-State financial arrangements requires systematic reforms to the revenue base of the States, which must include considerations of equity and efficiency so far lacking in the haphazard attempts of the States to overcome their fiscal constraints. In order to adequately evaluate the possibilities it is important to develop appropriate benchmarks of analysis and comparison.

6.2.1 What is a Good Tax Structure?

The three requirements for a good tax system are usually summarised in terms of equity, efficiency and simplicity (the latter embracing administrative considerations). In other words:

— The distribution of the tax burden should be equitable with everyone paying their fair share (equity objective);
— Taxes should introduce minimum distortion to the allocation of productive resources, and if possible correct for market failures (neutrality objective);
— The tax system should be administratively simple and easily understood, with the costs of administration and compliance being as low as possible (simplicity objective) (Musgrave & Musgrave, 1976, p. 210-211).

On the evidence presented so far it is clear that the system of tax collection and revenue distribution in Australia is in need of serious reform. The States rely on a range of narrowly-based taxes like stamp duties, payroll taxes and (increasingly) franchise taxes. It is self evident that this regime of taxes does not satisfy the principles of simplicity or neutrality. However, the principle of equity is also an important benchmark for analysing State taxes and charges. Some principles of efficiency and equity, which provide a framework for considering the various taxation options available to the States, are outlined below.

Equity
There have, in fact, been few attempts at assessing the success or otherwise of the States' taxes in meeting the equity objective.

This is, in part, due to both the paucity, and poor quality, of the available data. However, the Collins Report does provide an assessment of the New South Wales tax regime. Some of the Report's conclusions can be generalised to the other States.

As noted previously, payroll tax is the largest contributor to the States' tax revenue. Such a tax can be passed on in prices to consumers or users; it can result in lower wages being paid; or it can result in lower profits. *If passed on to consumers, the tax operates as a consumption tax; if passed on in the form of lower wages, it operates as a flat rate income tax; and if passed on in so that profits fall, it is a tax on profits levied on the value of wages paid.* Collins concluded that:

'the incidence of the payroll tax will most likely be a composite mix of a tax on sales, a tax on wage income and a tax on company profit but in every case levied on firms according to their payroll and not as a proportion of their sales or profits' (p. 197).

On the basis of this analysis, payroll taxes cannot be used to achieve desirable equity goals.

Generally, Collins concluded that '. . . State Governments have precious little influence open to them on . . . aspects of equity' (p. 197). It is clear, however, that a considerable amount of research needs to be undertaken on the issue of equity in the States' tax regimes. This would be an important task for a reformed Premiers' Conference as discussed in Chapter 4, Section 4.4.1.

It is important to realise also that the principle of equity need not always be adhered to. The use of inequitable consumption taxes on specific products may, in fact, be socially desirable. For example, taxes on tobacco or alcohol are designed to reduce their use and, in Victoria, the revenue raised from tobacco is diverted back into health funding.

The Distribution of the Tax Burden
The distribution of the tax burden across taxpayers is also important for equity in taxation. Determining who bears the burden of taxes or tax incidence must take into account two things:

— the effects of the individual taxes; and
— the effects of the system in general.

Taxes are legal obligations. Some individuals or corporate entities who are legally obligated try to avoid or pass on the burdens to others. To determine who pays, one must go beyond the meagre legal obligations. Two points are important here:

— the entire tax burden is always borne by individuals (or evaded), even if corporate entities are at the outset legally obliged to pay some taxes; and
— the final distribution of burdens is not likely to coincide with the distribution of initial legal obligations.

Economists distinguish between legal or statutory incidence (which relates to the legal obligation to pay tax) and effective or economic incidence (which considers who ultimately bears the burden of the tax). The difference between these two concepts arises because the legal obligation must always be paid to the Tax Department by the person or corporate entity concerned, who can then shift the burden onto other individuals through their pricing (and employment) behaviour. *In assessing the equity impact of a particular tax or taxes in general, it is the effective incidence which is relevant.*

Taxes are usually imposed on some aspect of economic behaviour. Economic transactions involve more than one person (or entity), and if taxes are imposed on the transactions, the legally obligated party may seek ways to reduce the economic activity in question, or alter the terms which define the conduct of the transaction. Either way, the behavioural changes impact on the other transactors.

Companies can forward shift taxes by increasing prices. The tax is therefore passed on in a sales tax form, which is regressive in impact. In summary, any forward shifted business tax is regressive. Companies can also backward shift taxes by reducing the prices offered for inputs. *A payroll tax, for example, which taxes labour costs, creates an incentive for the employer to offer lower wages (reduced wages growth) and/or less employment. It is claimed that this type of shifting would have a proportional*

impact across the workforce. However, to the extent that the firm has more discretion over the wages paid and employment variations for lower wage groups (less protected jobs) relative to salaried employees, the backward shifting would also be regressive.

Legal and effective incidence may coincide if no shifting occurs. In this case, profits, dividends and/or capital gains will be reduced, and it is possible that the incidence would be progressive, as a result of the type of individual income profiles which would be equity participants.

If the firm produces an intermediate good or service (that is, produces inputs for another firm(s) closer to the final product stage), then a forward shifted tax would spread throughout the economy (as burden impacts first on all the firms using the input) ultimately as a broad-based consumption tax.

The concept of tax burden must be outlined. Fiscal or budgetary policy, may or may not involve a transfer of resources to the public sector. If the government imposes a tax to finance its expenditure on goods and services, a resource transfer occurs because the private sector has less to spend. The resources utilised by the public sector represent the opportunity cost of the tax or the fiscal burden. Tax incidence considers how the burden is distributed across all the individual households in the private sector. The net burden considers, in addition to the tax burden, the benefits derived from the public expenditure.

Alternatively, if the tax finances transfers back to the private sector, no resource transfer to the public sector occurs. Tax incidence in this case seeks to determine the private households who gain from the transfers and those who lose as a result of the tax.

Progressive, Proportional and Regressive Tax Burdens
The distinction between progressive, proportional and regressive taxation can be made as follows:

— A tax is progressive if the ratio of tax to income rises with income. That is, the average tax rate increases with income;
— A tax is proportional if this ratio remains constant as income rises; and
— A tax is regressive if the ratio falls as income rises.

Empirical Estimation of Tax Incidence
In assessing the incidence of State taxes it must be acknowledged that considerable shifting of the incidence is exported to other States and/or to the Federal tax base (via Federal deductability of State charges). Conclusions made regarding the incidence of a tax system are extremely sensitive to the choice of incidence assumptions. A recent Australian study by N.A. Warren appears in Volume 2 of the Collins Report.

Warren estimated:

'the incidence of selected New South Wales taxes on New South Wales taxpayers on certain assumption as to the shifting behaviour adopted in response to these taxes' (Task Force Report, 1988, Vol. 1, p. 77).

The essential findings of Warren's Study into the incidence of some selected New South Wales taxes are worth reporting here.

Table 6.10

Incidence of New South Wales Taxes

Tax	*Incidence*	*Proportion Exported**
Payrolls	proportional	high
Franchise Taxes	mildly regressive	significant
Motor Vehicles	regressive	small
Stamp Duties:		
motor vehicles	regressive	small
property/contracts	mildly regressive	small
other	regressive	significant
Gambling	uncertain	small
Land Tax	mildly regressive	small

Note: * Indicates degree to which the tax burden is shifted interstate.
Source: Table 6.10 is based on Table 4.1 on p. 86 of the Collins Report.

Warren concluded that almost all the taxes imposed by the States are regressive in their incidence, with the exception of the payroll tax. The States have no current progressive tax instruments, although they could introduce progressivity into their tax structures by imposing (as is their constitutional right) either:

— a surcharge on the personal income tax imposed at the Federal level; and/or
— imposing a tax on the transfer of wealth in the form of death duties.

Tax Competition and its Implications for More Equitable State Taxes
The financing problem facing the States is significantly related to the constitutional constraints which prevent them from exploiting some desirable broad-based tax bases. However, even where valid tax bases (some with desirable efficiency and equity features) exist,

tax competition between the States has negated (or reduced) the revenue potential of these bases. A major goal of tax reform should be the increased harmonisation of the States' tax systems.

Tax competition can occur if a tax base is mobile, in the sense that the taxable activity can be transferred at a relatively low cost to another State, which imposes a lower tax burden on that particular base. Business activities and property are the two most mobile tax bases. Where a tax base is immobile (motor vehicles being a classic example), wide disparities in the tax burdens imposed on that base between the States can persist.

Tax competition (or the threat thereof) can lead to the abolition of taxation imposed on a particular base. *The States not only lose a potentially significant revenue source, but they are forced to rely more heavily on a narrower overall tax base.* The classic case of this destructive behaviour in recent history is the abolition in all States of the estate, inheritance and gift duties. This tax base represented a substantial revenue source, was progressive and allowed the States to redress severe inequities.

However, despite the case of death and inheritance duties, the competitive abolition of a tax base is rare and tax competition more often increases the administrative costs of enforcing compliance to the existing taxes imposed. In either case, the States lose revenue and are further forced to impose narrowly-based, discriminatory taxes.

The Collins Report (1988, pp. 379-380) concluded that it would:

> '. . . be very much in the interests of effective New South Wales tax policy to initiate a process designed to increase the degree of tax harmonisation and to reduce the degree of tax competition.

The distinction should be stressed between *tax harmonisation* and *tax standardisation*. There is no suggestion that States should be required to implement the same tax bases and apply to these bases the same tax rates . . . States should have the right to determine whether they wish to adopt high tax/high expenditure policies or low tax/low expenditure policies and to determine which tax mix is appropriate to their objectives . . .' (emphasis added).

The first recommendation regarding tax harmony within the Federal system is fully supported here. A Federal structure is appropriate where several separate jurisdictions share common interests in terms of national and international affairs, but who desire to preserve their individualism and where benefit-areas are smaller than the nation as a whole. It is difficult to conceive of tax competition as being a valid example of individualism. It is destructive to all the States.

The distinction between tax harmonisation and tax standardisation referred to in the quote from the Collins Report is not easy to make in practice. Standardisation does not necessarily mean equality of tax revenue. The different size of individual States would lead to unequal outcomes even where tax bases and rates were totally uniform. In the interests of harmony a large degree of standardisation is necessary and desirable.

6.2.2 Fiscal Equalisation

The previous discussion outlined the principles of equity and efficiency in tax collection. Such principles apply equally to the subsequent distribution of revenue back to the States.

As this book has repeatedly indicated, there is a marked imbalance between the Federal and State Governments in terms of revenue-raising capacity and expenditure responsibilities. Another imbalance occurs when the States are considered as a group (horizontal imbalance). Some States because of their size, location and/or economic structure suffer deficiencies in their revenue-raising capacity relative to their per capita expenditure responsibilities. The Commonwealth Grants Commission (CGC) is the principle administrative institution which attempts to redress the horizontal fiscal imbalance between States through the principle of fiscal equalisation.

The CGC allocates general revenue grants in order to redress the horizontal imbalances between the States. An important consideration is the extent to which horizontal fairness is achieved. Certain States (like New South Wales) have argued that in fact the process of fiscal equalisation discriminates excessively against the larger States. The consequence of the lower revenue grants is that more reliance must be placed on the States' own taxation revenue. The higher taxation burdens inhibits growth and prosperity in those States.

The Collins Report (1988, pp. 381-407) discusses this issue in detail. The 1976 Grants Commission Report indicates that the Commission redistributes resources:

> 'To enable a claimant State to function at a standard not below that of other States without having to levy taxation and other charges of greater severity than those in other States, its revenue needs to be supplemented because of:
> (a) its lower capacity to raise taxes and other revenues; and
> (b) its needs to incur higher costs in order to provide comparable government services.'

Of course, no State is forced to spend and/or tax in line with the average levels.

The Grants Commission adopts a tax-by-tax (or partial) approach when it assesses the revenue-raising capacity of each State, and aggregates these into an estimate of total State taxable capacity. An alternative method, the so-called global approach, has been suggested in recent years by New South Wales and Victoria, although the remaining States prefer the partial approach.

The global approach is based upon the view that a State's revenue-raising capacity is best measured by some overall indicator of State income and/or wealth. Collins (1988, p. 6) presents evidence, based upon the assumption that the State Gross State Product (GSP) per capita is the best indicator of ability to pay, that the Grants Commission's application of fiscal equalisation has not led to equity between the States. The Collins Report argues that:

'The fundamental issue here is the nature of the objectives of fiscal equalisation, an issue which appears not to have been squarely faced by the Grants Commission. The objective of fiscal equalisation should clearly be one of horizontal (that is, inter-State) equity . . . The Commission, in its fiscal equalisation process, has shown little interest in the achievement of horizontal equity in the sense of equal tax treatment of individuals (or families) in different States but having comparable capacity to pay . . . the equalisation process should put the States in the position of being able to arrange for the equal treatment of taxpayers in different States with comparable abilities to pay . . .

This approach to fiscal equalisation based on the similar tax treatment of individuals in different States having similar capacities to pay is at odds with the mechanistic approach taken by the Commission . . . the Commission assigns priority to achieving the capacity to levy the same rates of tax, rather than the same burdens of tax measured against some appropriate indicator of ability to pay' (Collins Report, 1988, pp. 386-387).

The Collins Report argues that fiscal equalisation should give the States the capacity to provide public services to individuals in the same family circumstances and having the same incomes at similar standards to those provided in other States, and with similar levels of taxes and charges.

The report recommends (Collins Report, 1988, p. 398) the global approach which reflects the true, calculable, and stable taxable capacity, and overcomes the problem arising from the States changing their assessed taxable capacity by manipulating their policy mix. The best measure of taxable capacity is Disposable State household income which is calculated from ABS State Accounts Data as total household income less direct personal taxes raised at Federal and Local levels, plus the State taxes, and then adjusted for company income undistributed or remitted overseas.

Table 6.11

Commonwealth Grants Commission Outcomes and Outcomes Under the Global Approach 1987-88

	CGC Recommendation		Global Outcome		Difference	
	$m	$ per capita	$m	$ per capita	$m	%
NSW	3356.7	630	3689.8	654	133.1	+3.7
Vic.	2645.2	625	2639.5	624	-5.7	-0.2
Qld	2398.9	888	2454.4	908	55.5	+2.4
SA	1294.8	925	1151.4	823	-143.4	-11.1
WA	1383.5	913	1395.5	921	12.1	+0.9
Tas.	477.1	1059	425.5	945	-51.6	-10.8

Source: Collins Report (1986) p. 406.

Calculations by the New South Wales Treasury comparing the CGC grants in 1987-88 based upon the tax-by-tax partial approach, and the grants which would be forthcoming under a global approach using the measure of taxable capacity defined above, are presented in Table 6.11. The implications of the figures in Table 6.11 are clear. Where a State is provided with higher grants under the global approach (New South Wales, Queensland and Western Australia), it would be able to reduce its taxes and charges and still provide the same level of public services. Alternatively, it could provide more public services at the current level of taxes and charges.

The change to the Global Approach, while not without problems (see Collins Report, 1988, pp. 402-406), would appear to have merit and, at the very least, clearly warrants more thorough analysis and assessment.

6.3 Some Options for Tax Reform

Taking into account the equity and efficiency principles outlined above, we are now in a position to evaluate the various tax options available to broaden the revenue base of the States. In addition to correcting the inadequacies in their tax regimes, the financing problems faced by the States must be overcome if they are to remain capable of meeting their economic, social and administrative goals as outlined in Part Three.

There are two available courses of action. First, the States could generate more revenue by innovations in the tax bases currently available to them. Several possible options can be identified, which include:

- taxes on business;
- personal income tax surcharge on Federal income tax liabilities;
- taxes on wealth; and
- resource taxes.

Secondly, the States could develop revenue-raising capacity in areas previously not available to them. In this regard an obvious answer is either to change the constitutional interpretation, or otherwise provide the States with some broad-based taxing power.

Options in each of these categories are outlined below. However, the current constitutional environment dictates the relative worth of each of these options and we begin with a summary of some recent High Court Decisions.

6.3.1 The Current Constitutional Environment

As *State of Siege* has already outlined, Section 92 (s92) of the Australian Constitution is a major constraint on the revenue-raising powers of the States, although it has recently been reinterpreted by the High Court in the Cole v. Whitfield (CvW) decision ([1988], 62 ALJR p. 303). The decision appears, at first glance, to increase the States' taxation discretion.

The focus in this case was 'on the notion of freedom from burdens of a discriminatory kind to which, in our view, the history and text of s92 point' (CvW [1982], 62 ALJR p. 303). S92 was plainly aiming to create free trade throughout the Federation, and to deny any governmental unit within the Federation the powers to inhibit this trade.

CvW is important because it reviewed the previously accepted interpretation of s92 (the so-called *fons et origo* doctrine espoused in Gilpin v. Commissioner for Road Transport and Tramways (New South Wales), (1935) 52 CLR 189, pp. 205-206).

In one case relating to motor vehicle charges (Finemores Transport P/L v. New South Wales [1938] 139 CLR, p. 338), while the charges were not intended to be discriminatory (being imposed on vehicles irrespective of their use), the High Court considered that such charges on vehicles registered exclusively to undertake interstate trade were invalid under s92. This was in effect discrimination in reverse (against local traders) because it provided protection for interstate traders.

CvW sought to remedy this 'protectionism' by focusing on the intention of the State law in question. CvW (p. 303) prohibits 'the discriminatory burdening of interstate trade.' Three points were made in the decision (CvW [p. 319]):

- a law which 'in effect, if not in form, discriminates in favour of inter-State trade' will offend against s92 'if the discrimination is of a protectionist character';

– a 'law which has as its real object the prescription of a standard for a product or service or a norm of commercial conduct will not ordinarily be grounded in protectionism and will not be prohibited by s92'; and

– 'if a law, is not protectionist in object, but discriminates against inter-State trade or commerce; it will offend s92'.

Discrimination must be of a protectionist nature to offend s92. CvW found that a State regulation (Tasmania) did burden interstate trade, but was not intended to be protectionist. The problem that is left by CvW is in deciding what constitutes discrimination upon protectionist grounds. A recent case, the first to apply the CvW principle of narrowing of s92 and increasing States' powers, is evidence that the decision is far from clear (Bath v. Alston Holdings P/L [1988]).

Accordingly, the legal straight-jacket that has constrained State taxation may be looser now than it has been in the past. The consideration of this factor is important because depending on High Court interpretations and decisions, some of the following proposals to rationalise and improve State taxes may become real alternatives, which no State will be able to ignore, in the near future.

6.3.2 Business Tax Initiatives

Groenewegen (1988) recently studied possible developments in the area of business taxation. He suggested four initiatives in business taxation:

– a State Corporate Income Tax;
– a State Retail Sales Tax;
– a State Business Tax; and
– a tax on Commonwealth Public Sector Business Enterprises.

After reviewing the overseas experience in the area of business taxation Groenewegen concludes (Collins Report, 1988, pp. 350-51):

'(i) business taxes internationally are an important component of sub-national taxation

revenue, particularly with respect to corporate business income.

(ii) Corporate business income internationally is most efficiently taxed if sub-national access is given to the federal base (Canada, West Germany) either through constitutionally guaranteed revenue-sharing or through *centralised piggy-backing*.

(iii) The other potentially significant forms of business taxes are the retail sales tax used efficiently in Canada and the US and the business *property* tax at the French, Canadian and German local and provincial level.

(iv) Canadian, German and US experience likewise suggests that there is a role for motor use taxes at the State level at least in part geared to motor fuel taxes' (emphasis in original).

A State Corporate Income Tax

A State Corporate income tax could be administered in an analogous fashion to the personal income tax surcharge allowed for in the 1978 Act (previously mentioned), which would be a low cost, proportional in incidence source of revenue. As long as the surcharges were similar, distortions in company location would be avoided. Certain problems might arise concerning the preparation of taxable income for companies that earn income across State borders, although the US experience shows that this problem can be solved.

The possibility of such a tax is, however, dismissed on the grounds that it is directly opposed to the current agenda of the Federal Government, which would be required to enact legislation along the lines of the personal income surcharge law. Certain other problems relating to dividend imputation, deductability of State taxes against Federal liabilities, reinforce the essentially political rejection of this attractive (and buoyant) potential source of State revenue.

Franchise Tax Growth

It has been shown that all the States (except Queensland), have vigorously expanded the contribution of franchise taxes by increasing tax rates; by reducing the period for which a licence remains valid; and by expanding the range of businesses subject to licensing and charges.

The range of products taxed by the States in this manner remains narrow, being confined (largely) to tobacco, alcohol and petroleum products, with small amounts gained from gas in New South Wales, Victoria, and South Australia. Franchise taxes bear similarities to retail sales or consumption taxes. An expansion of the contribution could involve more products and activities being subjected to the tax. A wider range of retail goods and services could be included by issuing licences and imposing the accompanying charges to retail establishments. Further, the States could introduce licensing (and charges) to providers of professional services such as tradespersons, medical practitioners, entertainment businesses, etc.

This is clearly a constitutionally valid area for the States to increase their revenue-raising capacity, and could be exploited in an administratively efficient and simple way. The degree of small business discrimination could be ameliorated by varying the licence period according to gross turnover.

The incidence of the franchise taxes are similar to a retail sales tax. The equity problems (lower income groups face a higher average tax rate than the higher income earners) may be reduced if forward shifting is not uniform, and is concentrated on luxury goods with higher margins. Warren's (1988) study confirms the regressive incidence of franchise taxes.

The expansion of the franchise tax by broadening the tax base reduces the possibility of distorting differentials, thus increasing the efficiency of the tax. Interstate distortions may occur (particularly at border locations) if the move to increase taxation is not uniform, although there would have to be substantial differences for capital to migrate. Evidence from the US indicates large variations in business franchise taxes between the States but only minor locational distortions arising (see Fox, 1986; Papke & Papke, 1986).

Efficiency is therefore most likely to be enhanced if:

– competitive incentives arising from differences in rates or coverage in franchise charges are minimised; and

– harmonisation of franchise taxes is a high priority of the States.

6.3.3 A State Surcharge on the Federal Income Tax

The Income Tax (arrangements with the States) Act 1978, introduced as an integral component of the Fraser Government's New Federalism strategy, gave the States powers to impose a surcharge on Federal personal income tax liabilities. Under current law, the tax would take the form of a percentage increment on the overall assessed income tax liabilities, rather than an increment on the marginal tax rates or a separate State income tax. All administration responsibilities would be retained by the Commonwealth.

Alternative State income taxation arrangements (which would require a further law change) could lead to percentage increments on each marginal tax rate, or an administratively separate State income tax structure. The latter would be administratively difficult and costly, and would increase the disharmony between the States.

What are the advantages of this option? First, the surcharge would have a similar incidence to the Federal income tax, and would give the States access to a progressive revenue source. This would overcome a major problem arising from the overriding regressivity of States' taxes.

Two qualifying points should be noted:

– it is usually accepted that State Governments should not try to redistribute income; and
– the progressivity of the present Federal income tax structure is questionable.

Second, harmonisation would be stimulated because all States would face the same tax-base and marginal tax rates, with the only State choice variable being the size of the surcharge.

Third, access to the Federal income tax base would expand the revenue-raising capacity of the States by a significantly greater degree than that arising from the feasible reforms to the existing States' tax bases.

Fourth, related to the advantage of increasing tax harmony between the States, the surcharge also satisfies the desirable objective of increasing the simplicity of the tax system. Other feasible reforms to existing State taxes would require more complex variations and subsequent learning difficulties by the taxpayers. A simple percentage surcharge is readily understood, easily calculated, and administratively tractable.

On the negative side three major shortcomings can be identified. First, a lack of flexibility is inherent in the current option because the only choice variable available to the States is the magnitude of the surcharge. The Federal Government would continue to determine the extent of the income base and the structure of the marginal tax rates. It has been suggested that 'the States would face a major problem of unpredictability of surcharge revenue' (Collins Report, 1988, p. 325), as a result of Federal Government changes to the income tax base and/or structure.

Of course, the fact that only one policy variable is available to the States under the current legislation, which the Federal Government intends to revoke (the surcharge), is an advantage because the States would only need a simple, low cost variation to the surcharge to protect their revenue.

Second, the surcharge imposed by the States increases the effective marginal tax rates, *ceteris paribus*. The Federal Government aims to further reduce the marginal income tax rates, and to introduce a greater degree of proportionality (reduce progressivity) into the direct taxation system. With the corporate tax rate currently set at 39%, it is inevitable that the top personal income tax rate will fall from 49% (having already been reduced from 60% in July 1987), to achieve a closer parity with the company tax rate.

The push for lower marginal tax rates and increased proportionality is based on the assertion that high marginal tax rates erode work incentives, encourage an increased reliance on the welfare system, and stimulate tax avoidance and evasion strategies. *It should be clearly stated, that none of these arguments has received any unambiguous empirical support*. The argument relating to welfare abuse (if such welfare abuse occurs in any significant proportion) is not a problem of the tax system. It would arise because of an inadequate or poorly enforced work test for example (assuming that employment opportunities are available).

The fact that the Federal Government is intent on reducing income tax rates is not, in itself, an argument against the States imposing their own surcharge. Indeed, decreasing Federal taxation provides the States with more room to impose a surcharge, without a net increase in the overall direct tax burden (compared to the present). Some argue that the Federal Government would feel thwarted and retaliate by reducing Federal payments to the States. This is tantamount to saying that there is some level of State revenue which the Federal Government has targeted. As a basis for federalism, such a view would be untenable.

Third, unless all the States imposed a more or less equal surcharge, the so-called double taxation might provide incentives for labour and capital to migrate to the States without a surcharge (or with a lower surcharge). This argument was used in the successful campaign to abolish death duties. In fact, little evidence is available to support the hypothesis that significant resource migration occurs between States as a result of tax changes.

It has already been argued that there is considerable disharmony among the respective State tax structures at present. The change in the degree of distortion between States would depend upon how the surcharge was introduced (for example, whether it was revenue-neutral or not; uniform or not). A revenue-neutral or a uniform surcharge would be an unlikely source of interstate migration.

Double-taxation already occurs in the States' taxation structures. What evidence is there to suggest that it is easier to evade direct taxation (through migration), than it is to evade indirect taxes?

6.3.4 Death Duties and Wealth Taxes

Wealth taxes can be imposed on an annual (or periodic) basis, or at the time of transfer by bequest or gift. Taxation of bequests (death duties) may take the form of estate taxes, or inheritance taxes which are imposed on the heirs. State Death Duties are no longer used by the States but are valid under the constitution. These taxes would enhance equity goals and would not promote major distortions in resource use.

States could impose a tax on the estate (prior to transfer) or on the heir (following transfer). Various objectives for death duties have been identified in the literature, and the specific form of the tax will depend on the objective chosen. First, society may choose to restrict wealth transfers following death. Thus a person relinquishes his/her right to use their property upon death. An estate tax with varying thresholds and rates of tax would be appropriate. Second, society may also wish to restrict wealth attainment independent of one's own labour. An inheritance tax would be the appropriate form of the death duty in this case. Third, inheritance contributes to the concentration of wealth, which suggests that a progressive tax on the heir is applicable if a more equal distribution of wealth is desired.

Most US States impose death taxes of an inheritance type with progressive rate structures. Progressivity is based on two considerations:

- the size of the individual shares in the estate; and
- the basis of the relationship between the deceased and the heir (the rate reducing as the closeness increases).

Death duties have both efficiency and equity effects. The main allocative effects include an increase in business mergers and property management distortions; distortions to labour supply; and effects on consumption decisions. The introduction of death duties may stimulate business mergers and distort the management of property. The uncertainty of the amount of tax and the problems of liquidity necessary to pay the tax may promote small business mergers with large corporations to avoid dissipating wealth in the form of cash. Liquidity worries affect the composition of asset holdings, with a bias towards marketable assets being introduced. These effects are sensitive to the administration of the tax, and where arrangements like the one-year instalment payment scheme are used (in the US) these distortions are small.

A death tax might change a person's decision to work or retire, in a similar way to an income tax. Economic theory is ambiguous here. The evidence is that the measured effect on work effort of income taxes does not appear to be large.

There are offsetting forces operating on consumption (savings). First, if a person desires to pass on wealth, they will save more rather than less to accommodate the tax. Alternatively, the anticipation of the tax may lead to a person avoiding accumulation and passing on the excess as consumption (for example, by increasing educational expenditure on children). However, as the tax is imposed at the end of life, severe behavioural changes are unlikely.

The distributional effects are likely to be progressive because the inequality of wealth is generally greater than for income, the size of estate transfers usually increases with income, and high exemptions are common. US evidence indicates that the burden of taxation is not shared evenly at the high income levels because of the different efforts undertaken to explore loopholes.

The design of the tax should attempt to achieve four main objectives:

- as an explicit device for breaking-up large fortunes, the tax structure should be progressive;
- the proximity of the heir to the descendant should be considered. Less taxable capacity is transferred to an immediate relative (for example, a spouse) than a more-distant heir;
- the tax rate should not discriminate according to the time of giving or the form in which the wealth is transferred. The death duty should minimise the effects on choice of methods of transferring wealth;
- the tax should minimise business effects, like those pertaining to liquidity problems of closely-held business assets.

If all these considerations are included in the design of the tax, the efficiency effects are likely to be small, while the equity effects are likely to be significant.

Death duties are a valid State tax and possess very desirable equity features. The problem is that they are highly susceptible to destructive tax base competition between the States, which led to the abolition of the tax across all States. They are also unpopular and subject to considerable evasion. For practical reasons alone it is hard to recommend them as a panacea for the States' financing problem. However, if a death duty was levied at the Federal level, and the proceeds returned to the States, the problems of tax competition could be minimised, while the effects on low-income earners could be avoided through the use of an indexed threshold. As the Collins Report concludes, even at the low rate of 2%, a wealth tax with a generous exemption level of $500,000 could raise $400m in the State of New South Wales alone (Collins, 1988, p 361).

6.3.5 Indirect Taxation

The Federal Government levies four taxes on goods and services: Customs Duties; Excise Duties; the Crude Oil Levy; and a Wholesale Sales Tax. These taxes contribute around 32% of total Federal taxation revenue. It is important to realise that the imposition of a particular tax can be motivated by a variety of non-revenue reasons. For example, Customs Duties are an integral component of Industry policy; excise duties are levied to inhibit the consumption of tobacco; and the Crude Oil Levy is aimed at assisting local oil exploration.

The existing Wholesale Sales Tax (WST) is a narrowly-based tax on commodities alone. *In 1987-88, the collections increased by a massive 18.9%, and the current Budget estimate for 1988-89 is for a 14.4% increase. Both these rises are well in excess of the inflation rate. The WST is beset with problems. Its narrow base requires higher tax rates to yield a given revenue level; consumption and production distortions arise from the differential rate structure; different tax burdens arise because individuals with equivalent incomes have different consumption patterns; and it is costly to administer the array of exemptions and tax rates.*

The States already impose an assortment of narrow-based indirect taxes, although not all of them are explicit. For example, the State franchise taxes (imposed on turnover generated in the previous financial year) are not legally considered to be sales taxes but are in fact quasi-sales taxes.

Warren (1987, pp. 87-88) concludes that:

'there is a strong case for a rationalisation of the Australian indirect tax system. Studies of tax incidence such as those by Warren (1987) highlight the potential to replace the current array of indirect taxes by a single broad based goods and services levy with only minimal effects on tax incidence.'

Australia's problem is it collects the same ratio of indirect to total taxes as the OECD, generally from a base of four commodity groups (tobacco, alcohol, petroleum and motor vehicles). There would be large gains from rationalising the maze of State indirect taxes; a broad-based State Goods and Services Levy (SGSL) would also provide a basis for further revenue neutral indirect tax rationalisations (See Warren, 1987, pp. 89-90).

Warren's conclusions together with the analysis above indicate the States' reliance on a narrow and regressive band of indirect taxes. Coupled with the Federal Government's increasing reliance on a somewhat ramshackle indirect tax regime, there is substantial potential for the reform of indirect taxation as a whole, in a program of rationalising and improving the revenue base of the States.

6.3.6 Resource Revenue and its Distribution

A significant source of tax revenue growth for the States could come from natural resource developments. Currently, all the States gain some revenue from this source.

Mineral wealth is unevenly distributed throughout Australia. There is a stark geographic separation between the mining and manufacturing industries, as a result of mineral discoveries well away from the populated areas.

The Constitution does not specifically discuss mineral resources. The States traditionally did not gain significant revenue from their natural resource deposits directly (by State royalties), preferring to use them to entice other industry. Rising international resource prices during the 1970s prompted the Federal Government to introduce mineral export controls (to inflate prices further), market sharing among the States, and used its foreign trade powers to control such things as foreign ownership. A landmark 1975 High Court decision gave the Commonwealth the power to own and control offshore oil and other resources. This was modified in 1979 and rights were shared with the States.

A resource rent tax (RRT) would begin at some threshold profit rate, which ideally would represent the opportunity cost of capital in projects of similar risk. It is not the same as a straight royalty because it allows for the recovery of capital costs before payments are required, thereby allowing for projects of differing scale and costliness.

A RRT could distribute net revenues (among the Federal and State Governments), with cash-bidding for rights to develop projects considered desirable. This system overcomes the major problem with a fixed front-end payment of ignoring different set-up and extraction costs.

A major difficulty in designing a RRT (or any taxing instrument) is the lack of clarity between Commonwealth and State taxing powers in this area. Resource developers, especially those from overseas, are likely to approach investment with a great degree of uncertainty, given the lack of clear agreements on taxation between the two levels of government.

The question arises, given the likely sharing of tax powers between the Commonwealth and the States, as to the most appropriate allocation of these powers between the two. For onshore resources which are owned unambiguously by the States, the auction system and subsequent revenue flow should be left to the States. This should be seen as a growth in revenue capacity for the States, rather than a revenue-neutral change achieved by reducing equalisation payments.

For efficiency reasons, the RRT should be harmonised across all States. Because of the uneven distribution of the mineral resources, the Commonwealth should collect the RRT (thereby ensuring tax harmony across all States), and adjust the equalisation accordingly.

6.4 The Tax Reform Package
6.4.1 Rationalising the Federal System of Indirect Taxation

'We accept that there is potential to rational-
ise the existing wholesale sales tax and extend into selected areas (sic) indirect taxation provided there is adequate compensation and that concerns about inflation and employment can be met.'
ACTU Policies & Strategies Statement, 1985, pp. 39-40

Of all the options available to overcome fiscal 'siege' of the States, the one offering the best mix of efficiency and equity is a reform of the Federal system of indirect taxation. This has the potential to achieve three major benefits. It could:

− rationalise economically irrational and distortionary taxes;
− provide a more stable and accountable fiscal base for the States; and
− ensure that a clear compensation package for regressive taxes is developed for low income and needy groups.

A State Goods and Services Levy (SGSL)
The best vehicle for reforming the Federal system of indirect taxation is through the introduction of a State Goods and Services Levy (SGSL), which would replace the Federal Wholesale Sales Tax and a range of State indirect taxes. The SGSL would be levied on forms of private final consumption expenditure (excluding residential accommodation, gambling, financial services, education, public administration and defence) with the Federal Government assuming responsibility for its collection and distribution back to the States. The SGSL would also involve a comprehensive compensation package in order to offset any inequities of the levy for low income groups.

In designing an SGSL to replace existing State tax bases, which are narrow and highly discriminatory, *the current proposal is clearly not equivalent in any form to Option C, which was correctly rejected at the Tax Summit in 1985. Option C sought to alter the tax mix at the Federal level away from direct taxation towards indirect taxation. The problems of regressivity that this move raised were sufficient to reject the proposal.*

Two of the most important aspects underlying the introduction of a SGSL are the maintenance of the progressivity of the overall tax/transfer system, and the imperative that a shift to indirect taxation does not give rise to an increase in Australia's underlying rate of inflation.

It is assumed, therefore, that the Federal Government would continue to pursue progressivity in the net budgetary incidence. Clearly, this was a vital concern at the 1985 Tax Summit because the question was one of changing the Federal Tax Mix from direct (progressive) to indirect (regressive) taxes. (As is argued below there are a number of initiatives which should continue to be undertaken in this regard and need to be investigated through a Wealth Inquiry.) In terms of our analysis, the suggestion is to alter the mix of indirect taxes per se, from more regressive (and discriminatory) to less regressive (less discriminatory) sources of taxes.

The SGSL would not increase the overall degree of regression. The crucial consideration is, of course, the degree of progression which applies in the taxation/welfare system overall. An SGSL would allow the States to rationalise the ragbag collection of indirect taxes that they currently rely upon for own-tax revenue, but which clearly are regressive and distortional. The extent to which the SGSL would allow a rationalisation of the existing State indirect taxes depends on the coverage, rate and other design features of the tax.

To generate some reasonable estimates of the proposal, the following assumptions are made:

 – the SGSL is collected at the retail level;
 – the current Federal Wholesale Sales Tax (WST) is abolished and the Commonwealth revenue loss neutralised; and
 – the SGSL covers all Private Final Consumption Expenditure (PFCE) except those listed in 1985 (Draft White Paper [DWP], 1985, p. 118).

A single-rate SGSL is considered here. However, there are trade-offs in the design and implementation of any tax reform which would have to be considered. Bearing in mind the fact that the present taxes involve considerable administrative costs, the simplicity gains alone of a broad-based retail sales levy on goods and services are worthwhile.

What should be included in the Base? This is a contentious matter which requires careful evaluation and discussion. In general, this comes down to the question as to whether essentials (food, clothing, heating, power and housing costs) should be included. On simplicity grounds and in order to reduce the discriminatory impact of the reform, the tax would be as broad as possible.

Table 6.12 shows some estimates of the revenue potential for various rates. The base is the PFCE for 1987-88. It should be noted that the available data for 1987-88 is not sufficiently disaggregated to decompose the expenditure according to the categories exempted. As an approximation, the base excludes dwelling rent; gas, electricity and fuel; post and telephone; and financial services.

The base includes food; cigarettes; alcohol; clothing, footwear, and drapery; household appliances; other durables; health, fares, motor vehicle purchases and operating expenses; entertainment and recreation; and other expenditure on goods and services. The total base subject to the State goods and services levy is $126, 277m, and it is assumed that the WST revenue ($7, 561.5m) is netted out.

Table 6.12

Sensitivity of State Goods and Services Levy Revenue to Different Tax Rates
1987-88
$m

	6%	8%	9%	10%	12%
Gross Revenue from SGSL	7576.6	10102.2	11364.9	12628.0	15153.2
Less WST Revenue Lost	7561.5	7561.5	7561.5	7561.5	7561.5
Net Revenue	15.1	2540.7	3803.4	5066.2	7591.7

There are important qualifications that must be made with respect to the estimates in Table 6.12. There is no attempt to estimate the price elasticity of the items in the base. It is likely that if the incidence of the SGSL is fully shifted to final consumers, various substitution and income effects will occur. The abolition of the WST would result in relative price changes and variations in the size of the base. Further, no attempt has been made to adjust beer excises to maintain a CPI neutral result in terms of beer (see DWP 1985, p. 124).

A major criticism of the Option C proposal which has some relevance to the current proposal relates to the CPI effects of the SGSL. For any good subject to the SGSL, but not currently subject to the WST, the retail price would rise in proportion with the tax rate. The price change for a good currently under the WST would equal the difference between the WST rate and the SGSL rate, with rises and falls occurring as appropriate.

While these effects would also occur under the current plan, several offsetting factors (which would reduce the pressure on the CPI) can be identified. These effects were absent in the Option C proposal. The current plan involves the substitution of SGSL revenue for revenue raised by the existing narrow-based taxes at the State level. The existing taxes vary in terms of their distortional impact. Distortions increase costs and reduce efficiency. The greater the revenue contribution from more efficient taxes (like the SGSL) the lower the pressure on the price level. So in the period following the transition, the CPI effects should be moderated as resources are reallocated and efficiency gains are made.

A broad view of the amount of revenue-substitution which can be achieved through the introduction of the SGSL can be gauged from Table 6.13, which shows in some detail the revenue contributions from the existing taxes imposed by the States in total. An SGSL levied at a rate of 9%, for example, would raise around 21% of total State taxation revenue after the WST revenue is given back to the Federal Government. A 10% SGSL raises around 27% of total revenue.

In specific terms, a 9% SGSL could, for example, completely replace all Stamp duties and Other Property tax revenue. Similarly, a 10% SGSL could replace all Payroll tax revenue and, say, a third of stamp duty revenue.

If the States were seeking to provide significant stamp duty concessions to first-home buyers to alleviate some of the burden of high interest rates, then this type of substitution would prove attractive. Employment would be stimulated if payroll taxes were abolished.

Table 6.13

Total State Taxation 1987-88
$m

Payroll Taxes	4033.1
Taxes on Property	
Immovable	4052.2
Stamp Duties	3507.3
Other	452.5
Taxes on Provision of Goods and Services	2482.8
Taxes on Use of Goods and Services	
Motor Vehicles	1884.8
Franchises	1567.2
Other	35.6
Fees and Fines	932.8
Total	18948.2

Source: ABS Government Financial Estimates, Australia 1987-88, Cat. No. 5501.0.

The question of which taxes would be abolished at a State level would have to be determined through the consultative mechanism provided by the new Premiers' Conference Secretariat. This consultative process would have to take into account:

- the relative contribution that each State tax makes to each individual State's revenue;
- the rate at which the SGSL is set; and
- the amount of revenue collected and distributed back to each State from the SGSL.

However, the following options are canvassed here for further debate. The introduction of the SGSL could result in a number of offsetting tax reductions. The analysis in this chapter has assumed the SGSL would replace the Federal WST and after compensating the poor for real income losses, the net revenue could then be used to replace (or reduce) a number of taxes currently levied by the States.

Option 1:
Assume that the SGSL is 10% and the WST is replaced.

The $5066.2m net revenue for 1987-88 (excluding a base figure of 20% of net revenue for compensation measures) could replace a package of taxes at the State level. If this option was taken up each State would determine its own basket of taxes to abolish in consultation with community representatives, the other States and the Federal government. Possible packages could include: the abolition of all State payroll taxation; or the abolition of all stamp duties with some cuts to payroll tax; or the abolition of selected regressive State taxes (such as FID and/or stamp duties for first home buyers); or the abolition of State taxes which most impact on families whose income is from $0 to average weekly earnings; or the abolition of State taxes which have the most dramatic impact on inflation and standards of living or finally, tax cuts of over $4 billion across all State taxes, fees and fines could be delivered. Studies of the desirable socio-economic effects of each package would need to be put forward and evaluated as part of the tax reform process.

Option 2:
The Federal Government could reduce the

equity impact of the SGSL by abandoning the WST but increasing its excises on luxury items. The States would then have more net revenue from the SGSL which means that the compensation packages could be more attractive; and/or the taxes replaced could be more wide ranging.

The increased excises would place a higher cost on luxury items so that equity would be achieved, not by reducing the taxes to lower-income groups, but by increasing them for higher-income groups. If the increased excises were targeted towards imported goods, disincentives to spend on imports would result. At a macro-economic level, such disincentives could help improve the current account problems without endangering equity.

Equity Effects
Two particular issues should be taken into account when considering the question of equity and the SGSL. First, as Neil Warren has recently argued, public finance analysts typically examine the reform of one tax in isolation from another, that is, they present arguments 'which might have substance if no other taxes were being considered'. However, he goes on to point out that '. . . if the tax change is part of a package of tax reforms, then it might be possible for the inequities of one reform to be offset by the equity improvement resulting from another' (Warren, 1987, p. 32). This point is particularly relevant to the option of the State Goods and Services Levy being used to replace regressive State taxes. The proposal for an SGSL acknowledges the need to fully compensate low income and needy groups who currently are not compensated for the regressive effects of indirect taxes.

Second, the SGSL is a vehicle of reform to the Federal system of indirect taxation. The evidence presented above indicates that there is already a move from direct to indirect taxation. Between 1981/82 and 1987/88, revenue from the Federally-levied Wholesale Sales Tax rose by 51% and the revenue obtained from business franchises at the State level rose by 93.9% and, while there is a need for further study of these rises, the possibility that *a consumption tax is being imposed by stealth* is of considerable concern. It is only by analysing the drift in different taxes across the levels of government that this event can be confirmed. However, there has been no debate or concern about this development and there is a clear need for public scrutiny of it. The inequity of the current regime of indirect taxes is also of considerable concern. There is currently no compensation accorded to low income and needy groups who carry the greater burden of paying levies such as the Federal Wholesale Sales Tax and other regressive State taxes and charges.

One of the purposes of an SGSL, as defined above, would be to eliminate the problems of a consumption tax by stealth and the temptation to increasingly rely upon a narrow and *ad hoc* range of taxes. It would make make any growth in the collection of indirect taxation explicit and ensure that there is no move away from the overall reliance on direct personal and corporate taxation.

Some Tentative Analysis of the Distributional Impact of the SGSL

The question of equity impact of an SGSL is not as straightforward as is often presumed. Certainly, the impact of the SGSL will be felt directly in the form of price rises of all goods and services which are included in the base. Lower income groups are disadvantaged disproportionately in relation to higher income groups because the expenditure on staples as a proportion of their income is higher. The CPI effects of the SGSL could be reduced by imposing price neutral conditions on goods currently subject to excise duties. This would have to be determined in the context of the previous discussion concerning the taxing of bads.

However, these equity-price effects are offset to some extent by the fact that the SGSL would replace (or reduce the impact of) a number of other regressive taxes. Currently, a person may have to pay small amounts to the States for a variety of reasons. For example, a person pays taxes or charges to obtain a licence to drive, to register a vehicle, to trade a vehicle, to buy a first or subsequent home, to obtain copies of birth and death certificates and the like.

Over time, these small regressive amounts add to considerable sums. It is therefore likely that the price effects of the SGSL would be substantially offset by a reduction in these imposts, if we analysed trade-offs over an extended period of time. Ensuring that price movements reflect the balance between the reduction of existing taxes and the introduction of the SGSL could be a role undertaken by State prices authorities (see Part Three).

In designing a State tax reform package centred around the SGSL, we must ensure that the taxes that we replace (reduce):

  − are not serving to reduce the production and/or consumption of bads;
  − are relatively distortionary with respect to resource allocation
  − are relatively regressive.

In this regard, a detailed study should be made to determine the relative allocative and equity aspects of the range of taxes currently levied by the States.

We have some information (Warren, 1988) which allows us to make some educated guesses about the likely gains from the introduction of the SGSL. However, the exact nature of the trade-off between the SGSL and the current taxes needs to be calculated after a detailed analysis is made of the complex effects that would result.

The 1984 Household Expenditure Survey, Australia (HES) is the most recent source of data measuring levels and patterns of expenditure on goods and services by private households in Australia. It allows us to analyse the distribution of household expenditure and income.

The HES provides data on household expenditure by household income decile group at the time of the survey. Some summary results are shown in the Table 6.14 below which relates the percentage of total expenditure for selected Gross Weekly Income (GWI) Groups for broad commodity or service groups.

The poorest (in terms of GWI) spend much more on current housing, fuel and power, food and non-alcoholic beverages, tobacco, household equipment, and medical and health than the average household. The top 10% GWI household spends more on alcoholic beverages, clothing and footwear, medical care and health, transport, recreation and miscellaneous, than the average household.

Table 6.14

Household Expenditure by Household Income Decile

	Lowest 10% ($0-113)	Third 10% ($172-235)	Six 10% ($388-472)	Top 10% ($861+)	All HH
			% of Total Expenditure		
Current Housing Costs	17.18	12.27	14.20	10.21	12.84
Fuel & Power	4.56	3.91	2.95	2.26	2.92
Food and Non-Alcoholic Beverages	23.40	22.94	19.83	17.87	19.68
Alcoholic Beverages	2.44	2.82	3.53	3.83	3.40
Tobacco	1.83	2.09	1.80	1.07	1.58
Clothing & Footwear	4.99	5.93	5.70	7.79	6.48
Household Equipment etc.	12.30	12.93	12.20	11.35	11.99
Medical & Health	4.13	3.59	4.05	3.55	3.89
Transport	10.11	15.83	15.88	17.17	16.31
Recreation	10.73	10.90	12.23	14.09	11.92
Personal	1.83	1.78	1.74	1.86	1.83
Miscellaneous	6.50	5.03	5.89	8.96	7.17

Source: (ABS, Cat. No. 6530.0).

A rough guide to the dollar loss as a result of different rates of the SGSL can be calculated. It should be noted that the expenditure categories used by the HES are not entirely congruent with the categories used in the Draft White Paper (DWP) produced for the 1985 Tax Summit or those used to assemble the estimates in Table 6.15. The estimates discussed in this Section are very broad and are intended to provide some ball-park numbers to help focus the debate.

The following figures are very much an overestimate of the real income loss because first, there has been no deduction for the savings to each household resulting from the abolition (reduction) of the WST, nor second, any deduction for savings resulting from the reduction or abolition of existing taxes. The calculations displayed in Table 6.15 assume that the SGSL is passed on fully to consumers in the form of higher prices. The average household GWI was $453.60 which would be placed in the sixth decile.

These estimates are based on 1984 prices and incomes. Two adjustments can be made to provide a rough guide to the net impact on real expenditure of the introduction of the SGSL and the abolition of the WST (measured as at 1987-88 which is the latest year that tax and national accounts expenditure data is available). First, the figures can be scaled up to reflect inflation. Second, the benefits of abolishing the WST can be estimated if certain assumptions are made concerning the distributional impact of the tax.

Table 6.15

State Goods and Services Levy — Estimated Real Income Loss

	Gross Weekly Income					
Rate of SGSL (%)	0-113 Lowest Decile	172-235 Third Decile	315-387 Fifth Decile	473-564 Seventh Decile	861+ Highest Decile	All Households
	Weekly Dollar Loss					
6	6.61	12.05	16.10	20.81	36.02	18.28
8	8.81	16.10	21.42	27.75	48.03	24.38
10	11.02	20.10	26.78	34.70	60.00	30.48
12	13.22	24.10	32.14	41.63	72.00	36.57

To get some idea of the WST savings, we assume that the total WST revenue for 1987-88 ($7, 561.5m) is spread across the households in the respective GWI groups in proportion to the HES expenditure distribution in 1984. This is an imperfect method of assessing the savings, but in the absence of actual data any method will be *ad hoc*.

The estimated annual savings from the abolition of the WST for each household in each GWI group are reported in the Table 6.16 below.

Table 6.16

Estimated Annual Savings — Abolition of Wholesale Sales Tax

Household Gross Weekly Income

0-113	172-235	315-387	473-564	861+
Lowest	*Third*	*Fifth*	*Seventh*	*Highest*
Decile	*Decile*	*Decile*	*Decile*	*Decile*
		Per Annum Dollar Saving Per Household		
587.69	987.94	1,363.25	1,724.33	2,954.20

Combining these savings with the dollar loss figures (inflated and annualised), a very rough guide to the extent of the distribution of the net loss arising from the introduction of the SGSL (based on 1987-88 data) can be calculated. The gross figures (ignoring any savings from the abolition of the WST) are reported in the Table 6.17 below.

Table 6.17

Total Gross Loss — State Goods and Services Levy

Gross Weekly Income

Rate of SGSL (%)	0-113 Lowest Decile	172-235 Third Decile	315-387 Fifth Decile	473-564 Seventh Decile	861+ Highest Decile
		Inflation Adjusted Gross Dollar Loss — 1987-88			
6	409.02	745.65	996.27	1287.72	2228.90
8	545.16	996.26	1325.47	1717.17	2972.10
10	681.91	1243.79	1657.15	2147.24	3712.80
12	818.05	1491.30	1988.82	2576.06	4455.36

The inflation-adjusted per annum net loss (taking into account the WST estimated savings) are shown in Table 6.18. While some questionable assumptions were employed in their derivation, the magnitudes involved indicate that poorer households would be worst-off once the SGSL reached 8%, whereas households on higher GWI would only suffer a disadvantage at SGSL rates over 10%.

Table 6.18

Real Loss — State Goods and Services Levy

Gross Weekly Income

Rate of SGSL (%)	0-113 Lowest Decile	172-235 Third Decile	315-387 Fifth Decile	473-564 Seventh Decile	861+ Highest Decile
		Inflation Adjusted Net Dollar Loss (Gain) — 1987-88			
6	+178.7	+242.30	+366.98	+436.61	+725.30
8	-42.6	-8.32	+37.78	+7.16	+17.90
10	-94.2	-255.85	-293.90	-422.91	-758.60
12	-230.4	-503.36	-625.57	-851.73	-1501.16

The annual cash grants which would make an average household in the lower deciles neutral to the change are indicated in these figures. For example the total annual cost of compensation for a 10% SGSL to every household in the lowest decile would be around $47.1m (using the HES estimate of the number of households in each decile). It is reiterated, however, that the price effects of reducing or abolishing certain existing State taxes have not been calculated, and the compensation required may, in fact, be less than that calculated above.

Compensation Options
As we have already seen, a State goods and services levy is tantamount to a flat rate tax on retail expenditure. If the index used to measure equality is income, then such a tax is inequitable (horizontal equity) because households with the same income have varying savings propensities and therefore pay different amounts of tax. Conversely, the tax is equitable if the index is expressed in terms of consumption. In terms of *vertical equity*, a SGSL would be proportional with respect to consumption and regressive in terms of income. Consumption as a percentage of income declines as income increases.

Regressivity can be moderated in a number of ways. The introduction of exemptions of necessities (like food and clothing) or, alternatively, multiple rates (higher rates on luxuries) are obvious methods. These complications may, however, add administrative difficulties and distort consumption and production choices. It is also difficult to assess the distributional impact of these variations. On this point it has been argued that:

'the tax revenue foregone by such a blanket concession . . . [exempting food and clothing] . . . would greatly exceed that required to compensate the low income earners for any regressive effects of the indirect tax on food and clothing prices' (DWP, 1985, p. 120).

In this regard, an alternative method of reducing regressivity is to provide certain income groups with credits against income tax (equivalent to tax-free expenditure). Various credit schedules could be used

(flat-rate, sliding-scale etc.). For zero income tax payers a direct refund is given (assessed at the tax-rate capitalised value of the per person credit).

Although a credit scheme can eliminate the regressive features of the SGSL, two problems arise:

- there might be difficulties in the direct payment provision for low income groups; and
- the regressivity at high incomes is unavoidable. Other taxes have to be relied upon to introduce the progressivity at this level.

The best alternative is for the States to use Federal support schemes like the Family Allowance Supplement as means of compensating for the SGSL because the costs of implementing compensation would be lower and easier to understand. In the same way the SGSL would have to offset the Federal loss of the Wholesale Tax revenue, the States could also offset the revenue required to implement the compensation package through the Federal transfer system.

The introduction of the SGSL would amount to a reduction in the purchasing power of disposable income. Two possible approaches to compensation include:

- compensation for the additional consumption required, or
- compensation for the reduction in real disposable income.

It is also important that low income groups dependent entirely on income support payments should be compensated fully through that system (that is, by increases in entitlements). Other low income groups not dependent on the income support system should be compensated either through a cash transfer or through an entitlements system which generates relief from the SGSL.

How it Could Be Implemented
A Constitutional amendment to facilitate the proposed introduction of an SGSL is unlikely, although the discussion above in relation to the recent Coles v. Whitfield decision in the High

Court certainly makes the situation more fluid. The s92 constraint in certain respects is not necessarily bad because separate State retail sales levies introduce the potential for disharmony. Different rates and exemptions across States could lead to locational distortions, particularly along border areas, although the US evidence suggests that the extent of such inefficiencies is minimal.

The most desirable arrangement, given the Constitutional rigidities, would be *a piggy-backing agreement* between the Federal and State Governments. In this case the Federal Government would impose the tax, and give the States access to revenue from a uniform base and rate structure. Minimal efficiency losses would occur, although some equity problems would persist. The problems could be redressed within the structure of the tax by exemption and/or credits (with some general efficiency losses at the national level); or could be solved by progression in, say, the income tax structure.

In the limit, the States could receive all the revenue (distributed as if the tax was imposed at the individual State level). Thus, the Federal Government would merely be acting as an agent of the States in order to bypass the Constitutional constraint.

The States would in turn abolish or downgrade some of the other more discriminatory taxes (like payroll taxes). The net gain in efficiency (with essentially neutral equity outcomes) would stimulate growth and stabilise revenue capacity. At a national level, there would be a once-off price level effect, reflecting the shifting of the tax onto the consumer, although the increased efficiency resulting from a replacement of more discriminatory taxes by less discriminatory taxes would help contain any adverse price rise.

The proposal certainly implies a substantial degree of uniformity between the States. This uniformity is in fact highly desirable. Importantly, the proposal would accomplish three desirable goals of tax reform:

- it would provide the States with a more reliable, buoyant, and neutral (less discriminatory) revenue source;
- it would negate any incentives for the States to compete away the revenue capacity from mobile tax bases; and
- it would maintain the individuality of the States in terms of their respective budgetary discretion.

In other words, standardisation of a significant portion of the States' overall tax base does not inevitably reduce their individual freedom to choose a particular budgetary stance. It is important to harmonise — with a high degree of standardisation — the mobile tax bases. While some divergences between the rates imposed by individual States are tolerable (given the costs of mobility), the States should accept that a substantial degree of tax base (and rate) consistency is preferred.

However, the States could still achieve fiscal discretion by imposing varying rates on the immobile tax bases. If a State desired to achieve a low tax/low expenditure outcome it could adjust its taxation on its immobile tax bases. A high tax/high expenditure State could overcome the uniformity arising from the broad-based (consistent) SGSL by levying higher relative charges on its immobile tax bases. Where size considerations interfered with such discretion, adjustments could be made via the process of fiscal equalisation.

However this sharing/choice trade-off is achieved, the implication of tax reform in each State is that all States and the Federal Government will have to increase the degree to which they cooperate on tax matters. *As Part Three recommends, the Federal and State Governments should establish some formal institutional framework through the Premiers' Conference to enhance the degree of cooperative federalism, through close consultation, aimed at developing shared tax bases, and non-competitive, individual tax initiatives at the State level.*

6.4.2 Other Tax Measures

Although the SGSL forms the major recommendation of this book, other tax initiatives should be investigated by the Premiers' Conference Secretariat. These include:

Wealth Tax
In the interests of social equity and public revenue generation it is vital that a national

inquiry into the distribution of wealth be established. The terms of reference for this inquiry should include consideration of: the adequacy or otherwise of the existing Federal capital gains tax as a wealth tax; and the scope for further wealth taxes, such as annual net wealth taxes and death duties. If this inquiry supported the introduction of additional wealth taxes, a proportion of the revenue so-gained should be returned to the States, as compensation for the loss of death duties.

Land Tax

State Governments should seek higher land tax payments from Australian non-residents and endeavour to plug the loopholes allowing transfer of ownership to other parties without the knowledge of State tax authorities.

Stamp Duties

Along with the possible abolition of stamp duties for homebuyers made possible through the introduction of the SGSL, the States should investigate the possibility of applying stamp duties to vendors rather than buyers. The abolition of stamp duties on cheques is also recommended as part of the SGSL package. Each State should also agree to significantly rationalise the multiplicity of minor duties applicable on documents such as Letter of Power of Attorney, Letter of Allotment and Letter of Renumeration etc which are not cost effective to collect.

Franchises on Petroleum Products

The equity impact of abolishing franchise taxes on petroleum products would be positive. As indicated in Table 6.14, lower income groups spend more on fuel and power than the average household. However, environmental factors should be taken into account when considering the rationalisation of petroleum franchises.

Motor Taxes

A distinction should be made between taxes specifically designed to finance expenditures relating to motorists and roads and other general revenue taxes on motor vehicles.

The costs of roads, road use, road damage and administration of motoring and roads should be met from various road user charges and taxes designed specifically to finance expenditures relating to motorists and roads, and their revenue, together with specific allocations from the Commonwealth, should cover the costs of road construction expenditure, maintenance and the administration of roads and motoring. Motoring taxes on heavy vehicles should be increased to the point where the costs of road damage inflicted by these vehicles are fully recovered.

Longer licence fees and reduced registration fees in all States should be considered as part of the package offered up to supplement the SGSL.

Alcohol & Tobacco Franchises

A greater percentage of the revenue from tobacco and alcohol franchises should be earmarked for health expenditure following the Cain Government's initiative in this area.

Financial Institutions Duty

As part of the SGSL package all States should immediately index and adjust the FID single receipt threshold to a new limit of $1.5m (see Collins Report, p. 266).

Interstate Tax Competition and Harmonization

The Premiers Conference Secretariat should pursue all avenues to promote harmonization of State and Federal taxes. In particular it should examine the merits of establishing an Interstate Tax Commission for promoting interstate tax harmonization.

Chapter 7

NON TAX REVENUE: STATE PRICING AND CHARGES POLICY

7.1 Introduction

State Governments also generate revenue through non-tax charges or payments to government bodies for the provision of a particular good or service. This revenue includes public transport fares, gas and electricity charges and rates for services such as water provision.

There is another reason, too, for considering government bodies' pricing policies. That is, some public undertakings provide inputs to downstream, private sector, industries. In this regard, electricity and telecommunications rank most highly (IAC, 1989, pp. C-5 to C-6). However, it is important that the impact of their costs on downstream industries is not exaggerated. In this regard, the Elcom discussion in Chapter Ten is particularly illuminating. Such undertakings are also significant in governments' capital spending programs and, as such, pricing policies are an important consideration for debt-servicing by government.

There have been some attempts to establish general principles for pricing and charges at a State level in recent times. The 1989 IAC Draft Report on Government Non-Tax Charges (IAC, 1989) advocated that charges should not be too high '. . . otherwise industry costs are necessarily increased and competitiveness is impaired', nor too low because '. . . charges which are below efficient costs of supply advantage user industries. However, the resulting implicit subsidies have to be compensated for by charging other users more, or through higher taxes or by reduced government spending'. According to the IAC, exposing public agencies to competition is the best means of ensuring that prices and charges were 'just right'

(IAC, 1989, pp. 79-80).

While the IAC cursorily summarises some of the administrative reforms which have been articulated in Part Three of this book, in the end it favours exposing public organisations to competition with the private sector and the privatisation option (IAC, 1989, p. 80). There are two fundamental problems with such a strategy. First, public trading enterprises are often used to cross-subsidise social functions which is only possible where the profits on the commercial operations are protected; and second (as noted in Chapter Five) there exist a class of public undertakings which meet the conditions necessary to justify a 'natural' monopoly (eg. large reticulation infrastructures like electricity, water and gas). Furthermore, as we have already established in Chapter Five, there are many contexts in which competition would not ensue through either privatisation or the breaking up of public enterprise markets. The text book world of competitive pricing rarely prevails in areas of public provision.

The fact is that there is no single principle for determining the prices and charges of government enterprises. State Government organisations vary in terms of the type of service that they provide: regulatory; public goods; private goods; mixed goods. The three broad methods of financing – governmental (taxes etc), market (user-charges), and mixed – follow logically from this distinction. For example, some organisations like public transport agencies offer services such as passenger transport which are financed partly by user-charges but which also attract a subsidy for public-good reasons, and other services like freight transport are essentially private goods and hence should so far as is possible be financed through user-charges. Table 7.1, based on the findings of the *New South Wales Task Force on the Classification of State Organisations*, provides a useful guide to the different types of government organisation and the role which prices and charges have in their operations.

Table 7.1

Classification of State Organisations	
A. **Public Service:**	Fully or almost-fully subsidised monopolistic bodies such as the Department of Mineral Resources, Business and Consumer Affairs, or central agencies such as Treasury and the Premier's Department.
B. **Community Service:**	Partly subsidised monopolistic bodies such as Registries of Births, Deaths and Marriages.
C. **Community Business:**	Partly subsidised semi-competitive bodies such as transport services.
D. **Commercial Service:**	Self-sufficient monopolistic bodies such as the Sydney Water Board and Electricity Commissions.
E. **Commercial Business:**	Self-sufficient semi-competitive bodies such as the New South Wales' County Councils or the TAB.
F. **Commercial Enterprise:**	Self-sufficient fully competitive bodies such as Insurance Offices and Banks.

Of all the tiers of government the States collect the greatest amount of revenue from government charges in Australia. Nearly 50% of such charges are collected by the States compared to 40% by the Federal Government and 10% by Local Government (IAC, 1989, p. 8). This breakdown indicates the relative importance of charges as a source of revenue for the States. Categories C, D, E and F are examined in the following section, and Categories A and B in Section 7.3.

7.2 State Public Enterprise Pricing and Charges

State public enterprises (ie. those organisations which generally fall into the categories of C, D, E and F in Table 7.1) contribute significantly to State revenue. However, it is difficult to calculate exactly how much revenue is raised from non-tax charges because revenue obtained though charges is netted-out in the net operating surplus of public trading enterprises. As a guide, the surpluses of public trading enterprises contributed around 7.1% of total States' revenue in 1979-80, 7.4% in 1985-86 and 10% in 1986-87, and the contribution of surpluses for public trading enterprises in each State is depicted in Table 7.2.[1]

It is clear from these figures that public trading enterprises represent a growing source of revenue for the States, but this development counsels caution for the equity element in the pricing policies of these bodies.

7.2.1 Principles and Practicalities

It has already been established in Chapter Four that public trading enterprises should be evaluated according to the principles of economy, economic efficiency, equity and effectiveness. Within this framework, financial performance and appropriate pricing strategies are crucial.

The public enterprise pricing literature suggests three main pricing guidelines:

– Prices should not fall below marginal (opportunity) cost levels and as far as possible should equal those cost levels (unless a divergence is warranted by the second or third guidelines);
– If there is a shortage of capacity (ie at times of peak demands) prices should be raised to higher levels (which reflect the

higher value users) to clear markets; when there is excess capacity, prices should be lowered to reflect the lower real opportunity costs of supply and to stimulate demand; and

− If prices determined by the first two guidelines do not generate the desired revenue, additional revenue may be raised by higher charges on less price-sensitive market segments. Thus, where additional revenue is required the optimal departure from marginal cost pricing requires higher additional charges on those users who are less sensitive to higher prices (so that distortions to marginal decisions are minimized). This policy is consistent with the better known commercial practice of price discrimination or charging what the market will bear.

Table 7.2

Contribution of Public Trading Enterprises to State Revenue
(81/82 Prices)

	81/82 $	81/82 %	82/83 $	82/83 %	83/84 $	83/84 %	84/85 $	84/85 %	85/86 $	85/86 %	86/87 $	86/87 %
NSW	483.5	(4.7)	760.5	(7.5)	702.6	(6.7)	860.6	(7.8)	822.0	(7.2)	768.0	(6.5)
Vic.	631.4	(7.9)	687.4	(8.2)	615.3	(7.1)	603.2	(6.7)	726.1	(7.8)	929.3	(10.4)
Qld	156.5	(3.5)	229.9	(4.4)	322.9	(6.2)	472.8	(8.8)	546.3	(9.5)	535.9	(9.3)
SA	190.5	(7.8)	209.1	(7.9)	227.8	(8.3)	205.8	(7.2)	235.2	(7.7)	216.8	(7.3)
WA	154.7	(5.8)	176.1	(5.5)	232.9	(6.7)	246.7	(7.2)	304.5	(8.6)	357.6	(9.9)
Tas.	97.7	(6.6)	102.8	(9.9)	122.7	(10.8)	138.3	(11.2)	143.2	(11.8)	154.8	(13.4)

Source: ABS 5504.0 'State and Local Government Finance, Australia', deflator CPI for each State capital.

The second guideline is relevant when peak/off-peak demand occurs. Thus, for a public enterprise subject to peak load demand, it is now well established that higher prices should be levied:

− to reflect the higher costs of meeting such demand (as in a multi-plant firm which caters for peak demand by using least efficient plants);
− for a single plant firm, to reflect the higher opportunity cost of satisfying the marginal consumer; and/or
− simply as a means of reducing peak (excess) demand towards a target level on the grounds that price rationing is more economically efficient than non-price rationing measures such as interrupting supply.

Where peak and off-peak demand are responsive to price, better load management and reduced pressure for capacity expansion (which is substantially occasioned by peak demand), including the accompanying effects of energy and environment conservation, would be amongst the more tangible benefits.

In practice, the concept of marginal cost can be used to justify any one of a number of pricing structures. The estimation of future costs, for instance, may be subject to large errors and historical costs, although more easily measured than future costs, do not necessarily provide a useful guide to the costs that will have to be incurred in the future. The diverse social and economic responsibilities of public sector activity mean that the application of marginal cost pricing in this sector is even more difficult than the complexities of a textbook model. The fact that many activities undertaken by public trading enterprises are more amenable to average cost pricing (eg electricity production) makes marginal cost pricing, as outlined above, still more problematic (IAC, 1989, pp. 33-34).

7.2.2 A Required Rate-of-return
From a practical viewpoint, it is useful to examine one approach to the problem of

pricing by the public sector, given that the textbook prescriptions are difficult to replicate. Since 1983, the Victorian Government has required its public enterprises to price their goods and services so as to meet a Required Rate-of-return (RRR). The principle performance criteria was a target rate-of-return on assets of 4%. This meant that public authorities were required to manage their internal costs and set prices to achieve a 4% real rate-of-return on the written- down current replacement cost of assets in service.

The Cain Government argued that:

'If lower rates of return are achieved . . . the result would be a misallocation of resources. Public authorities are required to recover all operating costs and capital costs and the real rate-of-return is a component of the capital costs of the public authority's operations. This means that public authorities performing commercial-type functions should achieve the same level of efficiency expected of private sector organisations.'

It was also maintained that a rate-of-return policy contributed to long-term price stability and provided flexibility to the utilities by lowering the cost of finance, consistent with the borrowing limits of State and Commonwealth Governments. Such an approach also avoided the problem of prices setting to achieve a fixed level of internal funding for capital expenditure and prevented significant price changes due to investment needs (Information Paper on Energy Pricing, 1985-86, p. 11).

How was the rate of 4% arrived at? The 4% RRR was derived from estimates of the long-term costs of debt and equity to the public sector, weighted by the extent to which these forms of finance (ie. debt and equity) are utilised by public enterprises (the debt:equity ratio).

To determine the long-term cost of debt to Victoria's public enterprises –

'. . . research was undertaken as part of studies conducted with the SECV and the Melbourne and Metropolitan Board of Works. These studies involved time-series analyses spanning more than 100 years to derive data on interest rates and inflation so as to determine the real interest rates on the debt of these authorities. The long-term average of these real rates, whilst subject to short-term fluctuations, was found to be around 3%. While acknowledging that at any particular point in time it is likely that the real interest rate would differ from this 3%, it was considered that this rate reflects the long-term average of the cost of debt which investors in these authorities would impute into their investment decisions as expectations of the long-term return' (Department of Management and Budget 1984, p. 42).

Is the 4% RRR defensible? On a positive note, the 4% RRR directly focuses attention on the opportunity cost of capital utilized, even if the actual amount may only approximate the true RRR required.

Australian studies have indicated that previously estimated average real rates-of-return in the private sector are substantially inflated. For instance, the Institute of Applied Economic and Social Research (1982) estimated that over the 9 years to 1977-78, private corporate trading enterprises in Australia achieved a real rate-of-return on all assets employed, before interest, of about 12% p.a. However, Ball and Davis (1984, pp 40-43) report recent estimates which show that in the 1970s the average real return was considerably less than 4%.

Even though a specific RRR may be questionable (if, for example, it does not take account of the community service obligation which the Public Trading Enterprise (PTE) may be required to meet) the use of a RRR as one of several financial and non-financial indicators is sound because it places an emphasis on the opportunity cost of capital used by a public enterprise.

Requiring a PTE to achieve a required rate-of-return can encourage increased efforts to lower costs of production. However, in the case of a monopoly supplier facing highly inelastic demand curves, alternative opportunities are available through price increases and/or quality of service deterioration. Thus constraints to limit these activities are required if pressures for cost reduction are to be sustained.

Price increases can be constrained by a CPI − X type system which is used in the UK to regulate British Telecom and British Gas (and which will be introduced in July 1989 to regulate Telecom Australia's price increases). Under this price-regulation system, if the X factor (the expected level of real price reduction per annum) is 2% and the increase in the Consumer Price Index is 7%, the level of price increase on average would be restricted to no more than 5% p.a. Incentives for cost reductions in excess of 2% are present since these better-than-expected cost savings are retainable (in the absence of other government decisions) by the PTE. Although difficult to develop and monitor, quality-standards performance indicators can be introduced to guard against cost savings achieved through lower quality.

Further, an appropriate RRR target, combined with a test rate of discount for investment projects helps to ensure that public enterprises do not absorb resources in unwarranted capacity expansion which might be more productively employed elsewhere. This enhanced cost-consciousness can serve to facilitate 'dynamic' efficiency.

7.2.3 Dividend Requirements

Since 1983 the Victorian Government has required its major public enterprises to make dividend payments (New South Wales introduced them in 1986). The Commonwealth and the other State Governments have announced their intention to pursue a similar policy. This development has clear implications for the pricing and financing of public enterprises.

The Victorian Public Authorities (Dividends) Act of 1983, requires that 'commercial statutory authorities' (public enterprises) pay to the State's Consolidated Fund each year a return on equity, in the form of a Public Authority Dividend (PAD) of up to 5% of the value of the public equity held in that authority.

PAD payments have important implications for State revenue. The Victorian Consolidated Fund receipts from PADs have increased from a total of $372.5m in 1983-84 to an estimated $589.3m in 1988-89 comprising about 5% of total Consolidated Fund receipts.

Since the community ultimately owns all public enterprises the PAD offers a means by which a return on that equity can be realised. This return should be paid to the Consolidated Fund and thereby made available for use in pursuit of the Government's overall programs and objectives, or to reduce State charges and/ or taxes elsewhere, thus distributing the benefits according to the priorities of the community as a whole.

The PAD payable by individual public enterprises could depend on a number of factors, including:

− the return on equity disclosed by RRR financial statements;
− historical cost profits (measured in accordance with conventional accounting principles);
− the availability of cash flow;
− the nature of the enterprise's capital program;
− conditions in money markets and the ability of the public enterprise to borrow;
− trends in the enterprise's debt to equity ratio; and
− community service or other obligations to be met by the enterprise.

Pricing and the PAD

The PAD requirement and the RRR guideline should be distinct aspects of public enterprise policy. The level of prices are affected by the target RRR but not the PAD because the RRR determines the enterprise's surplus out of which the return to equity remains after the cost of debt is met. The equity return is then available to meet PAD payments.

Many public enterprises are currently short of new capital. It might be argued that PAD payments, by depleting internal funding capacity (that is, by limiting the use of 'retained earnings' per capital expansion) promote a demand for increased borrowing, which in turn increases debt repayments and servicing charges and leads to price increases. It is therefore arguable that at least in the medium or longer term, (unless offset by sustained cost reductions) PAD payments will affect the level of public enterprise prices (and/or result in reductions in the range and quality of services).

As a matter of fact, real tariffs charged by Victoria's public enterprises have decreased in each year since 1983-84 and are expected to continue decreasing in the foreseeable future.

What Level of PAD is Appropriate?

One possible method of assessing the appropriateness of a given PAD level would involve a comparison with those prevailing in private enterprise. Table 7.3 indicates that private sector dividends paid as a percentage of average shareholder's funds have varied from year to year and for 1984 ranged from 3%, for resource-based manufacturing, to 8.3% for the services industry, averaging 4.8% for all non-financial industries. Thus, depending on which sector a public enterprise is considered comparable to, a PAD requirement of 5%, for instance, may be argued to be either excessive, appropriate or too low.

Table 7.3					
Dividends as a Percentage of Average Shareholders' Funds					
Industry Type	1979/80	1980/81	1981/82	1982/83	1983/84
Resource Based					
Manufacturing	4.3	3.6	2.8	2.8	3.0
Other Manufacturing	5.6	5.9	5.9	5.5	5.8
Total Manufacturing	5.1	5.0	4.6	4.4	4.7
Wholesale trade	5.1	4.7	5.2	4.8	4.5
Retail trade	5.2	5.4	5.8	4.8	6.8
Services	6.7	5.9	5.4	5.5	8.3
All industrials	5.2	5.1	4.8	4.5	5.2
Mining	7.3	4.0	2.1	2.5	3.0
Total Non-Financial	5.6	4.9	4.3	4.1	4.8

Source: Reserve Bank of Australia (1986), Bulletin Supplement: Company Finance (August) p. 6.

While other charts could be listed, such comparisons are problematic. Ergas (1986), writing of the telecommunications industry, warned that some of the factors underlying dividend policy in a private company (like the differential tax treatment of interest payments, retained earnings and dividends, and the disclosure element of company dividend announcements) are not applicable to the government and its commercial undertakings.

He suggested (p. 61) some factors which might be considered in setting PAD payments:

'It is reasonable, however, to suggest that the dividend policy of a public enterprise should perform two functions:
— reflect a capital structure, in terms of debt-equity ratios, which does not impose an excessive burden of fixed interest obligations on the enterprise, since (particularly in capital intensive industries) this will lead to unjustifiable price rises during cyclical downturns;
— take account of the growth prospects of the industry, of the need to provide for growth through adequate injections of equity, and of the fact that commercial equity capital would generally be available on favourable terms to rapidly growing private companies.'

In short, governments should decide which level of dividend payment is appropriate for the enterprise, taking into account the PTE's overall financial strategy and planning process rather than set a blanket, predetermined rate.

7.2.4 Equity Considerations

Efficiency concerns are important for any enterprise, but trading enterprises which are publicly owned have a particular obligation towards community equity and social justice considerations. The concept of universal service provision has evolved because of these obligations.

It has already been noted that the difficulties inherent in the marginal cost pricing system can lead to the conclusion that universal, subsidised provision of a particular service is the most rational decision to make. In reality, governments have a variety of criteria by which they make decisions regarding the way in which a service will be delivered, including the objective of income redistribution. For instance, should it be decided that neither full user-pays (for equity reasons) nor universal service (for efficiency reasons) is appropriate, then the use of cross-subsidisation is available. In Australia, for example, the provision of electricity facilities to non-metropolitan areas at prices which do not fully recover costs is commonplace. Reducing cross-subsidies between metropolitan and non-metropolitan customers by setting all prices to more accurately reflect costs would increase the electricity bills of currently subsidised customers. Such a decision may also militate against other policies (eg. decentralisation).

As Chapter Four has already argued, the specific community goals need to be clearly developed for each State trading enterprise. It is also important to note that, where the extent of cross-subsidisation does not meet the cost of Community Service Obligations (CSOs), the rate-of-return requirement will need to be adjusted. And while this is a controversial area for some economists, the work of public enterprise economists does provide some evidence that a more exact specification of community costs and subsidies is possible (De Ridder, 1989).

7.3 Charges for Other Government Services

In recent years there has been a marked increase in the application of policies of charging consumers of non-public enterprise services. There are clearly public services for which user charges can legitimately be levied. The arguments supporting this principle instead of financing free distribution from general revenue or borrowings are:

— the non-user is not penalised by having to support the service through taxation;

— the added funds reduce the revenue-gap, enabling more services to be provided for a given level of taxation (and borrowings);

— the costs of service provision will be partially offset by consumers who cross jurisdictional boundaries;

— where comparisons exist, charges could help to correct distorted prices in the private market; and

— since the buyer's response provides valuable information about demand, the allocation of resources within the government sector can be improved.

7.3.1 Industry Cost Recovery

Perhaps the most justifiable area for public service cost recovery lies in the provision of economic infrastructure and administrative services for industry. The increasing development and complexity of private economic activity has meant that new functions have been taken up by governments. In other cases functions which were undertaken privately have been increasingly taken over by governments. Examples of the former include such things as the provision of economic infrastructure for the aviation industry by government. Shifting responsibility for craft training to government is an example of the latter. *In these cases more pressure is placed on governments to expand their functions and put burdens on taxpayers which should properly be borne by industry* (cf. O'Connor, 1979).

At the Federal level the government has redressed these tendencies to some extent. Services for the aviation industry are fully funded by, in particular, landing fees and an excise surcharge on avgas. Agricultural services, quarantine, research and marketing, and other areas are funded by various levies and charges providing 100% cost recovery in some instances. Press reports suggest AUSTEL, the new Telecommunications regulatory authority, will be fully funded by some sort of industry levy. Meteorological services for specialised areas, particularly transport, are in part funded by industry charges. TV and radio operator licences contribute to the regulation of the broadcasting industry. The list could be greatly enlarged.

Many of the Federal initiatives seem to have

developed through Cabinet's Expenditure Review Committee (ERC). While the ERC may not have begun with a specific model in mind, the recovery proceeds from industries which require government infrastructure and activity. As far as regulatory activity is concerned, there are two main alternatives to the Federal model. First, taxpayers generally could fund the activity, which completely fails to address the historic problem of private activities generating the need for more government functions. Second, there is the option of relying on self-regulation, as for example occurs in some of the professions. For obvious reasons, self-regulation is unlikely to be a feasible option in most circumstances, the incentive of an industry body to turn a blind eye to the activities of a member being too strong.

An examination of the functions of State Governments in Part Three indicates many areas where some sort of industry cost recovery mechanism could and perhaps should be implemented. The examples include industry training, professional education, lands and legal records, agricultural services and regulation, conservation, regulation of industry and commerce, regulation of labour standards, health and safety functions, and infrastructure provided in mining towns, to name a few. In each example a strong case can be made for government activity but not necessarily taxpayer funding.

7.3.2 Social and Community Services
For some government provided services, charges are not practicable because it is not possible (or possible only at prohibitively high cost) to exclude those who are unwilling to pay the charge from benefitting from the service. In the case of the classical example of a 'Public Good', that of National Defence, everyone benefits, the externality is pervasive, and the 'non-excludability' characteristic prohibits the application of user charges.

For many other goods and services produced by the government which are designed to benefit the 'public purpose' but which are recognized also to yield significant individually appropriated benefits, the extent of cost-recovery through charges needs to be determined judiciously.

To summarise, charges are least justifiable when:

— they cannot be successfully employed at a relatively low cost (compared with the benefits);
— the benefits are not direct, so that charges, which reduce demand, will cause significant loss of externalities;
— demand (for the particular good or service) is highly inelastic, so that the application of charges does not aid resource allocation and does not help to eliminate excessive utilisation;
— charges result in inequities to lower income (or other groups) deemed by the government (or on the basis of accepted standards) to be in need of special consideration in the sense of not being required to pay for benefits received from the public services;
— a government service is deemed to be part of the social wage, and therefore should not be priced; and
— the government service is considered to be a merit good which consumers will demand too little of if user-charges are payable.

Under this model the approach of the Curran Commission (New South Wales) is simply untenable. This report contended that cost recovery should apply wherever possible to all public activities, including community services. For example, the Curran Commission recommends that performance indicators and target ratios of 'grant money to self raised ratios or paid hours to voluntary hours should be developed to evaluate recipients' qualification for grants' (Curran, 1989, p. 116).

7.4 Conclusion and Recommendations
7.4.1 Monitoring State Prices and Charges
Despite the importance of non-tax revenue for the States, the other tiers of government and for the economy as a whole, there is a dearth of information on the range of prices and charges provided levied by all the tiers of government. This lack of information and data should be addressed by the Premiers' Conference Secretariat proposed earlier in this book, for unless

the ABS or an alternative information agency is charged with collecting and analysing the relevant data in this area, then policy makers will have no firm basis upon which to develop the micro-economic policies which are appropriate for public trading enterprises. The 1989 IAC Draft Report is also correct to point out that the quality of inter-governmental relationships is also a factor which retards the performance of State trading enterprises and other organisations. This is also an important task which needs to be addressed by a central intergovernmental forum commissioned by the Premiers' Conference Secretariat.

7.4.2 User Charges
The States should continue to provide free and subsidised goods and services to users where they:

- generate systematic externalities,
- advance social equity

This principle applies to a large range of services within health, education, social welfare and public transport.

7.4.3 Industry Cost Recovery
In the areas where a user charge can legitimately be applied, we recommend strategies for increased self-financing and commercial performance of public services by extending the application of full and partial user charges and competitive pricing consistent with principles of social justice.

It should be stressed that unless the principle of industry cost recovery is endorsed, State Governments will find themselves unable, in the present fiscal climate, to respond to obvious new or increased needs thrown up by economic developments. However, it must be conceded that the exact mechanism which should be used in specific instances is not always obvious. It is therefore important that State Governments establish similar mechanisms to determine the appropriate means and level of industry cost recovery tailor-made to the specific circumstances involved. Not only must the incentive structure of the cost recovery mechanism be considered, but also the actual payment arrangements must be such

that they do not in any way compromise the body being funded.

Without the appropriate funding mechanisms there is a serious danger that necessary government functions will be provided at suboptimal levels or not at all. Of course, critics of government activity argue that Australian industry is already over-regulated. Generalities in this area are hard to establish. However, much of this regulation upholds the community's right to determine appropriate health, safety, product and other standards. It is axiomatic that industry bear the costs of both meeting and policing these standards.

It should be pointed out that genuine self-regulation, if it were adequate, could be expected to impose much the same costs on industry in meeting the same standards. In the absence of the obvious moral hazard problems, self-regulation funded by industry would have much to recommend it. In practice, that function should be a government responsibility — but there seems no logical reason why industry should benefit financially from the fact that self-regulation would not work.

7.4.4 Public Enterprises
Rate-of-Return Requirement
In principle, the imposition of a Rate-of-Return Requirement (RRR) for public trading enterprises is justifiable on economic and financial grounds. In the interest of an efficient allocation of resources, it is desirable that investments and resources utilized by public enterprises be required to earn a return comparable to their opportunity cost (what they would be able to earn in their best alternative use). At very least, an RRR would increase the capital-cost consciousness of management and staff, and provide an observable, monitorable focus for performance monitoring and evaluation.

An RRR also goes some way towards providing a surrogate for the discipline of a profit requirement in containing costs. It is true that many public enterprises face price inelastic demand schedules — at least for some services — so that cost increases might be easily passed on by way of higher prices. Nonetheless, where there are constraints on the ability of public enterprises to increase their prices, such as consumer resistance or the Victorian Government's policy guideline that price increases not exceed the rate of inflation, this restraint should preferably be formalised by a 'CPI − X' formula, where the level of X is the productivity improvement that might reasonably be expected of that enterprise. Such an arrangement would provide pressures to contain costs.

However, there are several questionable aspects concerning the use of a prescribed RRR:

− the RRR should not be regarded as a 'principal performance criterion' since this would be to claim or expect far too much of it. Other potential sources and incentives of improved performance for public enterprises need to be identified, developed, implemented and monitored;
− a uniform RRR applied to all public enterprises is not prescribed by economic theory, nor by the observation that rates of return vary widely between and among private and public sector enterprises. One must guard against the danger, though, that the prospect of rationalising a lower RRR for a particular public enterprise could provide a cloak behind which inefficiencies of various types might readily proliferate; and
− although in principle an appropriate RRR need not conflict with economic objectives, in practice it is difficult to identify the appropriate RRR for public enterprises. The RRR of 4% prescribed by the Victorian Government, which was determined by the 'weighted average cost of capital approach', cannot be demonstrated to be correct or superior on uncontentious theoretical grounds (see Chapter Five and Xavier & Graham, 1987).

Profit Measurement
The conventional historical cost accounting system is inadequate for facilitating measurement of a public enterprise's economic performance, for example, its RRR. A Current Cost Accounting (CCA) system, which takes into account the effects of inflation is more appropriate, particularly when the concern is to estimate real RRR. Hence the Victorian Government's requirement that public enterprises publish supplementary current Cost Accounting (CCA) information in their Annual Reports is to be commended. But the use of CCA is complicated by the fact that the choice of the appropriate CCA approach continues to be a controversial issue. Thus, Historical Cost Accounting information should continue to be published in Annual Reports. In particular, although it may be convenient to use the more objective and monitorable CPI index to calculate inflation-generated gains on debt, as done under the Victorian Government's Rate-of-return Reporting version of CCA, such a procedure can significantly understate or overstate the measure of profit and the dividend-paying capacity of the enterprise.

The Compatibility Between Economic and Commercial Objectives
A threat to the compatibility between commercial and economic objectives could arise if governments require unreasonably large dividend payments by public enterprises in the sense that the level of payments are insensitive to the need for these enterprises to pursue prudent financial and performance improving policies. In this context it is notable that some forms of Current Cost Accounting, including the Victorian Government's Rate-of-return Reporting approach, can estimate conceptual returns to equity which are far in excess of actual distributable profits (backed up with cash resources). Where such conceptual returns to equity are used to justify dividend payouts which, in the longer term, threaten the financial and economic performance of a public enterprise, the incompatibility between commercial and economic objectives can become quite stark. The Victorian Government's dividend requirement policy, which has at times required payments by an enterprise in excess of its conventionally calculated historical cost profit, should be reviewed in this light.

7.4.5 Revenue Issues
A further comment is required on the issue of public sector pricing. There are those who would prefer to see the public sector undertaking only those activites which cannot be commercially provided by the private sector

(see, for instance, Curran, 1988, p. 66). There is no rational justification for such a view.

It is the prerogative, and responsibility, of State (Federal and Local) Governments to use those of their enterprises for which commercial pricing policies are applicable (ie. where equity objectives will not be prejudiced) as revenue-raising instruments in order to ensure that other, non-commercial activites can be maintained. In Chapter Six we showed that levies on statutory corporations are becoming increasingly important in State revenues, and in Section 7.2 we showed that the Gross Operating Surplus of State Public Trading Enterprises represent a growing source of States' own-revenue. In this context, it would be extremely myopic for any State Government to relinquish ownership of these revenue sources, a fact that even the New South Wales Government seems

to have realised in its decisions to pull-back from the privatisation of the State Bank and the Government Insurance Office.

This point is also applicable to those (few, if any) public enterprises that are *exactly* identical to private sector enterprises, ie. where no social equity issue pertains at all. The onus is on the would-be-privatisers to justify ethically, economically and politically the alienation of such enterprises for the public sector. As we have shown in Chapter Five, such justifications do not exist.

Notes

1 Direct charges may also comprise part of Other Revenue. In 1979-80, Other Revenue was around 6.7% of Total State revenue and in 1986-87 this contribution had risen to 9.0%.

Chapter 8

FINANCING CAPITAL EXPENDITURE AND STATES' INDEBTEDNESS

8.1 An Introduction to State Debt

State Governments are responsible for the majority of public sector capital formation and the provision of capital infrastructure, which is partly financed by borrowings. Any analysis of public sector finance must therefore consider their borrowing and investment policies.

A number of misconceptions are commonly made concerning the role of debt finance in public expenditure by opponents of the public sector. For instance, the Executive Summary of the Curran Report (1988, p. 42) argues that 'public sector debt has grown significantly and represents one of the most serious issues for the New South Wales financial position.' They recommend debt reduction as a matter of high priority and 'strongly oppose the funding of capital infrastructure for social services through borrowings . . . [which should] . . . not be used to fund non-income generating activities such as schools' (p. 43). These issues are addressed following the presentation of some factual detail.

Capital outlays by State Governments as a proportion of total Commonwealth, State and local capital outlays have declined from 69% in 1980-81 to 64% in 1986-87. Over the same period, the Federal Government capital outlays to total Commonwealth outlays have declined from 11.6% to 10.9%, while the States' capital outlays to total State Outlays have declined from 27.7% to 25.4% (see ABS, Government Financial Estimates, Australia, 1986-87, Cat. No. 5501.0). Borrowing either in the form of Net Advances received from the Commonwealth Government, or Other Borrowing (domestic or overseas) provided about 17.5% of total funds received by the States in 1986-87

(rising from 15.9% in 1980-81).

The problem of debt management for State and Local Governments is somewhat different to that faced by the Commonwealth due to the Commonwealth's power over the level of State and Local Government borrowing. As an important aspect of stabilisation policy, aggregate debt management is an issue in which the the States are still expected to play a role.

Nevertheless, the States, even though constrained by the Commonwealth's overall macroeconomic policy, must still be cognisant of prudential limits and economic principles. The conservative approach is to ensure that public debt is in the form of long-term maturities, which protects the government from creditors imposing short-term calls on the loans. In modern times, however, it is assumed that maturing issues can always be refunded through new issues. The shorter the average outstanding debt, the larger is the refunding operation.

State Governments borrow primarily to finance capital works. Prudence suggests that loan finance is preferred to tax finance because capital formation yields benefits to successive generations. In some cases, capital formation generates income flows which can be used to service the debt, while otherwise, it provides enduring services to the community (like education) which do not directly generate revenue. In both cases, it is appropriate for the beneficiaries (the community in general) to contribute to the debt-servicing through general budget revenue (taxes and charges).

The notion of intergenerational equity justifies the use of debt-financing. Large-scale public works which yield services over a lengthy period tend to require large lumpy expenditures. If once-and-for-all capital expenditures were tax-financed a sharp tax increase would be necessary. Apart from the problem of fluctuating tax rates, this financing method also places an unfair burden on the current taxpayers. It is only fair to spread the burden across the generations which will enjoy the services. Thus, the initial cost would be covered by issuing debt, and tax revenue each successive year is used to service the debt.

The accumulation of debt therefore represents the cost to the future users of the services provided by the stock of public sector assets. In assessing the appropriateness or otherwise of any given level of debt it is necessary to have regard to the level of assets in place and their service potential; and the ratio of the debt to GDP.

From the Federal Government's perspective considerations of intergenerational burden transfer may be less important than the objectives of macro-economic stabilisation. The chosen mix between loan and tax-finance to satisfy these macro-economic goals may not be consistent with an ideal intergenerational burden distribution. However, the financing decisions of the States should consider the issues of intergenerational equity more carefully.

8.2 State Government Debt and Intergenerational Equity

To achieve an equitable transfer of the burden of financing the substantial capital expenditures between generations, the States should use debt rather than tax-finance. Of course, this proposition can be used to justify both positive and negative attitudes to borrowing:

— borrowing to provide services predominantly for the present generation might be excessive because the burden is transferred to the future generation; and
— borrowing is desirable in order to achieve intergenerational equity by spreading the costs of providing benefits among all the generations which enjoy them.

Musgrave & Musgrave, (1976, p. 606) note that the issue of 'intergenerational equity arises

most acutely at the State and Local levels where the bulk of public investment expenditures are made and financed.' A typical State expenditure might be the construction of a school building involving a substantial immediate (once-off) outlay for a resource which will provide services for twenty or more years. Tax financing would imply a sudden and large increase in taxes for a short period. Such a financing approach would place the burden of the provision of the school on the current taxpayers.

So debt-finance covers the initial cost of the school, and tax revenue (to service the debt) is raised in each future period according to the intertemporal distribution of benefits flowing from the school building. Musgrave & Musgrave (1976, p. 607) conclude that:

'A township which finances its school building by borrowing and amortizing the debt over the length of the asset life thus provides for an equitable pattern of burden distribution not only between age groups but also between changing groups of residents as the population of the jurisdiction changes in response to in-migration and out-migration.'

While debt-finance clearly facilitates a more equitable distribution of the burden of providing public goods over subsequent generations, it is clearly not an issue of financing exclusively. The expenditure side of the budget must always be analysed. Each generation should pay for the benefits they receive in accordance with the ability-to-pay of individuals within each generation.

8.2.1 Debt as Future Taxation

Economists antagonistic to debt-finance argue that the burden of all public expenditure must eventually be carried by taxation. It is argued that borrowings merely delay the inevitable tax raisings. Musgrave & Musgrave (1976, p. 603) summarise this view in the following way:

'The burden is thus postponed and future generations are born with a chain around their necks, ie., with the obligation to pay off the national debt.'

The fallacy in this argument is that the national debt need never be paid-off, and it is only the interest payments which generate future tax liabilities.

The opposing view argues that interest payments do not impose a burden on future generations because the future generation contains both taxpayers and interest-receivers (debt holders), and therefore, interest payments transfer resources from one group to another within the same generation. While valid, this view ignores, first, the costs of any inefficiencies arising from the tax distortions which could still lead to losses to the future generations; and, second, the issue of overseas debt which is particularly important in periods of exchange rate volatility. As a guide, economists believe that as long as the debt does not grow faster than GDP there is no cause for alarm.

8.2.2 The Effects of Debt-Financing on Savings, Capital Formation, and Growth

The debt burden may be shifted to future generations by reducing the growth of capital endowments passed on in time. Taxation tends to affect private consumption, whereas debt finance tends to affect the rate of saving and hence investment. If the present generation reduces its rate of saving as a result of debt-creating behaviour the growth in capital and future income will be reduced, other things equal.

Present saving is likely to be reduced if debt rather than tax financing is used because tax obligations are unambiguous to the present generation, whereas debt obligations involves a future commitment which is less clear. The declining savings rate would represent an indirect transfer of the burden from the present to the future generation, in the form of reduced growth potential (less productive capacity). But importantly, public capital formation provides vital infrastructure which may accelerate the growth potential of the economy.

8.3 Understanding and Defining State Debt

In examining trends in indebtedness of the States we must differentiate between gross indebtedness (the value of securities or other forms of debt outstanding) from net indebtedness (the gross figure less the value of the

financial investments held by the public sector). Further, the trend in real debt is more important than the nominal trend. In South Australia, for example, there has been a very large decline in the real value of indebtedness of the public sector. The composition of the debt is also of interest. Typically, there has been a decline in reliance on Commonwealth grants, and a commensurate rise in direct fund-raising from the capital markets.

For the purpose of this analysis, the public sector in each State is defined as the sum of the State Government itself (the Crown in right of the State) and the various corporate entities (semi-government authorities) created by Statute.

Certain financial intermediaries (for example, the State Bank of South Australia) are excluded. The framework follows the ABS national accounting definitions, which categorises government-owned banks, government-owned insurance companies, and public sector superannuation funds as being located in the finance sector rather than the public sector. In the South Australian data, the South Australian Financing Authority (SAFA) is included in the public sector, despite the fact that it is a financial institution (for a justification of this see South Australian Treasury [1985b], The Indebtedness of the South Australian Public Sector 1950 to 1985).

What is indebtedness? Public debt was traditionally defined in terms of the 1927 Financial Agreement, although this concept does not embrace the total stock of debt held by the entire State public sector. The latter includes the debt of the State Government and the borrowings of the semi-government authorities (whose debt activities come under the so-called Gentlemen's Agreement of 1936).

In the past, the debt raised under the Financial Agreement was for specific purposes, like housing, water supply, and urban development, and was subject to conditions stipulated by the Commonwealth. While still the most important source of debt, State Governments have increasingly accessed new capital sources independent of the Commonwealth. Following these trends, the concept of debt used in this section covers all financing arrangements 'which confer substantially the same rights and obligations as conventional borrowings' (South Australian Treasury, 1985, p. 7).

What is the relevance of the net indebtedness concept? First, consolidated relations are presented to avoid double-counting of transactions within the public sector. Second, the total stock of debt should not be viewed in isolation to the assets that it has financed. Not all of the public sector asset holdings are in the form of capital items. Some assets are held in the form of financial claims against third parties (cash or interest-bearing investment) and they directly offset a portion of the public sector's financial obligations. These offsets can be large and therefore the measure of indebtedness should be expressed in net terms.

8.4 Trends in Debt Management

In the period following the 1927 Financial Agreement, the States' borrowings and semi-government authorities' loan raisings, in both volume and form, were closely controlled by Commonwealth-dominated Loan Council arrangements.

Major changes followed the harsh cuts in Loan Council borrowings in the late 1970s, which provided incentives to the States to find alternative financing arrangements. The innovations which resulted included lease-back arrangements, security deposits, and trade credits. The cost of these funds was cheaper and their volume unrestricted by the Commonwealth, but they represented a transfer of funds from Federal to State in the form of Federal tax losses.

The Commonwealth recognising both its diminishing (though still substantial) control:

- varied tax legislation to eliminate the room for gains from lease arrangements; and
- developed the Global approach to public sector borrowing which essentially widened the public sector institutions who came under direct borrowing limits.

A summary of debt management since 1927 is as follows:

'(1) a long period between 1927 and the mid 1970s where debt management was seen as a joint (although largely Commonwealth) responsibility of members of the Loan Council;

(2) a period of about a decade when Loan Council controls became more stringent on the face of it but less effective and the States were able to take on financial liabilities on other forms; and

(3) the current period where greater flexibility is allowed with respect to forms of taking on liabilities, but where the volume controls are potentially more effective' (South Australian Treasury, 1988b).

8.5 Interstate Comparisons

In the past, comparisons between the States in terms of indebtedness have adopted the narrow concept of debt defined in terms of the Financial Agreement. In this section the more pervasive concept of debt is used.

Although the Curran Commission of Audit makes much of the indebtedness of New South Wales — without let it be noted, adequate reference to sources — the most meaningful indicator of the debt burden is ratio of debt to Gross State Product (GSP). This is because debt is usually incurred to finance a growth in productive capacity. Economists have long argued that rising debt levels should not cause alarm as long as it is associated with a proportional growth in output. Indeed, constructive use of debt finance is the principle source of growth. Table 8.1 expresses public sector net debt as a percentage of GSP in New South Wales, Victoria, and South Australia. The significant conclusion which can be drawn from Table 8.1 is that in New South Wales and Victoria the ratio grew in the mid 1980s, and is now declining. This is consistent with the suggestion that the debt has not been used to finance non-productive expenditure.

Another dimension of indebtedness is the trend in real debt holdings. Inflation reduces the value of nominal debt, and to gain an appreciation of the resource cost of the debt, price changes must be accounted for. Table 8.2 displays trends in various debt concepts in nominal terms and Table 8.3 indicates the real equivalents of these concepts.

The effects of price rises on the value of nominal debt are clearly shown. The rise in per capita debt since 1981 in South Australia and New South Wales has been modest in real terms, while Victoria's more substantial rise in

real debt reflects its more aggressive economic development strategy.

Table 8.1

Public Sector Debt as a Percentage of GSP

	1981	1982	1983	1984	1985	1986	1987	1988
NSW	n/a	n/a	20.2	22.5	24.4	23.0	23.8	17.9
Vic.	26.7	27.2	29.3	28.9	26.4	27.2	29.7	27.6
SA	22.4	22.4	23.0	21.1	19.6	19.3	19.3	17.2

Source: New South Wales Budget Papers, Victorian Treasury and South Australia Budget Papers.

Table 8.2

Total Debt Outstanding of State Public Sector
(Government and Semi-Government)
$m (Current Prices)

	1981	1982	1983	1984	1985	1986	1987	1988
NSW*								
Gross Debt	10943.8	12867.7	15296.0	18389.0	21104.1	22641.9	24714.1	26097.5
Net Debt	8575.8	9967.7	12185.1	14965.7	17791.4	18777.6	21341.9	18116.6
Per Capita	1638.2	1879.4	2276.3	2769.9	3255.8	3394.7	3802.8	3178.7
Victoria								
Gross Debt	10538.0	11846.0	13957.0	15738.0	17688.0	19857.0	21687.0	22962.0
Net Debt	10132.0	11428.0	13478.0	15034.0	17012.0	19319.0	21145.0	21951.0
Per Capita	2567.1	2867.1	3339.7	3687.9	4129.0	4642.9	5023.9	5152.5
South Australia								
Gross Debt	3379.7	3575.7	3969.8	4641.9	5533.9	6271.6	6990.8	9098.9
Net Debt	2367.0	2571.0	2917.0	3242.0	3387.0	3662.0	3958.0	3908.0
Per Capita	1794.8	1931.5	2167.5	2383.8	2470.1	2648.6	2838.9	2775.6

Note: * Includes debt of semi-government sector not directly and explicitly guaranteed by the New South Wales State Government.

Source: New South Wales Budget Papers; South Australian Treasury (1988), The Finances of South Australia; and Financial Paper No. 1 1989-89; Victorian Department of Management and Budget (1988), 'Victorian Public Sector Debt', Information Paper No. 2; Australian Bureau of Statistics.

The figures certainly do not indicate a massive blow-out in debt of the States. The Debt/GSP ratios are nowhere near critical and the trends summarised by Table 8.4 are also consistent with a controlled situation.

8.6 The Global Approach to Loan Council Borrowings

The borrowings by Commonwealth and State authorities are not subject to the Financial Agreement. The Gentlemen's Agreement in 1936 corrected this, and provided the framework until 1984 for Loan Council approval of

annual debt-raising for semi-government and local authorities. A major change occurred in June 1984 with the introduction of the Global Approach whereby these authorities are subject to global borrowing limits agreed annually by the Loan Council.

The Global Approach was introduced because the Federal Government realised that the Loan Council was progressively exerting less influence over the totality of authority borrowings. It aimed to broaden the ambit of Loan Council control over the totality of authority borrowings, by including all forms of borrowings by Commonwealth and State semi-government and local authorities, government-owned companies and trusts.The States all sought more creative sources of debt for their

authorities, and such techniques as financial lease-back arrangements were relied upon increasingly.

Table 8.3

Total Debt Outstanding of State Public Sector
(Government and Semi-Government)
(Excluding Financial Institutions)
Real Terms (1988 dollars)

	1981	1982	1983	1984	1985	1986	1987	1988
*NSW**								
Gross Debt	18718.0	19502.0	21364.0	23938.0	26050.0	25994.0	26451.0	26097.5
Net Debt	14668.0	15107.0	17019.0	19482.0	21961.0	21558.0	22842.0	18116.6
Per Capita	2802.0	2848.0	3179.0	3606.0	4019.0	3897.0	4070.0	3179.0
Victoria								
Gross Debt	18024.0	17954.0	19494.0	20487.0	21834.0	22797.0	23211.0	22962.0
Net Debt	17330.0	17320.0	18825.0	19750.0	20999.0	22179.0	22631.0	21951.0
Per Capita	4391.0	4338.0	4665.0	4801.0	5097.0	5330.0	5377.0	5152.5
South Australia								
Gross Debt	5781.0	5419.0	5545.0	6043.0	6831.0	7200.0	7482.0	9099.0
Net Debt	4048.0	3897.0	4073.0	4220.0	4181.0	4204.0	4237.0	3908.0
Per Capita	1319.0	1331.0	1346.0	1360.0	1371.0	1383.0	1394.0	1408.0

Note: * Includes debt of semi-government sector not directly and explicitly guaranteed by the New South Wales State Government.
Source: New South Wales Budget Papers; South Australian Treasury (1988), The Finances of South Australia; and Financial Paper No. 1 1989-89; Victorian Department of Management and Budget (1988), 'Victorian Public Sector Debt', Information Paper No. 2; Australian Bureau of Statistics.

The main features of the Global Approach are summarised in the 1988-89 Budget Paper No. 4, *Commonwealth Financial Relations with other Levels of Government 1988-89*, pp. 50-51. The major thrust of the Approach is to impose aggregate global limits on borrowings by Commonwealth and State authorities. In addition, there is a constraint imposed upon the ratio of overseas to total borrowings by State authorities.

Individual Governments have discretion to determine how global limit approvals are allocated among their respective authorities. The limits cover borrowings by semi-government and local authorities, government-owned companies and trusts. Excluded from the limits are borrowings by government-owned financial institutions and statutory marketing authorities except where their borrowings are on-lent to bodies subject to the limits.

Borrowings by other exempt institutions are also covered when on-lent to Government except where they are associated with temporary or unexpected fluctuations in outlays and receipts. New money borrowings are defined widely to include conventional domestic and overseas loan raisings; domestic deferred payment arrangements; overseas trade credits; financial leases including leveraged leasing, sale and leaseback, and similar arrangements; net changes in temporary purposes borrowings over the financial year and 'any other means of financing capital expenditures'. It excludes operating leases and temporary borrowings within the financial year.

Under the Global Approach, approval of the timing, terms and conditions and the form of all domestic borrowings undertaken by authorities is effectively delegated to the individual Loan Council members subject to the Council being kept appropriately informed. A ceiling on new money overseas borrowings by State authorities is set (currently at 22% of the total global limit with the distribution among the States to be determined by Loan Council and advised to the Commonwealth and the States to determine the allocation among their own authorities), and some controls operate over the access to public issues markets. Loan Council approval of terms and conditions of borrowings now only applies with respect to the sterling private placement market, although members are required to keep the Council informed of terms and conditions applying to borrowings in all other overseas markets.

Table 8.4

Percentage Growth in Real Gross, Net, and Per Capita Debt
Outstanding of State Public Sector
Annual (June on June)

State	1981/82	1982/83	1983/84	1984/85	1985/86	1986/87	1987/88
NSW							
Gross Debt	4.10	9.55	12.04	8.82	9.98	1.75	-1.30
Net Debt	2.99	12.65	14.47	12.72	9.82	9.82	-20.68
Per Capita	1.64	1.62	13.43	11.45	-3.70	4.40-	21.89
Victoria							
Gross Debt	-0.38	8.58	5.09	6.57	4.41	1.82	-1.07
Net Debt	-0.06	8.69	3.96	7.30	5.62	2.04	-3.00
Per Capita	-1.20	7.54	2.92	6.17	4.57	0.90	-4.18
South Australia							
Gross Debt	-6.76	2.33	8.98	13.04	5.40	3.92	21.61
Net Debt	-3.73	4.52	3.61	-0.01	0.55	0.78	-7.76
Per Capita	0.90	1.13	1.04	0.81	0.87	0.79	1.00

Source: New South Wales Budget Papers; South Australian Treasury (1988), The Finances of South Australia; and Financial Paper No. 1 1989-89; Victorian Department of Management and Budget (1988), 'Victorian Public Sector Debt', Information Paper No. 2; Australian Bureau of Statistics. 2 includes debt of semi-government sector not directly and explicitly guaranteed by the New South Wales State Government.

Significant discretion also lies with the States in operating domestic conversion and refinancing programs during the term of the debt, provided that there is no addition to the total level of outstanding debt. Debt conversion and refinancing programs are permitted as an addition to the new money overseas ceiling provided that there is no addition to the total overseas debt outstanding and that appropriate advice is given to the Loan Council.

Table 8.5 provides details of the annual borrowing limits set by the Loan Council since 1983-84, initially under the Gentleman's Agreement and from 1984-85 under the Global Approach. The significant increase which occurred in 1984-85, reflects, in part, the incorporation within the Global Approach of 'un-conventional' borrowings previously outside the Gentleman's Agreement. Some have argued that the limits under the Global Approach were initially set at generously high levels so enabling the States in following years to convert surplus borrowing capacity into financial assets, the so-called hollow logs. It is evident, however, that since 1984-85, the global limits have in total and for each State and the Commonwealth been cut significantly in real terms.

8.7 Borrowing Reforms: Commercial Authorities and Loan Council Controls
Should Commercial Authorities be exempted from Loan Council control? This question has stimulated considerable debate over the past

decade. Those who advocate the relaxation of Loan Council controls point to the detrimental effects that the restricted access to capital funds has had on the performance of these authori-

ties. *Limited access to borrowings may force greater reliance on internal funding of capital works and this may have to be achieved by excessive price rises* (Campbell Report, 1981).

Table 8.5

Australian Loan Council Limits for Annual Borrowings by Commonwealth, State and Northern Territory Public Bodies

$m

	83-84	%	84-85	%	85-86	%	86-87	%	87-88	%
NSW	1883.9	29	1940.6	28	2059.1	29	1845.0	29	1539.7	29
Vic.	1580.3	24	1984.8	28	2006.6	29	1858.9	30	1526.4	29
Qld	1652.0	25	1552.0	22	1538.9	22	1387.0	22	1160.5	22
WA	758.8	12	818.1	12	741.3	11	635.0	10	584.0	11
SA	481.0	7	493.0	7	400.0	6	350.0	6	300.8	6
Tas.	180.2	3	229.0	3	230.0	3	217.0	3	181.6	3
States	6586.2		7017.4		6976.0		6292.9		5293.0	
NT	16.6		50.0		65.0		86.3		65.0	
C'wealth	758.0		1200.2		1189.0		1459.0		1187.9	
Total	7360.8		8267.6		8230.1		7838.1		6545.9	

Source: Australia, Commonwealth Financial Relations with Other Levels of Government, 1987-88, Budget Paper No. 4, Table 99, p. 144.

Similarly, there is little to distinguish commercial authority investment from investment in the private sector. Therefore, it is discriminatory to control one and not the other. In most cases, commercial authorities could operable viably in the private sector and their investments are often complementary to the investment of private sector firms.

It is arguable that strict competitive neutrality between public and private sector enterprises requires not only that firms have equal access to capital markets, but that in other respects, firms do not have particular advantages or disadvantages arising from their ownership status (public or private), that would affect the cost of borrowing or the returns that could be obtained with borrowed funds. Whilst it would be relatively easy to free commercial authorities from Loan Council controls it may be considerably more difficult to achieve competitive neutrality in the wider sense.

Further, there are difficulties in using public capital works expenditures as an instrument of short-term counter cyclical policy. First, due to the long lead times between planning and actual expenditure, and constraints with con-

tinuing contracts, it is generally difficult to significantly reduce these expenditures in the very short-run. By the time changes become effective, the reductions may in fact be inappropriate. Second, in the rush to expand or contract expenditure, little regard may be had for project viability and the wider social costs and benefits. This may mean that projects with relatively low rates of return get higher priority, with consequential detrimental effects for long-term GDP growth.

Those who oppose the relaxation of Loan Council controls over the volume of borrowings by commercial authorities fear the loss of control and co-ordination of public sector borrowings in general (see disussion of Martin Committee below). While commercial authorities are only a subset of those authorities subject to global limits, they account for a very significant share of approved borrowings in total. It is argued that when controls were relaxed in the past there was a very large increase in borrowings (for example, in 1982, major electricity authorities were exempted from Loan Council controls and their borrowing increased rapidly).

Debate over the necessity for controlling the

level of public sector borrowings is influenced by the possibility that public sector investment and borrowings may crowd out private sector expenditures. There are various ways in which crowding out can occur in theory (see H.V. Evatt, 1988; Neville 1987). However, as Chapter Two shows the short to medium term crowding out effects are likely to be minimal.

In what way can commercial and non-commercial authorities be distinguished? The Campbell Committee (1981) failed to make this distinction clear, although it saw commercial authorities as being subjected to market disciplines, whereas non-commercial authorities would tend to be those with a strong social element. Suggested tests for commerciality included whether an authority had an adequate capital base; clear current and future cash flow to service debt; competitive pricing discipline, etc. The Campbell Committee considered that the small number of commercial authorities should be freed from Loan Council controls, and be subject to similar market disciplines experienced by private sector firms. In particular, there would no longer be a Government guarantee for their borrowings. Underlying these recommendations was the Committee's view that:

> '. . . the benefits to be derived from a market allocation of funds are sufficient to warrant at least, for those who clearly operate on a commercial basis, a limited move in the direction of borrowing freedom . . .' (p. 199).

The Campbell Committee considered that non-commercial authorities should remain subject to Loan Council controls over the volume of borrowings, but not the terms and conditions, and should continue to borrow under Government guarantee. It saw advantages in centralising the borrowings of non-commercial authorities under Commonwealth control, but, in light of the practical difficulties, recommended that State Based Central Borrowing Authorities be established to consolidate the borrowings of these authorities. The States, with Loan Council approval, subsequently moved to establish such organisations.

The Campbell Committee did note some practical difficulties with its recommendation to free commercial authorities from Loan Council control and subject them to normal market conditions. First, there was the problem that even when no explicit Government guarantee was given, the market might still impute such a guarantee. It would indeed be difficult for a Government not to become involved if one of its authorities could meet its debts.

Second, commercial authorities frequently do not have a totally free hand in their pricing policies, but must accommodate decisions taken at the political level. Third, the capital structure and profit requirements of the public commercial authorities could not be regarded as being strictly commercial in the private sector sense.

These difficulties were clearly seen as reducing the force of its recommendations notwithstanding the fact that the Campbell Committee also made other recommendations aimed at obtaining competitive neutrality with the private sector. These would involve the levying of fees to offset the borrowing advantages gained through Government ownership; a movement to full capitalisation to the standard of private sector competitors; recognition of any differences in taxation treatment between public authorities and private companies; the maintenance of operating efficiency; return on capital and dividend payments at comparable private sector levels; and appropriate disclosure of authority performance in commercial and non-commercial areas.

8.7.1 Other Developments Concerning the Relaxation of Loan Council Controls

In its 1982 report, the Advisory Council for Inter-Government Relations considered that there were potential advantages in freeing commercial authorities from these controls.

The Martin Committee (1983) supported the Loan Council's decision to eliminate its controls over the terms and conditions of domestic borrowings by local and semi-government authorities as previously recommended by the Campbell Committee. However, it rejected the Campbell Committee's recommendation to remove volume controls over commercial authority borrowings. It considered that direct control over the volume of public sector borrowing was necessary largely for macro-economic policy reasons (influencing aggregate demand via interest rates and private sector investment).

In 1987, the Commonwealth Minister for Finance issued a policy information paper which detailed broad guidelines within which Commonwealth statutory authorities and business enterprises were to operate in the future. Attention was given to the capital and financial structure of the enterprises. The paper specifically mentioned that consideration would be given to removing enterprise loan raisings from the requirement to obtain Loan Council approval. Clearly, if Commonwealth enterprises were to be exempt from Loan Council controls, State enterprises would also be affected. The issue has become somewhat controversial in light of broader discussion of the merits or otherwise of privatisation. It is probable that, even with the substantial management and accounting changes proposed for public enterprises, that the commercial aims and performance of the same will be impaired by the restriction in the access to funds for capital expansion by the limits set by the Loan Council. This loss of efficiency in turn has given rise to greater pressure for privatisation despite the erroneous logic of the latter strategy.

A major concern of the the House of Representatives Standing Committee on Transport, Communications and Infrastructure which reported to Parliament in November 1987 was a perceived shortage of public investment in Australia. It specifically recommended that the borrowings of commercial public authorities by excluded from the PSBR.

8.8 State Borrowings — A More Logical Approach

The arguments for exempting commercial authorities from Loan Council controls are stronger where those authorities have been established to compete with private sector organisations. Such authorities require this freedom if they are to provide a competitive stimulus in highly concentrated industries where firms have market power, either through dominance, or potentially, through cartel type behaviour. The case for exempting natural monopolies — in the main the large public utilities — is not as strong in this respect.

However, where such authorities are subject to rigorous guidelines concerning investment appraisal, borrowing practices, and pricing controls which require them to act as if they were operating in competitive markets, the case for exclusion from Loan Council controls is greatly enhanced.

On both efficiency and equity grounds, it would seem appropriate that commercial authorities (either operating in close competition with the private sector or subject to rigorous guidelines mentioned above) should be able to operate on the basis of competitive neutrality. This means that they receive no benefits or suffer disadvantages (like Loan Council controls) as a consequence of their public sector status, which are not similarly experienced by the private sector firms.

It is difficult to see why such public sector firms should be more restricted in their capital raising and investment policies than their private sector counterparts. Accordingly, commercial authorities in close competition with private sector firms, or subject to rigorous guidelines aimed at promoting effective market performance be no longer subject to Loan Council controls over the volume of their annual borrowings. This is especially relevant if investment is assessed according to the project's ability to generate a competitive rate-of-return.

8.9 State Financing Authorities

In the past, it was common for State bodies to arrange their own finance and develop expertise in-house or hire consultants externally. This lead to a number of diverse securities for a State's agencies being traded in the market. Thus, each agency may have become unfamiliar with the latest corporate finance techniques because it arranged and developed its own finance and financial expertise.

A centralised fund raising body for each State has the following advantages:

 — greater flexibility in structuring approaches to the capital market;

– ability to develop expertise in-house;
– opportunity to exploit modern structured financing techniques to obtain finance at lower rates than traditional sources;
– management of the State's financing and investment plans to achieve lower borrowing costs through planning;
– improved liquidity management, ensuring that the whole State's financing needs are met, without foregoing short term investment opportunities; and
– provide a mechanism to centrally fund economic development, infrastructure and provide venture capital.

All States have now established such centralised fund-raising bodies in recognition of the advantages they provide. Chapter Twelve provides a case study of a State central borrowing agency, the South Australian Financing Authority.

8.10 Conclusion

If the commercial trading authorities of the States are subject to market derived interest rates in the absence of guarantees, crowding out arguments diminish in strength. A public enterprise, paying corporate tax, when exposed to the capital market will face a cost of capital that ensures a socially optimum level of investment. That is, debt finance will be allocated between private and public sector enterprises at market derived rates. These rates will then be used in calculating the marginal cost of capital for use in investment evaluation. For all bodies the capital budget will then be determined by accepting all investment up to the point where the marginal efficiency of investment equals this marginal cost of the capital.

To work in practice, the debt:equity ratios (or leverage) of the statutory authorities need to be reviewed. In the absence of government guarantees, high leverage levels, with the associated high risk of liquidity difficulties (financial risk) will lead to the authorities being granted relatively poor credit ratings and hence high interest costs. So for the recommendations outlined here to work it may be necessary to accompany borrowing freedoms with an equity injection into some authorities.

The level of overseas borrowings is another important consideration. Australia, like any borrower, has a credit rating that is determined in part by the perceptions of the likelihood of default. As the level of overseas debt rises, the credit rating may fall, increasing interest costs. Increased overseas borrowings by authorities, while not necessarily crowding out private investment, may lead to a lower credit rating for the country. Accordingly, the new Premiers' Conference Secretariat should monitor, and publicise, the borrowing activities of commercial authorities freed from Loan Council controls, and the purposes for which funds are raised. Such 'transparency' will provide a means by which macro-economic stability can be safeguarded from excessive borrowing. Overseas borrowing also requires the acquisition of exchange rate risk management skills to avoid significant capital losses that may result from fluctuations in the Australian dollar.

Chapter 9

OTHER FINANCING ISSUES: EQUITY, VENTURE CAPITAL AND ECONOMIC DEVELOPMENT

Some of the more topical areas of State financial activity in recent times are private equity issues in State enterprises and the role of State Governments in venture capital and economic development. Given the tough era of fiscal constraint it is perhaps not surprising that particular States would be tempted to examine every possible means of raising revenue especially if such methods were outside the jurisdiction of the Loans Council and the Grants Commission.

The efforts of State Government in the area of venture capital and economic development are not new. For example, the Ryan and Theodore Governments took a leading role in providing venture capital to Queensland's mining industry from 1917-1920 (cf. Murphy, 1975, pp. 199-200). Usually, however, it is the spectacular failures in this area which attract attention, and there have recently been quite notable 'fractures'.

This chapter reviews the various initiatives in revenue raising from commercial activities over the last few years and provides some cautious recommendations on their worth.

9.1 Trusts

Unit trusts are taking on an increasingly important role in the Australian equity capital market. Although the legal nature of a unit in a trust is different to that of a share, it does represent direct ownership of the trust's assets and participation in the trust's profitability in the same way as share capital.

A trust's structure involves a trustee who holds the assets on behalf of the unit holders, and the management company which manages the assets using its skills in the relevant business activity. The major advantage of trusts is in avoiding company tax by distributing all of its taxable profits to shareholders, although the dividend imputation scheme reduces this advantage.

9.1.1 The Victorian Equity Trust (VET)

The VET was established in 1987 to raise equity capital for four major Victorian State authorities: State Electricity Commission, Board of Works, Gas and Fuel Corporation and the Portland Smelter Unit Trust. A unit trust was the capital-raising vehicle with the government holding majority control. A minority of equity was to be issued to the public in order to obtain stock exchange listing. Any funds raised from this initiative were propsed to be used to provide new capital to the authorities concerned.

The VET aimed to attract equity rather than debt to finance the investment of the PTEs concerned, and was consistent with financing developments in the private sector. The trust arrangement would have all of the characteristics of issued shares in that trust holders would receive dividend income and have voting rights (although voting rights were not forthcoming on issue of units). In this way, an element of private ownership would be introduced into the PTEs, while maintaining Government control with majority voting rights.

Five main factors influenced the decision to establish the VET:

- The Government already had substantial equity investment in the PTEs;
- The private sector was moving to equity rather than debt, including innovative equity instruments;
- A desire to reduce the debt levels in public authorities, primarily to reduce debt serving costs which were hampering long-term decision making;
- The VET supported their commercialisation strategy and placed financing, pricing, investment and dividend policies on a more commercial footing; and
- The Public Sector Borrowing Requirement would fall.

The trust structure adopted provides a holding company for investment in the participating authorities. It was argued that this would attract private sector investors by providing a desirable investment portfolio.

The prospectus stated that the trust aimed to achieve for its unit-holders an attractive and increasing level of distributions; security from a spread of investments in sound income-producing authorities; and long-term capital growth.

The choice of a trust over incorporation and sale of shares was not publicly addressed. There seems to be no commercial reason for favouring a trust over shares. Certainly, the issue of costs of the former are greater. Politically, however, the sale of shares may seem more like a form of privatisation than the sale of units in a trust, hence the avoidance of political costs may have been a key factor.

In any event the final form of trust chosen may eventually lead to its failure. The performance of the VET has been less than spectacular to say the least. Units were issued at $1 and are currently listed at below 90c. Part of the cause of this poor performance may be due to the fact that the trust is equity in name only. Unit holders only have a share in distributed income and lack equity in retained profits, the possibility of realising their capital through winding up or takeover, any voting rights, and imputation credits.

These features distinguish the trust from true equity. They also eliminate the possibility of significant capital growth since there is no equity in retained profits, only an interest in dividend. Accordingly the price of units will fall in the market until expected yields are in line with other investment instruments of equivalent risk. Recognising this, the government added a 'put option' to the units, whereby investors could redeem their investment in the future at a price linked to the share price index. The put option was a European type which allows for redemption on one particular day only, exposing investors to the risk that the index may be low on a particular date. A preferable approach may have been to use an American type of option allowing for redemption at any time up to expiry date.

There is also a further political risk dimension to the VET unit-holders. The government has the choice of either withdrawing funds by way of taxes and levies, or through dividends. However dividends must be shared with VET investors. The mix of tax versus dividend is a decision that may change over time in response to government policy and consequently private unit-holders may suffer.

Overall, the VET approach is a complex way of providing equity for public authorities. It requires either a trust structure granting all rights equivalent to share capital or it involves complex financing arrangements to achieve the same effect. In the absence of the true elements of equity, especially a share in the retained profits, the trust becomes, in effect, another form of debt.

9.1.2 South Australian Finance Trust Fund Limited

The SAFTL is a public company registered under the Companies Code and subject to all of the requirements of the Code. The company is owned by the Treasurer of South Australia through an arrangement whereby the shares are held in trust for the treasurer by the Bankers Trust Australia Limited. The Treasurer retains control of the company through control of the shareholders. The SAFTL is trustee for the South Australian Finance Trust which owns UK and Hong Kong resident companies. The SAFTL is also a beneficial owner or part-owner of several other limited liability companies.

The overall purpose of the SAFTL structure is to undertake cost-effective financing arrangements for the State. The trust structure is not a vehicle for selling equity to private investors (as in the VET), but is a vehicle for exploiting favourable financing conditions, especially tax concessions. It also provides the State with limited liability for its activities through the trust. This feature is not exploited since the government has agreed to guarantee all the obligations of SAFTL to give a marketing advantage to their issued debt paper.

9.2 State Development Activities

Although economic development agencies are not formed primarily for this purpose, in recent years a number of State Governments have pursued their revenue raising potential with some vigour. The austere fiscal climate of the 1980s has perhaps inevitably pushed governments down this path, since it offers a growing source of revenue to help maintain services.

The fate of this strategy in Western Australia is discussed at length in Chapter Thirteen, but it is important for the purposes of this chapter to include here an analysis of the revenue implications of economic development agencies. Armed with analysis, it is possible to disentangle revenue raising from development activities, and in so doing revive the legitimacy of the latter. In passing, it is relevant to note that the implementation of a States Goods and Services Levy, by stabilising State revenue, would help reduce the incentive for govern ments to pursue innovative – if not reckless – forms of revenue.

9.2.1 Victorian Economic Development Corporation (VEDC)

If entrepreneurial activities are to provide a source of future public revenues then the calibre of management is crucial to success. The Ryan Report into the VEDC found no evidence of fraud or dishonesty but found significant ineptitude in the management skills of those in charge. The VEDC provided venture capital and development finance through loans to, and equity investments in, ventures associated with new risky technologies that would have otherwise been denied finance. The nature of the venture capitalist's business is risky, but proper management of risk exposure

and lending procedures may have avoided the corporations ultimate insolvency. Ryan found that the Victorian Government failed to employ the correct people to manage the VEDC. Specific criticisms included:

– The financial information collected on client companies fell short of an acceptable standard for evaluating lending and investment proposals;
– Evidence that some board members had conflicts of interest because they sat on client companies' boards;
– Unwillingness to recognise bad investments, leading to additional loans that were not commercially sustainable; and
– Poor documentation of lending and investment guidelines and no policy on overdue loans.

The key element of failure, therefore, was in the recruitment of management. *For any public authority and especially commercialised authorities, to succeed appropriate management must be found which will involve paying market rates for proven private sector executives. It is unlikely that commercially orientated managers will exist within the public sector already. Accordingly, to attract the right management, salary packages in line with those paid to senior executives in large public companies would be appropriate. Clearly this is a conundrum for policy makers and government, implying as it does a challenge to public sector industrial relations practices.* The development of appropriate expertise within the public sector would be a preferable option for governments committed to this type of strategy.

The VEDC case also highlights the effect of risk management or in this case mismanagement. *The VEDC displayed a reluctance to foreclose in its bad investments and recognise a loss early.* Risk taking necessarily involves losses, but the key to effective risk management is recognising when to admit loss and avoid further losses. An environment is needed where managers are prepared to recognise losses quickly and to react in positive ways.

Other lessons for management of commercialised enterprises can be found in the Ryan Report's criticisms of the board:

– It did not properly fulfil its role in ensuring that normal procedures for a financial institution were developed, documented and observed;
– There was failure to adequately address the strategic direction of the corporation and a failure to adequately develop policies;
– A failure to respond to consultants' and the auditor's reports; and
– The board lacked balance, cohesion and apparently competence. The composition of the board of an enterprise should include a balance of expertise in line with the type of business.

In the aftermath of the Ryan Report into the VEDC the media has identified 'three issues of public interest' (*The Age*, 18 January, 1989). The first is ministerial responsibility for the public sector corporations such as the VEDC. The second asks whether the VEDC was a success or a failure. The Ryan Report was damning in its criticisms of the VEDC's management, yet the report did not address the positive side of the corporation's activities. Third, there is a philosophical issue of whether the State should be involved in high-risk venture and development capital. *State of Siege* contends that this role is defensible but it is more appropriate that a grants based model of funding provide this function, a recommendation which is developed below.

What of the positive side of the government involvement in providing venture capital? The Ryan Report points to losses to taxpayers from the VEDC's activities being $111m. However, it is likely that $50m or more of this amount will be recovered, leaving the State's loss, or investment in the ventures funded, at around $60m. The VEDC experience should also be set in the context of the Cain Government's broader and successful industry policy strategy. The returns from this investment are considerable including an extra 40,000 jobs in Victoria.

9.2.2 WA Inc.
Chapter Thirteen points out the issue of the risk exposure (based on complex property dealings) of government is highly relevant in a discussion of economic development and alternative revenue-raising strategies in

Western Australia. The actions of the Western Australian Government towards Rothwells Ltd. were the culmination of a development strategy which over-emphasised and over-valued the revenue potential of such activity and which in consequence mitigated against proper portfolio management. This weakness was exacerbated by the essentially immature nature of the Western Australian capital market, which had developed during a period of sustained bull-market stock exchange conditions and rapidly rising property values where a handful of large but highly leveraged corporations exerted political influence thanks to an element of popularism. Indeed other actions, such as the SGIC (Western Australia's) support for Bond and Bell Groups, represents a strong alliance between government and big business. SGIC have taken a shareholding in Bell Group and have held their shareholding in spite of the possibility to sell at a favourable price. SGIC appear to be mindfull of Bond Media's strategic interest in its share transactions. This situation has become even more complex as the relationships between the various Bond companies, the Bell Group and Bond's private company have been critically analysed by both the Australian Stock Exchange and the Australian Broadcasting Tribunal.

The Western Australian Government has also acted in favour of the Bond group's rescue plan in its action with regard to Rothwells Ltd. Following the 1987 stock market crash the Western Australian Government moved to rescue Rothwells and again in October 1988 it provided financial support to try to prop up the ailing bank. The government had provided a $150m guarantee for Rothwells Bank which it converted, in a complex deal, to a $175m equity holding in a proposed petrochemical plant.

WA Inc. is a tangled web of government-big business deals which a dedicated and accountable State development strategy would not have countenanced. In the process, the government has acquired interests in a diamond mine and a proposed petrochemical plant both purchased from Bond. In addition it made guarantees to support Rothwells in a support package organised by Bond.

The fall-out from WA Inc. may leave the State

with substantial losses to finance. It must be noted that the lesson is not that government should not be involved in business. The lesson is that government business ventures, that involve risk exposure, must be managed correctly.

The Western Australian experience with the merchant bank Rothwells, and as a risk-taking entrepreneur may hold some valuable lessons for the concept of commercialisation. As noted by Mr Cain following the report into the VEDC, the role of the government in enterprise may, perhaps, be ideally in the solid, less risky ventures that it has traditionally been involved in. While this may preclude the possibility of large profits, based on property speculation and the vagaries of the Stock Market index, it would also preclude the possibility of large losses of public money and the consequent adverse publicity. Failure in a government venture only serves the interest of those seeking to exclude government from the profitable activities in the economy.

9.3 Other Initiatives
9.3.1 Lease Finance
In recent years there has been a trend towards leasing as a source of finance for State authorities. Of particular interest are the leveraged lease used to finance New South Wales' Elcom's Eraring power station and ETSA's sale-leaseback-defeasance arrangement for some of its existing generating plant.

The main advantages of leasing are:

– for a public sector body, leasing permits the conservation of capital and reduces calls on Loan Council borrowing limits. However, finance leases are economically equivalent to debt leading to the situation where all forms of financing, including financial leases, are included in the State's global limit. Operating leases, however, may be used to supplement State assets. For example, vehicles may be leased at peak periods to supplement the State's fleet;
– Lease payments can vary over the term of a lease to better match the revenues generated by the asset under lease. Often assets do not reach their full earning potential until after several years of operation, whereas

cash flow requirements for debt servicing, (assuming that interest rate and adverse exchange rate movements are not built into the repayment conditions), are often uniform;
– In the past, tax benefits such as depreciation and investment allowances were not available to tax-exempt bodies, but lease arrangements were used to pass these benefits on to leasing companies in return for reduced lease payments. The leveraged lease of Eraring power station in New South Wales was one such arrangement, one which prompted a change in tax law to prevent tax exempt bodies from exploiting this arrangement. However, scope may remain for leases to generate tax benefits where the leasing company is foreign and subject to foreign tax laws that allow it to use depreciation and investment allowances. This appears to have been the case with the Electricity Trust of South Australia's sale and lease back of its generation plant. Further, creative financing techniques may be employed to generate tax-shields for private financiers that are shared with public enterprises in the form of lower borrowing costs Obviously, the probity of such mechanisms – which attract private capital by the lure of tax minimisation needs to be thoroughly examined;

The Electricity Trust of South Australia (ETSA) has been quite progressive in the use of constructive financing instruments employing lease arrangements. In relation to the Northern Power Station and Leigh Creek coal supplies, ETSA entered into an agreement where a private operator leases the station and purchases ETSA's coal supplies for use in generating electricity that is sold back to ETSA. The private contractor paid a $250m deposit for its coal purchases which was able to be applied towards the cost of the coal. Interest on this deposit is included as a component of the cost of the electricity along with the lease rent and a management fee. The net effect of the transaction was that ETSA received $250m and incurred a liability to provide this amount of coal, with the difference between payments for electricity and revenue from coal sales being economically equivalent to interest on the $250m. ETSA then entered into a defeasance arrangement whereby its liability can be removed from the balance sheet by placing assets and financial securities, that offset the quality and cash flow requirements of the debt, in the hands of a trust. This has lead to ETSA reporting only the interest component (the net expense) in its Statement of Revenue and Expenditure.

Why would ETSA enter such an arrangement? ETSA had effectively raised $205m at a lower interest cost than it could have through traditional arrangements. It has effectively turned a capital transaction into a revenue one, which in theory need not be included in the State's global borrowing limit. The interest cost may have been lower to ETSA since the $250m, as a deposit for coal supplies, would become a deductible expense for the private contractor generating a substantial tax shield and not seen as a capital advance. However, the private contractor's receipts from electricity sales to ETSA could be fully taxable, unlike a loan repayment where only the interest component is taxable. Overall, in total taxable dollars there would be no difference between this arrangement which is repaid over the period of the agreement, so a significant interest component accrues to the contractor. In addition, if tax rates fall, as they have, the full effect of the original deduction is never repaid. In this way ETSA and the private contractor are able to share in this benefit with lower effective borrowing costs for ETSA. The overall effect is that under such a scheme electricity consumers in South Australia are subsidised by Federal taxpayers.

In 1987, ETSA undertook a similar arrangement for the Torrens Island Power station and its related fuel supples. The total amount of financing raised under both arrangements was $543.3m, which was initially deposited in government securities awaiting use for capital funding requirements. In 1988, ETSA decided that the majority of these funds were not needed and set about arranging a debt defeasance of its liability. In doing so ETSA found that it needed to only deposit $490m worth of assets to defease the $543.3m, hence making an abnormal gain of $53.3m. This represented the interest savings over the life of the arrangement brought about mainly by the favourable tax arrangements.

ETSA also used some creativity in arranging a leaseback arrangement for the turbo-generators at the Northern Power Station. In this situation ETSA were able to obtain cheaper finance by exploiting investment allowances overseas. The overall gain to ETSA in this case was $9.5m which could be seen as a subsidy to South Australian electricity consumers from overseas taxpayers.

The Electricity Commission of New South Wales has also been involved in using leasing as a source of finance. A leveraged lease differs from an ordinary lease in that it involves a third party, who is a lender, in addition to the lessor and lessee. Under this arrangement the lessee borrows funds from the lender to acquire the asset, and then lends the leases to the asset to the leasee in the usual manner. In 1982, ELCOM announced that it would finance the Eraring power station with a leveraged lease worth over $1,600m which exploited the tax-exempt status of the authority and passed on investment allowances to taxpaying corporations. Not suprisingly, the Federal Treasurer moved quickly to stop arrangements that passed investment and depreciation allowances to the private sector, closing a loophole that effectively subsidised New South Wales electricity consumers from Federal funds.

9.3.2 Superannuation

Both employee and employer contributions to superannuation funds can be made available to fund an enterprise's capital works program. Telecom Australia, for example, has been able to retain its superannuation contributions for reinvestment in its capital works. In addition, the superannuation funds of large public companies have been used strategically in the battles for corporate control evident in Australia in the 1980s. Thus, superannuation funds need not be passive and can take a more active role in financing profitable investments and strategic actions.

9.3.3 Joint Ventures

An unincorporated joint venture is a form of association between parties in a project, where the assets are held in common, and income is usually received in mutually agreed shares rather than jointly receiving income. A joint venture does not constitute a separate body with its own assets, sales, profits, accounts and returns. It is merely an agreement to undertake a particular project for individual gain.

Where a joint venture is established to own and operate a project, several financing options are available. Firstly, each venturer could arrange separate financing and separate marketing of production. This arrangement preserves the joint venture for taxation purposes and provides flexibility in borrowing structure for each venturer. A second arrangement would involve a marketing/financing company that carried out the operations, marketing and financing of the project.

Joint venture arrangements are a method of financing desirable State activities. For example, the South Australian Urban Land Trust (SAULT) has entered into a joint venture with Delfin Property Group Ltd. to develop land in the Adelaide suburb of Golden Grove. The project is substantial and involves up to 10,000 dwelling over a 15 year time span. In 1987/88, the operating surplus from the joint venture contributed $2.7m to the Trust's revenue sources.

Under the joint venture agreement, the Urban Land Trust contributes an equal share of the development costs and receives payment for its land plus one half share of the profits (and losses) of the development. The alternatives to a joint venture in this case would have been to develop the land alone, requiring more expertise than the Trust possessed, or to sell the whole land to a developer and forego any profits. The joint venture enables the Trust to share in profits, build up its own expertise and achieve its aim of ensuring that adequate stocks of land are available for housing.

Joint ventures are a potentially important method of financing State activities and exhibit the following advantages:

– Enable public sector development with private investors participation;
– Are not subject to Loan council limits (private ventures' share only);
– Acquisition of commercial project management expertise; and
– Facilitate the expansion of State commercial activities.

9.4 Conclusion:
9.4.1 The Need to Separate Financing Initiatives from State Economic Development Strategy

The attempt by the Western Australian Government to use an economic development strategy as a growing source of revenue has already been surveyed and Chapter Thirteen considers this strategy in more detail. However, it is necessary to reiterate here that such an approach both badly damages the credibility of a legitimate State function (ie. economic development) and renders State revenues vulnerable to the potential losses in, a high risk activity.

It is not the intention of *State of Siege* to warn against ever again establishing commercial-oriented agencies like the Victorian Economic Development Commission because these can play a role in industrial development. As we have seen the VEDC's difficulties are management related, and not necessarily a function of the concept itself. However, the Western Australian experience clearly indicates that industry policy and revenue raising should remain distinct.

State Development Grants

Accordingly, the States should consider providing development finance through State Development Grants. These grants would provide a more appropriate standard of accountability and ensure that:

– high risk funding of a venture capital nature was viewed as a component of State economic development strategy;
– it was publicly understood that a commercial rate-of-return on this sort of investment cannot be guaranteed; and
– public funding to support the recapitalisation of mature industries took place;

The eligibility for State Development Grants might be based on a number of discrete and well understood criteria including:

– net export potential;
– an ability to add value to Australian raw materials; and
– job creation potential.

The Grants would not be tied, in the first instance, to short term profitability. However, should the enterprise involved become profitable with public assistance, provision should be made in the Grant conditions for the repayment of the grant in full, with interest.

It is possible to identify at least two types of innovative activity which would be targetted by such a scheme. First, the project related proposals, based on clearly recognised opportunities which have arisen from marketing surveys on new production processes. Second, are those proposals for which venture capital is required, perhaps to undertake market feasibility studies or, to convert the results of innovative research to a viable technology.

Appraisal of proposals for funding would need to be assessed by a body made up of (or with access to) representatives with relevant skills and expertise. In addition, and in relation to the conclusions of Part Three on community involvement and participation, the body would most appropriately be a tripartite organisation.

In terms of accountability, cognisance should be paid to the different purposes to which the funding would be put. for the first type of proposal, for example, explicitly defined and assessable components would be required before funds could be granted. The second type of proposal (venture capital), timetabled performance guidelines would be more appropriate.

Such a model would allow State Governments to continue their valuable economic development activities, without the odium which attaches to them if they are publicised as a new and stable source of State revenue, a promise which by their nature they cannot automatically fulfil.

9.4.2 The Limitations of Other Revenue Initiatives

This chapter in essence illustrates that no matter how innovative, substitutes for a stable tax base are risk prone and difficult to sustain. Although various initiatives like joint ventures and lease finance are worthwhile (provided they do not rely on questionable taxation arrangements), they do not offer any viable route out of the fiscal impasse which faces the States. Nowhere is this clearer than in the attempts to marry development programs to revenue raising, and in than in the attempts to marry development programs to revenue raising, and in the mediocre performance of the Victorian Equity Trust. In a genuine model of public sector renewal, the financial needs of public agencies should be provided through an appropriate taxation regime. Viewed from this perspective, the quasi privatisation of trusts and joint ventures are effectively an admission of failure.

Part Five

THE STATE
PUBLIC SECTOR

Chapter 10

NEW SOUTH WALES

10.1 Introduction

New South Wales is in the habit of characterising itself as the 'premier' State. In a number of respects — in addition to the obvious one (colonial history) — it actually is; New South Wales has the largest population, the highest Gross State Product, and also the largest State public sector (in absolute size). The predominant economic position of New South Wales, when combined with other pressing facts, greatly strengthens the importance which attaches to an analysis of the role of the New South Wales State public sector: the crisis of persistent external imbalance with which policy makers have struggled over recent years, and the imperative for economic restructuring consequent upon that crisis; and the election of a conservative State Government in March 1988 resulting in the prospect that New South Wales would serve as a 'laboratory' for an experiment in applying the political economy of the so-called New Right.

The role of the public sector is subject to scrutiny, question and controversy. This is not necessarily a bad thing — because a healthy political culture will ensure that nothing is beyond appraisal and criticism. However, it is unfortunate that public debate has been dominated by a resurgence of conservative (or economic liberal) doctrine concerning the State and public enterprise. As usual this recent intellectual fashion in Australia has uncritically imitated, with a lag, some overseas developments. The purpose of this study is both to expose the New South Wales application of this doctrine to critical appraisal and to project the essential and positive role which the State public sector does play — and, can increasingly play — in the economic and social life of New South Wales.

10.2 Demography and Economy

10.2.1 Demography

New South Wales' population in September 1988 was 5.7 million, over one third of the total Australian population of 16.6 million (ABS, 3101.0). At that time, no other State had a population over 4.3 million.

In fact, New South Wales' population has been over 5.0 million since 1981 (ABS, 3102.0). New South Wales has retained its position as Australia's most populous State despite net estimated migration to other States in every year since at least, 1971, and a rate of natural increase less than the Australian average. The net gain in population is accounted for by overseas migration to New South Wales, with nearly one half of all migrants settling in New South Wales. Table 10.1 illustrates this trend in more detail.

In 1986, about 60% of New South Wales' population lived in Sydney, and a further 15% lived in the cities of Newcastle and Wollongong. However Wollongong and the southern areas of Newcastle are both within commuting distance of Sydney.

The predominance of the State capital in New South Wales (in terms of population), is not as marked as Melbourne (70.6% of Victoria's population), Adelaide (72.3% of South Australia's population) or Perth (71.2% of Western Australia's population) (New South Wales Yearbook, 1988). However, the degree of urbanisation in New South Wales is still high, due to the larger number of urban centres in New South Wales compared to other States (ABS, 3102.0).

In common with the rest of Australia, the New South Wales' population is ageing. Graph 10.1 shows the change in the age of New South Wales' population between 1966 and 1988, and indicates that the New South Wales population is older than the Australian average.

These demographic trends place severe pressure on the New South Wales public sector. The urban sprawl associated with the growth of Sydney demands considerable infrastructure investment, together with a relocation of community services from the inner-city to the western suburbs. An active and well-funded public sector is required in these circumstances, if the quality of life in under-resourced regions in Sydney (and the State in general) is to be improved.

Table 10.1

New South Wales Population Trends: 1983-1988
% Increase

Year Ended 30 June	Natural Increase		Net Overseas Migration		Total Pop. Growth	
	NSW	Aust.	NSW	Aust.	NSW	Aust.
1984	0.77	0.84	0.39	0.32	0.93	1.21
1985	0.78	0.82	0.58	0.47	1.14	1.34
1986	0.72	0.78	0.75	0.64	1.23	1.46
1987	0.75	0.79	0.90	0.74	1.46	1.53
1988 p	0.75	0.77	p 1.05	0.88	p 1.55	1.65

Note: p – Preliminary data.
Source: ABS Catalogue 3101.0.

Graph 10.1

NSW Population by Age

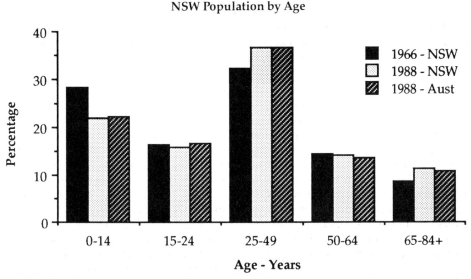

ABS Catalogue No. 3101.0, NSW Yearbook

10.2.2 Economy
Graph 10.2 shows the proportion of New South Wales' employment accounted for by each industry sector in 1966 and 1988.

The change in employment patterns illustrated in this graph is basically consistent with the structural changes which have occurred in the Australian economy as a whole, resulting in a decline in manufacturing's importance as an employer. About 40% of Australia's manufacturing production is undertaken in New South Wales. Metal and metal manufactures account for approximately 25% of New South Wales' exports, compared with about 10% of Australia's exports, reflecting the scale of the New South Wales manufacturing base (New South Wales Treasury, Budget Paper No. 2, 1988-89, pp. 4-7).

Graph 10.2

NSW Employment by Industry Division

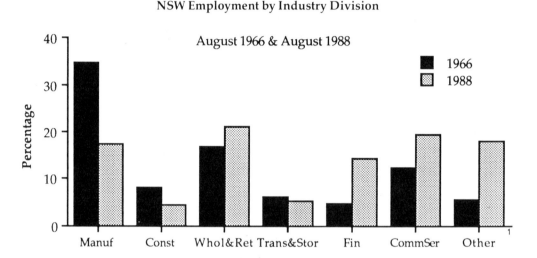

August 1966 & August 1988

1. 1988 includes Defence Personnel

ABS Catalogue No. 1305.1 & NSW Monthly Summary of Business Statistics, No. 396

Unlike the resource rich States of Queensland and Western Australia, mining contributes far less to employment in New South Wales (1.4%), and to New South Wales' export performance. Indeed, the mining industry is dominated by just one product, black coal. With the uncertainty of the world market (including changes in rates of energy requirements in manufacturing and the opening of internationally competitive mines elsewhere) the future performance of the industry is somewhat uncertain, despite recent signs of some improvement.

Overall, the New South Wales economy has lagged behind the performance of the national economy , as Table 10.2 shows. Despite relatively strong economic and employment growth in New South Wales in recent years, the State's 'misery index' (ie the sum of the unemployment and inflation rates) is still notably worse than the national figure, a point made in Table 10.3

10.2.3 Labour Market

The total number of full time employees in New South Wales in March 1989 was 1.67 million, comprising of 903,200 males and 469,000 females. Clearly, the participation rate for males (74.2%) is far higher than for females (51.4%), reflecting the discrimination which women experience in the workforce, and the institutional factors which still operate to exclude women from employment (including inadequate childcare).

The unemployment rates also provide evidence of this stratification of the workforce: in March 1989 the unemployment rate for men was 5.5%, and for women 6.8% (again it is worth noting that this higher unemployment rate occurs despite the markedly lower participation rate for women).

Table 10.2

Some Comparative Economic Trends

	Real Rate of Economic Growth*		Real Rate of Growth in Private Consumption Expenditure		Employment Growth	
	NSW (GSP)	National (GDP)	NSW	National	NSW	National
	%	%	%	%	%	%
1978/79	5.4	4.7	4.2	3.6	0.6	1.1
1979/80	2.8	2.7	3.0	2.5	4.4	2.9
1980/81	3.2	4.1	4.2	3.8	1.8	2.3
1981/82	3.9	1.7	3.0	3.2	-0.5	–
1982/83	-4.8	-2.2	-0.6	0.9	-3.3	-2.3
1983/84	4.0	5.0	1.8	2.7	3.6	3.7
1984/85	5.3	6.4	5.2	5.2	5.9	2.0
1985/86	3.5	3.1	2.7	2.6	-0.2	5.1
1986/87	0.9	0.8	-0.2	-0.2	1.7	2.0
1987/88	4.4+	4.4	3.6	2.9	4.3	3.4
10 Year Avg. Growth Rates	2.9	3.1	2.7	2.7	1.8	2.0

Notes: * For purposes of comparison these growth rates are calculated using the relevant CPI as a deflator.

+ Based on New South Wales State Treasury estimates in Budget Paper No. 2.

Source: ABS 'Labour Force' Cat. No. 62030, 6204.0, ABS 'State National Accounts' Cat. No. 5220, ABS 'National Accounts – Income and Expenditure, 1987-88' and ABS 'Consumer Price Index', Cat. No. 640/0.

Table 10.3

The 'Misery Index'*: Unemployment Plus Inflation

	NSW %	National %
1978/79	14.9	–
1979/80	16.3	16.3
1980/81	15.1	15.3
1981/82	15.9	16.6
1982/83	21.4	20.5
1983/84	16.4	16.5
1984/85	12.9	12.9
1985/86	17.0	16.3
1986/87	18.2	17.6
1987/88	15.7	15.1

Note: * Calculated by adding the average annual unemployment rate to the corresponding average annual inflation rate.

Source: ABS 'Labour Force, Australia', Cat. No. 6203.0 and ABS 'Consumer Price Index', Cat. No. 6401.0.

Women are also stratified in the workplace by industry. The following graph shows the proportion of total female employment by industry in New South Wales, in 1984 and 1988.

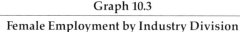

Graph 10.3

Female Employment by Industry Division

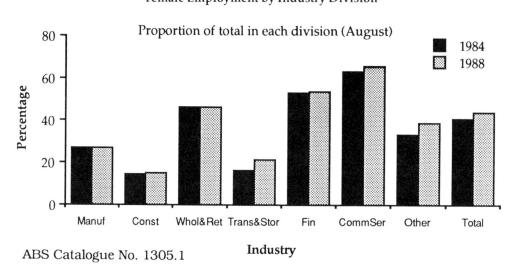

Proportion of total in each division (August)

ABS Catalogue No. 1305.1

10.2.4 Some Implications for the Public Sector. This brief outline of New South Wales' economy and society indicates that the New South Wales Government is confronted with a range of existing and emerging demands which will have to be met if living standards and basic human rights are to be maintained. To those special infrastructure needs outlined above can be added those needs readily identifiable from the discussion of the features of New South Wales' demography and labour market.

They include:

– the maintenance and extension of ethnic services;
– the provision of adequate services for an ageing population;
– the need to resource what positive reforms there have been in health and social welfare, and
– the need to provide the conditions whereby women would be able to fully participate in the State's economic and social life through, for example, the provision of child care.

The current status of the New South Wales public sector and the revenue-induced limita-

tions it faces are examined in the following sections.

10.3 The Functions and Structure of the New South Wales Public Sector

10.3.1 The Size of the Public Sector.

By various measures the New South Wales State Public sector is comparable in size to those of other large mainland States, in relation to the size of their economies (see New South Wales Budget Information Paper No. 2, p. 550). It is the State's largest employer, and its expenditures contribute importantly to capital formation in the New South Wales economy. Its considerable command over resources in the New South Wales economy is indicated by the magnitude of public sector outlays and revenue as a proportion of Gross State Product (GSP) at market prices which stood at approximately 19% and 15.8% respectively in 1986-87. Trends in revenues and outlays suggest that the size of the State sector has remained relatively stable over the past five years, during which economic growth and employment in the State have been in line with national performance. As illustrated in Table 10.4 the share of both outlays and revenue in GSP rose only marginally between 1981/82 and 1986/87, with slightly faster growth in revenue (12.5%) over outlays (11.0%) leading to a steady decline in the annual net public sector borrowing requirement over this period.

Table 10.4

Trends in New South Wales Government Revenues and Outlays

	Outlays		Revenues Grants Received		Net Public Sector Borrowing Requirement *	
	$m	% of GSP	$m	% of GSP	$m	% of GSP
1981/82	10,222	18.1	7,939	14.0	1,880	3.3
1982/83	11,253	18.7	9,406	15.6	1,349	2.2
1983/84	12,462	18.7	10,600	15.9	1,802	2.7
1984/85	13,625	18.7	11,753	16.2	1,094	1.5
1985/86	15,210	18.6	13,118	16.1	1,644	2.0
1986/87	17,185	19.0	14,293	15.8	1,354	1.5

Note: * Excludes funding provision from internal financial sources.
Source: ABS 'State and Local Government Finance, Australia 1986/87', Cat. No. 5504.0.

An important indication of the size of the public sector also emerges from its role as the largest employer in the New South Wales economy, employing nearly 374,000 persons, representing some 18.2% of total New South Wales employment. Since 1983/84 however, this ratio has fallen by about 1.5 percentage points reflecting the discernible slowdown in New South Wales State public sector employment growth over recent years.

Table 10.5

New South Wales State Public Sector Employment

	State Public Sector * Employment * (1) ('000)	Total NSW Employment (2) ('000)	(1) as % of (2)
1983/84	353.3	1,795.2	19.7
1984/85	358.1	1,845.7	19.4
1985/86	363.1	1,903.5	19.1
1986/87	369.7	1,959.4	18.9
1987/88	373.8	2,056.2	18.2

Note: * Average yearly figures.
Source: ABS 'Employed Wage and Salary Earners, Australia', Cat. No. 6248.0.

A broad picture of the structure of the New South Wales State public sector is provided in Table 10.6 showing a breakdown of employment by major departments and authorities as of 31 March 1986 (the most recent data available).

The relative contraction of the New South Wales public sector is confirmed by the declining contribution of the public sector to capital formation. This decline is revealed in Tables 10.7 which charts New South Wales General Government Investment for 1986/87 to 1987/88, comparing it to Australian General Government Investment and total Australian investment.

It is interesting to note that from these tables that, while New South Wales public sector investment has been rising as a proportion of Australia's public sector investment, it has been falling as a proportion of total Australian investment.

10.3.2 Economic Services and Strategy

As the largest manufacturing state in Australia, the economic services provided through the New South Wales public sector are of special importance. Table 10.8 indicates the range of departments and agencies which come under this classification.

The Greiner Government strategy for deploying its economic services and infrastructure is exemplified by its industry policy. While it is true to say that no New South Wales Government has developed an economic strategy as comprehensive as that in Victoria, the previous State Labor Government had formulated an Economic Development Strategy. This included a number of elements somewhat similar to elements in the Victorian Strategy, including the extension of the New South Wales Industrial Supplies Office's operations; the establishment of a Defence Industry Task Force to maximise New South Wales' industry involvement in defence projects; and the use of the Research and Consultancy Bureau to assist

local industry take advantage of State public sector R&D facilities (EPAC, 1988, p. 19).

It should be noted, however, that the New South Wales Strategy also bore some resemblance to the types of national economic policies in vogue in the 1950s and 1960s. That is, it was designed to create the conditions in which economic development could take place, rather than a coherent set of policies and programs designed to stimulate and support those industries judged to have greater value-added and export potential.

The Greiner Government appears to have lapsed even further into the myopia of a bygone era. While it has maintained the Department of State Development (now in the Deputy-Premier's portfolio), its responsibilities have little more substance than facilitating proposals brought to it by the private sector

Table 10.6

Composition of New South Wales State Public Sector Employment

As at 31 March 1986	Employment No.	Percentage of total Public Sector Employment
Departments		
Education	69,762	28.0
Health	14,763	5.9
Public Works	5,693	2.3
Social Welfare and Community Services	22,471	9.0
Economic and Industrial Services	12,764	5.1
Administrative Services	20,606	8.3
Total	*146,059*	*58.6*
Authorities		
Electricity Commission (Elcom)	10,876	4.4
Department of Main Roads (DMR)	9,105	3.6
State Rail Authority (SRA)	41,269	16.5
Urban Transit Authority (UTA)	6,561	2.6
Other Economic and Industrial Services +	35,306	14.1
Total	*103,117*	*41.2*
Other	379	0.2
Total	*249,555**	*100.0*

Notes: * The figure significantly underestimates the total number of New South Wales State Public Sector employment. It only includes employment identified by the Public Service Board of New South Wales in its personnel reports.

+ Includes an estimate of employees in the State Bank and Government Insurance Office.

Source: Public Service Board of New South Wales 'Personnel Management Data of Departments and Declared Authorities', 1985, 1986.

(Department of State Development, 1988), and the disposal of 'strategic government assets' (Department of State Development, 1989). Tripartite industry bodies, for instance, have been abolished. In addition, the failure of the Greiner Government to recognise the importance of coherence in, and co-ordination of, the

public sector's role in industry policy or economic development is evident in the duplication of activities between the Department of State Development and other portfolio areas, particularly those remaining in Business and Consumer Affairs (the old Department of Industrial Development and Decentralisation).

Table 10.7

Gross Fixed Capital Expenditure (GFKE)
1976/77 — 1987/88:

	NSW State & Local Govt $m (1)	Aust. Govt $m (2)	Total Aust. $m (3)	(1 as % of 2)	(2 as % of 3)	(1 as % of 3)
1976/77	841	3,316	21,055	25.4	15.7	4.0
1977/78	951	3,463	22,566	27.5	15.3	4.2
1978/79	1,005	3,482	25,933	28.9	23.4	3.9
1979/80	1,039	3,607	28,783	28.8	12.5	3.6
1980/81	1,162	3,725	35,176	31.2	10.6	3.3
1981/82	1,165	4,080	41,437	28.6	9.8	2.8
1982/83	1,185	4,562	41,035	25.9	11.1	2.9
1983/84	1,436	5,230	44,225	27.5	11.8	3.2
1984/85	1,713	6,128	50,859	27.9	12.0	3.4
1985/86	1,967	7,125	58,837	27.6	12.1	3.3
1986/87	2,328	7,807	63,161	29.8	12.4	3.7
1987/88	2,529	7,516	70,887	33.6	10.6	3.6

Sources: ABS 5206.0 Australian National Accounts, National Income and Expenditure & ABS 5220.0 State Accounts.

A feature of the new industry policy of the New South Wales Government is the extent of spending on decentralisation. Of a total $48m of recurrent funding allocated to Business Services by Business and Consumer Affairs in the 1988/89 Budget, $17m was allocated to 'payroll tax rebates and other assistance associated with the decentralisation of secondary industry in country areas' (New South Wales Treasury, 1988b, p. 226). Some of the components of the agency's decentralisation policies are laudable (for instance, the extension of the National Industry Extension Service's operations to regional centres to promote value-added production). However, much of the activity appears to have little or no focus; the range of products 'adopted' provide little opportunity for integration into a coherent industry plan. Such projects include promotion of Broken Hill

airport for export of primary products and bulk wool handling facilities at Eden, neither of which reflect any commitment to vertically integrated development (BACA, 1988, pp. 35-45). Such lack of coherence illustrates a lack of vision and appreciation of the changing patterns of resource utilisation and industrial production.

One of the key challenges for New South Wales public economic services, attested to by Sydney beach-goers, are the difficulties currently facing Sydney's water supply and sewerage system. There, market-based solutions to a pressing social and economic problem are conspicuous by their absence, leaving the public sector to undertake vital social and economic services. This challenge is magnified by the current inadequacy of the system which has failed to keep pace with expansion of Sydney.

Table 10.8

Economic Services

Departments	Functions, Services and Financing
Agriculture (and Fisheries)	Promotion of agricultural, livestock and fisheries resource development; Pastures Protection Boards; agricultural information services; quarantine services; research laboratories. *Large deficit.*
Business and Consumer Affairs	Regulation of corporations and capital markets; 'fair trading'; consumer information Affairs services; registration of businesses and agents; Corporate Affairs Commission; Consumer Claims Tribunal; Office of Small Business; Fair Rents Board. *Medium deficit.*
Industrial Relations & Employment	Industrial conciliation and arbitration; occupational health and safety; training and apprenticeship schemes; employment programs. *Large deficit.*
Lands	Public land management; land information systems; mapping and surveying services. *Small deficit.*
Mineral Resources	Promotion of mineral resource development. *Large surplus.*
Planning	Environmental planning; coastal protection; heritage agencies. *Large deficit.*
Public Works	Building and civil engineering works. *Medium deficit.*
State Development	Co-ordination and promotion of major private investment and employment programs.
Technical and Further Education	Post-school education. *Large deficit.*
Water Resources	Management of water and related resources. *Medium deficit.*

Authorities	
Electricity Commission (Elcom)	Electricity generation and bulk transmission. *Small deficit.*
Govt. Insurance Office (GIO)	Commercial insurer; third party vehicle insurer. *Small surplus.*
Grain Handling Authority	Bulk grain handling. *Small (operating) surplus.*
Maritime Services Board (MSB)	Port facilities; shipping; cargo movement; marine environmental protection. *Small (operating) surplus (before abnormal items).*
Marketing Authorities & Produce Corporations	Marketing of primary produce.
Metropolitan Waste Disposal Authority	Management of waste. *Medium surplus.*
Nat. Industry Extension Service	Promotion of Industry efficiency and international competitiveness (joint Commonwealth/State initiative).
Roads and Traffic	State road system; traffic management; driver *Authority* licensing, motor vehicle registration (amalgamation of DMR, DMT, and Traffic Authority).
State Bank	Retail banking *Small surplus.*
State Rail Authority (SRA)	Passenger and freight rail services. *Medium (operating) deficit (approximately 7% of Consolidated Fund receipts).*
State Transit Authority (STA)	Bus and ferry services; co-ordination of inter-*(STA)* urban passenger services; taxis for disabled scheme. Previously UTA. *Large (operating) deficit.*
Water Board(s)	Water supply; dams; sewerage; drainage systems. *Small surplus.*

Notes: The terms 'small', 'medium' and 'large' deficit/surplus refers to the agency's outlays, net of its own revenues, as a proportion of outlays (less than 20%, between 20% and 50%, more than 50%, respectively). Where deficits/surpluses are a significant proportion of total State revenues to Consolidated Fund (this percentage is indicated in parenthesis). The economic significance of these ratios needs to be treated with care because the agencies' revenues (particularly departments) commonly include charges and fees which are taxes or quasi-taxes (in so far as they are compulsory and bear no relation to the costs of any service provided), as well as asset sales.

This need was made clear by the Water Board in 1986, as was the fact that considerable expenditure would be required. The following quotes are from the *Interim Corporate Plan* of that year:

Water, sewerage and drainage infrastructure to cater for future urban expansion will increasingly become more expensive. The current Urban Development Program projects the need for an average of about 10,000 new lots each year over the next 5 years in the Sydney region (p. 18).

The backlog of urban properties supplied with water but without connection to the sewerage system is an ongoing priority and an important aspect of meeting community needs in a cost effective manner. The current backlog consists of about 16,000 properties which require extension of existing systems (p. 19).

Improved pollution control and environmental protection is increasingly becoming a major aspect of the Water Board's operation. However, qualitative programs to protect the environment are expensive particularly as they entail large capital outlays and generally do not contribute additional revenue (p. 23).

The recent moves made by the New South Wales Government to increase water and sewerage rates for industry in New South Wales are welcome as a means of raising revenue to combat the real pollution problems in New South Wales (*SMH*, 1/5/89). This positive move, however, needs to be contrasted with the capital amount allocated for water and sewerage in the 1988-89 budget, which amounted to a nominal cut of 2.7%; environmental protection fared even worse, with a cut in nominal terms by 24.0% (New South Wales Treasury, Budget Paper No. 2, p. 228). These spending cuts are a consequence of the Greiner Government's desire to cut the absolute size of the public sector, based on a belief that economic and social functions can be unproblematically shifted to the private sector. In many areas like water and sewerage, such a transfer of responsibility clearly will not take place, and yet the Government persists in denying the public sector adequate funds with which to meet its responsibilities.

10.3.3 Social Services

Chapter Three has identified a number of significant social problems which come under the direct jurisdiction of State social services. However, according to the New South Wales Council of Social Services, social welfare is one of the Greiner government's lowest priorities. In their analysis of the 1988/89 Budget NCOSS showed that welfare services in New South Wales received a decrease in recurrent funding of $98m or 17% on the previous years' appropriations (NCOSS News, Oct 88, pp. 2-3). Table 10.9 shows the major social service departments and agencies in New South Wales.

Despite some increases in capital spending on social services and welfare which are shown in Section 10.5, serious shortfalls in the social services area still exist, and under the current Government, are likely to deepen.The issue of housing is dealt with in some detail in a later case study, but shortages in this area are a source of widening social inequality in New South Wales. This inequality is not meeting with an appropriate policy response from the New South Wales Government which prefers to support home owners or to subsidise private developers rather than develop the public housing stock (New South Wales Treasury, Budget Paper No. 2, 1988-89, p. 229).

The deinstitutionalisation of psychiatric health care which has occurred in recent years also added to the demand for suitable housing while, at the same time, privately-owned boarding houses (which appear to be popular with people with disabilities) are closing due to higher rates of return available on other forms of property development (Benson, 1989, p. 28). Simultaneously, there has been a general rise in demand for public housing in New South Wales '. . . because of the rise in the number of people living below the poverty line' (Benson, 1989, p. 25). While the New South Wales Department of Housing appears to have made commendable efforts to meet demand for this specialised public housing, the fact is that '[The department] has funded this extra demand for public housing from mainstream public housing funds. As public housing funds are being extended at both the Commonwealth and State levels of Government there is major concern about people with disabilities gaining access to these depleted funds' (Benson, 1989, p. 27).

It is obviously not desirable for deinstitution-alisation to be reversed. But without adequate levels of support to complement these moves, the result can be both a personal, and social, disaster as volunteer agencies and families are again forced to undertake a role more adequately handled by the public sector.

Table 10.9

Social Services

Departments	Functions, Services and Financing
Arts (Ministry)	State Library; museums; archives; Opera House; historic houses; Art Gallery; cultural grants.
Attorney-General	Courts and other legal tribunals; law reform; Anti-Discrimination Board; registry of births, deaths and marriages. *Medium deficit.*
Education	Public primary and secondary schooling; registration and public funding of private schools; Ministry includes Adult Migrant Education Service. *Large deficit (approximately 15% of Consolidated Fund receipts).*
Family and Community Services	Community welfare programs – pre-school and day care; refuges; Home Services Care Service; child protection; youth projects; status of women. *Large deficit.*
Housing	Public housing; home finance; residential development; information and advisory services; Residential Tenancies Tribunal. *Small surplus.*
Health	Public hospital services; community and mental health services; dental and disability services; immunisation; ambulance service; pure foods and sanitation; regulation of medical practice. *Large deficit (more than 20% of Consolidated Fund receipts).*
Housing	As above.
Sport, Recreation & Racing	Development of sport, recreation and racing; State Sports Centre; sport and recreation centres. *Large surplus.*
Authorities	
Ethnic Affairs Commission	Cultural, educational and welfare assistance to ethnic communities.
Home Care Service	Home care for the elderly and disabled.
Nat. Parks & Wildlife Service	National parks; nature reserves; State recreation areas; historic sites; Aboriginal areas. *Large deficit.*
State Rail Authority (SRA)	Concessional fares and community service obligations.
State Transit Authority (STA)	Concessional fares and community service obligations.

Notes: See Table 10.8.

10.3.4 Administrative Services

One of the major areas of change between the current Greiner Liberal government and its Labor predecessor lies in its philosophy with regard to administrative services and particularly the sphere of law and order and social control. The 1988/89 Budget saw large capital expenditure devoted to police stations, juvenile courts, prisons, detention centres and other institutions on top of a rise over the previous years' appropriations of $288m. This represented an increase of 28% to law, order and public safety over the previous year. Table 10.10 shows the key administrative agencies and departments.

Reflecting another dimension of the New South Wales Government's philosophy of administrative services is the rationalisation of emergency services between fire, police and ambulance departments. While good coordination and efficiency are essential in such important public services this clearly cannot be achieved by cutbacks or by playing off one department against each other as if they were 'market competitors' (cf. 'Rescuers Row at Crash Site Alleged', *SMH*, June 28, '89, p. 2).

And yet another indication of the government philosophy of administration is exemplified by the June 27 Cabinet decision to shut down the Government Printing Office with the loss of some 700 jobs. Announcing the decision, the Minister of Administrative Services, Mr. Webster is reported to have said 'the closure was the only rational decision and that the majority of the employees would be able to get new jobs'. While this example cannot warrant a full scale case study in this book for reasons of timing, it appears the decision has been motivated by the views on privatisation and competitive tendering which have been criticised in Chapter Five. Apart from the publication of

Hansard, the government is reported to be 'contracting out' all the work of the Printing office (Media Release: The Hon. Robert Webster, MP, 27/6/89). The opposition challenged the financial merit of the sell off because it is clear that strategies of commercialisation and renewal can considerably reduce the current subsidy of the Printing Office (Carr, AFR, 28.6.89). It is unfortunate that this final option did not receive any attention since the printing industry with its changing technology has proven to be a fertile ground for strategies of renewal and development (Botsman & Rawlinson, 1986).

Table 10.10

Administrative Services

Departments	Functions, Services and Financing
Administrative Services	Administrative services to the public service; Government Information Service; Government Supply Office, Govt Printing Office. *Large deficit.*
Local Government	Administration of Local Government. *Small deficit.*
'Premier'	Two departments – Cabinet Office (monitoring of government policy); Premier's Office (administration, Aboriginal affairs). *Large deficit.*
Police	Enforcement of law and order. *Large deficit.*
Corrective Services	Custody of prisoners; community-based programs; post-custodial services (probation and parole). *Large deficit.*
Treasury	Economic policy advice to government; economic management of State public sector; revenue collection (Office of State Revenue). *Large surplus (more than 25% of Consolidated Fund receipts).*
Valuer-General	Valuation for rating and taxation. *Medium deficit.*
Agriculture (and Fisheries)	As above.
Business and Consumer Affairs	As above.
Authorities	
State Lotteries	Draw and instant lotteries. *Medium surplus.*
State Pollution Control	Air, water and noise pollution control; overseeing of waste disposal; environmental Commission protection. *Large deficit.*
Treasury Corporation	Loan raising for Budget sector, authorities and electricity county councils. *Zero deficit.*

Notes: See Table 10.8.

10.4.4 The Trend to Privatisation

Naturally, an outline of the range of public sector functions does not, in any manner justify the status quo, for it may be that those functions are not being adequately fulfilled; or that their benefit-cost ratios do not warrant them being carried out at all. Indeed the critique of

public sector activity by conservatives and economic liberals (as well as others) inevitably is a variation on one or more of these themes.

There is, in fact, great scope for reform, but any such change must recognise the role of the State sector, since this establishes the rationale or objective for reform. The position taken in this study is that the role of the New South Wales State public sector is to advance the material and social conditions of the citizens of the State, subject to constitutional limitations and the constraints of national policy. This objective points to the need for effective and efficient provision of State services, sound management of State assets (and liabilities), and a progressive system of State expenditures, taxes and charges, consistent with maintenance and advancement of real (social) wages and decent working conditions. This provides the basis for a program of progressive State sector reform and renewal.

Against this, the conservative government is instituting a program which is ultimately pernicious in its consequences for working people, and the community's disadvantaged. On the one hand, the government has moved to sell assets (enterprises and physical assets) which are profitable or capable of being made so, thereby reducing the asset base of the sector to the extent that the resulting funds are used for purposes other than asset purchases (or debt retirement). This deprives the State sector, and thereby the community of New South Wales, of a non-tax income stream (or potential income stream) which could be used to finance other (non-profitable) services (taken to the limit it would deprive the sector of any profitable activities). On the other hand, nonprofitable services are being run down and public provision narrowed via contracting out, State public sector abrogation and voluntarism. To the extent that this asset management and expenditure policy is part of a strategy to deliver tax reductions in the future (to whose benefit is unclear at this point in time), it involves running down the sector in order to finance consumption (public or private). In this respect the policy stance of the government involves a twofold abrogation of managerial responsibility: an unwillingness to manage the State sector capital stock so as to maximize pecuniary returns to the community, where appropriate (subject to socio-economic objectives); and an unwillingness to manage the sector so as to maximize non-pecuniary economic and social returns. The following is a (by no means complete) list of policies which the conservative government has initiated along these lines during the first year of its administration:

– sale of State Investment Corporation; 99 Macquarie Street (UTA, now STA), an Australian record auction price for a building ($69m); space above and land adjacent to St. Leonard's Railway Station (SRA), the former on a 99 year lease; industrial land, Homebush Bay (MSB);
– proposed sale of GHA; four power station sites at Balmain, Bunnerong, Pyrmont, White Bay (Elcom); harbourside properties (eg., Woolloomooloo Bay Finger Wharf) and coal loaders in Sydney, Newcastle, Wollongong (MSB); Transport House, Wynyard (SRA); New South Wales House, London; land vacated by closure of Homebush Abattoirs and State Brickworks (Homebush, Blacktown) – the Blacktown property has been sold already; 178-80 Phillip Street (Public Works); Sydney Showground; Prince Henry Hospital, Camperdown Children's Hospital, parts of Rydalmere and Parramatta Hospitals, Strickland House in Vaucluse (Health); Pyrmont Point, Mort Bay (Housing); 15 homes previously used for teenage State wards (FACS);
– inauguration of a number of private tollways; partial privatisation of electricity production (proposed); private sector 'Darling Harbour style' commercial/tourist/residential redevelopment of Pyrmont-White Bay area, using land now owned largely by Elcom, GHA and MSB (proposed); lease of navy base at South Head, for a private university; substantial staff cuts and expanded use of contract labour in Elcom (especially for maintenance), Public Works, and elsewhere; expanded private involvement in the Local Employment Initiatives program ('Business in the Community Ltd.', a subsidiary of Rotary) – grant from Department of Industrial Relations and Employment; increased use of community groups in provision of welfare services (eg., grants to the Volunteer Centre of New South Wales);
– abolition of 2,000 teaching positions; closure of approximately 15 inner city and North Shore schools; closure and cutback of country hospitals, rail services and court

houses; closure of one quarter of the State's community welfare offices and abolition of 350-400 positions (FACS); abolition of ethnic policy adviser position (FACS) and Ethnic Consumers Unit (BACA); abolition and reduction of a variety of employment assistance schemes (eg., Youth Employment Scheme); asset sales, equipment cutbacks and station closures (Police); abolition of in-dependent tenancy advice services; impo-sition of fees for legal aid.

— commercialisation of SRA freight div-ision; recommended shift towards commer-cial pricing in MSB; abolition of TransCover, with substantial increases in third party motor vehicle insurance premiums; removal of union representatives from Boards of statutory authorities.

Table 10.11

Trends in New South Wales Budget Revenue by Source

	81/82	82/83	83/84	84/85	85/86	86/87	Growth 81-87
Taxes, Fees & Fines							
%	28.2	29.6	29.7	29.8	30.2	30.5	
$m*	2,880.1	2,976.8	3,117.5	3,292.9	3,424.6	3,574.1	4.4
*NOS** of PTE's*							
%	4.7	7.5	6.7	7.8	7.2	6.5	
$m*	483.5	760.5	702.6	860.6	822.0	768.0	12.3
C'wealth Grants							
%	40.1	42.1	43.9	44.1	43.0	40.7	
$m*	4,095.9	4,226.0	4,602.4	4,867.7	4,889.8	4,769.9	4.1
*GG*** Net Borrowings*							
%	1.0	0.7	1.0	3.2	3.3	3.2	
$m*	100.0	66.4	101.7	354.6	371.8	375.0	75.0
PTE Borrowings							
%	17.4	11.3	13.5	4.8	7.5	4.7	
$m*	1,780.8	1,137.7	1,415.2	532.3	856.0	549.5	-9.8
Other Provisions							
%	8.6	8.8	5.3	10.3	8.8	14.4	
$m*	881.6	880.2	550.8	1,133.2	994.8	1,693.8	45.2
Total Revenue							
%	100.0	100.0	100.0	100.0	100.0	100.0	
$m*	10,221.9	10,047.6	10,490.2	11,041.3	11,359.0	11,729.8	2.8

Notes: * Average 1981/82 Prices.
       ** Net Operating Surplus.
       *** General Government.
Source: ABS 'State and Local Government Finance, Australia 1986/87', Cat. No. 5504.0 and ABS 'Sydney CPI', Cat. No. 6401.0.

It may be noted that not all of these policies are necessarily undesirable. In some excep-tional cases the asset-selling department may gain all (this is the case with Health Depart-ment asset sales) or part of funds realized — the usual procedure now seems to be divert approximately 50% of returns to Consolidated Revenue, and retained funds can be used for debt retirement or acquisition of new assets. However, as will be made clear the Govern-ment's program is not based upon the prin-ciples of sound asset management, but an ideological determination simply to wind back the public sector, regardless of the social or economic costs.

Table 10.12

Trends in New South Wales Tax Revenues

Average 1981/82 Prices

	1982/83	1983/84	1984/85	1985/86	1986/87	1987/88	Avg. Ann. Real Growth	1987/88 % of Total
	$m	$m	$m	$m	$m	$m	%	%
Payroll	983.3	949.4	1006.0	1019.0	1016.5	1010.1	0.5	25.1
Property	559.0	624.6	704.3	797.7	948.5	1335.8	19.5	33.2
Land Taxes	166.2	159.0	182.8	221.0	235.9	261.9	9.9	6.5
Stamp Duties	322.1	363.2	418.9	470.6	586.4	927.5	24.6	23.1
FID	49.6	94.1	99.1	102.5	112.4	117.1	22.5	2.9
Other	21.1	8.3	3.5	3.6	13.9	29.3	94.9*	0.7
Provision of Goods and Services	589.6	618.0	607.3	603.7	592.4	615.2	–	15.3
Levies of Stat Corps	9.7	10.4	11.9	12.0	10.8	17.8	15.1	0.4
Gambling	378.6	380.7	388.7	393.3	372.7	381.9	0.2	9.5
Insurance	201.3	226.9	206.7	198.4	208.9	215.5	1.7	5.4
Use of Goods and Services	689.7	759.7	809.9	838.2	834.7	842.1	4.1	20.9
Motor Vehicles	400.2	438.5	468.7	472.6	466.3	473.2	3.6	11.8
Business Franchise	282.7	316.2	336.3	361.0	364.3	364.6	5.3	9.0
Other	6.8	5.0	4.9	4.6	4.1	4.3	-7.7	0.1
Fees and Fines	163.4	172.5	178.8	177.6	198.7	220.2	7.2	5.5
Total	2985.0	3124.2	3306.3	3436.2	3590.9	4023.4	6.2	100.0

Note: * This growth is due to the introduction of the Statutory Authorities' Loan Guarantee Fee in 1986/87.

Source: ABS 'Taxation Revenue, Australia, 1987/88', Cat. No. 5504.0 and ABS 'Sydney CPI', Cat. No. 6401.0.

10.4. The Finances of the New South Wales Public Sector

10.4.1 Revenue

The main sources of revenue to the New South Wales State Government are Commonwealth Grants, which in 1986-87 accounted for 41% of total revenues, and State taxation which accounted for nearly 30%. Other sources of revenue include net operating surpluses of trading enterprises (6.5%) and other internal financial provisions (14.4%). The remaining source of finance to the State budget comes from net borrowing (both trading enterprises and general government) which accounts for nearly 8% of total revenues (see Table 10.11 below). There has been a marked reduction in the contribution of net borrowing to the budget over the past five years — particularly net borrowing by trading enterprises. The rapid growth in other provisions as a source of funding suggests greater use by the government of sinking fund facilities in meeting debt commitments. Although its contribution to revenue remains relatively small, nevertheless, the income generated by trading enterprises has been an increasing source of State funding despite the fact that government charges for public services have risen at a rate lower than the consumer price index over recent years (see New South Wales Budget Information Paper No. 2, p. 365). Perhaps the most important trend has been the strong growth in State taxes as a source of New South Wales budget revenue.

Table 10.13

New South Wales Consolidated Fund Recurrent Receipts

	1983/84	1984/85	1985/86	1986/87	1987/88	1988/89[a]
State Sourced: Taxation	40.5	40.4	40.6	42.0	44.6	46.3
Mining, Lands & Forestry	1.9	1.9	1.7	1.7	1.4	1.5
Receipts for Services						
Rendered	5.0	5.1	4.7	4.7	4.6	4.7
DMT[b]					1.7	1.8
Health					0.7	0.7
Other					2.2	2.2
Other	6.6	6.9	6.8	6.0	6.5	6.7
State Instrumentalities						
Contributions					1.0	1.6
State Lotteries					0.7	0.7
Other Recurrent Receipts					4.8	4.4
Total, State Sourced	54.0	54.3	53.7	54.4	57.2	59.2
Commonwealth						
Recurrent Payments	46.0	45.7	46.3	45.6	42.8	40.8
Total Recurrent Receipts	100	100	100	100	100	100

Notes: [a] Estimates.
[b] Now the RTA.
Due to rounding, in some cases percentages do not add to 100.
Source: New South Wales Budget Paper No.2, 1988/89, Tables 4.2,4.3.

As illustrated in Table 10.12 below the major sources of tax revenue are payroll tax (25.1%), stamp duties (23.1%), motor vehicle taxes (11.8%), taxation on business franchises (9%), gambling taxes (9.5%) and land taxes (6.5%). The reasonably strong growth in tax revenues over the past five years is attributable to a number of factors, primarily the rapid growth in stamp duty and tax collections arising from the buoyant activity in the stock exchange market in Sydney (Australia's major financial centre) and the escalation in Sydney housing and land prices. Resilient employment growth has ensured that payroll tax, the major source of tax revenue, also has remained a solid contributor.

Table 10.13 below shows that the declining share of Commonwealth payments since 1986-87 has been offset by a rising share of State tax revenues. State non-tax revenues are a small though significant component; but actually have shown some tendency to decline as a percentage of recurrent receipts. Commercialisation is about increasing this contribution (as well as reducing Budget outlays to a range of trading, or potential trading activities).

10.4.2 Expenditure
As Table 10.14 reveals, of total New South Wales Government expenditure in 1986-87, capital spending represented around 25%, consumption nearly 48%, interest payments 12.6% and other unrequited transfer payments 14.4%. Accompanying the compositional change in outlays has been a discernible increase in the allocation of own purpose expenditures towards interest payments and associated debt retirement. Since the early 1980s there has been a more subdued approach by government to public capital formation. This partly reflects an increased priority to wind back long-term government debt − particularly that of trading enterprises, which are the State agencies primarily responsible for the provision of economic and industrial infrastructure − so as to retard the growing allocation of expenditure to debt servicing costs. Although this development has been seized upon by policy makers sympathetic to privatisation, Chapter Eight has already demonstrated that the debt burden of New South Wales is entirely bearable, and cannot be used to justify the goal of a smaller public sector.

Table 10.14

Trends in New South Wales Government Expenditure

	81/82	82/83	83/84	84/85	85/86	86/87	Avge 81-87***
Capital Expend %	27.0	25.0	25.4	24.2	24.3	25.3	
$m *	2,762.4	2,513.3	2,663.7	2,667.8	2,761.7	2,971.6	1.6
Consmp. Expend %	49.6	48.6	47.8	48.8	48.3	47.7	
$m *	5,066.8	4,877.8	5,012.5	5,387.4	5,483.3	5,590.5	2.1
Interest %	9.9	11.3	11.4	11.9	12.8	12.6	
$m *	1,012.3	1,138.8	1,200.2	1,317.7	1,451.8	1,475.6	8.0
Other **%	13.5	15.1	15.4	15.1	14.6	14.4	
$m *	1,380.5	1,517.8	1,613.7	1,668.4	1,662.1	1,692.6	4.2
Total %	100.0	100.0	100.0	100.0	100.0	100.0	
$m *	10,221.9	10,047.7	10,490.1	11,041.3	11,358.9	11,730.3	2.8

Notes: * (average 1981/82 prices).
** Unrequited Transfer Payments.
*** Average Annual Real Growth.
Source: ABS 'State and Local Government Finance, Australia, 1986/87', Cat. No. 5504.0 and ABS 'Sydney CPI', Cat. No. 6401.0.

10.4.3 Functional Priorities

Table 10.15 shows that economic and industrial services (inclusive of transport and communication), which for the most part are carried out by statutory authorities, account for nearly 25% of total outlays in 1986/87, a figure which had steadily fallen over the preceding 5 years. In contrast, the social services area increased its share of total expenditure. Education (24%), health (17%) and social welfare and community services (22%) together accounted for nearly 65% of total expenditure outlays.

While total public sector outlays have grown at about the same rate as New South Wales GSP during the 1980s, there has therefore been a significant compositional change, reflecting the changing priorities of government in response to social and economic needs. The considerable slowdown in expenditure on economic and industry services evident from 1982/83, follows a period of large scale investment related to the installation of increased energy, transport and communication capacity. This slowdown can, in part, be explained by the reluctance (until recently) of government to raise charges in line with inflation. Governments were also responding to the demand to

minimise the rate at which long-term accumulated debt grew, particularly as interest rates were generally higher than historic levels. However, the main reason was the need to redirect expenditures towards social welfare and community and recreational facilities, arising from the growing demands in these areas, in turn due to lower real incomes, housing rental shortages and demographic factors related to the marked aging of the population. The average annual real growth in State public sector spending over the past five years has been particularly strong in social security and welfare (9.9%), public housing and community amenities (8.8%), health (5.9%), as well as recreation and culture.

These changes in spending priorities are mirrored by the pattern of capital expenditure. Although approximately 52% of total capital spending is directed toward economic and industry services (including transport and communication), the growth in capital expenditure in these areas has been slow or negative, whereas there has been strong growth in capital spending in the areas of health (20.9%) and social security and welfare services (14.2%). This pattern is revealed in Table 10.16.

Table 10.15

Trends in New South Wales Government Outlays by Purpose

	1981/82	1982/83	1983/84	1984/85	1985/86	1986/87	Avge Real Growth 1981-87
Education							
%	27.4	27.2	26.7	26.5	25.8	24.3	
(avg 1981/82 prices) $m	2,793.0	2,735.6	2,804.0	2,922.0	2,932.2	2,855.6	0.5
Health							
%	14.6	13.1	14.0	15.3	15.8	16.6	
(avg 1981/82 prices) $m	1,483.6	1,320.2	1,466.3	1,691.2	1,789.5	1,939.7	5.9
Soc. Welfare & Community Services							
%	18.6	17.2	18.1	19.5	19.8	22.3	
(avg 1981/82 prices) $m	1,890.8	1,727.4	1,894.7	2,160.5	2,252.9	2,615.5	7.1
Transport & Communications							
%	15.4	14.6	16.0	15.6	15.5	13.6	
(avg 1981/82 prices) $m	1,571.2	1,471.3	1,680.3	1,718.4	1,758.3	1,594.1	0.6
Economic & Industrial Services							
%		12.8	14.5	12.2	9.8	9.1	9.4
(avg 1981/82 prices) $m	1,314.4	1,453.8	1,282.5	1,084.4	1,034.1	1,101.7	-2.9
Other *							
%	11.2	13.3	13.0	13.3	14.0	13.8	
(avg 1981/82 prices) $m	1,137.1	1,339.0	1,362.3	1,464.9	1,591.9	1,621.4	7.5
Total Outlays							
%	100.0	100.0	100.0	100.0	100.0	100.0	
(avg 1981/82 prices)	10,190.1	10,047.3	10,490.1	11,041.4	11,358.9	11,728.0	2.9

Note: * Includes Public Debt Transactions.
Source: ABS 'State and Local Government Finance, Australia 1986/87', Cat. No. 5504.0 and ABS 'Sydney CPI', Cat. No. 6401.0.

Indebtedness

The level of outstanding (net) State sector debt as a proportion of GSP is also worthy of attention here. In New South Wales, this ratio is about 18%, somewhat down on its recent peak of over 24% in mid-1985 (see Table 10.17 below). According to figures compiled by State Treasury this is well below the ratio prevailing in other States (New South Wales Budget Information Paper, No. 2, p. 359). Although net debt has been reduced over recent years, debt servicing costs as a proportion of State Government receipts (including Commonwealth Grants) have gradually increased, reflecting the increased budget expenditure allocation to interest payments and provisions for the retirement of debt, as well as the relative decline in Commonwealth grants.

Table 10.16

Trends in New South Wales Government Capital Outlays by Purpose

	81/82	82/83	83/84	84/85	85/86	86/87	Avge 81-87 **
Education							
%	8.9	7.9	8.0	8.6	8.3	7.8	
$m *	247.2	199.4	213.4	228.8	229.1	233.0	-0.6
Health							
%	1.8	1.7	1.7	2.6	3.3	3.9	
$m *	49.5	43.6	44.2	69.8	89.8	115.3	20.9
Social Welfare & Community Services							
%	22.4	18.6	24.6	30.2	30.8	36.3	
$m *	618.5	467.9	655.0	806.7	849.5	1,078.8	14.2
Transport & Communications							
%	29.8	26.7	33.9	34.9	35.3	28.4	
$m *	822.8	671.8	904.2	932.5	975.7	842.6	2.1
Economic & Industrial Services							
%	36.9	45.0	31.7	23.5	22.9	23.9	
$m *	1,018.0	1,129.4	844.8	625.9	633.2	710.8	-5.2
Other							
%	0.2	0.1	0.1	0.2	-0.6	-0.3	
$m*	6.6	1.1	2.1	4.1	-15.7	-8.9	–
Total							
%	100.0	100.0	100.0	100.0	100.0	100.0	
$m *	2,762.6	2,513.2	2,663.7	2,667.8	2,761.6	2,971.6	1.7
General Government							
%	32.8	33.3	40.0	45.5	43.1	42.3	
$m *	906.2	836.3	1,065.9	1,214.3	1,190.6	1,256.0	7.4
Public Trading Enterprises							
%	67.2	67.7	60.0	54.5	56.9	57.7	
$m *	1,856.4	1,676.9	1,597.8	1,453.5	1,571.0	1,715.6	-1.2

Notes: * Average 1981-82 prices.
** Average Annual Growth Rate.
Source: ABS 'State and Local Government Finance, Australia 1986/87', Cat. No. 5504.0 and ABS 'Sydney CPI', Cat. No. 6401.0.

By way of summary the following points may be emphasized:

— the size of the sector has increased only marginally over the course of the 1980s with revenues growing slightly faster than expenditures as a percentage of GSP — though State sector employment has grown more slowly than total State employment;

— on the expenditure side, there has been an increased allocation of State own purpose expenditure to meeting debt servicing commitments over the past few years, though the present trend in (net) debt reduction suggests that the burden on the State budget of debt servicing costs in future years will fall; and,

— on the revenue side, the government has

over recent years reduced its reliance on external borrowings by increasing its 'internal' sources of revenue from tax receipts and charges on public services.

Finally it should be kept in mind that these trends in the State sector have occurred against a background of economic and employment growth in the New South Wales economy which is slightly below national performance, as Section 10.2.2 demonstrated.

Table 10.17

Trends in New South Wales State Public Sector Debt

As at 30 June	Outstanding State Public Sector Debt *	Debt Serv. Costs to the State Budget +	Gross State Product at Market Prices	Debt as a Proportion of GSP	Debt Servicing as a Proportion of State Govt. Receipts
	$m	$m	$m	%	%
1983	12,185.1	n.a	60,298	20.2	n.a
1984	14,965.7	732.3	66,531	22.5	17.7
1985	17,710.3	852.9	72,750	24.3	18.5
1986	18,862.6	1,081.2	81,726	23.1	21.0
1987	21,492.3	1,269.7	90,242†	23.8	21.9
1988	18,116.6	1,483.4	101,369†	17.9	21.4

Notes: * Debt is at its capital value, calculated as 'the amount of the loan proceeds, amortised over the life of the loan to face value' (Budget Paper No. 2, 1988-89, p. 319).
+ Refers to Debt Servicing Costs for the 'Inner Budget Sector Plus Transport Authorities' (Budget Paper No. 2, 1988-89, p. 322).
† Based on New South Wales State Treasury estimates of GSP growth.
n.a. Not available.
Source: Budget Paper No. 2, 1988-89, ABS 'State Accounts, 1986-87', Cat. No. 5220.0 and ABS 'Australian National Accounts − National Income and Expenditure, 1987-88', Cat. No. 5201.0.

10.5 Budgetary Policy − Revenues, Outlays and Debt

The purpose of this section is to provide an analysis of budgetary policy and its implications for the management and direction of the New South Wales State public sector, though at a number of points budgetary policy becomes inseparable from 'micro-economic' policy. For example, the scale of State sector outlays (expenditures) is inter-dependent with the amount of State revenues (receipts); but the latter is in part a function of the pricing policies applied to State trading enterprises, since these policies influence the size of non-tax revenues of the sector and hence the size of any net subsidy to (or from) trading enterprises, financed from other, essentially tax, revenues or contributing to other, essentially non-traded, State sector activities). (The micro-economic dimensions are taken up in detail in Section Five below). By way of preliminary, the logic of budgetary policy − as it particularly pertains to New South Wales under conservative government − may be indicated by considering two stylised cases.

I. A deficit between total outlays and recurrent revenues entails new borrowings and/ or asset sales. From the standpoint of maintaining and enhancing the State sector this might appear at first glance an undesirable situation, since it increases liabilities and/or reduces assets. However, there are two sides to these capital transactions and in themselves new borrowings or asset sales are not undesirable. Suppose that the 'outlay/recurrent-income deficit' is due to a capital outlay (asset purchase) to be financed by asset sales. In this case the composition of public assets is merely being changed; and if the priorities dictating the compositional change are appropriate, this would be desirable (taking as given the total scale of assets). If this reshuffling of assets involved a switch towards better utilized assets (eg., surplus or under-utilized land sales to finance increased public housing), then this restructuring would yield higher social and/or pecuniary returns to the State sector capital stock – in the latter case, subsequently adding to recurrent revenues. The same logic applies to new borrowings used to finance capital outlays – the addition to liabilities is matched by an addition to assets. If these capital outlays generate pecuniary returns which at least cover debt servicing costs, then the debt will be self-financing, generating recurrent revenue which at least covers the cost of capital. There is no compelling reason why use of borrowings should be limited to public sector projects which are (or are expected to be) self-financing in this sense: if the social returns from the use of borrowings are regarded as more than compensating for debt costs, then borrowings can also be justified. However, it should be evident in the latter case that if borrowings are used to finance capital outlays which do not generate a (sufficient) pecuniary return (eg. new schools), or consumption outlays (eg. more teachers), then debt servicing will have to be financed out of recurrent revenues (or asset sales). This involves a cross subsidy from those who provide the recurrent revenues (or benefited from the previously owned assets), most notably tax payers, to those who benefit from the outlay – which, of course, may be perfectly justifiable from the social standpoint.

II. Consider now a second case where a State Government pursues a budgetary policy aimed at reducing both taxes and State debt. To retire debt with a view to reducing total debt levels requires an excess of revenues net of new borrowings over outlays net of debt servicing costs, so that the resulting surplus can be used to service debt principle. If at the same time tax revenues are to be reduced, then this budgetary policy points to some combination of three options: reduce outlays net of debt servicing costs, so as to more than offset tax reductions; increase non-tax revenues; and/or sell assets. The first would include reduced public goods and services, running down the State sector capital stock, getting the same services at lower

outlays by altering wages and conditions of State sector workers, contracting for lower input prices for the sector, or improving technical efficiency. The second would include increasing the prices of State traded goods and services by extending the application of 'user pays' with a view to non-tax financed cost recovery. The third would include sale of assets which generate, or are potentially capable of generating, pecuniary returns to private wealth-holders (commercial or potentially commercial assets or enterprises), including public land. This case II budgetary policy is in essence the strategy of the Greiner State Government.

A number of subsidiary points may be added:

– at first glance it might appear to the lay person that debt retirement is always a good thing – the old-fashioned maxim, 'neither a borrower or lender be' – but this is not so. If the stream of (pecuniary and/or non-pecuniary) returns from debt-financed outlays exceeds debt costs then acquiring debt is desirable, subject to the viability of servicing debt costs. Asset sales to finance debt retirement may be desirable if the reduction in debt servicing costs frees up recurrent revenues for other purposes (eg., health, education and welfare); on the other hand, if the interest rate on a debt is less than the rate which can be earned on public funds invested, debt retirement will generate pecuniary losses. The retirement of Sydney Harbour Bridge debt by the Greiner Government was just such an error, probably designed to serve as a political stunt. Retiring debt may or may not be desirable – what is required in general to determine this is an analysis of the relation between outlay returns and debt costs, and debt costs and recurrent revenues (income);

(ii) case II above is a strategy which inevitably involves reducing the State sector capital stock and/or consumption expenditures, to the benefit of increased private consumption or capital accumulation – with all the macroeconomic and redistributional consequences likely to flow from this (Certainly tax reductions financed by public asset sales will increase consumption at the expense of total (public and private) capital accumulation);

– treating the New South Wales State sector as a corporation in the generic sense is quite harmless in itself; but there is a fundamental difference between a 'social corporation' like New South Wales and a private corporation. A private corporation has no other function or obligation than to maximize the private rate of return to private capital, within the law, the pecuniary rate of return being private wealth-holders' only interest in investment. *The function and obligation of government is to maximize social returns to social capital, of which, in a representative democracy, government is the mere custodian on behalf of the people.* Consider a case where government reduces outlays on home care. From the narrow standpoint of the State sector considered in isolation and purely in pecuniary terms, this 'improves' the balance sheet since (all other things being equal) consumption outlays have fallen. However this change increases costs to the individuals and families that previously benefited from this service – a new cost is added to their 'budgets' and so impacts adversely on their (notional) balance sheets. From the social standpoint – and this is the only legitimate standpoint for economic analysis as well as public administration – costs have simply been shifted from one balance sheet to others. From the social standpoint this exercise thus appears as a kind of fraud. For economic analysis what is required is a social calculus, not merely a pecuniary calculus. It is the 'budget' and 'balance sheet' of New South Wales society as a whole – where revenues (costs) and outlays (benefits), assets and liabilities, are conceived in the most comprehensive social and economic terms – which is the proper object of both economic analysis and socio-economically responsible government.

10.5.1 The Budgetary Strategy of the Liberal-National Government

Though the conservative government has been in power only since March 1988, there is little mystery about its medium term (3-4 year) strategy for the State sector. After coming to power the government established a 'Commission of Audit' (Curran *et al.*, 1988) with a view to establishing a 'true' balance sheet for the sector, so that the new 'sound (conservative) managers' could proceed with their task of placing 'NSW Inc.' on a proper financial footing. It may be said at the outset that this exercise has had a primarily political motivation, though the program has wide-reaching economic consequences (In particular, Curran's exaggeration of the State sector's exposure to liabilities set a tone of crisis – a kind of $1.5m public relations stunt, for justifying radical action (compare with the Auditor-General's comments in A-G II ([1988], pp. 111-13).

The government is aiming to reduce debt and taxes; and it is evident that this points, almost inexorably, to asset sales and expenditure reduction. Likewise it points to a strategy of generating more services for the same budget expenditures, or the same services for less expenditures. This aspect points to pervasive micro-economic consequences of the strategy: attempting to extract more work out of State sector workers by worsening conditions; contracting out to private sector agencies whose workers are denied similar wages and conditions to State sector workers; shifting social and welfare services on to private charitable agencies, including family units; wide-reaching structural changes to the pricing policies and operations of trading (or potential trading) enterprises, particularly the major deficit agencies which draw heavily on State revenues which the government would prefer to release for tax cuts (See Section 10.4.4 for examples). In the latter case the transport utilities are particularly under scrutiny (the UTA's deficit was much larger as a proportion of outlays than the SRA's; but the SRA's much larger outlays give it a greater budgetary significance). Nevertheless all trading enterprises are under examination as to asset (and debt) management, technical efficiency, pricing policy, and wages and conditions. It must be stressed that all this structural ('micro-economic') change, or projected change, is driven by a budgetary strategy; and behind this is a political strategy of seeking to ensure that the State sector after 3-4 years will have delivered up net revenues for the provision of tax cuts, with a view to the re-election of the conservative government

The strictly ideological character of much of Curran *et al.*, (1988) can be evidenced by the following statements – further examples of which could be multiplied many times over – with regard to the related issues of tax reduction, contraction of State expenditures and activities, and the abolition of State trading enterprise. It must be stressed again that no attempt is made to justify these propositions or the desirability of these policies, other than mere assertion:

– '. . . a more secure future for New South Wales . . . [is] a future offering a smaller, more responsible Government meeting genuine community needs, a lowered taxation impost on its citizens, all within a framework of productive effort and financial responsibility' (p. viii);.

– 'The . . . general presumption . . . should be that the private sector has a number of advantages over the public sector . . .' (p. 69).

'In the future, the State . . . sector would be much smaller with only those services being performed which cannot be provided commercially by the private sector' (p. 66);

– '. . . the Government should retain only that property necessary for its operations which cannot be economically provided by the private sector in a competitive environment. . . . Property which is not currently required, or by rationalisation [ie., sale] of activities can be made available, or is considered surplus, should be disposed [sic]' (p. 97); and

– 'The government should, as a matter of urgency, act to reduce significantly the size of Government based upon a review of services and activities in which it should properly be engaged. Possible areas for early rationalisation [ie., sale] of Government activities include:

Building maintenance
Bus services . . .
Elcom coal mines
Engineering Workshops

Ferries . . .
Government Insurance Office
Grain Handling Authority
Hydrofoil services
Land Development – other than genuine welfare housing
Maritime Services Board Coal Loaders
State Bank
State Lotteries Sales Offices . . .' (p. 109).

How far down this track the government will try to go, in part remains to be seen; but the Curran 'vision' certainly replicates the thrust of the government's program. What lies behind these views is a conviction that, as compared to the private sector, State service provision is invariably and inevitably inferior, if not an outright failure – and illegitimate if it occupies any ground which private capital could profit from. This is a view not arrived at by any empirical analysis of performance, but rather, an *a priori* belief from the catechism of the politico-economic theology of certain conservatives and economic liberals. It follows from this view that the government, rather than seeking to reform and revitalize the State sector in cooperation with the workforce, will be inclined, on the one hand to dismantle as much of the sector's trading enterprises as is politically and economically feasible, on the other hand to restrict those residual services which have no such commercial potential. The mere size of government becomes an irrational obsession, whereas the real issue of effective public administration is what is worth doing and how can it be done well, in the public interest and subject to budgetary and political constraints. Instead we witness a massive actual and prospective sell off of public capital assets which the government only controls on behalf of the public – a scale of sell offs for which the government sought no mandate at the 1988 election – to finance politically motivated tax cuts.

As mentioned above, in large part the Commission of Audit was an exercise in seeking to project a State debt crisis in order to 'soften up' community opinion for a sell off public assets and a reduction of State sector services. Our comments are not intended to convey the impression that State public debt should be treated as trivial to State sector management and reform; but the significance of debt must be grasped in the framework of a reasoned economic analysis.

It is in the nature of much State sector capital accumulation that it does not, or should not – and in many cases, could not conceivably – yield pecuniary returns in any way commensurate with costs (eg., capital assets such as schools, hospitals and police stations). In these cases borrowings cannot be self-financing but this does not mean that they are unjustified. From the social standpoint, which is the proper standpoint for economic analysis, a stream of non-pecuniary economic and social returns can warrant debt-financing of such investments.[1] The contrary Curran doctrine has no economic or ethical justification (it should be stressed that these non-pecuniary returns are not merely intangible, but include quite tangible economic returns – eg., from education – which are either not appropriated or non-appropriable by government). On the other hand, in general there is no warrant for borrowing for current public consumption (which by definition yields no future returns, pecuniary or otherwise) since this imposes the costs on 'future generations' who receive no benefits from the consumption. There seems no justification in general for such 'inter-generational' redistribution of net benefits.

In the case of State sector borrowings which are not self-financing the question of debt management becomes particularly important. The growth of debt increases debt servicing costs which must ultimately be financed out of recurrent revenues, thereby reducing revenues available for other budgetary purposes. It follows that continuous growth of debt may lead to a continuous rise in the proportion of State revenues devoted to debt servicing – a situation which would be unsustainable since it would eventually lead to debt charges consuming all of recurrent revenues. However, New South Wales is far from a position wherein the growth of debt, or debt service costs, would be alarming; notwithstanding the efforts of Curran et al. (1988) to project such a crisis. Their use of nominal and absolute debt magnitudes, gross rather than net debt, assisted in this misrepresentation. Nor is there

any recognition in their analysis of the fact that increase in debt service burdens primarily has been due to interest rate rises. As Groenewegen (1988, p. 8) has summed it up:

'. . . the Commission's debt story is designed to drum up public support for higher public utility charges and social expenditure restraint by instilling fears of the near bankruptcy of the New South Wales State Government. This overt political purpose was exploited so ably by the Premier that it caused problems for State security values in overseas financial markets. The Commission has also tended to ignore the State's low relative debt levels (with respect to GSP) as compared to the other Australian States . . .'.

Social responsibility finds no place in a framework of mere financial accounting, which seems to provide a model of good government for the conservative administration. This is not to indict accounting – it simply cannot be asked to perform a task for which it is not designed. This important point can be illustrated in the language of accounting itself. The government has moved to shift a number of welfare services 'off budget' by placing these functions under the responsibility of private agencies, including families (eg., child care and refuges). From the accounting standpoint this increases State receipts net of outlays (all other things being equal) and hence allows an improvement in the sector's balance sheet (net assets); but from the social standpoint this shifts new costs on to other social units (charitable organisations, families, etc.) thereby reducing their 'revenues' (including non-pecuniary benefits) net of 'outlays' (including non-pecuniary costs) all other things being equal, thereby impacting negatively on their (in many cases, purely notional) 'balance sheets'. If there are diseconomies of scale in decentralised private provision of any welfare services (as seems likely), relative to the public provision, total net social benefits actually will decline. The same kind of illustration could be given in other areas, for example the deterioration of teachers' working conditions in order to cut costs, the resulting deterioration in public education, and the impact of this on the 'balance sheets' of school children, and others (including in the future their employers and the Australian economy in general!). This kind of 'social audit' is essential to both economic analysis and responsible government. The 'corporate' model which apparently mesmerizes the Liberal Premier's administration is an abrogation of normal methods of economic assessment and normal social responsibilities of government.

Having said all this it should be added that there are aspects of the Commission of Audit's proposals and the government's program which deserve more serious consideration. These include: improvement of financial disclosure and accounting procedures, with a view to increasing the accountability of State sector agencies; related to this, reform of management practices, particularly with respect to asset management; and commercialisation of trading enterprises and explicit accounting and budgeting for cross-subsidisation. These will be discussed below.

10.5.2 Expenditure and Revenue Policies

With regard to the scale of State expenditure there are three basic accounting variables making up the budget identity: aggregate expenditure, recurrent revenues and net budget financing (consisting of net borrowings and asset sales). It is apparent, at least in the first instance, that for the purposes of budgetary policy only two of these three variables can be regarded as independent, with the remaining one treated as dependent on the prior policy setting of the other two. Of these three budget variables it seems more appropriate to treat the aggregate level of expenditures as largely dependent on prior determination of the amount of revenue raised and the size of net budget financing. The largest source of State revenues is Commonwealth Grants which depend in large part on the independent fiscal stance of the Federal Government, as well as how the Grants are allocated between the States, while Loan Council funds for capital works programs are subject to agreement under global borrowing limits. There is also at least a long term constraint on the State Government in raising loans because of the debt charges it implies,

which ultimately impact on the size of expenditures net of debt servicing costs. Given these parameters, the State Government can only alter the scale of expenditures by adjusting revenue contributions from State taxation and charges on public goods and services. In the current macroeconomic environment governments at both the Federal level and in New South Wales have given priority to controlling debt financing and revenue raising, and then adjusting the scale of aggregate expenditures accordingly.

As indicated above, the budgetary strategy of the conservative government is to reduce State sector debt and deliver tax cuts by 1991/92, implying a decline in budget expenditure as a proportion of GSP. In order to meet its aim of 'containing the size of the State Budget Sector and indeed to reduce it relative to the size of the economy' it intends to allow the level of expenditure to grow at only a zero real rate (New South Wales Budget Information Paper No. 2, p. 3). Part of its strategy is to procure productivity gains in the sector through administrative restructuring as well as altering the wages and employment conditions of employees so as to maintain services at lower dollar expenditures. However, as suggested in the above quotation, the main thrust of the government's medium to long term expenditure policy implies a decline in the quantity, range and quality of services provided by the public sector. *To justify this position, the government has enlisted the simplistic economic argument asserted by Curran (1988, ch. 1), that restraining State sector expenditure in real terms will decrease State sector demands on productive resources and so release a greater volume of community savings which will increase private sector investment, and in areas traditionally serviced by the State sector. This spurious argument neglects the fact that State public expenditures provide an important source of demand which stimulates production in the private sector.* In contrast to the conservative argument, there is every reason to believe that a real reduction in State public sector expenditures, particularly capital spending, will lead to a slowdown not an acceleration in capital formation and economic growth and employment in the New South Wales economy. There are no formidable economic grounds why the role of the State sector should be downgraded, nor why the scale of State public expenditures should be reduced in relation to the GSP.

The second aspect of expenditure policy is the composition of outlays, over which the State Government has fairly wide discretion, though subject to Federal constraints (Specific Purpose Payments in particular). The allocation of available funds for expenditure (net of debt servicing) cannot be regarded as based solely on objective criteria, it depends also on the political interests of the incumbent government. However, the government cannot easily ignore clearly recognized social and economic demands in the State; on the contrary, its political interests may well be best served, on many occasions, by giving priority to those areas of public demand. The conservative government's expenditure policy consists of giving priority to the areas of law, order, public safety, health, and roads in particular. These and other areas of social expenditures have been receiving increasing priority in budgetary funding over recent years, reflecting the acute need for such facilities and services in New South Wales. Demographic changes in the community, largely with respect to the aging of the population and the considerable shift in the distribution of population toward the Western and South-Western metropolitan regions of Sydney, has required both an expansion and relocation of public services, particularly in health, law, order and public safety, and education. In addition, the shortage of low cost rental housing in metropolitan Sydney and the general cuts in real incomes within the community over recent years has created a considerable need for public housing/community facilities including rental assistance programs as well as other welfare services to low income groups. The long-term trend in these demographic factors suggest that the provision of social welfare and community services will need to be a priority for some years into the future.

Given the government's commitment to reduce the overall level of expenditure and tax revenue, the increased allocation of expenditures to those priority areas mentioned above will be heavily dependent on obtaining expenditure savings in other areas of the New South Wales State public sector. Two main budgetary measures are to be adopted in order to obtain the necessary expenditure savings:

 — an outright reduction in capital works programs undertaken by the sector in relation to the provision of economic and community services; and
 — greater commercialisation of State trading enterprises, designed to increase their capacity to generate sufficient income to internally finance their operations and thereby remove or reduce reliance on the budget as a source of funds — if not provide a contribution to consolidated revenue. Some critical evaluation of these budgetary measures is warranted.

The reduction in State public works can to some extent be justified in the current circumstances, at least in the short-term, following the large-scale capital works program undertaken by the previous Labor Governments. The changing composition of Budget outlays since the early 1980s is outlined in Section 10.5 above, especially Tables 10.15, 10.16 and 10.17. The capital works program under Labor consisted of a marked expansion in infrastructure related to energy capacity (resulting in excess capacity) and public transport facilities, as well as the upgrading and the development of new recreational and cultural facilities (eg. the Entertainment Centre and Darling Harbour). These earlier capital works programs have provided scope for redirecting investment to other areas, in particular, the construction of public hospitals and other health facilities, public housing and community amenities, courts, prisons and police stations. While the conservative government has taken the opportunity to redirect capital spending in this way, its budget strategy clearly portends a long-term rundown in the capital stock of the State sector, particularly with respect to the public utilities.

The government's adoption of measures designed to 'encourage the private sector to play a greater part in infrastructure projects including transport links, energy and water systems, schools and hospitals' (New South Wales Budget Information Paper No. 2, p. 193) represents a serious attack on the capital spending function of the New South Wales State public sector. There is no economic reasoning which suggests that the community will benefit by transferring these investment functions from the State sector to the private sector.

The government's expenditure strategy is also motivated by a desire to reduce budget subsidies to trading enterprises through the expansion of non-tax revenue-raising via commercialisation and corporatisation of enterprises. The objective of commercialisation and corporatisation is to improve trading enterprises' commercial performance. There can be little objection to the adoption of budgetary measures which improve the cost-effectiveness of public trading enterprises, via improved management practices and investment decision-making, providing it does not entail an abrogation of legitimate social responsibilities of government. In this sense, there is no contradiction between economic performance and the pursuit of social objectives.

Turning to the revenue side of the Budget, it has already been indicated as a general principle that borrowings should be used only to finance capital outlays – though not necessarily revenue-generating capital outlays – or debt retirement. Borrowing for investment with non-pecuniary returns is legitimate because there are future returns and so a debt burden may reasonably be placed upon 'future generations'. There is of course no completely compelling reason why capital outlays should not be financed by recurrent revenues – this would be 'State sector saving' – or indeed by asset sales. It may be added that strictly symmetrical reasoning leads to the recommendation that asset sales also in general should be used only to finance capital outlays or debt retirement: to do otherwise involves incurring liabilities or shedding assets – ie., reducing net State sector assets – to finance consumption or outlays. This would be State sector 'dissaving'. The use of asset sales to finance capital outlays (or debt retirement) simply involves a change in the composition of State sector assets (or assets and liabilities). There is no reason why this should not be desirable as effective public administration seeks to adjust the composition of assets to more accurately reflect the sector's socio-economic objectives in changing circumstances.

Formally speaking, an asset sale for purchase of another asset (or debt retirement) will be desirable if the stream of pecuniary and/or non-pecuniary returns from the existing asset – actual returns, or potential returns from better utilisation of the existing assets – is less than the stream of returns from the prospective asset (or the stream of debt costs of some existing State debt). It is evident from Curran *et al.* (1988, Ch. 5) and other sources that a part of the property holdings of State agencies have at least actual returns which have been near zero. This is related to the poor management and accounting practices in parts of the sector.[2] Since some agencies have not even had a clear idea of what properties they hold, they could not possibly have been managing those assets effectively, so as to generate some social return or other. These assets should be put to full and effective use so as to generate adequate pecuniary and/or non-pecuniary returns to the community. If they generate pecuniary returns these can be used to service debt or finance recurrent outlays. If they cannot be put to any such use they should be realized with a view to debt retirement. Quite symmetric principles apply to the use of borrowings to finance capital outlays: debt should be used to finance only capital outlays, or purchase of other assets which yield at least a commensurate stream of pecuniary and/or non-pecuniary returns; where debt is used to finance investments which do not yield sufficient pecuniary returns to be self-financing, this must be subject to an overall (long-term) debt management policy which ensures that debt servicing does not impose an undesirable drain on recurrent revenues. A high ratio of debt service costs to recurrent revenues which reduced revenues available for other recurrent outlays, is not in the interest of the community or of State sector workers.

Given a prudent debt policy, and a responsible policy towards selling truly 'surplus assets', recurrent revenues will determine the level of consumption expenditures plus any additional capital expenditures. Of course, instead of determining expenditures in this 'residual' manner one could independently determine expenditures and then ensure that sufficient revenues are raised. Subject to broad economic constraints, the extent to which this can be done is essentially a political question.

New South Wales recurrent revenues divide into three fundamental categories:

- Commonwealth (general revenue and general capital purposes) grants and Commonwealth payments for specific recurrent and specific capital purposes;
- revenues arising from New South Wales non-tax charges, including fees for services rendered, revenue contributions by State trading enterprises (STEs) and the State Lotteries, minerals royalties, leases, interest receipts and rents; and
- New South Wales tax revenues, including receipts from stamp duties, pay-roll tax, land and racing taxes, licences.

Commonwealth grants do not lie within the power of State Government policy. It is also worth noting that via specific purpose payments, as well as the mix between general revenue and capital grants, the Commonwealth is able to exert a considerable influence on the composition of State expenditures. With regard to non-tax charges, these revenues arise primarily from pricing, profitability and sales of traded goods and services. The ability to generate revenues from these sources depends upon micro-economic policies pertaining to the extent of application of full or partial user pays, pricing policies of STEs, technical and cost conditions, management and so on. These issues will be dealt with below. It need only be pointed out here that to the extent that STEs and other user pays services generate net revenues they provide non-tax funds which can be used to finance other non-profitable or non-commercial State sector activities, reducing reliance upon tax and Commonwealth revenues.

Hence if we take borrowings and asset sales as determined by a prudent and progressive policy of debt/asset management, treat receipts from the Commonwealth as an external parameter, and take non-tax revenues as a given for the time being, then total outlays will depend upon State tax revenues.

As indicated above, tax reduction is part of the political program of the conservative government, serving as an axiomatic assumption for the Commission of Audit, not a conclusion of any economic or other argument. The proportion of tax revenues to Gross State Product (GSP) — and given GSP, the level of tax revenues — may rise or fall as a matter of policy decision. This is a political as much as an economic question. What we consider here is the tax mix, ie., the composition of any given level of tax receipts. The ratio of taxes to GSP can then be specified in accordance with politico-economic objectives and constraints, taken in conjunction with the possibilities offered by other sources of financing.

As it turns out, the issue of New South Wales tax mix has been capably and quite comprehensively examined by a Task Force established by the previous government (Collins et al., 1988). The changing structure and scale of New South Wales tax revenues over the decade 1976/77 to 1986/87 are indicated in Table 10.18 below).

Although New South Wales imposes a wide variety of taxes (in 24 of the 29 categories of State taxation identified by the Australian Bureau of Statistics) many of these are 'nuisance' taxes which make only minor contributions to revenue and offer little prospect of providing a much greater contribution, as well as imposing high compliance costs. The great bulk of tax receipts derive from three sources: payroll tax, stamp duties and motor vehicle taxes. New South Wales (apart from Queensland) has the most highly concentrated State tax base, with the 'big three' tax sources together accounting for 61% of tax revenues. The narrowness of the tax base is a long-term problem facing all States, in so far as it prejudices a steady growth of tax receipts per capita in line with GSP, as well as making revenue raising prone to cyclical disturbances. Furthermore, virtually all New South Wales taxes are regressive, or at least non-progressive, in their incidence. Since the abolition of death duties no progressive taxes have been in place in New South Wales, with the partial exception of land tax (a form of wealth taxation), and there are severe constraints upon bringing more progressivity to the structure (Collins et al., 1988, p. 86). But the most striking feature of the New South Wales tax system (shared with all other States) is that it amounts to an arbitrary and discriminatory regime of indirect taxes – a piecemeal ramshackle product of history – with no economic or ethical rationale. Its only possible rationale is a political one: the Constitutional limitation upon State imposition of a broad-based indirect tax; and even supposing this to be an insurmountable obstacle does not justify the current degree of narrowness. A major conclusion of Collins et. al., (1988) is that a mere change in the mix of current taxes can change little with regard to either incidence or base narrowness.

Table 10.18

Trends in New South Wales Tax Revenues, 1976/77 to 1986/87

	% of Total 1976/77	% of Total 1986/87	% increase in real tax revenues 1976/77 1981/82 *	% increase in real tax revenues 1981/82 1986/87 *	% increase in real tax revenues 1976/77 1986/87 *	Tax Revenue per capita 1986/87 ($)
Payroll	32.65	28.20	25.43	2.08	28.04	267.29
Property	13.73	6.61	-36.37	12.27	-28.56	62.70
Capital	10.65	19.40	60.66	68.00	169.91	183.87
Goods	0.00	0.62	**	108.07	**	5.83
Gambling	12.43	10.83	37.23	-5.85	29.20	102.65
Insurance	5.04	5.42	72.65	7.67	59.42	51.37
Vehicles	14.80	12.94	21.86	6.33	29.57	122.61
Franchises	5.56	10.22	134.51	16.19	172.47	96.89
Fees/Fines	5.15	5.76	66.39	-0.29	65.90	54.60
Total	100.00	100.00	32.63	11.76	48.23	947.80

Notes: * 1979/80 prices.
** No taxes imposed in this category until 1981/82.
Source: Collins et al. (1988), Tables 2.4, 2.5, 2.7, 2.8 (pp. 21, 27, 30, 31). Columns may not sum to Totals due to rounding.

10.6 'NSW Inc.' and Issues in the Reform and Development of State Public Services in New South Wales

The purpose of this section is to examine Premier Greiners' 'NSW Inc' in the light of micro-economic policy issues and the effective and equitable provision of State public services. By micro-economic policy in this context we mean policies pertaining to the structure, performance and methods of service provision of the sector. This involves a critical consideration of structural changes being pursued by the current government, as well as positive proposals for reform in light of the social objectives of the sector.

Section 10.6.1 provides an overview of the critical issues in micro-economic policy in New South Wales with regard to the State sector, since the election of the conservative government. This is followed by more detailed exami-

nation of three particular State instrumentalities: the Department of Health, Elcom, the GIO and housing. These case studies are followed by an analysis of the human services industry in NSW.

10.6.1 Issues in Micro-economic Reform

The link between budgetary policy and microeconomic policy was briefly indicated above. Restating the central point, a budgetary policy aimed at reducing State taxes and debt necessarily requires some combination of:

– reduced budget expenditures; and
– increased non-tax recurrent revenues and/or asset sales.

An additional point should be stressed here. Even in the absence of the conservative budgetary strategy State public administration in New

South Wales, as in other States, would be facing a difficult period of fiscal restraint. This is so because along with the impact of State Government policy, the State sector is coming under fiscal pressure from the Federal Government's strategy of fiscal restraint with respect to Commonwealth grants to the States (as well as pressure from restrictive monetary policy). The latter (Federal policy) is about as likely to go away as the former (State policy). Financing constraints, with all their attendant micro-economic implications, are likely to persist at least in the medium term (2-3 years).

Privatisation and Corporatisation
On the one hand, the doctrine of privatisation enunciated by Curran *et al.* (1988) and the government involves asserting that any profit-able (or potentially profitable) activities should be the preserve of private capital, so that in the extremity, public capital and expenditures would be left merely to service 'residual' wel-fare activities and social services. On the other hand, profitable assets which return revenues to the government – and these are the privatis-able assets of most interest to private capital – are difficult for a government to give up, since it thereby gives up a stream of income (albeit in return for a capital sum). The private con-sultants who examined privatisation of the State Bank for the government recommended against it – which amounts to concluding that the (discounted) stream of revenues from the Bank is worth more to the government than its marketable value (*SMH*, 30/11/88, p. 45), quite apart from any non-pecuniary returns. The GIO is likely to go the same way. The salutary lesson in this for the government is that it should get on with its proper business of managing its assets effectively, on behalf of the people and in pursuit of progressive social and economic objectives, rather than seeking to deprive the State sector of profitable and potentially profitable assets and enterprises. Obviously, this is conceptually distinct from that sale of truly surplus assets in order to pur-chase other more appropriate assets, or to re-tire debt, which is a legitimate and more or less continually necessary activity. *What privatis-ation is really about is a reduction in the net asset position of the sector as a whole.* Corporatisation

of State sector agencies, which is now proceed-ing in Elcom, the GHA, the GIO, the MSB, the SRA, the State Bank and the UTA, will create enormous pressure for ultimate privatisation, not least from the managements themselves, and should be as vigorously rejected as privat-isation. Corporatisation is only properly appli-cable to State trading enterprises which are exposed to systematic and substantial competi-tive forces; and which do not carry any social responsibilities which cannot be unambigu-ously reduced to financial flows.

The major agencies which have these charac-teristics – the State Bank and GIO – are in-deed already corporatised. On the other hand, the Water Board for example – which is a self-financing commercial agency – is not subject to significant competition and is being asked to pursue complex social objectives (of an environmental nature) which cannot be ex-pressed in transparent financial terms. Cor-poratisation would be inappropriate in this case. The dangers of corporatisation are well-illustrated by the experience of the GHA.

The Curran Commission's recommendation on corporatisation formed the starting point for the Steering Committee on Government Trad-ing Enterprises to explore the major issues which would be addressed in a corporatisation process. The Committee released its report ('A Policy Framework for Improving the Perfor-mance of Government Trading Enterprises') in September 1988. The recommendations made by the Steering Committee included that:

– Boards of Directors of the corporatised authorities should be appointed on the basis of commercial expertise;
– the objective of the boards should be to maximise the return on assets; and
– private sector analysts should assist in monitoring and assessing the corporatised authorities' commercial performance.

Consequently, Ernst and Whinney Services were appointed as consultants to undertake a review of systems and organisation structure for corporatisation of the Grain Handling Authority. The Report was released in March 1989. In fact, some of the recommendations made in the Report are desirable (for example, the establishment of an up-to-date asset register and that proper training be provided to staff). Somewhat paradoxically, the Report criticised the over-use of consultants in the GHA, but then goes on to recommend that consultants be used for implementing aspects of the corporatisation process many of which could be undertaken in-house.

Having received the recommendations as to what would be necessary for corporatisation, it is understood that the GHA has prepared a draft corporate plan for a corporatised body. As part of this corporate plan, it is understood that the GHA will be converted to a company – that is, become incorporated under the Companies Code. It is nowhere mentioned that, having done this, the government may lose control over the total operations of the GHA should it establish subsidiaries outside the Parliamentary discipline imposed currently. The Western Australian experience with aspects of WA Inc. should have offered a salutary lesson in this regard.

More specifically, Curran argued that corporatisation would form the basis of better service and greater customer satisfaction because 'exposing authorities to competition . . . is the best way to ensure that goods and services desired by the customer are provided at the lowest economic cost' (p. 70). In the case of the GHA its customers are primarily grain growers. Does corporatisation mean an improvement in the quality and efficiency of services provided to them? The simple answer is no.

The simplistic view adopted by Curran has, in fact, been refuted in a recent study of privatisation and corporatisation options for the Grain Elevators Board (GEB) in Victoria undertaken by Price Waterhouse Urwick which explicitly rejected corporatisation as offering no benefits to grain growers (*The Land*, 8/6/89, p. 5).

Economic services have not been the only area to undergo 'corporate review' in 1989, the State Minister for Education and Youth Affairs appointed a team of consultants (headed by Dr. Brain Scott) to review all aspects of his portfolio. The first 'briefing' from that review was released in June 1989 ('Schools Renewal: A Strategy to Revitalise Schools Within the New South Wales Education System'). A number of aspects of this Report indicate that corporatisation (and privatisation) for the Greiner Government is not limited to PTEs.

In respect of the roles of senior educational administrators, for example, the Report draws an analogy between the Assistant Director-General in each Region and the Chief Executive Officer of a subsidiary company of a large commercial enterprise with each having responsibility for the Region;s operations and performance (p. 17). In isolation, there may be no real objection to such an analogy, but when put in the context of other recommendations made in the Report, it takes on a more negative connotation. For instance, Regional plans would be developed, including Regional budgets, which would cover '. . . among other things, schools budgets, special grants, education programs, professional development programs, student welfare, minor and major capital works . . ., cyclical maintenance, and major plant and equipment purchases' (Scott, 1989, p. 17). This proposal seems to conflate two separate functions. The important function for any education system is the provision of quality education to students; a quite separate function is that of funds and resource management. It may well be that the quality of such management needs to be improved, but there is no justification provided in the Report for combining two roles. The distinction drawn here is, in fact, tacitly accepted by Scott when he urges the appointment of bursars for larger schools (p. 14).

There are a number of recommendations for privatisation in the New South Wales education system. The following are some examples:

– use of contracted externally-supplied curriculum support materials and services (p. 23);
– the establishment of Education Resource Centres to act as 'shop-fronts' for the sale and contracting of educational resources (p. 23);
– individual schools contracting cleaners and maintenance services (p. 31);
– tendering outside the Department of Public Works for construction (p. 31); and

– tendering for printing needs (p. 31).

The Report explicitly canvasses the option of privatising the Wetherill Park Furniture Complex, one of the largest furniture producers in the Southern Hemisphere (p. 32) In short, it gives a clear indication of the direction in which the Greiner Government is moving in its stewardship of the State's social infrastructure. That direction is consistent with its policies and programs outlined elsewhere in this Chapter, and is likely to have just as deleterious effect.

Contracting out and Tendering Processes

The expanding use of private contractors in the provision of public services – directly, or indirectly, through provision of inputs and services to the State sector – is a less visible but much more pervasive form of privatisation in New South Wales than enterprise and asset sales, with a multitude of instances throughout the sector; eg., in Public Works (*SMH*, 6/10/88, p. 1; see also Hogan, 1988a, pp. 35-37). While there is scope for sensible use of contracting out – in consolidating State sector activities and using outside contractors for peripheral or highly specialist activities which do not warrant a permanent State sector agency – in general contracting out has been motivated by an imperative for cost reductions as such, rather than any desire to increase efficiency. If however, the government believes that wages and conditions in the State sector are inappropriate it should negotiate that case with the unions which represent State sector workers, and before the relevant industrial tribunals (though it showed itself to be noticeably reluctant to do this in 1988, with regard to teachers), not circumvent these employment conditions by substituting private employees. The shift towards greater reliance upon private charitable organisations (and households themselves) for provision of welfare services (voluntarism) can only contribute to a declining quality and quantity of welfare services at a time when declining real incomes and increasing real housing costs are threatening the most basic needs of many. It obviously has the effect of simply shifting costs of welfare services 'off budget' and onto families, households and voluntary welfare agencies.

Commercialisation

It seems clear from the available evidence on tax incidence and the final beneficiaries of subsidies that the distributional impact of free-to-user services and subsidy-to-user services is by no means invariably to the benefit of 'widows and orphans', to use the old cliche; that is to say, there are extensive benefits to people who fall outside the objectives of a policy designed to benefit working people and the poor. In many cases it is desirable that the community in general derives the benefits from public services which are subsidised through the tax system. Nevertheless, as has been argued in Chapter Seven there is a strong micro-economic rationale for extending the scope of commercial practices in the State sector i.e. extending the application of cost recovery (including a rate of net profit) in the pricing of services, as well as reducing the rate of budget subsidy per unit of some services. Such commercialisation has a micro-rationale in terms of ensuring that the redistribution of income resulting from the State sector fiscal regime is not indiscriminate or ill-targeted. It also has a financial rationale since it will increase net non-tax revenues (fees for service) – or equivalently, reduce budget expenditures/subsidies – thereby generating funds for other more worthy purposes. Examples of areas where aspects of commercialisation usefully could proceed include the Water Board, Elcom and, to some extent, the SRA.

Pricing Policy and Cross-Subsidisation

Commercialisation has implications for the pricing policy employed in the State sector, the structure of cross subsidies, and the allocation of resources both within the sector and in the broader economy. Pricing services to ensure full cost recovery is synonymous with 'user pays' (ignoring externalities); and therefore, if universally applied to the sector, would be equivalent to abolition of all cross subsidisation. Attempts to widely or universally implement such a policy therefore would tend to abolish what has been described above as a fundamental (though not exclusive) objective of having the State sector at all: cross subsidisation is the mechanism for the redistribution of income which the sector brings about. *A generalised move towards full user pays should be firmly repudiated*. Certainly application of full user pays is inappropriate if applied to public services which are intended to overcome social inequities and ensure equality of access to essential goods and services, according to need; eg., health, education, welfare, legal aid, housing and public transport.

There are also resource allocation issues involved in pricing policy. It would appear to be desirable in general, for example, for households to face the full cost of electricity and water supply in deciding what quantity to use. This would encourage a more considered use of services and hence derivatively, also of State sector resources. The Water Board and Elcom are indeed (slowly) moving in this direction. Movement towards greater cost recovery in such areas should be combined with rebates and concessions which more accurately target specific groups deserving of subsidisation. Explicit cross-subsidisation through the Budget, as suggested by Curran et. al. (1988) would assist in accurately gauging the performance of enterprises by disentangling the financial impact of Community Service Obligations etc but is probably impracticable in many areas

Efficiency Costs and Performance
In discussing contracting out above, a distinction was drawn between cost reduction and efficiency improvement, in relation to the 'fiscal imperative' behind the conservative Government's micro-restructuring of the State sector. The point to be emphasised is that improved efficiency requires an unambiguously improved technical relation between inputs and outputs, such that the same outputs can be produced with an unambiguously smaller quantity of inputs; or the same inputs can produce an unambiguously larger quantity of outputs. As Chapter Four has shown, reduced costs on the other hand, can be a purely pecuniary phenomenon, not reflecting any technical improvement at all. The sad fact is that the fiscal imperative means that the government is concerned merely with cost reduction, not technical efficiency as such: a government can move a cost or an activity off its budget and simply enforce it upon someone

else's budget! This reallocates costs; it does not necessarily reallocate resources more efficiently. The litmus test for this issue is that the New South Wales Government will not be interested in any measures for increasing efficiency which do not contribute to cost reduction. However, in the current period of economic restructuring, the achievement of real efficiency gains in the public sector is essential if it wishes to maintain its economic and social relevance into the future. The present government's policies are not aimed at achieving such a result.

Management and Unions
Management of State sector agencies in general is a complex task, more difficult than the parallel management tasks in private sector corporations, as at least one advocate of privatisation recently has acknowledged (Hogan, 1988b). This is so because private sector management is required only to pursue a singular and relatively transparent objective — maximisation of the pecuniary rate of return on private capital invested — whereas State sector management often requires the pursuit of multidimensional objectives insusceptible of reduction to pure quantities. This necessary complexity is not something to evade by misspecifying objectives along private sector lines; but nor is it something to glory in. However, wherever possible management objectives should be clarified as much as possible, both to assist management and to better enable assessment of its performance.

State sector workers and their Unions have an important role to play in the process of reform and restructuring of public services provision; and a decent (and realistic) government and management will draw them into the process. Indeed it would be foolish and counter-productive to proceed without the support and cooperation of the workforce and their industrial representatives, the State sector unions. Government and management can either deny the legitimacy of the unions and seek to work around them; or accept their legitimacy as representatives of workers' objective interests and work with them. The conservative Government is naturally drawn to the former view, which is in nobody's interests, not least due to alienation of the workforce and destruction of worker morale. Whatever policies are pursued by government (at least, short of privatisation), it is the public sector workers 'on the ground' who will, in the end, be delivering the services.

10.6.2 Department of Health

Introduction

The recently released study by the Australian Institute of Health (April, 1989) estimates that the cost of public health care in Australia has declined by 1% per treatment since 1980. There has also been a 10% decline in public inpatients and a 45% increase in out patients. While these simple calculations cannot be a comprehensive measure of efficiency, it is clear that the public health system has become more cost effective and flexible over time. In national terms, it is also clear that the State hospital and community health system is the logical and cheapest place to develop comprehensive health services. Yet irrationally in NSW, the public hospital and community health system is being rationalised and is being forced to share its expertise and responsibilities with often 'immature', untried and ill prepared private hospitals and practitioners. These 'privateers' invariably provide only for the cheaper end of the health care system, they don't work in the unprofitable areas of health care and have benefited from public sector education and research paid for by taxpayers. One of the key questions to be posed of the NSW health system is: Is the course set by the Greiner Government destined to lead us towards the American model of profit oriented health care with its massive costs and inefficiencies?

The vital statistics of the Department of Health in NSW are as follows: under the Health Administration Act (1982) and the Area Health Services Act (1986) the Department of Health is responsible to the Minister of Health for the administration and delivery of a vast array of health care services to the people of New South Wales. These include the activities of public hospitals, mental health and development disability services, community health services, dental services, regulation of all hospitals (including private hospitals), forensic medicine, drug and alcohol programs, immunisation services, diagnostic and analytical laboratories and ambulance services. The Department is also responsible for the administration of Acts of Parliament relating to pure foods, the sale of therapeutic goods and medicines, sanitation etc. and through ten Professional Boards constituted under the various Acts for the licensing and control of practitioners of medicine, nursing, dentistry, optical services, pharmacy, chiropody, chiropractics and physiotherapy. In addition, the Department's administrative responsibilities encompass ancillary services such as hospital catering, laundry and other cleaning services etc. which are necessary to the provision of public health care.

Employment

As of 30 June 1988, public hospitals and other health care centres employ 74,949 persons of which 32,244 are nursing staff; while ambulance services employ 2,490 people, scientific services employ 283, and 991 are employed in departmental/regional administration.

Administrative Structure

Under the present structure, the administration of New South Wales public health is conducted by the Department through six country regional offices and ten Area Health Services in the metropolitan, Hunter and Illawarra regions where the mass of New South Wales population lives (This precludes some of the major metropolitan public hospitals which are managed by their own boards and have a direct administrative link to the Department). Each Area Health Service has a ministerially appointed board which is responsible for the day-to-day management of health care services in its designated region. Eighty per cent of departmental expenditures are through Area Health Services. With regard to funding allocation, based on annual returns furnished by the Area Health Services and hospitals indicating their financial needs the Department determines their level of subsidies after taking account of the population sizes, service requirements and objectives within a global budgetary framework.

Public Health Care Capacity

In New South Wales the provision of health care services is dominated by the public sector with the only major exception being nursing home care which largely operates on a commercial basis in the private sector. With respect to health care facilities (as at 30 June 1988), there are 232 public hospitals including the largest State hospitals providing general services, compared with 93 general private hospitals (New South Wales Department of Health, Annual Report, 1988). Interestingly, of the private hospitals only 21 are established in country regions compared to 170 public hospital establishments, reflecting the fact that general hospital services are less commercially viable in more sparsely populated areas. Of the twenty mental health and development disability hospitals in New South Wales fifteen are public; while of the 509 nursing homes 489 are private institutions. A more accurate picture of public health care capacity, especially as compared with the private sector, is the number of authorised beds in hospitals and other health related institutions. Table 10.19 below confirms the crucial importance of public health care capacity in the delivery of services other than those related to the accommodation and care of the aged in New South Wales (especially in country regions).

Table 10.19

Number of Authorised Beds in Public and Private Hospitals in New South Wales at 30 June, 1988

	Public No.	%	Private No.	%	Total No.
General Hospitals					
Metropolitan	13,141	74.4	4,512	25.6	17,653
Regional	9,901	88.3	1,308	11.7	11,209
Total	23,042	79.8	5,820	20.2	28,862
Mental Health and Development Disability Hospitals					
Metropolitan	3,265	91.6	299	8.4	3,564
Regional	2,326	100.0	0	0.0	2,326
Total	5,591	95.0	299	5.0	5,890
Nursing Homes					
Metropolitan	1,919	8.8	20,007	91.2	21,926
Regional	2,227	24.4	6,914	75.6	9,141
Total	4,146	12.3	26,921	86.7	31,067

*Note:** This total does not include two public hospitals which do not submit financial returns to the New South Wales Department of Health because they do not receive any State Government subsidy and two hospitals which are supervised by the Department of Veterans' Affairs — constituting 1,028 hospital beds.

Source: New South Wales Department of Health Annual Report, 1988, Appendix B2, p. 98.

Due to an increase in the construction of hospital facilities over the past few years there has been moderate growth in public hospital beds. Nevertheless it has not kept pace with the growth and changing distribution of the New South Wales population. Table 10.20 shows the decline in the overall number of authorised public hospital beds per 1,000 persons over the past four years as well as the low ratio persisting in the Western metropolitan region of Sydney where there has been a large shift in the distribution of the urban population.

These figures reflect the shortage of overall public hospital capacity in New South Wales to meet the rapidly growing demand for public health care (particularly since they tend to over-estimate actual hospital bed capacity). A major factor in this respect has been the large preferential shift from private to public hospital care following the introduction of Medicare which caused a significant reduction in the number of people electing to be privately insured. The Department of Health reported that between June 1983, prior to the introduction of Medicare, and March 1985, the proportion of the New South Wales population privately insured for hospital care had declined from 68% to 49% (New South Wales Department of Health, Annual Report, 1985, p. 1). Partially reflecting the shift from private to public hospital care, the proportion of non-chargeable patients to public hospital bed days occupancy increased from 47.3% in June 1983 to 67.6% in June 1985. The increasing access to public health provided by universal health insurance (Medicare) together with the significant ageing of the population has considerably increased the demand for public health care. These pressures on capacity have been moderated to some extent by the implementation of joint Commonwealth-State funded programs to reduce the average period of inpatient occupancy and so reduce outstanding hospital waiting lists. However, despite these measures

the severe pressures on public hospital capacity have persisted due in no small part to the shortage of nursing and other medical staff which also has contributed to a marked reduction in many kinds of services. In addition, the shortage of hospital facilities in many regions has reduced the effective delivery of health care services. This has been most severe in the Western and South-Western metropolitan regions of Sydney where the range and standard of health care services is well below the State average. *Indeed, a State parliamentary appointed taskforce (consisting of five Liberal-National parliamentarians) reported that hospital facilities in the Western metropolitan region were in a dilapidated State — a consequence of years of neglect. They estimated that $750m additional expenditures would be necessary to adequately upgrade health services in this region.* Given that some regions (eg., Eastern suburbs of Sydney) are relatively over-serviced there is a clear need for restructuring of hospital facilities in New South Wales to more appropriately (and equally) deliver health services to areas of need, in particular in Western Sydney where the mass of urban population is gravitating.

Table 10.20

Number of Authorised Beds per 1,000 Persons in General Hospitals in New South Wales *

	As at 30 June 1984	As at 30 June 1988
Northern Metropolitan	3.32 (1.83)	2.96 (1.73)
Southern Metropolitan	5.50 (1.57)	5.66 (1.57)
Western Metropolitan	3.25 (0.77)	2.83 (0.63)
Hunter Region	4.38 (0.91)	4.16 (0.78)
Illawarra Region	3.27 (0.85)	3.7 (0.85)
All other country regions	5.22 (0.58)	4.63 (0.61)
Total	4.48 (1.04)	4.04 (1.02)

Note: * Private hospital beds per 1,000 persons are in brackets.
Source: New South Wales Department of Health, Annual Reports 1984, 1988.

Financing
The considerable prominence given to the provision of health care services is reflected in the fact that the Department of Health now receives the largest allocation of funds in the New South Wales budget. This allocation consists of three main sources of finance: Commonwealth financial assistance, Department of

Health receipts and State budgetary revenue consisting of consolidated general revenue, Treasury receipts related to health care insurance and Treasury corporation approved borrowings. Table 10.21 provides a breakdown of the various sources of finance for the 1987-88 New South Wales health budget.

Table 10.21

Sources of Finance — 1987/88

	$m	$m	%
Commonwealth Contributions			
Medicare Compensation	444.3		
Hospital Grants	674.0		
Special Purpose Grants	75.2	1,193.5	32.8
Department of Health Receipts:			
Public Hospital Revenue	405.9		
Other	165.4	571.3	15.7
Treasury Receipts:			
Health Levies and Ambulance Insurance Plan Contributions	39.6		
Road Transport and Traffic Fund Ambulance Contribution	0.8		
Consolidated Fund General Revenue	1,691.2		
Treasury Corporation Approved Borrowings	138.2	1,869.8	51.4
Total Cost of Health Services		3,634.6	100.0

Source: Auditor-General of New South Wales (1988), Annual Report, Vol. 2, p. 250.

Commonwealth financial assistance represents a major source of revenue to the New South Wales Department of Health. Under a four year Commonwealth-State funding agreement associated with the introduction of Medicare, this assistance has consisted of an Identified Health Grant (under the States Tax Sharing and Health Grants Act 1981), Medicare compensation (for the loss to State hospitals of private insurance collections) and specific purpose grants encompassing a variety of health service programs. The introduction of this financing arrangement saw Commonwealth financial contributions increase significantly in 1984/85 such that it represented about 41% of the Department of Health expenditures, but has since gradually declined to 33% in 1987/88. At the May 1988 Premiers' Conference these funding arrangements were altered resulting in the discontinuation of the Indentified Health Grant and Medicare payment and the introduction of a specific purpose payment for hospitals. In 1988/89 under this new arrangement Commonwealth contributions are estimated to decline by 3.5% in 1987/88 so that as

a proportion of the total New South Wales health budget they are anticipated to fall below 30%. This gradual decline in Commonwealth assistance over recent years, which is one consequence of the Federal Government's fiscal austerity policy, has placed a greater burden on internal State financing out of consolidated revenues to finance New South Wales health services. *In 1987/88 State contributions to health funding rose by some 40%, including a substantial increase in Department of Health revenues arising from an increase in charges on the provision of services by public hospitals.* Continued fiscal contraction by the Commonwealth means that the expansion of public health care services in New South Wales will be increasingly dependent on New South Wales Government financing.

Key Policy Issues

The socio-economic benefits conferred on the community by public health services are often overlooked possibly because they are for the most part less transparent. The provision of health services by the State public sectors in Australia plays an essential role in Australian social and economic well being, not only by directly raising the quality of people's active lives but also by improving the health of the mass of the working population, thereby reducing days lost at work from sickness etc. and generally improving the physical and mental performance of workers and so contributing indirectly to labour productivity in the economy. Although difficult to quantify the external benefits to the economy of public health services is nevertheless obviously very significant.

In most OECD countries, especially Western European countries, there is a well established universal health care system with the delivery of services predominantly the province of the public sector, the notable exception being the US where health insurance and services are mainly provided by the private sector. In Australia the prominence of the public health system (as administered by State Governments) has been traditionally important in providing affordable health care services to the wider population. The introduction of the Medicare universal health insurance scheme by the Commonwealth Government in 1983 represented an important step in further widening the access to basic health services which, along with education, law and order etc. should be regarded as fundamental goods to which all citizens should have right of access. However, as already indicated, this initiative in conjunction with the implementation of a fiscal austerity program which has seen Commonwealth financial assistance to the States decline markedly over the past few years has placed considerable pressures on public health care capacity. In New South Wales these pressures have been exacerbated by long-term structural inadequacies within its public health system. These key problems afflicting the New South Wales public health system can now be dealt with in terms of the policy strategy of the present conservative Government.

Notwithstanding its overall contractionary strategy the New South Wales Government has given expenditure priority to health. However, much of its budgetary policy in health consists of financing an upgrading not an expansion of hospital facilities and an accompanying range of health care services through the attainment

of substantial cost savings. In accordance with the government's budgetary strategy, the Department of Health, along with the rest of the sector, is aiming to obtain productivity savings of 1.5% in 1988/89 and again in 1989/90. To obtain cost reductions supposedly through more efficient service delivery the New South Wales Department of Health, broadly following the recommendations of Curran et al., has introduced a corporate management approach to administration. It was indicated in Section 10.5.1 that there are considerable limitations to applying corporate management techniques to non-commercial socially oriented areas of the State sector, such as health, where performance can not be simply gauged by balance sheet results and performance criteria must take into account a myriad of qualitative factors. This is not to say that financial monitoring techniques such as program budgeting now used in the Department of Health is not relevant in the decision-making process. The point is that financial performance indicators are not sufficient on their own in making appropriate management decisions where qualitative social objectives are involved. The excessive reliance which the conservative Government places upon corporate management techniques in health administration indicates a greater concern with attaining cost savings per se rather than obtaining improvements in the quality and efficiency of health care service delivery.

The imperative to procure expenditure savings underlies the conservative Government's whole approach in solving the many problems in the New South Wales public health system. The over-riding problem is inadequate size and structure of health care service capacity in New South Wales of which there are a number of aspects. With respect to hospital facilities, the conservative Government's strategy is to fund an upgrading of facilities in areas of need (such as Western Sydney) by the closure of some public hospitals and the sale of surplus property sites. In 1989/90 the Department had earmarked six hospital property sites for sale which were estimated to raise $170m. The sale of unutilised assets is justified within a restructuring strategy, providing the funds raised are used to build facilities in areas in greater need of additional health care services and the process is associated with a net expansion in the capital stock of the whole public hospital system. *The New South Wales Government, however, has indicated that 'emphasis will be placed in future years on replacement and upgrading the existing capital stock, rather than increasing bed capacity' and that 'this policy is based on projections that the number of beds are adequate for future years, taking into account changing patterns of bed usage, a decline in the length of stay for inpatients and a greater role by private hospitals'* (New South Wales Budget Information Paper No. 2, 1988/ 89, p. 223, emphasis added).

The clear intention of this policy is to meet acute (regional) demands for hospital services largely through an expansion of private hospital coverage rather than through an expansion of the public hospital system. To this end the New South Wales Department of Health approved the construction of fourteen new private hospitals and the expansion of eleven existing ones in 1988/89; some on the sites of existing as well as closed public hospitals. This policy has been justified by arguing that it would assist in overcoming waiting lists at public hospitals as if there was no net loss to the public health system. As Professor S. Leeder has countered: '. . . it is not true that private hospitals "won't cost us anything"' because the 'Medicare money spent in private hospitals . . . comes off the Medicare allocation [by the Commonwealth] to New South Wales for public hospitals' (*SMH*, 4/10/88, p. 19). The policy therefore represents an insidious form of privatisation with the growth in private hospital institutions occurring at the expense to the public health system. *No efficiency gains will be made from such a privatisation policy as it will simply lead to an increase in private health costs (and eventually contribute to a rise in the Medicare tax levy) that in all likelihood will exceed the savings made in the New South Wales public health system. This policy portends a long-term reduction in public hospital capacity in relation to demand and hence represents a downgrading in the role of the public health system in New South Wales.*

Another major problem has been the shortage of medical personnel in the New South Wales public hospital system. The most notorious example is the long waiting lists for elective surgery following the withdrawal of ortho-

paedic and opthalmic surgeons from public hospitals in 1984 over a change in fees for service under Medicare. This long running saga revealed the severe shortage of permanently employed specialist surgeons in the public system and the corresponding over-reliance on Visiting Medical Officers (VMOs) who in many cases have a substantial competing interest in private hospital institutions. The agreement by which the New South Wales Minister for Health induced these VMOs back to public hospitals in 1989 cannot be regarded as a permanent solution. In the interests of a stronger public health system the number of permanently staffed medical officers and in particular specialist surgeons needs to be increased so as to minimise the reliance on VMOs who should only be used to overcome short-term demand pressures for services. In view of the prospective increase in demand for elective surgery which will accompany the ageing of the population this would be a sensible policy move.

Nursing staff shortages are also a major problem. These shortages have led to the under utilisation of public hospital capacity over recent years with many hospitals forced to close whole wards at various times because of the lack of nursing staff. The very high staff turnover which is no doubt associated with pay and work conditions (and been the subject of industrial disputation) is significant in this regard. Measures have been adopted in recent years to increase the supply of nurses. These measures are ineffective however if, as reported as recently as early 1989, many public hospitals with acute staff shortages cannot employ the additional nurses required to attain full hospital service capacity because of inadequate funding.

Conclusion
This study has focussed on the key problems in the New South Wales public health system as well as the conservative Government's privatisation oriented strategy to overcome them. *The government's strategy portends a long-term transference of health service provision from the public to private sector and will ultimately lead to higher health costs being borne by the community. It represents a fundamental attack on the public health*

system which is the vanguard of universal health care in New South Wales and for which the community has already demonstrated its strong support. A more responsible strategy which makes better use of its resources rather than divesting them is warranted. The renewal of New South Wales' public health system will require three essential ingredients:

— an overall expansion of public hospital capacity and community health(ie. facilities, better staffing levels and technology) and an accompanying increase in the range of health services to meet the strongly growing demand of the community;

— a restructuring of health care coverage, particularly in the metropolitan region, so as to more adequately distribute services to regions of greatest need (ie. Western Sydney); and

— a substantial increase in the levels of permanently employed medical and nursing staff to ensure fuller utilisation of hospital and other health care facilities.

10.6.3 Electricity Commission (Elcom)

The Electricity Commission of New South Wales (Elcom) was established in 1950 as a result of organisational restructuring which separated generation (production) and distribution functions with regard to electricity supply in New South Wales. Elcom is a statutory authority responsible for the production and supply of bulk electricity to 25 distribution agencies (23 county councils, 1 city council, 1 shire council) and 8 large industrial users (including the SRA); and is also empowered to engage in mining operations (The system of county councils was first established in 1919 and the Sydney County Council in 1935). This structure is unusual in Australia (Queensland has a similar system), in so far as generation is a State responsibility (and in minor part a Commonwealth responsibility, through the joint Commonwealth/New South Wales/Victorian Snowy Mountains Hydro-Electric Authority), and distribution is primarily a Local Government function. Elcom is responsible to the Minister for Minerals and Energy, the Department of Energy being the department of government primarily responsible for elec-

tricity supply policy. The following are some key statistics indicating the scope and significance of Elcom's operations (quantities are approximate).

Production Capacity
Total capacity is 12,100 MW (30/6/88). This is one third of total Australian generating capacity, involving seven major power stations. Coal fired power stations represent 95% of capacity. Additional capacity is available from the Snowy Mountains Scheme (2,500 MW of peak generating capacity) and through interchange with Victoria (typically 500 GWhr p.a.).

Output and Demand
Elcom is the largest electricity producer in Australia (approx. 40% of national output) and generates more than 90% of New South Wales requirements. In 1986-87 annual sales were 40,000 GWhr (1987-88: 43,000 GWhr), maximum New South Wales demand (winter evening peak) was approximately 9,000 MW (1987-88), and highest daily demand was 16783 GWhr. Almost 80% of total electricity output is sold into the Sydney, Newcastle and Wollongong markets.

Employment
Generation and transmission employs 10,350 people and a further 3,000 are employed in Elcom's coal mines. The distribution system (essentially the County Councils) employs 17,470 people.

Coal Supply
Elcom owns three coal mining companies which provide 55% of coal supplied to its power stations (1986-87). A further 21% of coal is supplied under contract by private companies from leases owned by Elcom, and the remainder from privately owned and operated mines.

Income and Expenditure
Income for 1987-88 was $2,376m, deriving from electricity sales ($2,278m), interest ($72m) and miscellaneous items ($26m). Expenditure was $2,355m, giving an operating surplus of $21m. The operating result after contributions, sub-

sidies, loan guarantee fee and dividend was minus $165m.

Distribution
Sales by the 25 distribution agencies (1986-87) were approximately $2,700m p.a., to an estimated 2.3m consumers. Business sales (excluding rural) are 59% of the total. Most of the distribution agencies are relatively small: the four agencies servicing Sydney, Newcastle and Wollongong account for almost 80% of State sales. Business sales into this urban/industrial market are more than 60% of total sales by the four agencies and more than 80% of total State business sales.

Throughout Australia electricity production and transmission is an important publicly owned industry, servicing both final ('domestic') consumers and providing a fundamental energy input to other production sectors ('business' consumers, commercial and industrial) (The electricity industry is publicly owned, or majority publicly owned in most OECD countries, Japan and Spain being notable exceptions and the US industry being 75% privately owned). As such the electricity industry exemplifies an important fact about State public sectors in the Australian Federal system: State sectors contribute to the economy fundamental economic and infrastructural services, particularly in the areas of energy

(including gas), transportation, water supply and waste disposal. *To this extent the State public sectors have a fundamental and quite direct role to play in the restructuring of the Australian economy, which has been consequent upon the problems of external imbalance of the 1980s, and is intended to revitalise Australian industrial and trading performance.*[3] In this regard public sector renewal is a necessary complement to industrial restructuring and revitalisation. With regard to electricity in particular, it accounts for approximately 18% of all public sector inputs to industry (based on 1980-81 input-output data) and is the first, second or third largest public sector input to 57, 22 and 12 industries respectively, of the 108 industries classified in the input-output tables. Electricity is the most significant public sector input to Australian industry – in terms of its total cost, its percentage of total public sector inputs, and the pervasiveness of its role in production (Industries Assistance Commission, 1988, pp. 3-7).

On the other hand, in terms of electricity's proportion of total costs of Australian industry a much less significant role emerges. Of the 57 industries for which electricity is the largest public sector input only two have electricity contributing more than 5% of total costs and only the top eleven have electricity costs in excess of 3% (IAC, 1988, pp. 18-19):

		$m Elect. Input Costs	%Total
1.	Cement	22.2	6.1
2.	Cotton Ginning, etc.	27.0	5.4
3.	Ferrous Metal Ores	49.5	4.8
4.	Basic Iron and Steel	164.4	4.3
5.	Other Basic Chemicals	66.0	3.9
6.	Water, Sewers and Drainage	67.9	3.8
7.	Restaurants, Hotels	128.9	3.6
8.	Non-Ferrous Metal Ores	78.3	3.4
9.	Clay Products, Refract's	21.6	3.4
10.	Veneers and Boards	10.3	3.4
11.	Worsted and Woollen Yarn	6.3	3.4

More recent data for New South Wales (New South Wales Government, 1988, pp. 135-38) indicate that for broad industrial sectors (agriculture, mining, manufacture, etc.), only mining has electricity costs in excess of 2% of the value

of sectoral output, at 3.15%. Coal mining uses approximately two thirds of the New South Wales mining industry's electricity input; but estimates suggest an average electricity input cost for coal of little more than $1.00 per tonne.

A breakdown of electricity costs to manufacturing industries in New South Wales (1984-85) indicates only two sectors with electricity costs as a proportion of turnover greater than 2%: basic metal products (4.33%) and non-metallic mineral products (2.49%) (These two sectors include industries 4 and 1,9 above, respectively). The moral to be drawn from this is that while public sector inputs as a whole are significant components of unit costs in some industries (vide IAC, 1988b, pp. 12-17), it would be a mistake to suppose that any possible restructuring of electricity production, costs and pricing by itself could offer any substantial contribution to the competitiveness of Australian industry. However it should be added that these data do not capture the indirect element of electricity costs (and public sector input costs in general) which are 'embodied' in other inputs to industry.

This is a cautionary tale, indicating that while public industrial inputs as a whole are significant for national economic performance, no satisfactory solutions can be found for Australian external problems by making public sector restructuring the cure-all — however ideologically seductive that may be to some. It almost goes without saying that this does not in any way diminish the importance of technical efficiency and minimising production costs for electricity generation in general and Elcom in particular. In this regard, movements in unit costs and productivity measures do not suggest a poor performance by Elcom or the distribution system in recent years. In the five years to 1987-88 Elcom's 'controllable costs' per unit of output (costs net of depreciation, government charges and contributions, finance charges) were reduced by 22% in real terms, resulting from a real reduction of 5.1% in fuel costs and 33.6% in other costs (Coal accounts for approximately 25% of Elcom's total costs). Total employment also fell, notwithstanding expansion of capacity during the same period. Elcom is of course also going through the same award restructuring process which is occurring throughout the Australian economy (vide Electricity Commission of New South Wales, 1989). With regard to the distribution sector, controllable costs per unit of output (costs net of electricity purchases, depreciation and finance charges) have decreased by 5.6% p.a. since 1985

and employment per unit of output has declined by 4.3% over the same period (New South Wales Government, 1988, pp. 144-48).

It is worth noting that when Curran *et al.* (1988, App. A.1, esp. pp. 6, 9, 21) consider Elcom's costs and productivity, using (unsourced) comparative data, they choose to compare Elcom's performance with the Queensland Electricity Commission (QEC). Indeed, when a favourable productivity comparison between Elcom and the State Electricity Commission of Victoria (SECV) is presented all that Curran et al. can find to say is that Elcom and the SECV have both shown little improvement compared to the QEC. No attempt is made to determine the quantity of private contractor labour employed in the Queensland system, which is certainly relatively much higher than in New South Wales and Victoria. A Federated Engine Drivers' and Firemen's Association response to the Commission of Audit's analysis of Elcom offers a pithy response to this strange oversight with regard to contract labour:

'On this basis of accounting if [Elcom] had a total contractor labour force the Curran Report would no doubt conclude that nobody was responsible for the generation of all power in New South Wales' (FEDFA, 1988, p. 7).

Curran *et al.* are also silent about the fact that this difference might have something to do with the vicious and successful attack on Queensland power workers' wages and working conditions in the infamous SEQEB dispute; but a little further on (p. 23) there is an extraordinary if somewhat coy statement on industrial relations, virtually inviting the New South Wales Government to proceed on similar lines: 'The Queensland experience suggests that long term benefits can justify short term dislocations' (!).

The accompanying Graphs indicate the level and broad structure of electricity prices in New South Wales, as well as Queensland and Victoria — the systems with which New South Wales is most closely comparable. Graph 10.4 maps average prices/kWh for 19 categories of electricity consumers. With regard to domestic consumers (1-4), New South Wales prices compare favourably with the other two States. For industrial consumers (8-19), New South Wales compares favourably with Queensland (except for small industrial consumers), but Victoria betters them both in all industrial categories (except 8). Queensland offers the best prices to commercial consumers (5-7), with Victoria setting extraordinarily high tariffs for low and medium usage. Put briefly, relative to New South Wales the Queensland tariff favours commercial and small industrial relative to large industrial, whereas the Victorian tariff relatively favours industrial as a whole. Relative to both Queensland and Victoria, the New South Wales tariff favours domestic as against business consumers.

Graph 10.4

Average Electricity Prices — NSW, QLD, VIC

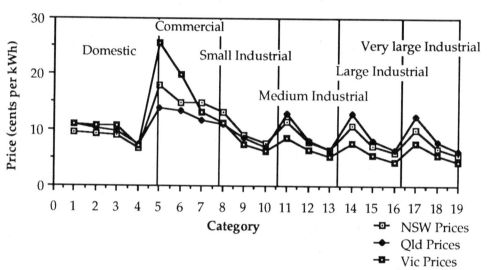

Graph 10.5 renders the scale and structure of the New South Wales tariff, compared with the other two States, somewhat more transparent. If tariff structures were identical overall, or in particular consumer categories, Graph 10.5 would map horizontal lines: the narrower the band of variation, the more similar the tariff structure. Hence comparing New South Wales and Queensland industrial prices, the levels of the former are lower except for small industrial; the structure of the two systems of industrial prices are similar (again, other than for small industrial). The rising curves indicate that the price advantage in moving from low to high usage in each category is less in New South Wales than Queensland. In the small industrial category the v-shaped curve indicates that New South Wales prices are more advantageous in the shift from low to medium usage but this is reversed in the shift from medium to high usage. Comparing New South Wales and Victoria, industrial prices are something of a mirror image of New South Wales versus Queensland. The levels of all Victorian industrial prices are lower than New South Wales. In the case of each industrial category except small industrial, the New South Wales tariff structure is more favourable in the shift from low to medium usage and less favourable in the shift from medium to high usage. In the small industrial category the New South Wales tariff is less advantageous throughout the transition from low to high usage. Tariff levels and structures are most markedly different in the

commercial category, with Victoria in particular, heavily penalising low and medium usage. For domestic consumers the New South Wales and Victorian tariff structure are almost identical except that the Victorian off-peak

tariff is relatively more favourable. The Queensland domestic tariff is more favourable to higher domestic usage, but this is reversed for off-peak use.

Graph 10.5

Average NSW Electricity Prices — % of Vic and Qld Average Prices

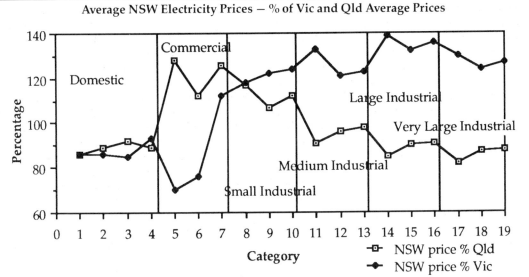

Source: Derived from NSW Government (1988), App. 20

The structure of the New South Wales tariff in relation to other States points to a feature which has received comment for some time: the cross-subsidisation of domestic consumers by business consumers, worth approximately $170m in 1987-89. There is no obvious justification for this practice — and indeed, the extent of cross-subsidy has been and is being reduced. To the extent that business consumers subsidise households, these costs will enter into business costs of production and hence will be forward shifted into business prices. The subsidy is thus akin to an indirect tax on production inputs: while formally it is paid by business, finally it is paid by consumers of all goods and services, in proportion to the electricity intensity of the various business outputs. There is no economic or ethical rationale for such a regime. It is of course necessary to the abolition of such cross-subsidies that Elcom and the distribution agen-

cies have in place adequate accounting structures to enable a correct identification of unit costs to various consumer categories.[4] Furthermore, reform of accounting structures is required for the implementation of any sensible system of rate-of-return (ROR) pricing in Elcom and the distribution agencies (Improvements to the accounting system have been taking place — see Elcom, Annual Report, pp. 36, 64-66). This is so because a rate of return can only be factored into the price system if depreciation and the replacement cost of capital can be accurately identified. New South Wales electricity prices do not look so favourable once differentials in ROR on capital are taken into account (cf. Industries Assistance Commission, 1989, pp. 7-9). Elcom is supposed to be moving towards a system of ROR pricing and appropriate dividend payments on equity, in consultation with State Treasury. (A dividend has been levied since 1986-87. It was $1.5m that year and

$10m in 1987-88. By comparison the very much smaller South Australian electricity authority – with about one fifth of Elcom's production capacity – generated a dividend payment of more than $50m in 1987-88. The SECV, with little more than half the assets of Elcom, paid a $103m dividend in 1987-88).

However, it must be stressed that given the considerable degree of monopoly enjoyed by Elcom, mere ROR pricing with accurate identification of costs will not be satisfactory: within some limits, costs due to inefficiencies etc. easily can be passed on to consumers (Elcom of course does face some competition – in particular, from alternative energy sources and for some 'mobile' business customers from other States). An independent external monitoring of technical and cost performance is essential. The distribution agencies are in the process (begun in July 1987) of adopting fully commercial accounting practices and Australian Accounting Standards, recognized as a necessary prerequisite for effective application of cost performance indicators to the distribution system. In the case of Elcom, monopoly power is the major reason why corporatisation should be avoided.

That the management of Elcom has been less than satisfactory is most strikingly evident from Elcom's extraordinary excess capacity – quoted variously at anything from 25% to 73%, though closer to the former on peak demand – which does not speak well for its investment decision-making and asset management. Related to this, much has been made of Elcom's debt burden by Curran et al., (1988) and others. Elcom itself blames the ill fated resources boom of the early 1980s for this excessive investment but even if this argument is accepted, this begs the question of whether Elcom has been adequate to the task of forecasting demand and planning (new capacity) as well as managing existing capacity).[5] Certainly its reserve capacity is much higher than for any other State (Industries Assistance Commission, 1989, pp. 10-18). Elcom apparently only recently has adopted formal investment appraisal procedures and one can only wonder how capital expenditure decisions were previously made. Its capital expenditure budgets are reviewed by Treasury, which hardly amounts to a vote of

confidence in management (and is, incidentally inconsistent with the government's corporatisation model). Elcom is also seeking to achieve the ongoing objective of funding 50% of capital works from internal funds, on a cumulative basis, by 1990. What these difficulties point to is that if Elcom is to be organized on an essentially commercial basis, as is entirely proper, then the reform of its management systems will be essential (cf. Industries Assistance Commission, 1989, pp. 29-31). This will require a management with the expertise to make investment decisions as economic decisions, not merely technical or engineering decisions, so that the cost of carrying excess capacity is fully taken into account; it will require a management with the economic expertise also adequately to manage assets and debt, including foreign currency exposure, so as to generate an acceptable rate of return on capital, and dividend on (government) equity; and it will require accounting systems which give decision-makers an accurate and pertinent information base for making these decisions (Elcom has been earning a negative real rate of return on capital). Finally, it may be doubted whether such a course can successfully be pursued unless senior management can be effectively made accountable for performance, by way of the 'ultimate' price: dismissal for failure. This is more viable now, in the New South Wales State public sector, than it has been in the past.

The Implications of Privatisation

The consequences of privatisation were thrown into stark relief by proposals put forward in 'Strategy Options for the Future: Overview of the Electricity Development and Fuel Sourcing Plan' (June 1989) which foreshadows further private sector involvement in the power generation industry. Key features of the proposed strategy include:

    – incorporating polices to encourage private investment in power generating plant bases on waste coal and other fuels; and
    – provides for the continued investigation of alternative options for future coal-fired power stations which 'may involve significant private sector participation'

The strategy is supposed to 'provide a sound basis for ensuring that the future needs of the State's electricity users are met reliably and in the most cost efficient way over the next 30 years' (Elcom, 1989, p. 5-6). The inability of this strategy to achieve this goal is evident in a confidential report prepared by a private team of consultants. The press reports of the report are as follows: 'Elcom would be subsidising the private companies, buying electricity from them at much higher prices than it costs the Commission to produce it' (*SMH*, 17 June 1989) It is in this context that the closure of the Tallawarra power station in June 1989 should be viewed; that is existing public sector capacity (which could be modernised) is being closed at the same time as the way is being made clear for private power stations to evolve. The destruction of the public sector's asset base as a consequence of such a strategy can only have negative effects for both economic efficiency and equity in NSW.

The implications of any privatisation of Elcom's functions which does occur (and the Greiner Government is certainly predisposed to such action) are evident from the international experience. The 3,000 electricity supply utilities in the US are predominantly owned by private investors. However, about three hundred of these account for approximately 75% of the electricity produced, and many of these are either subsidiaries of others or linked together in corporate groupings. There is a small publicly or co-operatively owned electricity generation capacity which sits alongside the private utilities (Electrical Power Engineers' Association [EPEA], 1986, pp. 13, 15).

In consideration of the market dominance achieved by a relatively few electricity generation corporations, there is an extensive regulatory system (encompassing both State and Federal Governments) designed to ensure that they do not abuse what is, in effect, monopoly power in the their markets. The power of the regulatory bodies (of which the State Public Utility Commissions (PUC) are the most powerful) is immense:

'. . . the PUC regulates (ie. controls) the price charged for electricity, the capital avail-able to the utility and the cost of that capital (by regulating the issue of stacks and bonds), the return it may earn on its capital and the agreements it may have with other companies. The utilities also have to obtain a Certificate of Need and Convenience prior to any major construction of generating plant or transmission facility, and prior to including the cost of any new plant in their rate-base they must have it declared "used and useful" by their PUC.

In some States there is an additional obligation on the utilities to submit regular advance plans (for up to 20 years ahead) to the PUC, which then rules whether or not the the proposed investments are in the "public interest" ' (EPEA, 1986, pp. 22-23).

One of the major rationales given for privatisation is that it will encourage competition thus leading to greater efficiencies and reduced costs. These efficiencies and cost savings, it is argued, will become evident in the pricing structures of the privatised bodies. *However, it is clear from the US example that private ownership is not necessarily accompanied by competition. This reality is borne out by the British experience of privatisation of the electricity generating capacity: there is nothing in the British Electricity Bill to provide for competition at the point of consumption* (Trade Union Congress, 1989, p. 11).

In addition it should be noted that, while those who advocate privatisation laud the qualities of private sector management, in the privately dominated US example, the fact is that:

'In many States, in spite of their best endeavours, the regulatory Commissions were effectively shadow managing the utilities. In a number of instances, the public interest requirements at the State level has led to the management prerogative passing in a number of key areas from utility to Commission' (EPEA, 1986, p. 27).

This is a clear example of the public sector undertaking those tasks associated with the generation of private sector returns, but which do not themselves generate returns to the public sector. The agenda for reform that we have put forward both in this Chapter and in Part Three provides a significantly more realistic means of resolving the problems that (undeniably) do exist in the New South Wales electricity generating industry than could be achieved by any process of privatisation.

10.6.4 Government Insurance Office (GIO)

The GIO owes its foundation to the Workers Compensation Act 1926, which provided for the first time in New South Wales labour history that employers undertake compulsory insurance for their employees against liability for injury sustained in the workplace. On its enactment many private insurance companies indicated a refusal to cater for the business of workers compensation insurance so the government was under an obligation to provide a vehicle via which employers could obtain such insurance so as to comply with the Act. The objective of the newly created Office was to offer workers' compensation insurance in competition with private insurers and through its operations exert competitive pressures on premium rates charged by private insurance companies. Prior to this initiative the New South Wales State sector had not been involved in commercial insurance activities, though it had conducted inhouse insurance business with respect to its own contingent liabilities since as early as 1891. The activities of the GIO were given legislative authority under the Government Insurance Act, 1927, though its commercial operations were to be restricted to workers compensation insurance and as a legal entity it remained a branch of Treasury. It is worth noting in view of the current discussion about privatisation that in 1933 the then conservative Government of New South Wales sought to effectively privatise the operations of the Office by requesting policy-holders to transfer their insurance business to private insurance companies. While this policy was never given legislative expression it did nevertheless result in a significant loss of business and materially reduced the capacity of the Office to universally maintain low cost workers compensation insurance to policy holders.

It was not until 1942, following a period in which the Office rapidly expanded its activities that amendments were made to the 1927 Act

establishing the GIO as a body corporate with power to carry on the general business of insurance, encompassing any class of commercial insurance activities and any other business activity whether the business of insurance or otherwise.

The Government Insurance (Amendment) Act 1985 conferred upon the GIO full corporate status with authority to have 'a subscribed capital and to pay dividends as provided for in Sections 7B and 7C'. Under Section 7B the GIO has a subscribed capital of $25m: the life insurance business division − $8m; insurance funds administration business division − $1m; and the general insurance business division, $16m. Pursuant to Section 7C,c the GIO pays dividends from these divisions 'as are determined by the Treasurer, after consultation with the Board, and after ensuring that sufficient profits are retained by the Office to maintain adequate solvency margins and to make such other provisions as may be considered necessary or desirable'. As a statutory body the GIO is not subject to Federal Income Tax and is exempted from government charges including Sales Tax and Stamp Duty. In lieu of these exemptions the GIO is required in addition to dividend payments to make a contribution equivalent to income tax payable and such other government charges payable to the New South Wales Treasurer. This source of income to the New South Wales sector is not discretionary (like dividends) though it clearly depends in large part on the profitability of the organisation.

Under its charter (as set out in the 1927 Act) the GIO is essentially regarded as a commercial profit-earning enterprise which should also fulfil a social purpose. The main ongoing social responsibility of the GIO − as directed variously by the New South Wales Government of the day − is to use its market share to exert a stabilising influence on the insurance industry particularly with respect to premium rates and to support State development through its investment activities (GIO Annual Report, 1987/ 88, p. 4). GIO management nevertheless has considerable independence in the conduct of its commercial activities and the pursuit of commercial objectives, though it remains ultimately responsible to, and subject to direction from, the Treasurer.

Structure and Performance

Insurance business conducted by the GIO is divided into three divisions — the Life Division which manages life insurance and related superannuation funds, the Funds Administration Division which manages insurance funds on behalf of the New South Wales Government and any body so directed by government, and the General Insurance Division encompassing the administration of funds for all other classes of commercial insurance operated by the Office. The operation of GIO's insurance funds depends heavily on services provided by other administrative related divisions for which the costs of operation are imputed to these three major insurance divisions. The Investment and Financial Services Division which incorporates retail and corporate funding as well as lending essentially acts as the inhouse banker for GIO's operations. Distribution (ie. retailing) which is an important aspect of GIO's commercial insurance business as well as accounting, personnel, information services and general administrative services come under the auspices of the Corporate Services Division. Overall GIO employs 2,483 people (30/6/88) mostly in the areas of insurance, legal, investment and financial, sales and information systems (GIO Annual Report, 1987/88, p. 64).

The GIO is a valuable income generating asset to the New South Wales sector. It has total assets under management of $116,178m (30/6/88) and in 1987/88 for example it earned total premium income of $1,268m — representing nearly a three-fold increase since 1983/84. In the past five years the GIO has contributed over $270m to New South Wales Consolidated Revenue in the form of dividend and income tax payments. Reflecting the growing profitability of the GIO these yearly contributions have escalated markedly over this period. Table 10.22 provides some important financial statistics relevant to GIO's performance.

General Insurance

General Insurance is the most profitable GIO Division. It conducts virtually all variants of commercial insurance with the main areas of coverage being motor vehicle, household property, small business insurance as well as specialist forms of high risk liability insurance for industry such as the insurance of museums and satellite insurance. The GIO has also a growing presence in the international reinsurance market. In 1987/88 this Division earned profits before tax of $103.6m, paid $14m in dividends and was liable to make income tax contributions of $45.5m.

Life Insurance

This division is also a fully commercial operation providing a range of life insurance and investment linked products. Despite the fact that its operations are confined to New South Wales, the GIO is the fourth largest life insurer in Australia thereby giving it a significant presence in the market. Policies in force as at 30 June 1988 numbered 105,597 with a total insurance value of $4,213m. The Life Division has experienced strong growth over recent years due to GIO's participation in a rapidly expanding life insurance market. Total assets were $2,479m as at 30 June 1988 representing a six-fold increase since 30 June 1984. In 1987/88 it earned net profits of $19.6m, paid dividends of $1m and taxable contributions of $30.6m.

Funds Administration

Although this division earns positive profits and pays dividends (in 1986/87 they were $6.6m and $1m respectively) its operations are not fully dependent on the pursuit of commercial objectives. The main insurance funds for which the division is responsible are the Transport Accident Compensation Fund covering compulsory third-party motor accident insurance, the State Compensation Board's Workcover Fund that services GIO's private sector clients, and the Government Workers Compensation Account that services New South Wales sector employees and various other statutory funds. Pursuant to the 1985 (Amendment) Act the GIO charges the New South Wales Government a management fee for administering these insurance funds on its behalf. In this regard the Funds Administration Division represents the key social function of GIO's operations. Illustrating this social role, in 1986/87 for instance when many private insurers temporarily withdrew from the market because of uncertainty surrounding an alteration in workers compensation liability following the introduction of Workcover, the GIO's strong presence in the market effectively stabilised premium rates. *This role is no more clearly demonstrated than by GIO's management of statutory funds (as required by government legislation) to meet outstanding workers compensation* *claims of failed private insurance companies.* The four workers compensation funds in Table 10.23 (named in each case after the failed insurance companies) have been established by Act for this purpose.

Table 10.22

New South Wales Government Insurance Office Financial Statistics
(As at 30th June)

	1988 $m	1987 $m	1986 $m	1985 $m	1984 $m
Life Division					
Premiums & Unit Trust Subscriptions	725.0	533.6	290.7	168.7	87.8
Life Cover in Force	4,287.3	3,235.0	2,564.4	2,158.4	1,821.9
Life Insurance Fund	2,114.5	1,460.1	871.3	490.7	325.6
Shareholders Capital & Reserves	93.9	75.2	53.7	–	–
Total Assets	2,479.0	1,768.8	1,037.7	650.3	434.9
General Insurance Division					
Premiums & Non Investment Income	497.4	611.4	422.5	384.4	368.8
Profit Before Tax	103.6	107.2	73.4	77.4	62.6
Net Profit	76.8	80.7	70.0	53.1	40.6
Shareholders Capital & Reserves	490.7	428.2	361.7	305.7	252.6
Total Assets	1,829.7	1,691.7	1,258.8	1,009.9	851.5
Funds Administration Division					
Management Fee	45.5	34.5	24.9	–	–
Profit Before Tax	6.6	4.5	3.0	–	–
Net Profit	3.1	2.8	1.8	–	–
Shareholders Capital & Reserves	8.1	5.2	2.6	–	–
Funds Under Management	1,869.3	1,416.7	1,409.9	1.474.5*	1,560.5*
Summary					
Tax Payable to State Treasury	85.2	36.8	13.9	44.0	32.7
Dividends	15.2	14.2	32.2	–	–
Assets Under Management	6,178.0	4,877.2	3,706.4	3,134.7	3,807.9
Total Premium Income	1,267.9	1,179.5	738.1	553.1	456.6

Note: * Assets of Transport Accident Compensation Fund and other Statutory Funds. The assets of these Statutory Funds came under management of Funds Administration Division as from 1st July, 1985.
Source: GIO Annual Report, 1987/88.

GIO and Privatisation

The GIO is a highly successful Australian commercial public enterprise whose operations are certainly not handicapped by any capital funding difficulties. It is therefore an asset which private insurance companies would be desirous of acquiring, especially offshore insurers wishing to obtain a substantial foothold in the domestic insurance market. As one of the participants in the Commission of Audit was reported to have said with respect to the privatisation of State sector assets, 'some of them such as the State Bank, the Government Insurance Office, the Maritime Services Board Coal Loader and the Lotteries Office are packaged with ribbons around them' (*SMH*, 3/8/88, p. 4). Among the recommendations made by Curran *et al.*, (1988, p. 109) was the privatisation of the GIO along with similarly profitable assets. While the notion of privatising the GIO *strongly appeals to the ideological instincts of the conservative Government, the substantial stream of income which could be foregone by its divestment, especially in light of the considerable budgetary pressures now operating, persuaded it on practical grounds to act otherwise. In this regard the privatis-* *ation of GIO (or any other profitable Statutory Authority for that matter) would mean foregoing not only dividend payments but also substantial income in lieu of Federal taxes, which would (in private hands) largely flow to the Commonwealth.*

Table 10.23

New South Wales Government Insurance Office Compensation Funds

Statutory Funds	Cumulative Claims Paid $
Riverina Insurance Company Ltd. and Other Insurance Company Act (Country Traders Mutual Insurance Company Ltd), 1971	712,625
Northumberland Insurance Company Ltd. Act, 1975	788,499
Associated General Contractors, Insurance Company Act, 1980	7,805,957*
Bishopgate Insurance Australia Ltd. Act, 1983	29,295

Note: * Loans advanced to liquidator, Associated General Contractors Insurance Co. Ltd.
Source: GIO Annual Report, 1987/88, pp. 156-163.

This exercise should serve notice to the government of the economic superiority of retaining a valuable income generating asset as against the attainment of a one-off capital windfall. Corporatisation of GIO that is now proceeding suggests that the government has not completely rejected the possibility of future privatisation. GIO management have already indicated their preference for eventual privatisation (*SMH*, 30/1/88, p. 45). This pressure for privatisation should be rejected, both on the basis of financial considerations and also social grounds. It is perhaps not readily appreciated that apart from being a significant source of revenue to the New South Wales sector, the GIO plays an important ongoing social role in the community. We have already seen that the GIO has historically played a crucial role in the establishment of universal workers compensation insurance and the development of third party motor accident insurance. It continued to be a medium by which to discipline private insurance companies from charging excessive premiums in socially oriented areas of insurance and by which the New South Wales

Government can introduce insurance schemes which have an important social objective. As a public enterprise the GIO therefore confers upon the people of New South Wales who are in fact its ultimate shareholders considerable socio-economic benefits.

10.6.6 Privatisation of Human Services in New South Wales: Housing
Introduction
Since 1988 the new philosophy articulated in the Curran Report has been felt not only in NSW commercial enterprises or in the general search for staff cuts and productivity gains, but also in the human services. Three areas which have been noticeably affected are housing, Family and Community Services and non-government organisations.

The latter are important, both because they are flexible and responsive deliverers of human services and because they are very likely to carry the ultimate burden of privatisation in the human services area. Such non-government organisation are funded by annual grants or specific project funding, often with a mixture of Commonwealth and State funds or jointly funded programs. This funding amounted to around $115m in 1987/88. The Curran Report noted that 19 State departments provide this funding. However, the largest funding source is the Community Welfare Fund administered by the Department of Family and Community Services.

Human services in New South Wales have been and continue to be the subject of a wide range of reviews intended to produce changes which fit under the general rubric of 'privatisation'. In particular there have been a number of instances of significant deregulation, a significant increase in user pays in services whose primary function is improvement of equity, the reduction (and in some important cases the elimination) of services in the belief that they are better provided in the private sector, contracting out, asset sales, lease back, shared equity and joint venturing. There has also been a stated policy of transferring funding to services with a higher use of volunteer labour. It should be noted, too, that the trends towards corporatisation and commercialisation in public enterprises have direct parallels in the non-government welfare sector. There are, however, important differences related to the different requirements of effectiveness and accountability in both management and services delivery in the welfare area. A recently released NCOSS discussion paper, 'Shifting the Balance – Public Responsibility and Privatisation in the Community Services Industry', takes up these issues in detail.

Transfer to the Private Sector
On 25 May 1989 the Minister for Housing announced that National Australia Limited had been awarded a mandate to establish a private partnership to construct housing for public tenants. The Partnership will effectively privatise a large part of public housing provision in New South Wales by moving the financing of $2m of rental accommodation for rebatable tenants to the privately run structure over the next five years. Unlike the existing New South Wales Rental Property Trust which depends on tax benefits to investors largely based on depreciation allowances, the new Partnership will be financed by a structure

based on borrowings and a range of new financial instruments offering lenders a AAA return on funds at a guaranteed real rate of interest. However, the return to investors comes from the capital gain realised by the sale of the stock. Because of the average length of public tenancies, all stock will have been sold by the end of twenty years. If the scheme is approved by the Commonwealth, the lower income generated by lower public housing rents will be subsidised by rebates made available through the Commonwealth State Housing Agreement.

A pilot program of 1,000 new units in 1989/90 at a cost of $120m will be undertaken (*AFR*, 25/5/89). New starts by the partnership are planned to rise to 3,000 per year by 1991/92, with a total of about 16,500 new starts over five years. To put this in some perspective, in 1987/88 the New South Wales Department of Housing achieved 3,611 commencements of new units in public housing. The same level of starts was announced for 1988/89. However, nine months into the financial year less than 1,000 units had actually been commenced. Against this should be set the planned sale in 1988/89 of the sites of around 760 planned units in the Sydney metropolitan area and the planned sale to tenants of 400 existing units throughout the State. Compared to this virtual standstill in public housing construction and coupled to the erosion of public stock through sales to tenants, the proposed Partnership clearly constitutes a dramatic privatisation of social housing provision.

The Minister's announcement of the agreement with National Australia Limited, pre-empts the report of the Client Services Review still being conducted by the Department. That review is primarily intended to restructure the direct management of public housing. It is, however, the platform from which the shift to privately financed, constructed and managed social housing has been planned. The pilot construction of 1,000 units was then, in effect, to be stage two of the Client Services Review. The announcement of a five year plan, however, is a dramatic step forward in the process.

In principle there is very little concern over the use of private funds to increase the stock of social housing. Already a substantial amount of public housing construction is financed by State borrowings (forced in part on the States by escalation of the rebate bill for public tenants as a result of reduced cross subsidisation from non-rebated tenants as the proportion of low income tenants has increased – from 56% in 1980-81 to 74% in 1986-87). Proposals also exist to gear public housing to provide much greater access to borrowings. Important innovations in social housing programs such as Community Tenancy Schemes (CTS) and housing co-operatives also use private rental market stock or private funds to provide subsidised local community based housing.

The crucial difference between the three models – public housing financed through borrowings, community housing financed at least partly on the private market, and a privately owned and financed scheme like the National Australia model – lies in the forms of management, pricing structures and decisions about resource allocation.

Public Housing is managed publicly. It also has a degree of tenant participation. It has provided security of tenure, using rents from those tenants whose income increases to cross subsidise rents from low income earners. It has also attempted to develop innovative programs to provide access to target groups such as women, single young people, Aborigines, people from non-English backgrounds and people with disabilities. In New South Wales the Department has also begun to develop a world reputation for design and urban renewal. All of this is about to change. The pricing structure of public housing has, until recently, been based on a cost rent formula (a formula which nonetheless can include interest repayments on borrowings, management and maintenance, and the market cost of the land in different locations). It does not include a component for profit.

Community housing provides far greater tenant participation in management, and hence far greater responsiveness to tenant needs such as maintenance. It is also able to target local populations and create the smallest possible housing dislocation. It, too, is intended to provide security of tenure. It's pricing structure is more vulnerable to market pressures since it often leases from the private

market. But by head leasing a substantial number of properties and providing its own management, it is able to substantially reduce the costs over the private market.

Rental property trusts or other commercial schemes, on the other hand, are managed purely to provide a return to investors. In the case of Trusts, they contract management to private real estate agents, excluding any tenant participation. They guarantee no security of tenure and are not able to target provision to meet low rental or special needs.

The National Australia scheme is presently different in an important respect. Rather than managing privately it will contract management and construction to the Housing Department (a somewhat ironical reversal of contracting out). This concession was only secured in order to gain access to Commonwealth subsidies. Security of tenure is also guaranteed, although the public utility of the stock is only secured for one, rather than sequential, tenancies. This raises the question of the cost effectiveness of the public subsidy (part of which goes to subsidise returns to lenders). In terms of tenant years of occupancy, it appears that the use of subsidy for direct construction would have produced greater public benefit.

The more difficult task of targeting specific areas of need will be left with the public housing sector. Even with the addition of public subsidies, the Partnership's pricing structure will be determined entirely by the private rental market. One effect of this is that, unless the public housing sector makes savings by reducing management and maintenance costs and by excluding the more expensive target groups such as people with disabilities, the cost of the rental rebate bill borne by the State and Commonwealth will increase to subsidise private profits.

Public Housing Sales Policy

The New South Wales Government has embarked on a program of sales, both of housing stock and of land, which it hopes will change the emphasis of the Department from construction to sales. This approach is underpinned by a policy often stated by both the Premier and the Minister to place the greatest emphasis on self reliance through home ownership.

In the 1987-88 Budget asset sales of public housing sites or of existing dwellings was estimated to raise $80m, with the possibility of increasing this figure as more potential asset sales are identified. One major effect of this policy has been to reduce the availability of housing stock in the inner city where infrastructure already exists, with the intention of replacing it in currently unserviced areas. Given the renewed emphasis on urban consolidation this policy is, at the least, contradictory.

The economic effectiveness of some sales must also be questioned with some tendering arrangements apparently ignoring higher bids, and with proposed asset sales including sites with facilities such as shopping centres which produce a very good income stream. In terms of overall government policy some housing department profits realised through asset sales must be seriously questioned. In particular, the site of the old Crown Street Women's hospital was sold to the Housing Department by the Health Department at well below market rates because of its intended use for public housing. The windfall profit of its current sale has therefore at least partly been at the expense of another government department.

Sales to Tenants

The New South Wales Housing Department has launched a major publicity campaign to induce public tenants to either buy their existing dwellings or to purchase other accommodation at substantially discounted rates. A number of financing options have been made available. As well as Affordable Home Loans and Premier Low Start Loans, the Ready to Buy program offers public tenants simplified contracts, and discounted mortgage interest rates (12.9% rather than 13.5%) which are exempted from stamp duty. Under a generalised Homefront program other options such as the purchase of part equity in public housing are being offered to tenants. The expected level of sales in 1988-89 is around 400. However the 1988-89 budget increased funding from $100m to $440m, $65m of which was to be allocated to the Ready to Buy program with the aim of enabling 1,000 public tenants to purchase their homes.

Commercialisation

Under the new government an explicit change in the emphasis has taken place. Construction has been reduced – with the elimination of a significant number of jobs in the production department – while land sales and joint ventures have substantially increased.

Joint ventures, of course, may provide a cost effective way of increasing both public and private rental accommodation. A typical model would be for the Department to provide the land while the joint venturer would construct the dwellings, with 50% being allocated to the Department for public housing. What is lost under this arrangement is the considerable expertise developed by the New South Wales Housing Department in the area of urban renewal and consolidation and innovative urban housing construction. It is probably no exaggeration to suggest that over recent years, the New South Wales Department has become a world leader in this field. Certainly no such expertise exists in the private sector.

In April 1989, the Department eliminated 102 positions (34 currently filled) from its production staff in a departmental restructure. The restructure has reduced the number of production teams from seven to five, a number of which already work exclusively on the preparation of land sales. Twenty of the positions lost filled by professional and technical officers (planners, architects and officers responsible for designs, overseeing planning submissions and supervision of contractors) will not be redeployed within the Department. It has been suggested that some technical staff may be redeployed as consultants.

The new emphasis on land sales is on line with a shift to more commercial areas of activity and to providing services mainly directed towards home purchase. The land acquisition and development program received a 68% boost in the 1988-89 budget with an increase from $49.5m to $83m.

Contracting Out and Client Services

The Housing Department has always made considerable use of contractors, both in construction and maintenance. However, it has maintained direct management of such areas and of basic client services such as rent collection. The current Client Services Review is set to change all that.

Although it has not yet reported, its initial recommendation is believed to be a transfer of all rent collection from Department offices to automatic collections through the banking system. The effects of such a change are not expected to be felt solely in rent collection. Since rent payment is the main point of contact between tenants and the Department, it is also the point at which maintenance requests are made. It is anticipated that the change to rent collection will also significantly reduce the extent of maintenance.

Combined with the initial impact of the Public Housing Rental Trust, the reduction of client services is expected to cut positions within the Department and is expected to accelerate once the Trust is beyond the pilot stage.

The Client Services Review was initiated, not simply to save costs, but to change the balance of the Department's functions. It is believed that the balance between services to existing tenants and to new applicants is inappropriately weighed in favour of existing tenants. Beyond this, it is argued that the Department should place more emphasis on the administration of programs such as the Mortgage and rent Relief Scheme which is designed to keep people in home ownership or the private market, than in servicing public tenants. Perhaps the clearest indication of this is the new official requirement to describe public housing as 'welfare housing'.

Increased User Pays
Pricing policy for public housing rents has never been straightforward. The Commonwealth State Housing Agreement (CSHA) has established a fairly comprehensive cost rent formula which includes management and maintenance costs as well as the cost of the property. In fact the States' discretion about how the components of the formula are calculated means that it is possible for cost rents and average market rents to be similar. Nonetheless, the cost rent model does provide a basis for State Governments to charge rents which are both more affordable to tenants, are not market driven (particularly in a period of volatile rent increases) and can act as a brake on

the private market.

However, the CSHA simply requires that *at least* the cost rent formula be charged. Some States, including New South Wales, have moved to a policy of charging market rents. The crucial point about market rents is that the notion is hard to measure in a practical sense. First, since there is no market in public housing accommodation, it is impossible to say what the market would determine. Comparisons are also impossible since the public housing estates are unique forms of housing and often the major development in a given region.

More importantly, the market rents policy means that rents are based on a periodical review of market rents. Since the only available data are the Real Estate Institute Rent Survey and Rental Bond Board data these become the benchmark for rent increases. However, they only measure rents for new tenancies. These are always considerably higher than actual rents for sitting tenants. Consequently, they do not represent the actual rents being charged. Instead of public being a brake on private rents, a market rents policy makes them market leaders.

New South Wales has just completed a market rent review with resulting rent increases of 30% or more. At least part of the explicit intention of this review is to encourage non-rebated tenants to move back into the private market or to take up home purchase assistance under the Ready to Buy program.

However, a second, and as yet uncompleted part of the government's review of public housing rents is equally significant. New South Wales public housing tenants receive a rebate which ensures that the amount of rent paid does not exceed 20% of income (and 18% in the case of pensioners). The current review is investigating a new scale which will increase these levels – possibly with a sliding scale from 20% to 27% of income. This alone would represent a rent increase of 35%, but the review is also examining which household members should be included in the calculation of the rent. Previously the household rent was increased by a flat $5 a head for each additional household member other than the lessee. Under the previous government this was changed so that all other adults paid 20% of income (like the lessee) and children aged 18 to 25 paid 10% of income. The Commonwealth also included 15% of the Family Allowance Supplement. The current review is considering increasing the contributions from other members by including income from those under 18 and including the full family income in the determination of whether the rent is calculated at the top of the sliding scale or lower down.

It is important to note that this arrangement treats public tenants quite differently from private tenants. Two very important considerations are whether it is appropriate to include the income of young people in the calculation of rents and the extent to which expanding the income base will mean that households are drawn closer to the full 'market' rent for the dwelling.

Deregulation

The Greiner Government has not only placed greater emphasis on the private market, it has also moved to deregulate that market. Five recent changes to legislation have had this effect or are currently being considered – the amendments to the Residential Tenancies Act 1987 (enactment of which was delayed by the new government); the amendments to the State Environmental Planning Policy No. 10 (SEPP 10) of the Environment Planning and Assessment Act 1979; an inquiry is being conducted in to Section 94 of the same Act; a similar inquiry is due to report on 'anomalies' in the Landlord and Tenant (Amendment) Act 1948 which concerns protected tenancies; and finally, changes to planning regulations which have reduced Local Government controls over a range of developments.

The amendments to the Residential Tenancies Act 1987 had the effect of increasing landlords' powers to enter properties and evict tenants while further reducing tenants' protections already watered down by the previous Labor Government. The inquiry into protected tenancies follows recommendations by the Government's Inquiry Inner City Homelessness, chaired by Max Raine of Raine & Horne Real Estate, that such protection be immediately removed. Changes to SEPP 10 and Section 94 weaken measures designed to slow the loss of boarding house stock or other low

income rental accommodation.

Community Tenants Advice

Just as deregulation has removed protection for private renters, particularly at the bottom of the market, so too has the removal of funding for the State's non-government Tenant's Advice and Housing Referral Services (TAHRS). In 1989 these services responded to 50,000 requests. They provided not only independent advice, but also representation and advocacy on behalf of tenants in dealings with landlords or agents.

As the services were funded from interest money from New South Wales Rental Bond Board, the cuts did not represent any saving to the Housing Department budget. However, it did represent considerable gains to the profitable operation of the private rental market. It has also meant an increase in cost in other areas as Local Government and neighbourhood centres as well as some church organisations (such as the Uniting Church Board of Social Responsibility) have attempted to replace some of the services. The 70 retrenched TAHRS workers have been replaced by four new department positions and one existing officer in each regional centre who will be trained to take on the purely informational aspects of this work as well as an additional duty.

Community Housing

Community Tenancy Schemes (CTS) were designed to proved a 'fourth tenure' which could increase the stock of low cost rental accommodation without putting extra strains on the public housing system, but offering comparable security and enhanced tenant access and control.

This year the 62 CTS in New South Wales (housing 7,000 tenants) were given a March 31 deadline to accept a radical restructure of the program or loose funding. The restructure made four important changes. It increased rents from 20% of income to 25%. CTS tenants have lower average income than other housing department tenants. It made the scheme a medium term accommodation program. Tenants will be annually reviewed for eligibility to remain. The intention is to encourage a return to the private market as soon as they are financially able. Existing Housing Department capital stock will be handed back to the Department (it is unclear what will happen to the current tenants) leaving almost all stock to be leased from the private rental market. Finally, the management load is to greatly increase, but with a dramatic reduction in tenant participation and facilities such as interpreter services. With no increase in management hours (in fact with a cut in 18 of the largest schemes, the number of households managed will increase from 2,257 to 3,148. Management workloads will increase from 2,257 to 3,248. Management workloads will increase between 43% and 82%.

Not only does this change the nature of the scheme to a temporary respite from the private market, rather than an innovative use of mixed public and private resources to provide a secure alternative to the private market, but it also is a particularly blatant example of the increased exploitation which governments can enforce when they devolve service to the community sector. Of course this is not necessary. The motivation for such devolution can be the provision of more responsive and effective services. In this case that objective has given way to cost cutting and exploitation.

10.7 Conclusion

This chapter has covered a considerable range of economic and social issues pertaining to the New South Wales State public sector under the management of a conservative government. Indeed the complexity of these issues has been increased by the frightening pace with which the Greiner Government is pursuing privatisation. In the process, the coherence and quality of the public sector is being broken down, as the principles of social justice are abandoned and economic services are being reduced. This is a model of public sector activity of a bygone era, not one capable of undertaking socially equitable, structural adjustment in an industrialised economy.

This chapter has often had cause to comment on the ideological intent of the conservative government, together with the broader national economic problems of external imbalance and economic restructuring. In con-

sequence, the role of the public sector has never been more subject to question. From this point of view the role of the New South Wales State public sector is at a crossroad. On the one hand it may head down the conservative path, whereby activities capable of profitability are removed into the hands of private capital; and even the remaining tax funded and unprofitable social and welfare services are straitened in the name of low taxes – or shifted as much as possible onto a user pays basis, thereby eliminating redistributive mechanisms. On the other hand the State public sector may take the path indicated by the renewal model: a rationalised tax system providing a secure basis for appropriately funded services; and the great majority of trading enterprises, and some other appropriately user-charge financed activities, organised on commercial lines, providing effective services, and generating net non-tax revenues for application in a progressive manner to free or subsidised services.

This model offers the best prospect for a New South Wales State public sector which will serve the interests of ordinary wage and salary earners, as well as the poor and welfare dependent, and at the same time enhance the life of the community in a multitude of ways which would be impossible in the absence of a vigorous and expanding public sector.

Notes

1 Analogies between societies and households, however beguiling, are notoriously misleading in economics. Nevertheless the state debt issue here may be compared with a common household debt issue: the fact that debt-financed purchase of a house for owner-occupation does not in general generate pecuniary returns which cover debt costs does *not* mean that it is in general economically irrational for a household to undertake such transactions. The same applies to the New South Wales Government.

2 Consultants to the State Government, Booz Allen Hamilton Inc., reported that 'the SRA's accounting system was the worst [railway accounting system] they had seen, including that of mainland China' (*Sydney Morning Herald*, 5-3-89, p. 2; hereafter cited as *SMH*).

3 As indicated above, other parts of the State sector – eg., education and health – also provide an 'investment in New South Wale's economic future, albeit less direct, less obvious, and in some cases less tangible'.

4   The abolition of the winter surcharge by the Conservative Government also amounts to an unwarranted subsidisation of peak domestic demand. (There are also regional cross-subsidies between urban and rural areas (favouring the latter) and within rural areas. These may well have an equity justification. There are also a range of (now) rather minor Community Service Obligations in electricity supply (New South Wales Government, 1988, pp. 105, 116). See also Industries Assistance Commission (1989, Apps. G and H), for a more detailed discussion of pricing policy.

5   The extension of interconnection between the state systems also has potential to reduce the margin of excess capacity required to satisfy seasonal and daily demand variations (*vide* Industries Assistance Commission, 1989, pp. 13, 31-32, App. E). Interconnection currently exists between New South Wales and Victoria, and will be extended to South Australia in 1990. It should be said that excess capacity is a particular problem for electricity producers, because the product cannot be stored.

Chapter 11

VICTORIA

11.1 Introduction

This chapter has three primary objectives, first, to reinforce some of the arguments made in Parts Two, Three and Four, by providing examples and evidence drawn from experience and circumstances in the State of Victoria; second, to review and appraise Victorian Government policies relating to the provision of State public services; and third, to consider the adequacy of Victoria's sources of finance available for the task of supporting renewal and development of State public services in the light of emerging demands.

11.2 Demography and Economy
11.2.1 Demography

Victoria is Australia's second most populous State. In 1988, the State's population numbered 4.2 million, which represents 25.9% of Australia's population. Over 70% of the population currently resides in Melbourne (Australian Year Books).

Since 1945, Victoria's population growth has gone through two distinct phases. The 1950s and 60s were years of quite rapid population increase, with the annual rate of increase in the 1950s exceeding that for Australia as a whole (2.5% cf. 2.1%). During the 1970s and 80s, however, Victoria's population growth slowed considerably to 1.1% from the 2% p.a. of the 1960s (Australian Year Books, various years).

The slowing of Victoria's population growth in the 1970s and 80s reflects declining birth rates, a slowdown in international migration, and large annual net outward migration to other States, particularly during the mid to late 1970s. One consequence of the decline in population growth is the ageing of Victoria's population structure over the last 10 years, a trend that is projected to continue into the 1990s and beyond (Ministry of Planning and Environment, 1988). This ageing of the population structure is particularly evident in Melbourne, where the number of people aged 65 and over is projected to increase from 302,700 in 1986 to 424,400 by 2001 (Victorian Ministry of Planning and Environment, 1988). As a consequence, the next two decades are likely to witness increasing demands on the State and Commonwealth Government to provide services required by the aged, especially those relating to medical and housing services.

The other demographic factor which will place an increasing burden on State Government resources during the next twenty years is the changing family and household structure. The most rapidly growing household and family types are single person households (often headed by an elderly person) and single parent families. The socio-economic characteristics of both household types suggests an increased demand for State public services, particularly in the areas of social and community services, labour market training schemes, public housing and health programs.

Melbourne's population in aggregate is projected to increase by 14.8% between 1986 and 2001, and household growth is projected to grow by 1.1%, or, in absolute terms, by 248,100 households (see Table 11.1). The demand for new housing and associated necessary residential infrastructure will therefore be substantial. With most of the land available in Melbourne's eastern corridor having been exhausted, much of this growth is likely to be channelled into two main corridors: the first in the south east of Melbourne (the Pakenham-Cranbourne Corridor), the other in the north west (the Plenty Corridor).

Table 11.1

Population Projections by Region
Melbourne 1981-2001

| | Year: | | | | Change 1981-2001: | |
	1981	1986	1996	2001	No.	%
Central	245400	234000	226700	215600	−29,800	−12.1%
Inner	628800	605800	588400	559300	−69,500	−11.1%
Middle	711200	708300	696400	660500	−50,700	−7.1%
Outer	824200	880300	937200	955000	130,800	15.9%
Fringe	396500	503500	644200	965300	568,800	143.4%
MSD Total	2806100	2931900	3093100	3356200	550,100	19.6%

Note: 1981 and 1986 are actual, the remainder are projections.
Source: Victorian Ministry of Planning and Environment, 1988.

The continuation of the suburbanisation process during the next two decades will place a considerable burden on State finances for two main reasons. First, with fewer people living in the inner and middle rings, existing public sector services in those localities will experience declining levels of utilisation. Second, and relatedly, a dramatic increase in the number of people living in the outer and fringe rings will require substantial capital expenditure to establish the infrastructure required in new residential areas. Sewerage, schools, public transport, day care centres, and roads will all have to be provided, particularly in the Plenty corridor, which at the moment consists basically of undeveloped greenfield sites. It is estimated that every household which moves to the suburban fringes rather than established urban areas produces a net infrastructure cost of approximately $29,000 (Victorian Government, 1987, p. 8). On the basis of the infrastructure costs associated with the development of previous corridors it is likely that the provision of infrastructure in the Plenty corridor will cost in the order of $1.6 to $2b, about half of which may have to be borne by the State Government.

11.2.2 Economy

In contrast to Queensland, Western Australia and Tasmania, the Victorian economy has long been characterised by a diversified industrial base in which the manufacturing sector has played a central role (Berry, 1984; Head, 1986). The diversified nature of the Victorian economy today is reflected in Table 11.2, which pro-vides data on employed persons by industry for Melbourne, the Rest of Victoria (ROS) and Australia in August 1988. The table demonstrates the importance of the manufacturing sector to the Victorian economy relative to the Australian economy as a whole. Whereas manufacturing employment accounts for 16.4% of employment throughout Australia, it accounts for 20.4% of employment in Victoria. Table 11.2 also shows considerable spatial concentration, with almost 80% of manufacturing employment being located in Melbourne.

The structure, conduct and performance of the manufacturing sector today is very much a legacy of public industry development policies. Of particular importance in this regard are, first, the high levels of protection for manufacturing which have been put in place and extended throughout most of this century; and second, the attempts by successive post-war conservative State and Federal Governments to encourage foreign manufacturing capital to invest in Victoria (Berry, 1984; Galligan, 1986; Ewer, Higgins & Stevens, 1987).

These strategies have resulted in the foreign ownership and control over one-third of Victorian manufacturing employment and value-added, and almost 50% of manufacturing fixed capital expenditure (ABS, Foreign Ownership and Control in Australian Manufacturing Industry, Cat. No. 5322.0). In addition, they served to guarantee the overseas firms concerned a high rate of profit whilst shielding them from any public or market pressures necessary to induce high levels of productive efficiency, investment and research and development (R & D) (Ewer *et al.*, 1987). The consequent low levels of Research and Development, the failure to update capital stock, the repatriation of profits and the lack of an export orientation which resulted are well documented (Ewer *et al.*,1987; Smith, 1986).

Table 11.2

Employed Persons by Industry Victoria and Australia
August 1988

	Melbourne		ROS		Victoria		Australia	
	No. ('000)	%	No. ('000)	%	No. ('000)	%	No. ('000)	%
Agriculture, Mining, etc.	12.5	1	88.4	17	100.8	5	527.7	7
Manufacturing	323.0	23	85.7	17	408.7	21	1199.4	16
Construction	97.9	7	34.6	17	132.5	7	526.4	7
Wholesale & Retail Trade	287.1	20	95.3	18	382.5	20	1496.1	20
Transport & Communication	72.1	5	18.0	4	90.1	5	376.7	5
Fin., Property & Bus. Services	181.4	13	6.6	7	215.4	11	801.1	11
Community Services	249.4	18	90.6	17	340.0	18	1304.9	18
Recreation	78.6	6	32.5	6	111.0	6	528.3	7
Other	112.9	8	42.0	8	154.5	8	569.6	8
Total	1414.9	100	520.6	100	1935.5	100	7330.2	100

Source: ABS The Labour Force, Cat. No. 6201.2.

During the 1950s and 60s, growth in Australian demand for Victorian manufacturing goods provided the foundation for relatively high rates of Victorian economic growth. However, the failure of manufacturing firms to undertake sustained levels of investment and R & D during the latter part of the 'long boom' found their expression during the late 1960s and 1970s in a declining ability to compete with cheap overseas imports and to tap export markets. Thus, between 1970 and 1980 employment in the Victorian manufacturing sector fell by 11%, from 446,000 to 397,000 (ABS Cat. No. 6201.2). In broader, spatial terms, the engine of Australian economic growth shifted from manufacturing to mining, and consequently away from the South-eastern States like Victoria to resource rich Queensland and Western Australia (Head, 1986; Stilwell, 1980).

The economic problems experienced by Victoria during the 1970s intensified during the early 1980s with global and national economic recessions exacerbating the decline in Victorian manufacturing employment. Between 1980 and 1984 manufacturing employment in Victoria declined by a further 11%, from 397,000 to 353,000 (ABS Cat. No. 6102.2). So severe was the economic contraction that Victoria's Gross State Product (GSP) declined in real terms in 1981/2 and 1982/3 (by 0.2% and 1% respectively).

Table 11.3 provides data showing the percentage change in Gross Domestic Product (GDP) for Victoria and Australia between 1977/8 and 1987/8. The Table indicates the resurgence which has occurred in the Victorian economy during the last five years. After experiencing rates of economic growth lower than for Australia as a whole between 1977/78 and 1982/3, Victoria has, over the last five years, consistently been one of Australia's fastest growing States.

The dramatic improvement in Victoria's economic growth rate has been accompanied by similar trends in private business investment. Between 1972/3 and 1982/3 the average annual growth in private business investment in Victoria averaged only 0.3%, a rate some 1.8

percentage points lower than that experienced by the rest of the Australian economy. Since 1982/3, however, the average annual increase in Victorian private business investment has been 7.9%, a rate of growth 3.4 pecentage points higher than that experienced by Australia as a whole (4.5%) (Department of Management and Budget, unpublished data).

Table 11.3

Gross Domestic Product Victoria & Australia
1977/8-1987/8
% Change
(Constant 1984/5 prices)

Year	Victoria		Australia	
	NFGSP*	GSP**	NFGDP*	GDP**
1978/79	3.3%	3.6%	3.9%	4.8%
1979/80	1.9%	1.4%	2.7%	1.9%
1980/81	3.3%	3.2%	4.0%	3.3%
1981/82	-0.1%	-0.3%	1.2%	1.8%
1982/83	-0.2%	-1.0%	-0.3%	-1.2%
1983/84	3.9%	5.4%	3.5%	4.9%
1984/85	5.6%	4.9%	5.1%	4.9%
1985/86	5.1%	5.0%	4.9%	4.6%
1986/87	3.3%	3.7%	2.5%	2.7%
1987/88	4.0%	3.5%	3.8%	3.6%

Notes: * Non Farm Gross State/Domestic Product.
                ** Gross State/Domestic Product.
Source: Victorian data: Department of Management and Budget; Australian data: Commonwealth Government Budget Paper No. 1, 1988, p. 11.

These relatively high rates of economic growth in conjunction with a relatively slow rate of population increase have resulted in Victoria experiencing for 69 consecutive months the lowest unemployment rate in Australia. In August 1988 the Victorian unemployment rate of 5.6% was more than one percentage point lower than Australian unemployment rate of 6.8% (ABS Cat. Nos 1303.0, 1303.2).

Employment growth in Victoria accounted for 24% of employment growth in Australia between August 1983 and August 1988. Over 25% of Australia's employment growth in manufacturing, construction and community services, and almost 33% of employment growth in finance, property and business services occurred in Victoria. Reflecting the deregulation of the Australian financial system, the sector which enjoyed the fastest rate of job growth in Victoria was finance, property and business services which increased its employment by 46%, a rate much higher than that experienced by Australia as a whole (39.4%) (ABS Cat. Nos 6201.0 and 6201.2).

Evidence of the turnaround in the growth of the Victorian economy over the last five years can be found in Table 11.4, which provides data on household income per head of mean population for all States expressed as a ratio of the Australian total. A relative improvement in household income for each individual State is indicated by an increase in the ratio, while a relative decline is indicated by a decrease in the ratio. Table 11.4 shows that between 1977/8 and 1981/2 Victoria experienced a decline in its household income per head relative to the rest of Australia, but since that time the opposite has occurred.

11.2.3 The Victorian Economy: Problems and Prospects

During the 1970s, Victoria's relatively large manufacturing sector was seen by some commentators as the State's main economic liability. With an increasing proportion of manufacturing production shifting to low paid developing countries, it was considered that, in the absence of larger and larger protective trade barriers, the future of manufacturing in Victoria, and, accordingly, of the Victorian economy itself, was bleak (see for example Stilwell, 1980; Berry, 1984).

Table 11.4

Household Income per Head of Mean Population
(Expressed as a Ratio of Australian Total by State)
1977/8 − 1986/7

Financial Year	NSW	Vic.	Qld	SA	WA	Tas.	Aust.
1978	103.1	103.0	91.8	94.2	96.7	90.9	100.0
1980	105.0	101.4	91.4	93.8	94.6	91.1	100.0
1982	105.8	101.5	92.5	90.3	95.0	87.9	100.0
1984	103.5	104.2	91.1	96.9	92.8	87.9	100.0
1986	103.8	104.5	88.3	95.7	96.0	90.1	100.0
1987	104.1	105.9	87.5	94.4	93.9	90.3	100.0

Source: ABS Australian National Accounts, States and Territories, Cat. No. 5502.0.

However, during the mid to late 1980s, the dramatic devaluation of the Australian dollar, low levels of industrial disputation and moderate wage growth have combined to convince many commentators that Victoria's diversified industrial base is in fact a valuable asset. Australian manufacturing industry has improved its international price competitiveness, and the opportunity has emerged for the creation and expansion of an internationally viable, export-oriented manufacturing sector. Given the dramatic changes which have taken place in manufacturing production during the last decade, with computer assisted manufacturing systems, robotics, and new inventory systems it is now possible for firms to compete internationally despite the absence of a large domestic market.

While the absence of current, detailed data makes it difficult to be precise, there are signs that during the last four years, Victorian manufacturers have begun to take up the export challenge, and this in turn has had a significant influence on Victoria's economic performance. While Victorian export volumes increased in real terms by 30% between 1984/5 and 1987/8, manufacturing export volumes increased by a massive 52.9%. Both these increases are significantly higher than those recorded by the rest of Australia (19.8% and 19.2% respectively) (Victorian Government, Trading on Achievement, VGPS, Melbourne, 1988). Reflecting these trends, manufacturing exports have over the last five years come to account for an increasing proportion of total Victorian export volumes, increasing from 23% of total exports in 1984/5 to 28% by 1987/8 (ABS Cat. No. 1301.2).

This is not to suggest, however, that Victoria's new found international price competitiveness in manufacturing will translate into a prolonged period of economic prosperity. Clearly, the long term viability of the Victorian manufacturing sector will depend on the degree to which Victorian firms can successfully enter and maintain a significant presence in the fastest growing segment of world merchandise trade, namely, high value added, elaborately transformed manufactured goods. In this market, international competitiveness is affected by a variety of factors, only one of which is price. Those other factors are summarised in Figure 11.1

In Australia over the last five years, most academic and media attention has focussed on the environment within which firms operate rather than the latter set of factors. And within this category, most attention has focussed on the level of taxes and wages. However, as both DITR (1986) and Ewer *et al*. (1987) make clear, these environmental factors are the least important of the constraints facing the establishment of an internationally viable manufacturing sector in Australia.

A far more important 'environmental' constraint on Victorian manufacturing industry is the variety of deficiencies in the Australian capital market which have limited the supply of venture and development capital to small to medium sized, entrepreneurial companies (in the form of equity and debt capital) necessary to finance the production of new, high value added manufactured goods (see for example Esprie Committee, 1983; Valentine, 1984; Ewer *et al.*, 1987). Ewer *et al.* (1987, p. 91) suggest that

the three main weaknesses in capital markets involve a shortage of venture capital, a limited supply of long term debt capital, and a shortage of specific forms of development capital such as export pre-shipment finance. The Victorian Government's attempt to deal with the problem of a shortage of venture capital is outlined in Section 11.8.

Figure 11.1

Factors Affecting 'Dynamic' International Competitiveness

1. The Environment Within Which Firms Compete

a) private   *b)* public

i) wages   *i)* taxes and charges
ii) nature of firms with   *ii)* public and
which input/output   social infrastructure
relationships exist
iii) availability of   *iii)* industry policy
seed and development
capital
iv) structure of market   *iv)* fiscal and monetary
within which firm exists   policy

2. Management Practices: the Ability of Firms to Compete

Management interest and concern with:
i) quality control
ii) marketing
iii) after sales service
iv) co-operative labour relations
v) quality and quantity of
past and present investment
decisions
vi) strategy planning
Source: Adapted from DITR (1986).

Deficiencies in the capital market notwithstanding, DITR (1986) argues that the main impediment to the establishment of an internationally viable manufacturing sector are the management practices which affect a firms ability to compete. Of particular importance in this regard is the failure of managers to give due regard to quality control, marketing, R & D, investment in new plant and equipment, after sales service, and modern co-operative, participative forms of labour relations, all of which are of vital importance to successful penetration of world trade in elaborately transformed manufactured goods (DITR, 1986, Ch. 6).

The foregoing discussion should not be interpreted to mean that the quality of management is merely a matter of individual choice and voluntarism. As Ewer *et al.* (1987) point out, poor management has as its source deficient economic, cultural and political institutions which reward, rather than discourage, bad management, and which impede, rather than encourage, export orientation.

A particularly important institutional impediment on the ability of Victorian firms to compete internationally is the very structure of the Victorian manufacturing sector. The problem here is twofold. First, the high levels of foreign ownership and control in manufacturing reduces the prospects of R & D expenditure so necessary to the development of new, high valued added manufactured goods capable of penetrating international markets. This is because, in the absence of well targeted assistance and encouragement by governments, subsidiaries of multinational corporations typically undertake most of their R & D expenditure in the countries in which their headquarters are located (Ewer *et al.*, 1987; Massey, 1986).

Second, a very large slice of the Victorian manufacturing sector is composed of firms which have emerged and grown in the context of broad, untied forms of trade protection (see EPAC, 1986; Warhurst, 1986). The ill-conceived 'protection at all costs' strategy responsible for such high levels of protection has for decades discouraged manufacturing firms from taking an export oriented outlook and it would seem highly implausible that the lowering of protection levels alone will equip them with the necessary skills and abilities necessary to compete internationally. On the contrary, much will depend on the degree to which Commonwealth and Victorian Governments can in a relatively short time period successfully develop and implement programs necessary to equip Victorian managers with the knowledge and ability to compete in global markets for manufactured commodities.

A large survey of trade exposed manufacturing establishments in the North Eastern Region of Melbourne suggests that the managers of Victorian manufacturing establishments themselves recognise that capital market failures and 'skill' deficiencies of Victorian managers represent the major obstacles to long term growth of trade exposed manufacturing industries in Victoria. The survey results show that the main forms of government assistance that the respondents to the survey felt was required to assist in their firms expansion in coming years were the provision of development and working capital, the provision of advice and assistance in the areas of marketing, business planning, the acquisition of modern technol-

ogy, and the identification of export opportunities. Reduction in State taxes and charges or labour market deregulation did not rank in the 18 forms of assistance (North West 2000, Stage II, 1986).

The provision of venture and development capital and the ability of Victorian managers to adopt the necessary export oriented and innovative outlook, however, are not the only obstacles facing the establishment of a viable, export oriented manufacturing sector in Victoria. The highly skilled nature of modern, elaborately transformed manufacturing and its associated flexible manufacturing production systems requires an education and training system capable of equipping people throughout their lives with the knowledge and skills necessary to use modern, advanced, continually changing forms of manufacturing technology. The structure and nature of public education and training systems which are responsible for the provision of skills to employees in the manufacturing industry have grown and matured to service the needs of what is now an outdated, but rapidly restructuring manufacturing sector.

The need to restructure the Victorian education and training systems does not, however, rest simply with the requirements of the manufacturing sector alone. The rapid developments in computers and information technology in general and their increasing use in all types of work will place additional pressures for change, and will require Victorians to have a longer, more broadly based education than in the past.

Achieving the requisite increased education retention rates, however, will not be an easy task. This is because retention rates in both Australia and Victoria vary considerably according both to socio-economic status and gender. In 1985, for example, while the overall retention rate in Victorian schools was 58% for males, it was only 42% for females. Moreover, while the retention rate for females and males from a low socio-economic status background was 41% and 50% respectively, for females and males from high socio-economic status backgrounds it was 66% and 84% respectively (Department of Employment, Education and Training, 1987). This suggests that it will be difficult to achieve increased retention rates amongst children from high socio-economic status backgrounds simply because their retention rates are already very high. Much, then, will depend on the degree to which governments can develop programs which target children from low socio-economic status backgrounds and girls in particular. This in turn will require finely attuned regional education policies, principally because socio-economic inequality in Melbourne is reproduced spatially, with the resource deprived West standing out as a region in particular need of more educational resources. The recently announced University for the Western Suburbs is an important initiative in this context.

11.2.4 Summary and Conclusion
Victoria's relatively high rate of economic growth over the last six years has by no means resolved the variety of economic and social problems which have bedeviled the State for well over a decade. Although Victoria's unemployment rate has declined considerably during the last 5 years, the improvement has not been consistent across the State. While the unemployment rate in Melbourne fell between 1985 and 1987 from 5.6% to 4.7%, in the rest of Victoria the unemployment rate increased from 7.6% to 8.1%. Moreover, much of the improvement within Melbourne has occurred in the Inner Eastern (3.5% unemployed in August 1988), Southern (3.5%) and North Eastern (4.2%) Regions. The Western Region, however, continues to experience unemployment rates (6.8% in August 1988) well above the Victorian average of 5.6% (as at August 1988) (ABS The Labour Force, Victoria, Cat. No. 6201.2).

In addition, despite the overall decrease in unemployment and the increase in per capita household incomes over the last six years, the legacy of the recessed years of the 1970s in combination with the demographic and other changes outlined earlier have meant that the level of poverty and social inequality in Victoria remain unacceptably high. In June 1986, 22.7% of all Victorian households in private rental housing were in housing related poverty (that is, living below the poverty line after housing costs are taken into account) (Burke, Leigh, Hayward, 1989).

Furthermore, there is no guarantee that the relatively high rates of economic growth in Victoria over the last six years will continue in the coming decades. There are a multitude of cultural and institutional constraints impeding the economic development of the State, and these constraints will not be solved by − nor can they be left to − the vagaries of market forces alone. Well chosen, carefully designed and closely targeted public sector initiatives are required to break down these constraints, to foster improved competitiveness, and to enhance social justice in Victoria.

11.3 The Functions and Structure of the Victorian State Public Sector
The previous section indicated that there are major economic, demographic and social changes occurring in Victoria which have placed and will continue to place considerable demands on the services provided by the Victorian public sector. This section examines the nature of these public services: in essence, the previous section considered the demand side of the public service problem, this section begins the focus on the 'supply' side.

11.3.1 The Victorian Public Sector in Context
Two useful indicators of the size and importance of the Victorian public sector are, first, public sector outlays, and second, public sector employment. Table 11.5 provides per capita outlay data which indicate the distribution of Victorian public sector resources in terms of functional categories in comparison with the Consolidated Australian State Public Sector. The Table demonstrates that the majority of Victorian public sector resources are concentrated in the key social service/social wage functional areas, with 63% of outlays being accounted for by education (28.7%), health (16.3%), housing (6.1%), recreation and culture (2.2%) and transport and communications (11.9%). The data show that, on a per capita basis, Victorian public sector outlays were higher than outlays by the Australian State Public Sector as a whole in the key social service/social wage functional areas of education ($840 for Victoria compared to $796 for the State sector as a whole), and social security ($96 cf. $89), but were lower than the Australian State

public sector as a whole in health ($476 cf. $494), housing and community facilities ($178 cf. $184), recreation and culture ($65 cf. $90), transport and communications ($349 cf. $394), and in most areas of industry assistance.

Table 11.5

Outlays by Government Purpose Category
Per Capita 1986/7

	Victorian State Public Sector		Australian Consolidated State Public Sector	
	$	%	$	%
General Public Services	148.5	5.1	138.4	4.3
Public Order & Safety	160.7	5.5	186.9	5.8
Education	839.6	28.7	796.0	24.5
Health	476.4	16.3	494.0	15.2
Social Security & Welfare	96.1	3.3	89.9	2.8
Housing & Community Amenities	177.8	6.1	184.3	5.7
Recreation & Culture	65.3	2.2	89.9	2.8
Fuel and Energy	44.5	4.9	173.3	5.3
Agriculture, Forestry, Fishing & Hunting	43.4	1.5	92.7	2.9
Mining, Manufacturing & Construction	2.6	0.1	16.1	0.5
Transport & Communications	349.0	11.9	393.9	12.1
Other Economic Affairs	55.5	1.9	59.5	1.8
Other	633.8	21.7	533.8	16.4
Total	2,921.0	100.0	3,248.7	100.0

Note: Australian Consolidated State Public Sector includes six States plus the Northern Territory.
Source: ABS Cat 5504.0.

These variations in part reflect the different social, economic and cultural institutional structures of the States, but they also indicate that there is scope for expansion of public sector activity in Victoria.

In 1986/7 outlays by the Victorian public sector were equivalent to 18.8% of Gross State Product, and approximately 26% of total Australian State Government outlays. Although the overwhelming majority of the outlays were current (15.1% of GSP) rather than capital (3.7% of GSP), the public sector in 1986/7 still accounted for over one quarter (33%) of Victorian New Fixed Capital Expenditure.

Between 1983/4 and 1987/8, Victorian public sector employment averaged 304,000 per year, or approximately 20% of the total Victorian workforce. Although public sector employment increased by 10.1% during this period, the rate of growth was less than private sector employment growth and, as a consequence, the proportion of total employment accounted for by the public sector declined from a high of 22% in 1984/5 to a low of 19% in 1987/8 (see Table 11.6).

In both employment and outlay terms, the size of the Victorian public sector is not large by comparison with the other States. In 1986/7, for example, Queensland (22.2%), Western Australia (23.1%), South Australia (22.5%) and Tasmania (26%) all had a larger proportion of their workforce employed in the public sector than Victoria (19.6%), and all States contained public sectors whose outlays were equivalent to a higher proportion of Gross State Product than was the case in Victoria.

A striking aspect of the Victorian public sector is not so much its size — the Australian public sector in total is, after all, relatively small by international standards — but its sheer complexity. One way of making sense of the complex, heterogeneous nature of the Victorian public sector and to comprehend the myriad of ways in which the public sector underpins Victoria's economy and society is to divide its component parts according to the categories we have used elsewhere: economic, social services and administrative functions.

Table 11.6

State Government Sector Employment and Total Employment Victoria
1983/4 – 1987/8

Year	State Government	Total	State as % of Total
1983/4	282.2	1373.3	20.6%
1984/5	315.1	1432.6	22.0%
1985/6	302.2	1528.1	19.8%
1986/7	308.5	1575.5	19.6%
1987/8	310.6	1636.4	19.0%
% change			
1983/4 – 1987/8	10.1%	19.2%	

Source: ABS Cat. No. 6248.0.

There are three main functional areas in which Victorian public sector organisations have a beneficial effect on the Victorian economy and society. The first is primarily an economic one, including stabilising the macro-economy, the provision of industry assistance, and the construction and maintenance of public infrastructure; the second primarily involves improving the quality of life in Victoria through the provision of key social services, many of which compose the social wage; and the third is essentially an administrative one, encompassing the regulation of industry and commerce, labour standards and the enforcement and maintenance of law, order and public safety.[1]

11.3.2 Economic Functions

The economic role of the Victorian public sector can be further broken down into three sub-components. The first of these is a general economic stabilisation function, in which the Victorian Government can organise budgetary decisions in a way that enables the public sector to assist in stabilising excessive cycles in Victorian economic activity. In times of economic recession, for example the government can increase its borrowings as a means of funding increased capital outlays, thereby stimulating economic growth. Alternatively, in periods of excessive aggregate demand, the government can decrease its level of borrowings and capital outlays (or increase taxation) and thereby decrease the State's contribution to aggregate demand. Up until relatively recently, this counter-cyclical role of the State Public Sector has not received much attention. During the depressed years of the 1970s, for example, successive Victorian Governments reduced both the level of public sector borrowings and the level of capital works expenditures thus accentuating the recession. In 1982, however, having inherited from the previous government an economy in severe recession, the Cain Labor Government implemented in its first budget a 70% increase in budget sector capital works expenditures in an attempt to stimulate the economy out of its recessed state. As discussed in Section 11.5, by 1985/6, when private sector investment activity had begun to pick up, the Cain Government adopted a conscious policy of reducing capital works expenditure so as not to precipitate excessive demand pressures. The success of this strategy should give economic liberal theorists and privatisation advocates pause for thought, many of whom have rejoiced in the supposed death of Keynesian demand management and its counter-cyclical role.

The second component of the Victorian public sector's economic role involves the construction and maintenance of Victoria's public infrastructure (public transport, roads, bridges, sea and air ports, electricity and gas, sewerage and water, etc.). This infrastructure is of vital economic importance, affecting, for instance, both the cost and the time that it takes Victorian firms to circulate both consumer and producer goods between markets. To compound the problem, parts of the existing infrastructure are ageing and will require increased levels of maintenance and replacement expenditure. For example, most of the States 10,200 bridges were constructed during the 1950s and 1960s and, according to the Road Construction Authority, the level of maintenance expenditure needs to be sharply increased from the current $20m p.a. to an estimated $55m (*The Age*, 8/5/89, p. 17). There are also reports of expected sharp escalation in maintenance costs in many other areas including buildings and water supply (*The Age*, 8/5/89, p. 17).

Table 11.7

The Major Victorian General Government and Public Trading Enterprises which Undertake Primarily Economic Functions

Name	Officers Employed in 1987/8[1]	Expenditures (1987/8 $m)[2]
a) Economic Stabilisation		
Department of Management and Budget	1,565	$2,500
Associated Government Financial Enterprises:		
State Bank of Victoria	9,300	
State Insurance Office	702	
b) Public Infrastructure/Industry Policy		
Ministry of Transport	132	$2,067
Associated Statutory Authorities/PTE's:		
State Transport Authority (V/Line)	11,399	($561)
Metropolitan Transit Authority (The Met)	12,000	($683)
Road Construction Authority (RCA)	4,100	($532)
Road Traffic Authority (RTA)		($153)
Port Authorities (Melbourne, Geelong & Portland)		($18)
Department of Industry Technology and Resources	516	$113
Associated PTEs:		
State Electricity Commission	21,710	$2,870
Gas and Fuel Corporation	5,926	$861
Department of Water Resources	134	$151
Associated Statutory Authorities/PTE's:		
Melbourne and Metropolitan Board of Works (MMBW)	7,371	
Rural Water Commission (RWC)	1,170	
Department of Agriculture and Rural Affairs	1,565	$125

Notes: [1] Employment for General Government Departments relate to permanent part and full time employees employed under the Public Service Act as at 30/6/88.

[2] Expenditure data in brackets indicates overlap with government department program expenditures. Department of Management and Budget Program expenditures include moneys on-passed to other government agencies.

Source: Budget Paper No. 5, 1988. Victorian Government Directory, Public Service Board Annual Report; Annual Reports of Statutory Authorities.

The final way in which the Victorian public sector positively influences economic activity is through its range of industrial development policies and programs. These range from the provision of information and advice, through to the provision of financial assistance for particular industries. Particularly important agencies in this area are the Department of Industry, Technology and Resources, and the Department of Rural Affairs.

Table 11.7 summarises some of the principal general government departments and Public Trading Enterprises of the Victorian public sector which are responsible for these economic functions.

11.3.3 Social Wage & Social Services
The second functional area in which the Victorian public sector is involved is primarily concerned with the provision of key social services, most of which form important components of the social wage (education, health, public housing, public transport, community services etc.). It also encompasses the provision of a variety of services designed to enhance the cultural and recreational opportunities available to Victorians. Table 11.8 indicates the principal general government departments responsible for this functional area.

Table 11.8

**Some General Government Agencies which Undertake Primarily
Social Service/Social Wage Functions**

Name	Officers Employed[1] 1987/8 (Number:)	Expenditures[2] 1987/8 ($m)
Ministry of Education	1,641 (42,000 teachers)	$3,130
Associated Statutory Authorities/Agencies: (Govt. Schools; Technical & Further Education; The Victorian Curriculum Advisory Board; The Victorian Post Secondary Education Commission)		
Department of Health	5,432	$2,400
Department of Community Services	2,783	$574
Ministry of Housing and Construction	2,013	$768
Department of Conservation, Forests & Land	2,137	$197
Associated Authorities: (Zoological Board; National Parks Advisory Board)		
Ministry for the Arts	464	$122
Associated Authorities: (The National Gallery; State Film Centre, Library & Museum)		
Department of Sport and Recreation	166	$43
Associated Authorities: Totalizator Agency Board; National Tennis Centre		
Ministry for Ethnic Affairs	60	$4

Source and Notes: See Table 11.7.

11.3.4 Administrative Functions
Foremost among the administrative and co-ordinating agencies of the Victorian public sector are the Department of Premier and Cabinet, the Public Service Board and the Department of Local Government. The principal 'regulatory' agencies include the Ministry for Police and Emergency Services, the Attorney General's Department, the Ministry for Consumer Affairs, the Department of Labour and associated authorities (see Table 11.9).

11.4 The Finances of the Victorian Public Sector
Section 11.2 of this chapter suggested that the future of the Victorian economy will be determined by the degree to which the State's diversified industrial structure capitalises on the new international price competitiveness to produce the high value-added, elaborately transformed manufactured goods, and high value-added tertiary products, which represent the fastest growing components of world trade. This in turn will depend on whether

appropriate public sector initiatives are put in place to encourage Victorian firms to become export oriented. Recognising this, the Cain Labor Government, on coming to office in 1982, set about establishing an economic

strategy designed to provide clear objectives and harness the various parts of the Victorian public sector into a collective thrust towards achieving those objectives.

Table 11.9

Some General Government Agencies which Undertake Primarily Administrative Functions

Name	Officers Employed 1987/8	Expenditures 1987/8 ($m)[2]
a) Co-ordination		
Department of Premier and Cabinet	191	$36
Associated Statutory Authorities:		
(Public Service Board; Audit Office; Office of the Solicitor General; Promotions Appeals Board)		
Department of Local Government	67	$173
Associated Statutory Authorities:		
(Victorian Grants Commission; the Local Government Commission; the Local Authorities Superannuation Board)		
b) Regulatory		
Ministry for Police and Emergency Services	1,490 (9,229 Police)	$665
Associated Agencies:		
(Country Fire Authority; Metropolitan Fire Brigades Board; State Emergency Services; Adult Parole Board; Office of Corrections)		
Attorney-General's Department	940	$142
Associated Agencies:		
(Public Prosecutions; Chief Parliamentary Counsel; Corporate Affairs Office; State Trust Office.)		
Ministry of Consumer Affairs	214	$12
Associated Authorities:		
(Small Claims Tribunal; Residential Tenancies Tribunal)		
Department of Labour	692	$80
Associated Authorities:		
(Industrial Relations Commission; Conciliation & Arbitration Boards; Occupational Health & Safety Commission)		
Ministry of Planning and Environment	710	$56
Associated Authorities:		
(MMBW; Soil Conservation; Council; Historical Building Council)		

Source and Notes: see Table 11.7.

As the previous section pointed out, however, economic management tasks are only one set of activities undertaken by the Victorian public sector. Equally important is the Victorian

public sector's role in effecting a more equitable distribution of income through the provision of key social services and many components of the social wage. Thus in 1987, the Cain Government introduced a Social Justice Strategy to complement the already existing Economic Strategy.

Although the Economic and Social Justice Strategies have been used as a basis for reforming the nature and operation of parts of the public sector (particularly the Economic Strategy), they have primarily functioned as a framework for guiding the development of annual budgetary initiatives. Overlaying these strategies, the State Government has played a distinctly Keynesian macro-economic stabilisation role.

The purpose of this section is to document the nature of this strategic approach by outlining the key features of the government's overall macro-economic strategy and the Economic and Social Justice Strategies. In so doing, the section provides the background for understanding the trends in Victorian public sector spending and funding which are examined in the following sections. This section is primarily descriptive with an evaluation of the Economic and Social Justice Strategies provided later in Section 11.8.

11.4.1 The Macro-Economic Strategy: Opportunities and Constraints

Although the Victorian Government has pursued a 'Keynesian' counter-cyclical strategy, the design and implementation of this stabilisation strategy has not been easy because of the various constraints which face budgetary planning at the State level. There are two main constraints affecting State budgetary planning. First, the State Government has direct control of less than half the funds available to it in any one year. A large proportion of the Consolidated Fund's current and capital receipts are from Commonwealth grants, with a further proportion of capital receipts from Commonwealth Government borrowings raised on behalf of the State Government. Moreover, the level of borrowings by State Trading Enterprises is controlled by the Global Borrowings limit agreement between the Commonwealth and State Governments. The main consequence of this is that the State Government is limited in the degree to which it can use borrowings to finance capital expenditure as a means of 'pump priming' the economy out of

recession, particularly because under the Financial Agreement, the State Government is not allowed to borrow to finance a deficit on the Consolidated Fund, which arises during the course of a particular year.

This latter restriction is important because State Government receipts – especially those stemming from taxes – fluctuate with the level of economic activity. Current expenditures, on the other hand, are largely inflexible on a year to year basis, particularly in a downward direction. This is because the main components of recurrent spending are in the form of wages, interest on debt, the operating deficits of the public transport authorities and superannuation payments.

The problem facing the State Government is that when the economy enters an unforeseen recession, tax receipts will decline more than was anticipated, but current expenditures will remain unchanged. As a result, the Consolidated Fund will tend to move into deficit on current transactions with the State Government prohibited from borrowing to fund such a deficit. The solution to the problem is either to cut back on works and services expenditures or to increase taxes. But both measures will worsen the recession.

On coming to office in 1982, the Cain Government sought to address this situation by putting in place a macro-economic strategy which would substantially enhance the government's ability to use the State budget in a positive, counter cyclical way (for details see Victorian Government Budget Papers, various years; Victoria, The Next Step, 1984, pp. 15-19). The key components of this strategy involve winding down borrowings and works and services expenditures during the mature stage of the economic cycle. It also involves restricting the rate of increase in current expenditure initiatives to below the trend rate of economic growth. Both measures reduce the pressures to redirect monies available for works and services expenditures into the current account of the Consolidated Fund during an unforeseen recession.

11.4.2 The Economic and Social Justice Strategies

While the macro-economic strategy represents

the main framework for medium term budgetary planning in Victoria, the composition and nature of annual spending and funding initiatives is primarily determined by the government's Economic and Social Justice Strategies.

The Economic Strategy
The Economic Strategy was first released in 1984, and has since been updated twice. The three Economic Strategy documents released to date are: *Victoria, the Next Step* (April 1984); *Victoria, the Next Decade* (April 1987); and *Victoria, Trading on Achievement* (August 1988). In marked contrast to the small government rhetoric of the New Right, what underpins the Economic Strategy is a commitment to the proactive role of the public sector as a facilitator and catalyst of economic growth and industrial restructuring.

The objective of the economic strategy is primarily to maximise Victoria's long term trend rate of income and employment growth, particularly through the expansion of those sectors of the economy which generate exports (the trade exposed sector) and/or which compete with imports. Targeted for special attention are small to medium firms (defined as firms employing less than 200 people and which have a net worth less than $5m) producing high value added services and manufactured commodities (Victorian Government, 1984, pp. 2-4; 1987, p. 207; 1988, pp. 2-3).

The Economic Strategy concentrates on increasing competitiveness in the trade-exposed sector, both through normal market processes and through government activity. In seeking to improve the competitiveness of the trade-exposed sector in Victoria, the government embarked on two levels of policy action. One level relates to the overall economic environment. This includes areas such as wages policy and industrial relations, business costs, regulation, efficiency of the public sector and of capital markets, and the availability of assistance to growth firms or firms undertaking structural change. Accordingly, the government has developed facilitative policies in four areas:

— reform of the public sector and of business regulation;
— support for export development;

— promotion of growth firms; and
— enhancement of the education and training system.

The second level of policy identified particular areas where Victoria possesses a competitive strength. Specific policies were then developed to enhance these capacities. Some of Victoria's key realisable and potential strengths included:

— an industrial skill base;
— world-class scientific and technological research institutions;
— high quality brown coal deposits;
— oil and natural gas reserves;
— a diverse agricultural base including the State's timber resources;
— Port Phillip as a major transport, distribution and communications hub;
— Melbourne as an international commercial centre;
— Melbourne's national role as a major trading, cultural and sporting centre; and
— Victoria's tourist destinations.

The government reaffirmed this direction in 1987 with the release of the document, *Victoria, The Next Decade*. In August 1988, the Victorian Government released a further document *Victoria: Trading on Achievement* which outlined an integrated approach to Victoria's long-term development and set out the government's plans to continue the development of its Economic Strategy to maximise internationally competitive growth in Victoria.

The document announced several new initiatives and programs ranging from strategic research and venture capital through to education. Wherever possible, the provision of State public services gives priority to these themes, in the context of the ongoing development of the government's Economic Strategy and the Victorian economy itself.

The Social Justice Strategy
The Victorian Government's Social Justice Strategy was announced in 1987. Like the Economic Strategy, it is a government-led plan to harness resources and public sector initiatives

across departments as a means of achieving common goals.

Victoria's Social Justice Strategy is based on the belief that efforts to ensure equitable distribution must accompany policies designed to create new job opportunities and increase aggregate economic welfare.

The Social Justice Strategy has four major social objectives:

- reducing disadvantage caused by unequal access to economic resources and power;
- increasing access to essential goods and services according to need;
- expanding opportunities for genuine participation by all Victorians in decisions which affect their lives; and
- protecting, extending and ensuring the effective exercise of equal legal, industrial and political rights.

The strategy is designed to ensure that when government agencies allocate resources or plan initiatives in public expenditure/services, they do so with the above social justice objectives in mind.

The Social Justice Strategy measures seek to tackle the underlying factors generating disadvantage, rather than simply addressing the symptoms. The distinction is that between retraining parents to enable them to gain access to jobs, and providing emergency financial relief to families in poverty. It is the more active measures such as retraining which actually get at the cause of the problem; such measures provide the opportunity for people to help themselves rather than becoming the passive recipients of welfare payments.

Both the Economic and Social Justice strategies receive further attention in later sections of this chapter. The discussion here has been largely descriptive and concentrated on the underlying rationale of the strategies in order to provide requisite background information to an examination of Victoria's public sector expenditure and financing programs in recent years – the subject of the following two sections.

11.5 Financing Victoria's State Public Services

11.5.1 Trends in Victoria's Public Sector Finances

As indicated in Tables 11.11 and 11.12 the Victorian Government has direct control over the level and composition of less than half of the total funds available to it in any one year. Table 11.10 shows the main sources of finance between 1981/82 and 1986/87 in nominal dollar terms, as a percentage of total State public sector finance and as a percentage of Victoria's Gross State Product. Table 11.11 shows the sources of finance in constant 1981/2 dollars.

The Tables demonstrate an increasing reliance by the Victorian public sector on its own sources of revenue between 1981/2 and 1986/7. Continuing cuts in Commonwealth Government grants and advances between 1984/5 and 1986/7 in combination with declining levels of State borrowings since 1985/6 (as a consequence of the global borrowings limit) have resulted in State taxes, fees and fines and net operating surpluses of public trading enterprises accounting for an increasing proportion of Victorian public sector finance: from 34.7% of total finance in 1981/2, to 39.2% by 1986/7. During the same time period Commonwealth grants have declined from 40.5% of all funds to 39.3%, and Commonwealth advances have declined from 2.5% to 0.9% of all funds. The decline in Commonwealth advances has been particularly severe. In 1986/7, Commonwealth advances were equivalent in real terms to only 39.7% of their 1981/2 level. The tighter global borrowing limit resulted in a real decline in borrowings of 12.5% in 1986/7.

The increasing contribution of the State's own sources of finance to offset declines in the Commonwealth's contribution has been assisted by the relatively strong rates of economic growth in Victoria during the last 6 years (see section 11.2), which have boosted taxes and charges and enabled public trading enterprises to significantly increase their operating surpluses. Continued real cuts in Commonwealth grants and advances to Victoria in combination with declines in Victorian global limit borrowings means that the adequacy of Victorian State finances will become increasingly dependent on these high rates of economic growth continuing. A slow-down in the Victorian economy (due, for example, to macro-economic contractionary measures) would result in declines in State generated revenue which may lead to a major contraction in the funding available able for the provision, improvement and development of public services.

Table 11.10

Source of Finance: Victoria
1981/82 − 1986/87
($m)

	1981/2	1982/3	1983/4	1984/5	1985/6	1986/7
Taxes, Fees & Fines	2148.8	2639.2	2783.2	3140.7	3431.7	3844.5
% of Total	26.8%	28.0%	27.1%	27.7%	27.4%	28.8%
% of GSP	5.1%	5.7%	5.3%	5.5%	5.3%	5.4%
Operating Surpluses						
of PTEs	631.4	772.4	732.5	763.5	981.2	1387.0
% of Total	7.9%	8.2%	7.1%	6.7%	7.8%	10.4%
% of GSP	1.5%	1.7%	1.4%	1.3%	1.5%	1.9%
C/W Grants	3107.5	3599.2	4113.2	4586.1	4900.9	5254.9
% of Total	38.7%	38.1%	40.0%	40.5%	39.2%	39.3%
% of GSP	7.4%	7.8%	7.9%	8.0%	7.6%	7.4%
Property	311.8	317.3	387.6	495	520.8	495.6
% of Total	3.9%	3.4%	3.8%	4.4%	4.2%	3.7%
% of GSP	0.7%	0.7%	0.7%	0.9%	0.8%	0.6%
Other	66.8	59.5	117.8	75.5	132.9	147.4
% of Total	0.8%	0.6%	1.1%	0.7%	1.1%	1.1%
% of GSP	0.2%	0.1%	0.2%	0.1%	0.2%	0.2%
C/W Advances	198.3	236.8	231.0	181.4	177.7	117.0
% of Total	2.5%	2.5%	2.2%	1.5%	1.4%	0.9%
% of GSP	0.5%	0.5%	0.4%	0.3%	0.3%	0.2%
Borrowings	1129.2	1534.2	1326.9	1556.4	1769.5	1694.1
% of Total	14.1%	16.3%	12.9%	13.7%	14.2%	12.7%
% of GSP	2.7%	3.3%	2.5%	2.7%	2.7%	2.4%
Other	431.2	279.2	586.6	536.6	590.6	418.2
% of Total	10.1%	6.9%	10.6%	9.8%	9.9%	7.9%
% of GSP	1.9%	1.4%	2.1%	1.9%	1.9%	1.5%
Total	8024.9	9437.7	10278.7	11335.2	12505.3	13358.8
% of Total	100.0%	100.05	100.0%	100.0%	100.0%	100.0%

Source: ABS Cat. No. 5504.0; GSP data from Victorian Department of Management and Budget.

The next part of this section examines in more detail the Victorian public sector's financial circumstances for 1987/88 and 1988/89 expressed through information presented in the State's most recent budgets.

Payments To Victoria By the Commonwealth Government
Table 11.12 shows that in 1987/88 and 1988/89, the trend of declining Commonwealth payments to Victoria continued. Indeed, in 1988//89, the increase in payments in nominal terms is estimated at only 2%, a decline of about 5% in real terms. It is estimated that Specific Purpose Payments will fall by an estimated $256m or 46.6% in 1988/89.

As Part Four outlines, there is a clear need for a longer-term agreement for sharing the national revenues to be made between the Commonwealth and the States based around the State Goods and Services Levy.

State Taxation
Australian State Governments have a narrow

revenue base the reasons for which have been well documented. Due to constitutional and other practical constraints, Victoria has access to only a small number of low-yielding and narrow-based taxes such as stamp duties of various descriptions, motor vehicle taxes, gambling taxes, and land taxes. The narrow interpretations by the High Court of Sections 90 and 92 of the Commonwealth Constitution have on a number of occasions disallowed revenue measures introduced by the States. For instance, in 1983, the High Court declared Victoria's Pipeline Licence Fee unconstitutional. More recently, in the Alston Holdings case the Court declared that certain provisions of Victoria's Business Franchise (Tobacco) Act 1974 were invalid under Section 92.

Table 11.11

Sources of Finance 1981/82 — 1986/87
(1981/82 Prices)
($m)

	1981/2	1982/3	1983/4	1984/5	1985/6	1986/7
Taxes, Fees & Fines	2148.8	2204.8	2325.1	2511.2	2529.3	2589.4
% Change		2.6%	5.5%	8.0%	0.7%	2.4%
Operating Surpluses						
of PTEs	631.4	694.2	611.5	610.3	723.1	934.0
% Change		9.9%	-11.9%	-0.2%	18.5%	29.2%
Grants	3107.5	3236.7	3436.3	3665.9	3611.6	3538.7
% Change		4.2%	6.2%	6.7%	-1.5%	-2.0
Advances	198.3	212.9	193.0	145.0	131.0	78.8
% Change		7.4%	-9.3%	-24.9%	-9.7%	-39.8%
Borrowings	1129.2	1379.7	1108.5	1244.1	1304.0	1140.8
% Change		22.2%	-19.7%	12.2%	4.8%	-12.5%
Other	809.7	589.8	912.2	884.3	916.5	714.1
% Change		-27.2%	54.7%	-3.1%	3.6%	-22.1%
Total	8024.9	8487.1	8587.1	9060.9	9215.4	8995.8

Source: ABS Cat. No. 5504.0; CPI data from Australian Year Books.

Table 11.12

Commonwealth Recurrent Payments to Victoria
($m)

	1983/4	1984/5	1985/6	1986/7	1987/8	1988/9 (est.)
General Revenue Assistance	2312.3	2395.1	2619.4	2906.3	3108.8	3438.3[a]
% change		3.6	9.4	11.0	7.0	10.6
Specific Purpose Payments	279.5	428.9	449.5	487.3	548.1	292.6[a]
% change		53.5	4.8	8.4	12.5	-46.6
Total	2591.8	2824.0	3068.9	3393.6	3656.9	3730.9
% change		9.0	8.7	10.6	7.8	2.0

Note: [a] In 1988-89 the general revenue assistance includes the newly created hospital grant which replaces the former general purpose health grant and the specific purpose medicare grant. Since the introduction of the medicare grant on 1 February 1984, the annual grant has been $80.0m in 1983-84; $249.2m in 1984-85; $256.0m in 1985-86; $265.7m in 1986-87; and $284.9m in 1987-88.
Source: Victoria, Consolidated Fund Receipts, Budget Paper No. 4 (various years).

Table 11.13 provides a breakdown of State tax receipts in each year from 1983/84 to 1988/89. In 1987/88, the last year for which data is available, State taxation increased strongly by about 15.6% and provided revenue of about $3.9b which comprised about 42% of Victoria's total Consolidated Fund receipts. Amongst the most important State taxes in terms of revenue are pay-roll taxes, stamp duty and land tax.

Table 11.13

State Taxation
($m)

	1983/4	1984/5	1985/6	1986/7	1987/8	1988/9 (est.)
Pay-Roll Tax	963.5	1064.2	1179.3	1264.7	1389.6	1562.3
Stamp Duties	564.2	752.1	840.2	982.3	1294.0	1442.5
Tattersalls Receipts	202.7	201.9	198.1	228.1	249.1	279.2
Land Tax	143.1	153.3	183.0	195.3	209.5	224.0
Petroleum Franchise Fees	151.6	192.4	210.8	214.6	237.5	249.9
Totalizator Taxation Revenue	72.9	81.9	93.0	102.9	115.3	132.5
Liquor Licence Fee	70.2	72.5	77.4	84.7	90.9	103.2
Motor Registration Fees	48.7	50.8	54.8	57.9	56.8	39.4
Tobacco Franchise Fees	83.8	104.6	111.5	113.4	112.5	117.0
(FID)	80.9	90.7	105.0	119.5	139.4	159.0
Motor Drivers Licence Fees	33.7	34.9	32.1	27.2	29.4	29.4
Environment Protection Authority	3.6	3.7	2.8	2.9	2.8	3.0
Miscellaneous Taxation	1.7	3.1	4.4	7.0	5.0	5.1
Total	2420.6	2806.1	3092.4	3400.5	3931.8	4344.5
% change		15.9%	10.2%	10.0%	15.6%	10.5%

Source: Victoria, Consolidated Fund Receipts, Budget Paper No. 4 (various years).

Recurrent Receipts From State Sources Other than Taxation

In 1987/88, recurrent receipts from sources other than State taxation amounted to about $1.8b or 19% of Consolidated Fund receipts. Table 11.14 provides a breakdown for each year from 1983/1984 to 1988/89.

Total revenue raised from Departmental fees and charges amounted to only 2.9% of Consolidated Revenue in 1987/88. The case for Departmental fees and charges has been discussed in Part Four. As it concluded there are instances, where for social or economic policy reasons, charges which achieve less than full cost recovery may be appropriate. However, this limitation is not applicable to all goods and services provided by the public sector. The Victorian Government has set constraints on the pursuit of increasing revenue from this source.

11.5.2 Recurrent Receipts: Policy Restrictions

The Victorian Government has established policies to limit increases in taxes. Specifically:

— it has undertaken to restrain the increase in taxation revenues in line with the increase in Victorian non-farm gross domestic product; and

— it has made specific tax reductions/concessions over the last four years which have removed about $431m from the tax base for future years.

The Victorian Government has also set annual guidelines which require that increases in fees and charges including those set by public trading enterprises not exceed the rate of inflation.

Taxation Revenue
Table 11.15 compares taxes, fees and fines for both Victoria and the consolidated Australian State Government sector for the years 1981/2 and 1986/87. The Table demonstrates the importance of payroll taxes (29% of total taxation receipts in 1986/87), and stamp duties (18%) as sources of State taxation.

Table 11.14

Recurrent Receipts from State Sources Other Than Taxation
($m)

	1983/4	1984/5	1985/6	1986/7	1987/8	1988/9 (est.)
Recoveries of Debt Charges	224.1	218.4	286.4	329.5	293.8	326.5
Land Revenue	194.0	217.8	228.5	171.8	172.1	153.7
Harbour Revenue	9.8	11.3	11.7	10.9	10.6	10.2
Departmental Fees and Charges	200.5	238.7	273.0	305.3	331.8	354.0
Forestry Revenue	31.7	37.8	37.1	42.0	43.9	48.8
Rural Water Commission	81.7	72.3	73.2	56.6	67.3	73.0
Public Authority Receipts	372.5	371.7	415.0	462.2	507.0	589.3
Miscellaneous Receipts	111.0	176.8	145.6	155.0	168.5	173.0
Cash Management Account	–	–	–	15.0	–	171.0
Recurrent Revenue Previously Paid to the Trust Fund	196.1	208.5	216.2	228.9	223.0	191.8
Total	*1421.4*	*1553.3*	*1686.7*	*1777.2*	*1818.0*	*1931.3*
% change		*9.3*	*8.6*	*5.4*	*2.3*	*6.2*

Source: Victoria, Consolidated Fund Receipts, 1988-89 Budget Paper No. 4.

One of the main differences between the structure and composition of Victorian taxation relative to the Australian State Government sector as a whole is the greater reliance on levies on statutory corporations. In the case of Victoria, these excises take the form of a Public Authority Dividend on the Gas and Fuel Corporation, which involves some of the revenues generated from the exploitation of Victoria's gas reserves in Bass Strait being paid into the Consolidated Fund to finance recurrent initiatives. These excises or dividends accounted for 6% of Victorian tax receipts in 1986/87, and for over two thirds of State Government revenue derived from this source.

Also noticeable is the greater reliance by the Victorian public sector on the Financial Institutions Duty and stamp duties relative to the Australian State Government sector as a whole. Between 1981/82 and 1986/87, total receipts from taxes, fees and fines in Victoria increased by 20.5% in real terms, which was a lower rate of growth than that experienced by the Australian State Government sector as a whole (22.7%). This lower rate of growth can be attributed, firstly to the Victorian Government's pledge not to increase the level of taxes and charges at a rate faster than the growth in Non-Farm Gross State Product (NFGSP), and secondly to a variety of tax concessions or 'tax expenditures' introduced by the government over the last five years at a cumulative and on-going annual cost to the Consolidated Fund of

$431m (See Table 11.16) (Victorian Government Budget Paper No. 2, 1988/89, pp. 42-43).

In 1986/87 the Victorian Government's taxation receipts increased considerably as a consequence of a surge in property prices (particularly in 1988) and share market activity (during the second half of 1987). Between 1986/87 and 1987/88, receipts from stamp duties and land tax increased by 27%, and are likely to increase by 10% during 1988/89 (Victorian Government, Budget Paper No 4. 1988/89, pp. 9 & 14). The importance of the property boom in recent years in swelling State tax receipts from stamp duties cannot be underestimated: whereas stamp duties on property transactions accounted for 37.4% of total stamp duty receipts

in 1983/84, by 1985/86 they accounted for 43.2%, and by 1987/88 they accounted for approximately 50% (Victorian Government Budget Paper No. 4 1988/89, p. 9). A slow down in the property transactions and/or in the rate of growth of property values has already materially affected the Victorian Government's financial situation: Consolidated Fund figures to end-April 1989 show that only $107m has been raised from land lax, whereas $224m had been expected. This is placing considerable strain on the government's fiscal, economic and social policies, and clearly indicates that windfall revenue gains cannot substitute for the sort of stable revenue base available from reforms discussed in Part Four (see AFR 8/6/89).

Table 11.15

Taxes, Fees and Fines by Type, Victorian and Total Australian State Public Sectors, 1981/82 and 1986/87

| Type | Victorian State Public Sector | | | | Total Australian State Public Sector | | | |
| | 1981/82 | | 1986/87 | | 1981/82 | | 1986/87 | |
	$m	% of Total	$m	%of Total	$m	% of Total	$m	% of Total
Payroll Tax	696.0	32	1108.4	29	2434.0	34	3682.9	28
Property Tax*:								
Land Tax	115.9		159.3		340.0		703.8	
Other	79.4		32.1		164.1		95.8	
Total	195.3	9	227.4	6	504.1	7	799.6	6
Capital Tax**:								
Stamp Duties	289.9		699.5		1123.7		2213.5	
FID	0		119.5		0		354.3	
Total	289.9	14	819.0	21	1123.7	16	2567.8	20
Excise Tax on Stat Corps	88.0	4	217.9	6	138.4	2	327.9	3
Gambling Taxes	210.3	10	353.2	9	718.8	10	1245.3	10
Insurance Taxes	153.6	7	208.2	5	435.5	6	711.0	5
Vehicle Taxes	256.9	12	394.4	10	996.7	14	1699.9	13
Franchise Taxes	213.2	10	431.7	11	548.2	8	1455.0	11
Fees and Fines	45.6	2	86.0	2	329.4	5	561.8	4
Total	2148.8	100	3845.3	100	7228.7	100	13051.2	100

Notes: * Other Category composed mainly of Estate and Gift Duty.
    ** FID: Financial Institutions Duty.
    Totals may not add due to rounding.
Source: ABS Catalogue 5506.0.

Table 11.16

Taxes, Fees and Fines: Victorian State Public Sector and Total State Public Sector
(1981/82 Average Prices and as Percent of Gross State Product)

	Victoria		Australian State Total	
	% of GSP	% Change	% of GDP	% Change
Year End June		1981/82 prices		1981/82 prices
1982	5.1		4.6	
1983	5.7	10.5	4.9	4.0
1984	5.3	−2.0	4.9	3.8
1985	5.5	8.0	4.9	7.8
1986	5.3	0.7	4.9	1.5
1987	5.4	2.4	5.0	3.9
Percent change 1981/82 − 1986/87		20.5		22.7

Source: ABS Catalogue 5504.0. GSP data from Victorian Department of Management and Budget (GSP in market prices). CPI for Melbourne from ABS Catalogue 3301.0.

Specific Reductions in Taxes and Charges

Over the four years 1984/5 to 1987/88, the government has made discretionary exemptions and cuts in taxes and charges which have reduced the revenue base by about $313m a year. A further set of revenue cuts was introduced for 1988/89 at an estimated cost of $118m in a full year, bringing the cumulative reduction in the annual revenue base to $431m. The major reductions are to Payroll Tax ($120m), motoring charges ($133m), stamp duties ($87m), and Land tax ($94m).

Despite the constraint on public trading authority price increases, the government has received an increasingly important proportion of Consolidated Revenue from dividend payments made by these public authorities. We turn our attention now to these payments.

11.5.3 Dividend Payments by Victorian Public Authorities

Since 1982, the Victorian Government has introduced a number of important reforms to the State's Public Trading Enterprise (PTEs) in an attempt to ensure that such enterprises operate more efficiently. In broad terms these reforms have involved a concerted attempt to commercialise and corporatise the State's PTEs in a way that encourages them to operate more like private companies. A key part of this reform process already dealt with in Part Four, has been the requirement for the PTEs to pay a Public Authority Dividend (PAD) of up to 5% of the opening value of the 'public equity' in the

relevant authority. The government's requirement that most of the State's PTEs do not increase their charges at a rate in excess of the rate of inflation effectively prevents this from occurring (see Victorian Government Budget Paper No. 4 1988/89, p. 40).

Table 11.17 summarises the level and source of PADs in the State.

As the Table indicates, public authority payments received by the Consolidated Fund have increased significantly from $372.5m in 1983/84, to an estimated $589.3m in 1988-89 − an increase of 58% over five years. Indeed, receipts from this source during 1987/88 comprised 5.3% of total Consolidated Fund recurrent receipts or an important 27.8% of the State's own-sourced, non-taxation revenue in that year. Although the practice of requiring dividends from public trading enterprises has been open to some dispute on the grounds that the definition of equity seems unclear in the case of public (by comparison with private) enterprises, the requirement to pay dividends is quite defensible as a matter of government policy judgement pertaining to the distribution of public enterprise earnings.

Since dividend payments required of a public enterprise will affect its borrowing and subsequent debt servicing requirement, they are likely (in the medium or longer term, at least) to affect the level of prices charged by a public enterprise (unless offset by sustained cost reductions). In this regard it should be noted, however, that thus far, the major Victorian public enterprises subjected to the reforms in question have increased their prices by less than CPI increases in each year.

11.5.4 Financing Transactions: Borrowings and Advances

In 1986/87, approximately 50% of Victorian public sector borrowings were used to finance capital outlays by State PTEs, while the remainder was used to finance generally non-commercial activities such as the building of schools and hospitals. The borrowings which finance capital outlays by the PTEs are generally self-financing in the sense that they gener-

ate income which is more than sufficient to cover the interest on the debt. While the non-commercial borrowings are not directly self-financing, the public infrastructure which they finance typically add to the productive capacity of the economy, and thereby underwrite future economic growth and private sector profitability. To the extent that such economic growth finds its expression in increased taxation receipts, the borrowings are at least partially (and indirectly) self-financing. As Chapter Eight also pointed out, borrowing for such purposes is also desirable on the grounds of inter-generational equity.

Table 11.17

Consolidated Fund Receipts from Public Authority Payments (PAP)
($m)

	1983-84	1984-85	1985-86	1986-87	1987-88	1988-89 (est.)
PAP *	183.9	154.4	171.1	173.7	218.7	233.8
Other Public Authority Receipts	188.6	217.3	243.9	288.5	288.3	355.5
Total	*372.5*	*371.7*	*415.0*	*462.2*	*507.0*	*589.3*

Note: * Public Authorities in which the VET holds 8% of the equity.
Source: Victorian Government, 1988/89 Budget Papers, Budget Strategy and Review Paper No. 2.

The main sources of funds available to the Victorian public sector to finance capital outlays, other than Specific Purpose Capital Grants and any excess of current revenues over current outlays, are General Purpose Capital Payments from the Commonwealth and Victorian public sector borrowings. Importantly, both sources of funds are under Commonwealth control.

Table 11.18 summarises trends in the net indebtedness (ie. gross debt less holdings of financial assets) of the Victorian public sector expressed as a percentage of Non-Farm Gross State Product. The Table distinguishes between the net indebtedness of budget sector authorities (which are predominantly non-commercial in nature), and non-budget sector agencies (which are basically commercial in nature, eg. the SECV). The Table shows that the net indebtedness of the Victorian public sector increased markedly between 1980/81 and 1985/86, primarily because of a substantial increase in borrowings by the non-budget sector agencies.

Since 1985/86, however, the net indebtedness of the public sector has declined significantly in real terms, falling from 30.7% of NFGSP in 1985/86 to an estimated 27.9% of NFGSP in 1988/89.

11.5.5 Central Borrowing Authorities

To overcome the competitive disadvantage for smaller statutory authorities resulting from the relaxation of maximum interest rates at Loan Council and the development of a market in semi-government securities, most States set up central borrowing authorities to handle their borrowings. In 1983 the Victorian Transport Borrowing Authority (VTBA) was established to borrow on behalf of the transport authorities.

In 1984, VicFin was established to borrow on behalf of the smaller non-transport authorities. The two authorities were combined in 1986. The advantage of such centralised borrowing is that the securities can be freely traded in financial markets, which was not possible for the smaller authorities. VicFin has now become the State's largest borrowing agency.

Centralisation of statutory authority debt creates economies of scale in the management of fewer and larger packages of securities, and the use of techniques to mitigate against interest rate volatility. Fluctuations in future debt service obligations and in maturity structures can also be more effectively managed.

11.5.6 New Sources of State Finance

The Victorian Equity Trust

Chapter Nine has evaluated the performance of the Victorian Equity Trust (VET) which was launched during 1988. It was established to provide selected authorities with access to private sector sourced equity while enabling the government to retain control over the authorities' operations. It raised a total of $500m for the Portland Smelter Unit Trust ($100m) and three major public trading authorities, the State Electricity Commission of Victoria ($240m), the Gas and Fuel Corporation of Victoria ($50m) and the Melbourne and Metropolitan Board of Works ($100m). None of the amount raised was directed to the Consolidated Fund.

Table 11.18

Recent Trends in Borrowing and Net Debt
(All Figures Expressed as a Proportion of Victorian NFGDP)

	Net Government Borrowings[2]	Public Sector Net Debt	Net Debt Budget Sector[1]	Net Debt Non-Budget Sector
1980-81	2.8	27.7	15.8	13.6
1981-82	3.5	28.1	15.0	14.5
1982-83	4.2	29.9	15.3	15.9
1983-84	3.8	29.8	15.0	16.0
1984-85	3.3	30.4	15.1	16.3
1985-86	3.0	30.7	15.3	16.2
1986-87	2.7	30.4	15.5	15.2
1987-88	1.8	28.5	15.0	13.9
1988-89 (est.)	1.7	27.9	15.0	13.2

Note: [1] Because of transactions between sectors, data for budget and non budget sector net debt do not add to total for Victoria.

Source: Victorian Government, 1988/89 Budget Paper No. 2, p. 20.

The proposal to establish VET came at a time of severe Loan Council restraint over global limit approved borrowings. However, while the Victorian Government was initially optimistic that what it considered to be equity raisings would be considered to be outside the global limits by the Commonwealth, this did not turn out to be the case. In short, the Commonwealth considered funds raised through the VET to be more akin to borrowings than equity and therefore falling within the global borrowing limits. Thus the VET was unsuccessful in raising additional funds for the authorities.

Sale of Assets

The Victorian Government has undertaken a policy of selling surplus assets, particularly land, to generate revenue to finance investment in new capital assets. In 1987/88, Consolidated Fund receipts from the sale of assets were $200.2m, more than double the previous year's receipts of $96.5m, though this source of finance, too, has not met the government's expectations (AFR 8/6/89), adding to the Victorian Government's difficulties consequent on the slowdown in the property market.

11.5.7 Expenditure

Table 11.19 summarises the trends in Victorian State Government current, capital and total outlays between 1981/2 and 1986/7, compared to the Australian State sector as a whole. The table shows that total outlays of the Victorian public sector increased in real terms by 12.1% between 1981/2 and 1986/7. This was considerably less than the 18.3% increase in outlays of the total Australian State Government sector during the same time period. Moreover, because of the relatively higher rates of economic growth in Victoria relative to the rest of Australia, Victorian public sector outlays have declined as a proportion of GSP between 1981/2 and 1986/7 from 19.1% to 18.8%, while total outlays of the Australian State Government sector have increased as a proportion of gross domestic product from 19.0% to 19.8%.

Table 11.19 also shows that most of the expenditure restraint by the Victorian public sector has been borne by capital outlays, which fell in real terms by 21% between 1981/2 and 1986/7 (it fell by 11.5% in 1986/7 alone). This real decline stands out in sharp contrast to the 4.4% real increase in capital outlays by the total Australian State Government sector during the same time period.

Expenditure Categories

Table 11.20 summarises, by government purpose category, per capita outlays by the Victorian and Australian State public sectors.

Table 11.19

	State Public Sector Outlays, 1981/2 − 1986/7 $m − 1981/82 % of GSP					
	Victorian Public Sector			*Aust. State Public Sector*		
	Current	Capital	Total	Current	Capital	Total
	Outlays in Constant Dollars					
1981/2	5802.2	2222.8	8025.0	21507.1	8109.7	29616.0
1982/3	6246.0	2241.2	8487.1	22601.0	8823.5	31424.5
1983/4	6405.9	2181.2	8587.1	23705.6	8739.9	32445.6
1984/5	6969.9	2091.0	9060.9	25543.1	8349.3	33892.4
1985/6	7229.3	1986.2	9215.5	26385.4	8600.3	34985.7
1986/7	7237.6	1758.2	8995.8	26571.3	8470.0	35041.3
	% Change on Preceding Year					
1981/2						
1982/3	7.6%	0.8%	5.8%	5.1%	8.8%	6.1%
1983/4	2.6%	−2.7%	1.2%	4.9%	−0.9%	3.2%
1984/5	8.8%	−4.1%	5.5%	7.8%	−4.5%	4.5%
1985/6	3.7%	−5.0%	1.7%	3.3%	3.0%	3.2%
1986/7	0.1%	−11.5%	−2.4%	0.7%	−1.5%	0.2%
	% change					
1981/2						
1986/7	24.7%	−20.9%	12.1%	23.5%	4.4%	18.3%
	Outlays as % of GSP					
1981/2	13.8%	5.3%	19.1%	13.8%	5.2%	19.0%
1982/3	15.1%	5.4%	20.5%	14.8%	5.8%	20.6%
1983/4	14.7%	5.0%	19.7%	14.8%	5.5%	20.3%
1984/5	15.2%	4.5%	19.7%	15.0%	4.9%	19.9%
1985/6	15.2%	4.2%	19.4%	15.1%	4.9%	20.0%
1986/7	15.1%	3.7%	18.8%	15.0%	4.8%	19.8%

Source: ABS Cat. No. 5504.0. CPI data from Year Books. Victorian GSP from Department of Management and Budget. Australian GDP from ABS Cat.To facilitate comparisons, the corresponding Australia-wide State public sector information is also presented in the Table.

The Table shows that, in general terms, the areas of the Victorian public sector which have experienced the fastest rates of outlay growth per capita between 1981/82 and 1986/87 were those associated with the social wage, with outlays on health (22%), and social security and welfare (58.2%), standing out in this regard. Outlays on public order and safety also increased considerably (by 18.7%). The functional areas to have borne the brunt of expenditure restraint were those associated with industry services, with outlays on fuel and energy (-59.8%), agriculture etc., (-23.3%) and

mining manufacturing and construction (-60.2%) all declining significantly. Much of this decline can be attributed to the completion of large capital works programs for electricity generation in the early 1980s, together with the end of the severe drought in rural Victoria in 1983/4. Whilst the increase in social expenditures and public order and safety outlays and the decline in industry services outlays in Victoria mirror the trends in outlays for the consolidated Australian State public sector, it is notable that the changes were much larger in Victoria.

Table 11.20

Outlays by Government Purpose Category
Per Capita
$m – 1981/2
1981/2 – 1986/7

	Victorian State Public Sector			Australian Public Sector		
	1981/2	1986/7	% Change	1981/2	1986/7	% Change
Public Service	$77.2	$100.0	29.6%	$81.5	$94.0	15.4%
Order & Safety	$90.8	$107.7	18.7%	$114.8	$127.0	10.6%
Education	$564.1	$565.4	0.2%	$537.4	$540.7	0.6%
Health	$262.9	$320.8	22.0%	$282.5	$335.6	18.8%
Social Sec. & Welfare	$40.9	$64.7	58.2%	$41.6	$61.1	46.8%
Housing & Com. Amenities	$117.3	$119.7	2.1%	$108.9	$125.2	14.9%
Recreation & Culture	$37.3	$44.0	17.9%	$37.0	$61.1	64.9%
Fuel & Energy	$242.3	$97.3	-59.8%	$188.3	$117.8	-37.5%
Agriculture Forestry, etc.	$38.1	$29.2	-23.3%	$52.0	$63.0	21.0%
Mining, Manufact. & Construction	$4.4	$1.8	-60.2%	$10.3	$10.9	6.0%
Transport & Communication	$212.5	$235.0	10.6%	$258.3	$267.6	3.6%
Other Econ. Affairs	$38.2	$37.4	-2.2%	$26.2	$40.5	54.1%
Other	$295.9	$426.8	44.3%	$258.7	$362.6	40.2%
Total	$1854.8	$1967.0	6.1%	$1997.8	$2207.0	10.5%

Source: ABS Cat. No. 5504.0 (unpublished tables); CPI from Australian Year Books; Population Data from Commonwealth Government Budget Paper No. 4, 1988, p. 17.

Capital Expenditure
A recurring theme of this book is the contribution that the States make to infrastructure development in Australia. In fact, as Part Three indicates, the States are responsible for a larger

proportion of total government expenditure on economic services than the Federal Government, notwithstanding the Commonwealth's greater revenue raising capacity. It is therefore worthwhile examining the Victorian Government's capital expenditure in more detail.

The decline in capital outlays indicated in Table 11.20 in part reflects the State Government's macro-economic strategy of winding back on capital spending during periods of relatively strong economic growth in order to reduce the level of borrowings and, therefore, interest on debt. However, more prosaically, they also reflect the completion during the early to mid 1980s of large scale capital works projects such as the Loy Yang Power Station and the Thomson Dam. By 1987/88, public authority capital spending was some 40% lower in real terms than its level in 1981/82.

11.5.8 Expenditure Priorities in Recent State Budgets

The 1988-89 Budget was designed to assist families to adjust to recent falls in after-tax incomes; develop new and expanded measures to improve social justice in Victoria; undertake new Economic Strategy initiatives; and hold taxes down and to reduce borrowing and debt as a proportion of Non-Farm Gross Domestic Product (NFGDP) (1988-89 Budget Paper No. 2).

The total estimated cost of current account initiatives in 1988-89 is $360.5m. Of this total, $118.0m is in the form of 'tax expenditures' ie.

tax concessions/cuts or other reductions in revenue which otherwise would have been available to the Consolidated Fund.

The last two Budgets taken together involve initiatives with a cost of $674.1m. The family assistance package, with a cost of $198.4m, involves complete abolition of motor registration on Private 'A' vehicles, the introduction of an Education Expense Allowance available to families in receipt of Family Allowance at an annual level of $100 per child aged between 4 and 16 years, and the introduction of stamp duty and mortgage duty exemptions for first home buyers who meet the income test under the Commonwealth first home owners scheme and who have dependant children. Social Justice Strategy recurrent initiatives have a total cost of $97.3m, while works and services initiatives in this area total $28m. These initiatives are focused on the needs of old people, children in poverty, the long term unemployed and the protection of basic rights. Most of the Economic Strategy initiatives, in terms of budgeted cost, have focussed on the pay-roll tax, with a major restructure of the scale, and the enhancement of pay-roll tax concessions for exporters (Victorian Government, 1988-89 Budget Paper No. 2). Table 11.21 summarises these developments.

Table 11.21

Recurrent Budget Initiatives, 1987-88 and 1988-89
($m)

		1987-88	1988-89	Total
1.	Family Support Measures	85.1	113.3	198.4
2.	Social Justice Strategy	29.4	67.9	97.3
3.	Other Social Expenditure	47.1	118.5	165.6
4.	Economic Strategy Support	96.5	35.1	131.6
5.	Other Revenue Initiatives	55.5	25.7	81.2
Total		313.6	360.5	674.1
of which:				
Expenditure		130.0	242.5	372.5
Revenue Forgone		183.6	118.0	301.6

Source: Victorian Government 1988-89 Budget Papers No. 2, Budget Strategy and Review, p. 2.

Debt Charges

The indebtedness of, and the level of interest payments by, the Victorian public sector has been a matter of public concern (see, for example, The Australian, September 24/25/88,

p. 28). However, the debt servicing ratio of both the Victorian and Australian State public sectors could hardly be considered as excessive, with interest accounting for less than 15% of total revenues (Davidson, 1988).

Between 1985/86 and 1986/87, in fact, the interest on debt of the Victorian public sector declined in both constant dollar terms and as a proportion of Gross State Product — 2% and 0.1% respectively. This real decline in interest costs can be expected to have been maintained during 1987/88 and 1988/89 due to continuing real reductions in capital outlays and in the level of borrowings.

11.5.9 Conclusion
The overview of spending and financing trends of the Victorian public sector provided in this and the previous Section together with the overview of economic and demographic trends provided in Section 2 neatly summarises the variety of problems facing the Victorian State public sector. It has been shown that the public sector plays a crucial role not only in providing key elements of the social wage but in augmenting the State's infrastructure.

The financing difficulties currently being experienced by the Victorian Government are partially explicable by reference to Commonwealth Government policy, and partly by the government's own policies. The ability of the State to rely on its own revenues in recent years can be accounted for by Victoria's relatively high rates of economic growth in the last six years, which have simultaneously resulted in a surge in tax receipts and the net operating surplus of PTEs. No State Government can afford to rely on the continuation of such an environment. The slow-down in the Victorian economy is already having its consequences on the Victorian public sector and Victorians in general.

11.6 Case Studies of Privatisation in Victoria
11.6.1 Introduction
As Part Three of this Report has illustrated, the case for privatisation is unconvincing. There is a considerable body of empirical evidence to show that, in practice, many of the alleged benefits of privatisation are illusory, while the social costs which often result are both real and large. In this Section we examine examples of privatisation which have taken place in Victoria. The Victorian experience of privatisation to date warns strongly against any attempt to

implement a substantial privatisation program in the State.

11.6.2 Privatisation in Victoria: Some Examples
While the Victorian Government remains publicly opposed to a comprehensive privatisation program, over the years various programs have been put in place which embrace each form of privatisation identified in Part Three. Some of these policies date back to the 1950s (eg. the sale of public housing). Others are of more recent origin. Table 11.22 provides a summary of examples of each form of privatisation currently to be found in Victoria.

It should be recognised that there may be a case for implementing on an individual basis some privatisation initiatives. For example, the Victorian Government has over the last few years implemented an asset sales program in which surplus government buildings and land have been sold, with the proceeds of the asset sales being used to finance new capital expenditures on projects yielding higher net benefits to the public sector. The revenue gains from such policies do not, however, provide a solid basis from which to plan medium to long term spending policies.

As the following case studies make clear, there have been individual cases of privatisation in Victoria which, in the long term, have led to an unjustifiable and costly dismantling of parts of the public sector, and this in turn has compromised the ability of the public sector today to meet emerging social needs. Moreover, while the proponents of privatisation claim that greater use of the private sector will necessarily result in a more efficient use of resources, the Victorian case studies suggest that this is not the case.

11.6.3 Case Studies
Asset Sales: The Case of Public Housing
A key component of Margaret Thatcher's privatisation program in the UK during the last ten years has been the sale of public (council) housing to sitting tenants. The program has so far proven to be a 'popular' one (Saunders, 1986), with some 750,000 public housing units being sold between 1979 and 1986 (Forest & Murie, 1986) at a considerable

(and increasingly large) discount price (as high as 60%) (Ball, 1985). For housing analysts in Australia, the research findings on the British privatisation program have been treated with a sense of *deja vu*.

Far from being a new-comer to privatisation policies, Australian Governments in fact have been world 'leaders' in the privatisation of housing. Indeed, the Thatcher Government's privatisation of public housing – often hailed as a new privatisation initiative – lagged behind, by over two decades, the privatisation of public housing in Australia. Had the British Government examined the Australian experience prior to launching its own privatisation program it would have drawn the same con-

clusion that most commentators reached in Australia: in the long run, the consequences of the privatisation of public housing produce costs which far outweigh the benefits. It is indeed ironic that the implementation of the public housing sales program in Britain in 1979 occurred only 12 months after the conservative Fraser Government had decided that the costs of the program could no longer be tolerated in Australia. In 1978, the Fraser Government moved to restrict the ability of State Governments to sell public housing at discount prices. In 1981 it prevented them from doing so altogether, and the widescale sale of public housing in Australia was effectively brought to an end.

Table 11.22

Examples of Privatisation in Victoria

Form of Privatisation	Selected Examples
Asset Sales	Housing Commission (Ministry of Housing) Ministry of Transport; Department of Health; Ministry of Planning & Environment. Sale of public housing; surplus land and buildings.
Contracting Out	Ministry of Housing and Construction (Housing Commission/Public Works Department); Road Construction Authority; Metropolitan Transit Authority; V Line; Gas and Fuel Corporation; State Electricity Commission.
	Contracting out of: housing construction & maintenance; construction and maintenance of roads, bridges; up-grading and maintenance of gas and electricity services (in peak periods).
Deregulation	Estate Agent Industry.
Commercialisation	Government Printer; State Bank; State Insurance Office; Gas and Fuel Corporation; State Electricity Commission.
Corporatisation	Ministry of Housing and Construction; Ministry of Education, Department of Community Services. State Electricity Commission; Gas and Fuel Corporation.
Voluntarism	De-institutionalisation of mental health.
User Pays	Government primary and secondary schools. Technical and Further Education. Imposition of 'voluntary' charges on primary and secondary school students; fees for TAFE courses.

Victoria was a particularly enthusiastic participant in the Australia wide policy of selling off public housing. Between 1950 and 1981 some 28,500 publicly rented housing units in this State alone were sold to sitting tenants (Burke, Campbell, Hayward & Nisbet, 1985).

This represents 51.5% of all public housing units constructed or purchased in Victoria during this time period. The enthusiasm of Victorian Governments toward this program was so intense that, between 1974 and 1981 approximately 50% of publicly rented housing stock sold in Australia was accounted for by Victoria alone (Burke, Hancock & Newton, 1983).

The key ingredient to the 'success' of the public housing sales policy in Victoria (and, indeed, Australia) was not simply allowing tenants to purchase their homes – something which tenants have been consistently entitled to do since the establishment of public housing in Victoria in 1945. Rather, it was the decision by the Menzies Government in 1956 to encourage State Governments to sell publicly rented houses at discount prices, often with the assistance of cheap housing loans provided by the Commonwealth Government (Berry, 1988). Discount pricing was necessary because tenants could not otherwise have afforded to purchase the houses (nor would there have been much sense in them doing so because their public housing 'cost' rents were relatively low, and they also enjoyed the security of tenure offered by public housing).

Through a 'discount' pricing policy, the public housing sales program effected a redistribution of income and wealth from the public sector to the purchasing tenants, and the Victorian Housing Commission (now the Victorian Ministry of Housing and Construction [VMOHC]) did not generate sufficient revenue to finance a complete asset replacement program. Hence, the net level of additions to the public housing stock fell from an average of 2,619 units p.a. between 1945 and 1956 (prior to the sales program being introduced), to an average of 460 units p.a. between 1956 and 1976. In some years (1960, 1961 and 1977) the size of the public housing stock actually declined! To give some indication of the impact of the sales program on the size of the Victorian public housing sector, had the sales program not been implemented, by 1976 the Victorian public housing stock would have consisted of 115,000 units instead of only 36,674 units. Instead of accounting for only 3.3% of the total stock of housing, public housing in Victoria would have accounted for over 10% (Kemeny, 1983, pp. 12-16; Berry, 1988).

Of course, the houses that were sold simply passed from the public to the private sector: the size of the public housing stock fell, but the home ownership rate increased. However, by

failing to charge full market or replacement prices for the houses, the sales program resulted in under-investment in additional (new) housing units, with the funds which otherwise could have been used to finance the building of additional houses by the public sector being transferred to the purchasing tenants. The consequence of this 'leakage' of funds from the housing system manifested itself in 1981 in a public housing waiting list in Victoria of approximately 17,000 households. The tenants who were allowed to purchase their homes undoubtedly benefited, but they did so at the expense of other low income households, the majority of whom remained trapped in insecure, unaffordable, dilapidated private rental housing.

The cost of the sales program did not end here, however. The establishment of a nationwide public housing system in Australia in 1945 was premised on the view of tenure neutrality, in which public housing would stand alongside home ownership as a viable housing alternative for all Australians. Rents for public housing would be determined not on strictly commercial criteria, but according to the historical costs of constructing the housing (amortised over 53 years) plus a mark-up for maintenance and administration (Berry, 1988). Over time, the average value of the debt on the stock would decline in real terms and rents would not only remain below market prices, but would probably decline in real terms. Public housing would therefore be an affordable, acceptable and secure alternative for those households who could not afford or did not wish to buy their own homes. The sales program undermined these original aims because, by selling dwellings – and the better quality stock at that – the rents charged did not fall in the way originally envisaged. During the 1970s the problems faced by the Victorian Housing Commission and its clientele were exacerbated, first, by the decision in 1973 to implement a 'means test' for access to public housing, and second, by the decision in 1978 to move from cost to market rents (a decision which was reversed in 1983), with rebates being applied to low income tenants. In combination, the sales policy, the means test requirement, and the implementation of market rents transformed public housing in Victoria (and Australia generally) into welfare housing, in which only the very poor could live (Kemeny, 1981; 1983; Paris, Williams & Stimson, 1985; Berry, 1988).

This has had three undesirable consequences which together have served to undermine the viability of public housing in Victoria today:

— public housing estates are characterised by high rates of poverty, a high proportion of single parents, and high levels of unemployment (see for example Victorian Ministry of Housing, 1985). Households in public housing are now clearly identifiable as being poor simply by virtue of their housing tenure. This has led to problems of discrimination and victimisation, and has resulted in the VMOHC experiencing difficulty in providing more accommodation because of the opposition by private householders to having public housing and therefore poor people located in their neighbourhood. It is now increasingly common for Local Councils, under pressure from local action groups, to oppose the building of additional public housing units, and for the building program consequently to be delayed by many months until, as is usually the case, the Planning Appeals Tribunal orders that the program should proceed;

— the increasing proportion of public tenants on very low incomes has meant that a decreasing proportion of tenants can afford to pay the relatively low cost rents now charged by the VMOHC. The Ministry's policy is that tenants should not have to pay more than 20% of their base income in rent. The difference between the actual rent and the rent that can be afforded is made up by a rental rebate. In 1984, 31,129 households, or 73% of all public tenants, were in receipt of rental rebates. By 1988 the number of recipients had increased to 42,586 households, which represented 79% of all tenants in that year (Ministry of Housing and Construction Annual Reports). With such a large proportion of tenants on rental rebates, it is now impossible for the Ministry of Housing to operate its public housing pro-

gram with an operating surplus. In 1987/8 the cost of the rebates to the Ministry was $79m, which was almost four times the value of the Ministry's operating deficit in that year ($20m) (VMOHC Annual Report, 1987/8); and

— consequent on these privatisation policies there remains a considerable spatial imbalance in the location of public housing. This is primarily because, as Table 11.23 shows, the sales policy operated in a spatially uneven way. For example, while approximately 50% of the public housing stock in the metropolitan area was sold between 1956 and 1981 (the discount sales policy ended in 1981), the proportion of stock sold in each of Melbourne's regions varied from over 70% in the North Western Region to 50% in the North Eastern Region, and to less than 4% in the Inner Urban and Outer Eastern Regions.

Compounding this problem is that house price inflation, particularly in the Inner, Inner Eastern and Southern Regions, now makes it virtually impossible for the VMOHC to afford to purchase in those municipalities additional stock to replace that which has been sold. In some municipalities it is impossible for the Ministry even to contemplate re-purchasing stock that was sold only ten years ago!

The final consequence of these privatisation policies is related to the previous one. One of the reasons for the spatially uneven nature of the sales program was that the dwellings most likely to be sold were good quality detached and semi-detached houses, often of solid brick construction, which tended to be concentrated in particular parts of the metropolitan area. Hence, not only has the Ministry of Housing and Construction been saddled with a stock distributed in a spatially uneven way, but it has been left with a large proportion of its stock consisting of dwelling units which are either difficult to maintain (eg. high rise flats) or are of poor quality, often being made of inferior materials (eg. concrete and fibro cement dwellings). The latter is particularly the case in country regions and in some metropolitan estates (eg. West Heidelberg). The poor quality of the dwellings that were not sold off has further contributed to the erosion of public confidence in public housing. It has also resulted in the Ministry experiencing a rapidly increasing maintenance bill. For example, in 1983/4 the Ministry's maintenance bill accounted for approximately 15% of total operating expenses, but by 1987/8 it had come to account for approximately 25% (Ministry of Housing and Construction Annual Reports).

Table 11.23

Public Housing Stock and Public Housing Sales
(by Melbourne Metropolitan Region)
(1987)

Region	(1) Stock at 30/6/88 No.	(2) Stock sold 1956-1981 No.	(1) + (2) Potential Stock No.	(2)/(3) % of Stock Sold	Waiting List Applicants 30/6/88
Inner Urban	12,439	441	12,880	3.4%	1,435
Western	5,279	8,595	13,874	62.0%	918
North Western	2,914	7,302	10,216	71.5%	2,979
North Eastern	5,033	5,069	10,102	50.2%	2,133
Inner Eastern	2,009	2,636	4,645	56.7%	3,140
Outer Eastern	2,062	15	2,077	0.7%	3,337
Southern	1,850	1,621	3,471	46.7%	6,783
Westernport	5,001	7,106	12,107	58.7%	6,599
Total	36,587	28,579	65,166	43.9%	27,324

Note: waiting list figures include transfer applicants.
Sources: Burke, Campbell, Nisbet and Hayward, 1985: Tables 2.8.1-2.8.6; Victorian Ministry of Housing and Construction Annual Report, 1987/8.

This overview of the privatisation of public housing in Victoria is more than just of historical interest. In recent years some leading New Right figures have been arguing strongly in favour of a renewed commitment to the privatisation of public housing. However, rather than simply advocate a repeat of the sales policy of previous decades, the call now is for governments to redirect monies currently used to build or buy public housing into a housing allowance scheme, which would be made available on a means tested basis to all households in need of housing assistance. Perhaps the most disturbing aspect of this proposal is the way that the history of public housing in Australia is fundamentally distorted in order to justify a renewed attack on public housing. Walsh (1988), for example, manages to provide an overview of the history of post World War II housing policy in Australia without even mentioning the public housing sales program. Having overlooked this major privatisation housing policy initiative, he not surprisingly draws the conclusion that the Australian experience of building public housing has been a failure: 'Despite the continued funding of public housing programs, government tenancies represented only about 5.1% of all tenancies in 1981 . . .' (1988, p. 8). Equally understandable, given his failure to acknowledge the sales program, is his conclusion that the history of Australian housing policy is 'characteristic of, and symptomatic of, the problem of the growth of government' (1988, p. 2).

As has been argued above, the problem facing public housing provision today is not a consequence of too much government. Rather it is a direct result of decades of a privatisation policy that in the long run has produced more costs than benefits.

Just as the sale of public housing has generated long term net costs, the housing allowance proposal too could have such effects. In a recent evaluation of the likely long term effects of a housing allowance scheme in lieu of the direct provision of public housing in

Melbourne, *Econonsult* (1989) have concluded that:

> 'In terms of cost effectiveness in providing poverty relief . . ., even under the most unfavourable assumptions, public housing emerges as the lowest cost long term strategy' (1989, p. iii).

As an example, they cite the case of the likely long term effects in the outer Melbourne suburb of Cranbourne of maintaining public housing investment instead of pursuing a housing allowance scheme. Through an econometric model, they project that by year 20 the direct provision of public housing would yield 65% more accommodation to low income households than would have been the case if all government funding was directed to a housing allowance scheme. By year 30 the model projects the difference to be a massive 200% (1989, p. 29)! In explaining why their results contradict the projections made by those in favour of the housing allowance proposal, Econsult point to the tendency of New Right writings to focus on the short rather than the long term consequences of their policy proposals (1989, p. iii).

In summary, the privatisation of public housing in Victoria has generated costs which are still being felt today and will continue to be felt by the next generation of Victorians. Moreover, it provides a striking illustration of the way that privatisation policies can lead to a pernicious and self reinforcing process of public sector decline in which some private individuals benefit, but the majority of ordinary citizens lose. The 33,000 households currently waiting for access to public housing in Victoria serve as a tangible and vivid reminder of a short sighted privatisation policy that failed to take into account the longer term consequences (see Table 11.24).

Table 11.24

Waiting List Applicants for Public Housing
(1978-1988)

	No. of New Applicants[1]		No. of New Applicants[1]
1978	12,863		
1979	12,836	1984	20,992
1980	12,190	1985	23,729
1981	16,813	1986	28,772
1982	14,260	1987	30,076
1983	19,886	1988	33,000

Note: [1] These data exclude transfer applicants. The total number of applicants in 1988 was 37,472.
Source: Victorian Ministry of Housing and Construction Annual Reports.

The Case of Contracting Out in the Victorian Ministry of Housing and Construction

Contracting out has the potential to be one of the most far reaching forms of privatisation. It can be applied to 'internal' operations of a public sector agency (eg. cleaning, research, catering), or it can be applied to 'external' operations (eg. bus services, the running and administration of prisons). It can embrace the provision of labour only (eg. hiring a contractor to perform a particular task using publicly owned assets) through to the provision of labour and assets (eg. hiring a contractor to provide buses and bus drivers).

According to its advocates, contracting out offers the public sector a convenient vehicle for achieving significant gains in productive efficiency. This is because the 'function' can be effectively 'auctioned' through a tendering process to a private contractor who agrees to perform the function at a cheaper price than either the public sector or any other private contractor. Providing the competitive tendering process is on-going and comes up for renewal periodically contractors are said to be provided with an incentive to continually improve the level of output for a given level of input, to ensure that the service provided is of adequate quality, and to perform the activity at the lowest possible price.

Contracting out of public sector functions in Victoria is by no means a new phenomena. The operation of some bus services, and both housing construction and maintenance have been contracted-out since World War II. In this case study we examine the use of contracting out of maintenance work and house building by the VMOHC. We do so because these functions have been contracted out for over four decades now, so they provide an important demonstration of the costs and benefits of this form of privatisation.

Each year the VMOHC uses contractors for a variety of purposes associated with its public housing program. These include the construction of new housing units, the design of new housing (or the modification of existing housing), and the rehabilitation and modification work on recently purchased existing dwellings which need to be altered in order for them to be suitable for various programs. Contracting out thus embraces architectural services through to construction and maintenance work. In 1987/8 the Ministry employed contractors to construct over 1,550 units, and to rehabilitate a further 250 dwellings. While it is difficult to be precise, it would appear that over $100m of the Ministry's program expenditures were allocated for these purposes (VMOHC Annual Report, 1987/8, pp. 35-39).

In addition to construction work, the VMOHC employs contractors to undertake maintenance work on its public housing stock.[2] As is the case with private rental housing, maintenance of public housing rests quite properly with the legal owners of the dwellings, in this case the public housing authorities. The maintenance work can range from single skilled (eg. plumbing) to multi-skilled tasks (eg. repairing a damaged bathroom, which would require plumbing, tiling, plastering and carpentry work). Because of the size and geographical dispersion of the public housing stock the Ministry's maintenance task is far more complex than that confronting a private rental landlord. In Victoria there are some 55,000 public housing units throughout the

State, 36% of which are spread throughout country regions (VMOHC Annual Report 1987/8). Moreover, due to the sales policy mentioned above, almost 30% of the stock is over 25 years old, almost one in three units is constructed with concrete (a building material subject to a variety of maintenance problems), and a further one in three metropolitan units consist of high rise or walk-up flats. The stock has therefore increasingly become maintenance intensive, and the Ministry's maintenance bill has (as the previous section demonstrated) increased (VMOHC Annual Report).

Unlike some other States which use various combinations of day-labour and private contractors, in Victoria virtually all maintenance work on public housing currently is contracted out. As with general construction work, the procedure involves competitive tendering of work to be done either through advertisement or preferred tender in which a small number of specific contractors are invited to tender. On completion of the tasks by the contractor, the job is inspected by VMOHC staff to assess the adequacy and quality of the work done.

During the last six years an increasing level of concern has been generated over the quality of the work done by Ministry contractors, and the way that they have achieved alleged cost savings. In 1982 an investigation (the Seabrooke Report) was launched into the extent of 'pyramid contracting' and 'cash-in-hand payments' by contractors to the then Public Works Department, which has since been merged with the Ministry of Housing. Pyramid contracting involves a contractor hiring out some or all aspects of the tasks to be undertaken to other sub-contractors, who in turn engage the services of other sub-contractors. Cash-in-hand payments involve paying workers in cash, so that the workers do not have to pay income tax on their earnings (usually as an offset to receiving sub-award wage and working conditions). The investigation was undertaken because both practices involve an attempt by contractors to avoid paying payroll taxes and to avoid meeting their statutory obligations such as regularly providing contributions to the State's Building Industry Long Service Scheme and the State's workers compensation scheme (then known as the Workers Compensation

Scheme, now called WorkCare). In addition, pyramid sub-contracting enables the workers employed to lower their income tax payments. This is achieved by the workers involved forming companies with spouses and then splitting their income to lower the amount of tax due. The Seabrooke Report found that contractors to the Public Works Department engaged in all forms of tax avoidance mentioned above on a large scale (contractors who were involved in one of these avoidance activities usually engaged in all avoidance activities). Altogether, the Report identified 289 incidents of cash-in-hand payments of which 189 involved government departments (105 being associated with the Public Works Department) (For a summary of the Seabrooke Report, see Building Industry Investigation Committee, 1983, p. 44).

Shortly after the release of the Seabrooke Report, the then Ministry of Housing undertook a similar investigation (the Sneath Report), which agreed with the conclusions reached by Seabrooke (for a summary of the Sneath Report see The Building Industry Investigation Committee, 1983, p. 47).

Following the release of these reports, the Victorian Government established the Building Industry Investigation Committee (BIIC) in 1983 to examine the level and extent of 'pyramid sub-contracting' and 'cash-in-hand payments' in the Victorian construction industry in general. The BIIC, too, found that tax

evasion in the construction industry was extensive, and expressed particular concern that government agencies had for many years been hiring contractors who, through an intricate system of sub-contracting and cash-in-hand payments, achieve cost savings by avoiding the payment of payroll taxes, long service leave contributions, and workers compensation contributions; by eroding working conditions (including health and safety standards) in the building industry; and by engaging in shoddy workpractices (1983, pp. 72-92, 117-125). The BIIC referred to submissions by some contractors who claimed that it was not possible for a contractor to successfully tender for work with a government agency without engaging in the forms of avoidance and evasion practiced by other contractors (1983, p. 93). It also drew attention to the considerable long term costs being borne by the building industry because of the tendency for the contractors not to hire apprentices (a task left up to the 'sub-contractors', whose insecure job tenure acts as a strong incentive for them not to assume this responsibility). The Committee was especially concerned that Victorian Government agencies had no mechanism in place for preventing contractors from engaging in tax avoidance and the evasion of their statutory obligations. Table 11.25 summarises the results of investigations by the Committee into the extent of these practices in government agencies.

Table 11.25

Number of Cases of Tax Avoidance and Cash-in-Hand Payments by Contractors Working for Government Agencies

	Number of workers Investigated	Number of cases of tax avoidance:			
		Cash-in-Hand	PAYE	Workers Comp.	Long Service
Public Works Dept.	65	34	26	30	34
Housing	164	94	80	94	66
Health	14	12	5	12	12
Transport	130	13	13	8	13
SEC	7	1	1	–	1
Total	380	154	125	144	126

Source: Building Industry Investigation Committee, 1983: Appendix 17, Table 2.

In 1985 the Victorian Government established the Building Industry Inquiry Implementation

Committee (BIIIC) to examine ways of implementing the recommendations of the earlier

Committee, and to further investigate the extent of tax avoidance in the construction industry. A key point made by this Committee on the basis of intensive interviews with key public sector personnel was that government agencies considered it to be in their economic interest to hire contractors who engaged in tax avoidance, the evasion of workers compensation and long service leave contributions and to hire workers under sub-award conditions. This is because, in an era of fiscal austerity, the individual agencies were keen to have work completed at the lowest possible short term cost to their own program budgets. The problem with this view is that the 'savings' to the program budgets do not derive from 'efficiency' gains, but simply represent a redistribution of income: the agencies get their work completed at a lower price than otherwise would be the case, but the costs are borne by Consolidated Revenue (in the case of tax avoidance), other 'legitimate' construction contractors (who faced higher workcare premiums and Long Service Leave contributions), and those building workers who suffer an erosion in their working conditions.

From our investigations,[3] it would appear that tax avoidance and evasion, as well as the evasion of other statutory obligations by VMOHC contractors is still considerable. Two of the largest builders of public housing in Victoria hire no direct labour at all (all building work is sub-contracted out) and it would appear that many other contractors have, until relatively recently, made only token contributions to the Long Service Leave Scheme and to WorkCare. Recent estimates indicate that the extent of avoidance and evasion remains considerable. This is particularly so amongst contractors hired to do maintenance work on government buildings (ie. those who work for the former Department of Public Works), with anywhere between 30% to 40% of workers hired by these contractors being employed in a way that enables the contractors not having to pay appropriate levels of government taxes and charges.[4]

In addition to contractors engaging on a large scale in tax avoidance and the evasion of statutory obligations, there is also evidence of overservicing and overclaiming for work done. The Victorian Auditor-General referred in his

1986/7 Annual Report to two specific cases. The first involved a contractor who between December 1985 and December 1986 overserviced by $108,000. As the contractor had been employed by the VMOHC over a 20 year period, the Auditor-General suggested that the total monies involved far exceed the $108,000 so far identified. The second involved a contractor who both duplicated claims and overcharged on time taken. The total bill in this case was $120,000.

Our research findings, and those of the Committees mentioned above, suggest that any attempt to compare the cost differences between a government agency employing direct labour and contractors must be done with extreme care. This is because while it is not possible for government agencies employing direct labour to avoid paying taxes and to employ workers on sub-award conditions, contractors, by virtue of 'market forces', seem to do so as a matter of course.

The problems with the contracting experience of the VMOHC do not end here, however. On the basis of the available evidence, the quality of maintenance work undertaken by contractors appears to vary considerably. The Ministry of Housing and Construction has, until recently, made no systematic attempt to monitor the adequacy of work undertaken by contractors or to prevent contractors who perform poorly from being re-hired. The only comprehensive evaluation of tenant satisfaction with the quality of the contracted out maintenance work was conducted in 1983 on the West Heidelberg Housing Estate, which consists of large numbers of brick, wood, concrete and prefabricated dwellings constructed during the 1940s, and 50s. The findings of this evaluation are instructive, however, because the housing on this Estate was poorly built (by private contractors), and was constructed on extremely poor quality soil. In conjunction, these two problems have ensured that maintenance problems are considerable, with, for example, over 90% of dwellings having cracked walls including one fifth of the dwellings with cracks over one quarter of an inch wide (Tenants Action Project, 1984, p. 14). The tenants therefore have had extensive first hand experience with the

Ministry's maintenance system. The findings of the evaluation are worth quoting:

> Over half of the tenants (53%) were dissatisfied with the maintenance system. The common complaints were: poor quality repair work, rude and inefficient contractors and long delays. Tenants complained that the contractors work was of a very poor standard and was often not completed properly. One tenant commented: 'How they get paid for what they do has got me tossed'. Another stated: 'You wait for ages and when they come they don't do the job properly, in fact they leave an even greater mess behind'. This last statement represents the sheer frustration that tenants have experienced with the maintenance system (Tenant Action Project Team, 1984, p. 21).

Tenant dissatisfaction with VMOHC contractors also appears to extend to the work completed by house builders. (cf. CSH, 1987, p. 89.) Interviews we conducted with Public Housing Tenants' Associations and Regional Housing Council's revealed that it was not uncommon for new public housing units to suffer major structural flaws within five years of the dwellings being built. The most common problems cited were that of inadequate bathroom fittings (particularly showers, which tended to leak), and poor foundations, with the latter eventually resulting in cracked walls and ceilings.

These severe and continuing problems which plague the contracting out of building work by the Ministry of Housing and Construction have their origins in the private, not the public sector, and can be traced as far back as the late 19th century (Hayward, 1987). For house builders today, the sub-contracting out of building work is a convenient method of employment for several reasons, which together have ensured that few builders employ any direct labour. First, competition between subcontractors for work keeps wage rates relatively low. Second, pyramid sub-contracting and cash-in-hand payments keep wage and on-costs lower than would otherwise be the case. Third, it provides a convenient vehicle for keeping control over a labour force which can

be spread over a number of different building sites. And finally, and most importantly, it provides the builders with a flexible form of employment contract, so necessary in an unstable industry such as house building: when the housing market experiences a recession, builders can shed labour at will (Hayward, 1987).

It is these features of sub-contracting which result in building workers having to endure episodic, rather than continuous, employment, often on a very low wage. It also results in the building industry tending to be chronically short of skilled labour. During market downturns, building workers frequently leave the industry, while builders cut back significantly on their intake of apprentices (see for example the apprenticeship data provided in Indicative Planning Council, 1988). Hence, when the building industry subsequently experiences an upturn, builders quickly experience a shortage of skilled labour (Hayward, 1989).

The most disturbing aspect of our research on the contracting out of building and maintenance work by the VMOHC is not, then, that the public sector is responsible for the problems which bedevil the contracting out of public sector housing work: the problems experienced by the public sector in actual fact are a private sector problem which the public sector has inherited. Although it is likely that the VMOHC will continue its practice of contracting out (particularly for the purpose of housing construction), the serious and continuing problems associated with the maintenance system has recently resulted in the Ministry reaching the same conclusion as this report: that contracting out has not proven to be an efficient or effective exercise, particularly in the area of maintenance. As a result the Ministry has agreed to undertake a pilot program with a view to assessing the feasibility of replacing maintenance contractors with its own direct labour force.[5] By so doing, the Ministry now has the opportunity to assume a pace setting role in the area of building industry employment. By expanding its use of direct labour, the Ministry will be in a position to offer to building workers pay and conditions to which they are entitled, but which they frequently are denied due to the dubious employment practices which characterise the private house building industry. Moreover, it offers the Ministry a unique opportunity to hire more apprentices, and thereby help overcome the shortage of skilled labour which regularly afflicts the building industry. It is a welcome and long overdue initiative.

User Pays in the State Education System
One of the implications of the emerging pressures on State finances noted in Section 6 is that the Victorian Government will increasingly consider reducing outlays on some parts of the public sector. One of the government's potential candidates for real declines in funding is education. First, as Section Five made clear, education outlays are the single most important expenditure item in the Victorian State budget, accounting for over 28% of total State outlays in 1986/87. Of this, almost 60% goes to State schools. Second, Victorian education outlays are much higher than education outlays by most other States.

One option adopted by government is to jettison the principle of direct government provision of education funded by taxation, and to move towards a system of user pays, in which at least part of the cost of attending State schools would be borne by parents. The British experience of privatisation — to initially introduce a 'nominal' charge for attendance at government schools and then to gradually increase the level of fees until a significant proportion of expenditure on education on public education has been shifted on to the budgets of individual households — has been emulated in Victoria over the last five years.

State schools in Victoria have long been permitted to charge parents a fee to cover some of the costs associated with their children's education, although parents have the right to refuse to pay the fee charged. During the 1970s, most schools took advantage of this by charging students for the costs of materials used for 'practical' subjects such as woodwork. During the 1980s, however, an increasing number of State schools have introduced a generalised 'voluntary' fee imposed on all students in order to cover some of the costs of the schools operating expenses (eg. maintenance of yards, photo-copying and payment of wages for first aid officers).[6] The simple reason for the imposition of such fees is that government funding of education has been declining in real terms (Victorian Government Budget Paper No. 4 1988/89, p. 13).

The government provides no published information on the amount of money raised by schools through these fees. In an attempt to assess the extent to which government schools have come to rely on fees to cover their operating costs (excluding wages), the Victorian Association of Principals surveyed 300 Victorian secondary schools in 1988. Because of the variety of forms the fees take, and the low response rate to the questionnaire, the results of the survey must be treated with caution. However, in aggregate the respondents indicated that they accounted for 30% of school non-salary operating costs by 1988, up from 15% in 1982.

To verify these findings, and to assess the level of fees charged by schools in 1989, we interviewed bursars and Principals at 13 State secondary schools in the Melbourne Metropolitan region. Each school was asked whether they charged a fee; if so, how much per student; and the uses to which the fees were put. With the one exception of a disadvantaged school, all had either introduced fees during the last five years, and all agreed that it would not be possible for their schools to operate effectively without the fees.

Two of the most striking aspects of the information obtained was the variation in the fees charged, ranging from nil (the disadvantaged school) to $175 p.a.; and the variation between schools in the more affluent Eastern and Southern regions relative to the fees charged in the poorer Western regions. The Principals and bursars gave the clear indication that the need for more funds existed in the poorer suburbs, but that they were unable or unwilling to impose additional costs onto the already relatively impoverished families whose children attend those schools.

The implication of this is clear: the more that schools are required to fund their operating expenses from fees, the greater the spatial disparity in the quality of education provided in the metropolitan area. Seen in this way, the 'voluntary' fees are in clear contradiction with the aims and objectives of the government's Social Justice Strategy.

Interviews we conducted with the Principals and Federation of State Schools' Parents Association leave little doubt that, in practice, in many State schools the fee is anything but 'voluntary'. Fee notices sent to parents often imply that the 'voluntary' nature of the fee only applies to those parents in financial hardship. Given the contraction in education funding, should schools emphasise that fees are voluntary, they would undermine an important source of revenue.

Some schools resort to questionable tactics to ensure that most parents pay the fee. The Federation of State School Parents Associations has received numerous letters from aggrieved parents whose children have been singled out at school assembly or who have had their school reports withheld because of non-payment of the fee.[7] In response to these complaints, the Ministry of Education has publicly rebuked those schools which have engaged in these practices, and continues to maintain that fees are voluntary, which appears a device for deflecting criticism rather than a genuine attempt to solve the problem. In some cases, the fees have produced considerable local conflict. In the Southern region, a prolonged and highly public dispute between a high school and a group of aggrieved parents has resulted in considerable negative publicity in local newspapers towards the government education system.

A most disappointing aspect of this privatisation policy is that the government could quite easily have resolved the problems by increasing the level of recurrent school funding, without increasing the level of overall school funding. In the 1987/88 Budget the government introduced an 'Education Expense Allowance' (EEA) to be paid to families in receipt of Family Allowances with children aged from 5 to 15 at a rate of $60 per child. In the 1988/89 Budget this EEA was increased to $100, and coverage was extended to families with children aged between 4 and 16. For 1988/89 the cost of this initiative was estimated at $72.9m. In many ways, this EEA is a form of education voucher because it is paid to all parents in receipt of

family allowances who have children of school age regardless of whether the children attend State schools. The irony of the EEA is that for most families whose children attend State schools a considerable proportion — if not all — of the EEA would be used to cover the cost of fees.

The problems experienced in some schools with the fee could quite easily be resolved by the government using the funds for the EEA to finance the abolition of fees for State schools. In this way the government would abandon its flirtation with the privatisation of State school education and demonstrate its support for free and universal government-provided education.

Deinstitutionalisation

Deinstitutionalisation refers to the process of moving people with disabilities out of large segregated institutions into community-based living arrangements. It is not merely about finding alternative accommodation, but also about developing a more appropriate support system. Funding and planning remain the responsibility of the State but community groups become responsible for the delivery of services. The process raises the issue of the role of the public sector, and also the issues of voluntarism and trade unionism.

The large formal psychiatric or intellectual care institutions (such as Willsmere) have their origin in nineteenth century attitudes towards the care of the intellectually disabled or psychiatrically disturbed. Those who did not conform to the prevailing social norms were incarcerated, and it was this attitude which dominated the State's policies until the 1980s.

The momentum for de-institutionalisation in Victoria gathered strength throughout the 1980s and reflected greater community awareness of the human rights of the disabled, and that the needs of the disabled would be best met within the community. This philosophy, often called 'normalisation', became reflected in the Victorian Government's 1986 Disability Services, and Mental Health, Acts, which encouraged and facilitated the relocation of intellectually and psychiatrically disabled into the community.

Since 1985, the Department of Community

Services (CSV) has been responsible for the people with intellectual disabilities and the Health Commission (later, the Department of Health) responsible for psychiatric difficulties. The specific offices responsible for these areas within the Departments are the Office of Intellectual Disability Services (OIDS) and the Office of Psychiatric Disability Service (OPDS). In 1987/88 the CSV spent $147m on services, and the Department of Health, $249m. There were some 6,600 intellectually disabled or psychiatrically ill people in institutions in 1987, and it is intended that a large proportion of this number should be de-institutionalised over the next ten years.

The process of de-institutionalisation has the potential to go enormously wrong if it is not properly resourced, planned and managed by the government, as the US experience illustrates. Thirty percent of the homeless in the US are estimated to be former psychiatric or intellectually disabled persons (The Economist, 6-12 May 1989, pp. 36-36).

However, in contrast to the 'hands-off' model adopted in the US, the Victorian Government has created the conditions for a successful de-institutionalisation process albeit not without some continuing problems in at least two areas. They are in the areas of resourcing, and industrial relations. In terms of resourcing, a recent study on de-institutionalisation in Victoria found that:

'a positive feature of the Victorian scene is the number of non-government organisations providing accommodation and services provided by the Victorian Government Department's of Health and Community Service' (Neilson, 1988, p. 144).

The involvement of community groups in human service activities requires sufficient funding to ensure, first, that there are an adequate number of agencies to provide services; and second, that the quality of services offered is consistent with the needs of clients and the expectations of the community. While the level of government funding has been sufficient to attract community involvement with a reasonable level of quality, there remain a number of areas of financial shortfall identified in a

management review of Regional Residential Associations (Management Review of Regional Residential Associations 1988). De-institutionalisation means finding houses for the former patients. The management committees and staff Residential Associations have spent considerable time in identifying and maintaining stock. This role is a new one for the committees, and additional resources are required for training, both formal and in-service. There are indications that such resources may be made available in 1988/89.

At least part of the funding for the process of de-institutionalisation will come from the sale of existing institutions: for example, Willsmere has been valued at $25m. However, in the long-term, the funding of such initiatives cannot rely on such one-off 'wind-fall' gains. There is also the problem that such sales may meet opposition from resident action groups, who see the vacating of the institutions as a means of obtaining community resources.

In the area of trade unionism, one of the major factors affecting the quality of community-based human services delivery is the fact that the social and community sector is a recognised industry in terms of industrial conditions and awards. While the management committees are elected volunteers, staff are professionals employed under the award wages and conditions in the public service. The scope for exploitation of workers, while limited, still remains due to the lack of management expertise on the committee. However, this problem has been formally identified and a recommendation is before the Department of Community Services for management committees to have access to relevant training.

Another continuing problem involves the co-ordination of the activities of the Ministry of Housing with those of the Departments of Community Services and Health. The Ministry has a fairly strict policy of providing public housing to people who are 'capable of independent living', which precludes direct access to housing for many disabled people. Moreover, there is no Disabled Persons' Unit in the Ministry of Housing to respond to, or initiate programs with, disabled people. Conversely, Health and Community Services have embarked on a program of property acquisition without consideration to the impact of their policies on public housing: the various bodies could be competing for the same stock but for different reasons.

So far, the Victorian experience of de-institutionalisation remains a positive one, which stands in marked contrast to the US experience. In large part this appears to be a result of the Victorian Government having a commitment to community health principles embodied in de-institutionalisation. Credit must also be given to the positive role of community services workers and their unions in contributing to the design and implementation of the program. These three factors seem to be the essential ingredients to a successful de-institutionalisation program.

11.7 Developing Improved, More Equitable, Efficient and Effective State Public Services

Part Three of this report considered the advantages of reforming, renewing and developing State public services at some length. Part Three, and the previous section of this chapter, also argued that the case for less State Government services and widespread privatisation is not persuasive. Indeed, the previous section provided examples of significant broader and longer-run costs of privatisation often overlooked by proponents of this policy. More equitable, efficient and effective provision of the services in question can derive from efforts to reform the public sector. This is the primary conclusion of this section which discusses and appraises various initiatives to improve the performance of Victoria's public services introduced by the Victorian Labor Government since it commenced its administration in 1982. Although not without deficiencies, overall these initiatives have resulted in a significant improvement in public sector performance and serve to indicate an alternative to the program of the New Right.

11.7.1 A Review of the Economic and Social Justice Strategies

Part Three has made clear the need for governments to adopt explicit and co-ordinated policies designed to achieve greater flexibility and responsiveness in the public sector. This is necessary in order to ensure that both the economic and social goals of the public sector are achieved. This Chapter has drawn attention to the Victorian Government's Economic and Social Justice Strategies which manifest a commitment to a proactive role of the public sector in economic renewal and social justice. In the light of the priorities identified in Part Three, this Section provides as assessment of the achievements of the two strategies.

The government has demonstrated its ongoing commitment to the Economic Strategy in particular by setting monitorable quantitative targets, and by providing in the budget papers details of the way new initiatives are consistent with the objectives of the strategies. However, a similar commitment needs to be demonstrated with respect to the Social Justice Strategy. In fact, recently announced reforms suggest that this may be occurring.

The Economic Strategy

The long term nature of the Economic Strategy makes it difficult at this relatively early stage to conduct a comprehensive and systematic evaluation particularly in quantitative terms. Nevertheless, it is worth attempting to make some assessment of progress to date. Towards this end, Table 11.26 summarises the Economic Strategy's quantitative targets (Victorian Government, 1987) and compares these targets with the actual rates of growth in Non Farm Gross State Product, investment and exports for both Victoria and the rest of Australia (ROA). Victoria's performance appears to have been strikingly good.

Of course, it is difficult to establish the extent to which these performance outcomes were due to the Economic Strategy's various initiatives. Nevertheless, it is possible to make some general observations.

Since it is the primary objective of the Economic Strategy, the long term rate of economic growth through expansion of the trade-exposed sector is the main benchmark against which the Strategy should be reviewed. Thus, successful initiatives are those which improve Victoria's competitiveness.

As Section 11.2 of this Chapter suggested, 'competitiveness' must be seen as a dynamic, multi-faceted concept, which embraces two main sets of factors: those which form the competitive environment within which firms compete, and those associated with the ability of firms to compete. In Section 11.2 it was argued that the main environmental factors which have constrained improved competitiveness in Victoria (and Australia generally) are, first, the inadequate venture and development capital available to small and medium sized firms seeking to develop and market new, elaborately transformed, high value-added products; and second, deficiencies in the educational system which impede the process of skill formation. The main factors identified as impediments to the ability of firms to compete were the variety of institutional and historical processes which have for decades prevented private sector managers from engaging in high levels of research and development, and investment, and from taking an export oriented outlook.

Table 11.26

Comparison of Targets and Outcomes of the Economic Strategy

Dimension:	Target[a]:	1982/3 – 1987/8		Outcome: 1988/9[b]	
		Vic.	ROA[c]	Vic.	ROA
Gross State Product	4% p.a.	4.3%[d]	3.9%	3.3%	2.6%
Employment	2% p.a.	2.7%	2.5%	2.8%	2.8%
Exports	10% p.a.	11.9%	7.9%	8.0%	5.4%
Private Investment	5% p.a.	7.9%	4.4%	12.8%	4.7%

Notes: (a) Targets are in real terms and are averages for five years period, 1986/7 – 1991/2.
(b) Forecast by D.M.B.
(c) Rest of Australia.
(d) Target is for Gross State Product; the data are Gross Non Farm Product.
Source: Jolly, R. (1988) Budget Strategy and Review, Budget Paper No. 2, Melbourne; *Victorian Government (1987) Victoria. The Next Decade*, Melbourne.

To an extent, the Victorian Government's Economic Strategy has focussed on problem areas. For instance, by targeting assistance to small to medium sized firms, the Strategy has sought to encourage growth of those firms least likely to be foreign owned and controlled, and which are most likely to engage in innovative forms of research and development and product development.

However, as DITR (1986) points out, Economic Strategy initiatives have tended to focus on improving the competitive environment within which firms operate, and too little attention has been given to programs and initiatives which have as their principal objective the task of assisting the ability of Victorian firms to compete internationally through encouraging Victorian managers to acquire the skills and expertise necessary to participate in world markets for high value added products. In the early Strategy documents in particular, attention focussed on reforms to Victorian Public Trading Enterprises (see above) and to tax

initiatives (see below) as major reforms which, by reducing the cost structure of Victorian firms, would improve the competitiveness of Victorian industry. As was argued above, the reforms to Victorian Public Trading Enterprises on balance do appear to have effected significant efficiency improvements, and can be justified as necessary public sector reforms. It is questionable, however, the extent to which these reform do improve competitiveness. As DITR (1986) points out, even if the government were to reduce by one third all taxes and charges on, for example, the Victorian metal fastener industry, the industry's return on assets would only increase from 9.9% to 11.3%.

This is not to suggest that all of the government's 'competitive environment' initiatives cannot be justified in terms of the Economic Strategy's objectives. Some very important reforms have been made, particularly in the area of education and in the establishment of a scientific and technical infrastructure, with important reforms having been introduced to the secondary education system (the new Victorian Certificate of Education), to Technical and Further Education (the latter involving tripartite mechanisms of decision-making and reform), and to higher education (the Victorian Education Foundation, which provides a vehicle for harnessing private and public funding for new courses required by industry). Much has also been done to increase the level of research and development in Victoria. In 1988, the government announced the introduction of a *Strategic Research Fund*, which has as its main objective the support of basic research of long term significance to Victoria.

Venture Capital
Until recently, the government has also striven to facilitate an increased supply of venture and development capital to firms which engage in activities consistent with the Economic Strategy's objectives. The three agencies given primary responsibility for this task were the Victorian Economic Development Corporation (VEDC) (which was absorbed by the Rural Finance Corporation in late 1988), the Victorian Investment Corporation (VIC), and the Victorian Venture Capital Fund (VVCF). The Department of Industry Technology and Resources was also given a relatively minor role in providing venture and development capital.

In brief, the history of the Cain Government's role in providing venture and development capital can be traced back to 1984 when the VEDC was restructured with a view to it becoming the government's principal agency for the provision of loan funds, in particular, and, to a lesser extent, of equity capital to new, small to medium sized, Victorian firms. The VIC was subsequently established in 1986, with the primary objective of providing equity funding, particularly for companies involved in high technology based business ventures. Thus, while both the VEDC and the VIC have provided venture capital, the former has primarily been concerned with the provision of loans, whereas the latter with equity finance. In late 1988, the State Government announced the establishment of the VVCF, which was to supplement further the provision of venture capital in Victoria by investing funds in companies operating as part of the Federal Government's

Management and Investment Companies (MIC) scheme. Funding for the VVCF was to come primarily from State Government Superannuation Funds, which would be allowed to invest, on the basis of commercial criteria, up to 5% of their funds in approved MIC companies (which provide venture capital to fledgling, high technology companies seeking access to equity capital and marketing and management advice and assistance). In contrast to the VEDC and the VIC, therefore, the VVCF was to operate essentially by contracting out to the private sector the function of managing the provision of venture capital funds. Over a three year period the government sought to supplement by up to $200m the provision of venture capital in Victoria through the VVCF (an amount equivalent to the total funds so far invested in MIC companies).

Following months of media speculation concerning VEDC mis-management and financial malpractice during mid-1988, the government merged this agency with the Rural Finance Corporation. Following further allegations of mis-management, in late 1988 the government commissioned an Inquiry (hereafter the Ryan Report) into the VEDC, and, in early 1989, the Auditor-General released his report on the government's Industry Policy initiatives, which also included an examination of the VEDC (Auditor General of Victoria, 1989). These two reports leave little doubt that the VEDC was badly mismanaged. The Ryan Report concluded that as at November 1988, the VEDC was technically insolvent with a deficiency of shareholders funds of approximately $78m, a recorded loss of $105m for the year ending June 1988, and provisions for bad debts in excess of $100m.

But there were broader reasons why the VEDC performed so badly. The Ryan Report and the Auditor-General's Report have identified the main contributing factors. They include: the VEDC's objectives and loan targets, which were too broad to be an effective guide and evaluative benchmark for its operations; the VEDC's grossly inadequate loan assessment, loan approval and loan monitoring procedures by key Board members and, in particular, senior managers failing to perform their duties adequately; the private accounting firm hired to audit and oversee the VEDC's lending and investment practices not adequately discharging its responsibilities; the VEDC experiencing extreme difficulty in hiring a properly qualified and experienced General Manager; the VEDC's failure to hire more loan officers despite a rapidly increasing number of loan applications and approvals; and the VEDC's functions being compromised by the practice of providing loans at interest rates which did not properly reflect the risks involved, whilst simultaneously being required to earn a profit on operations and to pay the Victorian Government a Public Authority Dividend on its equity base.

Shortly after the release of the Ryan Report, it was announced that the VIC recorded a $9.5m loss on its operations during 1987/8. Considerable media coverage of the failings and mismanagement of the VEDC and the recorded loss of the VIC took effect in March 1989, when the government announced that it would substantially reduce public sector involvement in the capital market. In short, the government will no longer provide venture capital to Victorian industry. The RFC/VEDC, the government's primary vehicle for providing venture capital in the form of loans, will provide only development capital (loans for existing companies seeking to grow); lending activities will no longer be tied to any specific industry targets or objectives; and the agency's lending portfolio will shift from high to low risk ventures. The government has also decided to end its involvement in the VIC. At the time of writing, no decision has been made as to whether or not to proceed with the VVCF (Cain, 1989).

In some ways the government's decision to reduce substantially its role in the provision of high risk venture capital is an understandable reaction in view of the intense and, at times, misleading media coverage of the operations of the VEDC and VIC. In addition, the criticism by the Opposition was relentless. Particularly problematic from the government's point of view is that the provision of venture capital, especially when in the form of equity, is a high risk activity in which the financial returns only become evident after approximately five years of operation. The 'lemons', in other words,

generally appear earlier than the 'plums', with years two and three being the time when many losses occur (United Kingdom Venture Capital Journal, July 1986). By the very nature of their activities, new public sector initiatives in this area (such as the VIC) must expect to incur losses in their early years of operation, and this in turn would be likely to prompt negative media reaction.

Nevertheless, media assessment should not be the main criterion against which Economic Strategy initiatives are evaluated. Since the government itself has pointed out that it is the tendency for the 'lemons' to appear before the 'plums', and not VIC mis-management, which explains the $9.5m loss incurred by this agency in 1987/8 (see Cain, 1989, pp. 13-14), it is arguable that the government's decision to end its involvement in the VIC was premature. Few commentators seemed to reject the principle of government involvement in the venture capital market. An alternative model with which to pursue this objective is provided in Chapter Nine, where a system of development grants is sketched.

The government has sought to defend its decision to reduce its venture capital role by claiming that the private sector must assume primary responsibility for this task (The Age, 18 January 1989, p. 3; Cain, 1989, p. 15). This, however, is to ignore the very reason why the government became involved in the provision of venture capital in the first place, namely, the variety of institutional flaws in Australian capital markets which inhibit the private sector from undertaking this function satisfactorily. The government itself has produced no evidence to show that private sector financial institutions are now more willing and able to provide venture capital. Indeed, only five months prior to the retraction of its commitment in regard to the provision of venture capital, the government was arguing forcefully that there remained a continuing and substantial need for public sector initiatives in this area (Victorian Government, 1988, pp. 31-36). Finally, should the government completely withdraw from the provision of venture capital − whether in the form of debt or equity − it will have undermined its ability to undertake industry policy initiatives which, in the medium to longer term, are potentially directly self financing.

Payroll Tax Initiatives

While the government is currently reviewing its industry policy initiatives (including the status of the VVCF), one option being canvassed is the extended use of payroll tax cuts to encourage private sector initiatives in this area (*The Age*, 18 January 1989, p. 3). Adoption of this option would further increase the level of tax expenditures currently in place which seek to achieve Economic Strategy objectives. In all three Economic Strategy documents, a variety of initiatives have been introduced which seek to lower the level of taxes and charges payable by Victorian industry. These include raising payroll tax exemption levels and introducing and subsequently increasing payroll tax deductions for firms achieving more than 20% of their sales from exports. As was pointed out in Section 11.6.5, the cumulative cost of all 'tax expenditures' to the government's revenue base in 1988/9 is estimated at $431m. It should be recognised that tax expenditures are blunt instruments of industry policy. Ewer *et al.*, (1987) and Collins *et al.*, (1988) point out that the broad nature of tax expenditures makes it difficult to monitor their impact and effectiveness in terms of their objectives. Collins *et al.*, (1988) and Ewer *et al.* (1987) criticise the use of tax expenditures, and recommend instead the use of specifically targeted grants based on the condition that the recipients can demonstrate that they have performed a particular activity (eg. implemented an adequate business plan or marketing program designed to increase exports).

Although the focus of the Economic Strategy reforms has centred on the 'competitive environment', some attempt has been made to implement more initiatives which seek to improve the ability of Victorian firms to compete internationally. The Department of Industry Technology and Resources, for example, has implemented a number of programs which provide financial support and advice to firms seeking to expand into overseas markets (eg. The East Asia Market Entry Program; The Pacific North West Market Entry Program; and the Export Marketing Familiarisation Pro-

gram), and which encourage Victorian firms to source their supply needs from local firms (eg. the Industrial Supplies Office). In addition the Victorian Heavy Engineering Program has also achieved some success in what is a strategic sector of any advanced economy. These programs are estimated to have increased the value of Victorian exports by $514m in the three years to June 1989 (for further details see Victorian Government, 1988b, p. 95; and Ewer *et al.*, 1987, pp. 156-60). Also worth mentioning are the various initiatives which attempt to revitalise Victorian industry by providing expert advice and/or financial assistance in an attempt to improve quality performance (eg. The Quality Victoria Program), investment in advanced manufacturing techniques (The Strategic Firm Investment Program), and business planning (The Business Planning Scheme) (for further details see Victorian Government, 1984, pp. 74-80; 1987, pp. 72-76; Budget Paper No. 5, 1988, pp. 197-206). These types of initiatives deserve a much more prominent role in the Economic Strategy.

The Social Justice Strategy

The Social Justice Strategy, outlined in Section 11.4.2 provides an indication of the government's commitment and plans to address social inequality in Victoria. However, this strategy must be further developed.

The Social Justice Strategy should require the continual development of concrete targets and time frames for achieving them. Here it should be noted that some Victorian social justice goals are so broad in scope they can be used to justify a range of budgetary initiatives which seem only tenuously related to the concept of social justice. For example, as was pointed out in Section 11.5.2, in the 1988 budget the government announced as one of its major social justice initiatives the progressive abolition of private motor registration fees at an annual cost of $66m. The Victorian Council of Social Services has criticised this initiative because of its untargeted nature: for example, relatively affluent families with two or more cars or who regularly purchase new, expensive vehicles will benefit, while poor families dependent on public transport will not.

A further arena of developing social justice

objectives concerns reforms to government agencies. Government agencies should be required to consistently and systematically develop ways in which Social Justice Strategy objectives can be achieved. The Social Justice Strategy should also do more to address the regionally specific nature of many social justice issues. For example, in Section 11.2 it was pointed out that Melbourne's western suburbs have consistently experienced higher rates of unemployment than the rest of Melbourne, and are relatively deprived of key urban resources such as recreational and educational facilities. A serious commitment to reducing disadvantage would involve a 'spatial' targeting of social justice programs, and the increased availability of key public services.

Attempts should also be made to integrate the Social Justice and Economic Strategies. This avenue of development is currently problematical because many economic initiatives are designed to facilitate market processes. However, it should be noted that market outcomes may accentuate social inequalities, particularly in a spatial context. For example, although employment growth in Melbourne has been strong over the last six years, for every 40 jobs created in the eastern and southern suburbs of Melbourne, only one is created in the west (Victorian Government, 1987, p. 13). This is thus an area where Economic Strategy and Social Justice Strategy should combine to address such problems as private sector locational decisions and investment strategy.

The government should further develop Social Justice targets, and a more comprehensive social justice data base which will improve monitoring of social justice issues in Victoria. In addition, government agencies should be encouraged to further develop performance indicators to be used at central, management and service delivery levels, which will integrate the activities of government agencies with the goals of the Social Justice Strategy more tightly. It will also enable the agencies themselves to monitor the impact of their programs in terms of social justice principles.

While these reforms will be useful and important, other changes will also need to be made. As a matter of priority the Social Justice

Strategy should develop mechanisms for enabling community participation in the implementation and evaluation of Strategy initiatives! Government agencies should be required to establish consultative process with consumers of public services. Consultation with recognised social service organisations such as the Victorian Council of Social Service as well as public sector trade unions such as the Victorian Public Service Association in the formulation of social justice objectives, and in the identification of initiatives would also be important.

11.7.2 Appraising Reforms to Victorian Public Trading Enterprises

Section Three has already noted the efforts of the Victorian Government to improve the performance of its major public trading enterprises. The aims of public enterprise reform in Victoria have extended beyond improved financial performance and have included improvements in: Economy; Allocative, Productive and Dynamic Efficiency; Equity; and Effectiveness. Since 1983, the Victorian Government has required the State's major public enterprises to (amongst other things): earn a real (inflation-adjusted) rate of return on assets of 4%; publish supplementary Current Cost Accounting information in their Annual Reports (based on the so-called Rate-of-Return Reporting); adjust prices to more closely reflect the marginal (incremental) costs of supplying the service; pay dividends of up to 5% of the estimated 'public equity' in the enterprise; engage in more open consultations with consumers and the public; use formal Cost-Benefit Analysis procedures to evaluate investment projects; and develop and use a broad range of performance indicators to facilitate monitoring and evaluation of, and encourage improvements in, performance.

Our overall assessment of the Victorian Government's initiatives to improve the efficiency and effectiveness of public trading enterprises is favourable, and, as Chapter Seven also makes clear, should be seriously considered by other State Governments. Moreover, these enterprises now appear to be much more customer and community conscious. Such successful reforms under continued government ownership need to be realistically compared with the alleged cost efficiency benefits of privatised enterprises, particularly in the regulated environment they are likely to operate within. The evidence from the US, and, more recently the UK, about regulated public utilities does not instill much enthusiasm for this alternative.

11.7.3 Improving The Performance of Victoria's General State Public Services

Apart from reforms to the State's trading enterprises discussed above, the Victorian Government has also been concerned to enhance the performance of the State's public services within the budget sector by the introduction of corporate planning and program budgeting.

(a) Public Sector Management Reforms
Corporate Planning

One of the major reforms of the public sector flagged in Part Three was better organisational structures. In Victoria the Labor Government embarked upon a reform of the organisational structure of the public sector, particularly at the managerial level. Foremost amongst these reforms was the introduction of 'corporate planning' (Department of Management and Budget Program Development and Review Division, 1986).

In essence, corporate planning is a more systematic approach to decision making, and involves: specifying long term objectives after 'taking stock' of the external climate; a continuous process of monitoring and review; and a management structure capable of planning and making decisions consistent with these plans.

In the process of implementing corporate planning, government Departments have typically appointed new departmental heads, undertaken organisational restructuring, appointed or promoted specialist staff, and developed new organisational procedures and practices. Without a systematic and comprehensive review of managerial reforms it is difficult to evaluate success or failure. Nevertheless, some observations can be made.

The managerial reforms in practice have often involved an almost incessant process of organisational restructuring, particularly

where there has been a turnover of senior management or Ministers who wish to impose their particular interpretation of corporate planning through organisational reforms. As Bryson points out:

> 'organisational change in the Victorian public service has taken on the appearance of an end in its own right' (1986, p. 364).

One of the major destabilising effects of restructure which has been endemic for almost a decade is the minimisation of intra-departmental and inter-departmental communication and collaboration (Econsult, 1988, p. 522). Incessant restructuring has undermined interagency co-ordination, even with respect to programs that are clearly interdependent. For example, at the end of 1988 there was no liaison between the Ministry of Housing and the office of Psychiatric Services regarding support services for relevant clients in Ministry units or between the Education Department and Community Services regarding suspensions from school of children in Community Services care (Econsult, 1988, p. 528).

Given the emphasis on senior management in the government's corporate planning manual, it would appear that one of the outcomes of the managerial reforms in Victoria is that, contrary to Wilenski's advocacy of a flatter organisational structure (see Part Three), public sector agencies in Victoria have become more hierarchical. For example, senior officers and chief administrators accounted for 62% of the total increase in public service officers between 1985 and 1988 (Annual Reports of the Public Service Board).

The 'corporatisation' of Victorian public sector agencies seems also to have involved the assumption that business administration skills are all that is required for effective management of government Departments. Thus, for example, no knowledge of human services is seen to be required to manage a human service delivery agency. Indeed as Bryson (1986) suggests, an excellent knowledge of the service or product of an agency seems not to be an important consideration in making senior appointments. In such circumstances, the possibility of insensitive and inappropriate policy decisions is increased considerably. This problem appears most evident in the human service areas, housing, community services, health etc., which do not lend themselves as readily to the management philosophy initially designed, and most appropriate for, commercial public sector agencies.

To date, the focus of most of the key agency reforms in Victoria has been on senior management and the 'specialist planners'. The need for skill formation and training of operational rather than corporate planning staff can be neglected given this focus. A recent review of the training requirements of housing workers in Australia including those of the Victorian Ministry of Housing and Construction found that lower and middle level staff including counter staff had very inadequate levels of skill training and virtually no broader education as to the problems and characteristics of the client groups requiring public housing or of public housing policy (Burke, Dalton & Paris, 1989). Also indicative of the problems that can attach to corporatisation is the downplaying of operational activities versus management activities. In the Ministry of Education it can be argued that a hierarchical managerial philosophy has moulded a context in which salaries and career paths now make it more lucrative to administer and manage outside of, rather than actually teach in, schools.

Program Budgeting
Program Budgeting was introduced by the Victorian State Labor Government in 1983, with a view to improving the use of resources in the public sector through the adoption of more rational criteria for decisions on resource allocation. The steps below illustrate the specific stages required of program budgeting for Victorian Government agencies:

— define and delineate their objectives into measurable areas of expenditure, identified as programs;
— describe their program operations, and in the process identify performance indicators;
— prepare annual budgets and forward estimates at program levels, with budgets allocated and funds appropriated to programs,
— adapt their accounting systems to record

program and program element costs, with costs being allocated at this level; and
— integrate their recurrent and works expenditures within the program framework. (Department of Management and Budget, Program Development and Review Division, 1986).

Program budgeting does appear to have improved the budgetary process, and has also assisted the implementation of the Economic and Social Justice Strategies. Indeed, it is difficult to see how a social justice strategy could be adequately achieved in the absence of program budgeting.

It would be all to easy, however, in any discussion of State public sector reforms, to be over enthusiastic and optimistic about what program budgeting promises. Certainly its principles are consistent with the broad goals endorsed by many public sector reformers: efficiency, effectiveness, accountability, flexibility, etc. In practice however, there are a host of problems associated with it, some of which have been experienced in Victoria.

One major problem flows from the expectation that objectives can be specified and ranked in a measurable form and that effective performance indicators can be developed to monitor and evaluate program success. In the Victorian Government's guide to corporate planning and program budgeting, the State Electricity Commission of Victoria is used to illustrate the application of program budgeting concepts and techniques (Department of Management and Budget program Development and Review Division, 1986). Performance objectives and indicators for a commercial public sector body providing a physical output (eg. gigawatthours of electricity) often are quite different to those relevant to a non-commercial public sector agency providing, for example, extended family care to low income families where performance is more about quality of service than quantity. This problem is illustrated by the Department of Community Services which has been handicapped in developing needs indicators for allocating program resources by the absence of adequate client statistics (Burke *et al.*, 1989). In this context, it is worth noting one initiative of the Victorian Public Service Board towards the development of better information bases for resource allocation which emerged out of a review of library funding in Victoria. The review recommended that a percentage of a library's funding should be based on its performance in setting up a library information system appropriate for on-going performance monitoring (Public Service Board, 1987).

A second difficulty in the program budgeting process is identifying and explaining 'program conditions'. Program conditions are the factors creating the demand for a service, for example, changing demographic, economic, technological, attitudinal, locational processes. Identification of changing program conditions is essential if program objectives and indicators are to be defined. Such conditions in effect provide the rationale for funding. While program budgeting provides a framework for establishing resource priorities, there is no point in funding programs or policies which are themselves misconceived or based on false premises because inadequate thought, consultation and research has gone into the 'conceptualisation' stage of program delivery.

11.7.4 Conclusion

This section has reviewed some major aspects of reforms and renewal in Victoria's public sector. Overall, the principles underpinning these reforms are commendable. Public trading enterprises would appear to be operating more efficiently and effectively with a more open and responsive attitude to their customers and the community. The Economic Strategy has served to facilitate industrial restructuring and economic growth and thereby revive the Victorian economy from the doldrums of the early 1980s in a quite dramatic way. Victoria now leads the other Australian States in terms of many economic growth indicators. While not without problems, the more recent Social Justice Strategy has provided an important 'first step' along the path to ensuring that State Governments play a much more strategic and considered role in facilitating a more equitable distribution of income. Finally, since 1983, the Victorian public sector at large (including community services and social policy agencies), has been undergoing substantial renewal including organisational, management and ser-

vice delivery aspects. While these latter reforms do not appear to have been as successful as the reforms to public trading enterprises, the results of all these developments in State public services are providing increasingly persuasive evidence of the equity, efficiency, effectiveness and growth benefits that a strong public sector can deliver. For Victoria in the 1980s at any rate, the thought of the alternative scenario of a small, public sector preferred by the New Right is a chilling one.

11.8 Some Issues in Financing the Renewal of Victorian Public Services

Section 11.5 reviewed the current financing of Victoria's State public services and raised the question of the future adequacy of finance for the State's public services. This section considers the question further and discusses longer-term issues relating to the various sources of finance required to support the renewal and development of Victoria's public services including: Consolidated Fund Receipts (encompassing Commonwealth Payments, State Taxes, and State Non-tax Revenue); and Capital Expenditure Funding for both the Budget and Non-Budget Sectors.

11.8.1 Consolidated Fund Receipts

Section 11.5 outlined Victoria's Consolidated Fund Receipts for 1987-88. The major components are discussed in turn below (more detailed information is included in Parts Three and Four).

Payments By The Commonwealth Government
There is a clear need for a longer-term agreement to be made between the Commonwealth and the States for sharing the national revenues. Indeed, the practice of *ad hoc* decisions about the level of Commonwealth payments from one year to another is applied even more starkly in regard to the system of Commonwealth capital payments to the States. General Purpose Capital payments to the States, including global borrowings for State authorities, are determined each year, without any indication of their likely levels in future years. Fiscal planning especially for capital projects, becomes extremely difficult for the States under these circumstances. The uncertainties

about Commonwealth funding also seriously undermine a State's ability to follow a medium to longer term economic strategy. And, finally, the uncertainties make it difficult to develop and implement a financial strategy for an improved system of State public services. For all these reasons the Victorian case offers strong support for the tax reform measures outlined in Chapter Seven.

State Taxation

State Government taxation provided about 35% of total Consolidated Fund finances in 1987-88. As a result of stringent constraints on State powers to raise revenue combined with Commonwealth dominance of income tax, Victoria and other States have been left with recourse to a miscellany of taxes which are open to major criticism as being an irrational mix, with an overall regressive character. A strategy for reform to Victoria's State taxes should obviously be considered within the context of the nation's wider tax structure.

There are also strong pressures on a State Government to restrain increases in State taxation. One reason for this is the Cain Government's appreciation of the narrow and regressive nature of State taxes and charges. Tax competition has also led some State Governments to self-impose restraints on tax receipts growth. Indeed, as was noted in section 11.6 of this chapter, the Victorian Government has established explicit policies to limit increases in taxes by: undertaking to restrain the increase in taxation revenue in line with the increase in Victorian non-farm gross domestic product (NFGDP); and by making specific tax expenditures over recent years which (as discussed earlier in section 11.6) have removed an estimated $431m from the tax base for future years.

However, if there is no reform of the State tax base through a major reform of indirect taxation the Cain Government's initiatives in these areas will almost inevitably have to be reversed. This is because tax expenditures (tax concessions which in effect provide subsidies similar to those provided by direct government expenditure) result in a narrowing of the tax base which necessitates the implementation of discriminatory tax rates and increases adminis-

trative and compliance costs. At the same time, tax expenditures are a blunt instrument which is difficult to cost accurately, and with which specific targeting of beneficiaries is also a problem.

Longer Term Tax Mix Issues

Consideration of Victoria's tax reform strategy has to occur within the context of the rigid Constitutional and practical constraints to which State tax policies are currently subject.

As Part Four of this report argues, the preferred approach by far would be for a State Goods and Services Levy, while, at the same time, abolishing or reducing existing State taxes. Nevertheless, any State action to expand into this area would obviously need Commonwealth support.

These proposals for changes in State taxation have been supported in principle by various Victorian committees of inquiry into State taxation (see, for example, Committee of Inquiry into Revenue Raising in Victoria [1983]). The major concern is with the tax mix. Similarly, the New South Wales Review of the State Tax System (1988) strongly recommended a further extension of State tax bases, for example, by the introduction of a personal income tax surcharge. However, the Review proposed that the additional tax revenues thus generated be used to reduce other taxes eg., payroll taxes (so as to encourage investment activity and State employment growth).

11.8.2 Recurrent Receipts From State Sources Other Than Taxation

User Charges in Victoria

In 1987/88, about $332m (or 2.9%) of total Victorian State finances was generated by user charges. User charges are not only a growing source of Consolidated Fund receipts, they are also controversial.

As Part Four of this report explains, the user-pays or benefit principle is difficult to apply in practice across the broad range of State public services. Indeed, assessment of its appropriateness is not easy because: it depends partly on the extent to which it is considered that, by imposing user charges for public services, resource allocation will be improved; the extent to which movement towards the user-pays pricing principle will detract from distributional objectives (which cannot/will not be met by the use of other policies); and the extent to which distributional attainments of departures from user charges are counterbalanced by efficiency losses from pursuing such a practice.

The basic point being made here is that any departure from the user-pays principle should be a considered decision not taken lightly since if there is considerable potential for increased cost recovery, this could considerably reduce the pressures on State finances. On the other hand, on a case by case basis, there may well be good social or economic reasons for not requiring users to meet the full costs of public services.

As discussed in section 11.5, the Victorian Government has exercised tight control over fees and charges in recent years by setting an annual guideline percentage increase. Generally, fees and charges have been permitted to increase by no more than the Consumer Price Index. Where user charges are appropriate, however, such blanket restraints may impede the ability for charges to be adjusted to more closely reflect the cost of providing particular services (which is a policy prescribed not only by revenue raising, but by efficiency considerations).

Dividend Payments by Victorian Public Authorities
As Section 11.5 has noted, the Public Authorities (Dividends) Act 1983, provides for a dividend of up to 5% of the opening value of the public equity in the relevant public trading authority to be paid into the Consolidated Fund. Public authority dividends received by the Consolidated Fund are now significant having increased from $372.5m in 1983-84 to an estimated $589.3m in 1988-89 – an increase of 58% over five years. Receipts from this source during 1987-88, comprised 5.3% of total Consolidated Fund Recurrent receipts or 4.5% of total Consolidated Fund receipts.

Economic theory seems of limited assistance in deciding the appropriate level of dividend payments. Certainly a doctrinaire or simplistic view that the level of dividend payments should be guided primarily by a predetermined rate, for example, the Victorian Govern-

ment's 'up to 5%' would be unwarranted. This seems particularly so since the 5% figure was determined on the basis of an arbitrarily chosen risk premium of 2% added on to a questionable estimate of 3% for the long term cost of debt.

Rather, the extent of dividend payments by individual public enterprises should depend, among other things, on the particular circumstances faced by a public enterprise including the requirement to retain earnings to finance a planned investment program, to improve a cash-flow position, the expected return on equity both in the short and longer term, the level of accumulated profits, the actual and desired debt: equity ratio, the prevailing constraints on borrowing, and so on.

We conclude that whilst dividends should continue to be paid into the Consolidated Fund as they provide a legitimate return to public equity, the actual level of dividends required by the government should be sensitive to the obligations of an enterprise to pursue prudent financial policies as well as improvements in efficiency and effectiveness.

Sources of Funding for Capital Expenditure
Capital outlays by the Victorian Government was $3.453m in 1986-87 and an estimated $3.478m during 1987-88. In 1986-87, 57.2% of capital expenditure was made by budget sector agencies and 42.8% by public trading authorities. Section 11.5 provided a discussion of borrowing as a source of capital funds.

In regard to borrowings by Victorian Government trading authorities, the conclusion offered in Chapter Eight and repeated here, supports that drawn by the Victorian Economic and Budget Review Committee (1987):

'On both efficiency and equity grounds it would seem appropriate that such commercial authorities should be able to operate on the basis of competitive neutrality, ie. that they receive no benefits or suffer penalties through their public status that their private sector competitors do not also experience. It is difficult to see why such public sector firms should be more restricted in their capital raising and investment policies than their private sector counterparts' (p. 83).

11.9 Conclusion

This Chapter has made clear the key role of the public sector in Victoria's economy and society. The public sector is a major source of capital expenditure on which the State's economic activity is founded; the public sector plays the major role in guaranteeing social justice and equity in the State; and the State's administrative functions ensure the smooth running of the economy and also protect citizens from the excesses of an unregulated market.

In meeting these objectives the Victorian Government has been at the forefront of public administration, both in terms of social justice and in the operations of the State trading enterprises. It has shown great initiative in designing strategies to overcome its financial restrictions. Unfortunately, it did not have the foresight to ensure the institutional safeguards necessary to meet the high standards demanded of public bodies.

The sustained decline in Commonwealth payments to Victoria which provide some 40% of Consolidated Fund Receipts) has forced the State to rely increasingly on own-sourced revenue from tax and non-tax sources. However, State revenue being vulnerable to economic downturns is uncertain in the medium term, which increases the problems of formulating and implementing a strategy for renewing and developing State public services. Part Four argues the preferred way to reform the State taxation system is for the States and the Commonwealth to co-operate on the implementation of an entirely new tax regime at the State level, and also to more realistically assess the revenue raising potential of the State's public enterprises. The major role played by the public sector makes such initiatives not only desirable but necessary.

Notes

1 The dividing line between these functional areas is not an easy one to draw. Many components of the social wage, for example, can have a substantial impact on economic growth (eg. education), and conversely, many of the economic functions of the public sector can have an influence on the quality of life in Victoria (eg. the provision of public infrastructure).

2 The contracting out of maintenance work is quite complex. There are three main maintenance requirements of the public housing stock: cyclical, vacancy, and responsive. Cyclical maintenance tasks involve the performance of routine tasks designed to address normal wear and tear experienced by dwellings from the weather and occupation; vacancy maintenance involves bringing a dwelling up to standards appropriate for re-letting; and responsive maintenance involves solving problems which pose a threat to health or well (eg. repairs to toilets, broken windows, etc.). In 1987/8, the Ministry spent $30.2m on responsive maintenance, $10.9m on vacated maintenance and $6.9m on cyclical maintenance.

3 The data that this discussion is based upon comes from research undertaken by the Victorian Trades Hall Council, involving approximately 100 workers employed by maintenance contractors working for the VMOHC on tasks formerly undertaken by the Department of Public Works.

4 The Victorian Trades Hall Council and the Operative Painters Union cited to us numerous recent cases involving contractors employing 'sub contractors' on sub award conditions (eg. recently arrived Vietnamese carpenters being paid $10 per hour on a cash in hand basis).

5 This information has been provided to us by the Trades Hall Council and has been confirmed by the VMOHC. The pilot program has been made possible by the merger of the former Ministry of Housing with the Department of Public Works in 1987 to form the Ministry of Housing and Construction. The pilot program will involve the use of the direct labour force previously employed by the Public Works Department.

6 Schools typically refer to the fee as a voluntary contribution.

7 Interview with Federation of State School Parents Association held 8 May 1989.

Chapter 12

SOUTH AUSTRALIA

12.1 Introduction

The history of the South Australian public sector illustrates the importance of public economic and social provision in Australia. Due to the particularly poor natural resources of South Australia the very fundamentals of an industrialised economy were not readily to hand. However, the State public sector provided basic infrastructure, and through its own enterprises, created supplies of essential resources like water, coal and power generation. In the absence of this activity the South Australian economy could never have reached its current state of development and a continuation of these functions is required if the State's growth potential is to be realised.

State Governments of both political persuasions have been active in encouraging investment in the State by offering benefits to potential investors in the form of land, housing and other basic infrastructure. Furthermore, the State public sector has developed significant social welfare mechanisms, including a first rate health system.

12.2 Demography and Economy

12.2.1 Demography

South Australia is the second smallest populated State in Australia, although in per capita income it out performs the more heavily populated Queensland, trailing only behind New South Wales, Victoria and Western Australia. Table 12.1 provides summary comparative demographic and economic information about the Australian States.

Table 12.1

Summary Demographic and Economic Data for the States

	NSW	Vic.	Qld	SA	WA	Tas.	Total
Population (000s) June 1987	5605.3	4207.7	2675.3	1393.8	1496.1	449.1	16248.8
% Total (inc. Territories)	34.5	25.9	16.5	8.6	9.2	2.8	
% Six States	35.4	26.6	16.9	8.8	9.5	2.8	
*GDP $m 1986-87 *	89477	73708	38056	20491	24289	6087	260367
% Total (inc. Territories)	34.4	28.3	14.6	7.9	9.3	2.3	
*GDP per capita($) **	5963	17517	14225	14702	16235	13554	16034

Notes: * Estimate of South Australian Treasury.
      ** June 1987 population.
Source: South Australian Treasury (1988a), Appendix 1.

Table 12.2 summarises the relative rates of population growth for the Australian States. Population growth in South Australia has been well below the national average during the 1980s, although it has been stable. The only time the South Australian growth rate has exceeded the national average was between 1947 and 1966, when the rate of net-migration rose steeply (following mineral and manufacturing developments). Since 1966, the State's growth rate has been below the national average.

Census data for 1981 and 1986 provides some insight into the changing nature of the age distribution. Large absolute changes occurred in the age groups 35-39, 40-44 and 60-64, which increased by 23,994, 13,821, and 9,264 respectively, and 5-9 which fell by 9,571 (South Australian Year Book 1988). The median age was 27.5 years in 1971, 28.7 in 1976, and is estimated at 32.0 years for 1986, which is the oldest in any Australian State. South Australia also has the highest proportion of its population aged 65 years and over (11.6%) of any Australian State.

Table 12.2

Population Growth by State 1982-83 to 1988-89
(% Change)

	NSW	Vic.	Qld	SA	WA	Tas.	Total
1982-83	1.2	1.1	2.9	1.0	2.6	0.6	1.6
1983-84	0.9	1.0	1.9	1.1	1.9	1.0	1.3
1984-85	1.1	1.0	1.8	0.9	1.7	0.8	1.3
1985-86	1.2	1.0	1.9	0.8	2.4	1.0	1.4
1986-87	1.3	1.1	2.1	0.9	2.9	0.6	1.5
1987-88[e]	1.6	1.2	2.1	0.9	2.7	0.1	1.6
1988-89[e]	1.4	1.2	2.4	1.0	2.5	0.1	1.5
Average *	1.1	1.1	2.1	0.9	2.3	0.9	1.4

Notes: [e] Forecast.
          * Period.
Source: South Australian Treasury (1988a).

In terms of geographic distribution, South Australia is highly urbanised and increasingly so. In 1927, 51.6% of the population lived in Adelaide, 8.4% in other urban areas, and 39.4% in rural areas. By 1986, the proportions were 68.1% in Adelaide, 16.4% in other urban, and only 15.3% in rural areas. Thus only 16% of South Australia's population is located in other urban centres, which is very low compared to the three eastern States. In New South Wales, Victoria and Queensland, there are at least 6 centres outside the capital city with more than 20,000 residents, whereas, Whyalla and Mount Gambier are the only such centres in South Australia.

South Australia's aging population and its changing demographic profile has implications for the future demand for public services like education, hospitals and other social infrastructure. In addition, the continuing trend towards a very high degree of urbanisation, also has implications for public service provision and assistance. It might be argued that the public sector will, increasingly, have to rationalise rural facilities (as evidenced by the current hospital mergers), and increase the availability of urban land and infrastructure.

While the stable yet below average population growth in South Australia suggests that marked increases in public expenditure will not be demanded by an increasing population, it also means that the revenue base will not expand rapidly. The restricted size of the market does not provide incentives for business to develop, which also retards the tax base.

12.2.2 Economy

The performance of the South Australian economy in recent years has been mixed. Table 12.3 provides information about real changes in the GSP of the States since 1982-83. In 1983-84, South Australia appeared to recover more quickly from the recession of the early 1980s than the larger eastern States (and the national average). However in recent years, the larger States (New South Wales, Victoria, Queensland and Western Australia) have experienced strong real GSP growth rates, whereas the growth in the South Australian economy has been subdued and well below the national average.

Major developments like the Submarine Project at Port Adelaide, in addition to the strong recovery in private new home construction, and the rising demand for motor vehicles should enable the State to experience a rising growth in GSP. The South Australian Treasury estimates that the State GSP should maintain growth at the current national average forecast of 3.5%.

It is important to emphasise the role that the State Government has played in facilitating economic growth through initiatives like the construction of the ship lift at the Port of Adelaide for the Submarine Project. The success of public sector activity such as this underlines the vital importance of maintaining a vital and aggressive public involvement in the economy.

Table 12.3

Real Gross State Product — 1982-83 to 1987-88
(Percentage Change)

	NSW	Vic.	Qld	SA	WA	Tas.	Total
1982-83	-3.2	-0.9	-0.8	nil	4.7	-1.2	-1.1
1983-84	3.2	5.7	3.8	13.0	1.1	3.1	4.6
1984-85	3.7	4.5	5.7	6.6	12.4	6.0	5.4
1985-86	4.6	4.9	2.3	2.7	4.0	4.6	4.3
1986-87	3.3	2.6	2.9	0.6	1.7	2.6	2.6
1987-88[e]	4.8	5.0	3.0	2.8	5.3	2.5	4.4

Note: [e] forecast.
Source: South Australian Treasury (1988a).

Table 12.4 focuses on the changing rural contribution to economic activity in each State. The year to year fluctuations in real farm GSP which result from the exposure of commodity exports to world price movements are obvious, and reinforce in a State perspective the external vulnerability of Australia's economy discussed in Chapter Two.

Table 12.4

Percentage Change in Real Farm GSP

	NSW	Vic.	Qld	SA	WA	Tas.	Total
1982-83	-33.3	-22.0	-16.6	-36.5	12.4	12.4	-19.9
1983-84	82.1	57.4	27.0	59.1	-26.6	-1.8	37.7
1984-85	-4.9	-16.3	2.8	-0.3	73.8	-8.1	2.3
1985-86	3.9	11.1	-3.8	-5.0	-23.8	19.6	-1.3
1986-87	-3.6	12.8	3.2	2.6	3.4	7.4	3.3

Source: South Australian Treasury (1988a).

Table 12.5 presents a broad summary of economic activity in South Australia. It can be seen that consumption expenditure absorbs around 56% of total turnover, investment 15%, with the remaining 29% satisfying export demand. Total exports account for 42% of State GSP, whereas they only comprise 15% of total Australian GDP. Exports from South Australia to other States represent 31% of GSP, a higher proportion than for Queensland, Western Australia, and Tasmania. The overseas exports (11%) from South Australia is well below the proportion for Queensland and Western Australia. Exports of goods dominate total export receipts (over 90%), the remainder being largely due to interstate and overseas travel credits.

Imports represent approximately 46% of GSP, with only 13% being directly from overseas. Of the total imports, 51% are intermediate goods, and 11% are capital equipment.

In summary, these figures indicate that South Australia is more closely linked to the domestic (national) economy, than the States of Queensland, Western Australia and Tasmania.

Table 12.5

Transactions in South Australia 1984-85

($b)

	Purchases Turnover by local Industry (1)	Consumption Total Private (2)	Consumption Total Public	Investment (3)	Investment (4)	Exports of Final G & S (2+3+4)	(1+2+3+4)
Sales							
Imports	3.9	3.0		1.0	0.01	4.0	7.9
Local	9.1	10.9		2.7	7.2	20.8	29.9
Total	13.0	10.5	3.4	3.7	7.2	24.8	37.8

Source: South Australian Treasury (1988a), Appendix 2.

12.2.3 The Composition of Industry in South Australia

The South Australian economy has a similar diversity of industry to the other States. Table 12.6 presents per capita figures for GSP by industry, and shows the relatively significant contribution of South Australia's rural sector South Australia generates the second largest per capita contribution from Public Administration, Defence and Community Services (with Victoria a close first). South Australia is well behind the larger eastern States in terms of financial and business services. One problem that the South Australian economy faces is the reluctance of large corporations to locate their office operations in the State. The larger financial markets of New South Wales and Victoria (in terms of the scale and range of financial services available) create favourable scale economies which attract head office locations.

Table 12.6

Gross State Product by State by Industry 1986-87

($ Per Capita)

	NSW	Vic.	Qld	SA	WA	Tas	Aust.
Agriculture*	480.6	587.3	833.2	713.2	923.1	665.8	626.5
Mining	335.4	716.3	1026.8	422.5	1368.2	394.1	667.1
Manufacturing	2542.6	3187.5	1793.8	2580.5	1842.1	2124.2	2439.0
Electricity Gas & Water	520.4	593.4	479.6	414.7	455.9	745.9	518.0
Construction	939.8	927.8	1044.7	886.8	1093.5	868.4	1081.4
Wholesale & Retail Trade	2034.5	2141.8	1664.5	1729.8	1756.6	1614.3	1929.8
Transport, Storage & Communication	1402.2	1209.0	1249.2	1137.8	1453.1	1068.8	1291.4
Finance, Property & Business Services	1196.2	1106.8	712.1	959.2	1385.6	645.7	1081.8
Public Admin., Defence & Community Services	2200.2	2432.7	1928.8	2404.2	2197.0	2306.8	2364.7
Recreation, Personal & Other Services	600.1	502.6	487.8	543.1	637.7	529.9	553.0
Ownership of Dwellings	1445.9	1358.0	1082.9	1173.8	935.8	766.0	1274.7
General Government Gross Operating Surplus	310.2	326.1	364.1	315.7	391.7	436.4	349.3
All Industries	14008.0	15089.0	12667.4	12983.2	14440.2	12166.5	14064.8

Notes: * Includes Forestry, Fishing and Hunting.
       Population figures as at June 1987.
Source: South Australian Treasury (1988a), p. 3.

The relatively large percentage contribution from Public Administration, Defence and Community Services is due to:

— the large Federal Defence Projects located in South Australia (particularly the Weapons Research Centre at Salisbury); and
— the strong commitment by the State Government to Community Service provision.

12.2.4 The South Australian Labour Market

On the employment front, it is well known that Australia has experienced continued strong growth in jobs since 1983. Table 12.7 compares employment by industry in 1982 to 1987 for Australia and South Australia. It also presents the annual compound percentage rate of growth for each industry over the 6 year period. Overall, South Australia has lagged rather behind the national trend having a annual growth in total employment of 0.79%

compared to 1.02% for Australia. The growth in manufacturing employment of 0.47% p.a. in South Australia is better than the national performance of 0.29% p.a., but overall the evidence does not support any contention that rapid restructuring is occurring.

There are two notable features of the specific industries performance. While the national economy has experienced rapid growth in finance, property and business services (1.65% p.a.), and recreation, personal and other services (1.57% p.a.), South Australia has not shared in the growth.

Further, the growth in general public administration and defence in South Australia has been around 4 times that of the national rate (1.21% p.a. compared to 0.34% p.a.). This reflects, as noted earlier, the large defence establishments located in South Australia, but in fact, total *State Government* employment fell by -0.03% between 1982 and 1987 (ABS Cat. No. 6248.0).

Table 12.7

Employed Wage and Salary Earners by Industry

	Australia (000s)			South Australia (000s)		
	1982	1987	%*	1982	1987	%
Mining	83.8	86.4	0.51	5.0	6.2	3.65
Manufacturing	1052.6	1070.8	0.29	95.5	98.2	0.47
EGW[a]	135.6	129.0	-0.83	11.3	10.9	-0.60
Construction	261.1	281.5	1.26	19.1	22.6	2.84
Wholesale and Retail	1132.8	1196.4	0.91	90.7	99.8	1.6
Transport and Storage	290.3	294.7	0.25	22.2	21.5	-0.53
Communication	136.7	132.3	-0.54	10.8	10.3	-0.79
Finance etc.[b]	666.9	735.5	1.65	50.5	53.3	0.90
Public Administration	313.6	320.0	0.34	20.1	21.6	1.21
Community Services	1191.6	1229.9	0.53	114.8	118.5	0.53
Recreation[c]	404.1	443.8	1.57	34.0	34.3	0.15
Total[d]	5577.2	5928.3	1.02	474.7	497.7	0.79

Notes: * signifies the annual compound percentage rate of growth, calculated as exponential of the [log(1987/1982)/6].

[a] Electricity, Gas and Water.
[b] Finance, Property, and Business Services.
[c] Recreation, personal and other services.
[d] Total includes government employees in agriculture, forestry, fishing, and hunting.

Source: ABS Cat. No. 6248.0.

South Australia's relatively poor job growth record is reflected in a worse than national average unemployment rate. Table 12.8

illustrates South Australia's recent unemployment rate compared to the Australian average.

Table 12.8

South Australian Unemployment
(Seasonally Adjusted)

	Unemployed Persons	Unemployment Rate	
		SA	Aust.
	(000s)	(%)	(%)
1987			
December	57.8	8.7	7.8
1988			
January	57.8	8.7	7.8
February	61.0	9.2	7.4
March	56.8	8.5	7.4
April	62.0	9.3	7.9
May	59.5	8.9	7.5
June	61.0	9.1	7.4
July	58.2	8.6	6.9
August	57.8	8.6	7.0
September	56.0	8.3	7.0
October	54.6	8.0	6.9
November	51.9	7.6	6.7
December	52.6	7.7	6.9

Source: ABS Cat. Nos. 6202.0 and 6203.0.

According to ABS Cat. No. 1304 South Australia has the second highest proportion of its population receiving unemployment benefits of all the Australian States, and its relative position is worsening. South Australia's relatively weak labour market is reflected on the earnings side where the evidence is mixed. Although male and female average weekly earnings (AWE) in South Australia have grown substantially in excess of the national growth rate since the latter part of 1987, it is important to note that the levels of average weekly earnings of all employees for males, and persons in South Australia were the lowest of all the States in May 1987, with females AWE the second lowest.

Male AWE in May 1987 were $411.80 compared to the Australian average of $450.90. The next lowest was Tasmania with $438.20, while the other States were New South Wales $455.60, Victoria $451.10, Queensland $433.50, and Western Australia $480.20. By August 1988, South Australian male AWE were $457.90, Tasmania $475.50, New South Wales $493.30, Victoria $486.30, Queensland $464.40, Western

Australia $510.30, and Australia $486.20. Similar results apply to females.

So even if the growth has been relatively high in South Australia, the base levels are still very low compared to the other States. In short, the labour market in South Australia indicates a twofold need for public action : first, social justice initiatives to deal with the relatively lower standards of living revealed by the higher unemployment and lower earnings; and, second, active industry development programs to generate jobs.

12.3 Functions and Structure of the State Public Sector
12.3.1 Overview of Functions and Departments

The South Australian public sector can be divided into a number of categories. In South Australia, a number of significant functions including water and sewage, forestries, and highways are administered through ministerial departments and not the statutory authority structures employed in other States.

The major activities of the State public sector

are discussed below using the following classification: agencies concerned with resource management, economic development, conservation, social service, the regulation of industry, commerce and agriculture and internal administration. There is considerable overlap in this classification in that many of the agencies have objectives that fit into several of these categories. Figure 12.1 summarises the portfolio of government departments.

Figure 12.1

South Australian Government Departments:
Classified by Main Activity

	Resource Management	Economic Develop.	Social Service	Law & Regulation – Commerce – industry – Agriculture	Admin.
Agriculture	*	*		*	
Arts			*		
Attorney-General				*	
Auditor-General					*
Community Welfare		*			
Corp Affairs				*	
Correctional Services				*	
Court Services				*	
Education			*		
Electoral					*
EWS	*	*	*		
Envir. & Planning			*	*	
Fisheries	*				
Highways		*			
Housing & Construction		*	*		
Labour			*	*	
Lands	*			*	
Local Govt.					*
Marines/Harbours		*			
Mines/Energy	*	*			
Police				*	
P & IR					*
Premier/Cabinet					*
Public/Cons. Affairs			*	*	
Recreation & Sports			*		
Services & Supply					*
State & Develop. & Tech.		*			
TAFE		*	*		
Transport		*	*	*	
Treasury					*
Woods & Forest		*			

Table 12.9 summarises the State Government employment performance. It is clear public sector employment has been very stable in the last 6 years. Another interesting aspect of Table 12.19 relates to the ratio of full-time to part-time work in the public sector. The number of full-time equivalent (FTE) Departmental jobs has risen by 3.7% between 1982 and 1987, while the number of persons employed has risen by 6.1% over the same period. Similarly, the FTE jobs

for the Public Sector as a whole has risen by
8.1%, while the corresponding number of persons employed has grown by 13.4%. In other
words, the expansion in employment has been
largely in fractional jobs.

If the full-time/part-time ratio had have remained constant over the 5-year period, the
total number of State Public Sector employees
would have been around 104,103 persons, a fall
of 5063 on actual outcomes. It is difficult to provide a qualitative interpretation to this finding.
The South Australian Government has actively

promoted part-time employment opportunities, particularly in the area of education
(ancillary staff especially). While more people
are being employed the average income is reduced. Further, it would be undesirable to
expand part-time jobs at the expense of full-
time opportunities if this meant the decline in
stable career-oriented employment. Casualis-
ation is often associated with the fractionalis-
ation and deskilling of a complex task,
previously performed by a full-time skilled
employee.

Table 12.9

Employment in the South Australian Government Sector

June	1982	1983	1984	1985	1986	1987
Departmental Employees						
Full-time Equivalents	46292.5	46652.7	46932.1	47102.1	48663.7[1]	48013.3
Persons	49410.0	50363.0	50805.0	51328.0	52819.0	52425.0
Public Sector Employees						
Full-time Equivalents	89444.0[2]	90314.2	90437.5	92196.5	96238.9[3]	96750.3[4]
Persons	96259.0	98681.0	99507.0	102473.0[5]	107160.0	109166.0[4]
Percentage of Total SA Employment	17.3	18.3	17.8	17.7	17.9	18.1

Notes: [1] *In July 1985, 790 FTE employees were re-classified as departmental, as a result of transfers from the*
Kindergarten Union to the Children's Services Office.
[2] Excludes around 300 FTE in Health Commission for June 1982.
[3] Includes 2308 FTE in Health Commission organisations which were not previously classi-
fied as part of the Commission, due to a change in the funding status of these organisations.
[4] Includes 767 FTE employees (1063 persons) not previously counted in the Health
Commission.
[5] Includes 582 persons not previously counted in CAEs.
Source: South Australian Treasury (1988a), p. 76.

12.3.2 Economic Development

South Australian Governments have a tradition of active industry development policies.
The Department of State Development and
Technology is currently the principal agency
involved in this field. Its main objectives are
the creation of a growth environment for business, although it has devoted the greater part
of its resources to the revitalisation and growth
of the State's existing industries and companies
and particularly the State's traditional manufacturing base – motor cars and consumer
durables.The Department administers the

South Australian Development Fund which
has directly contributed to the creation and
retention of some 2,700 jobs and almost $160m
in capital expenditure.

State Development has also been active in
attempts to reduce the vulnerability of local
companies to interstate and overseas takeover.
Accordingly they have been developing skill in
consolidating control and ownership in South
Australia through management buyouts, the
encouragement of local investors and through
takeover defense strategies including submissions to the Foreign Investment Review Board.

Some of the other Government activities initiated to promote economic development include:

— Technology Park Adelaide Corporation, to develop and promote a technology park that attracts high technology industries.
— Centre for Manufacturing, to facilitate the introduction of new manufacturing technology into South Australian industry.
— Manufacturing Advisory Council, to provide a forum for consultation on manufacturing issues for unions, the public sector and private industry.
— Industrial Supplies Office, to act as an intermediary between major purchases and local suppliers of goods and services.
— Industries Development Committee, to review applications for assistance to new and existing industries.
— Regional development councils/committees, to plan the economic development of several South Australian regional centres (The Riverland, Port Pirie and Whyalla).
— South Australasia Pty. Ltd., a company formed to encourage trade between South Australia and Malaysia.
— Tourism South Australia

Technology Park provides the essential infrastructure for the expanding micro-electronics industry. It was established in 1982 as a 'campus-style', multi-tenanted development. Related high-technology research and development ventures benefit from the proximity. Co-operation between firms at the Park is already generating rewards (eg. the development of satellite instrumentation products).

Tourism South Australia has been established to increase the value of tourism to the economy by developing and marketing the State as a tourist destination. South Australia attracts approximately 7% of the Australian international tourist market and 8% of the domestic market. Given the emerging importance of tourism in Australia, the South Australian Government is committed to ensure that these levels are maintained or increased. Tourism is currently one of Australia's fastest growing industries representing approximately 7% of Gross Domestic Product. Tourist

arrivals is forecast to reach 5 million p.a. by the year 2,000 with domestic tourism expected to maintain 3% growth p.a. The South Australian Government's actions to encourage tourism include: the Grand Prix, the Casino, the Adelaide Hyatt Regency Hotel development, the Adelaide Convention Centre and a number of regional restoration projects.

The State Government has been extremely active in creating locational advantages to prospective manufacturing industries, through the Department of State Development. The State Government has played an important role in the the provision of industrial land, worker accommodation (under the aegis of the South Australian Housing Trust — the most active public housing authority in Australia), and the development of public infrastructure.

Table 12.10 presents data for the relative payroll tax levels across the States by size of annual payroll. The data shows that although the burden of payroll taxes is similar across the States, South Australia provides strong incentives for larger payroll firms, relative to New South Wales and Victoria.

State Governments also impose charges on business for the provision of energy, usually in the form of electricity and gas. Table 12.11 reports typical annual electricity charges for various size industrial users in capital cities, while Table 12.12 outlines the typical gas tariffs for commercial and industrial usage. The States have similar electricity charges, although Victoria provides advantages to large users. In terms of gas tariffs, South Australia is the cheapest State for all except the largest volume consumers, where again Victoria provides advantages.

South Australia's achievements in the area of electricity generation are all the more remarkable when the absence of a significant high grade coal resource is considered. This is an exemplary indication of the ability of State public sectors to undertake crucial economic services which the private sector declines to tackle. In so doing, the South Australian public sector has overcome fundamental resource constraints on the State economy. Without this intervention it is doubtful whether the industrialisation of South Australia could ever have been achieved.

Table 12.10

State Payroll Tax Burdens for Selected Payroll Size
May 1988 ($)

	$1.0m	Payroll Size $3.0m	$10.0m
NSW	42,000	180,000	500,060
Vic.	42,000	177,732	597,732
Qld	45,067	150,000	500,000
SA	45,625	150,000	500,000
WA	36,250	172,500	575,000
Tas.	50,000	150,000	600,000
ACT	50,000	150,000	500,000
NT	50,000	180,000	600,000

Table 12.11

Representative Annual Electricity Charges
(as at July 1988)

Industrial Category	Sydney	Melbourne	Brisbane	Adelaide	Perth	Hobart
Small (low voltage)	1,530	2,120	1,340	1,930	1,690	1,210
Medium (1 shift)	15,920	14,820	13,310	12,970	14,760	11,560
Large (3 shifts)	567,680	702,400	618,100	684,700	757,900	593,300

Source: ETSA.

Table 12.12

Gas Tariffs for Industrial and Commercial Usage (Feb 1988)
$ Per Month

	Megajoule Usage	Sydney	Melbourne	Brisbane	Adelaide	Perth
Small	9,000	89.16	76.02	95.47	78.16	124.84
Meter	30,000	284.35	236.42	304.07	221.06	362.07
Medium	30,000	284.35	236.42	304.07	221.06	362.70
Meter	50,000	470.25	389.18	492.07	347.06	584.90
Large	50,000	470.25	408.30	492.07	347.06	584.90
Meter	90,000	754.37	680.78	860.07	557.56	1029.30
	200,000	1535.70	1341.20	1782.07	1096.56	2249.51
	500,000	3666.60	3118.10	4092.87	3402.06	5579.51

Source: Report of the Working Party to Review Energy Pricing and Tariff Structures by the South Australian Government.

The Electricity Trust of South Australia (ETSA) was created with the acquisition by the Government of the Adelaide Electric Company and a number of regional electricity suppliers. ETSA is vested with the responsibility to generate and distribute electricity for consumers and industry in South Australia. ETSA also operate a light, brown coal mine at Leigh Creek for use in power generation. This development and other research directed at finding alternative coal supplies within the State, have been undertaken to avoid the State being vulnerable to supply and price fluctuations from the Eastern State suppliers.

The competitive advantage of South Australia's gas tariffs is in part due to the development activities of the State public sector. Although the provision of energy is a mixed private/public sector activity, the public sector is heavily involved in direct provision and in addition maintains strong legislative control over private industry.

Cooper Basin Natural Gas output which supplies around 36% of Australia's total output, is largely private with the State Government (through the South Australian Oil and Gas Corporation Ltd. – SAGASCO), owning less than 15%. The dominant private holdings are owned by Santos.

Up until recent times, the private South Australian Gas Company has reticulated gas to both industry and households, under the controlling influence of the Gas Act. A new arrangement will see gas supplied under the aegis of SAGASCO Holdings (which will be 82% public owned).

In other area of resource provision or extraction, South Australia's economic development has been hampered due to the lack of a most basic resource-water. Again public sector provision has overcome the deficiencies of nature in a way the private sector could not.

The Engineering and Water Supply Department (EWS) has responsibility for the provision of water and sewerage facilities to the State. The EWS has a crucial role in managing the key water-related services in a State often dubbed, 'the driest State in the driest continent'. Water has played a significant role in both economic development and politics in South Australia. In terms of economic development, water supplies provided by the EWS have been crucial to the development of the City of Whyalla with its heavy engineering industries and in agriculture, especially in the irrigation areas adjacent to the River Murray. Thus the creation of whole towns and industries has been conditional upon the activities of the State public sector.

A further case in point is provided by the creation of a competitive Forestry Industry in South Australia. *Private sector involvement in the forestry operations has been sought unsuccessfully several times leaving the development of the industry in public hands.* The Woods and Forests Department of South Australia was created in 1882 as a replacement for the Forest Board which was established in 1875. Its charter was to develop a forest resource to meet the timber needs of the State and to provide the raw material for a wood processing industry. The first forest plantings of pinus radiata were undertaken in the 1880s, and led to significant forests being ready for harvesting by the 1920s. Woods and Forests operate their own milling and logging operations and have developed their techniques to the extent that they are now recognised as a world leader in softwood plantation management and utilisation methods.

Woods and Forests operate with a view to profit while recognising that the assets under their control are public assets. This is evidenced by their published social responsibility objectives to act as responsible corporate citizens in matters affecting the community and to allow use of their lands for public activities.

In the three aforementioned cases of coal, water, and forests the State Government has undertaken to create or develop and manage resources that were not readily available. *The record and current operations of the State public sector in these areas is impeccable by any standards of technical or economic efficiency – an achievement which denies the basic rationale of those wishing to dismantle public economic functions.*

South Australian Governments have accepted the need to create a competitive advantage through policy instruments and public enterprises where none existed. This tradition remains alive for example, through a number of joint partnerships between the public and private sectors. In so doing the public sector can underpin State economic and regional development.

The South Australian Government's current business portfolio contains a mixture of equity and debt investments as well as wholly owned subsidiaries. The principal agents involved in the Government's business portfolio are the

State Government Insurance Commission (SGIC), the State Bank (SBSA), South Australian Government Financing Authority (SAFA), and the South Australian Superannuation Fund Investment Trust (SASFIT). The Government also has a number of trading enterprises including: Central Linen Service, State Clothing Corporation, South Australian Timber Corporation, Adelaide Convention Centre, South Australian Film Corporation and South Australian Meat Corporation.

SAFA was established to raise and manage most of the public sector's debt and has in recent years expanded its investments activities to earn revenue for the State. SAFA is considered in depth below, however at this stage consider its current investments in local South Australian companies:

The major holdings are:

— 45% of Sybiz Software, which specialises in developing a range of accounting software for small business.

— 42% of the Plas-tec Group, an innovative manufacturer and marketer of injection-moulded products and tooling for the plastics industry.

— 37% of Wine Technologies South Australia Ltd., a joint venture including Petaluma Wines that is developing a new system for the storage of premium wines in oak.

— 26% of Mineral Control Instrumentation Ltd., a successful manufacturer of sophisticated analysing equipment for the mining and processing industries.

— 25% of Disposable Products Australia Ltd., the Technology Park manufacturer of biotechnological and medical products which is well established in the Australian and export markets.

— 18.5% of Forensic Science Technology International, which is developing image and audio-processing computer systems and services for the forensic science, law enforcement and security fields.

— 15% of IPL Datron, a Sydney-based Distributor of computer hardware and peripherals which is expanding into computer communications.

— 50% of Flinders Technologies, a company

formed with Flinders University to commercialise the results of research.

SAFA recently took control of Enterprise Investments, a venture capital company and its portfolio will grow as Enterprise Investments and the subsidiary South Australian Ventures expand activities. To grapple with this mishmash of interests, SAFA has recently hired merchant banker Ayers Finniss, a subsidiary of the State Bank, having first sought submissions from the private sector.

The SBSA was created in 1984 with the merger of the Savings Bank of South Australia and the State Bank. It was created in a climate of concern for the banking needs of South Australia following the collapse and subsequent takeover of the Bank of Adelaide.

The Bank's general objectives are focussed on South Australia. It seeks to promote balanced development of the State's economy including ensuring the availability of housing loans. It looks to operate with a view to profit and provide a broad range of services and facilities. In this way, the SBSA has developed a portfolio of banking, property and financial enterprises. At balance date, June 30 1988, the State Bank listed the following subsidiaries among total assets of more than $11,000m with capital and reserves of $1,000m:

— Beneficial Finance Corporation (100%), finance company.

— Executor Trustee and Agency Company, trustee company (100%).

— Ayers Finniss (100%), merchant bank.

— Oceanic Capital Corporation (100%), funds manager.

— SVB Day Porter (50%), stockbroker.

— Myles Pearce and Co. (50%), real estate agent.

Since 1984, the State Bank Group has built up its operating profit to $66.4m in 1988 when it paid a dividend to the Government of $46m. Total assets of the Group as at 30 June 1988 were over $11b including $968m of investments, mainly in Government and Semi-Government securities.

SASFIT invests the superannuation funds of State Government public servants. It has an

80% holding in Fairey Aviation, wholly owns Thorn EMI, has invested $165m into the ASER and Adelaide Casino projects and holds another $22.9m in assorted shares. The total value of investments at June 30 1988 is listed as $614m which yielded investment income of $67.9m.

The State Government Insurance Commission (SGIC) was established in 1970 at a time when the majority of funds from premium income was invested outside the State by the private sector insurance companies. The SGIC is now one of Australia's largest insurance organisations with premium income of $217m and total assets of $1.2b. Although initially excluded by law from the life assurance market, SGIC now provide general, life and health insurance, as well as being the sole provider of compulsory third party motor insurance. In 1987, SGIC also became the sole agent for Workcover, the State's uniform workers rehabilitation and compensation fund. SGIC receive premiums that are invested to provide income to offset what insurers call 'underwriting losses'. This means claims by policyholders generally are not covered by the premiums received so the investment income makes up the shortfall and provides any profit that may be earned.

The SGIC is a major contributor to the South Australian economy through its substantial shareholdings in South Australian based companies and in property development, through provision of funding to a number of the major construction developments currently underway in Adelaide. SGIC owns 20% of South Australian Brewing, 14.2% of Coca Cola-Bottlers, 13.5% of Fauldings Ltd., 10% of Adelaide Brighton Cement, 9% of the troubled Health and Life Care, 100% of Bouvet Pty. Ltd. (which operates the Gateway Hotel in Adelaide), 80% of developer Durham Trust and 100% of SGIC Health. Direct investments are worth $453.9m with another $4.7m locked up in subsidiaries. A major motive in these investments has been to ensure that companies with Head Offices in Adelaide are protected from takeover.

While SGIC's liabilities exceed assets by $23.7m, the weak financial position has been improving in the past two years. SGIC report that if investments were revalued to market value this deficiency would become a surplus. Subsidiary operations incurred losses of about $600,000 last year but the insurer closed the year with a net profit of $24m.

SAFA, SBSA, SASFIT and the SGIC are the main financing aims of the Government. Their activities have been directed towards the investment activities detailed below. That is as an active investor making investments for revenue and strategic purposes and as a provider of development and venture capital.

The State's role in economic development is not limited to direct commercial or resource development but also includes the maintenance of services crucial to the competitiveness of the private sector. For example, a major State Government innovation in shipping services has occurred at Outer Harbour of the Port of Adelaide. There, competitive public cargo handling facilities, are able to handle the largest cellular-type container ships, roll-on/roll-off and break-bulk vessels. Recently, the Australian, New Zealand, Eastern Shipping Conference decided to double the frequency of container shipping to the Port of Adelaide from Japan and Korea. The decision to establish such modern cargo handling facilities, taken by the State Government in the mid-1970s has now been vindicated. The Port of Adelaide will now handle 95% of the container trade between Japan and South Australia, instead of the shipping being initially handled at the Port of Melbourne. A spinoff is that exporters will be able to ship their output with greater surety and reduced transport costs.

Once again, the economic well-being of the State, particularly the private sector is enhanced by the provision of infrastructure by the public sector.

The continuing operation of the State public sector in economic development is required because South Australia continues to face the need for structural adjustment. In particular the State suffers from a narrow manufacturing base where a few industries dominate the industrial activity of the State economy. The largest manufacturing employers in South Australia are food and beverages (17.2%), transport equipment (15.0%) and machinery and equipment (13%) (1984/5 Manufacturing Census).

The relative dominance of a few industries is also revealed when the South Australian Manufacturing Value Added is compared to National Data. Table 12.13 is based on Manufacturing Census Data which was last available in comprehensive form in 1984-85.

Food, beverages and tobacco account for 17.1% of South Australian Value Added in 1984-85; Metal products (which comprises basic and fabricated metals) 16.2%; Transport equipment 15.9%; Other machinery and equipment 12.8%; Paper, paper products, printing and publishing 9.0%, are the leading output contributors.

Table 12.13

Manufacturing Value Added for South Australia and Australia
1984/85
($m)

	SA ($m)	Aust. ($m)	SA/Aust. (%)
Food, Beverages & Tobacco	529	6835	7.7
Textiles	64	1026	6.2
Clothing & Footwear	98	1659	5.9
Wood, Wood Products & Furniture	224	2190	10.2
Paper, Paper Products, Printing etc.	279	4045	6.9
Chemical, Petroleum & Coal	139	3542	3.9
Non-Metallic Mineral Products	182	1971	9.2
Basic Metal Products	287	3996	7.2
Fabricated Metal Products	214	2912	7.3
Transport Equipment	490	3809	12.9
Other Machinery & Equipment	396	4366	9.1
Miscellaneous Manufacturing	192	2037	9.4
Total Manufacturing	3095	33387	8.1

Source: ABS Cat. Nos 8203.0, 8203.4.

These figures show that the State public sector must actively intervene to encourage a more diversified and higher value added industrial structure for South Australia. This is a task which the private sector unaided will not be able to achieve within a satisfactory time scale.

As noted in Part Three, the provision of Occupational Health and Safety services is an important function for the States. There are two primary components of such a service: first, to deal with workplace injuries which do occur (compensation); and second, to ensure, through a system of adequate regulation and training, that the incidence of workplace injury

is minimised. South Australia has established the Workers Rehabilitation and Compensation Corporation which is responsible for workers compensation insurance and services to injured workers. At the same time, the data base which such an organisation is able to develop enables it to identify those employment categories in which workers are most at risk, and to target them for special prevention programs. The scheme operated by the Corporation is known as WorkCover and is intended to be fully funded from workers' compensation insurance premiums. The actuary believes that the scheme will reach this stage by 30 June 1990

(Workers' Rehabilitation and Compensation Corporation, 1988, p. 11) The South Australian Occupational Health and Safety Commission is responsible for ensuring the occupational health and safety of the South Australian workforce. This is done in conjunction with both employers and unions. For example, the Commission runs occupational health and safety courses for both workers and employers. In 1988, under these two categories, 1002 and 183 people attended respectively. The United Trades and Labor Council of South Australia has described the Commission as 'an important step forward in health and safety reform' (South Australian Occupational Health and Safety Commission, 1988, p. 12).

12.3.3 Social Services

The South Australian State public sector also plays an important role in the provision of social services. Public employment in the community services area is above the national average (see Table 12.14). However, this is offset by the diseconomies of small scale in certain community service areas compared with the two largest States and the greater coverage of community service functions by the State rather than Local Government in South Australia.

There are a number of State agencies that provide services that form part of what is termed the social wage. It is these services that most come under fire in periods of fiscal restraint, but it is these services that deliver social justice in the community. The future of these agencies and their funding at appropriate levels is crucial to the maintenance of the social wage and to overall social justice. The South Australian State Government has a policy of social justice and has established a unit within the Department of the Premier and Cabinet to facilitate the policy's introduction. The main thrust of a social justice strategy is to ensure that Government agencies direct on equitable share of their resources and programs to those most in need (see below). It follows then that Government resources are to be aimed at preventing disadvantage. Other related areas include: facilitation of re-entry into the workforce by sole parents; consideration of the social impact of transport planning

and provision; assessment of the problems of credit over-commitment; provision of income support for young people; and assessment of the effect of the current distribution of concessions.

The main elements of the social wage provided by the State Government are health, education, transport and welfare. In addition the State provides law and order, consumer protection, environmental protection, monitoring of labour conditions and support for the arts, recreation and sports bodies. Overall, the State Government is the main provider of social services to the community.

The South Australian Education Department is the main provider of primary and secondary education in the State. In July 1987, there were 187,831 students enrolled in the State's 717 government schools. In addition there were 53,988 students enrolled in non-governmental schools. Average class sizes in 1987 were 23.1 for primary and 18.1 for secondary. The Department's overall goal is to provide the best possible educational opportunities for young people. A key aim in this endeavour is to provide for the different needs of young people and to give them equal access to educational opportunities.

South Australia's education system provides for compulsory schooling in the 6 to 14 aged group with primary and secondary levels ranging from Reception to Year 12. The Year 12 Certificate of Achievement provides the educational standards necessary for entry to tertiary education at the State's two universities, the Institute of Technology and the College of Advanced Education. Students may also undertake Certificate and Associate Diploma studies in the TAFE system. Year 12 has also developed to allow for more general studies for those entering the workforce on completion. The retention of students to complete secondary education has been increased by making the final years attractive to those less academically inclined. Fifty-three per cent of those completing Year 8 continued to Year 12 in July 1987 which was up from 29.6% in 1977. Female retention rates (58.3%) are significantly higher than male (49.0%) reflecting that the drive towards retention has been more successful for females (30.6% in 1977) than for males (28.7% in 1977). These statistics highlight the important role that the Education Department plays in the State in preparing students for further studies or for the workforce. The existence of a

well-educated population is vital for economic development and the development of society in general.

Table 12.14

Public Sector Employment and Employed Wage and Salary Earners by State
(Average 3 Months to Dec 1987)

	Public Admin.	State Government Comm. Servs.[a]	State Government Other [b]	Total	Local Gov't	State/ Local	C'wealth Gov't	Total Gov't	Total W & S[c]
NSW									
000s	24.7	224.4	124.0	373.1	63.4	436.5	135.3	571.8	2053.5
% of Total	1.2	10.9	6.0	18.2	3.1	21.3	6.6	27.9	100.0
% 6 States	34.6	31.4	35.7	33.0	40.6	33.9	37.9	34.7	36.1
Vic.									
000s	19.8	202.5	89.7	312.0	43.3	355.2	98.8	454.0	1639.3
% of Total	1.2	12.4	5.5	19.0	2.7	21.7	6.0	27.7	100.0
% 6 States	27.7	28.4	25.8	27.6	27.7	27.6	27.7	27.6	100.0
Qld									
000s	11.0	107.5	57.4	175.9	26.5	202.4	50.2	252.6	839.1
% of Total	1.3	12.8	6.8	21.0	3.2	24.1	6.0	30.1	100.0
% 6 States	15.4	15.1	16.5	15.5	17.0	15.7	14.1	15.4	14.7
SA									
000s	*6.0*	*73.9*	*30.8*	*110.7*	*8.7*	*119.3*	*36.0*	*155.3*	*526.2*
% of Total	*1.3*	*15.2*	*6.3*	*23.0*	*2.0*	*25.1*	*5.1*	*30.1*	*100.0*
% 6 States	*8.4*	*10.2*	*8.9*	*9.9*	*5.6*	*9.3*	*10.1*	*9.4*	*8.5*
WA									
000s	6.6	79.6	35.0	121.2	10.6	131.8	26.7	158.4	526.2
% of Total	1.3	15.1	6.7	23.0	2.0	25.1	5.1	30.1	100.0
% 6 States	9.2	11.2	10.1	10.7	6.8	10.2	7.5	9.6	9.2
Tas.									
000s	3.2	25.8	10.6	39.6	3.7	43.3	10.3	53.6	151.7
% of Total	2.1	17.0	7.0	26.1	2.4	28.5	6.8	35.3	100.0
% 6 States	4.5	3.6	3.1	3.5	2.4	3.4	2.9	3.3	2.7
6 States									
000s	71.4	713.8	1347.2	132.4	156.1	1288.5	357.3	1645.8	5695.5
% of Total	1.3	12.5	6.1	19.9	2.7	22.6	6.3	28.9	100.0
% 6 States	100.0	100.0	100.0	100.0	100.0	100.0	100.0	100.0	100.0

Notes: [a] Health, education and welfare.

[b] Includes electricity, water, finance, manufacturing, construction.

[c] Total wage and salary earners.

Source: ABS Cat. No. 6248.0, and unpublished data available to South Australian Treasury.

The South Australian Social Justice Strategy
As part of its commitment to the provision of social services, in August 1987 the South Australian Government introduced a Social Justice Strategy, the basic goal of which is 'to redress disadvantage and inequality' (Social Justice Strategy, 1987, p. i). The Strategy is designed to

ensure that each public sector agency pays due regard to social justice considerations in its decision-making and activity. At the same time, the Strategy incorporates a commitment to community liaison. A notable feature of the Strategy is the co-ordination which occurs between the public sector agencies, and also between government Ministers.

In the public sector, a Social Justice Unit has been established within the Cabinet Office, which has responsibility for liaising with a responsible senior staff member within each Department and Authority. Within the government, a Cabinet Human Services Committee has been established to which Department and Authority heads will report.

The introduction of this Strategy marked a major change in emphasis in the government's approach to social justice issues. As the Strategy document noted:

'Much of our social policy has been concerned with the treatment of *symptoms* of poverty. Now, because of the increasing concern about the number of people in poverty and the curtailing of resources, it is shifting to a concern for *preventing* inequalities rather than shoring them up.

The problems of disadvantage and poverty have been left to 'welfare' services. This has tended to compound disadvantage itself and turn recipients of welfare services into second-class citizens. Yet it is obvious that all spheres of socio-economic activity from housing industry policy to energy tariff structures have a profound impact on standards of living for everyone' (p. 5).

Three levels of activity are required by the Strategy. These are, first, the continual assessment of the effectiveness of programs in meeting social justice objectives; second, the support for community initiatives and the fostering of debate; and third, '. . . agencies will be required to devise active, interventionist policies and practices which can act as a springboard out of poverty for people who are in financial or personal crisis' (Social Justice Strategy, 1987, p. 14).

It is significant that the Strategy makes particular reference to the social justice impact of both pricing policies and rebate systems. In addition, it makes reference to the role of transport authorities and the need to ensure that public transport travels where it is most needed.

The United Trades and Labor Council of South Australia has expressed support for the initiatives embodied in the Strategy. However, it has also pointed out the need for continual effort to guarantee an integrated social justice strategy rather than a series of *ad hoc* decisions. In 1988/89, the Social Justice Unit will undertake an analysis of budget distribution and expenditure designed to assess the degree to which the government's policies have been integrated into public sector activity.

In 1988/89, $15.2m has been allocated to the implementation of social justice initiatives, and a further $4m for additional projects (Government of South Australia, 1988/89, p. 19). Such expenditure includes $1.3m to ensure that remote Aboriginal communities have access to to electricity services, and $900,000 to ensure that they have access to water services.

12.3.4 Administrative Services

The benefits of State public sector regulation have already been alluded to in the discussion of South Australia's comparative advantage in gas tariffs. A number of State agencies and departments perform similar regulatory functions. For example, the Department of Agriculture plays a pivotal role in protecting the States orchards from fruit fly infestation through powers conferred on it by a specific Act of Parliament. In 1987/88 fruit fly outbreaks were eradicated in a number of localities at a cost of nearly $250,000 (South Australian Department of Agriculture, 1988, p. 41). In addition, the Department was successful in intercepting infested fruit on 31 occasions. The Department also has some responsibility for the State's involvement in the Murray Darling Basin Commission, the role of which was outlined in Part Three. However, it is not just South Australian primary producers who benefit from the Department's functions. For example, the Department appears to have some success with biological control of the introduced black Portuguese millipede which infests the homes of people in urban areas. The States' fisheries are maintained on a sustainable basis through the supervision and management measures of the Department of Fisheries.

The rights of the people of South Australia are also a State public sector responsibility. This includes the provision of a an effective courts system, and a well developed regime of consumer protection agencies, in addition to the provision of civil rights to the less well-off.

Equal opportunity, ethnic affairs, consumer protection, residential tenancy rights and obligations, and the monitoring of standards of licensed people and premises are the responsibility of the Department of Public and Consumer Affairs. This Department provides a broad range of services directed at protecting the individual from a range of undesirable practices. For example, equal opportunity is intended to provide remedies against unlawful discrimination on the grounds of sex, marital status, pregnancy, sexuality, race or physical impairment.

The promotion of multiculturalism is encouraged through the Ethnic Affairs Commission which promotes the full participation of ethnic groups in the social, economic and cultural life of the community. The consumers' rights are protected through consumer education programs and through the activities of the Consumer Affairs Division which acts in the interests of non-business consumers and as a conciliator in disputes between purchasers and suppliers. The State Residential Tenancies Act and the Retirement Villages Act are administered by the Residential Tenancies Division with the aim of advising tenants and landlords of their rights and responsibilities.

The State also establishes minimum standards of competence and probity for people engaged in, for example, the building industry. In addition, standards of trading practice are enforced to minimise the incidence of unfair practice, but at the same time all legislation is regularly reviewed to avoid over-regulation. The Prices Division reviews prices at three levels of surveillance: price fixation, price justification and price monitoring. The Department also provides a central register of all births, deaths, marriages, adoptions and changes of name occurring in South Australia as well as providing a facility for civil marriages.

Finally, it is worth noting that other administrative functions of the State can also have a marked economic value. The South Australian Traffic Inspectorate, for example, plays a role in reducing the cost of damage to the State's roads caused by overloaded commercial vehicles

(estimated by the National Association of Australian State Road Authorities at $400m per year nationally). The South Australian Public Service Association has conservatively estimated that the cost in South Australia at $4m (ie. 10% of the total) (South Australian Public Service Association Inc., 1989, pp.3-4). Thus, the actual and potential service provided cannot just be seen in terms of maintenance of 'law and order', but also in the considerable community and economic benefits that a properly resourced Inspectorate could provide. In terms of the public sector itself, the Inspectorate raised $900,000 through Court Awards of successful prosecutions in the year to 30 June 1988.

12.4 The Finances of the South Australian Public Sector
12.4.1 Federal-State Financial Relations
The finances of South Australia are dominated by the relations with the Federal Government. The major aspects of this relationship are briefly described below (see South Australian Treasury 1988b, p. 5):

— in Constitutional/legal terms, there exist equivalent taxation powers between the two levels of government, with the exception that duties of custom and excise are reserved to the Commonwealth;
— in practical terms, income taxes (both personal and corporate) are levied exclusively at the Commonwealth level. The absence of broadly-based indirect taxes at both levels leads to a high proportion of taxation being collected at the Commonwealth level;
— there exists broad equivalence between the two levels of government in the level of their outlays, excluding transfers between them;
— a high level of transfers from the Commonwealth to the State occurs with heavy dependence by the latter upon the former, and with the bulk of these transfers taking the form of 'untied' (general purpose) grants;
— there exists a very sophisticated and detailed system of financial equalisation between the States, based largely on the recommendations of the Commonwealth Grants Commission; and

— there are close inter-relationships between the two levels of government in borrowing arrangements under the Financial and Gentlemen's Agreements through the operations of the Australian Loans Council.

While the above summary might suggest that the State is highly constrained by the Federal level, there is no evidence to support the view that the Commonwealth would ever leave a State without financial support. Even in times of Federal stringency, which leads to reductions in the funds available to the State, the Constitution still provides the State with access to a variety of revenue-raising sources, in addition to the commercial opportunities the State might develop.

12.4.2 The State Government Budget

The budget is the central instrument of public finance in South Australia, in that it details the proposed expenditures from, and revenue into the Consolidated Account (CA). The CA on the one hand, records the majority of State public sector recurrent spending, directly or in terms of the required deficit funding. Excluded from the CA is recurrent spending by ETSA, the Housing Trust, and the Department of Woods and Forest. While capital spending also appears in the CA, a large part of capital expenditure is financed by the internal provisions and borrowings by public trading authorities (PTAs), which does not appear in the CA. Table 12.15 records the recent history of recurrent and capital spending shown in the South Australian CA.

Table 12.15

Consolidated Account Expenditures

	Recurrent Spending			Capital Spending			Consolidated Account		
	Actual	Variation from Budget		Actual	Variation from Budget		Actual	Variation from Budget	
	$m	$m	%	$m	$m	%	$m	$m	%
1981-82	1766.8	-44.4	-2.6	181.0	5.5	2.8	1947.7	-39.2	-2.1
1982-83	2032.8	-106.9	-5.6	242.0	-5.9	-2.5	2274.8	-112.8	-5.2
1983-84	2190.4	-7.9	-0.4	389.5	-10.9	-2.9	2579.9	-18.8	-0.7
1984-85	2626.2	-2.4	-0.1	414.5	0.3	0.1	3040.7	-2.1	-0.1
1985-86	2955.4	12.2	0.4	501.7	-12.7	-2.6	3457.1	-0.5	—
1986-87	3214.9	-2.4	-0.1	563.4	2.6	0.4	3778.3	0.2	—
1987-88	4215.2	-13.6	-0.3	617.8	-1.0	-0.2	4833.0	-14.6	-0.3

Source: South Australian Treasury (1988b), p. 26.

The variations of the actual from the amount set down (in advance) in the Budget for each financial years usually not large, and are explained in the following years Financial Statement of the Premier and Treasurer, which accompanies the Budget Papers. The only abnormally large error in the budget forecasts occurred in 1982-83 and was due to an extraordinary combination of drought, bushfires and floods which placed great demands on both components of expenditure in the CA.

Variations from the budgeted receipts for any year also occur. Table 12.16 presents data for the CA in terms of the overall variation in the recurrent revenue and receipts and capital outlays and receipts. Again the large deficit in

1982-83 arose due to the unforeseen natural calamities which occurred in South Australia, and as such can be ignored for the purposes of establishing trends. The strong recurrent surpluses in 1984-85 and 1987-88 were attributable to a large contribution on the receipts side from stamp duties as a result of the buoyant property markets in those years. The overall CA has increasingly moved to surplus positions. In 1986-87 and 1987-88 the forecasted (small) deficits became in actual terms robust surpluses due to less than planned expenditures and greater than planned receipts (largely taxation). In fact the PSA in South Australia has claimed that these results are part of a Government strategy to overstate expenditure demands and understate revenue-capacity, in order to avoid Drastic Federal cut-backs, and

demands from constituents within the State for increased benefits and lower charges.

Table 12.16

Variations in the Consolidated Account

	Recurrent			Capital			Consolidated Account		
	Actual		Variation from Budget	Actual		Variation from Budget	Actual		Variation from Budget
	$m		$m	$m		$m	$m		$m
1981-82	61.3	deficit	-14.3	61.8	surplus	+17.8	0.5	surplus	+3.5
1982-83	109.0	deficit	-67.0	51.9	surplus	+9.9	57.1	deficit	-57.1
1983-84	29.7	deficit	+3.3	28.1	surplus	+0.	1.6	deficit	+3.4
1984-85	13.7	surplus	+38.7	0.0	balance	-25.0	13.7	surplus	+13.7
1985-86	11.0	surplus	+11.0	0.1	surplus	+0.1	11.1	surplus	+11.1
1986-87	2.3	surplus	+9.6	7.7	surplus	+7.7	10.0	surplus	+17.3
1987-88	10.4	surplus	+61.7	24.0	surplus	-13.0	34.4	surplus	+48.7

Source: South Australian Treasury (1988b), p. 27.

Table 12.17

Consolidated Account Presentation for 1987-88

	1986-87 Actual	Revised 1987-88 Forecasts	Variation between 1986-87 and 1987-88 adjusted for changes to CA presentation
	$m	$m	%
Recurrent			
Total Payments	3,214.9	4,215.3	9.7
Total Receipts	3,217.2	4,225.7	11.7
Surplus (deficit)	2.3	10.4	
Capital			
Total Payments	563.4	617.8	-15.0
Total Receipts*	154.9	301.4	-10.0
Total			
Payments	3,778.4	4,833.0	6.0
Receipts	3,372.1	4,527.1	10.7
Financing Requirement	406.3	305.9	
Consolidated Account Result			
Borrowing	416.2	340.3	
less Financing Requirement	406.3	305.9	
CA Surplus/Deficit	9.9	34.4	

Source: South Australian Treasury (1988b), p. 28.

The public sector in South Australia comprises the activities of the government departments and agencies which are recorded in the published accounts of the Treasurer (CA, Deposit and Trust Accounts), and the activities of a

variety of Statutory Authorities (SAs) created by South Australian legislation. The Local Government sector is conceptually distinct from the South Australian public sector.

The major trends in South Australian public

sector finances closely resemble those found in the other Australian States. First, recurrent payments are typically less than cash receipts and Federal grants (that is, gross capital payments are partly funded by recurrent receipts). Second, payroll tax revenue provides the largest source of tax receipts, with stamp duties and franchise taxes (in that order) the next largest. Third, a large proportion of recurrent outlays (>50%) go to education and health; while capital expenditure is largely absorbed by road transport, housing and energy provision (the three accounting for more than half of the total). Finally, the financing requirement in any year is highly variable because of lumpy capital demands

and fluctuating revenues (especially related to stamp duties as real estate prices rise and fall).

Table 12.18 presents a summary of the South Australian public sector finances for the years 1983-84 to 1987-88, while Table 12.35 presents the same data in real terms (using the Non-Farm GDP deflator except for recurrent payments which used the Government Final Consumption Deflator, and capital payments which were deflated by the Total Public Gross Fixed Capital Expenditure Deflator). Recurrent expenditure in 1987-88 accounted for 76.4% of total outlays, with capital outlays around 18%. Financing the PTE deficits absorbs the remainder.

Table 12.18

South Australian Public Sector Accounts

Year Ending June	1984	1985	1986	1987	Rise	1988	Rise
	$m	$m	$m	$m	%	$m	%
Recurrent Outlays	2115	2435	2750	3018	9.7	3343	10.8
Capital Outlay	714	686	765	780	2.0	783	0.4
Deficit of the PTEs[1]	148	150	182	236	29.7	247	4.7
Total Outlays	2977	3271	3696	4035	9.2	4373	8.4
Commonwealth Grants	1796	2010	2095	2242	7.0	2368	5.6
Taxation Receipts	659	787	830	899	8.3	1001	11.3
Other Receipts[2]	94	120	177	179	1.1	166	-7.3
SAFA Surplus	5	83	189	220	16.4	250	13.6
Total Receipts	2554	3000	3291	3540	7.6	3785	6.9
Provisions[3]	131	148	169	198	17.2	203	2.5
Net Borrowing[4]	292	123	236	297	25.8	385	29.6
Total Financing	423	271	405	495	22.2	588	18.9

Note: [1] Net Operating Deficit of the Public Trading Enterprises.

[2] Comprises mining royalties, land rent, interest, statutory contributions from banks and other financial institutions, and other minor items.

[3] Comprises depreciation allowances and other allocations to internal reserves.

[4] Includes other financing arrangements.

Source: South Australian Treasury (1988b), p. 33.

12.4.3 Public Sector Spending in South Australia

An analysis of the functional distribution of South Australian public sector spending reveals the common fact across all States, that the bulk of public expenditure is accounted for by Education and Health. Smaller but still significant areas of expenditure are Housing and Community Amenities and Transport and

Communications. Together these four areas absorb more than 60% of the total. The fact that this is common across most States is largely due to the constitutional division of spending responsibilities between the State Governments and the Federal Government.

Table 12.19 details the trends since 1983 in the real public sector financial aggregates. Fluctuations in capital expenditure in South Australia are driven largely by the timing of electricity infrastructure developments. The rapid growth in the early 1980s reflected the expenditure associated with the construction of an new power station. If we excluded expenditure by ETSA from the figures in Table 12.20, a quite different picture emerges in terms of the real growth in State public sector expenditure.

Table 12.19

South Australian Public Sector Accounts in Real Terms

Year Ending June	1983	1984	1985	1986	1987	1988	Rise
	$m	$m	$m	$m	$m	$m	%
Recurrent Outlays	2652	2741	2978	3151	3242	3343	3.1
Capital Outlays	904	978	879	893	842	783	-7.1
Deficit of the PTEs[1]	243	196	186	211	253	247	-2.4
Total Outlays	2268	2374	2498	2430	2407	2368	-1.7
Commonwealth Grants	2268	2374	2498	2430	2407	2368	-1.6
Taxation Receipts	776	871	979	963	965	1001	3.7
Other Receipts (2)	144	124	149	205	192	166	-13.6
SAFA Surplus		7	103	219	236	250	5.9
Total Receipts	3188	3376	3728	3817	3801	3785	-0.4
Provisions[3]	211	173	184	196	213	203	-4.7
Net Borrowing[4]	480	386	153	274	319	385	20.6
Total Financing	690	559	337	470	532	588	10.5

Table 12.20

Real Growth in Main Public Sector Financial Aggregates

Year Ending June	1983	1984	1985	1986	1987	1988
			% Change On Previous Year			
Recurrent Outlays	4.5	3.3	8.7	5.7	2.9	3.1
Capital Outlays	12.1	8.2	-10.1	1.6	-5.7	-7.1
Total Outlays	7.8	3.0	3.3	5.2	1.9	0.8
Commonwealth Grants	7.7	4.7	5.2	-2.7	-0.9	-1.6
Taxation Receipts	-0.8	12.3	12.3	-1.6	0.3	3.7
Total State Revenue	-1.0	9.0	22.8	12.8	0.5	1.7
Total Receipts	5.0	5.9	10.4	2.4	-0.4	-0.4

Table 12.21 shows this clearly. The year ending June 30 1984 is abnormal for reasons previously noted. In 1987-88 capital works associated with linking power grids between Victoria and South Australia, was undertaken. The forecasted fall (7.1%) in total capital outlays for that year reflects a massive 17.1% decline in real terms in the non-ETSA capital outlays.

Table 12.21

Real Growth in Spending (Net of ETSA)

Year Ending June	1983	1984	1985	1986	1987	1988
		Percentage Change on Previous Year				
Capital Outlays	-0.4	27.6	1.7	7.6	-4.0	-16.9
Total Outlays	5.3	4.9	6.8	6.8	2.1	-0.5

Capital Outlays (around 18% of the total) reflect the pattern of functional dominance described above. Housing absorbs 29.0% (in 1987-88), which is divided between 10.8% for advances to concessional home loans, and 18.2% for other housing/works; ETSA 15.9%, Roads 10.9%, and Education 8.1%. The current State Budget strategy is to maintain real outlays at the existing level. With recurrent expenditure expected to grow in real terms by a small margin, this objective means that capital works have been cut fairly harshly over the last few years.

12.4.4 Public Sector Revenue-Raising in South Australia

The trend in receipts is negative (0.4% decline in real terms in 1986-87, and 1987-88), despite an earlier growth of 6% over the period 1983-84 to 1985-86. The robust growth was largely attributed to a strong contribution by stamp duties as property values boomed. The overall decline in the current period which is expected to endure into the future is largely due to Federal restraint and a failure of non-tax income to show positive growth.

The dominance of the Federal Government is summarised by the fact that around 66% of total State public sector revenue is derived from the Commonwealth. This source of funding declined by 1.6% in real terms in 1987-88 (-2.7% in 1985-86, and -0.9% in 1986-87). To help maintain the revenue of the State, taxes and charges grew by more than 3.7% in real terms in 1987-88.

An important contributor to the revenue side of the CA is the SAFA surplus. In 1987-88 this increased by more than 6% in real terms, and accounted for more than 7% of total public sector receipts in that year.

Revenue from Taxes and Charges are dominated by four categories: Payroll tax, around 30%; taxes on property, around 20%; franchise taxes, around 14%; and motor vehicle charges around 13%. The growth source of tax revenue is the franchise charges (see Chapter 5 for a full comparative treatment of the State tax mix).

12.4.5 A Comparison of South Australian Public Sector Finances With the Other States

Data for State finances is available from the individual Treasury Departments, and the ABS. The only basis for a comparison is provided by the ABS data which uses common definitions and concepts. The major publication in this regard is the ABS, Government Financial Estimates 1987-88, and State and Local Government Finance 1985-86 which cover all public sector transactions except government owned financial institutions. In other parlance, the data covers the general government (GG) sector and the PTEs.

Table 12.23 shows that the ratio of Total State Government Expenditure to GSP for all States (except Tasmania) is fairly similar. This proportion has exhibited stability over the period shown. The feature to note about Table 12.40 is the relationship between the ratio and the size of the respective States. Smaller States have higher ratios because the per capita costs of providing services is higher, and the small economic base produces less GSP.

For South Australia, (second smallest population) the ratio is significantly higher than the larger States. The South Australian Treasury (1988b, p. 43) cite Grants Commission analysis which shows:

'that in South Australia there is above average real social service provision, but below average administration spending and above average recovery of business undertaking costs (adjusted for levels of service).'

Of course, there is no optimal ratio of Total Outlays to GSP. Clearly, the ability of a State to raise financing revenue is an important constraint on the size of the Total Outlays. In addition, the economic and resource base of the State will influence the GSP outcome. It is important to emphasise that a large part of State expenditure is of a recurrent nature which historically has been difficult to prune. The day to day level of welfare of the population who depend on State services is very sensitive to cuts in State spending. In South Australia's case, the overhead component of outlays is low relative to the actual in-kind dollars that are transferred to social welfare recipients spending.

Table 12.24 provides comparative data on the Net Borrowing Requirements to GSP. This ratio gives an indication of the ability of each State to support a given level of expenditure from current revenue. It would be problematic if the ratio of Spending to GSP (Table 12.40) was associated (for any particular State) with a rising Net Borrowing Requirement to GSP ratio. The evidence is that most States are reducing this ratio, some faster than others. In the early 1980s the 6 States average was 3.1%, whereas it had declined to 1.9% by 1987. Over the same period, the 6 States Total Outlays to GSP ratio had risen from 17.8% to 18.3%. Although this rise is modest, it indicates that the States are moving away from debt financing, and finding growing sources of current revenue.

Table 12.22

Financial Data for the South Australian Public Sector

Year Ending June	1983		1984		1985		1986		1987		1988	
	$m	%[a]	$m	%	$m	%	$m	%	$m	%	$m	%
Expenditure												
1 Consumption	1615	58.3	1763	57.1	2007	59.2	2208	73.2	2408	57.0	2674	59.1
2 Net Interest-GG	47	1.7	63	2.0	100	3.0	160	5.3	185	4.4	244	5.3
3 Net Interest-PTE	203	7.3	258	8.4	281	8.3	305	10.1	374	8.9	400	8.8
4 Benefits/Grants*	136	4.9	171	5.5	187	5.5	209	6.9	238	5.6	239	5.3
Local Gov't Grants:												
5 Current Grants	43	1.6	46	1.5	51	1.5	55	1.8	60	1.4	64	1.4
6 Capital Grants	17	0.6	38	1.2	36	1.1	33	1.1	29	0.7	31	0.2
7 Other Transfers**	40	1.4	42	1.4	42	1.2	47	1.6	33	0.8	47	1.0
8 Current Outlays												
(1+2+3+4+5+6+7)	2101	75.9	2381	77.1	2704	79.8	3017		3227	76.4	3699	81.7
9 Capital-GG	195	7.0	245	7.9	255	7.5	302		380	9.0	394	8.7
10 Used Assets-GG	-16	0.5	-22	0.7	-12	0.3	-18		-38	0.8	-52	1.1
11 Capital-PTEs	430	15.5	409	13.2	384	11.3	409		409	9.7	388	8.6
12 Used Assets-PTE	8	0.2	23	7.4	11	0.3	7		7	0.1	-3	0.0
13 Advances Paid	50	1.8	52	1.7	47	1.4	95		138	3.3	99	2.2
14 Capital Outlays												
(9+10+11+12+13)	667	24.1	707	22.8	685	20.2	795		896	21.2	826	18.2
15 Total Outlays (8+14)	2768		3088		3389		3812		4525			
Revenue												
16 Taxes/Fees/Fines	537	23.3	659	24.6	788	25.8	835	25.3	903	25.0	998	25.7
17 PTEs Surplus***	129	5.5	183	6.8	154	5.0	181	5.5	186	5.2	228	5.9
18 Income from PFEs	8	0.3	5	0.2	47	1.5	103	3.1	204	5.6	279	7.2
19 Other	41	1.8	42	1.7	54	1.8	82	2.5	60	1.7	61	1.6
20 C'wealth Grants	1590	69.0	1791	66.8	2011	65.8	2095	63.6	2256	62.5	2321	59.7
21 Total Revenue												
(16+17+18+19+20)	2305		2680		3054		3296		3609		3887	
22 Financing Transactions (15-21)	463		408		335		516		614		538	
23 Depreciation	57		63		74		89		99		125	
24 Other Provisions	24		20		78		46		61		62	
25 Deficit (22-23-24)	383		325		183		381		454		451	
26 Net Borrowing Requirement												
(25-13)	33273		136		286		316		352			
27 GSP	12676		15353		17280		18935		20491		22752	
28 Household Income	11347		13313		14609		15977		17184		n/a	
29 Population (000)	1346		1360		1372		1383		1394		1405	

Notes: [a] percentage of relevant total.
  * Personal Benefits and grants to non-profit institutions.
  ** All Other transfers excluding subsidies to PTEs.
  *** Net Operating Surplus of PTEs excluding subsidies.

Table 12.23

Ratio of Total State Expenditure to GSP
(%)

Year Ending June	1982	1983	1984	1985	1986	1987
NSW	16.9	17.3	17.6	17.3	17.3	17.2
Vic.	17.3	18.5	17.8	17.6	17.2	16.9
Qld	18.1	21.2	20.8	19.8	20.5	19.7
SA	19.7	21.8	20.1	19.6	20.1	20.6
WA	18.5	21.1	22.6	19.5	19.4	20.1
Tas.	26.4	28.1	28.5	29.2	28.3	26.5
6 States	17.8	19.3	19.1	18.6	18.5	18.3

Source: South Australian Treasury (1988b) p. 44 (based on ABS Data).

Table 12.24

Ratio of Net Borrowing Requirements to GSP
(Per Cent)

Year Ending June	1982	1983	1984	1985	1986	1987
NSW	3.6	2.4	2.1	2.0	1.9	2.0
Vic.	3.6	3.8	3.4	3.0	2.9	2.2
Qld	2.0	4.1	3.1	1.4	1.6	1.5
SA	2.0	2.6	1.8	0.8	1.5	1.5
WA	1.6	4.3	3.9	2.0	1.7	1.7
Tas.	3.8	4.9	2.9	3.9	4.2	2.6
6 States	3.1	3.3	2.8	2.1	2.2	1.9

Source: South Australian Treasury (1988b) p. 44 (based on ABS Data).

South Australia in particular has the lowest (with Queensland) ratio of all States, although its Total Outlays to GSP ratio is well above the larger States. This indicates a healthy, well managed budget process.

One consequence of borrowings is that it places a debt-servicing burden on future generations. The oft-quoted value of gross interest paid ignores the fact that the State hold financial assets from which interest is earned. The more relevant measure of the debt-servicing burden of the public sector is the net interest paid as a percentage of total revenue after the distribution of surpluses from PFEs which is provided in Table 12.25.

Table 12.25

Total Net Interest Paid as a Percentage of Total Revenue
(After Allowing for the Distribution of the Surplus from the PFEs)

Year Ending June	1982	1983	1984	1985	1986	1987
NSW	10.7	12.6	12.1	12.3	12.0	14.0
Vic.	15.9	17.6	17.8	19.0	20.9	20.3
Qld	6.8	8.8	10.8	11.2	9.6	9.9
SA	9.9	10.5	11.8	11.1	11.3	10.4
WA	8.9	10.4	12.8	13.5	13.3	14.1
Tas.	15.2	16.2	16.7	17.0	17.5	18.2
6 States	11.4	13.1	13.6	14.0	14.1	14.8

Source: South Australian Treasury (1988b) p. 51 (based on ABS Data).

Once allowance is made for the surplus contribution of PFEs to the Budget and the income from financial asset holding by the State, South Australia has the second lowest debt-servicing burden. Importantly, while the general trend for all States is to suffer significantly higher burdens, South Australia has recently experienced a rapid diminution in the servicing commitment. In the main this is because the overall level of net debt is relatively low in South Australia due to the reduced relative reliance on net borrowing.

Another way of appraising the Budget is to compare total outlays to total revenue on an adjusted basis. The adjustment involves netting out the advances received from total outlays. Table 12.26 shows the adjusted total outlays to total revenues. In a similar vein, Table 12.27 reports data for the ratio of total current outlays to total revenue including capital grants.

Table 12.26

Ratio of Adjusted Outlays to Total Revenue

Year Ending June	1982	1983	1984	1985	1986	1987
NSW	1.34	1.22	1.21	1.19	1.19	1.21
Vic.	1.31	1.31	1.30	1.29	1.30	1.23
Qld	1.46	1.28	1.22	1.11	1.13	1.13
SA	1.15	1.18	1.13	1.09	1.13	1.13
WA	1.14	1.33	1.26	1.17	1.16	1.15
Tas.	1.20	1.21	1.14	1.18	1.21	1.14
6 States	1.26	1.26	1.23	1.19	1.20	1.18

Source: South Australian Treasury (1988b) p. 45 (based on ABS Data).

Both tables show that all States generate higher receipts than their recurrent cash outlays. South Australia was committed to cash outlays of some 92% of revenue in 1986-87. In other words, around 8% of non-borrowed revenue (about the same magnitude as capital grants received from the Commonwealth) was available for capital outlays.

It is important to note that the ABS definition of current outlays exclude accrued liabilities like unfunded superannuation and depreciation in the GG sector, and offsets like inflation gains on nominal debt held.

Table 12.27

Total Current Expenditure to Total Revenue
(Per Cent)

Year Ending June	1982	1983	1984	1985	1986	1987
NSW	96.2	90.6	89.4	89.9	88.7	91.5
Vic.	94.1	95.6	97.7	99.5	101.5	99.4
Qld	78.6	82.4	83.0	78.7	77.8	78.8
SA	90.6	91.1	88.8	88.5	91.5	92.2
WA	86.0	89.6	88.2	88.0	88.7	86.8
Tas.	92.0	88.3	84.9	85.0	89.4	90.4
6 States	91.0	90.5	90.1	89.9	90.4	91.0

Source: South Australian Treasury (1988b) p. 46 (based on ABS Data).

An important qualification should be made to the preceding ratio analysis. While instructive, the figures are quantitative and therefore cannot say anything about the quality of services provided or capital formation undertaken by the spending, on the one hand; and the regressivity and discriminatory severity of the taxes and charges, for example, on the other side. A high expenditure to GSP ratio might be related to a strong growth in quality capital infrastructure which says the basis of sustained growth in future GSP per capita; whereas, alternatively, it might reflect a large unproductive consumption commitment financed by debt, which might imply a large taxation burden in future years to service the debt.

The South Australian Treasury (1988b, p. 46) argue that:

'For example, high capital expenditure to current expenditure is not by itself an indicator of financial soundness – a judgement needs explicitly to be made about the quality and productivity of a State's total expenditure in creating an economic and social environment involving both physical infrastructure and human capital ie. job skills, labour satisfaction, work attitudes,

etc. which will most readily permit future growth in Government revenues.'

South Australia, like all the States, relies heavily on Federal grants. In recent years, Federal restraint has led to a substantial reduction in Commonwealth Grants to the States. South Australia has suffered restraint in two ways:

– the total funds available to the States collectively has been trimmed; and
– the per capita share of this total for South Australia via the process of fiscal equalisation has been cut as a result of the Grants Commission decision.

Table 12.28 summarises the recent trends in the ratio of Commonwealth grants to GSP for the individual States.

Table 12.28

Total Commonwealth Grants to GSP
(Per Cent)

Year Ending June	1982	1983	1984	1985	1986	1987
NSW	7.2	7.9	8.3	8.3	8.2	7.9
Vic.	7.1	7.5	7.6	7.7	7.3	7.1
Qld	9.5	10.0	10.5	10.4	10.1	9.9
SA	11.6	12.5	11.7	11.6	11.1	11.0
WA	10.6	10.3	11.0	10.3	9.9	9.8
Tas.	15.0	15.9	17.3	16.6	14.9	14.0
6 States	8.3	8.9	9.2	9.1	8.8	8.6

Source: South Australian Treasury (1988b) p. 47 (based on ABS Data).

The problems with the Grants Commission assessment of a State's need have already been discussed in Chapter 5 of the main Report. In brief, the Grants Commission assessment of a States revenue-raising capacity may not reflect the true capacity. The effects of equalisation are clearly shown in Table 12.28. New South Wales and Victoria have below average Federal contributions.

Table 12.29 shows the extent to which the States raise their own taxation revenue, while Table 12.30 adds the effects of non-tax revenue-raising activities to derive the Total Own Revenue as a percentage of GSP. South Australia is the second lowest taxing State (relative to GSP). The explanation for this can be traced

to smaller payroll tax base (relative to Victoria and New South Wales), and less available and cheaper real estate. A recent calculation by the Grants Commission suggests that South Australia could raise the overall tax burden by 4% before it would equal the average 6 State burden.

The contribution of non-tax revenue to total State revenue has been increasing across all States over the period covered. New South Wales and Victoria have experienced below average increases in their respective revenues from this component, whereas Queensland, Western Australia and Tasmania have witnessed substantial increases in the contribution. South Australia is between the two extremes (slightly above the average rise).

12.5 The Indebtedness of the State Public Sector
12.5.1 An Overview
South Australia is:

'a stable political entity operating with a system of Parliamentary democracy subject to the rule of law and orderly administrative processes' (South Australian Treasury 1988b, p. 3).

The debt management by the State Government has been prudent throughout its history. The State Government has used debt to finance the purchase and development of physical assets or increase the holdings of financial paper, and has avoided raising debt to support recurrent cash needs. This use of debt helps to achieve inter-generational equity in terms of the distribution of the burdens involved in the purchase of capital items (see Part Five). In recent years the real per capita net indebtedness of the public sector has fallen. In terms of the publicly-owned assets (physical and financial), and the projected debt-servicing burden, South Australia is well placed. Several independent agencies including the Auditor-General and the Public Accounts Committee of the Parliament monitor the expenditure and revenue-raising activities of the State.

Table 12.29
Taxation as a Percentage of GSP

Year Ending June	1982	1983	1984	1985	1986	1987
NSW	5.2	5.6	5.6	5.6	5.7	5.8
Vic.	4.9	5.5	5.1	5.2	5.1	5.2
Qld	4.1	4.1	4.1	4.1	4.0	4.1
SA	4.2	4.2	4.3	4.6	4.4	4.4
WA	4.1	4.0	4.5	4.3	4.2	4.8
Tas.	4.4	4.3	4.3	4.6	4.6	4.9
6 States	4.7	5.0	5.0	5.0	5.0	5.1

Source: South Australian Treasury (1988b) p. 49 (based on ABS Data).

Table 12.30
Total Own Revenue as a Percentage of GSP

Year Ending June	1982	1983	1984	1985	1986	1987
NSW	5.5	6.2	6.2	6.4	6.4	6.3
Vic.	6.2	6.7	6.1	6.0	5.95	6.6
Qld	5.9	6.0	6.2	7.2	7.4	7.0
SA	5.5	5.6	5.8	6.0	6.3	6.6
WA	5.6	5.5	6.6	6.3	6.6	7.4
Tas.	6.9	7.1	7.5	8.0	8.1	8.8
6 States	5.8	6.2	6.2	6.4	6.5	6.7

Source: South Australian Treasury (1988b) p. 49 (based on ABS Data).

The South Australian Treasury has recently published an analysis of State public sector debt entitled Trends in the Indebtedness of the South Australian Public Sector 1950 to 1985. In this section we draw on aspects of that report, but extend it to the present and include comparative data from New South Wales and Victoria.

Table 12.31 is a summary of the Debt situation in the South Australian public sector.

Table 12.31

Summary Data on Indebtedness of the State Public Sector
($m)

Period Ending	Gross Debt	Financial Assets	Net Debt
1949-50	314	32	281
1959-60	826	90	736
1969-70	1,691	229	1,461
1979-80	3,226	1,003	2,223
1980-81	3,391	1,013	2,378
1981-82	3,587	1,004	2,583
1982-83	4,005	1,053	2,952
1983-84	4,653	1,400	3,253
1984-85	5,546	2,139	3,407
1985-86	6,280	2,596	3,683
1986-87	6,999	3,024	3,975

Source: South Australian Treasury (1988b), p. 53.

The growth in gross debt averaged 16.3% p.a. through the decade ending 1960, 10.5% p.a. for the decade ending 1970, 9.1% p.a. to 1980, and in recent years has been around the 11% mark. The corresponding growth in financial assets has been 18.1% p.a. to 1960, 15.4% p.a. to 1970, 33.7% p.a. to 1980, and in recent years varying from around 50% in 1984-85 to a more modest but still strong 16.4% in 1986-87. The rapid growth in financial assets in recent years is attributable to the expanding role of SAFA.

Three phases in financial asset accumulation can be noted. First, until the 1980s strong growth was achieved. Second, the nominal growth in the stock of financial assets was effectively zero for the first three years of the 1980s. Third, the already noted robust growth in the following years to 1987.

The combination of these trends has resulted in the fact that net debt (gross debt minus financial assets) has not grown as fast as gross debt.

In terms of the range of financial assets held by the State public sector (as at 30 June 1987), the dominance of SAFA is highlighted by the fact that it holds in liquid and non-liquid assets more than 38% of total financial assets.

More specific data for the Net Indebtedness of the South Australian public sector are provided in Table 12.33. The increase in real indebtedness from 1950 to 1970, was followed by a large decline until 1980. After that time the real level has been roughly maintained, with some annual fluctuations. As a ratio to GSP the debt level has declined since 1983.

No one factor explains the changes in net indebtedness. This change reflects net borrowing, by definition, which is the difference between total taxation, Federal grants, or reductions in financial asset holdings and outlays. While these factors interact in a complex manner, short-term fluctuations are often driven by major infrastructure spending.

Included in the Net indebtedness figures for the public sector are many non-budget agencies which meet a portion of their debt-servicing (and general operating costs) by imposing user charges. The agencies concerned include: ETSA, Pipelines Authority of South Australia, South Australian Timber Corporation, Lotteries Commission of South Australia, Urban Land Trust, Totaliser Agency Board, Racecourses Development Board, E & WS, Woods and Forests Department, and the South Australian Housing Trust.

The implications for the level of net debt raised by self-financing agencies is different from those related to the debt raised by the Budget supported sector. The latter does not generally seek to recover recurrent outlays by imposing user charges. Table 12.34 displays the Net Indebtedness of the Budget supported public sector.

It is clear that the ratio of net debt as a percentage of GSP is falling, although this is due to a GSP growing faster than the real and nominal levels of net debt. Overall, the bulk of the per capita burden is due to self-financing borrowings by agencies (72%). The other notable aspect of the Budget supported public sector indebtedness relates to its substantial real decline over the last twenty years. This has been counter to the trend in the overall public sector indebtedness in South Australia, and suggests that the Government is mindful of the need to match financing commitments with appropriate revenue flows.

Table 12.32

State Public Sector Financial Asset Holdings
($m)

Equity in the State Bank	43.6
Interest Bearing Subscribed Capital to State Bank	306.4
Loans to the State bank	329.1
Loans to the SGIC	108.0
Loans to LGFA	101.4
Interest Bearing Subscribed Capital to LGFA	50.0
Loans to SAFTL	62.9
Loans to SAFL	158.9
Loans to Primary Producers	89.4
Equity in SAGASCO	33.5
Loans to SAGASCO	230.5
Liquid Assets held by:	
SAFA	1027.5
Treasurer	5.0
Semi-Government authorities	140.6
Other Non-liquid assets held by:	
SAFA	134.8
Treasurer	30.0
Semi-Government authorities	172.4
Total Financial Assets	3023.9

12.5.2 Debt Management in South Australia

Borrowings under the 1927 Financial Agreement, have over the years represented the largest source of debt finance to the State. The Financial Agreement was instigated to coordinate the total borrowing of the public sector at all governmental levels. In practice, the Commonwealth Government has dominated the operations of the principal lending institution, the Loan Council. The total debt borrowed from the Loan Council (Financial Agreement or Public Debt) represents a less than comprehensive measure of the total State public sector indebtedness. This is due to the developments since the Agreement, which have seen the number of statutory authorities expand, and the diversity of debt sources used by the public sector agencies increase.

The State have also introduced some new financing arrangements, principally by establishing central public sector financing authorities. SAFA was set up by the Government to increase the volume of financial reserves available to the State public sector. The objective was to reduce the inflexibility in public sector financing arising from large periodic capital outlays, sudden changes in Federal funding, natural disasters, and rigidities in Loan Council lending.

The State also exploited a high credit rating to earn positive margins on borrowing and lending. A rise in gross indebtedness has accompanied the increased holdings of financial assets. This is not a problem because the assets have been earning income.

This strategy (which effectively reduces the net interest costs incurred by the State) has been referred to as the hollow logs strategy and criticised by the Federal Government. Of course, any attempt to eliminate the financial assets held by State Governments would be identical in effect to a rise in borrowings.

Table 12.33

South Australia Public Sector Net Indebtedness

Year Ending	Money* Value $m	Real** Value $m	Real Per Capita $	Per cent*** of GSP %
1949-50	281	3,496	4,927	n/a
1959-60	736	5,129	5,426	n/a
1969-70	1,461	7,426	6,412	n/a
1979-80	2,223	4,007	3,063	23.3
1980-81	2,378	3,900	2,958	22.5
1981-82	2,583	3,739	2,814	22.5
1982-83	2,952	3,928	2,928	23.3
1983-84	3,253	4,002	2,956	21.2
1984-85	3,407	3,957	2,904	19.7
1985-86	3,683	3,962	2,886	19.5
1986-87	3,975	3,975	2,873	19.4

Note: * Real value is nominal value deflated by the non-farm GDP deflator (June 1987 prices).
    ** Per capita figures based on estimated resident population.
    *** South Australian Treasury Estimates.
Source: ABS Quarterly Estimates of National Income and expenditure; ABS Australian Demographic Statistics Quarterly.

Table 12.34

Budget-Supported Public Sector Net Indebtedness

Year Ending	Money* Value $m	Real** Value $m	Real Per Capita $	Per cent of GSP %
1949-50	213	2,646	3,729	n/a
1959-60	388	2,707	3,255	n/a
1969-70	742	3,770	3,255	n/a
1979-80	900	1,638	1,252	9.4
1980-81	992	1,627	1,234	9.4
1981-82	1,017	1,473	1,109	8.8
1982-83	1,125	1,497	1,116	8.9
1983-84	1,251	1,539	1,136	8.1
1984-85	1,229	1,428	1,047	7.1
1985-86	1,370	1,473	1,073	7.2
1986-87	1,514	1,514	1,094	7.4

Note: * Real value is nominal value deflated by the non-farm GDP deflator (June 1987 prices).
    ** Per capita figures based on estimated resident population.
Source: South Australian Treasury (1988b), p. 58.

12.5.3 Fixed Assets Held by the State Public Sector

The other often neglected side of net indebtedness is the stock of fixed assets held by the State public sector which facilitate the provision of public services. Data in this area is very sparse. In part this reflects the cash-based accounting systems used by non-trading departments, which reduces the need for asset-registers. Where data has been available (PTEs) the use of historical-cost valuation has reduced the usefulness of the figures.

Over 1986 and 1987, the Public Accounts Committee of the South Australian Parliament investigated these problems and as a result calculated the current replacement cost of the major public sector infrastructural assets. In summary terms, the total current cost of replacing the assets was (1984-85 dollars) around $21b. Asset valuations drawn from the Public Accounts Committee report, adjusted by the South Australian Treasury to account for inflation and new acquisitions, reveal that Total fixed asset values in the State public sector as at 1986-87 were $29.1b (written down value $17.7b). Water and sewerage, electricity and highways were the dominant asset areas.

Table 12.35

Replacement Cost of Major Fixed Assets in State Public Sector 1986-87

	Current Replacement Cost ($b)	Written Down Current Cost ($b)
Highways (inc. Local Roads)	3.8	1.8
Housing	3.0	2.0
Electricity	5.1	2.9
Hospitals	1.8	1.4
Transport	.0.6	0.2
Education	2.8	1.2
Water and Sewerage	8.6	4.6
Woods and Forests		0.4
Marine and Harbours		0.1
Other	0.8	0.5
Total Improvements	26.5	15.1
Land Value	2.6	2.6
Total Asset Values	29.1	17.7

Source: South Australian Treasury (1988b), p. 69.

The importance of the asset register relates to the need for the State Government to monitor and correctly measure the rate at which assets are used in providing public services. It could be argued that the cash-based and historical-cost accrued accounting methods are inadequate, and lead to sub-optimal decision making.

One of the major aspects of the State public sector financing problem is the need to generate funds which can maintain and replace these assets as they become obsolete. While capital outlays are easier to cut in the short-term, because they are not readily identified by the public, it is crucial that Governments resist this policy. The long-term damage of this expediency would be very costly to the nation as whole in terms of community living standards.

12.5.4 Management of Liquidity

The State public sector also holds substantial cash and liquid assets. SAFA utilises temporary cash (liquid) surpluses to generate investment income over and above the borrowing costs related to the assets. Public sector liquidity is the main form of flexibility that the Government has to fulfill its responsibilities. On top of the cash assets held by the public sector, various credit facilities ($20m overdraft with Reserve Bank; $20m overdraft limit with Commonwealth Bank; Promissory note facilities with assorted banks to $600m, etc.) allow the State Government considerable flexibility.

Almost 90% of public sector liquid investments are held by SAFA (with continued increases anticipated). The benefits of this centralisation (discussed in detail elsewhere) are briefly as follows:

— higher rates of return can be earned over a broader range of maturities;
— lower administrative costs;
— improved overdraft and short-term credit flexibility; and
— improved reporting and accounting of all public sector liquidity.

Table 12.36

Public Sector Liquidity
($m)

	Government	SAFA	Semi-Government Authorities	Total Marketable Investments
June 1985	171	719	146	1,037
June 1986	128	780	147	1,055
June 1987	5	1,027	141	1,173

Source: South Australian Treasury (1988b), p. 73.s

12.6 Selected Case Studies of State Public Sector Activities in South Australia
12.6.1 Introduction
The South Australian case studies that follow cover a broad cross section of public sector activities and are intended to outline the various functions of government and approaches to the financing and management of entities involved in these functions. The main elements to emerge from the cases are commercialisation, investment performance, the provision of development and venture capital; and asset replacement needs.

The bodies covered by the case studies are the Department of Lands (Lands), the Electricity Trust of South Australia (ETSA), and the South Australian Government Financing Authority (SAFA). Lands are an example of a government department undertaking a program of commercialisation and consequently the case looks to the methods adopted and any results of the process in terms of improved efficiency and cost effectiveness. ETSA face a large asset replacement program and has adopted innovative financing and accounting policies. Several of ETSA's financing schemes have called on the services of SAFA, the State's financing authority. In looking at SAFA emphasis is on the role it plays in the South Aus-

tralian economy. SAFA's activities have included the direct financing of government activities, the management of an investment portfolio and the provision of venture and development capital.

12.6.2 Department of Lands
The South Australian Department of Lands (Lands) provides an example of a traditional government undergoing a process of introducing modern management practices. Features of this process include corporate planning, business planning, a user pays principle and the emergence of marketing to expand the revenue base. For the purpose of this section this process is referred to as commercialisation.

The mission of the Department of Lands is:

'To ensure that government land information and management policies are implemented, statutes administered and authorised services provided effectively and efficiently within a co-ordinated structure supporting the Director of Lands.'

The principal land related services provided by the Department include surveying, registration services for property and land, valuation services, crown land and government real estate services, major land information systems, and Mapland, a commercial outlet.

The services provided by Lands offer ample scope for low-risk, commercialisation. Its valuation, surveying and information services are able to be offered on a commercial, for profit basis. In addition, its role in managing government real estate enables it to act as a land development company offering subdivisions that can achieve both financial and social justice objectives.

In implementing recommendations from the Guerin Report, designed to effect a leaner more efficient approach, a Performance Agreement was prepared between the Chief Executive Officer and the Minister of Lands. The Performance Agreement identified targets for the Department to achieve, which must be reported on in the Annual Report. In 1987/88 Lands achieved all targets identified in the Performance Agreement.

Financially, Lands achieved an increase in Recurrent Receipts of $3.8m which was far in excess of its budgeted increase figure of $0.75m. In addition, the Department obtained receipts from freeholding Crown land totalling $8.3m which was far in excess of the target of $4.3m.

Lands have also entered into marketing arrangements with another Semi-Government body, SAGRIC International, to market their services overseas. Overseas marketing of Government skills has potential to raise significant revenues for a number of agencies and allow them to subsidise their domestic activities.

The process of commercialisation requires effective accounting systems to ensure control and hence the achievement of commercial objectives. In this regard, Lands have refined its management planning process and is developing its performance reporting system based on performance indicators derived from this process.

A strategic plan has been completed by Lands for its information systems and long-term computing strategies completed. This commercialised approach has led to the investigation of non-traditional methods such as joint ventures

The commercialisation process does not mean that social objectives and labour relations are neglected. In a commercial environment such objectives become an integral element for success. At Lands equal opportunity issues are identified and integrated into management plans and explicit occupational health, safety and welfare programs have been implemented, reducing time lost through injury to very low levels. Commercialisation does not involve deterioration in working conditions, but looks to a harmonious work environment and its consequent improved efficiency.

Lands are also focusing attention on product development whilst maintaining a thrust to improve productivity.

Business Planning

The management of Lands have produced a Statement of Intent outlining the future direction that it will be taking. The main elements are:

- recovering the full cost of services provided (by adopting the user pays principles except where government determines otherwise);
- increase income by forceful marketing of existing products and identifying new products to market;
- improving productivity by efficiency and effectiveness programs, thereby reducing the unit cost of activities; and
- marketing technical expertise overseas at a profit.

The business plan reflects a commercialised approach with a movement towards user pays, improved productivity and marketing. Applications of the plan can be seen in land development, the freeholding of Crown land, the management of Government real estate and in overseas marketing.

Lands' development activities include 61 projects in country towns, Regency Park and Grand Junction Industrial Estate and the major development projects of Roxby Downs and Lincoln Cove. The role of Government in land development is one that has met with considerable debate over the past 20 years. One approach calls for a high level of Government involvement in sub-division and sale of both residential and commercial sites. In this way the Government ensures an even supply of land at reasonable prices with a surplus or profit being available to fund other community services. Arguments against Government involvement are based mainly on the philosophy that the Government ought not be involved in risky business ventures and that the private sector is more efficient. South Australia has a history of involvement in land development through both the Lands Department and the South Australian Urban Land Trust.

The freeholding of Crown land involves granting perpetual leases for pastoral properties and the sale of holiday shack sites where appropriate. Management of Crown land may involve sales where the sites concerned are considered acceptable as in the case of shack sites, and should not be confused with asset sales with the aim of transferring public sector functions to the private sector.

Lands have been involved in the area of disposal of Government real estate. While land development and eventual sale is one course, another would involve sale to private developers, an action somewhat against the main thrust of commercialisation. Property disposal has also increased as a result of development of the Land Resource Inventory, and the rationalisation of Government agencies' stocks. Once again asset sales in this context are an element of improved public sector management and not a form of privatisation.

However, there have been some sales of properties which foreshadow a movement of some functions to the private sector. The Raywood Inservice Centre was a conference centre operated by the South Australian Education Department and used for teacher professional development programs and available for hire by other organisations. The sale of the centre, planned for 1989, will see this asset, and a public sector function, transferred to private ownership. Other sales of significance in 1987/88 included:

Health Commission properties	$4.212m
Education Department primary schools	$1.800m
Department of Lands	$2.235m

The total realised from the sale of 89 properties in 1987/88 was $11.840m.

There are plans for sales in 1989 of Woods and Forest Department reserves, two hospitals, a Technical and Further Education campus and a development at the country town of Goolwa. Most of these sales are routine, buying and selling in the process of managing the State's asset base.

The Department of Lands and SAGRIC International, the South Australian Government's technology transfer company, have been actively marketing the Department's expertise. Bids were submitted for a $19.23m Philippines land resource management project and an Indonesian valuation project. In addition, work has been undertaken in Vanuatu and Yemen. These opportunities not only earn valuable revenue for the State, but also provide important staff development opportunities that enhance productivity domestically and strengthen the skill base for future overseas assignments.

Lands have also created a new Business Manager's position whose role is to identify and develop new product opportunities. Much of this activity is currently focused on providing information services to the real estate industry and to Local Government.

Accounting and Reporting
The Department of Lands still maintains its account on a cash basis, employing fund accounting for Recurrent Receipts and Payments and Capital Accounts. The Department operates on a loss with the net cost of recurrent operations being $16.229m in 1987/88 down from $18.368m in 1987. Although the result was acceptable to achieve the targets of the Performance Agreement it must be borne in mind that a cash basis of accounting ignores accrued revenue and expenses, depreciation and the incurrence of employee benefit liabilities, such as superannuation and long service leave.

The failure to provide commercial accounting to report on the results of a commercialised entity is unfortunate.

Operating Performance
Lands have traditionally operated with an excess of payments over receipts, however, through a process of commercialisation the net cost of operations has been reduced over the

past three years. The commercialisation process has lead to greater emphasis on the provision of services that are marketable and when coupled with a user-pays basis of pricing, has led to significant increases in revenue. Further, emphasis has also been placed on cost control and reduction through computerisation and reassessment of work methods.

The commercialisation approach adopted in Lands can be compared and contrasted with the approach adopted by the Greiner Government in New South Wales. In New South Wales, Land dealing information is supplied, on a daily basis, to CLIRS (Computerised Legal Information Retrieval System), which has been given monopoly control over computerized legal information by the Federal, Victorian and New South Wales Governments. CLIRS is a wholly owned subsidiary of Computer Power Group Pty. Ltd. in which Rupert Murdoch retains a major interest. Accordingly, information which is essentially public in nature is sold to private interests and will only be accessible through payment of a subscription fee. However, the issue is not really one of whether a fee is appropriate or not, but one of who should be responsible for the maintenance and distribution of public information. The Department of Lands in South Australia has shown that it has the necessary technical knowledge and skill to develop information systems and indeed its skills are being recognised overseas. The alternative approach is to privatise all public information services which may lead to the abandonment of social objectives, price levels that discriminate against small users and the provision of a limited service.

12.6.3 The Electricity Trust of South Australia

The Electricity Trust of South Australia is a body corporate operating under the Electricity Trust of South Australia Act, 1946. ETSA's broad purpose is to serve its customers in South Australia through the provision of a reliable, safe, efficient and competitive supply of electricity and associated services.

It generates and transmits electricity and distributes it to approximately 640 000 customers in South Australia. The available capacity of the generators in the ETSA system totalled 2380

megawatts at 30 June 1988. ETSA employs about 5900 people.

ETSA finances its capital works program and meets its operating expenses through revenue received from its customers and repayable loans. It has been involved in some innovative financing arrangements in recent years which can be seen as a feature of commercialised bodies. It has also been innovative in its accounting for fixed assets and depreciation which have enabled it to expand the user-pays principle to recover the current cost of providing electricity from consumers. The combination of these factors has enabled ETSA to finance $145.3m of new capital works in 1987/88, while reducing its debt level by $9.3m.

ETSA have been using pricing based on notions of current cost accounting to provide funds for the acquisition of fixed assets and to reduce borrowing levels. ETSA values its power stations and charges depreciation on the basis of the cost of replacing generating plant. In this way ETSA plan to recover 85% of the ultimate replacement cost of its power stations of $1,367m. As noted in Chapter 4 such a policy is not optimal. It leads to a transfer of wealth from this generation to the next and by guaranteeing replacement of plant does not encourage innovation and efficiency improvement.

For Federal Statutory Authorities like Telecom, attention is often focused on the level of investment in new fixed assets funded by internal sources. Internal sources of funds are Net Operating Surpluses plus the expenses that do not require cash outlays: depreciation, employee's retirement benefits, long service and annual leave liabilities, self insurance and any other deferred costs. Telecom has an objective of funding 50% of its capital works program from internal sources. ETSA's level of internal funding was 163.7% and 136.3% in 1987/8 and 1986/7.

In looking at the operating performance of ETSA since 1980/81 it becomes obvious that increased depreciation charges have been used to justify price increases and reduce politically sensitive profit levels. In 1981/82 ETSA's profit was 10.4% of its revenues, while depreciation was 10.1%. In the next year depreciation jumped to 16.7% of revenue, forcing profit down to 2.1% of revenue. Depreciation has continued to be based on current replacement cost and still remains at 16 to 17% of revenues.

Notwithstanding the fact that ETSA's price rises in recent years have been below the CPI, it may be argued that prices should have in fact been lower. Given the creative finance and accounting techniques of ETSA it is possible that electricity prices could be 10-15% below their current level. A reduction in energy prices of this magnitude would assist the State in attracting industrial investment and indeed strengthen existing industry. ETSA's policies have not been debated publicly and appear to have avoided parliamentary scrutiny. A not insignificant factor has been the ample dividend paid to State coffers by ETSA, $51.3m in 1987/88.

ETSA's position is defended on the grounds that it will lead to a lower debt burden for future generations and hence lower future electricity costs. In doing so it will avoid the foreign exchange management problems of other Australian electricity suppliers. As an approach to financing capital needs, it is akin to a taxation option, albeit a hidden tax option. Politically it is less sensitive than 'real' taxation or borrowing options. Economically, it may have a negative impact on current economic growth in particular industrial investment. Overall, ETSA's accounting methods are considered inappropriate since they are intended to hide their pricing policies' effects.

ETSA have also been involved in 'cost effective' financing arrangements through SAFA. While it is apparent that some of these transactions involve receiving tax benefits from overseas, it is not clear that they do not involve the undermining of the Federal income tax base. Both ETSA and SAFA are reluctant to discuss details of their 'structured financing deals'. The activities of SAFA are discussed in more depth below.

12.6.4 South Australian Financing Authority
The South Australian Financing Authority (SAFA) commenced operations in January 1983 initially as a central borrowing agency and has developed to encompass a broader role for the South Australian public sector's fund raising, debt management, cash management and in-

vestment. SAFA is subject to the control and direction of the Treasurer of South Australia and any liabilities incurred by it are guaranteed by the Treasurer. In centralising the corporate finance or treasury operations of the Government, SAFA is able to exploit commercial financing techniques to improve the borrowing and general financial management of the State.

Organisation
SAFA is organised into seven main functional units which are discussed below with analysis of their major activities.

Financial Policy
This section is mainly involved in advising on borrowing and investment strategies aimed at minimising the State's net borrowing costs. This involves managing the State's debt portfolio through a variety of modern financial instrument, for example:

- the physical trading of securities;
- interest rate swaps;
- interest rate futures' trading.

The risk exposure created by these dealings is managed through limits on certain activities such as futures trading. The leverage effect of futures trading requires careful management to ensure that large losses are not incurred. Instruments such as interest rate swaps can exploit the State's good credit rating and can be used to reduce borrowing costs for short term funds. For example, SAFA might enter into an agreement with another borrower with a lower credit rating who is unable to obtain long term funds. Assume SAFA only requires additional short term funds but has access to long term funds. An interest rate swap agreement might be entered into whereby SAFA borrows long and the other borrower borrows short and both parties swap the terms of their finance. In this way SAFA would obtain short term finance at a cheaper rate than that readily available in the market and the other borrower accesses long term funding.

The Financial Policy section is also responsible for advising on strategies for managing SAFA's equity investments. As noted in Chapter 4, SAFA has taken up the entire Loan

Council borrowing limit of the State even though it was not all required to fund capital works. In this way SAFA has financed an investment portfolio of $1,373m. The composition of this portfolio is shown in Table 12.37.

Table 12.37
SAFA Investment Portfolio

	1988 %	1987 %
Local/Semi Government Securities	41.2	25.0
Commonwealth Government Securities	–	1.9
Letters of Credit	–	1.6
Corporate Securities and Loans	16.0	14.9
Offshore Investments	3.7	9.5
Bills of Exchange	22.7	40.6
Deposits with Banks	0.9	1.1
Short-term Money Market	–	4.7
Equity Investments	7.7	0.5
Units in South Australia Finance Trust	7.5	–
Other	0.3	0.2
	100.0	100.0

Of particular note is the increase in equity investments and the investment in the South Australian Finance Trust. The increased equity investment reflects SAFA's allocation of shares in South Australian Gas Company Holdings Limited and the takeover acquisition of Enterprise Investments (South Australia) Limited. SAFA has also subscribed $99.7m for units in the South Australian Finance Trust, which is discussed below. SAFA has foreshadowed an increase in its equity investment which may reflect a move towards a more aggressive portfolio management approach. SAFA also reduced its offshore investments significantly from 1987 to 1988.

Overall, the activities of this section involve a more commercial approach to financing the State, which ultimately leads to reduced net borrowings.

SAFA's debt instruments total $5,823.1m and are summarised in Table 12.38.

Table 12.38
SAFA Borrowings

	1988 %	1987 %
Promissory Notes	13.4	12.8
Inscribed Stock	32.1	31.0
Debentures, Unsecured Deposits[1]	8.5	2.5
Overseas Borrowings	17.6	28.0
Floating Rate Notes	0.9	4.2
Deferred Annuities	2.2	3.6
Liability Assumptions	2.0	3.4
Lease Financing	0.6	1.3
Deposits from Treasurer and Semi-Government Authorities	8.9	13.8
Structured Indexed Bonds	2.7	–
Other	1.1	0.2
	100.0	100.0

From 1987 to 1988 SAFA's debt increased by 87.7% mainly in the areas of Inscribed Stock and Debentures. These funds were mainly used in Loans and Capital investments to Semi-Government Authorities, in particular the Electricity Trust of South Australia ($507.9m), the South Australian Finance Trust ($899.1m), the South Australian Finance Trust Limited ($610.3m, net) and the State Bank of South Australia ($250m, capital).

International Finance
The International Finance section of SAFA is involved in analysing overseas investment and borrowing opportunities, managing foreign currency exposure and control of SAFA's offshore affiliates.

SAFA has $1,025.8m in overseas borrowings and $50.5m in offshore investments. SAFA also has a policy of having no foreign currency exposure which is quite expensive to maintain. Studies have shown that an optimum policy is likely to be one where risks are managed and not one where risks are completely covered, hence SAFA's policy appears overly conservative.

Domestic Finance
The Domestic Finance section has the function of raising capital funds in the domestic market and employs four main methods:

— promissory notes issued to institutional investors through an underwritten tender panel;
— medium to long term inscribed stock issued to institutional investors through a dealer group;
— inscribed stock issued to retail investors through a 'tap' issue; and
— private placements of inscribed stock or debentures.

From the Table above, these instruments have raised 64% of SAFA's borrowings. They can be seen as traditional sources of debt finance.

Cash Management and Debt Administration
This section is responsible for managing the public sector's cash resources, co-ordinating

financial arrangements between SAFA, the State and Commonwealth Governments and semi-government authorities, Loan Council guidelines administration and overseeing SAFA's short term $A Euro-note borrowing facility in Hong Kong.

Cash management involves holding an optimum balance of cash and investing any surplus amounts in investments, whose terms depend upon estimates of future cash needs. It is a balance between ensuring solvency and maximising possible gains from investment. Effective cash management requires the development of expertise and by SAFA taking a centralised cash management role the need to duplicate necessary skills throughout the public sector is avoided. Further, larger amounts of funds are available for investment under the centralised approach.

Linked to the cash management function of SAFA and its whole financial planning role is its short-term Euro-note facility. Such a facility enables SAFA to issue short-term Euro-notes in Australian dollars to assist in its liquidity management in Australia. The attraction of an off-shore facility is that it spreads the risk exposure to short-term interest rate fluctuations within Australia.

Structured Finance and Commercial Assessment
This section adopts a finance consultancy role in searching for alternative financing techniques and in the analysis and design of structured financing packages. The unit also advises agencies on aspects of the financial structure and in investment decisions. In this way SAFA is able to offer services that would normally be purchased from outside the public sector.

Examples of structured financings that lead to reduced borrowing costs to the State agencies were:

— $239m through liability assumptions and other structured transactions;
— defeasance arrangements entered into with ETSA (see Chapter 4);
— $9m refinancing of a woolstore;
— a structured financing was arranged to fund the privately-run 'Island Seaway'.

These techniques have raised finance at rates between 0.5 and 4.0% below conventional borrowing costs.

Creative financing techniques are also being planned for:

- refinancing of major State assets to raise $270m;

- funding new capital projects from non-conventional sources;

- proposals to finance or refinance major sporting bodies;

- proposals to undertake a number of off-shore structured finance transactions.

Other Sections
SAFA's other functional areas are Accounting and Administration and Affiliated Companies and Trusts, which is responsible for the day to day management of SAFA's associated bodies.

Fund Raising Activities
SAFA is subject to Loan Council State borrowing limit arrangements, however some of its borrowing is excluded from this limit, for example temporary, short-term borrowing (within year only) and borrowing on behalf of Government-owned financial institutions. SAFA's 1987/88 fund raising authority is summarised in Table 12.39.

Table 12.39

SAFA Fund Raising Authority
1987/88

	Domestic $Am	Overseas $Am	Total $Am
Loan Council	195	66	261
New	628	28	656
Refinancing	823	94	917
Rural Adjustment Scheme	10	–	10
On behalf of Financial Institutions	1,501	126	1,627
Repurchase of SAFA Securities etc.	298	–	298
Total	2,632	220	2,852

SAFA's $261m new finance limit was 86.7% of the State's global limit, emphasising the key role intended for SAFA in State financing.

Under the Rural Adjustment Scheme, SAFA was permitted to borrow $10m for the purposes of making advances to primary producers. These borrowings are exempt from Loan Council Limits.

During 1987/88, SAFA repurchased a number of its own securities and since new securities were not issued additional borrowing authority of $284m was generated.

SAFA raised $2,846m of its $2,852m borrowing authority in 1987/88.

Domestic Fund Raising
In domestic fund raising activities, SAFA raised $1,077m through the institutional fixed-interest market in SAFA's Inscribed Stock Dealer Group. The Dealer Group was established in February 1987 to be responsible for the orderly placement of SAFA stock into the market and for making two-way prices in the Stock. In this way, the Dealer Group's commitment to quoting 'buy' and 'sell' prices has enhanced the liquidity and turnover of SAFA stock.

SAFA has also improved the marketability of its stock by supporting the dealers' activities in repurchasing stock when demand is weak and lending stock on a short term basis when supply is not. SAFA also holds a supply of trading stock in key maturities to facilitate its dealer support.

The relationship between SAFA and the dealers in its inscribed stock can be seen as one reason why SAFA's stock price has risen relative to other government securities. SAFA stock has consistently traded at a 0.1 to 0.2% margin over the prime semi-government bond rates. This margin, however, not only reflects market-ability but also reflects market perceptions of differing risks between SAFA and statutory authorities such as Telecom.

SAFA are very active in the promissory note market, making issues totalling $1,800m in 1987/88 and with an average daily amount on issue of $320m. Being a non-taxpaying body and hence immune from the cash flow pressures of periodic tax payments, SAFA is able to time its promissory note issues to take advantage of market conditions. Accordingly, SAFA has not had to rely on underwriters to take up their notes. SAFA's use of this area of financing is likely to increase in the future.

The tap issue public loan arrangement for SAFA Bonds is proving to be a cost-effective method of raising finance from smaller corporate investors and the general public. This facility offers investors a variety of maturities with interest rates that vary in line with market conditions. The State Government guarantee and improved liquidity for investors through an early 'cash-in' facility add to the attractiveness of this form of investment.

Overseas Fund Raising
SAFA has now made nine successful public Eurobond issues. The two issues made in 1987/88 were:

 — Euro $A50m 13% Notes
 — EuroYen 7b 7% Index Linked Notes

The EuroYen issue was linked to interest and cross currency swaps which converted the Yen notes into a $A72m floating rate borrowing at a rate lower than the Bank Bill rate.

The following example illustrates the mechanics of an interest rate swap. Assume that another borrower only has access to short term Bank Bills at the bank rate plus 0.5% while its long term funds cost 14%. Assume that SAFA can obtain short term finance at the bank bill rate and long term finance at 13%, fixed rate. A swap agreement could be entered into whereby the two parties obtain cheaper finance, with the term desired.

In its borrowing overseas SAFA's has a policy of avoiding foreign exchange risk exposure. It achieves this by either fully hedging its borrowings or using natural hedges, that is, off-shore asset holdings that match its liabilities and hence cancel out any risk exposure.

SAFA operates with a AAA credit rating for transactions in Australian dollars and a AA + rating for issues in foreign currency.

Common Public Sector Interest Rate
The Common Public Sector Interest Rate (CPSIR) is the rate charged on all loans to Government and authorities, except specific undertakings. It is based on a weighted average cost of SAFA's debt plus implicit guaranteed fee margins and an administration margin. The average cost of SAFA's conventional inscribed stock issues of all maturities during 1987/88 was around 13.25% which is reduced to 13% after allowing for interest rate swaps. The cost of structured financings was considerably lower.

Overall SAFA's use of modern corporate financing techniques enable it to provide finance to Government agencies at rates lower than the individual agencies could achieve alone. By centralising finance in this manner, SAFA is able to employ specialists and affords the economies of scale available in making fewer, larger approaches to the capital market. The effect is demonstrated dramatically in the effect of one instrument — interest rate swaps — which reduced the average cost of debt by 0.25%, a significant amount when considered in relation to total borrowings of $5,823.1m.

At issue here is the extent to which SAFA is able to reduce its borrowing costs at the expense of the Federal company tax base. That is, to what degree do the financing techniques involved result in the creation of tax deductions for private sector financiers generated through tax-exempt bodies. While from a State point of view such techniques are defendable, from a Federal point of view the erosion of the tax base will not be greeted with enthusiasm. Federal action in the past has been to close loopholes as they become known, as in the case of leveraged leases and in the tax position on gains and losses on foreign exchange dealings.

Operating Performance
Since inception SAFA has displayed dramatic

growth in its net income. In 1987/88 it returned net income of $279m including extraordinaries of $23m. It has built its return on equity to over 12% and has paid dividends to the State, $205m in 1987/88.

The key position in evaluating the operating performance of SAFA is whether the profits earned are real or whether they are simply internally generated. If SAFA has merely made profits by borrowing and on-lending at a guaranteed margin to government agencies, then the profit may not be real, being only internal generated (internal to the public sector). However, the evidence is in favour of SAFA's profit being real. Its on-lending rate is below the semi-government borrowing rate for the public enterprises concerned – a real gain to those bodies. Further it has created value by centralising funds management, ensuring that cash is not left idle in bank current accounts. These are real gains to the public sector. A final element of SAFA's profit is from its investment portfolio. SAFA is able to borrow as a low-risk borrower and invest in riskier private businesses. Provided such risk is managed then such an approach generates real returns to the public sector.

In its six year history, SAFA has earned $771m profit and paid almost $500m into general State reserve. Its dividends are now a significant and growing contribution to State revenue. Its performance is so good that Federal tax authorities may soon look at its activities for evidence of Federal tax base erosion and question the tax exempt status of SAFA especially given the status of the financiers that it competes against.

Investment Portfolio

As noted, SAFA invests funds surplus to its current requirements in a number of financial securities. Graph 12.1 displays the composition of SAFA's investment portfolio over the past few years.

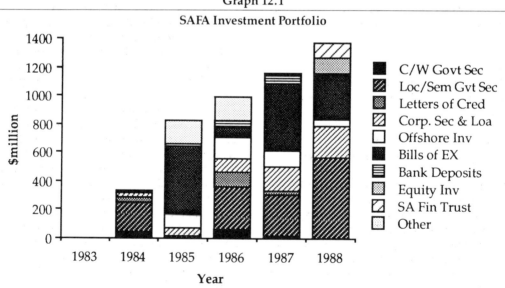

Graph 12.1
SAFA Investment Portfolio

Of particular interest is the emergence in 1987/88 of a significant level of equity investment. In that year this item went from $5.3m to $106.4m. Much of this increase was due to the takeover of Enterprise Investments and its investment in the South Australian Gas Company Holdings Ltd. ($88.6m). The investment in Enterprise Investments has been written down from $5.3m to $2.0m reflecting the fall in value of the company concerned.

The key issue in looking at an investment portfolio like SAFA's, is that of risk. Investment markets are characterised by risk and return. Striving for increased returns may involve taking increased risk. There are significant political costs involved in making losses which will occur if risk exposure is increased. To overcome political costs, the public must be made aware of the benefits to the taxpayer of an efficiently managed investment portfolio like SAFA's.

Strategic Investment

SAFA do not appear to have been involved in a large amount of strategic investment, that is, investment in companies with the aim of protecting those with a head office in Adelaide from takeover. This role has fallen on the State Government Insurance Commission.

Venture and Development Capital

SAFA owns 100% of the venture capital company Enterprise Investments, which is involved in funding a number of ventures with growth potential. In addition, it was involved in arranging finance for the private operators of the Island Seaway, a ferry between Adelaide and Kangaroo Island. In South Australia, the Government also owns the State Bank of South Australia (SBSA) and the State Government Insurance Office (SGIC) which have also been involved in the provision of finance (debt and equity) to local companies.

In any undertaking involving the provision of venture and development capital there will be risk involved. Government bodies involved in this process must ensure that they operate in a commercial manner employing all of the procedures used by conventional financial institutions. The key therefore is risk management and involves controls on lending, monitoring of risk exposure and the ability to act quickly to minimise losses in the event of collapse of one of the debtors. If these measures are implemented correctly then there is no reason why the Government cannot act as a provider of both debt and equity venture and development capital.

12.7 Conclusion

South Australia is characterised by a high level of GDP per capita, but with high unemployment and the lowest level of male average weekly earnings in Australia. The earnings figure can be linked to high unemployment and the absence of a large executive class brought about by the fact that the State has failed to attract a significant proportion of the growth in employment in the finance, property and business services segment of the Australian Labor market. The State's manufacturing base is heavily dependent on factors in the Australian economy, while agricultural success is heavily dependent on climactic conditions and global community prices. Demographically, the South Australian population is an ageing one with a median age of 32 years and the highest proportion of over 65 year olds in Australia.

The picture painted of South Australia dictates an important role for government in the provision of health and welfare services and in the facilitation of economic development. The demand for health and welfare services will increase over time as the effects of an ageing population are felt. The government's role in economic development has also become more crucial as the State undergoes a process of restructuring and the establishment of a broader industrial base, geared to take advantage of overseas export opportunities and exploiting high technology market niches. In all development ventures the government is also vested with responsibility for protection of the environment, an increasing concern into the 1990s and one that will require the commitment of resources to assess environmental impact and in monitoring such impact.

The State Government must look to maintaining its services and expanding them as demand increases over time. The financing of these activities is hampered by a continuing reduction in the tax base of the States and restrictions in their ability to raise new taxes. The South Australian response to these problems has been to introduce measures designed to improve public sector efficiency and effectiveness through introduction of the principles of commercialisation and in streamlining financial management through SAFA. These efficiency on cost minimisation strategies will not provide sufficient finance for the public sector to maintain the level of services demanded. Accordingly, a means of supplementing State

finances is needed. Given the need to redress the imbalance of the tax mix between
direct and indirect taxes, the most effective financing initiative for the State is a
broadly based State levy on consumption
expenditure.

Chapter 13

WESTERN AUSTRALIA

13.1 Introduction

Like all the Australian States Western Australia has endured a declining revenue base in recent years. In attempting to overcome this constraint, the State Labor Government embarked on a high risk strategy of commercialisation, which in the narrow − if not immature − capital market of Western Australia has failed. This sanguinary experience, and the lessons it provides for public policy, is the central theme of this chapter.

At the outset it is essential to distinguish between the Western Australian strategy which was driven by revenue raising motives, and active industry development policies which are motivated less by the requirement for an immediate commercial return and more by a long term commitment to State economic growth. Before embarking on this analysis Section 13.2 provides some necessary statistical background.

13.2 Demography and Economy
13.2.1 Demography

Despite the falling birth rate Western Australia registered a 2.7% increase in total population in 1987, which compares favourably with an average increase of 2.3% over the past 5 years. More strikingly, the 1987 figure is the highest population growth rate of any State, and is significantly higher than the national growth rate of 1.6%. Indeed the rate of population increase in Western Australia has exceeded the national rate in each of the last 10 years (see Table 13.1). It is the high rate of net overseas and interstate in-migration which is responsible for this relatively fast population growth rate (Treasury of Western Australia, 1988).

Table 13.1

Population Growth: Western Australia and Australia

	WA %*	Australia %*
1978	1.95	1.177
1979	1.528	1.09
1980	1.801	1.237
1981	2.442	1.551
1982	2.988	1.749
1983	2.252	1.378
1984	1.621	1.208
1985	1.964	1.341
1986	2.852	1.457
1987	2.539	1.439

Note: * Change on Previous Period.
Source: ABS Cat. No. 3201.0.

There are a number of interesting features accompanying these demographic trends. As Table 13.2 demonstrates, Western Australia's population is relatively younger than the Australian population and has become increasingly so between 1978 and 1987. In addition, the size of the resident population who are not in the labour force has increased at a rate exceeding the national rate of increase in each of the years 1980 to 1987.

Table 13.2

Age Composition: Western Australian & Australia

Age	30th June 1978		30th June 1987	
	WA %	Aust %	WA %	Aust %
0-14	27	24	26	23
15-24	18	17	18	17
25-54	39	42	38	41
55+	16	17	18	20

Source: ABS Cat. No. 3201.0.

Neither of these features is surprising given the principal sources of Western Australia's population growth. However, they are of interest in view of Western Australia's State ranking in terms of household income per capita. Despite relatively rapid economic growth, Western Australia's ranking has fallen from fifth highest amongst the States in 1981/82 (Petridis, 1984), to sixth highest in 1986/87. The relatively young population and the rapid rise in the non-labour force participating resident population (See Graph 13.1) are in part responsible for this decline.

Graph 13.1

Resident Population not in the Labour Force

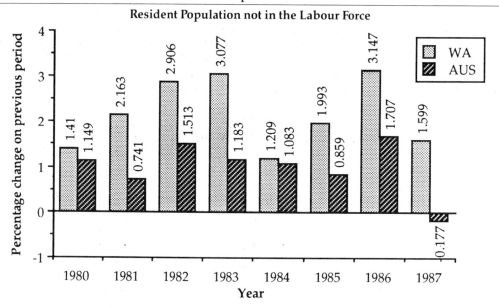

Source: ABS Cat. Nos 6101.0, 6202.0.

The demographic trends revealed in this analysis point to specific demands on State services, with infrastructure developments to support housing needs and social services like childcare being in particular demand.

13.2.2 Economy

The past decade has seen strong growth in State Gross Domestic Product (SGDP) both in absolute terms and relative to the performance of the Australian economy. By 1985/86 real

SGDP was 32.6% above its 1977/78 value as compared to a 24.5% increase for the nation's real GDP over the same period. In this section we examine the structural trends in the Western Australian economy and their relationship to the strong growth in SGDP. Our investigation suggests that the strength of the external sector is an important factor explaining the expansion of the State's economy. However, the Western Australian export base is narrow and this

means that economic development is particularly vulnerable to shifting world trade patterns.

Western Australia SGDP growth has averaged 3.6% in real terms over the period 1977/78 to 1985/86. This expansion has enabled Western Australia to lift its share of national GDP from 9.0% in 1977/78 to 9.5% in 1985/86, and SGDP per capita is becoming significantly higher than that of Australia as a whole (see Graph 13.2).

Graph 13.2

GDP Per Head Mean Population

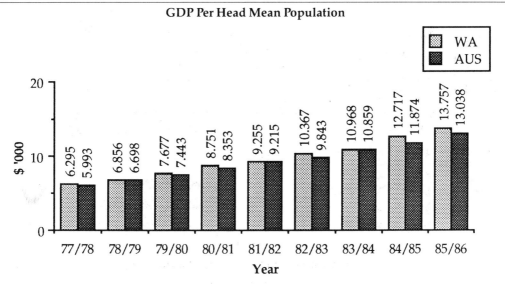

Source: ABS Cat. No. 5220.

Nevertheless, the real SGDP growth rate exceeded the national growth rate in only 4 years during the period 1978/79 – 1985/86 (see Graph 13.3). These divergent features can be reconciled by noting that Western Australia's growth rate is much more volatile than that of Australia as a whole. This volatility can be attributed to the importance of primary product industries in the Western Australian economy. As this book has noted on many occasions, such industries are very exposed to fluctuations in world commodity prices.

Reflecting the buoyant economic conditions in the State, investment expenditure has exhibited a relatively strong performance in recent years. Following the recession years

1981-1983 real private new capital expenditure remained flat in Australia. In contrast there has been a significant recovery in Western Australia (see Graph 13.4).

In addition private new capital expenditure has maintained a healthier profile in relation to Western Australian SGDP, than in Australia as a whole (see Table 13.3).

A striking feature of the Western Australian industrial structure is the prominence of the primary product industries. In 1985/86 this sector accounted for 16.9% of SGDP (see Table 9.4), and between 1977/78 and 1985/86 its average contribution amounted to 17.8%. This is the highest proportion of any Australian State. Since 1986 much of the impetus behind growth in primary products' output has come from wool, meat and gold production, as prices of these commodities improved substantially from the latter half of 1986 (IMF, 1988).

Graph 13.3

Growth in Real GDP

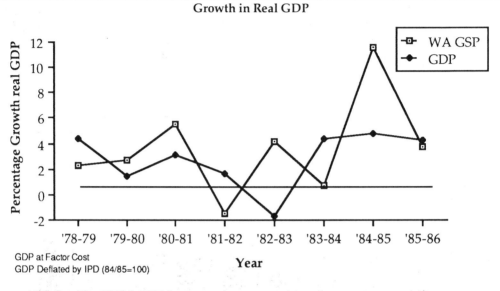

GDP at Factor Cost
GDP Deflated by IPD (84/85=100)

Source: ABS Cat. Nos 5220.0, 5206.0.

Graph 13.4

Private Investment in New Capital Equipment
$ Mil (thousands)

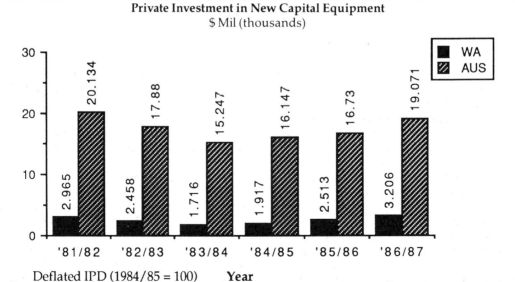

Deflated IPD (1984/85 = 100)   **Year**

Source: ABS Cat. No. 5646.0.

Table 13.3

Private New Capital Expenditure[a]

	Western Australia % of GSP	Australia % of GDP
81/82	19.4	11.6
82/83	15.5	10.6
83/84	10.7	8.6
84/85	10.7	8.7

Note: [a] Deflated by IPD (1984/85 = 100).
Source: ABS Cat. No. 5646.0.

Table 13.4

Western Australia Gross State Product: Proportion by Industry

Manufacturing	12.7
Mining	10.7
Agriculture, Forestry, Fishing, Hunting	6.2
Ownership of Dwellings	6.2
Public Admin, Defence & Com Services	18.3
Finance, Property & Business Services	8.4
Transport, Storage & Communications	9.8
Wholesale & Retail Trade	12.7
Construction	7.5
Other	7.4

Source: ABS Cat. No. 5220.0.

While iron ore remains the most important commodity in terms of value of output, gold production is not far behind. With traditional export markets such as Japan not buoyant, there are attempts to diversify into new markets. Developments with the Republic of China, Romania, Czechoslovakia and Hungary represent potentially fruitful export initiatives (Treasury of Western Australia, 1988), and such diversification may help to stabilise production patterns. Table 13.5 and 13.6 illustrate the extreme volatility of the real value of rural and mineral production in the period 1978/79 to 1987/88.

Table 13.5

Mineral Production — Western Australia

Year	% change
78/79	-0.12
79/80	18.82
80/81	2.07
81/82	-3.61
82/83	9.84
83/84	0.76
84/85	15.51
85/86	5.84
86/87	7.38
87/88	4.81

Deflated by Gross Non-Farm Product IPD (1979-80 = 100).
Source: Department of Mines, (WA).

Table 13.6

Rural Production — Western Australia

Year	% change
78/79	3.02
79/80	-12.59
80/81	-2.29
81/82	27.02
82/83	18.59
83/84	-20.23
84/85	34.73
85/86	-15.37
86/87	11.32
87/88	-7.02

Deflated by Gross Farm IPD (1984/85 = 100).
Source: ABS.

While primary product industries are relatively important in Western Australia, it is exceeded in size by public administration, defence and community services (which includes general government ie. State budget). This sector averaged an 18.5% contribution between 1978/79 and 1985/86. However, since 1982/83 the relative contribution of public administration, defence and community services has declined sharply from 19.8% to 18.3% in 1985/86. As Section 13.3 shows, there were reductions in real State Government expenditure on community and social services between 1984 and 1986, which helps explain this relative decline. The same pattern is exhibited by manufacturing which has fallen from 15.2% of SGDP in the recession years of 1981/82, to 12.7% by 1985/86. Not surprisingly, Western Australian manufacturing industry contrasts with Australia as a whole, with a significantly higher incidence of primary product based manufacturing industries. This is being encouraged by the Western Australian State Government which has entered into joint ventures to construct a Gallium extraction plan at Pinjarra and an integrated petrochemical plant at Kwinana (Treasury of Western Australia, 1988). State Government industrial policy is discussed in more detail below in Section 13.5.

13.2.3 The External Sector

Exports and interstate trade (the export base) are regarded by many analysts as a significant determinant of regional growth (Armstrong & Taylor, 1978; Thirwell, 1980). The relatively strong performance of the Western Australian State economy in the past decade and its healthy export base is consistent with this view.

Graph 13.5 compares exports per capita in 1986/87 between the 6 States and two territories. Western Australia is by far and away the most export intensive. Overseas exports are $4,506 per capita with Queensland the next highest at $2,918 per capita. On the other hand, imports per capita at $1,720 are exceeded in both New South Wales and Victoria.

The overseas orientation of the Western Australian economy is further emphasised by Graph 13.6 which compares Western Australian overseas exports as a percentage of SGDP, with Australian overseas exports as a percentage of the nation's GDP. The Western Australian figure has hovered at and above the 30% level as compared to a 15% and below for Australia over the period 1981/82 to 1985/86. These comparisons underline the observation that trends in world trade are of even greater importance to the health of the Western Australian economy than that of the nation's.

In contrast to overseas trade Western Australia has traditionally experienced a deficit on interstate trade. Indeed, in 1981/82 this deficit outweighed the surplus on overseas trade (Petridis, 1984). However, as Graph 13.7 shows, an overall surplus on overseas and interstate trade was registered in each of the three years 1984/85, 1985/86 and 1986/87.

Graph 13.5

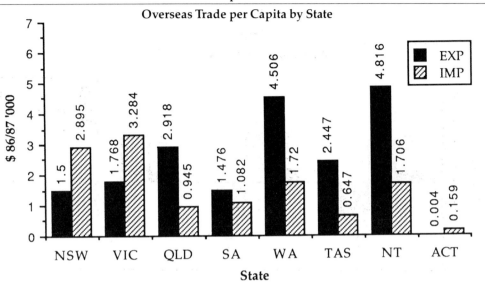

Overseas Trade per Capita by State

Source: ABS Cat. Nos 5424.0, 5426.0, 1304.0, 8502.3,4,5,6 & unpublished ABS data for Victoria, NSW, & NT.

Graph 13.6

Exports as a Percentage of GDP

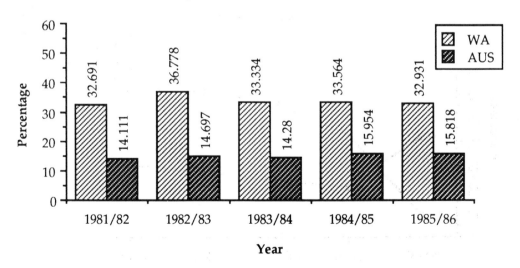

Source: ABS Cat. Nos 1304.0, 1305.5, 8502.5.

Trends in the Western Australian external account position are depicted in Graph 13.8. Here the interstate trade deficit and overseas trade surplus are expressed as a percentage of SGDP for the period 1981/82 to 1985/86. These graphs indicate early signs that the previously healthy external account position could be reversed in the future. While the overseas trade surplus improved in these years, it began to tail off towards the end of this period, and since 1982/83 the interstate trade deficit has deteriorated.

Graph 13.7

Trade Balances Western Australia

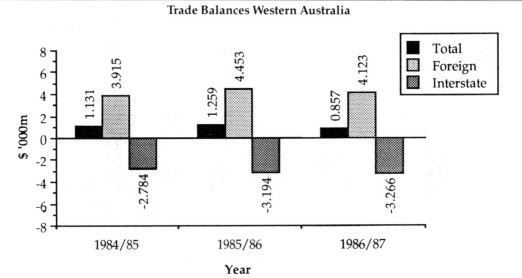

Source: ABS Cat. No. 1305.5.

Graph 13.8

Interstate and Foreign Trade

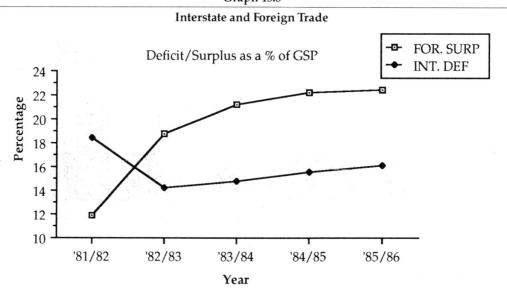

Source: ABS Cat. Nos 1305.5, 5220.0.

While the flattening of the overseas trade surplus curve reflects weakness in world commodity markets at that time, it is also consistent with structural adjustment in the

Western Australian industrial base. The strongly export oriented sectors of the Western Australian economy – manufacturing and primary product industries – accounted for a declining share of SGDP in the ten year period 1977/78 – 1985/86. Equally importantly, the strongest growth sector in this period proved to be the financial, property and business services sector. A substantial proportion of the goods and services supplied by this sector are not internationally traded. Unless continued expansion of this sector reduces interstate imports, a weaker external account position can be expected. Initiatives designed to diversify the manufacturing and primary products export base are desirable in view of these trends, and are examined below.

13.2.4 The Labour Market

During the 1982/83 recession Western Australia, in common with the rest of the nation, experienced a sharp rise in the unemployment rate. This increase was particularly severe with respect to males. The unemployment rate amongst males rose from 5.4% in April 1982 to 9.5% in April 1983 as compared to an increase from 9.6% to 10% amongst females (Confederation of Western Australian Industry, 1983). The pattern reflects particularly poor employment opportunities in mining, transport and storage and building and construction where employment is male dominated.

Since the recession of 1982/83 there has been a steady rise in employment with an average increase of 3.3% in Western Australia between 1983/84 and 1987/88, as compared to a national figure of 2.6% (Treasury of Western Australia, 1988). Part-time employment has provided much of the impetus behind this employment expansion with a rise of 48.3% in male part-time employment in the period February 1983 – July 1988, female part-time employment increasing by 37.0% in the same period (ABS Cat. No. 6203.0).

Despite this strong growth in employment, the Western Australian unemployment rate has fallen only 2.0 percentage points between 1983/84 and 1987/88 (from 9.7% to 7.7%). During this period the Western Australian unemployment rate has averaged 8.3% as compared to a national figure of 8.4% (Treasury of

Western Australia, 1988). Whilst Western Australia's relatively strong economic position is reflected in most economic magnitudes, this is not the case with the unemployment rate. This in part reflects a more rapid rate of population increase in Western Australia, a younger labour force and a higher rate of labour force participation. Graph 13.9 graphs the Western Australian and Australian labour force participation rate between second quarter 1978 and second quarter 1988. Whilst the participation rate has increased slightly in Western Australia and Australia, the rate has remained 2 percentage points or more higher in Western Australia. The increase in the participation rate has been most prominent amongst females (see Graph 13.10).

Whilst the relatively strong economic performance of the Western Australian economy is not fully reflected in the unemployment rate, it is evident when examining the trend in real average weekly earnings. In the fourth quarter of 1981 real average weekly earnings in Western Australia averaged 93% of the Australian figure. However, since the 3rd Quarter of 1986 real average weekly earnings in Western Australia have exceeded those in Australia as a whole (see Table 13.7). The change in earnings differentials will mirror changes in the earnings attracted by occupational categories, as well as employment shifts between occupational categories that are caused by structural adjustment in the Western Australian industrial base. We now turn to these structural adjustments.

In order to examine longer run structural adjustments in the Western Australian economy, Tables 13.8 and 13.9 calculate the difference between Western Australian employment growth and the employment growth which would have transpired had it been at a pace equal to the national rate. This exercise is accomplished both at the aggregate level and across sectors of the Western Australian economy. The results are indicative of emerging long run trends in the structure of the State's economy, as well as strengths and weaknesses of the various sectors relative to their national counterparts.

In the ten year period 1978-1988 total Western Australian employment rose from 519,200 to

689,200, an increase of 170,000. If Western Australian employment had grown at the national rate, the increase would have been only 115,000. This implies a positive differential employment growth of 55,000 and underlines the comments above concerning the strength of employment growth in Western Australia. However, Table 13.8 reveals that the rate of differential job growth is slowing. Whereas the period 1978-1983 saw an average of 6,917 differential employment growth per annum, the more recent five year period 1983-1988 exhibited an average differential job growth rate of 2,873 per annum. This is less than half the figure in the earlier period, and is primarily the result of stagnation in community services employment and job losses in transport and storage (see Wood & Bushe-Jones, 1988).

Graph 13.9

Labour Force Participation Rate

Quarter

Source: ABS Cat. No. 6203.0 (Original Series).

Table 13.9 lists differential employment growth across 12 sector categories and between the industry and service sectors. A number of important points emerge from an examination of Table 13.9. These are:

(i) The Finance, Property and Business Services sector is the most significant source of differential employment growth.

(ii) The Western Australian economy has traditionally been heavily dependent upon the primary product industries. Reliance upon those industries as a source of employment growth has diminished.

(iii) The manufacturing, construction and public utility industries in Western Australia have failed to match national employment growth rates.

(iv) The service sector has become the dominant source of differential employment growth.

There is evidence here that the Western Australian economy is maturing as it catches up with the more diversified industrial structures of the eastern States. The structural adjustments are also consistent with a slowdown in the growth of the Western Australian overseas trade surplus (see above), as the service sector has a more limited exposure to export trade. Whilst this may suggest a flatter growth profile in the future for Western Australia, the more diversified industrial structure should result in a less volatile pattern of growth.

Graph 13.10

Female Labour Force Participation Rate

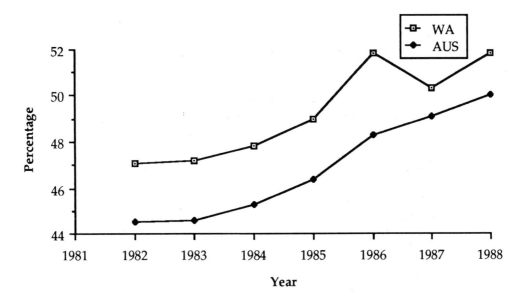

Source: ABS Cat. No. 6203.0 seasonally adjusted (August).

Table 13.7

Average Weekly Earnings
All Employees
$ 1980/81

Quarter	Western Australia	Australia
'4/81	217.5	232.6
'2/82	235.2	243.0
'4/82	231.7	238.0
'2/83	227.3	233.3
'4/83	227.4	235.0
'2/84	246.1	252.0
'4/84	239.5	246.8
'2/85	235.2	243.9
'4/85	237.8	241.7
'2/86	238.3	239.5
'4/86	239.7	235.7
'2/87	237.3	231.9
'4/87	241.6	232.8
'1/88	239.2	232.3

Source: ABS Cat. No. 6203.

Table 13.8

Differential Employment Growth
WA 1978-1988

1978-1988	1978-1983	1983-1988
55.1	34.6	14.3

All Figures in 000s.
Source: ABS Labour Statistics: Australia Cat. 6106.0.

Table 13.9

Differential Employment Growth By Industry Categories
WA 1978-1988

Industry	Employment Growth
1. Agriculture, etc.	11.163
2. Mining	1.102
3. Manufacturing	-3.337
4. Electricity, Gas & Water	-1.794
5. Construction	-3.776
Total Industry	*3.358*
6. Wholesale & Retail Trade	7.825
7. Transport & Storage	-5.843
8. Communication	-4.181
9. Finance, Property & Business	25.314
10. Public Admin & Defence	3.793
11. Community Services	10.140
12. Recreation & Other Services	14.632
Total Services	*51.680*

All figures in 000s.
Source: ABS Labour Statistics: Australia Cat. 6106.0.

13.3 The Role of the Public Sector in the Western Australian Economy
13.3.1 Introduction

In recent years it appears that the relative size of the State public sector has fallen. Table 13.10 depicts State Government employment as a percentage of total employment, and it is evident that there has been a significant decline from around 26% in 1984 to around 23% in 1988.

Table 13.10

State Government Employees
Percentage of Total WA Employed Persons

1983	25.5
1984	26.3
1985	24.7
1986	24.0
1987	23.0
1988	22.8

Source: ABS Cat. No. 1305.5.

Perhaps the best indication of fiscal restraint in the Western Australian public sector is the annual average growth rate of total expenditure since 1979-80 of 2.9% compared with the growth of gross State product of over 5% in the same period. This implies that the State Government's share of resources has declined, while the government has serviced an increasingly larger economy. If the last five years of Labor Government in Western Australia are considered, the point can be made with very great force – government expenditure grew at under 3% p.a. while gross State product grew in excess of 7% p.a.

Within this environment of slow or stagnant growth in the public sector the relative shares of expenditure between a selection of functional activities is depicted in Table 13.11.

Table 13.11

Total CRF Expenditure
All Major CRF Expenditure Groups
Relative Share of Total

	79/80	80/81	81/82	82/83	83/84	84/85	85/86	86/87	87/88
Education	28.1	28.0	28.9	29.2	27.5	28.4	28.1	27.9	26.8
Rec. & Culture	1.7	1.5	1.4	1.4	1.4	1.6	1.7	1.9	1.9
Health	19.8	20.1	18.9	17.0	16.9	17.7	18.0	19.5	19.9
Welfare	3.4	3.5	2.5	4.1	5.0	5.3	5.1	5.6	5.6
Public Order	6.0	6.1	6.4	7.3	6.7	7.0	7.4	7.4.	7.5
Housing	1.4	1.3	1.2	5.2	5.0	5.1	3.6	3.3	3.2
Trans. & Comm.	3.6	4.6	4.9	15.0	14.9	14.5	13.1	11.1	10.2

Source: Western Australian Budget Paper 79/80 – 88/89.

13.3.2 Economic Services

In a rapidly growing economy it is surprising to find that economic services for agriculture, forestry and fishing, for mining and mineral resources, and transport and communication have barely grown at all in the last decade. As a result economic services now account for about 19% of total expenditure, down from 25% a decade ago.

While these traditional measures of public economic services have fallen in relative terms, nevertheless the actual level of public economy activity has if anything increased. State Governments of the 1960s and 1970s intervened in the economy through the direct provision of infrastructure, fiscal incentives to encourage private investment and the granting of State guarantees and concessions specific to individual projects. The Burke Labor Government elected in 1983 envisaged the need to diversify and modernise the State's economy, and included in its platform the promise to set up a Western Australian Development Bank and a South East Asian Marketing Corporation as vehicles to pursue these policy objectives.

The policy platform for the 1986 election saw the need for:

'direct government involvement in commercial activities to stimulate economic growth and *to return financial benefits to the whole community through the capacity to reduce taxation and extend public services*' (Australian Labor Party, [Western Australian Branch], 1986, p. 70, emphasis added).

It is clear from the subsequent fate of this strategy that the goals of economic development and revenue-raising are not easily reconciled within public development agencies. Again, it is important to distinguish between public trading enterprises, which are capable of operating along commercial lines, and development agencies which are more properly concerned with economic growth in the long term.

While the creation of the Western Australian Development Corporation (WADC) was the direct outcome of the 1983 platform, the acquisition and creation of a group of limited liability companies could not have been anticipated from the 1983 policy platform. We now describe the background to the creation of these enterprises.

(i) Western Australian Development Corporation

The WADC was a statutory body corporate created by the WADC Act 1983. Its principal function, as defined by Section 9 of the Act, was:

'to promote the development of economic activity in Western Australia . . . and to operate subject to this Act as a commercial business undertaking and to generate profits (and thereby dividends) for the benefit of the shareholders of the Corporation.'

The authorised capital of the corporation was $30m and the Treasurer acquired $15m of issued capital in 3 tranches; $5m was paid from the State Development Fund and $10m from the General Loan Fund. The Corporation was not authorised to borrow without the prior approval of Parliament, funds in excess of 8 times the sum of issued capital and reserves. In addition, it was unable to lend sums to one business undertaking exceeding $50m and 50% of the sum of issued capital and reserves. The WADC is currently in the process of being dismantled by the State Labor Government (for a more detailed discussion refer to Section 13.5.2).

(ii) Western Australian Government Holdings (WAGH)

WAGH evolved out of the purchase by the State Government of Northern Mining Corporation No Liability (NMC, registered in Victoria) under the NMC (Acquisition) Act (1983). The act enabled purchase of 100% of the shares in the no liability company from the Bond Corporation along with its main asset, a 5% share in the Argyle Diamond Mine. The Argyle Diamond Mine interest was subsequently sold to WADC and in 1985 NMC changed its name and status to WAGH Ltd., which was a public company limited by shares under the Company (Western Australia) Code.

The authorised capital of the company was

$50m; issued and paid up capital comprise $7,080,000 ordinary shares held by the Treasurer. The NMC Act (1983) contained no provisions limiting the lending and borrowing powers of WAGH. The principal investments of WAGH were:

– a 43.75% stake in Petrochemical Industries Company Ltd. acquired for $175m. The purchase was funded by the issue of debentures purchased by the State Government Insurance Commission.

– 100% ownership of Aboriginal Enterprise Company Ltd. which funds loans to Aboriginal business ventures.

– 100% ownership of the shares in Business Services (Belgium) NV, which provides commercial services to the Western Australian Diamond Trust, which is managed by WADC and holds the 5% share in the Argyle Diamond Mine previously held by NMC.

In 1985/86 the Exim Corporation was established as a wholly owned subsidiary of WAGH.

(iii) The Western Australian Exim Corporation

The Exim Corporation was created as a statutory corporation by the Western Australian Exim Corporation Act of 1986. The Corporation was vested with the responsibilities of developing the activities formerly carried out by the Western Australian Overseas Project Authority. However, the Corporation was also given the wider responsibilities of achieving a return on the resources invested in the various services of government, with WADC concentrating on managing the assets of the State Government. Three areas prominent in the activities of Exim were Educational Marketing, Business Migration and Investment and Pastoral Re-construction. A plethora of subsidiary companies were created or absorbed by Exim and these are listed in Figure 13.1. Exim had an authorised capital of $30m and issued and paid up capital of $7m were held by the Treasurer. The Corporation was not subject to limitations upon its borrowing and lending by any provision of the 1986 Act.

Figure 13.1

Exim Companies

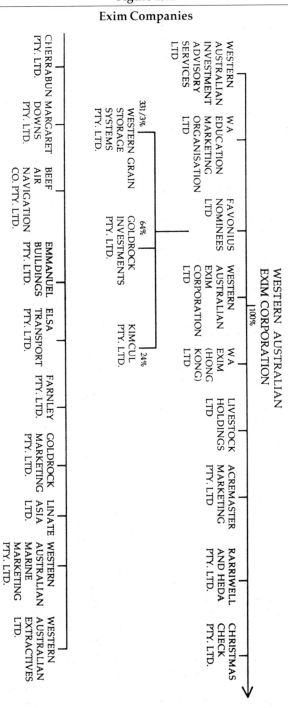

Source: Burt Commission (1989)

(iv) The Gold Banking Corporation (GBC) and its Subsidiaries

GBC is a statutory body corporate created by the GBC Act 1987. However, the corporate structure established by the act effectively consists of 3 corporations:

- a banking corporation;
- a precious metals processing and manufacturing corporation, namely Western Australian Mint;
- a marketing arm, GoldCorp Australia.

The principal function of the corporations is that of generating export income by promoting and developing industries and markets for gold. To this end the authorised capital of GBC is $100m of which the Treasurer holds $25m fully paid. Each of the corporations has unlimited power to borrow and invest money. Whilst no authority from the Commonwealth is required for a State Bank, the Board of GBC was seeking formal recognition from the RBA as this is considered necessary for international competitiveness. Since the February 1989 State election the GBC's future is also now in doubt. It has been suggested that GBC will become a wholly owned subsidiary of the R&I bank, though this remains to be officially confirmed (The West Australian, 14-3-89).

An Appraisal

These corporations have been labelled hybrid enterprises (Harman, 1986) as they represent an unusual degree of interpenetration of government and business in Western Australia. Three motives are primarily responsible for their creation:

- a widely perceived need to augment existing sources of State Government funding;
- the aim of modernising and diversifying the industrial base of the Western Australian economy;
- a desire to increasingly expose the management of government activities to the influence of commercial business practices.

To some extent these three goals are subject to conflict and tension. For example, the task of economic development may require the recapi-

talisation of mature industries where government should make a non-commercial investment for the sake of economic externalities (the public assistance rendered to the steel industry is a case in point at the Federal level). Accordingly a coherent model of public sector development must separate revenue raising from the application of these funds to meet social and economic goals. The proposed SGSL is an instrument capable of achieving this coherence.

The activities and performance of the four corporations are given a detailed examination in Section 13.5.2. Here we concentrate on a general treatment of the issues, which are extensively illustrated in that case study.

(i) Accountability and the Concentration of Power

Accountability procedures in Western Australia (and elsewhere in Australia) conform to the Westminster model, where any agency that has the capacity to create liabilities which may be a charge on Consolidated Revenue should be subject to the control of a Minister of the State, and accountable through that Minister to Parliament for all its activities. The accountability and auditing procedures for Western Australian State corporations are set out in the Financial Administration and Auditing Act 1985. A common feature of the hybrid enterprises is that they are not subject to this act. Rather, they are incorporated under the company (Western Australian) Code. Though WADC must gain parliamentary approval for borrowing and lending which exceed statutory limits, the other three corporations are not accountable to Parliament in any way whatsoever and this includes the creation and acquisition of subsidiary companies. Indeed the introduction of confidentiality provisions within contracts entered into by these corporations may even deny ministerial scrutiny (The Burt Commission [1989] documents such a case, pp. 114-115).

These institutional arrangements place conflicting responsibilities and considerable influence on the shoulders of a small number of politicians and business persons. The Western Australian State executive must balance the need to ensure that the enterprises operate in the public interest, with the flexibility required to pursue business objectives. This conflict of interest is unavoidable as both regulatory and commercial responsibilities are vested in the executive, and since there is a loss of parliamentary control, the boards of these enterprises become relatively more influential than the boards of other government agencies.

The board of the hybrid enterprises are drawn almost exclusively from the private sector. It is reasonable to assume that they are fully aware of their obligations under the companies code, and familiar with the management style of profit seeking private companies. Whilst the hybrid enterprises have as their overriding objective the pursuit of profit, there are obligations *implicit* in the quasi-public nature of the enterprises which can be complex and obscure. The private sector management style can be ill-suited to these obligations (Hogan, 1988a). For example, normal commercial practices such as reliance on a trusted network of suppliers and professional advisers, can become associated with political patronage (Harman, 1986).

(ii) Privileges and Immunities
By being incorporated under the companies code, the hybrid enterprises' flexibility in commercial decision making is not impaired by the accountability and auditing procedures that pertain to public enterprises subject to the Financial and Auditing Act 1985. The Corporations are placed in a preferential position vis a vis their private sector counterparts by a number of privileges and immunities. These are (Harman, 1986):

— the intangible benefits arising from closeness to executive government, whose source is inside knowledge about government policy developments and contracts;
— provisions enabling unqualified and closed access to State Government guarantees;
— as an agent of the Crown WADC has intergovernmental immunities, eg. Trade Practices Act.

It should be emphasised that public trading enterprises do not require preferential models of accountability or financing. The problems of

WA Inc. was that its model of public sector development was not sufficiently accountable in its financial or economic undertakings. The analysis contained in this book demonstrates that PTEs should be accorded a commercial but neutral flexibility which places them on the same competitive footing as their private sector rivals. In situations of natural monopoly, it should be recognised that publicly owned and accountable enterprises are the most desirable option.

(iii) Social Considerations
The rationale for WA Inc. stemmed from a need to diversify State revenues. In pursuing this fiscal imperative, the strategy lost sight of the genuine social functions of the sector. This omission stands in contrast to the public sector model proposed in this book where the various strands of public sector activity receive their own recognition. For example, in such a model the social functions of government are formulated into an intergrated social justice strategy which accords with and complements economic development policy.

13.3.3 Social Services
Turning to some of the major items of the State social wage, Graph 13.11 shows the expenditure growth rates of the health and education portfolios.

Clearly, education expenditure grew steadily until 1986 when it fell by more than 5%, and was followed by a further fall in 1987-88. Its average growth rate was 2.1% p.a. compared to a growth rate of total expenditure of 2.9% p.a. As a result the share of education in total expenditure has tended to decline, from 28.1% in 1979-80 to 26.8% in 1987-88. Expenditure on health has also grown at a lower rate (2.4%) than total expenditure and health's share of total expenditure has also tended to decline. On average, health and education are now accounting for about 45% of total expenditure, about 3% less than a decade ago.

Three areas appear to have absorbed the resources released by the slower growth of health and education expenditures (see Table 13.11 and Graph 13.11). These are welfare (defined as expenditure on family and child welfare, aged and handicapped welfare), public order and safety (covering police services, prisons and corrective services, law courts and legal services, and fire protection services) and housing and community services (including housing, community development, water and sewerage services, and protection of the environment).

Of these categories, welfare has had the most consistent growth, with its share of total expenditure rising from around 5.7% in 1979 to 8.7% in 1987-88.

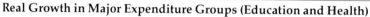

Graph 13.11

Real Growth in Major Expenditure Groups (Education and Health)

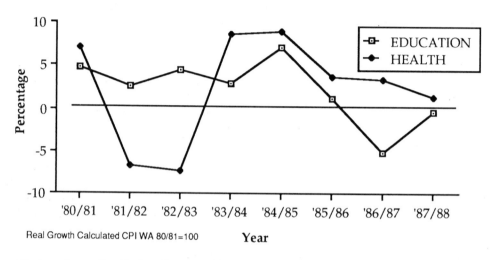

Real Growth Calculated CPI WA 80/81=100   **Year**

Source: Western Australian Budget Papers 79/80 — 88/89.

Graph 13.12

Growth in Major Expenditure Groups (Welfare and Housing)

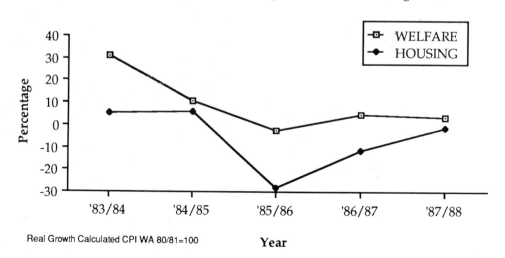

Real Growth Calculated CPI WA 80/81=100   **Year**

Source: Western Australian Budget Papers 79/80 — 88/89.

Finally, housing and community amenities has fluctuated very widely, as public housing expenditure has been adjusted according to both the economic and political cycles. Its share of total expenditure now stands at around 5% compared to under 3% a decade ago

13.3.3 Administrative Services

In the area of administrative services, public order and safety has also grown consistently and now accounts for over 11% of total expenditure.

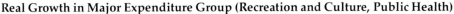

Graph 13.13

Real Growth in Major Expenditure Group (Recreation and Culture, Public Health)

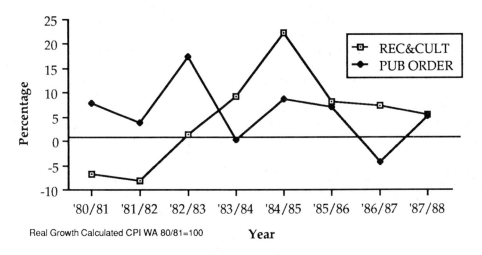

Real Growth Calculated CPI WA 80/81=100   **Year**

Source: Western Australian Budget Papers 79/80 — 88/89.

13.4 Financing and Spending Western Australian State Public Services
13.4.1 Introduction

Sustained efforts to transform the Western Australian economy through industrialization met with only limited success up to the early 1960s. The relaxation of the iron ore export ban by the Federal Government saw the take-off of the mining industries and the acceleration of economic growth rates past the Australian rates. By 1968 the time was ripe for Western Australia to relinquish its 'claimant State' status under the Commonwealth Grants Commission. In the early seventies the relatively generous allocation of funds to the States by both conservative and Labor Governments, and the transfer of an apparent growth tax in payroll tax to the State meant that Western Australia was relatively less revenue constrained. But the onset of deep recession after 1974, the

pressure for greater fiscal restraint at all levels of government, and the election of the Fraser Government completely changed the picture.

The 'new federalism' of the Fraser Government only paid lip service to its avowed objective of decentralization, and Western Australia like the other States was reluctant to use the newly legislated income tax powers. As a result, the progressive reductions in Western Australia's share of Federal tax collections began to place increasing stress on the State's finances. The search for a viable growth tax began in earnest, especially as the employment inhibiting effects of the payroll tax were increasingly recognised. Prolonged recession also cut deeply into other sources of State revenue, and it was not until the recovery after 1983 that the fiscal stress eased at all. This section reviews the pattern of revenue growth over the last decade, followed by an examination of the manner in which expenditures have been adjusted to the revenue constraint, and concludes with an analysis of the revenue and expenditure priorities in the 1988-89 budget.

13.4.2 State Revenue
(i) Revenue Growth and Revenue Constraint
In common with most other States, the somewhat misleading approach also adopted in Western Australia is to refer to revenue and outlays on the Consolidated Revenue Fund (CRF) as if they referred to all the activities of the State Government. In fact in the last decade they have accounted for between 61% and 73% of all revenues available to the government in any year. It has then been a simple matter for governments of both political persuasions to transfer funds from other sources into the CRF in order to create the impression of sound economic management by balancing or running a tiny surplus on the 'budget' (as the CRF is euphemistically described). In fact outlays have exceeded revenues by a low of $290m (11.9% of outlays in current prices) and

a high of $846m (20.8% in current prices) in different years in the last decade. These figures are from the Australian Bureau of Statistics publication Cat. No. 5501.0 and provide a broad indication of the deficits generated by the Western Australian Government. However, because of time lags and because the classification of data are not appropriate for the purposes of this chapter, the data which follow have been derived from the Budget papers and accompanying Statements of the Western Australian Government.

(ii) CRF Revenue and Total Revenue
Revenue taken to the Consolidated Revenue Fund has usually been applied to recurrent expenditure only and rarely to capital works programs. As Table 13.12 shows in 1979 total revenue on the CRF was just over $1.6b (in current prices) and by 1988 it was estimated to rise to $4.04b. The growth rate of State sources of revenue on the CRF has been in excess of 5% p.a. over the last decade, including 1986-87 when revenues actually declined in real terms by 8.04% (see Graph 13.20).

Table 13.12

Total Revenue of the CRF
from State & Commonwealth Sources

	State $m	Real % Change	C'wealth. $m	Real % Change	Total $m	Real % Change
79/80	787.74	–	853.44	–	1641.18	–
80/81	906.01	5.73	954.55	2.82	1860.56	4.21
81/82	1023.20	1.58	1038.69	-2.12	2061.89	-0.32
82/83	1183.12	4.94	1141.75	-0.24	2324.87	2.33
83/84	1393.68	10.17	1266.19	3.72	2659.87	7.01
84/85	1502.09	3.70	1340.98	1.90	2843.07	2.84
85/86	1673.71	3.13	1425.70	-1.60	3099.41	0.90
86/87	1692.69	-8.04	1591.53	1.50	3284.22	-3.65
87/88	2052.83	13.19	1757.56	3.07	3810.39	8.29
88/89	2465.12	13.30	1558.87	*	4044.00	6.11

Note: * Commonwealth Health Grants absorbed into Hospital Grant from 1 July 1988.
Source: Western Australian Budget Papers 79/80 – 88/89.

By contrast Commonwealth revenues on the CRF grew by just over 1% in the same period, including three years when there were substantial reductions in real terms. Thus revenues from the Commonwealth to be applied to recurrent expenditures have declined in

importance, which is consistent with the increasingly stringent approach followed by the Commonwealth. In the 1979-80 financial year the Commonwealth contributed 52% of funds on the CRF, in 1987-88 this proportion had fallen to 46.13% (see Graph 13.14). The falling share of the Commonwealth also reflects the relatively faster economic growth rate in Western Australia as well as the success of revenue raising efforts by the State Government.

Graph 13.14

Growth of Revenue on the CRF

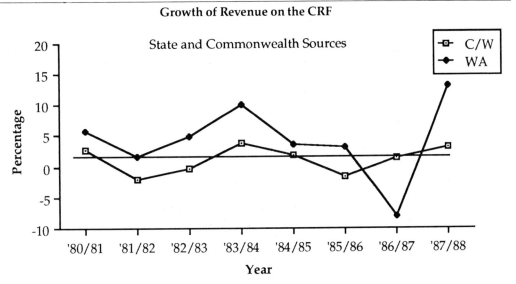

Source: Western Australian Budget Papers 79/80 – 88/89.

The total revenue available to the State from all sources is in Table 13.4, which also shows that CRF revenues as a proportion of this total have declined in importance. Additional revenues not in the CRF are usually committed to the capital works program. State funds for this purpose are classified somewhat inconsistently, sometimes according to their destination and sometimes according to their origin. These non-CRF State revenues comprise funds in the General Loan Fund, internal and other funds, and borrowings by State authorities, all of which are directed towards capital works. An analysis of the growth pattern of these funds in Table 13.13 shows that non-CRF funds have fluctuated more than CRF funds. As a result column 4 of Table 13.14 shows that the real percentage change in total State funds has ranged from an increase of 32.21% in 1982-83 to a decrease of 4.73% in 1986-87 during the last decade. By contrast, non-CRF funds provided by the Commonwealth while also fluctuating more widely than CRF funds, have also grown faster than CRF funds (except for the last two years). As a result total Commonwealth funds grew in real terms by about 1.7% p.a., tending to offset the slower growth rate of Commonwealth funds on the CRF. Only in 1986-87 and 1987-88 have substantial declines in total Commonwealth funds occurred.

Movements in Commonwealth non-CRF funds reflect the tendency of successive Federal Governments to make specific purpose capital grants, and to a lesser extent general purpose capital grants. Despite this faster growth of non-CRF funds from the Commonwealth, Graph 13.15 shows the widening gap between the contributions of State and Commonwealth sources to total State revenues. Financial stringency imposed by the Commonwealth has led Western Australian Governments to make greater revenue raising efforts, to look for new forms of taxation, and on the expenditure side, to look for a variety of improvements in efficiency and to make some other related but less desirable attempts at economising on resources.

Table 13.13

Total Revenue

	Total Revenue $m	Real % Change	Total CRF $m	CRF Rev As Prop of Total	CRF State Rev Prop of Total
79/80	2255.81	–	1641.18	72.75	34.92
80/81	2564.96	4.52	1860.56	72.54	35.32
81/82	2866.42	0.52	2061.89	71.93	35.70
82/83	3679.10	16.49	2324.87	63.19	32.16
83/84	4371.61	11.13	2659.87	60.84	31.88
84/85	4502.44	-0.90	2843.07	63.15	33.36
85/86	4898.12	0.69	3099.41	63.28	34.17
86/87	5202.93	-3.41	3284.22	63.12	32.53
87/88	5481.82	-1.66	3810.39	69.51	37.45

Source: Western Australian Budget Papers 79/80 − 88/89.

Table 13.14

State & Commonwealth Funds
Real Growth Rates

	State CRF	State Other	State Total	Real % Change	C'wealth Total	Real % Change
79/80	787.74	268.97	1056.71	–	1199.10	
80/81	906.01	290.76	1196.77	4.11	1368.19	4.89
81/82	1023.20	352.94	1376.14	3.43	1490.28	-2.03
82/83	1183.12	821.56	2004.68	32.21	1674.42	1.97
83/84	1393.68	1041.03	2434.71	13.59	1936.90	8.19
84/85	1502.09	909.96	2412.05	-4.68	2090.39	3.84
85/86	1673.71	935.17	2608.88	0.11	2289.24	1.36
86/87	1692.69	1040.85	2733.54	-4.73	2469.39	-1.92
87/88	2052.83	854.30	2907.13	-0.74	2574.69	-2.68
88/89*	2465.12	1139.72	3604.84	17.00	–	–

Note: * Estimates of Commonwealth funds for 1988/89 not yet available in a comparable form.
Source: Western Australian Budget Papers 79/80 − 88/89.

(iii) Changing Patterns of Taxes and Charges
A trend to an increasing reliance on taxation as a revenue source which began in the mid-1960s has been continued during the last decade. If anything, the reliance on taxation has been increased. Table 13.15 shows that there have been very substantial increases in taxation in real terms in all but two years (1982-83 and 1985-86) when the change in real terms was negligible. At the same time taxation revenue has steadily grown in relative importance by contributing over 28% of CRF revenue in 1987-88 compared to less than 20% in 1979-80.

Territorial revenue, about 90% of which is accounted for by mining royalties, was at one time in the late sixties thought of as the 'growth tax' with greatest potential. But in the seventies it ceased to grow, and began to display great annual volatility related to international economic and financial conditions. This volatility is clearly visible in the data for the eighties, with real increases of 36.8% in 1985-86 being followed by declines of 23.0% in the following year. Nevertheless, Table 13.16 clearly shows that territorial revenues have increased their share of total CRF revenue by about 1% in the last decade. The remaining revenues, departmental and public utilities are best considered together because revenues from organisations previously classified as public utilities are now more likely to be included under depart-mental revenues, denoted as profits and surpluses of business undertakings. Depart-mental and public utilities revenues accounted for about 22% of total CRF revenues in 1979-80 and despite wide fluctuations from year to year the trend has been for their share to decline. This trend appears to have accelerated since 1985, but the figures are affected by the reclassification of some revenues as non-CRF, associated with increased commercialis-ation of some government activities. Neverthe-less, the indisputable conclusion is that State taxation has been the most important contri-butor to the growth in revenues in the last decade.

Graph 13.15

Relative Shares of Total Revenue

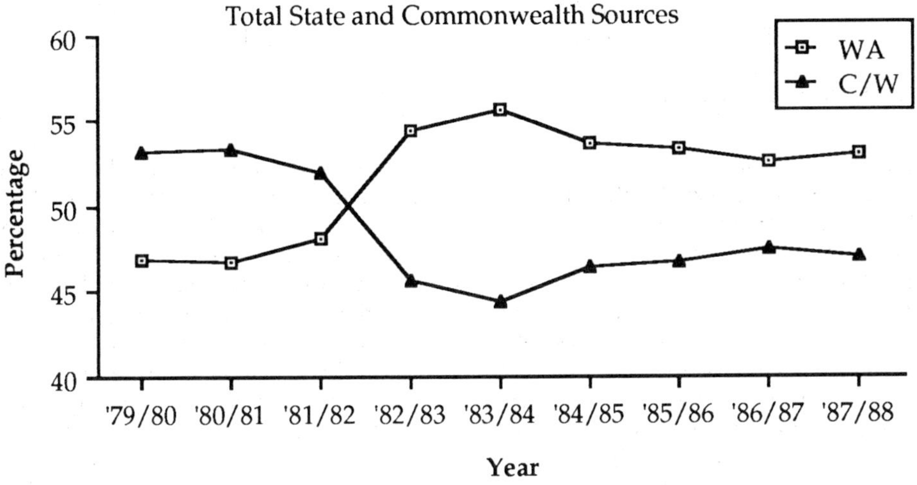

Total State and Commonwealth Sources

Source: Western Australian Budget Papers 79/80 — 88/89.

Table 13.15

Growth in Taxes & Charges on CRF Revenue
Real Growth & Relative Contributions to Total CRF

	Taxation		Territorial		Departmental	
79/80	—	19.90	—	5.21	—	11.13
80/81	6.43	10.32	9.86	5.49	9.73	11.71
81/82	2.72	20.94	-3.35	5.32	-4.43	11.23
82/83	-0.08	20.44	12.82	5.87	15.91	12.72
83/84	15.04	21.98	4.57	5.73	23.04	14.63
84/85	11.47	23.82	10.53	6.16	-18.12	11.65
85/86	-0.54	23.48	36.78	8.35	22.00	14.08
86/87	4.04	25.36	-22.98	6.68	-19.09	11.83
87/88	19.95	28.09	2.18	6.30	15.08	12.57
88/89*	3.34	27.36	-4.23	5.69	54.38	18.29

Note: * Budget Estimate.
Source: Western Australian Budget Papers 79/80 — 88/89.

Table 13.16

Growth in Taxes & Charges on CRF Revenue
Real Growth & Relative Contributions to Total CRF

	Law Courts		Public Utilities		Total State	
79/80	–	0.63	–	11.14	–	48.00
80/81	-0.14	0.60	-1.12	10.57	5.73	48.70
81/82	11.39	0.67	8.05	11.46	1.58	49.62
82/83	13.07	1.74	-0.77	11.11	4.94	50.89
83/84	4.46	0.73	-10.17	9.33	10.17	52.40
84/85	6.74	0.75	15.18	10.45	3.70	52.83
85/86	-6.32	0.70	-28.70	7.38	3.13	54.00
86/87	7.71	0.78	-9.99	6.90	-8.04	51.54
87/88	1.33	0.73	-2.87	6.19	13.19	53.87
88/89*	25.06	0.86	-8.44	5.34	13.30	57.53

Note: * Budget Estimate.
Source: Western Australian Budget Papers 79/80 – 88/89.

(iv) Regressivity of State Taxes

Most State taxes are levied without regard to the level of income of the taxpayer, and most taxes are flat rate percentages of the value of an asset or the value of a transaction. These taxes display the greatest degree of regressivity. Liquor, tobacco and gambling taxes fall into this category. On the basis of other information these taxes cover activities in which low income earners may be relatively more important.(see Groenewegen, 1984; New South Wales Tax Task Force Report, 1988). Of course, some of these taxes may be justified on the grounds that they increase the cost of 'anti-social' activities. This is clearly visible in the huge increase in the tobacco tax in 1983-84 (see Table 13.17). The tobacco tax has grown faster than liquor and gambling taxes in the last decade, although the growth rates of the latter have fluctuated as governments have adjusted the rates down and then up according to general financial conditions. On a per capita basis all three taxes have increased substantially in real terms.

Table 13.17

Net Collections of State Taxation
Real Growth, Real Growth Per Capita, Share of Total

	Liquor Tax			Tobacco Tax		
79/80	–	–	5.00	–	–	2.98
80/81	1.50	-0.61	4.76	-3.24	-5.26	2.70
81/82	-2.91	-5.58	4.50	5.41	2.51	2.77
82/83	-2.41	-4.89	4.40	28.78	25.50	3.58
83/84	5.86	3.88	4.05	157.87	153.06	8.01
84/85	-0.88	-2.54	3.60	2.09	0.38	7.34
85/86	8.62	6.10	3.93	6.44	3.97	7.85
86/87	37.49	33.56	5.19	-1.28	-4.10	7.46
87/88	12.28	9.22	4.88	-1.88	-4.55	6.12

Source: Western Australian Budget Paper 79/80 – 88/89.

In the case of some strongly regressive taxes, such as stamp duty and to a lesser extent, land tax, successive State Governments have attempted to moderate the degree of regressiveness. In the case of land taxes this has been done by varying the tax according to the area of land on which the taxpayer's principle residence has been located, and by exempting very small areas of land from tax altogether. Stamp duty rates have been varied according to the type of transaction ostensibly to protect low income earners. For example a lower rate of stamp duty has usually been levied on the purchase of low cost housing. Such concessions have been relatively minor in recent years, and Table 13.19 shows that stamp duties have

become an increasingly important source of revenue. The pattern of increasing reliance on regressive taxes is reinforced by the history of two other taxes, probate duty and the financial institution's duty. Probate duty (in economic terms, a relatively efficient tax) began to be phased out in 1977 and completely disappeared by 1985.

Table 13.18

Net Collections of State Taxation
Real Growth, Real Growth Per Capita, Share of Total

Gambling Tax

79/80	–	–	4.74
80/81	3.34	1.19	4.60
81/82	-1.92	-4.62	4.39
82/83	-2.39	-4.88	4.29
83/84	9.63	7.58	4.08
84/85	9.61	7.77	4.02
85/86	14.02	11.37	4.60
86/87	7.58	4.51	4.76
87/88	3.41	0.59	4.12

Source: Western Australian Budget Paper 79/80 − 88/89.

Table 13.19

Net Collections of State Taxation
Real Growth, Real Growth Per Capita, Share of Total

Stamp Duty

79/80	–	–	23.56
80/81	19.74	17.24	26.48
81/82	4.53	1.66	26.95
82/83	-3.84	-6.29	25.93
83/84	20.63	18.38	27.19
84/85	20.62	18.60	29.43
85/86	2.21	-0.16	30.21
86/87	12.73	9.51	32.78
87/88	47.16	43.14	40.32

Source: Western Australian Budget Paper 79/80 − 88/89.

Confronted by financial stringency in 1983 the newly elected Labor Government, substantially increased most rates of stamp duty, and followed the example of the other States in introducing another regressive tax, in the form of the financial institutions duty. Within a year this new tax was accounting for 5% of total tax revenues, more than the government expected, and under pressure from the financial sector, the rate of duty was reduced. Since 1985-86 the financial insti-

tutions duty has provided around 3% of tax revenues.

Payroll tax is the last important tax, once regarded as the 'growth' tax to solve all the financial problems of the State, when that other 'growth' tax from mineral royalties went into decline. In the first full year after the transfer of payroll tax from the Commonwealth, the tax accounted for 40% of tax revenues, it peaked at 56% in 1974-75, and stayed in the low fifties until 1983-84 as Table 13.20 shows.

Table 13.20

Net Collections of State Taxation
Real Growth, Real Growth Per Capita, Share of Total

Payroll Tax

79/80	—	—	51.63
80/81	8.02	5.77	52.35
81/82	4.76	1.88	53.38
82/83	0.19	-2.36	53.53
83/84	-1.65	-3.49	45.76
84/85	3.38	1.65	42.45
85/86	-1.63	-3.91	41.94
86/87	-3.32	-6.08	39.02
87/88	8.05	5.10	35.24

Source: Western Australian Budget Paper 79/80 — 88/89.

Conservative Governments complained that this 'growth' tax had turned out to be a tax on employment, but their budgets did little more than adjust the rates of payroll tax and the threshold of its application more or less in line with inflation. It was left to the Labor Government in its first budget in 1983-84, and to a greater or lesser extent in each budget since, to reduce the rates of payroll tax and to substantially increase the payroll threshold before any tax is levied. Table 13.11 shows how the growth of payroll tax slowed in 1982-83 as a result of the deep recession in the economy, and how the rate of growth in payroll tax was negative in three out of the next five years because of the reductions in the rates of tax. Growth in payroll tax per capita has slowed even further between 1983 and 1988, and this in the context of growth in employment in excess of 3% p.a. So the share of payroll tax in total tax fell sharply in 1983-84 (and that of stamp duty rose) and these changes in share have continued in each year to the present. Clearly stamp duties (and other regressive taxes) have substituted for payroll tax.

Western Australian Governments have been compelled to place greater reliance on State taxes as a source of revenue in recent years. These taxes have tended to be more regressive than if the same amount of revenue had been collected by the Commonwealth through taxes on income. Most changes to State taxes and the introduction of new ones have also been regressive. Changes in the mix of payroll tax and stamp duties has an ambiguous effect on regressivity. Without a more detailed analysis it

is not possible to draw conclusions on this issue. Economists have usually pointed to the very rapid growth in employment since 1983 as one of the benefits of the cut in payroll tax. But equally the level of aggregate demand is of great importance. With a lower increase in regressive stamp duties (and also motor vehicle taxation and licences) the level of aggregate demand might have been even higher.

(v) The Decline of Non-Tax Revenue Sources

As noted earlier, according to the figures in Tables 13.15 and 13.16, departmental and public utilities are now contributing about 18% of CRF revenues compared to 22% a decade ago. Only the railways are now classified under public utilities, so that the revenues received by the government from other utilities now appear in the CRF under departmental revenue. In addition, departmental revenue is generated from the very wide range of services provided by government departments. Successive governments have instituted reviews of departmental fees and charges for most services, many of them of a minor nature, in order to ensure that the charges reflected the cost of providing them. This has been the guiding principle for over a decade, except for those fees and charges involving political decisions, but with an avowedly economic end. For example country water supplies, railways and other freight services, and metropolitan transport have been provided at consistently lower charges than the cost of provision. Thus many departmental revenues have not even increased at the rate of inflation in the last decade. This partly explains their declining contribution to total revenues.

In the case of the three most important charges, for energy, water and housing, successive governments have made strenuous efforts to keep increases in charges below the rate of inflation. On average that has been achieved in the last decade, but rather unevenly, as the timing of increases has been influenced by the election cycle. There has also been an increasing emphasis on 'user pays'. For example water rates and fees accounted for almost 83% of gross earnings in 1979-80, but by 1987-88 they were accounting for around 55% of gross earnings of the Water Authority. There was a corresponding increase in the proportion of gross earnings related to water sales and other services from 17% in 1979-80 to 45% in 1987-88. These changes were undoubtedly economically 'rational' and may well have led to the economising of scarce water resources but they also shifted the burden from business to households. Many businesses with low water consumption had previously paid large water rates. With the emphasis in charges shifting to quantity of water consumed, the cost of water rose substantially for most households.

With respect to energy prices there has been a divergence in the pattern of increase during the last decade. Electricity prices have increased at around or below the rate of inflation, and their share of gross earnings of the State Energy Commission have declined from 92% in 1979-80 to 67% in 1987-88. This decline has been due partly to actions to change the pattern of demand towards the abundant, but relatively costly supplies of natural gas. While natural gas accounted for just 6% of gross earnings in 1979-80 it had increased rapidly to almost 33% in 1987-88. The price of natural gas has increased faster than the rate of inflation, including very steep increases in 1984-85. Financing and servicing the capital expansion plans of the State Energy Commission has proved an extremely difficult management task. The huge areas over which energy has to be supplied and the consensus about the need for cross subsidization, has led to relatively high energy costs for urban consumers in Western Australia. As in the case of water

supplies, the contribution to the State's revenues by the State Energy Commission have been quite small.

Providing low cost housing for rental or purchase seems to have been one of the success stories of the last decade. Increases in rents have certainly been below the rate of inflation, and many rents appear to be below market values as well. More recently some increases in rents have been above the inflation rate as governments have tried to move rentals closer to 'market' rents. Nevertheless, State housing is being provided with a substantial subsidy to income earners in the lowest quartile of the income distribution. The precise size of the subsidy cannot be determined without a more detailed study. Certainly the provision of housing has been a negligible contributor to net State revenues.

Two other source of revenues remain to be examined. First is territorial revenue which consists of mineral royalties (about 84%), timber royalties (about 10%) and the remainder accounted for by various forms of leases of land. In the late sixties it was assumed that mineral royalties would provide the State with a long sought after growth tax. But this optimism about mineral royalties evaporated in the seventies. Early in the 1980s political discussion focused on the rate of mineral royalties, and the Liberal Government of the time, responded in the 1981-82 budget by implementing the only significant increase in royalty rates in the last decade. As Table 13.6 shows, despite that increase in rates, territorial revenue has increased its share of total CRF revenues only slightly, from 5.2% in 1979-80 to 6.30% in 1987-88. Of course, the amount of royalties is highly sensitive to export volumes, which have fluctuated widely according to the State of the international economy. Shortly after the Labor Government came to power in 1983 it instituted a major academic inquiry into mineral royalties.(see Bradley, 1986). This report recommended a shift to a profits based determination of royalties, and argued that the State's revenues could be increased substantially as a result. None of the recommendations have yet been implemented.

Second is the issue of asset sales. The Western Australian government has announced plans to sell assets as a means of overcoming its revenue difficulties. Three reasons have been advanced by the government to explain its proposed asset sales. First, it has developed in response to the 1989 Premiers' Conference and Loan Council decisions to cut Western Australia's access to finance;. Second, there are a range of emerging demands in Western Australia which its current revenue sources will be inadequate to meet. These include basic needs such as hospitals and schools in new suburbs established in the recent property boom. And third, the State's own revenue sources have begun to dwindle as increased stamp duty revenues are falling away as a result of the slump in the property market (AFR 20/6/89).

The rationale for this action is very similar to that proffered by the Victorian government when it announced a program of cuts in services for State revenue purposes (see Chapter Eleven for more details).

13.4.3 Western Australian State Expenditure
(i) Expenditure Restraint
The review of revenues has shown a pattern of increasing financial constraint in the 1980s because of the declining proportion contributed by the Commonwealth. Since 1986-87 Commonwealth funds received by Western Australia have been substantially reduced in real terms and alternative sources of revenues have not compensated for these reductions.

Overall, the State's expenditure has increased in real terms in each year in the last decade, except for a decline of less than 0.5% in 1981-82 and 1985-86, and a decline in excess of 3% in 1986-87. In 1987-88 a real increase of around 5% was made possible by the substantial increases in State taxation and departmental revenue. There is a strong possibility that some functions previously classified under economic services are now covered by the remaining major category, general government services. This category has a small sub-item of legislative affairs, accounting for less than of expenditure, while the remainder classified in the 'other' category covers a wide range of government services. Taking general government services and economic services together, suggests only a small decline of around 3% in their share of total expenditure.

In Section 13.2 data was presented which showed that the ratio of State Government employment to total employment has consistently declined since 1984. It is well known that this ratio usually declines as an economy approaches a peak in economic activity, but the phenomenon usually lasts for a period of 4 to 6 quarters. This time the decline in the ratio of State Government to total employment has been maintained for 16 quarters, and there is no sign that it is about to rise again. Even after taking into account the prolonged, and very strong recovery in Western Australia, it does not seem possible to dismiss this slowing in the growth of State Government employment as a cyclical phenomenon. To what extent has this slower growth in government employment led to a curtailment of government services?

The question can be partially answered by examining the details of the expenditure plans outlined in the State budget. As a first step a strong contrast may be drawn between the conservative government in power until February 1983, and the approach of the Labor Government thereafter. Between 1979 and 1983 in successive State budgets, the government indicated that it was pursuing expenditure restraint because of the difficulties posed by Federal-State financial relations. It also argued that it was aiming to reduce the tax burden, and that the other major expenditure problem it faced, was the persistent rise in its wages bill each year. For this it blamed the arbitration system.

In the period considered here, 1979 to 1983, the State Government responded to the perceived need for expenditure restraint in an unimaginative and conservative manner. A special plea for more Commonwealth funds was repeated year after year. The plea was supported by arguments about the size of the State, the dispersion of its population, and on the more positive argument that Western Australia made a disproportionate contribution to the generation of export income. Rhetoric on calls for expenditure restraint was not matched by appropriate action. In 1981 a Cabinet Expenditure Review Committee was established. Its recommendations for cuts in expenditure amounting to 0.7% of total expenditure were spread across education, health and other unidentified areas. But in general, until 1983, the incremental approach to budgetary policy was dominant, with few or no new programs or innovations. The remarkable fact is that these governments rarely if ever referred to efficiency in government, and hardly any of their expenditure decisions were made with the objective of increasing efficiency.

By contrast the Burke Labor Government's response to expenditure restraint was to implement a totally different approach to budgetary and management policies. There were three strands to these policies. First, the pruning of expenditure on a selective basis, on some occasions without any apparent regard to its popularity or political consequences. Second the establishment of a functional review procedure. Third, the increased participation of the State Government in a variety of productive activities via some form of equity participation, leasing and profit sharing arrangements, increased participation in private sector activities and/or the application of private sector skills and principles to government activity.

Over the five year period 1983-88 the pruning of expenditure in various budgets involved among other things, pay cuts for ministers, members of parliament and senior public servants. On two occasions, there were direct attempts to cut public service numbers, the first in 1983, by the operation of a selective non-replacement policy for departmental staff. In 1986 a 3% reduction in public service employment was gradually implemented with its effects being most strongly felt in 1987-88. Other measures involved economies in the use of government vehicles and the identification and cataloguing of government statutory boards, committees, etc. with a view to reducing their numbers and their maintenance costs. These attempts to rein in expenditure are fairly conventional and invariably confront interest group opposition. As a result governments have a tendency to gradually relax or phase out such measures. In any case, the impact of these measures on the public service cannot be considered independently of the other policy changes which were implemented.

In September 1983 the Burke Government announced the establishment of the Functional Review Committee and a month later reinforced the announcement in its first budget by laying great stress on the importance of the functional review process for efficiency in the public sector. The cynical outsider might have been tempted to dismiss the government's announcements on public sector efficiency as typical first term grandstanding. But the next four budgets contained a specific section devoted to a discussion of the progress of various functional reviews and to their impact on efficiency. Further reinforcement of the government's intentions was signalled by the Financial Administration and Audit Act which came into operation in July 1986. The Act aimed to increase accountability in the spending of public funds, allowed the Auditor-General to comment on how organisations spent funds, and also provided a mandate for the Auditor-General to examine the efficiency and effectiveness of government departments and statutory authorities. While there appears to be some potential for overlap or conflict in the review functions of the Auditor-General and the Functional Review Committee (FRC) this has been avoided in practice for two reasons. The Auditor-General must report to Parliament unlike the FRC which reports to the Premier. So far the Auditor-General under this Act has tended to concentrate on accounting and audit functions, although there are signs that reviews of the efficiency and effectiveness of government expenditure will be increasingly undertaken. Although not publicly announced, it is expected that a set of co-operative procedures for the exchange of information and other aspects of review will be developed between the two reviewing authorities.

So far it is the work of the FRC which has most impinged on government expenditure. The guidelines for functional reviews laid down that comprehensive reviews would be made of all functions, activities and services of government. Although much of the information relating to reviews is not publicly available, information has emerged at the stage of implementation of recommendations. It appears that the reviews have focused on the major functions performed by organizations rather than looking at organisations or departments as a whole. The FRC recommends to the Premier on whether a particular 'activity should be modified or abandoned and whether the mechanism for carrying it out is operating efficiently' (Budget Speech, 1985-86, p. 2).

Well in excess of fifty reviews have been undertaken since the first, of the Architectural division of the Public Works department (revamped as the Building Management Authority) began in late 1983. As noted earlier, information about reviews has usually become available because of implementation difficulties, leading to personnel and other industrial relations problems. But after the rather insensitive handling of the redeployment and early retirement proposals for the Building Management Authority, implementation of subsequent reviews have confronted fewer problems. Other reviews have looked at many of the functions in the areas of education, health, prisons, water authority, lands, rail and bus operations, etc. Some observers have argued that the overriding objective of the reviews has been to reduce the numbers employed in the performance of a particular function. In the case of the Building Management Authority and Homeswest (which provides public housing) FRC recommendations have adversely affected the standard and quantity of services. It is difficult to gauge the extent of any offsetting improvements in efficiency, although on a crude employment basis there has certainly been an increase in efficiency. Broadbanding and award restructuring has also been implemented as well as the introduction of a senior executive service and a comprehensive executive development program.

The government's drive to apply private sector skills to the public service has undoubtedly produced some efficiency gains. However, that the functional reviews have sometimes recommended privatisation, contracting out, the sale of some government assets, and the reduction of day labour forces. The case studies in Section 13.5 consider some of these developments in more detail.

Finally, a related response to expenditure restraint (alluded to in Section 13.4) was the application of private sector management principles emphasising an increased 'entrepre-

neurial role' for government. Thus in its first budget for 1983/84 the Burke government purchased interests in two diamond mining ventures and announced the establishment of the Western Australian Development Corporation (WADC). At the time the well intentional purpose was:

'. . . to utilise the private sector mode to increase our community's share of the benefits of our State's development through, for example, equity participation, sophisticated leasing arrangements and profit sharing arrangements' (Budget Speech, 1983/84, 13th October 1983, pp. 5-6).

In every subsequent budget speech the treasurer referred to the success of the WADC and in 1987/88 claimed that in less than four years of operation the Corporation had paid a dividend of $23m to the State which had subscribed $15m in capital (Budget Speech, 1987/88, p. 12). While these figures are confirmed by the published information, considerable doubt exists (see Section 13.5, case study 1) on the extent to which the activities of the WADC have involved genuine value added activities. More recently the State Government Insurance Corporation (SGIC) has also increased its private sector involvement (see below). While the official published results so far indicate a net gain to revenue some of these activities are clearly subject to a high degree of commercial risk associated with cyclical fluctuations in the economy and with managerial competence. In 1987 large once-off profits were made, but these profits were due to financial strength of a government corporation and could hardly be attributed to increases in output or productive capacity in the economy. So the profits represented a redistribution of income, which fortuitously in this case, was towards the State Government.

(ii) The Election Budget, 1988-89
The requirement that a State election should be held before the end of May 1989 quite naturally influenced the drafting of the budget presented to parliament in August 1988. On the revenue side, apart from the need to offer

moderation in taxes and charges, as compared to the previous two years the government's problems were compounded by a further reduction of 10% in nominal terms in Commonwealth payments to the State. However, the government optimistically forecast a rise of 13% in nominal terms in State revenue collections on the CRF and was thus able to budget for a 'balance' between revenue and expenditure on the CRF. This 1988-89 forecast of a 'balance' followed five years in which the Labor Government had ensured that the CRF outcome was a small surplus of a few million dollars. Thus, like its predecessors, the Dowding Government preserved the impression of competent economic management.

At the time the budget was bought down in September 1988 it was possible to draw the conclusion from the speech and accompanying papers that revenues would receive a substantial boost from the government's involvement in a range of business undertakings. By March 1989 it had emerged that potentially large losses of revenue (approaching $400m) might result from government involvement in the proposed petrochemical plant, the SGIC, and the government's direct and indirect role in the attempted rescue of Rothwells. So the government began to step back from its involvement in a wide range of commercial or semi-commercial activities, an approach which it had confidently espoused right up to the presentation of the 1988/89 budget.

In fact during most of 1988 the government had presented its approach aggressively by identifying areas of expenditure which it claimed were being funded by the profits and surpluses of business undertakings. The Budget Speech emphasised a new Social Strategy which provided for the construction and upgrading of Family Centres and child care facilities, and provided a variety of subsidies for family and school related activities. This was the only major change in the 1988-89 budget, and it was a change of emphasis not direction. The capital works program was to rise by a massive 48.4% in 1988-89 boosted by a carryover of funds due to an apparently deliberate underspending in the previous years. Major items of expenditure included housing (which had fallen by a large amount in the previous year) on schools and related educational facilities, on hospitals, and on the electrification of suburban rail.

For the first time in six budgets no reference was made in the 1988-89 budget to the question of efficiency of the public sector. However, the functional review process discussed earlier is continuing. Pressures for commercialisation and moves in that direction clearly have emanated from these reviews. Equally clearly (as noted in Section 13.2.2), the government has signalled its intention to continue to be involved in joint activity with the private sector by taking a minority interest in a $1b petrochemical plant. The argument in the 1988-89 budget was that without government involvement such a project might never be developed by private enterprise in Western Australia.

State budgets are extremely difficult to assess not only because they depend on forecasts of the State of the economy over which the State Government has very little control, but also because accounting procedures complicate the interpretation of data especially on the expenditure side. The 1988-89 budget is not free of these problems. Nevertheless, this budget is even more difficult than usual to evaluate because it seems to be based on optimistic forecasts of revenue generation by the State outside the bounds of previous experience. Some revenues have been generated by the special circumstances of the 1987-88 financial year (including the October 1987 crash) while some business undertaking activities particularly housing and construction are especially susceptible to fluctuations in financial markets. Some activities in which the government is involved are subject to a relatively competitive environment, which may not matter when the economy is growing rapidly, but may depress revenues equally rapidly when the economy slows. On the expenditure side the financing requirements of some development projects is unclear and more resources may be called for in a rising interest rate environment. By the end of March 1989 according to a progressive financial Statement (State Treasury, 1989) revenue, especially from departmental sources which includes business undertakings was lagging well behind the estimates, and expenditure was running well ahead of the estimates, as compared to the same nine month period in 1988. Grave doubts are emerging about the ability of the government to achieve its plans and there is no doubt that expenditure restraint will be more stringent than at any other time during the six year reign of the Labor Government. The Dowding budget of 1988-89 is a direct descendant of the five previous Burke budgets, and appears to be a less reliable budget document because of its legacy from that period. It may well be that with the usual financial gymnastics the 1988-89 budget will be 'balanced', but the amount of revenue generated and expended may fall short of the budget estimates.

13.5 Case Studies: Privatisation and Commercial Performance
13.5.1 Introduction
One definition of privatisation as provided by George W. Wilson, Distinguished Professor of Business and Economics at the Indiana University School of Business reads as follows:

'The broader and more relevant meaning of privatization must refer to nothing more or less than greater reliance upon *market forces* (my emphasis) to generate production of particular goods and services' (Miller & Tufts, 1988, p. 102).

The interest in the concept of 'market forces' stems partly from its presumed descriptive power and partly from its implications for economic efficiency. People trading in competitive markets exchange goods and services that results in a position after trade which is efficient in a narrowly defined sense. For instance, an allocation of resources through the workings of 'market forces' is said to be efficient if there is no other feasible allocation that would make at least one individual in the economy better off without making anyone else worse off. However, what is often not pointed out is that this may have nothing at all to do with creating social benefits because initially, a very unjust allocation of resources, with vast wealth for a few, and poverty for many, will be efficient if there is no way of improving the lot of the poor without injuring the wealthy few in some measure. It is this fact

which is crucial to our understanding when discussing the privatisation of public resources.

Further, while it is clear that market forces have many virtues, they also have serious limitations which are too often ignored. Markets should not be made the complete arbiter of social life because they do not always work as the textbooks say they should. Discussions about this point, within the discipline of economics, have pointed out that the strict conditions which usually ensure competitive markets in textbooks are not typically fully met in the real world. This points to the limits on the validity of 'market forces', whereby certain actions while leading to the private benefit of certain individuals may also lead to social ills or breakdown.

What is left unsaid by Wilson in the above definition, and anyone else who would agree with him, is that efficiency criteria of 'market forces' are valid only under very specific assumptions about the economic world and the many social and private preferences which exist in that world. The fact that privatisation may provide more efficient and effective service is a necessary but not sufficient condition for it to take place. A more crucial and complex question that must be answered is whether or not privatisation is socially beneficial (Arrow, 1985, pp. 107-123).

Australian State public services are now faced with serious problems. State Government revenue has been radically reduced, in real terms, at a time in which the States have assumed increased financial and social responsibilities, which in turn has led to a general emphasis on 'privatisation'. In the long term, we argue, this process threatens the development of viable State public services.

Case study examination of the funding and development of public services in Western Australia most clearly reflects the information provided in Section 13.4 of this chapter. The data and figures in Section 13.4 show a pattern of increasing financial constraint for the State in the 1980s due to the declining proportion of revenues contributed by the Commonwealth Government to the Consolidated Revenue Fund of Western Australia; and the limited ability of the State to compensate for these reductions in Commonwealth contributions. It is this pressure which has forced the State to seek new revenue sources, to come up with new forms of taxation, and to increase the efficiency of expenditure and service delivery. While there is nothing remiss in these activities, in and of themselves, the concern is that government administrators and politicians have acted hastily and somewhat haphazardly, given the budgetary pressures faced during this decade.

Since the State Labor Government took office in 1983, there have been quite substantial increases in State taxes. Given the nature of State taxation as indicated in Section 13.4.2, the overall effect of these increases has been to increase the regressivity of their impact on income earners, relative to what would have been the case had the same amount of revenue been collected and distributed by the Commonwealth Government via the personal income tax. On the expenditure side, the government has been forced to service an increasingly larger economy from a reduced resource base. This has been directly responsible, as shown in Section 13.2, for a consistent fall in the ratio of State Government employment to total employment since 1984.

Until recently, political representatives in Western Australia have defended the need for government to be more innovative and to find additional finances without adding to the existing tax burden. However, specific types of innovation utilised in this endeavour have led others to suggest that the Western Australian Government bears an ironic resemblance to the Stuart kings' search for sources of revenue outside parliamentary control (Black, 1988, p. 37). The unaudited profit of the State Government Insurance Commission of $137.2m for 1987/1988, is one example of the magnitude of funds available from extra-parliamentary sources. For State Governments whose tax base is invariably regressive, alternative sources of revenue are important both politically and economically, but without full accountability for these sources to parliament, they may enhance executive power at the expense of the legislature, thereby dissembling the balance of powers deemed essential in democratic governance. The ramifications then of States being

cut loose from the purse strings of the Commonwealth Government, at least in the short run, can be quite dramatic.

These pressures are reflected in each of the Case Studies below. Case Study 1 identifies a dimension of State activities (which has come to be known popularly as WA Inc.) in a variety of private sector dealings involving equity participation in private enterprises, investment of State Government Insurance funds in high risk ventures, the bonded guarantee or subsidisation of failed entrepreneurial enterprises to protect small investors and soften the shock of capitalist mis-adventure, and the increased application of private sector efficiency principles to the management of government departments and statutory authorities. This process of corporatism has enhanced the integration of State Government activity and the Labor Party itself with organised groups of capital in the State, with the goal of promoting a realm of consensus and co-operation within a capitalist ideological framework. Case Study 2 examines the sale of the State Engineering Works as an example of asset unloading by the Labor Government under tremendous pressure from private industry and the Opposition parties. Case Study 3 portrays the increased level of 'contracting out' of government activity to non-government institutions and the private sector, particularly in the area of Community Services. Finally, Case Study 4 examines what appears to be an innocent, but which in fact is an insidious increase of volunteer workers in the State education system being used to replace paid school assistants.

13.5.2 Corporatism In the Public Sector — Western Australia Incorporated

Shortly after the 1983 State election and the victory of the Labor Party, Laurie Connell and Partners, under contract to the new government, successfully completed a complex and unique set of negotiations to vary the Argyle Diamond Mines Joint Venture Agreement Act, restructuring the royalty payments to the advantage of both the government and the companies which were involved (CRA Ltd., Ashton Mining, and Northern Mining). The companies did not want to build a $70m township for workers, to which they had already agreed, preferring instead a fly in-fly out scheme to carry out the production process of diamonds. To avoid their original contract obligations, the companies agreed to pay the Burke Government $50m as a pre-payment royalty. Forty-two million of this was then used by the government to purchase the 5% stake in the diamond venture which was held by Alan Bond's company, Northern Mining Ltd.

In 1983, the Labor Government also enacted the Western Australian Development Corporation Act, which established a statutory corporation aimed at promoting economic development in the State. This corporation was set up to operate on 'commercial principles' being put under the direction of management and a board of directors drawn almost completely from the private sector. Upon formation of the Western Australian Development Corporation (WADC), under chairman John Horgan, the government stake in Northern Mining was sold to the WADC which in turn sold the 5% share of the Argyle Diamond Mine to a trust at a profit of $2.7m, ostensibly so the public could also invest in a Western Australian project. WADC then bought 5 million units in the trust at $1 each and became the trust manager. Forthwith, the shell of the Northern Mining Corporation was transformed through an amended memorandum and articles into Western Australian Government Holdings Ltd. which was to be used as a parent company for subsidiary public enterprises wholly or partially owned by the government.

The following year, at the request of the government, experts from Rothwells Bank, which was established by Laurie Connell, reviewed the activities of the Motor Vehicle Insurance Trust and the State Government Insurance Office (SGIC). The Bank recommended merging the two to form the State Government Insurance Commission. Further, it was suggested that the Commission's funds be moved away from fixed-term, low-yielding investment into the buying of shares and property. Subsequently, this master plan was put into effect and the SGIC entered into the big league with 39.2 million shares in BHP at $7.25 each, a number of properties in the central business district and shares in the Bell Group of Robert Holmes à Court (Sunday Times, 6/11/88, p. 5). Con-

currently, Price Waterhouse was recommending that the State Superannuation Board look to increase its stockmarket outlays on more speculative and young growth-oriented stocks. Later the Board did invest in a number of 'high-technology' companies controlled by Laurie Connell, as well as ventures in the Bond and Holmes à Court empires (Ibid.).

The network of ties being cemented between the Labor Government and a number of high-flying entrepreneurial capitalists of Western Australia is also demonstrated in the fact that Laurie Connell received a $250,000 spotters fee for the purchase of Fremantle Gas and Coke by the State Energy Commission; and was appointed chairman of the Western Australian Meat Marketing Commission and the Western Australian Meat Commission.

The ramifications of this restructuring provided the Burke Government with access to big pools of cash in government trust funds through a chain of new government organisations. Thus, immediately following the election, the government had created a nexus between itself and the entrepreneurial giants of the Western Australian economy; although it was evident from the beginning that the government was walking a tightrope by encapsulating itself in these new activities and by the formation of alliances which sit very uneasy with a Labor Party. With the crash of October, 1987, when both the economic activities and political alliances began to unravel, the vultures were waiting to pounce on the evidence of contradiction which had been in existence for five years:

'The Burke model, based on cronyism, elitism, the abuse of fiscal responsibility and the denial of public accountability, is a political mutation on the basic characteristics of 1980s Labor — pragmatism, corporatism, and the rich mates syndrome. It was the ultimate alliance between new Labor and new money' (Kelly, 1988, pp. 1-2).

From this point on, the Labor Party and government under Premier Dowding were to come under continuous attack from friends and foes alike.

In the earlier halcyon days of Labor Government restructuring, Brian Burke called the West Australia Development Corporation (WADC) the 'jewel in the crown'. EXIM, established in 1985, was another of his government's proud creations. WADC was to be run on private business lines to make profits from managing government assets (including monetary assets previously handled by the Treasury, State-owned city properties, the Mint, and public forests) and to promote economic development in the State. EXIM Corporation was seen to be the State's version of a giant trading company which could be used to open vast export markets for both Western Australian products and new industries. EXIM was established as a wholly owned subsidiary of Western Australian Government Holdings Ltd.; and itself set up a variety of subsidiaries of its own in the floricultural, livestock, metals and advisory services industries, as well as a number of pastoral properties. Many of these ventures were failures, and EXIM, in particular, was severely criticised in the media.

In any case, both WADC and EXIM were originally touted by Burke as typical examples of benefits which could be gained by binding the private and public sectors in a partnership. It should be evident by now that these new enterprises, established by the government, had nothing whatsoever to do with the principles of nationalisation or even democratic socialism. Quite the contrary, the main goals were to identify and get access to alternative sources of revenue as quickly as possible, as well as overcome the deficiencies in financial markets which were not providing funds to a number of projects in Western Australia; the danger being, in walking this knife's edge, that in time the government would be accused of losing touch with its base amongst traditional Labour voters.

Following the election in February, 1989, the Cabinet was not enthusiastic about either WADC or EXIM, although the right-wing Labor Unity faction and members of the Left within the ALP caucus, jointly, but for different reasons, continued to argue strongly for retention of WADC. Irrespective of the political support, the claims of WADC and EXIM to continuing profits and economic success began to have a hollow ring, although some benefici-

aries did reasonably well. Chairman John Horgan in 1987/88 earned almost $300,000 in director's fees from WADC alone plus a so far undisclosed amount from EXIM and Gold Corp. Many of the corporate investments had gone sour, and criticism regarding the validity of stated profitability was causing the government political problems. In October, 1988, WADC released its annual report promoting its $10.7m profit. Yet the accounts were, to say the least, lacking in detail.

For instance, WADC had to admit it lost $590,000, making provision for an unknown amount, after agreeing to guarantee a $3m bank loan to McLean Brothers and Rigg Ltd., an old unlisted Western Australian company. In 1972, Metro Industries Ltd., then managed by the present chairman of WADC, John Horgan, bought control of McLean Brothers and Rigg (MB & R) and merged it with another business, Sandovers. In September, 1985, the shell of MB & R was sold to a group of investors led by businessmen Roy Annear. Annear Investments bought 58% of the company and WADC took a 16.6% share for more than $1.5m. Laurie Connell was included among the other investors. Early in 1986, WADC went guarantor for a $3m loan from the Australia Bank to MB & R which was borrowing funds to buy a sports and leisure business. In April, 1987, Annear was in financial difficulties, and the WADC guarantee was shown as a $3.1m contingent liability in the 1986/87 annual report. In early 1988, WADC paid a sum into a trust account, administered by the Australia Bank and itself, while attempts were made to restructure the deal. Part of that restructuring involved the Bank agreeing to lend Annear $900,000 to buy back the WADC's 16.6% stake, a loss to the Development Corporation of $590,000. The contingent liability of $3.1m does not appear in the previous years' WADC report and John Horgan would not reveal the amount provided, claiming it was commercially confidential. He said it has been accommodated in the profit and loss account, but had not been itemised (Hewett, Loxley & Smith, 1988, p. 15).

Overall, in 1987/88, it can be calculated that WADC lost $1m on its investments. The claimed profit on 'projects and investments' of $2.85m was only made possible by including

$3.85m of the $5m WADC received from the sale of Gold Corporation. Land Corporation, which buys, sells, and develops government land, made $5.48m for WADC, and Funds Corporation, set up as a money market operator to manage Treasury cash surpluses, earned $2.36m for WADC. As a result of the Burt Commission Report on Accountability released on January 22, 1989, Funds Corporation was immediately disbanded due to legal doubts which were raised about the right of WADC to borrow the State Treasury's short-term surpluses for investment purposes. This left WADC with two main operating arms – Landcorp and Eventscorp – as well as equity in projects such as Underwater World and the Cable Beach Club at Broome.

On February 9, 1989, immediately following the State election, WADC announced a half-yearly operating profit of $15.2m. As usual, the bulk of the latest profit results were made up of one-off land sales, particularly the State Engineering Works site in North Fremantle (see the case study below on the State Engineering Works), and the Buckland Hill site, in nearby Mosman Park. Buckland Hill was sold to the Melbourne-based company Analed Pty. Ltd. for $5.4m and the State Engineering Works site was sold to JIMWA Pty. Ltd. for $12.4m.

Gold Corp.,was set up to provide services to the gold industry, investors, and the international market. It's terms of reference were to assist with every stage of gold production from the giving of technical advice on starting a project to financing it, processing gold, trading, turning gold into value-added products and marketing them. The Corporation had made a profit of $2.5m in its first year. Then it made a loss of $1.4m in the first 6 months of the 1987/88 fiscal year. This trend apparently continued in the second half (it was requesting a tax holiday from the government) when it was spun off from WADC. After discussions with the Reserve Bank, Gold Corp. delayed its plans to move to full banking status until it has built up its capital base and fulfilled all other requirements the Reserve Bank expects of a bank.

After struggling for four years to prove itself, EXIM lost the battle for survival. EXIM began operations in 1985 with $2m and a plan to borrow more in order to help establish new Western Australian business ventures geared for overseas markets. Its performance was marred by several poor investment decisions in the areas of horticulture, jewellery and agricultural machinery and, because of this, was attacked vociferously by business and industry groups.

The 1988 annual report of EXIM confirmed what the critics were saying. The report announced a $911,740 post-tax profit for the year to June 30, 1988, which was down from the $1.94m post-tax profit posted in the previous year. However, the full set of accounts indicated clearly that EXIM traded at a substantial loss. EXIM's post-tax 'profitability' did not lie in revenue, but in the reinstatement of capital expenditure previously written off ($553,976) and income tax credits ($889,820). Without these items, EXIM would have faced a trading loss of more than $500,000. Further, a post-extraordinaries profit of $1.69m was offset by a $1.94m contingency loss booked under Western Australian Government Holdings as a provision for falls in the value of EXIM's investments in its subsidiaries. The report also showed director fees of $301,992 for the six-man board for the year, as well as pre-paid director's fees of $93,332.

Towards the end of its life EXIM had, with limited success, concentrated its efforts in three areas: promoting business migrants; attracting overseas students; and rationalising the Kimberley pastoral industry. This did not prevent a strong push, coming from within the Cabinet, to disband the corporation. It is understood that Premier Dowding and Deputy Premier Parker supported an anti-EXIM move for both political and economic reasons prior to the February election. On November 7, 1988, Premier Dowding announced that the WADC would be put under the umbrella of the auditor general and a review would be made of WADC and EXIM. Following the election, and given the review, it was determined, and announced in March 1989, that EXIM's operations would be brought back inside the parliamentary arena under the Ministry of Economic Development and Trade; with the R & I Bank taking over the business migration scheme. The equity holdings were to go to WADC for disposal. In any case, EXIM ended up as the first sacrificial lamb for a general policy of corporatism that had gone terribly wrong in political and commercial terms.

Following the stockmarket crash of October, 1987, Laurie Connell's Rothwells Bank was on the verge of collapse. The government, in cooperation with Alan Bond, developed a rescue package to try and pull Rothwells back from the brink of collapse. The government's contribution to the package was to provide a guarantee of $150m to the National Bank of Australia so that loan backing could be provided to keep Rothwells going. As it turned out the rescue package was insufficient. The Bank failed and was placed in the hands of a provisional liquidator.

To make matters much worse, the Teacher's Credit Society in Perth, the largest credit union in Australia, had collapsed in August, 1987, and government representatives, in that instance, had also committed themselves to save the investments of depositors. In an agreement with the government-owned Rural and Industries Bank, the Teacher's Credit Society was totally absorbed by the bank and the government helped to pay for the losses incurred. According to the Minister for Budget Management, the total cost to the government of this endeavour was $125m plus $6m in interest and administrative expenses.

Therefore, when it became evident that Rothwells was not going to survive, the government, in order to prevent the massive political embarrassment of having the $150m guarantee called upon by the National Bank of Australia, concocted another deal with Alan Bond. In this deal, the $150m guarantee for Rothwells was transformed into a $175m 43.75% equity stake in a proposed petrochemical plant.

Petrochemical Industries Company Ltd. (PICL) was a joint venture between Laurie Connell, Rothwells founder and Dallas Dempster, one of the original founders of the Burswood Casino. Both Connell, as indicated above, and Dempster had been closely involved with the government in a number of business dealings. The transformation from Rothwells to PICL was based on a $400m payment to Connell and Dempster ($350m to Connell and $50m to Dempster) by the State

Government and the Bond Corporation. Of the $400m, the State Government put in $175m for its share in PICL as well as a commitment to provide cheap gas to make the project work, with Bond covering the rest. The money for the government's share was borrowed from the SGIC at 13.9% interest and channelled through Western Australian Government Holdings. Connell then used his $350m to buy a portfolio of Rothwells' non-performing debts and balance the books so the National Australia Bank would allow the State Government's guarantee to be retired. In this way the government appeared to have rid itself of any involvement with Rothwells. However, one ironic twist is that PICL, in January, 1989 had to pay four Local Shire Councils $3m on bills of exchange which matured at the end of December, 1988. The shires had invested in Rothwells and the investment was secured against PICL by Connell and Dempster. At the time of writing this chapter, lawyers for PICL were seeking repayment of the $3m from Connell and Dempster.

A review by First Boston Corporation of New York has indicated that PICL is a viable project with 100% debt funding at nominal interest rates of 13 to 15% for the $800m in construction costs, and once operational in the financial year 1992-93, the business will be more than worth the $400m price tag. Based on future sales and cash flow, the plant has been valued by Price Waterhouse at more than $1b. The catch is that the PICL project is only worth the purchase price and attractive to bankers because the government is involved. So government involvement raised the value of the project, which was then used as the basis for the share price paid by the government for its stake. Bond had only agreed to buy out Connell and Dempster on the understanding that the government would also take equity (Hewett & Loxley, 1988, p. 13). If the government finds it necessary to sell, then presumably the project would no longer be worth as much and the selling price would fall!

The questions, of a commercial nature, which remain include:

1. If the government pulled out of the project, would any of the world's major

petrochemical producers be interested in taking over the responsibility?

2. How is Western Australian Government Holdings to meet the annual $24.3m interest bill and the redemption payments to SGIC on its borrowings?

3. Will these payments be a future charge against revenues of the State?

4. What is the expected interest rate on the $800m required for construction costs?

5. Given a two year construction period and a nine year loan period, how long will it be before a cash return can be reasonably expected?

6. Exactly how much more (approximately) was paid to Connell and Dempster over and above fair compensation for work done to date on the project, given the fact that the government gave them an exclusive concession, at no cost, in 1986 to develop the plant?

7. What is the value of the gas subsidy promised PICL by the State Energy Commission?

8. What further liabilities will the government incur during the construction and start up period? For instance, it is known that the Bond Corporation will receive a management fee of $29m from PICL for managing the construction phase of the project. The environmental issue is also crucial to this question. Speculation has it that PICL will be prepared to fund a Workers' Health Centre in Kwinana as one of the conditions for union support of the project.

Most recently, it is the environmental issue, which has raised a great deal of citizen and trade union attention to questions of social benefit. After supporting the government's involvement in the PICL deal in October, 1988 by a vote of 91 to 41, the Trades and Labor Council had a rethink in December and called for full public inquiry into health and environmental safety at the proposed complex. The Trades and Labor Council junior vice-president, Claire Howell said that the inquiry should be taken out of the hands of the government because of its involvement in the project:

'The safety of the plant, and in particular the suitability of the proposed site, needs a much more thorough examination. The fact that the government has a major financial stake in the project suggests it is less than impartial on the issue.'

In response, Premier Dowding established a special task force to report directly to him on the environmental and safety questions.

The PICL project will manufacture the very hazardous intermediate products of Vinyl Chloride Monomer and Ethylene Dichloride, as well as the safe and inert plastic Poly Vinyl Chloride. The economic benefits are that the products will provide value-added returns to exports from the VCM and EDC products, and import substitutes for the alumina industry in the form of caustic soda; a valuable plastics industry would be created; and an enhanced range of technology as well as increased direct and indirect employment would be created. The negative effects include the health and safety risks involved in establishing the plant close to a large metropolitan area, as well as the possibility of worker subjection to carcinogenic materials and respiratory afflictions as part of their conditions of employment.

Finally, it should be remembered that the petrochemical industry on a global scale is continually affected by cycles of boom and bust. Prices for petrochemical products are presently increasing. For instance, ethylene was $US292 per tonne in April, 1987 and in early 1989 it was selling for $US725, which is a 150% increase in less than two years. However, within the past year there has been a rush of plans in newly industrialising countries such as Taiwan, Thailand and Korea to build petrochemical facilities; Malaysia, Indonesia, Canada and Saudi Arabia have finalised plans to establish their own petrochemical industries with the product mostly meant for export; and Mitsubishi has just signed a $9.6b deal with the Soviet Union to build a chemical production facility in Western Siberia (The West Australian, 9-12-88, p. 79). Singapore has a petrochemical industry, established as a $2b joint venture with Japan in 1978, which is now considered a major national liability due to the fact that it is unable to find sufficient markets for its products (Tzong-biau Lin, 1987, p. 176).

Upon reflection, corporatism in Western Australia has not been a success. Premier Dowding, continually referred to the fact that 'WA Inc. is now dead' in his pre-election speeches during January and February, 1989. Many of the previous activities, are now being placed under the control of various Ministers. EXIM has been abolished and WADC will cease all activity by September 30, 1989, subject to normal commercial requirements. Western Australian Government Holdings will become a statutory authority subject to accountability requirements, ministerial direction and scrutiny by the Auditor-General. It will be renamed the Western Australian Petrochemical Industries Authority. There will also be greater ministerial scrutiny of investment activity by the SGIC and the Superannuation Board. In making the announcement of closure of WA Inc., Premier Dowding said:

> 'In many ways it is unfortunate because we will lose a source of revenue and an ability to stimulate the commercial environment.'

The 'Rothwells saga' became a major economic and political embarrassment for the government and created the necessity for a distance between the government and its entrepreneurial allies. And while the transformation from Rothwells to PICL allowed the government to recover a large part of the taxpayer's funds, the re-investment of these same funds in a petrochemical industry appears at present to be a very risky enterprise. If and when PICL gets off the ground, one should not be too surprised if, given the possibility of further political embarrassment, the government tries to extricate itself from the project.

In March, the Premier, Mr Dowding dismissed Mr Kevin Edwards (another sacrificial lamb!) from his positions as executive co-ordinator of the PICL project and director of Western Australian Government Holdings on the basis that he had 'ceased to be beneficial to the government' (The West Australian, 11-3-89, p. 12). Mr Edwards had been one of the 'high fliers' in the Burke administration in establishing WA Inc. Under Burke, he was chief executive of the Department of Cabinet, deputy chairman of the State Government Insurance Commission and a member of the State Superannuation Board. Dowding had continued his status by appointing him as executive co-ordinator of the PICL project when it was originally established. The dismissal of Edwards flags the process by which the Dowding Government is attempting to move out of the shadow of WA Inc. and change direction (at least superficially) away from the legacy of his predecessor, Brian Burke.

It is also not yet clear that the government is totally free of major encumbrances. On March 30, 1989, the National Bank refused in the Queensland Supreme Court to support the plan of the provisional liquidator of Rothwells to see unsecured creditors get 100 cents on the dollar back from their investments. Under the scheme, 'mums and dads' would get paid in full, while major creditors would receive about 66 cents in the dollar. For this to occur the National Bank would have to return the $150m which is seen by the liquidator as a preference payment. If the National Bank is forced to pay the $150m back to the liquidator on the basis that it was given preferential treatment when Rothwells was known to be insolvent (which retired the government's guarantee of Rothwell's), the bank will surely call for reimbursement by the government. This amount will be added to the $20m which will have to be paid back by the State Government Insurance Corporation which is said, by the liquidator, to have received a preference payment from Rothwells; and the $40m of unsecured investments in Rothwells which was lost by government Instrumentalities in the 1987 crash. However, government representatives have argued that the original guarantee is no longer valid and that the government would be prepared to fight the matter in court.

In other words, most of the activity outlined above during the past six years has been unplanned, haphazard and ill-advised. It has not been an example to remember or recommend by proponents of 'corporatism'. However, Western Australia has not been alone in the corporatist fiasco. The Victorian Economic Development Corporation, for different reasons, but with similar results has been responsible for the loss of $105m of taxpayer's funds in 1987/88, the resignation of the Deputy Premier of Victoria in 1989, and a series of embarrassing criticisms of the role of government vis-a-vis corporatist ventures.

To some degree, the above problems can be explained away by the budgetary pressures created by the decline in Commonwealth funding which caused the unnecessary haste to restructure and consolidate government authorities in order to provide another revenue base. But more likely, when a government establishes close ties with capitalist entrepreneurs and is guided by their principles at the expense of social benefits carried forward by a well-considered policy of social planning with maximum participation, the resulting problems might be expected.

13.5.3 Asset Sales — The State Engineering Works

In 1913, the decision to establish an agriculture implement works at Rocky Bay resulted in the transfer and re-erection of all of the workshops, operated by the Public Works Department, at the new site in North Fremantle. Originally known as the State Implement Works, the institution primarily serviced the agricultural sector in the early years. It was the first enterprise in the State to make oil engines, ploughs, harvesters, seed drills, chaff-cutters, binders, cultivators, and among the first to make windmills, irrigation equipment and water well drilling machines. By 1922-23, agricultural parts and implements accounted for 50% of total sales, but by 1929, this figure had fallen to 20%. In 1926, the State Works invented and then manufactured the 'stump-jump' plough until the government sold the patent to a private manufacturing firm causing a major public scandal. It was only a year after the loss of the 'stump-jump' plough patent that the 370 workers were told that the Works had showed a $40,000 loss and the government of the day was threatening to close it down (Historical information for this section has been gathered from a variety of sources including the State Engineering Works Annual Reports; The Civil Service Journal, 18-4-86, p. 1; Wainwright, 1987, pp. 32-33).

In 1930, a restructuring took place. The Works became a major general engineering operation and foundry, primarily servicing the requirements of the various State Government departments. Throughout the first 17 years of the Works' existence support for its activities were based on a drive to replace interstate and overseas imports of engineered goods with local manufactures. In the 1930s, production was largely concerned with government orders for bulk wheat handling equipment, shipping repairs, State Steamship Services maintenance, heavy road construction machinery, harbour craneage and other machine equipment installation for government concerns. Agriculture implement work had declined to about 1% of sales by 1940.

During World War II, Allied naval activities in the South East Asian and Pacific war zones gave rise to a strong resurgence of trade at the Works. The production of Bren gun carriers, floating docks and propeller shafts for US submarines based at Fremantle, as well as emergency work in hospitals, airfields and harbours were only part of the new responsibilities for what was now known as the State Implement and Engineering Works. Post-war economic growth was associated with farmland and infrastructure development which stimulated demand for engineered products. Everything from wharf cranes and the merry-go-round at the zoo to the development of the new Wundowie charcoal, iron and steel works were handled by the Works production facility.

Growth of sales and profits continued in the 1950s in response to needs of government departments; and through the ability to manufacture specialised items outside the capability of local private engineering firms such as bulk handling equipment, heavy land clearing equipment, and marine overhaul and servicing, in addition to the regular work associated with water supply pipes and fittings. The value of the Works to the people of Western Australia was shown when in 1959, the government again threatened to curtail the activities of the Works based on a declared policy of removing government from business-oriented activities. However, within a matter of days the government realised the folly of its policy when it became obvious that the engineering capacity and jobbing services, which epitomised the Works, were not available from the local private sector.

Towards the end of the 1970s, a change in government purchasing methods began to occur. Departments and Instrumentalities began attempting to reduce costs by examining other sources of supply by 'contracting-out' through open tendering methods. The Works responded to the challenge and maintained its level of government business by competitive tendering at about 80% of turnover; but in doing so had to drastically reduce its cost/revenue margin.

In the early 1980s, a program of Works re-habilitation commenced. Over many years, profits generated by the SEW were paid into the Consolidated Revenue Fund at the direction of the Treasurer. This action, coupled with the traditional practice of depreciating assets on the historic cost basis, meant that the Works virtually made no provision for asset replacement until the mid-1970s. The rehabilitation exercise proved to be a lengthy one, principally due to the formalities required before commencement, the limited funds available, the need to avoid disruption of trading and the rapid changes in technology.

The first part of the modernisation program was the construction of a new foundry, which was completed in 1982/83. This put an end to an expensive and frustrating period of trying to operate foundry activities on two different sites and cleared the way for the demolition of the old and very unsafe foundry building. Progress was made with the replacement of high tension electric power supply lines and sub-stations; and a start was made on the conversion of patterns to suit the requirements of the new automatic mould-making system. Also, in 1982, the government decided that control of the Works under the State Trading Concerns Act and as an appendage to the Public Works Department was no longer appropriate. It was argued that this form of control may have been suited to the 'government's Workshop' image which surrounded the Works from the 1930s onwards, but was not suitable for a modern organisation serving and surviving in the more sophisticated and competitive industrial and commercial environment existing at that time. It was decided that steps should be taken towards the creation of a new body in the form of a statutory authority with full corporate powers and its own Board of Management.

With the subsequent change of government in the State from the Liberal/National coalition to Labor in 1983, the Interim Management Committee was endorsed and approval given for legislation to be drafted for the rest of the proposed Authority. With the legislation coming into effect, the Committee was replaced by a Board of Management and a new general manager was named on January 1, 1985. The State Implement and Engineering Works ceased to be and the State Engineering Works (SEW) was brought into existence. Management now believed that the most difficult stage had been completed: namely the replacement and modernisation of the foundry and the changing of management and employees' attitudes from a government workshop with a captive market in the public sector, to a commercially oriented environment in which the Works must lift its productivity, efficiency and economy of operation. Optimism was to be quickly dampened when almost immediately, in August, 1985, the State Government's Functional Review Committee initiated a review into the structure and viability of the SEW.

Between January and August, 1985, tremendous pressure was being brought to bear on the Labor Government to get rid of the SEW by both the Liberal/National Party Coalition which was, at the time, riding the crest of a popularity wave around the issue of 'privatisation'; and by representatives of private enterprise whom the government itself was wooing in the interest of its own commercial ventures.

A meeting was held by the Foundry Section of the Metal Industries Association of Western Australia at Confederation House on April 23, 1985. At that meeting, according to the Minutes, it was pointed out to the government in no uncertain terms that the government could best help the Foundry industry in difficult times by not competing with it through the SEW and the Midland Railway Shops. The meeting also made it clear that Statements by the Minister, that the government would not fund any deficits incurred by SEW foundry ventures, were not acceptable to the industry, as the SEW would be able to hide any losses in this area by book-keeping methods. It was then argued that the correct role for government would be to assist the Industry (in addition to the removal from the market-place of government-owned manufacturing enterprises), by funding a lobby to solicit business for Western Australian Foundries, provide incentives for marketing 'out of State', and give a reimbursement of certain costs and taxes.

While cause-effect is not proved by any means, it is a fact that the Functional Review Committee in August, 1985, concluded that:

'approval in principle be given for the disposal of the SEW, subject to preservation of employment for existing employees' (State Government Task Force Report, 1986, p. 1).

The tricky part was yet to come as the government was going to have to go to the polls in the following year and had to avoid looking to the trade unions as if it was caving in to the immense pressure coming from industry representatives and the opposition political parties. So, on September 23, 1985, Cabinet requested that a Task Force, including industry and trade union representatives, be established to assist in the restructure of SEW operations. The Task Force had eight members including the general manager of SEW, one union representative, a nominee for the Minister of Works, a nominee of the Deputy Premier, a representative of the Department of Industrial Development, a representative of EXIM, a representative of the Western Australian Foundry Industry Council, and was chaired by the Director of the Policy Secretariat of the Premier.

Of most concern to the unions involved at work in SEW, was the fact that while the Functional Review Committee was deliberating and shortly before the Task Force was established, the SEW reported a loss of $1.3m for the fiscal year 1984/85, which was the first reported loss in 30 years. The two reasons for this occurrence, according to union officials, was that the Fabrication industry is typically a cyclical industry and during the lead up to the closure it was in a trough of depression, which was part of the reason for the outspoken industry attacks on the SEW. Since the closure however,

the industry has recovered, and in 1989 there has been insufficient capacity in the State for the work required. The second reason was that the SEW was required to operate both commercially and as a government instrumentality, eg., doing the public sector work in which the private sector was not interested at a minimal rate. All the public sector work that was not profitable was still expected of the SEW (Information based on interviews with Alan Stafford, Foundry Sub-Branch Secretary of the Australian Society of Engineers, Moulders and Foundry Workers' Union and John Sharp-Collett, Assistant Secretary of the Amalgamated Metal Workers' Union, January, 1989).

In fact, the decline in profitability had begun in the early 1980s about the time that the new foundry was put in place. In 1982/83, net profit amounted to $308,506, down from the $398,565 recorded in 1981/82. Profits collapsed dramatically to $33,850 in 1983/84; and then in 1984/85 a loss of $1.3m was reported. Further losses of $642,000 and $936,000 respectively, were recorded for 1985/86 and estimated for 1986/87. The Task Force argued that without severe restructuring of the SEW, losses of $1m annually could be expected (Information extracted from various State Engineering Works Annual Reports and the State Government Task Force Report).

For their part, the unions were never opposed to restructuring, even to the point of accepting a tighter, integrated facility at a new location. In the submission by the trade unions to the Task Force, their recommendations and conclusions incorporated the following (Siddons, 1986):

1. The SEW must continue to exist as a publicly owned facility;
2. It should not continue to operate in its current form, halfway between a government department and an independent authority without an overall plan;
3. The workforce must be protected;
4. The SEW requires re-structuring into a facility based around the foundry, machine shop and fabrication areas. The foundry is the heart of SEW's future. Its uniqueness is best demonstrated by the fact that it was the only place in Australia able to cast the Aus-

tralia II keel, and was asked to cast other keels as well;

5. The management and administrative structure is too large and cumbersome for an integrated engineering facility;

6. The SEW has played one of the most important roles in the State in training young apprentices in the metal trades and this function must be preserved;

7. Although the new Act set up the SEW as a separate entity it still is tied to public service provisions, and a large superannuation debt was inherited which had been accumulated before the facility was made independent by the government which was devastating to cash reserves.

The Civil Service Association pointed out that although totally ignored by the Task Force, it was opposed to the closure or privatisation of the SEW; and made the case for the foundry as the most sophisticated in the southern hemisphere, thereby able to overcome short-term difficulties faced by all firms operating in the industry at very low capacity at that time (The Civil Service Journal, 18-4-86, p. 1).

The general manager of the Works, who took up his position in January, 1985, argued before the Task Force that the rot for the SEW had set in when an increasing number of government departments, (the Water Authority, Electricity Commission, Main Roads, Prisons and Agriculture and Forests Departments, Westrail, the Port Authority and the Buildings Maintenance Authority) all began expanding their own workshops from ones established as purely maintenance shops to those for fabrication and other work (Western Australian Business World, 1986, 4-5).

After due deliberation of all the submissions and information internally generated, the SEW Task Force brought down its recommendations for restructuring in May, 1986. Three options were spelled out:

(1) complete shutdown;
(2) retain the status quo; or
(3) re-establish the SEW as a profit-making company at a more appropriate location, sell off the land and dispose of any surplus assets to the private sector.

Although, quite alarmed by the deteriorating profitability and cash flow situation, the Task Force developed the third preferred option which was to relocate the foundry section to a new location where it would form the basis of a 'lean and hungry' company with a substantial reduction of the workforce and would incorporate the Westrail foundry orderbook. As the Committee saw it, given industry expansion during the 1960s and 1970s the services provided by the SEW were now available from the private sector; and by the 1980s the State Electricity Commission and the Water Authority of Western Australia (who together contributed on average 70% of the SEW work) had developed substantial in-house engineering and jobbing capability and had also embarked on a procurement policy of open tender. Together with having to compete for work that had been traditionally captive, thereby suffering major market erosion, the SEW would, in the future, be subject to increased costs. Except for the foundry, completed in 1982 at a cost of $1.5m, the other buildings were 70 years old, in poor condition, and the subject of adverse safety reports. Furthermore, the SEW Act, 1984, required the SEW to operate on commercial principles and to pay all local authority and government rates, charges and taxes as well as the full provision for the employers' share of superannuation liability. The superannuation burden alone was seen by the Task Force as totally incompatible with any concept of SEW functioning as an independent, self-funded and competitive organisation. After all of this, the SEW still had to pay 50% of any profits into the Consolidated Revenue Fund! (State Government Task Force Report, 1986, pp. 4-6 and 13).

Following the election, at the end of 1986, the government announced its decision to reject the Task Force's analysis, thereby accepting the original decision of the Functional Review Committee (initiating a great deal of cynicism amongst the trade union representatives with reference to the amount of time spent dealing with the Task Force during the previous year), to sell the foundry, re-deploy workers and develop the land for property development. The foundry was sold to Wigmores Tractors Pty. Ltd. (owned by Robert Holmes à Court company Bell Resources) in September, 1987 for $650,000, and henceforth transferred to Midland with 75 of the foundry and pattern-shop employees. In October, an auction for the remainder of the equipment took place and the buildings were demolished. Nineteen workers in the Fabrication shop were redeployed, most of them downwards because the retraining scheme didn't work; and the rest of the workers took retirement and/or severance pay. The land itself, was found to be contaminated and the sale had to be delayed until the site was cleaned up and the contaminated material removed (The Civil Service Journal 23-9-88, p. 3). Finally, in November, 1988 the 8.4 hectares, with a 500 metre frontage to the Swan River, were sold by the WADC to JIMWA Pty. Ltd., a property developer, for $12.4m. As late as April, 1989, the land was still sitting idle and vacant due to a decision by the Fremantle council to reject a proposal by the developer to establish a low density 'millionaire's row' housing sub-division.

The attempt by the unions to save industrial capacity not duplicated anywhere else in the State, the high quality and unique skills of all the workers (particularly those in the fabrication shop), and one of the major apprentice training centres in Western Australia, had failed, but not for lack of trying. Just before closure, clients of the SEW had required the provision of crushing equipment to the iron ore industry; pipes in iron, steel and plastic and irrigation metering equipment to the Water Authority; coal handling equipment to power stations; bridge beams and guard rails for highways; drilling equipment, quality cabinets and joinery to hospitals and schools; components for dams, harbours and defence services; and shipping repairs. All of the recipients of the SEW products and services would now have to look elsewhere.

The SEW could melt and pour more steel or alloys at one time than any other foundry in Western Australia. The size of the boiler shop, the size and layout of the fabrication area, and the heavy duty cranes meant that the SEW could handle heavy jobs which were not possible for any other foundry in Western Australia. Loss of the SEW meant the loss of a unique industrial capacity which has yet to be replaced by private enterprise.

13.5.4 Contracting Out Public Services
Department of Community Services and the
Authority for Intellectually Handicapped Persons

> ' "Contracting out" refers specifically to the purchase of an end product which could otherwise be provided "in-house" by the purchaser' (Ascher, 1987, p. 7).

The contracting out of public services to the private sector has existed on a small scale for many years in Western Australia, as was made evident in Case Study 2; and has probably been the most closely examined approach to privatisation in the world. However, other than solid waste collection, very few trials of contracting out have been adequately evaluated to permit government agencies to learn the conditions under which it may work (Hatry, 1983, p. 24). Its recent growth in popularity, like other forms of privatisation, is generally attributed to the ideological wave of fiscal conservatism which has characterised the rebellion against 'big government' in many industrialised nations in the West, rather than to any scientific analysis of its benefits.

The objective of contracting out, as normally stated in most privatisation exercises, is to introduce greater competition, thereby improving the efficiency of service delivery and reducing the cost to the public. Competition is seen as important in circumscribing the extent of Leibenstein's notion of 'X-inefficiency', which describes the failure of firms (or governments) to make maximum use of inputs in producing a given level of output (Leibenstein, 1966, pp. 392-415). Other objectives may include the lack or inadequacy of in-house expertise, the need to reduce overheads, greater administrative convenience or the need to increase flexibility to respond to changes in market conditions (Ascher, 1987, p. 8). But, unlike several other forms of privatisation, contracting out does not signal an end to public sector control, because the State agencies continue to both plan and finance the services involved, although opponents argue that indirect delivery reduces accountability, democratic control, and the quality of the service.

In the case studies below, it appears that the State's purpose for contracting out the specific services indicated was multi-faceted, including cost-effectiveness, greater administrative convenience, and in particular, the need to increase flexibility in the workforce. However, in general, as well as in the instances cited below, governments normally fail to include in the cost-effectiveness equation, the relevant costs associated with the tendering process, including both administrative and transitional costs. The administrative costs, which include the opportunity costs of personnel undertaking tasks associated with individual tendering exercises, are considerable. Transitional costs associated with terminating in-house provision and the commencement of the new private contractors have also been significant as will be shown.

Other than the obvious opportunity and transitional costs not included in the cost-effectiveness equation of contracting out, O.E. Williamson has identified five qualitative situations in which the internal provision of a service offers significant advantages over contracting in the market, even where it is found to be a less cost-effective option (Williamson, 1975, as cited in Ascher, 1987, pp. 254-256):

1. Where flexible sequential decision-making is needed to cope with uncertainties in the environment;

2. Where only a small number of competitors are present, and there is a likelihood of opportunistic and predatory pricing behaviour;

3. Where a divergence of expectations is likely to occur between the internal purchaser and the external seller;

4. Where operational or technological information gained from experience is likely to give one external supplier a strategic advantage over all others, thereby reducing competition;

5. Where a transaction-specific 'calculative relation' between parties is inappropriate and 'quasi-moral involvement' between those supplying and organising the service is necessary to effective provision.

Since we are speaking below of the provision of contracted services by non-profit organisations, the connection to the points raised by Williamson is not perfectly relational; but the reader will immediately be aware of the fact that numbers 1, 3 and 5 are relevant to the relationship between the non-profit organisation as seller and the government as purchaser of the contracted services discussed.

Finally, all government representatives should keep in mind the story attributed to John Glenn when he returned from the first human space flight which is decidedly relevant to the process of open tendering or contracting out.

'A reporter asked what was the biggest danger in space travel. Supposedly, Glenn answered that it was being hundred of miles above the earth in a ship made up of 50,000 component parts, each purchased from the lowest bidder' (Wesemann, 1981, p. 59).

Department of Community Services
It was pointed out by the State Government Minister of Community Services in August, 1988, that during the fiscal year 1988/89, a much bigger part was to be played by non-government agencies in providing welfare services. During the year, of the total $101.4m allocated to the Department of Community Services, $23.3m (23%) was to be directed to non-government groups (The West Australian 31-8-88, p. 20).

As part of this effort, a pilot project was announced for the tendering of an Employment and Training Support Program by the Minister for Community Services. This program would assist young repeat offenders to find suitable employment or training and provide them with intensive follow-up support to help them retain their employment or training positions. The Department of Community Services (DCS) allocated the sum of $250,000 to any reputable group which could show that they were able to provide a program for young offenders which satisfied the Department's selection criteria (The YMCA ended up to be the successful tenderer for the contract). As part of the contract, over and above the $250,000, DCS would make available a liaison officer from the Department; departmental staff and facilities for the training of personnel involved in the program; the premises known as Watson Lodge and all necessary office furniture to accommodate the administration; as well as pay the water and shire rates and the electricity.

In return, during the year, 250 males and females between the ages of 15 to 18 were to be assisted within the program. The agency was to employ 1 co-ordinator, six employment placement officers and clerical support staff from monies in the allocated grant. Staff were to be contracted for 12 months with no guarantee that the contract would be extended as the funds were fixed and non-recurrent with no guarantee of funding after the first year.

The activity contracted out to the YMCA had been a part of the total responsibility of 'Group Workers' and After-care Officers employed within the public service at three hostels located in the city, one of which was Watson Lodge. The hostels had been closed in early 1988, with 3 'After-care Officer' and 5 'Group Worker' positions being abolished as items on the payroll and the people transferred to other duties. In fact, what happened at Watson Lodge is that, of the seven positions to be filled by the YMCA, five were filled by seconded Group Workers on yearly contract. The internal positions remain lost and when these people return to the Department they will fill different positions. But it is important to note that Group Workers were more than capable of filling the roles required by the YMCA and DCS duty Statement for the contract, as they had been doing much the same work previously, as well as fulfilling other responsibilities. Relatively high administrative and transitional costs had been incurred by the Department to have the work done by almost exactly the same group of people that had been doing the work previously.

Concurrently, let us keep in mind the qualitative points raised by Williamson above in situations where the internal provision of services may offer significant advantages over contracting out even if they are less cost-effective. An internal report was circulated within the Department in August, 1987 which made the following points:

'Watson Lodge is staffed by 5 Group Workers, who offer a life skills program to youths, facing difficulties at work, school or alternative activity options. Activities also include a weekly group for the young women who are pregnant or mothers. Most of the adolescents require intensive input and individual attention.'

'The two major problems with the change-over to a non-government agency in terms of services provided include: teenage girls who are pregnant and/or mothers and having difficulty managing their young children; and Aboriginal adolescents who will experience greater discrimination. Watson Lodge is very popular with Aboriginal teenagers because of its structure.'

'Group Workers, supported by other professional staff, are seen to be the best qualified people for the work required. They have been selected for their abilities in understanding and relating to adolescents and have been trained to work with difficult behaviours. The terms of their employment also allow for flexible rostering so that teenagers and their caregivers can be provided assistance 24 hours a day, seven days a week as needed. Generally, they are practically oriented people who prefer to work directly with clients and are prepared to spend large amounts of time doing this. There is also readily available within the system a clinical psychologist, senior social worker, occupational therapist, teacher, and psychologist/social worker administrators who provide supervision.'

'Job rotation is recognized by the Department (Human Resources Policy and Procedures Manual) as a method of improving work skills, preventing stagnation and stress, increasing morale and accommodating personal needs. If the hostels are closed opportunities for rotation would be drastically reduced with consequent negative results.'

To begin with it is evident that the Program was being discussed and formulated with no consultation at all with the workers or the Civil Service Association. It was not until the tendering process had begun that the union became aware of the implications, and to no avail, expressed its concern to the Director of Human Resources in September, 1988.

Without more information, which is not forthcoming, it is not entirely clear that DCS has reduced total costs in the above situation. It is clear that the decision provides greater flexibility in the labour force in that funding requirements for much the same work has been changed from tenured employees in the public service to contract employees hired on a yearly basis. And it is most likely that given the fact that at least 8 positions have been lost in the shuffle at this one hostel, that natural attrition will reduce the salary requirement at some point in the future.

In qualitative terms, it does appear according to the internal memo that working conditions for all Group Workers have been reduced; the functions of the hostels have been reduced in that they no longer fill the role of specific assistance to young pregnant women or mothers, nor does the hostel structure exist which was previously so popular with Aboriginal teenagers; the focus of attention is on employment and training which omits the previous functions of assistance with school or alternative activities; and the impressive professional support structure of psychologists, therapists and teachers is no longer available. In view of the above, even if costs have been reduced overall for the DCS (which has not been shown), it is not necessarily due to a greater level of efficiency in the delivery of services at all, but rather the omission of a number of direct and indirect services to young people, as well as reduced working conditions for the staff. To reiterate the introduction to this particular case, this is only one small example of the tendering process in the Department which has allocated $23.3m overall to these types of activities.

Authority for Intellectually Handicapped Persons
Another interesting case study, within the realm of this form of privatisation, is the hybrid 'voluntarist-contracted out seed' of Project Employment Personnel (PEP), which was planted in the Western Australian Authority for Intellectually Handicapped Persons (AIHP). In February, 1984 Project Employment Personnel

was established, and then incorporated in August of the same year as a non-profit association offering open employment opportunities for persons with disabilities of any type or severity.

Three professionals working for AIHP set up PEP (on a voluntary basis) in response to the relative paucity of vocational training programs for this particular population. The only other program then in existence was the Work Preparation Program operated by the Commonwealth Department of Community Services; but this organisation only catered for those individuals who were mildly disabled. PEP developed a program that was equally applicable and available to those persons with severe intellectual disabilities and was the only such service in Australia. According to representatives of PEP, the challenge is in locating a job which approximates the individual's abilities and interests. The closer the job match, the less training resources that will be expended. Similar work had been carried out by the professionals and social trainers within AIHP, but no where near to the extent envisaged as necessary by the sponsors of PEP.

While PEP had its origins within the Authority for Intellectually Handicapped Persons, it is now a separate incorporated body with which the Authority maintains close links and provides major funding. In fact, the Director of AIHP himself, worked very hard to get PEP Commonwealth funds as well as exemptions from guidelines of Commonwealth funding groups, not always successfully, it might be added. In June, 1986, PEP got off the ground with grants from the State Department of Employment and Industrial Relations of $29,218 and the Commonwealth Department of Social Security. In 1987, funds were also received from the Commonwealth Departments of Employment, Education and Training and Community Services and Health ($150,000).

From the very beginning AIHP agreed to provide State assistance to PEP, both to get it started, and to provide organisational credibility in applying for Commonwealth assistance. AIHP allocated 8 Social Trainer staff full-time to PEP as part of the deal with an increase anticipated with success over time. The formula used, and applied on a yearly basis, was one Social Trainer for each 5 workers placed in employment. No limit was placed on the time that AIHP staff would participate. Also, AIHP provided an eight-room house, with three installed telephone lines, for office space and agreed to meet all rates, taxes and insurance accruing on the premises. The total value of AIHP's 'in-kind' contribution was calculated at $145,000.

In the first year of operation as an 'independent', incorporated body the projected budget was $290,024, one-half of which came from the Western Australian Government through AIHP. At present, the 1988/89 funding is as follows: AIHP contributes $324,000; the Commonwealth Department of Community Services and Health $180,000; and a further Commonwealth Government grant of $120,000; the total being $624,000 of which AIHP contributes over one-half. In return, PEP has 670 people on their register, from which 220 employment placements have been made on award wages. It is calculated that this has saved the taxpayer up to $15,000 per person annually in unpaid pensions, unemployment benefits and subsidies, not to mention the taxes paid by the workers themselves. On the other hand placing and maintaining an intellectually disabled person is costing approximately $4,800 per person. Of course, it is now a matter for conjecture as to whether or not the calculated savings would be any greater or less if the service was provided by AIHP internally rather than subsidised (contracted out) by AIHP and Commonwealth funds.

In the years before sufficient funding was available, the professional staff of AIHP — two psychologists and a occupational therapist — were carrying out their work for PEP in addition to allocated duties in their respective paid positions; and field support was provided by the AIHP Social Trainers. A management committee was selected to provide competent management for PEP in order to gain access to funding in order to provide autonomy. It so happens that Brian Burke, then Premier of Western Australia was Chairman of the management committee.

Ultimately, it was the view of the Director of AIHP that the three professionals could not carry out their duties and their volunteer work

for PEP in the long term. Therefore, the Director and the professionals pursued 'outside' funding to establish the operations in facilities external to AIHP.

With the establishment of PEP 'the three professionals became the Managing Director, Job Support Manager and Job Search Manager of the new non-profit, non-government agency at a total salary cost of $110,000, with the 8 Social Trainers, and office facilities being provided on loan by AIHP. The Commonwealth Funds provided the operating expenses of the organisation. In 1986, the Social Trainers resigned from AIHP and joined the permanent staff of PEP. At a later date, three Assistant Managers, a Technical Advisor, and Administrative Assistant and four additional Social Trainers were added to the staff. Overall, at present there are twenty positions lost to the public service and transferred to a non-profit organisation — positions and people which could have provided the service from within AIHP.

As in the previous case study, with reference to the State Department of Community Services, it is difficult to identify the total real cost-effectiveness in the decision to transfer a partial function of AIHP into a separate agency, which in this instance, did not even have to tender to get the business. While cost reduction for the State may have had something to do with the decision to establish PEP, given the transfer of 8 Social Trainers and 3 professional positions out of the public service, it appears that administrative convenience in order to increase the possibility of funding for an important service was a major factor in the decision. Manifestly, a decision was made within the Authority to emphasise and increase one particular aspect of its operations which appeared to be in great demand within the community. This could only be accomplished by devising a method whereby the service would be granted a substantial subsidy (approximately 50%) by the Commonwealth Government. By applying for grants as an 'independent' enterprise with State backing, the Commonwealth Government would look favourably upon the enterprise and provide the assistance required. That is, a very specialised scheme to assist intellectually handicapped people was devised by the group of professionals within AIHP. Since total funding of the activity was approximately twice what AIHP could afford at the time given the fiscal constraints of the State, it was decided, with support at 'the highest levels' in the State, to cut the scheme away from the State public service and get the Commonwealth to provide a share of the necessary funding. The entire affair ended up as a quite ingenious, but complex way for the State to replace the loss of funds brought about by the decline in Commonwealth Government contributions to the Consolidated Revenue Fund. There is also an engaging lesson here in attempting to delineate the blurred line of demarcation between 'subsidisation' and 'contracting out' of public services in this peculiar example of 'privatisation'.

13.5.5 Volunteer' Labour: School Assistants and the Western Australian Department of Education

A 'Volunteer' is defined as:

'a person who, on a regular basis, contributes services without receiving remuneration commensurate with the economic value of the services rendered. Volunteer work fulfils an essential economic and ideological function for the State in providing social welfare services which could be paid for by governments. These functions become of crucial importance during times of economic crisis when governments reduce welfare spending and the voluntary sector is placed under considerable pressure to increase services in these welfare areas' (Baldock, 1983, pp. 279-280).

But it is only very recently that attention has been directed to the contribution made by unpaid, non-domestic labour to capitalist social formations (See for instance Redclift & Mingione [Eds.], 1985; as well as Baldock & Mulligan, 1987).

Baldock makes the valid, and obvious point pertinent to this particular case study, that volunteer work is only able to satisfy the changing and ever-increasing demands made upon voluntary agencies, (or in this instance the State Government), because of the avail-

ability of unpaid female volunteers who combine volunteer labour with other unpaid work, namely that carried out in the domestic setting. Because much of the social service volunteer work is also labelled 'caring work'; and present government priorities seem increasingly to shift responsibility for provision of many of the services in this sector back to private and community/family provision, the distinction between community provided charity and individual rights as citizens to minimum community standards, is befogged to say the least (Roberts, 1988).

In a survey carried out by the School Assistants, and analysed in this particular study, the euphemism regularly used by respondents to describe the volunteers was 'mothers'. This should prompt us to keep in mind that a 'double-edged sword' exists in this distinctive case study. On the one hand, community involvement in schools, particularly primary schools, is generally seen as something which should be commended. This is one of the reasons for P & C Committees which provide a great deal of volunteer assistance to schools across Australia. Altruism is seen as a desirable human trait and has been recognised as such by the Department of Education, the School Assistants and the Civil Service Association in this particular dispute. Moral pressure does exist and is exercised by various authorities in order to get citizens to donate their labour time freely for the benefit of their children, the school, the neighbourhood, the community, etc. However, again as Baldock makes clear, given the structure and ideology of patriarchy, it seems logical to assume that only women, and especially married women, have the characteristics which guarantee their availability for regular volunteer work; and altruism, the alleged basic requirement for volunteer work, is commonly assumed to be a typical feminine trait (Baldock, 1983, p. 289).

Finally, the last point to remember regarding this complex area of unpaid labour, is that many of the paid School Assistants were themselves, at one time, volunteers. They became concerned, and took union action, against volunteers in this instance, because an increased use of unpaid labour by the schools was coincident with a cutback by the Department of Education in hours of paid time worked by School Assistants. While the paid labour time and wages of School Assistants were declining, they almost insultingly, were also being asked to supervise the volunteer labour being welcomed into the schools by the Ministry of Education and Headmasters to do the work of School Assistants for free.

In the State school system there are about 1,500 School Assistants. Their jobs are divided into three classes:

Class 1 designated for typist receptionist;
Class 2 for Library Aid;and
Class 3 for Registrars.

The salary scales range from $14,767 to $16,306 for Class 1; $16,819 to $18,331 for Class 2; and $18,935 to $20,213 for Registrars. There is no promotional or career structure. Up until 1983, many of the Library Aid jobs were done by volunteers and many of these volunteers were hired at that time as School Assistants. Historically, there does seem to be a de facto system in schools that when a School Assistant position becomes vacant, the longest serving and/or 'most competent' volunteer is in line for the job.

The current primary and secondary staffing formula for non-teaching staff was the subject of a review by the Education Department in 1984. The review found that the present formula lacked detail, was inadequately flexible and was insufficient to cover the variations in demand for service, within and between the State schools. The conclusions and recommendations of the Committee were never acted upon. The result is that a staffing formula is in existence which was designed decades ago to meet the needs of an education system which was quite different from what prevails today. Consequently, schools are inadequately staffed and under resourced, even though more is expected from the system in terms of both the range of services offered and the quality of output expected (State School Teacher's Union, Western Australia, 1988).

In November, 1987, the Director of Human Resources of the Education Department sent the following notice to a number of School Assistants in schools which 'exceeded their entitlement to School Assistant Library time'. It read in part:

'In accordance with the provisions of the Education Department Ministerial Officers Salaries, Allowances and Conditions Award 1983, one month's notice of variation of contract is given and will be effective from January 28, 1988. Regrettably therefore, it will be necessary to reduce your hours of employment per fortnight.'

Shortly, after that variation came into effect in 1988, the Ministry of Education suggested volunteers as a way of relieving the situation of overwork for the School Assistants. In other words, it wasn't that there was insufficient work for the School Assistants whose labour time was being reduced. To the contrary, the work load for School Assistants in the libraries was increasing at a very rapid rate, but was given a low priority by the Ministry in circumstances under which the State budget was being tightened.

A survey of 121 School Assistants carried out by the union discovered that unpaid hours were worked by 74% of the respondents, and 76% had volunteer assistance. Seventy-five per cent of the School Assistants had experienced an increase in their workload in recent years and felt that increased staff or working hours was essential to improve the work situation (Civil Service Association, 1988).

By the middle of the year, however, the situation had become totally out of control. At one school there were 13 volunteers to one library School Assistant (Minsie, 1988, pp. 10-11). At Kingsley Primary, '10 mothers averaged 17 hours per fortnight volunteer labour while the School Assistant was hired for 13'. East Maddington had '13 mothers working unpaid for 27 hours per fortnight and the School Assistant was employed for 19½ hours'.

In the survey, one of the School Assistants was quoted as saying:

'I have to turn to my 81 year old father (who is an ex-school teacher) at times in order to catch up with my work. The school only allows me to work 13 hours per fortnight. I'm not doing a satisfactory job as I just don't have enough time to perform all that is expected of me. I try to keep the displays interesting and the children and teachers happy but I'm finding it very difficult to do so'.

Another School Assistant, who worked 33 hours per fortnight for pay and 5 hours per fortnight unpaid overtime said:

'I have been extremely lucky. My resource teachers have been hard working and our mothers are a responsible and happy lot. It does take a lot of thought and planning to ensure there is enough work for mothers to do while they are here'. This school received 30 hours per fortnight unpaid volunteer time!

Of the primary schools sampled, they received, on the average, volunteer help of about 15 hours per fortnight; and at two-thirds of the schools, School Assistants averaged 4 hours per fortnight of unpaid overtime. Remember that the salary range for the position of Class 1 and 2 School Assistants is $14,767 to $18331. Using an average salary of $17,000 or $654 per fortnight; and assuming overtime paid at time-and-a-half; then on average, according to data provided by the survey, each school received $262 in unpaid volunteer time and $105 in unpaid overtime each fortnight. Over the year for 570 primary schools this amounts to a total subsidy of approximately $5.4m in unpaid labour time to the State by 'mothers' and School Assistants.

Time is the key factor in running an efficient resource centre (primary school) or library (high school). Duty Statements could not be carried out in the time allocated before the cuts took place, much less after, with regard to activities such as maintenance, repairs, catalogue preparation, library displays and stock checking. Schools used to include a librarian or school teacher in the library to be with the school assistant. In many schools this is no longer the case. When the school does not have a resource teacher the School Assistant is expected to run the centre and make important supervisory decisions when children are sent to the centre to do research. All the while the workload continues to increase and cover a wider spectrum from the technical to the psychological, as the centre now not only houses books, but also teacher resources, video equipment, games, audio-visual equipment, computers and software; as well as the School Assistants being required to run book club fairs and provide awards to the children for excellence and diligent behaviour in the library.

On July 25, 1988 the Secretary of the Civil Service Association, on behalf of the School Assistants, notified the Ministry of Education that:

'while recognising the valuable contribution of volunteers in schools, the CSA does not sanction their use in performing work normally done by our members. The use of volunteers has now reached an unacceptable level, posing a real threat to the security of our members' jobs in the future. The problem arises from inadequate staffing formulas which do not allow proper school administration without voluntary assistance. Therefore, our members will have adopted a policy of non-cooperation with volunteers and will not do any work outside the scope of their normal duties; will not work overtime or take work home to complete.'

This position was supported wholeheartedly by officers of the State School Teacher's Union who accused the Ministry of using volunteers as a substitute for employing paid staff; and who directed their members not to undertake any work that has been declared black by the CSA in the School Assistants work to rule campaign (The Western Teacher, 9-9-88, p. 3).

In response, the Chief Executive Officer of the Ministry of Education wrote the Secretary of the CSA on August 4 stating:

'Schools are seeking volunteers presumably to assist the school assistants who are under pressure. To refuse help to these volunteers to acquire the training to make their assistance productive, is inimical to the interests of the people who are invoking the bans. By imposing bans school assistants increase the pressures on themselves and force schools to increase their reliance on volunteer staff.'

The interesting, but convoluted logic provided here by the Chief Executive Officer, that School Assistants were responsible for their stress and the increasing workload because they would not train or supervise people who were doing their work for free, at the instigation of the Department of Education, should not require further comment.

Immediately following the union announcement of the 'work to rule' campaign, the Ministry of Education carried out a Staffing Formulae Review to identify problems within the school system. Submissions to the review committee indicated 'pressure point' areas which should be addressed immediately. Of top priority was a 20% increase in classroom teaching staff. Next came the School Assistants for which a 15% increase was suggested (Ministry of Education, 1988). The government acted on the review at the end of 1988 by suggesting an increase in the full-time equivalents of School Assistant positions by 150 in 1989.

The Civil Service Association did not believe that this new staffing formula (which was related to the number of teachers rather than the number of students) solved the workload and staffing problems. Given 570 primary schools and 150 secondary schools in the State, the increased staffing, divided up equally amongst the schools, adds up to approximately one-fifth of a full-time equivalent School Assistant per school. However, in the spirit of compromise, the union agreed to the numbers in November, 1988, on the condition that the additional time allocated be offered first to current staff so that volunteer workers would not be rewarded by employment; that the allocation be on the basis of need; and that schools with laboratories be given priority.

In any case, the work to rule decision remained in effect in a number of schools at the beginning of the 1989 school year, but the militancy tended to decline over the summer months. The hesitant agreement by the Civil Service Association to the limited amount of additional resources provided by the government for 1989, has provided a hiatus, not a solution to the predicament faced by School

Assistants. It is very possible that the dispute will continue to boil and the School Assistants will again take action this school year.

Volunteer or charitable work for one's community is a praiseworthy act. But the State must not manipulate the community, so that certain vulnerable groups such as 'mothers' and 'dedicated School Assistants' are providing important social services for free, in order to solve a fiscal crisis. Baldock and May (1985) wrap up their analysis of unpaid labour very succinctly:

'It would be a retrograde step if government assumed that many welfare functions could be left to undemanding female volunteers while resources for paid work were directed elsewhere. Clearly, the social implications of volunteerism are complex. To say for instance, that work now voluntary should be paid, would be to ignore the grassroots practicalities and financial realities involved, not to mention the actual preferences of some groups and individuals. However, we feel that government policy makers need to be aware of the ramifications of having a substantial part of the welfare burden born by unpaid workers.'

13.6 Public Sector Renewal in Western Australia
13.6.1 Introduction
Renewal of the Western Australian public sector will require a resolution of funding uncertainties. It also requires a more considered and deliberate use of the public sector in State social and economic development. Such an approach must encompass a vision of organisational reform for public sector agencies, which might, for example, build upon the already extensive efforts of the Civil Service Associations award restructuring program.

13.6.2 Economic Strategy
In this section reform proposals are advocated which represent a significant change in direction from present State Government economic policy. In the space and time available, detailed blue-prints for change are not offered. Rather, the principles upon which reforms should be based are elucidated, and the chief insti-

tutional and policy mechanisms for bringing about change are outlined.

In Sections 13.2 and 13.5 the State Government's economic strategy was subjected to detailed scrutiny. An alternative approach to economic development involves targeting assistance and intervention to sectors where higher value added and net export growth could be expected. Such an approach should also involve in the case of Western Australia, a regional development program where the economic potential of disadvantaged communities and regions is maximised. The principles of a strategy along these lines should include:

- protecting and creating employment and skills;
- investment in production processes with a long-term perspective in mind, and in the interests of regional economic development.

The vehicle for the pursuit of these goals are Regional Economic Development Boards (REDB), located in strategically relevant sub-regions of the State, funded from the Consolidated Revenue Fund or Loans Fund, and subject to the accountability provisions contained in the Financial and Audit Act (1985). The policy instruments which the REDBs are expected to avail themselves of include:

- the provision of financial assistance through equity, loans and loan guarantees to existing and new small to medium sized firms, made conditional on pre-commitments to further training, investment or Research and Development goals. Such pre-commitments to be negotiated in advance between employers, Trade Unions and/or Community group representatives;
- to subject investment projects to social accounting methods of rate of return appraisal, whereby the net return should include the lost rate income, increased social services and foregone tax revenues which would have accrued if the investment was not made;
- the creation of information and technology networks based on modern communications and data processing technology.

Each network specialises in a given region, with firms and public agencies being paid a fee to supply information on their identity, major product lines and investment projects for which they seek a specified list of inputs. The networks aim to reduce the transaction costs associated with firms or public agencies identifying suitable trading partners and market opportunities, thereby facilitating the co-ordination of investment within the State's sub-regions, and enhancing the local multiplier effects of investment projects. Users of the network would be charged a fee, and provisions preventing the breach of commercial confidentiality would be needed.

- where return on investment is possible without jeopardising the broader social and economic goals of State development such funds should be returned to the development program.

It is evident from the stipulated objectives and policy instruments of this approach, that the thrust of the strategy is to promote economic development. Instead of relying on the uncertain and poorly targeted 'trickle-down' effects of the investment activities of Western Australia's 'hybrid' enterprises, the REDBs embody a 'bottom-up' notion of intervention which directly seeks to release the States resources and skills.

Though the Boards are expected to make investments in existing and new firms, their activities should not be granted autonomy from State executive and legislative scrutiny. While this requirement might impair short-run flexibility, this must be viewed as an inevitable and desirable consequence of the implicit and explicit public obligations of the REDBs. In short, the REDBs are not expected to act as a purely commercial undertaking, nor to have a relationship with government which is akin to that between shareholders and private companies. Such an arrangement provides the basis of a coherent model of public sector activity in which different functions are linked to a general social and economic strategy but remain relatively autonomous in their operations. More detailed comments on these issues of accountability are offered in the following section, where we discuss the relationship between government and public trading enterprises (PTEs).

The Relationship Between Government and PTEs
In Western Australia we can draw a distinction between two types of PTE. First, those utilities occupying natural monopoly positions and/or possessing statutory monopoly rights eg. Western Australian State Electricity Commission. These enterprises' relationship with government is defined by the Financial and Audit Act (1985), and ensure that corporate strategy is subject to Ministerial approval and Parliamentary scrutiny. Whilst accountability provisions are satisfactory, the control mechanisms whereby the social and economic efficiency of these enterprises is furthered, requires discussion. Second, those entities that were labelled 'hybrid' enterprises in Section 13.3 (ie. WAGH, WADC, EXIM and GBC), which have been created as vehicles to further the State Government's corporatist strategy. These corporations are not subject to the accountability provisions contained in the Financial and Audit Act (1985), and in all but one case, are incorporated under the Companies (Western Australian) Code. Serious accountability issues are evident in respect of these corporations, and their future status must be examined given the changed role of the public sector envisaged in this document.

The 'Hybrid' Enterprises
The present relationship between government and the 'hybrid' enterprises is akin to that between shareholders and private companies. As has been dealt with at length in Sections 13.1 and 13.3, the lack of accountability, interpenetration of government and business and the privileges and immunities of these enterprises is unacceptable. Furthermore, the shareholder − private company relationship is flawed as a model for government − PTE relationships as there are a number of important features which distinguish the latter relationship, and which warrant more stringent monitoring and policing provisions;

− unlike shareholders who voluntarily take an equity stake in private companies, and

can relinquish this stake, the shareholders in PTEs (taxpayers) are 'locked in'. The principle of accountability to Parliament, as the electorate's representatives, should then be observed;
− whilst the 'hybrid' enterprises have profit as their primary objective, there are duties and obligations which their boards must meet and which are intrinsic to the quasi-public nature of these enterprises. The executive and legislative must be seen to discharge their responsibility to monitor and police the fulfillment of these obligations;
− the executive's position in relation to PTEs is compromised by conflict between regulatory responsibilities and their commercial interest in the profitability of PTEs. Parliamentary scrutiny and the independence and powers of the State Government Auditor General, serve as a check on any inclination of the executive to use PTEs as a source of short term revenue gain, for reasons of political expediency and to the detriment of social obligations.

The obvious response is to make the 'hybrid' enterprises subject to the Financial and Audit Act, as advocated by the Burt Commission. This will be problematic as the management of these enterprises have been accustomed to an autonomy which has enabled them to develop the businesses along commercial lines, free from the government interference normally associated with PTEs. They are likely to view this development with concern, as their roles will be perceived as much more circumscribed than has been the case. Some erosion of morale and loss of personnel can be anticipated. Furthermore, the future role envisaged for State Government economic policy entails intervention and assistance in disadvantaged regions/communities. A gradual winding-down, perhaps involving the floating of the more commercial ventures, would be the most sensible approach as it would facilitate the funding of REDBs which now become the important vehicles of State Government economic policy.

As described in Sections 13.1 and 13.3, the Labour Government has begun to wind-down the operation of the 'hybrid' enterprises, whilst ensuring that what remains will be subject to the Financial and Audit act. Whilst these moves are to be applauded, an alternative approach to economic development has yet to emerge. We advocate serious consideration of the proposals outlined above.

(i) Public utilities
The political scrutiny which PTEs are subject to, and which limits their autonomy, is not in itself a bad thing, indeed it is desirable in the context of public utilities. A primary rationale behind public ownership, accountability and control of utilities is that of preventing private or public exploitation of the monopoly powers possessed by utilities such as electricity, gas and water. To relax or remove those accountability and control procedures is to abrogate the duties of government in this regard. In addition, the public utilities have a crucial developmental role to play in the State's economy, and a control environment is necessary to foster this role.

In practice, the government and PTEs relationship is characterised by an unavoidable and uneasy compromise between:

— a control environment that stimulates efficient production;
— accountability to ministers, Parliament, the workforce and customers;
— simultaneous fulfillment of financial targets and social and economic development obligations.

In Australia and overseas PTE managements have experimented with marginal cost pricing rules, discounted cash flow methods of investment appraisal, external financing limits, target rates of return and price-productivity formulae (See Part Five). Social obligations can be many and varied but have rarely been explicitly and tangibly incorporated in the performance goals of PTEs (See Part Four). With the exception of the hybrid enterprises discussed earlier, accountability procedures have been based on the Westminster model, and remain so.

The management of PTEs and suggestions for its reform are extensively discussed in Part Five of this book. Here we outline a few comments that relate to the Western Australian

experience concerning the recent fashion of stressing financial performance and rate of return targets. Whilst frequently justified on the grounds of stimulating efficient production, the imposition of rate of return targets can have spurious validity on these grounds, as the monopoly powers of public utilities enable them to meet targets by cuts in output and increases in prices which are unaccompanied by gains in productivity. Indeed, the motives which spawned 'hybrid' enterprises can also play a role in pushing rate of return targets into a prominent position in the control environment. The Public Account Dividend (PAD) is a potentially fruitful source of revenue to the Consolidated Revenue Fund (CRF), though this once again rests on the tenuous assumption of additionality.

Critics of the use of Rate of Return targets and PADs to augment the CRF have referred to the practice as implicit taxation. Instead of aligning these magnitudes alongside the investment requirements and social obligations of PTEs, the implicit tax practices 'milks' the PTEs as source of revenue dictated by the demands of the CRF account. There are potentially serious economic consequences which deserve attention:

— unless realised by improvements in productive efficiency, implicit taxes must involve rising public utility charges and/or cutbacks in service. As the goods or services supplied by utilities are generally regarded as necessities, the impact is regressive.

— government charges for supplies to industry amounted to $13b in 1980-81, which is 6% of total industry costs (IAC, 1988). Implicit tax driven public utility charges risk significant 'knock-on' effects in Australian industries, with potentially significant employment losses.

There is no evidence to suggest that Western Australian public utilities have been used in this way. The CRF contribution of public utilities declined in each of the fiscal years 1985/86 – 1987/88 (see Section 13.3). However, reliance on traditional public utilities if the fiscal problems of the State intensify.

13.6.3 Social Justice Strategy

Unlike South Australia and Victoria, the Western Australian government has not implemented a Social Justice Strategy. This is a major oversight considering the demographic trends peculiar to Western Australia, and the identified need for greater service provision which has become obvious as a result of the recent property boom and the opening up of new suburban areas in Perth.

In fact, the government itself alluded to these needs in early 1989 when it issued a housing and land issues document. The initiatives announced in that document included the granting of stamp duty rebates for first home buyers and the subsidisation of home purchase by very low income earners. The document made no reference to the provision of public housing (WA ALP, 1989).

Further, there has been no recognition of the need to co-ordinate the programs of government departments and authorities into an overall strategy designed to maximise community welfare, which is a central feature of the South Australian Strategy. There is a clear need for such initiatives, for instance, in an environment of increasing revenue pressure on State Public Trading Enterprises which would ensure that the revenue raising strategies adopted do not prejudice their social justice or community service obligations.

13.6.4 Funding

Of all the States, Western Australia exemplifies the social and economic dislocation of Federal fiscal austerity. By placing the States on a sounder financial footing through the implementation of an SGSL the damage caused by this dislocation can in time be repaired.

13.6.5 Organisational Reform

Chapter Four of this book outlines an argument that an important issue confronting public sector managers is greater responsiveness of service delivery to user needs. Reference is made to Wilenski's proposal to 'flatten' the organisational structure of public agencies responsible for service delivery (Wilenski, 1988). The Western Australian State Government in announcing its position on managing change in the public sector, stressed the need

for public sector agencies to become more 'adept at interpreting changing community needs and attitudes and incorporating such changes in their service programs' (Government of Western Australia, 1986, p. 4).

These aspirations are in part the response to a widely held belief in Australia and overseas, that welfare State institutions can become insensitive, inefficient and unduly bureaucratic. In view of the threat which privatisation poses to these institutions, defenders of public service provision have urgently sought and investigated new policy instruments which are designed to ensure more effective service delivery. Perhaps the most important development along these lines are arguments favouring the decentralisation of public service provision, and encouragement of citizen participation in public agency decision making. Proposals of this kind are now discussed.

13.6.6 Decentralisation of Service Provision: The Rationale

Decentralisation involves delegating major administrative tasks and/or financial decision-making responsibilities associated with the delivery of services to the local level. The fundamental proposition upon which decentralisation proposals rest is that:

> 'the closer decision making is to those affected, the more responsive it will be in recognising needs, co-ordinating responses and deciding priorities between competing demands' (OECD, 1988, p. 19).

Clearly, the greater proximity between decision making and clients afforded by decentralisation is critical to the argument. This is because service delivery mechanisms are not so likely to be viewed as distant and insensitive. Hence information concerning client aspirations is more readily elicited. The devolved administrative and financial responsibilities facilitate a more rapid response to changes in these aspirations, and citizen participation in decision making can be promoted by such measures. Finally, an area based approach to service delivery can encourage integration of services and yield efficiency gains.

The Logistics of Decentralisation

The practicalities of a decentralisation policy raises a host of questions, including:

- what services can be readily decentralised?
- which administrative tasks and financial functions should be delegated?
- what is the appropriate size of area to which services are devolved?
- is a gradualist or instantaneous approach warranted?

Services provided by State Governments vary considerably in respect of their capital requirements and scale of their impacts. For instance, infrastructure services such as railway construction and operation, road construction, water and sewerage services are characterised by large capital requirements, economies of scale and widespread spatial impacts. These features render such services inappropriate for decentralisation as effective delivery requires consideration of area interdependencies, and centralised provision enables realisation of economies of scale. Experience amongst OECD member countries indicate that social services and cultural functions such as child care, housing, programs for the youth and elderly, recreation, parks and library services are likely to be more effectively and efficiently provided on a small scale (OECD, 1988, p. 20).

The functions devolved by decentralisation programs vary widely; they can range from major administrative and financial decision making responsibilities in which area units control a budget and differentiation of service delivery is encouraged, to simply delegating administrative tasks and the delivery of services to the local level. But in most cases, decisions regarding the allocation of resources between area units remain central. It needs to be borne in mind that simply devolving the administrative tasks of delivery to the local area, limits the gains in flexibility and responsiveness as decision making remains predominantly centralised.

Just as the devolution of functions varies considerably, so does the size of decentralised units. So for instance, decentralisation measures in Sweden and the Netherlands have involved the creation of units comprising 50,000-100,000 people in cities, as compared to 2,000-10,000 in provincial towns (OECD, 1988, p. 34). General criteria determining the devolution of functions and size of units are not evident, and decentralisation programs tend to be gradualist in nature, with lessons learned from experience gained. Whilst there are cases in which a range of services are decentralised at the same time and in the same manner, thereby facilitating integration of service delivery, it has been suggested that no particular service necessarily produces an ideal model for practice across the range of public services (Fudge, 1984).

The Impacts of Decentralisation

The greater access to services afforded by decentralisation fosters expectations of rising public demands, resource requirements and costs. Whilst it is self-evident that decentralisation requires additional resources to initiate implementation, there are credible claims that in the long term these are offset by improvements in the effectiveness of service delivery. The efficiency gains are primarily attributable to two sources.

First, greater flexibility in resource allocation. Experience is beginning to suggest that the information benefits which accrue due to the greater proximity of decision takers to clients, tends to alter the pattern of spending between services rather than raise overall demand. The implication is that centralised service delivery mechanisms are particularly prone to misallocation of resources in relation to user needs.

Second, greater integration of service delivery mechanisms can be achieved via decentralisation programs. For example, in Sweden it is increasingly common for local social housing authority centres to offer laundry, recreation and child care facilities. However, a word of caution is warranted about the generality of such claims, as integration can be impeded by the organisational structure of governments divisionalised by service functions.

13.7 Summary and Concluding Comments

Decentralisation programs involve the delegation of administrative tasks and/or financial decision making responsibilities to area based service delivery units. The greater proximity of decision takers and clients offers the potential of realising a more effective and responsive public service delivery system. Whilst ex-perience is beginning to suggest that these benefits can be sizeable, the change in attitude and role of public agencies is a significant one and warrants serious consideration before embarking on such a program of reform.

Chapter 14

QUEENSLAND

14.1 Introduction

Queensland is the third most populous State and the second largest in area. Over recent years it has experienced rapid growth in the tourist industry and continues to rely on the expansion of extractive industries to achieve rates of economic growth comparable to the rest of Australia. Its manufacturing base is small.

Successive Queensland Governments have attempted to 'curb the power' of the trade unions in Queensland. Public sector trade unions have been used as a target for this attack. Predictably, this confrontational approach to public policy has achieved little save ideological tokenism. This chapter outlines the structure of the Queensland economy and public sector, and provides a critique of government policies which have materially disadvantaged the Queensland population.

Only by properly understanding the nature of the Queensland economy and public sector is it possible to develop a set of policies designed to overcome Queensland's low rates of school retention, inadequate stock of public housing, and its serious unemployment problem.

14.2 Demography and Economy
14.2.1 Demography

Queensland's divergence from the demographic patterns of other Australian States indicates, in part, the social impact of the State's particularly precarious economic circumstances. Economic dependency and the nature of Queensland's privileged economic sectors have produced a dynamic and volatile population profile. This peculiarity is evident in three indicators: urbanisation; population growth rates; and regional mobility.

Urbanisation

While Australia's level of urbanisation (86%) is one of the highest in the world and is not expected to change dramatically in the medium term, Queensland's economic dependence on agricultural, mining and personal service industries has resulted in a significantly lower level of urbanisation (79%). Moreover, only 46% of the State's population lives in the capital, whereas the average for all the Australian States is 64%. By national standards Queensland is highly decentralised, and Queensland's relatively large number of moderately sized urban centres have absorbed much of the State's urban growth since 1921. The physical distance between these major population centres is considerable, and the challenge for public sector functions is further increased by a comparatively large and very scattered rural and provincial population.

Population Growth Rates

Queensland's population profile has in recent decades been subject to considerable, albeit gradual, change. Firstly, over the last twenty years, the average annual population growth rate (2.3%) has been almost double the Australian average. All of this difference is due to net interstate and overseas migration gains (Barker and Reinders 1983). These gains have been uneven both in terms of destination and age.

There has been some evidence of a 'turn-around' in the urbanisation trend characteristic of Australia since the late 1940s. The effects of the rural-urban migration flow have been partially offset by significant population growth in particular rural areas — although this does not appear to be the result of any resurgence of agricultural or pastoral industry.

While Brisbane's growth rate has been two-thirds the State average, those of the Sunshine and Gold Coasts have been around three and four times the average respectively.

High growth centres fall into three categories:

(i) *coastal resort areas*: Landsborough, Noosa, Maroochy, Hervey Bay, Gold Coast.
(ii) *urban areas surrounding* Brisbane and major provincial centres: Caboolture, Moreton, Redland, Logan.
(iii) *resource development areas*: Broadsound, Peak Downs, Calliope, Nanango, Emerald.

At least two influences would seem to be at work here: the success of tourist promotion attracting people for lifestyle and occupational opportunity reasons; and the development of (principally coal) mining projects in Central Queensland.

These region-specific population trends are expected to continue to accelerate over the next twenty years (Barker, 1984). The State's population will continue to grow much faster than that of the nation as a whole such that the State's share will increase from 16.3% (1989) to 19% (2006). Brisbane's share of the State's population will continue to decline from 46.8% to 43.7%, primarily because of the expansion of coastal resort and retirement centres epitomised by the Moreton division's expected growth of share from 13.3% to 18.1% (Barker, 1984). Moreover, while most rural divisions are expected to continue their slow decline, population will be maintained in particular central State mining areas such as Fitzroy (the Bowen Basin), subject of course to the maintenance of healthy mineral commodity prices.

Mobility
In the context of a State economy dependent on an unstable agricultural-mining-tourism base in conditions of continuing if uneven growth, it is unsurprising to find the population is highly mobile. More than half the State's population appears to change its residence in any five year period and for all regions except Brisbane these shifts are overwhelmingly inter-regional (McDonald, 1984).

Population gains from interstate and intra-state mobility should be distinguished. While the former represent an increase in absolute terms in demands made on State services, the latter represent a need for the reallocation and reorganization of the provision of State services. Generally, with respect to growth regions, most net migration gain in the resort-retirement regions is due to interstate mobility, while most gain in the resource development regions is due to intrastate shifts. Regardless of the cause, the strain placed on existing services — education, housing, employment, amenities — in any growth region is especially great (McDonald, 1984).

The most mobile age cohort in Queensland is the 25-34 group with a net inflow being recorded to all growth regions, particularly the resource development areas. This suggests particular strains on educational, child care and family relocation facilities in those regions. Thus, for example, while school enrollments will steadily decline in the inner Brisbane area, they will increase disproportionately in the growth regions favoured by these 'family' cohorts (Warry & Butler, 1984).

While the elderly cohort is not especially mobile, those who do move shift overwhelmingly to the resort-retirement regions, very often from interstate. This indicates the probability that demands on existing health and specialised welfare facilities will increase for some time.

While people are attracted to regions of economic diversification because those areas normally offer a range of employment opportunities and services (Widdows, 1974), this imagined security is often absent in Queensland regions. Queensland's historic dependence on an agricultural and pastoral economy resulted in a low level of capital accumulation, a generally high rate of poverty and low per capita incomes for a widely spread and underserviced population (Mullins, 1980). In short, Queensland's contemporary demographic profile is as unstable and uneven as the economic profile which underlies it.

14.2.2 Economy
A general impression of the comparative economic profile of Queensland is given by Table 14.1. Labour force participation is notably

lower than the national average suggesting the impact of retirement age and pre-employment age migration gains as well as the failure of labour market policies to encourage participation by marginalised groups. The State's unemployment rate also reinforces the points made above concerning the weakness of the State economy. While the State is abnormally productive for its population the dependence of its production on raw material export markets is evident. Queensland's very low rate of private fixed capital expenditure indicates both the paucity of manufacturing capital and the fiscal demands on the government to provide permanent infrastructural investment support. Finally the rate of existing Federal funding suggests Queensland's dependency on the revenues raised from the 'richer' States.

Table 14.1

Major Socio-Economic Indicators and Policy Expenditure
Queensland as a Proportion of Australia (%) 1986-87

Population	*16.3*
Labour force	15.9
Gross State product	18.2
Exports	22.6
Private fixed capital	13.4
Unemployment	17.7
Electricity generation	17.5
Manufacturing establishments	12.3
Manufacturing employment	10.8
University enrollments	14.0
Existing Federal grants	17.8
Household income	14.4
Expenditure on:	
General public services	15.9
Public order and safety	16.1
Education primary and secondary	15.5
Health	13.0
Social security and welfare	20.3
Housing and community amenity	3.8
Total social expenditure	14.9
Agriculture, forestry, fishing and hunting	26.0
Mining, manufacturing and construction	18.7
Transport and communications	22.5
Other economic affairs	14.4
Total of all Expenditure	*15.5*

Source: Drawn from ABS Cat. No. 5504.0 1986-87; Year Book Australia 1988.

Two enduring features distinguish the Queensland economy from the economies of other States:

(i) a dependence on primary production, specifically agriculture and mining; and
(ii) high levels of foreign and interstate ownership and control.

These two features make Queensland particularly sensitive to fluctuations in world commodity prices, patterns of international demand and the decisions of foreign entrepreneurs. In short, the Queensland economy is dependent. The social cost of this dependence is manifested in insecurity of employment, a largely unskilled labour force and relatively limited prospects for the development of local capital.

Primary and Extractive Industries

Queensland, unlike New South Wales and Victoria, has been highly dependent on agriculture for employment and economic growth. While agricultural production constitutes 4.3% of Australia's GDP, it accounts for 6.5% of Queensland's GSP (Queensland Government, 1988a, p. 25). The bulk of this agricultural production has traditionally consisted of sheep, beef and sugar cane (Mullins, 1980). This profile has endured little recent structural adjustment or innovation such that for 1987-88 72% of the value of the State's agricultural production was derived from meat, grain, sugar and wool (Queensland Government, 1988a, p. 26).

Sugar, grains and horticultural produce comprise the bulk of the State's farm crops. While fortunes have been mixed, crops are steadily contributing less to the gross value of rural production, constituting 56% of value in 1983-84 but only 46% by 1987-88 (Queensland Government, 1988a, p. 27). The medium-term prospects for the sugar industry appear somewhat doubtful, with the rise in prices over the past two financial years subject to considerable fluctuations.

Grain and cotton fortunes and prospects in Queensland have also been dangerously uneven in recent years. While the cotton crop for 1987-88 was double that for the previous year, world prices have been falling steadily since August 1987. The value of the State's wheat crop has declined at an annual average rate of 20.8% over the past five years. Although the value of horticultural production has been steadily increasing over the past five years it remains a highly vulnerable sector being particularly prone to unseasonal weather and fluctuations in export markets. These sensitive commodities now represent 12% of the value of the State's rural product.

The sheep and cattle industries seem similarly subject to cyclical fluctuations as production outputs and prices continue to vary. After a 26% increase in the value of beef production for 1986-87 the following year saw no increase with higher prices being offset by lower

production (Queensland Government, 1988a, p. 28). The strengthening of the Australian dollar, the uncertainty of US conditions and markets and some quality problems appear to threaten any sustained recovery in the beef industry.

The important point to note is that farming, especially export oriented farming as found in Queensland, is always a fragile basis for an economy. Queensland's traditional reliance on these products is continually affected by recurrent drought conditions, downturns in world commodity prices, and the pricing effects of the (increasingly protectionist) agricultural and trading policies of competitors.

The rural sector in Queensland is clearly in relative decline having contributed 13.7% to the Queensland economy in 1960 but only 6.5% today. Similarly, while the rural sector is a (proportionately) larger employer in Queensland than in any other State, its labour force is declining. Rural employment accounted for 21% of workers in 1960, but just over 8% in 1988 (ALP, 1988, p. 3).

The Queensland economy is also distinguished from the southern States by its dependency on basic mineral extraction industries such as black coal, base metals, gold, bauxite, and sand mining. While mineral production currently contributes 8.6% of Queensland's GSP it should be noted that, as the State's industry centres simply on the extraction rather than on the extraction and processing of the raw materials, mining in Queensland is very capital intensive employing only 2.5% of the State's workforce (ALP, 1988, p. 4).

As at June 1986 some 416 mining enterprises operated in Queensland constituting almost 30% of all establishments in Australia. Although coal accounts for over half of all mineral value produced, its structure and ownership are especially concentrated with only 28 or less than 7% of the State's establishments being involved. Most other mining establishments are relatively small operations concerned with the extraction and basic processing of construction materials (ABS, 1988d, p. 160).

Minerals, like farm products, are produced and exchanged in very unstable conditions.

Mineral exploration is a high risk investment and has required extensive technical and capital development assistance from the public sector. Mineral production also shares with farming a sensitivity to shifts in world prices. This economic sensitivity is exemplified by the recent decline in the value of mineral production which, after a number of years of growth, fell 4.1% in 1987-88. Some marginal increases in the value of metals production were more than offset by a considerable decline in the value and quantity of the fuel minerals.

Given that black coal accounts for 56% of the State's total mineral production value, the importance of its decline since July 1987 should not be underestimated. While the Treasury cites unfavourable exchange rate conditions as principally responsible, other more fundamental forces appear to be at work (Queensland Government, 1988a p. 35). A 4.1% fall in output, lower domestic prices, increased industrial disputation and the failure to secure adequate price increases with the Japanese has seen a 16.6% fall in the value of the State's coal. As the viability of more mines is jeopardised and as the competition from Western Europe, China, Columbia, South Africa and Canada increases, revenue from Queensland coal production can be expected to continue to decline.

While the practice in Western Australia has been to allow the private mineral developer to build and own their own rail facilities, since the Theiss Peabody Mitsui Agreements of 1965, the Queensland Government has retained ownership of lines used exclusively for bulk coal haulage. The financial risks associated with the enormous capital outlay required and the possibility of the project being aborted have been lessened by the negotiation of massive security deposits which have eventually proved large enough to cover the entire capital establishment cost. The profit component in the rail freight charges negotiated with the Utah Development Company (which followed Theiss into the Bowen Basin after 1967) have been progressively increased. Being a rail freight charge individually negotiated, rather than a royalty, this arrangement has allowed the magnitude of these profits to be kept secret. According to Galligan's research however, about two-thirds of the freight charge is a rent-like profit. 'The Queensland Coal Association maintains that it costs the State $2.30 to $5.30 per tonne to rail coal from the new mines in the Bowen Basin, yet it is charging $13.30 a tonne' (Galligan, 1987, p. 92).

Tourism
Queensland's traditional reliance on primary production has recently been supplemented by rapid growth of the tourist industry. 'It is one of the State's most valuable industries, second only to mining' (ABS, 1986a). The public sector has played a significant role in expanding tourism, particularly in the area of marketing. In five years, the money generated by the Queensland Tourist and Travel Corporation has more than doubled. A recent study commissioned by the Queensland Travel and Tourist Corporation reveals that, since 1979:

a) those employed in tourist accommodation establishments has increased from around 12,000 to 22,000;
b) 37% of new jobs created have been 'tourism related';
c) the proportion of the workforce engaged in tourism related employment has increased from 10% to 15% (Queensland Government, 1988a, p. 53).

Manufacturing
Although Queensland has not traditionally been a 'manufacturing State' a distinctive feature of the State's economy has been the steady erosion of the manufacturing base. Manufacturing in Queensland is dominated by the food, beverage and tobacco division which accounts for around 30% of the value added and just under 30% of the employment in the manufacturing sector (Queensland Government, 1988a, pp. 44-6). Meat processing, with abattoirs concentrated in Brisbane, Toowoomba, Townsville and Rockhampton, and raw sugar milling, with operations along the north Queensland coast, account for half of all production within this division. Employment generated by this sector has fallen sharply from 20.8% of employment in 1959-60 to just 12.8% by 1985-86 (ALP, 1988, p. 4). Numbers employed within manufacturing industry have remained static over the past five years.

The infrastructure of the industry is a combination of a small number of large establishments, (principally in food, beverages and tobacco, metal products, chemical, petroleum and coal product and transport equipment) and a large number of very small establishments. It is important to note that the moderate growth in the past five years in Queensland's manufacturing industry has been almost exclusively in very small establishments.

Foreign Ownership and Control in the Queensland Economy
The distinctive pattern of foreign ownership of the Queensland economy is perhaps most evident in mining. In 1974-1975, foreign investors controlled 59% of the value added in Australia, but 85% of the value added in Queensland. The potential for instability resulting from foreign control is exacerbated by the tendency for these enterprises to be larger and more capital intensive. In Queensland in 1981-1982 foreign ownership accounted for 15% of all mining establishments but 71% of fixed capital

expenditures (Head, 1984).

The fast expanding tourist industry also features foreign ownership of the largest enterprises. International hotel chains are typically extensively foreign controlled. Notable examples include Daikyo Kenko, Iwasaki, ANA, Hilton and Sheraton corporations. The entry of these operators into the Queensland market accounts for much of the State's recent tourist growth. The possibility that the size and resort nature of these establishments might have the effect of dominating the (smaller) existing, local operators and of suppressing the normal multiplier effects of tourist development cannot be discounted.

14.2.3 Labour Market
As Graph 14.1 shows, growth in the number of employed wage and salary earners in Queensland over the five year period of the Australian Bureau of Statistics Survey has been concentrated in the private sector. Over the same period very little growth has occurred in State Government employment.

Graph 14.1

Queensland Employment — State and Private Sector

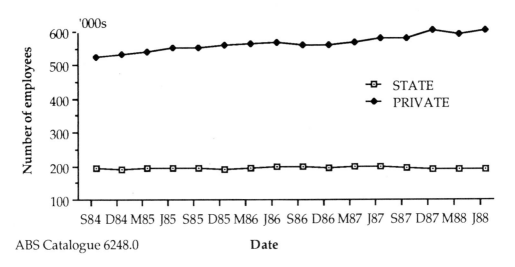

ABS Catalogue 6248.0   **Date**

A more detailed examination of the pattern of employment change in the Queensland public sector in the two year period to June 1988 is provided in Table 14.2, which shows that

employment in the private sector increased by 37,700 or 6.8% to 588,700 during this period, while public sector employment underwent a significant decrease of 15,100 or 5.6% to

253,500. Much of the decline in employment has occurred in the area of State Government activity where 5,500 fewer wage and salary earners found employment in the two year period. Moreover, as indicated in Graph 14.2, the Queensland Government's approach toward the public service contrasts sharply with that of most other States which generally maintained or showed modest increases in public sector employment.

Table 14.2

Employed Wage and Salary Earners by Sector
1986-1988
(000s)

	1986	1987	1988
Total Queensland	819.5	822.2	842.2
Private	551.0	563.1	588.7
Public	268.6	259.1	253.5
Commonwealth	58.7	51.1	50.2
State	182.0	181.3	176.5
Local	27.8	26.7	26.9

Source: ABS 6248.0.

Graph 14.2

Change in Private and State Government Employment (%)

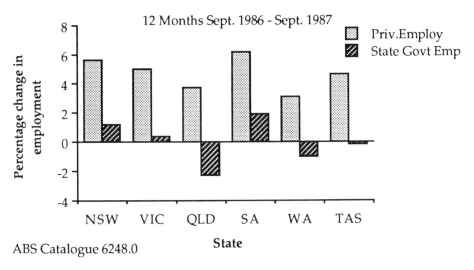

ABS Catalogue 6248.0

Data on the employment rates of the age groups 15-19 and 20-24 in the State Public Service is available for seven years and is included in Table 14.3 which indicates a significant downward trend over almost the entire period.

Graph 14.3 which shows that Queensland clearly trails the other States in bringing women into the ranks of the public service.

Perhaps more significantly, little emphasis has been placed on issues of occupational segmentation which seriously disadvantage women employees (Bryson, 1987). While the data on public sector employment indicates that 43% of State public servants are women, this figure disguises the fact that the nature of much government employment is in areas which have been traditionally attractive to female labour such as teaching, nursing and secretarial work. The overall figures for female public sector employment in Queensland also need to be viewed together with a breakdown of State Government employment by wage levels as shown in Graph 14.4 These data demonstrate clearly that women are locked into the lowest rungs of the service as stenographic and secretarial staff, occupying 68.7% of the positions at salaries below $20,000 but only 2.8% of the positions at salary levels above $50,000.

Table 14.3

Youth Employment and the Queensland Public Service
Change in Percentages in Age Cohorts Over Five Years

Year	15-19 Years	20-24 Years
1981	11.3%	24.0%
1982	11.5%	21.8%
1983	13.9%	21.7%
1984	9.3%	19.8%
1985	8.5%	19.2%
1986	7.7%	17.7%
1987	6.4%	16.8%

Source: Government of Queensland, Public Service Board, Annual Report, Brisbane, QGPO, 1982-1986.

Graph 14.3

State Government Female Employment

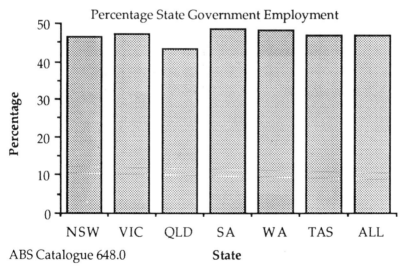

Percentage State Government Employment

ABS Catalogue 648.0

High unemployment has been accompanied by a relative fall in average weekly earnings in Queensland. The increase in average weekly hours worked by males has been less than the Australian average, while the relative increase in part-time work masks a high level of hidden unemployment. Lower labour costs and a more flexible labour market have not induced manufacturing employment in Queensland. They have led to the expansion of secondary labour markets in tourism and the personal service industries which have contributed further to the vulnerability of economic activity in the State.

Graph 14.4

Queensland Government Female Employment by Income

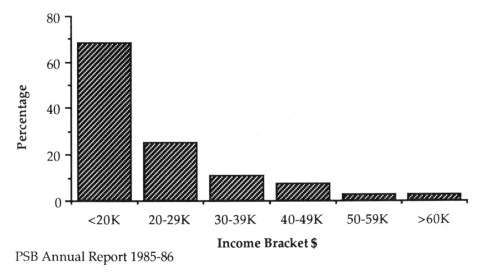

PSB Annual Report 1985-86

14.2.4 Summary

The three central pillars of the economy – agriculture, mining and tourism – are representative of one general characteristic of the Queensland economy: its orientation to foreign markets. In January 1988, the then Under Treasurer, put the point thus:

'Because of its export orientation, the Queensland economy is particularly susceptible to the volatility which characterises the markets for many of its exports' (Hielscher, 1988).

It should be stressed that the State's economic dependency does not mean that Queensland's potential for economic growth is limited; only that this growth is typically marked by significant instability. The instability of economic activity in Queensland has historically been offset by the public sector's active participation in investment, marketing and regulation.

The social costs of Queensland's economic dependence have previously been limited by the involvement of the public sector as an active participant in distribution and investment. Marketing boards, capital development programs and industrial regulatory bodies have all ameliorated the major fluctuations and volatility of economic activity.

Three broad conclusions emerge from this profile of the Queensland economy:

(i) What is produced in Queensland makes the economy unusually sensitive to external market forces. Export oriented primary production has enjoyed periods of rapid growth but also periods of damaging recession.

(ii) Levels of foreign ownership and control compound this instability. Mobile capital is much more likely to disinvest, putting economic security substantially beyond the control of Queenslanders whose livelihoods depend on the favour of foreign entrepreneurs.

(iii) The public sector, as a vigorous participant in distribution and investment has insulated Queenslanders from the most harmful effects of a dependent and precarious economy. This role foreshadows important policy options involving the public sector in stable long-term growth.

14.3 Functions and Structure of the Queensland Public Sector
14.3.1 Introduction

The history of public sector activity in the Queensland economy reflects three interrelated influences:

- the effect of the size of the State and the distribution of a comparatively large proportion of the population across a number of distant regions;
- the effect of the continued dependence on primary production and extraction industries often located in distant and/or inaccessible regions; and
- the effect of a chronic shortage of private capital investment.

These factors have generated a significant role for the public sector in the provision of infrastructural and social services, magnified by successive governments' attempts to attract capital.

The extent of the State's public sector commitment to infrastructural and service support particularly in relation to the mining industry is notable. The Department of Mines has traditionally been the source of direct State assistance by way of aid, grants and loans for construction. More significantly however, the development of mining in Queensland has always relied on considerable public service support in terms of providing social facilities – schools, hospitals, roads, electricity and water supply – for new or expanding population centres. Only in recent times have the costs of such provision been offset by the financial cooperation of the private partner in joint venture projects.

The Queensland experience also demonstrates that the public provision of infrastructural support may provide opportunities for surplus revenues or profits which can then be used to subsidise other areas of public service. Since the mid 1960s mineral boom, 'Queensland has used super rail freights to extract economic rent from its export coal industry' thereby arresting the decline of the overextended and under-utilised rail system (Galligan, 1987, p. 77).

Although this novel use of the State's rail monopoly raises questions of 'political accountability, economic efficiency, public propriety and administrative practice' (Galligan, 1987, p. 93), it is a major instance of diverting some of the benefits of lucrative private projects to the public purse. Since 1980 Utah and other developers have been waging a campaign against what they see as excessive charges in Queensland and this may have the effect of threatening Queensland's already low rate of private fixed capital investment. The case of Queensland coal development indicates both the possibilities of 'creative' public sector infrastructural support and the potential economic benefits from using a monopoly to subsidise other publicly demanded services.

In more general terms an examination of the activities and policies of post-war Queensland Governments reveals a contentment to oversee an existing pattern of growth which can only be characterised as uncoordinated development without planned diversification. Government policy has concentrated on the encouragement of large scale private developments which exploit existing natural strengths and resources – agricultural production, mineral extraction and, more recently, tourism. Strengthening of the manufacturing sector, broadening the economic base of the State and extending the possibilities of tertiary development and processing of the raw materials extracted and produced have never been serious governmental priorities. The economic strategy of concentrating on adding value to resources within the State remains undeveloped.

Despite references to a 'vision of excellence' and a 'new direction', the 1988-89 budget speech suggests very little change in these primary development priorities. The accent on attracting private capital investment through tax incentives, tax competition, privatisation and promises of immunity from 'excessive' regulation is prominent. Thus amongst the government's stated key budget objectives are 'smaller and more accountable government, including commercialisation and marketisation of appropriate government activities' and 'improving the economic and business outlook through less government intrusion, [and] support for private sector initiatives . . .' (Queensland Government, 1988b, p. 8).

The government's approach to the agricultural industry continues to be marked by a stress on increasing levels of production of existing commodities by encouraging the placing of more land under cultivation and the increased slaughter of livestock. Thus the principal rural industries initiative announced by the Ahern Government for 1988-89 is a three-year, $50m Primary Industry Productivity Enhancement Scheme designed to improve the productivity of present agricultural techniques (Queensland Government, 1988b, pp. 14-15). Notably absent is any proposal to extend the range of production, into, for example, exotic and tropical fruit production or to further the extent of food processing. Similarly, the Queensland beef industry is dominated by the export of bulk meat supplies and largely ignores the possibilities of increasing product specification, diversification and advanced processing.

Per capita expenditure on industrial development in Queensland ($5.00) remains well below the national average ($10.68) (ALP, 1988, p. 5). Despite the present government's claim to activate a 'campaign to broaden and deepen the economic base of Queensland' the major initiatives announced involve the extension of payroll tax concessions to employers, a freeze on electricity tariffs and a statement of strong support for the mooted 'Cape York Space Port' (Queensland Government, 1988b, p. 16). The government's obsession with large scale glamour projects requiring injections of foreign capital and massive taxation and regulatory concessions remains.

The industrial structure of Queensland has suffered under successive governments with only limited commitments to diversified manufacturing and processing industries, extensive welfare provision, higher education or a tradition of a civic tolerance. The State is simply not a successful one if the level of publicly provided services, average weekly earnings, employment security, private sector investment or

educational attainment are the criteria.

14.3.2 Economic Services
Queensland's size and relatively high level of decentralisation make its transport and infrastructure providers particularly important. The Transport Department and the Railways Department together constitute the transport ministry and provide rail construction and maintenance, control of land and air transport and planning and coordination of public transport. The Department of Main Roads together with its present ministerial relative the Department of Works provide massive contributions to the State's economic and industrial infrastructure as well as the more obvious social service provision.

The Ministry of Mines and Energy encompasses the Mines Department which regulates and assists the mining industry, for example, through research conducted by the Queensland Minerals and Energy Centre. The Queensland Coal Board regulates the coal industry in particular, and energy generation and supply is administered by the Queensland Electricity Commission.

Reflecting the State's traditional reliance on primary production, there are a number of departments and authorities which have specific responsibilities in this sector. The Land's Department, the Valuer-General and the Department of Geographic Information are responsible for land management, with the Department of Environment Conservation and Tourism and the Department of Forestry being central in the coordination and provision of land usage. The Department of Primary Industries provides extensive advisory, regulatory and infrastructural support to primary production in the State. The DPI is also particularly notable for its responsibility for hundreds of primary produce marketing boards, councils and authorities. Since the First World War marketing boards as established by the then Labor Government have been crucial in their regulation of agricultural production and distribution. The boards which consist of 'growers representatives' and a member of the DPI compulsorily acquire all the produce grown within the State, provide pooling, grading and marketing of the produce and providing

growers with advance payments. The boards
have the power to determine prices, impose
levies for specific planning and place quotas on
production quantities. This system thus enables, in theory at least, the effects of market
volatility to be dampened and in combination
with the research expertise of the DPI and the
economic priorities established, permits longer
term planning of production strategies.

The Department of Harbours and Marines
and the Harbours Corporation of Queensland
regulate port and harbour usage which, given
the export orientation of the Queensland economy, have a pivotal role to play. In connection
with the Queensland Water Resources Commission hold responsibility for the range of
drainage boards, river improvement trusts and
rural water supply boards which plan, coordinate and control water supply.

The provision of economic services to the
private sector is largely conducted by the
Department of Industry Development. The
department administers the National Industry
Extension Service, provides consultancy subsidies and other financial assistance and provides advisory services to business through
the Small Business Development Corporation.
Two other agencies which provide extensive
economic services to the private sector are contained within the Finance Ministry: the
Queensland Industry Development Corporation and Suncorp Insurance and Finance. The
Department of Environment, Conservation
and Tourism services the tourist industry in its
responsibility for the Queensland Tourist and
Travel Corporation.

The power and importance of Queensland's
public bodies has recently been expressly
recognized by the government in its publication of an updated Register of Statutory
Authorities and a Statutory Authorities
Manual which, for the first time, outlines
policy directives and administrative guidelines
for the establishment, conduct and termination
of authorities. The Manual states that Queensland's Statutory Authorities are of considerable
economic significance. Collectively: –

  – they pursue a diversity of strategic
  development-oriented functions;
  – they exercise a wide range of powers;

  – they constitute a significant financial
  force in the State economy; and
  – they constitute a major source of
  employment.

Particularly through their investment
decisions, revenue raising capacities and employment policies, the aggregate activity of
these authorities has a significant impact on
the State Government's ability to coordinate
and implement policy (Statutory Authorities
Manual, 1986, p. 2).

The 1987 Register identifies 663 Statutory
Authorities. The Register does not include
Local Authorities, Aboriginal or Islander
Councils or over 250 individual authorities
which operate under the Primary Industries
Ministry. Public bodies in Queensland considerably extend the range of public sector
activities. Many of the authorities, such as the
Hospital Boards, contribute to the provision of
social and welfare services, while others, such
as the Electricity Boards, assist in the provision
of economic infrastructure and general public
utilities. The Commodity and Marketing
Authorities are devoted to the coordination of
the production and distribution of primary
produce. The importance of this structure in
the economic planning of the State's development cannot be overstated.

14.3.3 Social Services

The two largest public service departments in
Queensland both in terms of budget and personnel, the Health Department and the Education Department, are central to the social
service responsibilities of the State although
both clearly play a major role in the provision
of human capital infrastructure. Beyond the
provision of the State hospital system the
health department provides community
health, home care, psychiatry, dental, nursing
and occupational health services. The department also regulates private sector health
activity through licensing and registration
processes as well as overseeing health and
safety standards in a wide range of occupational and community settings under its
Divisions of Environmental and Occupational
Health and Community Medicine. Extensive

medical research is coordinated by the Institute of Medical Research and health education programs are pursued throughout the State. On a similar scale the Education department maintains the State education system but also administers grants to non-government youth and community groups, conducts community recreation and fitness programs and sponsors educational research.

The public sector also plays a key role in the provision of public services via the operation of social and welfare service agencies. The Department of Family Services provides child protection, disability, fostering and residential care and juvenile corrective services as well as providing grants to the numerous community organizations which are forced to provide many of the welfare services needed for Queenslanders. This Ministry is also responsible for the Queensland Housing Commission which conducts the planning, construction, acquisition, maintenance, leasing and sale of public housing, as well as the granting of loans for home ownership. The Department of Community Services and Ethnic Affairs is responsible for Aboriginaland Islanders' development, the Ethnic Affairs Advisory Committee, and State responsibilities for migration.

In the increasingly important area of environmental services, which has both a social and economic value, the Department of Environment, Conservation and Tourism which is concerned with the monitoring and control of water, noise and air pollution as well as with the administration of the large Queensland National Parks and Wildlife Service are major agencies. The Rural Fires Board and the State Fire Services operate under the authority of the Minister for Administrative Services and the State Emergency Service is the responsibility of the Minister for Police, Administrative Services and Emergency Services. Cultural services are coordinated by the Arts Division of the Premier's Department which administers the Cultural Centre and Performing Arts Trusts as well as the Queensland Art Gallery, Museum, State Library and the Royal Queensland Theatre Company.

14.3.4 Administrative Functions

The most powerful central responsibilities of planning, co-ordination and financial administration rest with three departments which have since 1983 fallen under the responsibility of the Premier and Deputy Premier. The Premier's Department which controls the co-ordination of the public works program (State Projects Division), strategic economic planning (Economic Development Strategy Division) and general State planning (Office of State Affairs). The Treasury is charged with financial administration, planning and budget and notably is classified as part of the finance ministry which assists the Premier and Treasurer in economic administration. Similarly although the Department of Works is the responsibility of the Deputy Premier the principal policy function of coordination remains with the Premier. Thus the splitting of the central portfolios characteristic of most of the years of coalition executive incumbency (Wiltshire, 1985, p. 186) has been greatly overcome and the role of the Premier considerably enhanced with the recent assumption of the previous Public Service Board's responsibilities by his own ministry and the Finance Ministry.

The State's responsibility for the maintenance of law and order is discharged through a number of departments and agencies: the Police Department and the Corrective Services Commission are the most obvious examples the latter organisation having recently assumed responsibility for the functions of the former Prisons Department and the Probation and Parole Service. The Attorney-General's Ministry administers the legal system generally through the Justice Department and a number of offices – Solicitor-General's, Director of Prosecutions, Corporate Affairs Commissioner's, Law Reform Commission, Licensing Commission, Public Defender's, Titles, etc. – are responsible for legal services which are of considerable economic value in guaranteeing property and personal rights and obligations as well as of more obvious social value.

A number of departments and agencies exist to supply infrastructure to the public sector itself. The Works Department, discussed earlier, is the principal agency although the Administrative Services Ministry is responsible for the

Government Printing Office and the State Stores Board. The responsibilities for overall coordination and planning for public service personnel which previously fell to the Public Service Board have been divested to the newly formed Office of Public Service Personnel Management and the Office of the State Service Superannuation Fund within the Finance Ministry.

Reflecting the government's adherence to conservative economic policies, the recently formed Private Sector Economic Advisory Committee is made up of private sector figures and has responsibility for providing the government with recommendations on privatisation.

In respect of the preservation of working conditions and consumer rights, the Ministry of Employment, Training and Industrial Affairs which consists of, first, the Department of Industrial Affairs, conducts industrial inspection and regulates occupational safety, industrial conditions and has responsibility in relation to trade unions and; second, the Consumer Affairs Bureau, the Price's Office, the Workers' Compensation Board and the Department of Employment, Vocational Education and Training, investigates and regulate consumer affairs, profiteering and trade and business protection, trading hours and other day-to-day business activity, employment promotion, workers' compensation, manpower planning, apprenticeships and the administration of technical and further education.

One of the most significant functions performed by Queensland's system of Statutory Authorities relate to the regulation of a range of private sector activities. Professional and occupational registration authorities regulate the standards of conduct of certain professions – from barristers to veterinary surgeons – to both the social and economic benefit of all citizens. Given the specialized nature of many professional services provided by private practitioners the normal operation of the market (eg.: consumer preference) will tend not to control these standards adequately. Here the State's role in coordinating and enforcing expert surveillance is crucial. Similarly, industry control agencies regulate the conduct of specific industries – from agricultural chemi-

cal distribution to wheat quotas – so that standards of both product and business conduct are maintained. These agencies also provide a structure which can usefully bridge the planning and coordination gap between the executive and the private industrial sector ensuring that industry practices accord with development policies.

14.4 The Finances of the Queensland Public Sector

14.4.1 State Revenue

Introduction

State Government revenues consist of payments received from the Federal Government (called, at various times, Income Tax Reimbursement Grants; Tax Sharing Entitlements, Tax Sharing Grants, Financial Assistance Grants and General Revenue Grants), as well as internally generated revenues from State taxes, railway revenues, mining royalties, etc.

Table 14.4 shows the relative contribution of these different sources of revenue in recent years.

Commonwealth-State Financial Relations

As in other States, Queensland relies heavily on Commonwealth payments. In 1987-88 Commonwealth payments to Queensland were $2.8 billion or 45% of total revenue (Queensland Government, 1988, p. 31). Over 90% of Commonwealth payments to Queensland are general purpose grants, with the remainder being specific purpose grants, relating to areas such as primary and secondary education, natural disaster relief, child-care and so on.

Table 14.5 shows that Federal revenues in the immediate post-war period were just over 30 % of Queensland's total revenue, the figure increasing to 40 % in the 1960s, reaching almost 50 % in the 1980s. This upward trend is also indicated by Graphs 14.5 and 14.6. Despite the post-war increase in the proportion of Queensland's revenue derived from Federal taxation a declining proportion of Federal outlays are forwarded as assistance to State and Local Government, and the Commonwealth's contribution to total State revenue has been in decline since 1984.

Table 14.4

Components of the Total State Government Revenues

	80.81	81.82	82.83	83.84	84.85	85.86	86.87	87.88
Commonwealth Payments to Qld	47.0	48.7	48.4	49.3	47.6	45.5	46.8	45.4
State taxation	23.2	22.3	21.3	20.8	20.1	19.8	22.7	26.2
Railways	15.7	15.0	15.2	16.4	18.6	18.6	17.8	16.2
Royalties, etc.	4.2	3.7	3.5	3.5	4.0	4.7	3.5	3.3
Property income	4.6	5.2	5.7	4.3	3.7	5.4	5.2	4.4
Services rendered	2.5	2.3	2.2	2.2	2.3	2.2	1.9	1.9
Other	2.8	2.8	3.7	3.5	3.7	3.8	2.1	2.6
	100	100	100	100	100	100	100	100

Source: Summary Tables Relating to the Public Accounts (Consolidated Revenue Fund), various years.

Table 14.5

Federal Government Contribution to Queensland Budget Revenues

1947	31.2%	1969	43.9%
1949	31.5%	1971	50.7%
1951	33.0%	1973	46.0%
1953	36.8%	1975	47.7%
1955	34.2%	1977	47.5%
1957	34.8%	1979	48.5%
1959	36.2%	1981	47.0%
1961	40.4%	1983	48.4%
1963	43.0%	1985	47.6%
1965	39.7%	1987	46.8%
1967	44.3%	1989	45.7% (est.)

Source: Summary Tables Relating to the Public Accounts (Consolidated Revenue), various issues.

The static or declining Commonwealth payments to States have improved the financial performance of the Commonwealth in recent years. It is an exaggeration however to claim that Federal fiscal rectitude has been achieved at the expense of Queensland (Queensland Government, 1988, p. 82). However, an increasing proportion of Federal taxation receipts are spent directly by the Federal Government leaving a smaller proportion of total government revenue to be disbursed by States. The static or declining Commonwealth payments to States are hence likely to continue in the future.

Relatively, and historically, Queensland has benefitted from the existing 'fiscal equalisation' formula for allocating Commonwealth payments to States. The objective of fiscal equalis-

ation is 'to give each State . . . provided it were to make a comparable revenue effort, the fiscal capacity to provide services to its residents at a standard not appreciably different from the standards of other States' (Commonwealth of Australia, 1987a, p. 26). Queensland has always received above average revenue assistance per head of population from the Commonwealth and has received a higher proportion of total Commonwealth revenue assistance than is warranted by its 'population share' of 16.3%. The State has received effective subsidies from the populations of New South Wales and Victoria, though the rate of increase in these subsidies has slowed and the larger States have been able in recent years to demand and receive a larger proportion of the total Federal disbursements. This means a continuing pressure on the State's own budget and revenue raising strategies.

Queensland however, continues to be relatively advantaged even in the environment of fiscal restraint imposed by the Commonwealth at the Premiers' Conference in 1988. Premier Ahern was quoted as saying that '. . . the Hawke Government would force Queensland into new tax areas because of its reprehensible, bully boy tactics to restrict the States global borrowings for capital works' (Courier-Mail 13 May 1988). Queensland refused to accept at the Premiers' Conference that the State cut back by $367m its global borrowings over and above other States.

Graph 14.5

Commonwealth Payments to Queensland Government

Percentage of Total Revenues 1973/78 - 1988/89

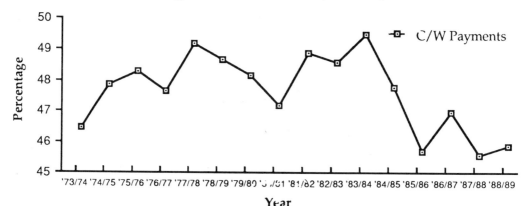

Consolidated Revenue Fund : Estimates & Probable Ways and Means
1988/89 estimates

But if we examine total Commonwealth payments to States as opposed to global borrowing requirements and total Federal funding for Queensland as a proportion of total State and territory allocation (Graph 14.7) we find that Queensland received the highest increase, over 3%, in total Commonwealth payments and once again received a higher proportion of Commonwealth payments than its population warranted (17% relative to 16.3%) (The Professional Officer, Sept/Oct 1988, p. 125).

There is little doubt that in a situation of a static or declining revenue the Queensland Government has cause for complaint even though relatively it is doing better than other States. The real question is can revenue strategies be changed at the Commonwealth or the State level to either expand existing revenue (ie., increase taxes, broaden the taxation base) or disburse recurrent revenue such that new sources of revenue are opened up or developed (ie., planning for employment and growth).

A methodology has been developed for the Commonwealth Grants Commission to base its assessments of General Revenue Grants (specific payments are treated as a separate case) on historical data (in 1988 this related to the years 1984-85 to 1986-87) and on categories drawn from the standard budgets of the States. A rotating standard on a population-weighted basis has been devised to compare distribution supplied by the Commission's assessments from State to State. In 1988 the Grants Commission, in response to its terms of reference varied the methodology in a number of respects. In particular, it decided to include the Northern Territory in the rotating standard against which comparisons were being made.

New South Wales and Queensland were the only parties to argue against this proposition. The Commission claims that as the Northern Territory has only one percent of the six States and Territory total this had a marginal impact on the States (Commonwealth Grants Commission, 1988, p. 37).

Other changes in 1988 include on assess-

ment of temporal policy changes in standard budgets of the States such that discontinued and revised program arrangements in the future would be taken into account. As well, a number of categories in the standard budgets – Non-metropolitan Transport-Freight Services, Coastal Shipping Services and part of Tourism – were assessed as zero needs.

Graph 14.6

Queensland Government Revenue by Source

Percentage Contribution 1973/74 - 1988/89

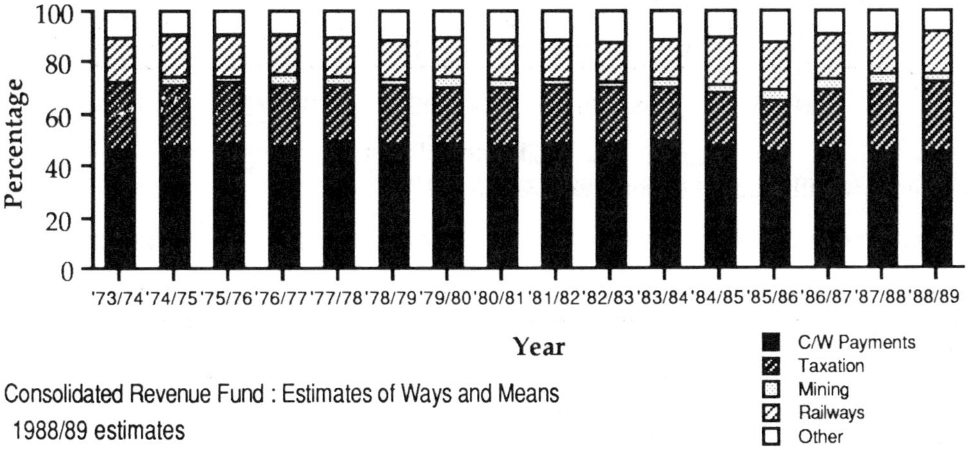

Consolidated Revenue Fund : Estimates of Ways and Means
1988/89 estimates

Legend: C/W Payments, Taxation, Mining, Railways, Other

Some of these changes had a specific impact on Queensland. For example, as part of its decision to assess zero needs in the Non-metropolitan Transport-Freight Services category, the Commission decided to treat part of the revenue derived from the haulage of black coal in Queensland as mining revenue.

Queensland, and other States, were also affected by amendments the Commission has made in its procedures for measuring the revenue base for payroll taxation. Were the Commission to assess pay roll tax solely on aggregate figures in the standard budget, it would fail to take into account variations in State administration and collection policies. The Commission decided to measure the pay roll tax base by reference to data, in particular ABS data, which were not influenced to the same degree by differences in State policies.

This change discriminated against States that had stepped up their revenue-raising efforts prior to 1988 and subsidised those such as Queensland which had been tardy in their efforts to raise State revenue.

The biggest problem the Commission has however, is to define the Standard budget. The Commonwealth Grants Commission faces precisely the problem faced by the authors of this document in that there are no standard accounting procedures across States; State budget descriptions of recurrent revenue and expenditure vary enormously and the process of Grants Commission assessment of general revenue may not only encourage inefficiencies within and between States but may generate incentives to distort recording and account procedures of revenue and expenditure.

As the Commission notes:

Graph 14.7

Queensland – Federal Funding

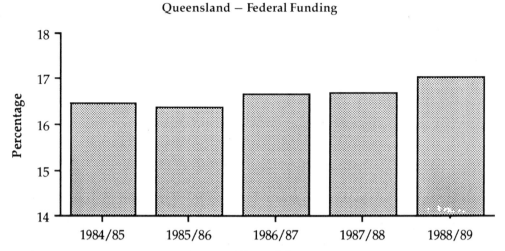

Commonwealth Budget Papers 1988/89 No.4

'. . . in practical terms recurrent budgets seldom exist in their traditional sense. Taxes and charges have been raised for financing capital works and services; borrowings and profits derived from the sale of major government assets have been introduced as recurrent receipts; and other recurrent receipts have been held in suspense accounts pending allocation to the revenue budget. Likewise, expenditures in revenue budgets have included substantial end-of-year transfers to reserves and provisions for use in later periods, and significant outlays of a capital nature. These have included loan transactions; expenditures on major plant, and equipment, especially computers and other communication facilities; compensation payments arising from deferral of capital projects or for assets acquired by government; land acquisition and development costs; capital financing transactions such as working capital advances and payments made under guarantee arrangements; and substantial supplements to capital works programs. Conversely, capital budgets have been credited with recurrent items, such as interest earnings, and have expended funds on items of a recurrent

nature, such as the maintenance of government assets, the purchase of light motor vehicles, debt servicing and grants to private organisations' (Commonwealth Grants Commission, 1988, p. 126).

One implication of the variations in the methodology adopted by the Commonwealth Grants Commission in 1988 for Queensland is that Queensland's implied difference from equal per capita distribution increases. This is in marked contrast to other States such as Victoria and to a lesser extent New South Wales which move closer to an equal per capita distribution under the Commission's 1988 assessment. The implication of this increase from per capita equalisation for Queensland in 1988 is that it will be redressed in future years further eroding general revenue grants to Queensland.

A further implication of the changes in 1988 for Queensland and other States is that the 'fiscal equalisation' formula is becoming very difficult to manage and losing its legitimacy in some circles.

14.4.2 Taxes and Charges
Queensland collects proportionately less tax

than other States, and also raises revenue from a small number of taxes which accentuates the problem of narrow indirect tax bases:

'During recent years, Queensland has engaged in tax competition to attract residents and business activities to the State. It thus led the charge in abolishing death duties, threatened to withdraw from the uniform arrangements for taxing conveyances and marketable securities, did not follow other States in imposing statutory corporation payments, franchise taxes and financial institutions duty and granted longer exemptions for payroll tax than most other States.

Its overall tax effort, standardised for differences in taxable capacity, is only about 80% of the six-State average' (Mathews, 1985, p. 13).

Table 14.6 suggests that Queensland collects less tax and that this poor revenue effort reduces the implied service level in Queensland. Queensland raises less tax per capita than all other States except in the areas of General Insurance, Mortgages and Loan Securities and liquor taxation. It is notable that payroll taxation is well down even compared with other small States (except South Australia).

Table 14.6

**Commonwealth Grants Commission Calculation
Of Tax Efforts and Implied Service Levels 1980-81**

Total Revenue Effort			Implied Service Level	
		Education	Social Services	Total Exp.
NSW	104.8	99.1	100.4	103.0
Vic.	107.0	108.6	103.6	103.8
Qld	79.4	81.6	80.2	81.8
SA	76.5	111.9	108.8	103.9
WA	81.7	93.4	108.3	102.2
Tas.	96.8	113.9	113.4	107.3
Six States	100.0	100.0	100.0	100.0

Source: adapted from Mathews et al., 1985.

Although Queensland has been tardy in increasing its taxation capacity (falling from 96.56 in 1985 to 92.61 in 1988 according to the Commonwealth Grants Commission, 1988, p. 66) its general revenue grant from the Commonwealth has not been reduced. This is explained by the big increase in the assessed revenue capacity voted for Queensland in Other Revenue. This Other revenue increased dramatically from 102.40 to 130.69 (Commonwealth Grants Commission, 1988, p. 66). This shows clearly that Queensland's lower taxation effort has been offset by revenue from resources, particularly, black coal in recent years.

While Queensland is, in relative terms, a low tax State, it relies heavily on a small number of taxes and gains a relative contribution from fees and fines which is more than double the six State average. As a consequence of raising revenue from a small number of taxes, Queensland exacerbates the problem faced by all States that the taxes available to it are '. . . narrowly based and fragmented, and therefore do not necessarily rate highly either in terms of efficiency or equity criteria' (Queensland Government, 1988, p. 31). Over 86% of tax revenue is derived from payroll tax and stamp duties. The range of other taxes, including land tax, totaliser and betting tax, gold lotto tax, casino tax, bookmakers tax and soccer pools, in relative terms, make only a modest contribution to tax revenue.

Queensland is in the same position as the other States in that its expenditure responsibilities are not matched by its revenue raising capacity. This 'vertical imbalance' relates to the 'fiscal equalisation' formula adopted by the grants Commission to disburse income tax funds and other payments from the Commonwealth to the States. The 'vertical imbalance' is 'caused' by the fact that the Commonwealth raises about three quarters of total taxes collected by all levels of government in Australia, but accounts for only about 49% of total expenditure. In contrast, the States raise only about 20% of taxes, but account for about 45% of total expenditure. As noted above, Queensland is being forced to adjust to the reality that Commonwealth payments can not be expected to increase and that the Queensland Government will have to fund services out of its own, expanded, revenue base.

The Queensland Government has adopted a policy of generating as much revenue as possible from resource-based industries. Railway fares and freight charges and mineral royalties are an example of this. Tourism through equity holdings and a series of leisure-related taxes is also a component of this policy.

Yet, the principal source of taxation revenue for the Queensland Government is payroll tax and stamp duties. This situation is unlikely to change. Payroll tax and stamp duty are receipts generated by productive activity – manufacturing and employment – in the context of a growing economy. It is therefore doubly mysterious that the Queensland Government has done little to plan for industrial growth and has overseen a State economy that has a high rate of unemployment: 7.3% in April 1989.

The problem is not, as we will see in the following sections, that low taxation requires low levels of service delivery and therefore cutbacks in government spending (as, for example, the IPA Review, Nov/Jan 87-88, p. 40 recommends) but rather that planning for growth will require a reorientation and increase in government services directed toward value added production and employment generation.

14.4.3 Funds Management
The major borrower and fund manager for State authorities is the Queensland Government Development Authority (QGDA). The QGDA operates in a more volatile domestic

and offshore financial market as a result of continuing deregulation of the Australian financial system. The QGDA would prefer to have the flexibility to borrow whatever mix of domestic or offshore funds that markets had to offer rather than have limits placed on the proportions to be raised in either market.

The experience of recent years highlights the cost and benefits of borrowing activities such as QGDA. Though QGDA has been able to generate enormous sources of funds for Treasury there is an element of risk when the markets turn down.

The Queensland Government has not been deterred however and in May, 1988 the Queensland Treasury Corporation was established to broaden the investment front for government funds' and was given a free hand by Treasurer Ahern '. . . to move into property, probably buying into the CBD or outlying shopping centre development' (AFR November 9, 1988).

14.4.4 Analysis of Revenue Collection Strategies
The Queensland Government has at least four possible alternative revenue collection strategies available to it

> (i) it could increase administrative efficiency in taxation collection
> (ii) it could increase the levels of taxation received in existing areas
> (iii) it could broaden the tax base by introducing new indirect taxes
> (iv) it could begin to disburse current revenue such that new source of revenue are opened up (ie., planning for employment and growth).

The first three alternatives would generate an increase in revenue in the short term, the fourth alternative would generate revenue in the longer term. We look at each alternative in turn.

(i) Increase Administrative Efficiency in Taxation Collection
We do not have accurate figures for efficiency in administration across States therefore it is difficult to judge whether Queensland could or

could not generate further revenue by this method.

However, it is clear that improvements in departmental efficiencies in such areas as telephones and motor vehicles, as proposed in the 1988/89 budget, could take some pressure off the need to raise additional revenue.

Also, exemptions on State taxes could be reviewed to ease the revenue shortfall. There are exemptions from stamp duty on some classes of documents, particularly in relation to educational, charitable and religious organisations and for government departments. Under the Land Tax Act (1915-1985) exemptions are allowed under certain conditions to proprietary companies using land solely for the business of agriculture pasturage or dairy farming (ABS, 1988d). These exemptions could be reviewed.

In the 1988/89 Budget, Premier Ahern announced that Payroll tax exemptions will be progressively raised from $324,000 to $500,000 to produce tax savings for an estimated 300 employers and boost small business employment. It would appear unwise to reduce revenue accruing from the main source of State taxation at this time, without the revenue compensation available through the implementation of the State's Goods and Services Levy outlines in Chapter Seven.

(ii) Increase the Levels of Taxation Received in Existing Areas

This is the main revenue collection strategy adopted by the new government of Premier Ahern in his first budget of September, 1988.

Premier Ahern introduced at 30% tobacco tax, to cost smokers an extra 45c to 50c a packet, and a 2% increase in liquor licence fees that will raise beer prices 1c to 2c a glass in 1989. The tobacco tax, which took effect on January 1, 1989 will earn the government $45m in the 1988/89 financial year and about $100m in the full year.

However, Premier Ahern also introduced significant exemptions on the main sources of revenue. The payroll tax exemption has already been mentioned. The Budget also contained cuts in Stamp Duty on insurance business (already higher than other States, as we have seen).

The result is that in the 1988/89 budget total estimated revenues are up only 2.9% to $6492m, compared with the Budget's working inflation rate of about 6% while total departmental expenditure will rise only 5.5% (The Australian, 9 Sept., 1988). This strategy is unsound because it merely works the existing narrowly-based taxes more intensively. The problem is that the States impose indirect taxes which are particularly detrimental in terms of equity and efficiency.

(iii) Broaden the Taxation Base by Introducing New Indirect Taxes

The most desirable direction that tax reform can take is to introduce fairer, broad-based indirect taxes, and replace a range of existing discriminatory indirect taxes. The current strategy of increasing taxation in areas that are already high (eg. liquor taxation which was higher than Victoria's before the recent budget) and increasing exemptions in main sources of revenue, eg. payroll tax and stamp duty tax must be reversed.

Queensland claims that the taxes available to it are '. . . narrowly based and fragmented, and therefore do not necessarily rate highly either in terms of efficiency on equity criteria' (Queensland Government, 1988, p. 31). In some instances, this is true. For example, Queensland's lower per capita collection of payroll tax could be a result of the weaker manufacturing and business base in Queensland and a reflection of the decentralised and small-scale nature of most of the States workshops and enterprises.

However, the Queensland Government, as a result of policy decisions, has deliberately chosen to narrow its taxation base. This is particularly true of indirect taxation.

The Queensland Government has chosen to narrow its taxation base in areas of indirect taxation such as Financial Institutions duty, fuel tax, statutory corporations payments and has collected a very small amount of revenue compared to other States in areas of transfers of shares and marketable securities.

All these indirect taxes could be introduced to broaden the taxation base in Queensland and to introduce equity across States. However, merely expanding the revenue-raising capacity of these narrowly-based taxes is not the best solution. The Queensland Government will have to stop thinking of the State taxation system as an alternative to industry policy. It will need to devise ways to stimulate business growth in Queensland while at the same time standardising its direct and indirect taxation efforts with other States.

(iv) Disburse Current Revenue Such That New Sources of Revenue Are Opened Up (ie. Planning for Employment and Growth)

Apart from the introduction of a State Goods and Services Levy, the Queensland Government's revenue shortfall will also be alleviated by economic growth, employment and economics of scale in all areas of business activity.

It is only in an economy where economic activity is deeper and broader, where value added activities predominate that the main sources of taxation revenue – payroll taxation, stamp duties, land tax – and new indirect tax – finance institutions – will generate the volume of revenue the Queensland Government needs. The exact revenue potential of this strategy depends on the range of State taxes and charges which are abolished under the terms of the SGSL agreement with the Federal Government. Such an economy will also generate substantial revenue from a low rate of indirect tax, and low rates of tax have the advantage of reducing equity problems.

Hence, in order to alleviate revenue short fall, the Queensland Government must begin to plan programs that sponsor value-added activities and employment. The public sector should take a lead in these activities.

Program budgeting could, if properly implemented provide a means of more accurately assessing the performance of government policies. It could also alter the existing situation where departments are 'topped-up' according to inflation and the previous year's allocation.

Instead, departments would be funded by program. Many social justice programs such as education and health would be considered as making major contributions to training and employment and thus would receive extensive funding.

Program budgeting would break the nexus between those departments, such as Treasury

that have high earning potential and therefore spend a lot and those departments such as health and education which rely on Commonwealth funds and therefore have an incentive to go cap in hand to the Commonwealth each year. Instead, Treasury's financing operations may be drawn on to fund education programs. Also, education could engage in more extensive financing transactions.

Premier Ahern has already moved some direction toward program budgeting. Treasury has moved some distance toward removing global limits on departments and has accepted the idea of departments being funded according to programs. However, it remains to be seen how this will affect the revenue-side of the department's activities.

Program budgeting, properly introduced, requires quite extensive planning at both the budget stage and in terms of a department's own priorities.

14.4.5 Recent Trends in Public Sector Expenditure

State expenditures are a key indicator of government priorities and the importance ascribed by governments to the various Public Service activities. In turn they produce a public sector policy-making and administrative structure firmly implanted with government perceptions of what is, or is not, to be undertaken. This section examines the broad pattern of State expenditure in Queensland since 1981-82. Briefly, in recent years Queensland has reduced the percentage increases in Budget outlays. In particular, Queensland has made big reductions in recurrent spending rather than simply reducing total outlays by reducing capital expenditure as some other States have done.

On initial inspection, as shown in Table 14.7, the average annual real growth rate of government expenditure in all forms in Queensland (5.2%) is very strong, being faster than population growth (2.1%) and, perhaps more significantly, being considerably stronger than gross State product growth (3.9%) (Queensland Government, 1988, pp. 11-13).

However the exact pattern of that growth as revealed by Table 14.8 requires qualification. The rate of growth of public expenditure was far stronger in the first half of the decade than it is proving to be in the second half with an absolute decline in expenditure growth being recorded for the first time in 1986/87 (-0.5%). Notably, for the same period GSP grew by 3.6%. Furthermore, growth in the direct public service provision part of the budget — capital (4.1%) and consumption (3.5%) expenditure — has been moderate and uneven with absolute declines in capital outlays being recorded for three of the last five periods surveyed and an absolute decline in recurrent expenditure occurring in the budget for 1986/87. Thus in real terms there has been a recent contraction in direct public service provision with most of the expenditure growth being generated by increased outlays on interest payments and unrequited current transfer payments.

Table 14.7

Trends in Queensland Government Expenditure

	1981/82	1982/82	1983/84	1984/85	1985/86	1986/87	Average Annual Real Growth
Capital Expend							
%	33.5	37.1	32.4	29.6	31.2	30.5	
80/81 $m	1363.2	1734.9	1539.3	1447.2	1635.4	1592.1	4.1
Consump. Expend							
%	49.6	44.9	46.7	47.7	45.6	45.8	
80/81 $m	2016.5	2101.8	2216.6	2333.9	2394.6	2392.4	3.5
Interest Payments							
%	11.7	12.6	14.4	16.6	17.3	18.1	
80/81 $m	477.0	589.7	681.2	809.6	909.1	944.9	14.8
Other (Unrequited Transfer Payments)	5.1	5.3	6.5	6.1	5.7	5.6	
80/81 $m	208.2	251.2	307.9	298.3	298.4	292.7	7.7

Source: ABS 5504.0 and ABS 1303.3 and 1307.3.

While interest payments to the Commonwealth on advances have been gradually declining payments to other creditors have ballooned from $280m in 1981/82 to over $750m by 1986/87. Interest payments have been increasing at an annual average growth rate of 14.8% in real terms. Thus Queensland now has the highest rate of public debt transaction of all States with that cost increasing from 17.7% of current outlays in 1981/82 to 26% in 1986/87. Similarly, expenditure on subsidies, personal benefit payments and current grants has increased from 7.7% of current outlays in 1981/82 to 8.1% by 1986/87. While the existence of considerable public debt is certainly defensible and indicates the important role of the State public sector in the provision of financial infrastructure in an era of Commonwealth fiscal restraint, other sectors of the budget which cater directly for public service provision have not increased commensurately. Nevertheless the ratio of capital to recurrent expenditures has remained stable and in the order of

6:9, although there has been a marginal increase in favour of consumption expenditures over the past five years. Profiles of recurrent and capital expenditure for the Queensland public sector are presented in Tables 14.8 and 14.9 according to public service purpose.

The central social and welfare services of education, health and social security and welfare have consistently consumed around two-thirds of the final consumption expenditure for the State and while keeping pace with expenditure growth in general, health (2.9%) and education (3.4%) consumption expenditure has remained below the rate of GSP growth. Most average real growth in this purpose area has been recorded in the small social security and welfare sector which has increased its share of the current outlays from 2.6% to 3.3% since 1981/82. Nevertheless there has been a significant growth in the 'general public services' sector and this clearly contributes to social and welfare service provision.

Table 14.8

Trends in Queensland Government Final Consumption Expenditure by Purpose

	1981/82	1982/83	1983/84	1984/85	1985/86	1986/87	Average Annual Real Growth 81/82 − 86/87
Education							
%	40.0	39.5	39.1	39.6	40.0	39.8	
80/81 $m	806.4	830.4	865.9	924.7	957.9	951.5	3.4
Health							
%	25.0	23.6	24.0	24.2	23.9	24.2	
80/81 $m	503.9	496.3	531.4	563.9	572.1	579.6	2.9
Social Security and Welfare							
%	2.6	3.3	3.3	3.2	3.2	3.3	
80/81 $m	52.1	69.2	72.1	74.8	76.0	78.0	9.0
Transport and Communication	5.0	4.8	5.8	5.3	5.1	4.9	
%	99.8	102.6	129.5	124.2	122.7	118.4	-0.7
*Economic and Industrial**							
%	6.5	6.5	6.5	6.1	5.8	5.7	
80/81 $m	130.8	137.1	144.9	141.9	139.1	136.7	0.9
Total Consump. Exp.							
%	100	100	100	100	100	100	
80/81 $m	2016.5	2101.8	2216.6	2333.9	2394.6	2392.4	3.5

Note: * Includes Fuel and Energy sector, Agriculture, Forestry, Fishing and Hunting sector and Mining, Manufacturing and Construction sector.
Source: ABS 5504.0 and ABS 1303.3; 1307.3.

Although the 1981/82 − 1986/87 period reveals overall growth in expenditure on existing social services it must be noted that that growth has recently slowed to the point where education endured a cutback and health only a very marginal increment for the most recent period. This contraction must be considered serious in the context of the State's poor record in social service provision throughout the 1970s, as well as in the context of significant population growth and ageing in contemporary Queensland. Thus although the State ranks third behind Victoria and South Australia in recurrent funding for education as a proportion of all current outlays (ABS, Cat. No. 5504.0 1986/87, p. 9) a massive education funding shortfall persists (QTU, 1988). It is notable that Queensland ranks as the lowest of all States in terms of health funding as a proportion of all current outlays (ABS, Cat. No. 5504.0, 1986/87, p. 9).

The most significant contraction in consumption expenditure has been in the provision of economic infrastructure: whereas this economic service part of the recurrent budget accounted for 11.5% of consumption in 1981/82, it now accounts for 10.6%. The most significant single element of this contraction has been the decline in the expenditure on electricity and other energy generation despite Queensland's apparent over-capacity in this area.

The pattern on the capital outlays side of the budgets is broadly similar with the comparative advantage to the social service sector less pronounced. Overall spending growth on fixed capital assets has been slow (3.1%) with a 4.5% reduction in capital outlays being recorded for the most recent (1985/86 − 1986/87) period. This is a key indication that public sector investment in the State is far from dynamic and that pressure for capital will increase with the recent contraction in investment taking its effect on the extent and quality of social and economic services.

Fixed capital expenditure for social service purposes tended to steadily increase through to the middle year of the 1980s and decline quite sharply thereafter resulting in marginal overall growth for the period. Social service capital expenditure increased from 17.5% of all capital expenditure in 1981/82 to 18.2% by 1986/87. While the education sector enjoyed strong growth for all periods but the last, the health sector was the hardest hit of all suffering

an average annual decline of 2.8% in real terms. While the steady increases in the 'Housing and Community Amenities' sector appear impressive it should be noted that it still accounts for only 4.4% of all capital expenditure by the public sector and that even when combined with Local Government spending Queensland is by far the lowest spending State on housing and community capital projects as a proportion of total capital outlays: 11.2% in Queensland compared with an average for all States of 20.5%.

Table 14.9

Trends in Queensland Government Fixed Capital Expenditure by Purpose

	1981/82	1982/83	1983/84	1984/85	1985/86	1986/87	Average Annual Real Growth
Education							
%	7.2	5.9	7.1	8.8	11.1	9.5	
80/81 $m	87.1	85.9	96.5	112.5	158.2	128.5	9.7
Health							
%	3.7	3.0	4.6	5.9	4.7	2.2	
80/81 $m	44.4	43.3	62.9	75.7	66.1	30.3	-2.8
Social Security and Welfare							
%	0.2	0.2	0.3	0.4	0.3	0.2	
80/81 $m	2.9	3.0	3.6	5.1	4.2	2.8	0.0
Housing and Comm. Amenities							
%	3.9	4.5	5.8	6.0	5.3	4.4	
80/81 $m	47.4	65.2	78.9	77.3	75.8	59.5	3.8
Public Order and Safety							
%	2.5	2.1	2.1	1.7	1.6	1.9	
80/81 $m	30.0	30.8	28.5	22.1	23.4	26.3	-1.8
Transport and Communication							
%	42.2	39.3	35.6	32.5	36.0	37.2	
80/81 $m	506.9	575.6	483.4	415.0	510.9	504.6	1.1
Economic and Industrial*	35.3	40.8	37.6	37.2	33.7	36.1	
80/81 $m	424.6	596.9	509.6	473.7	478.3	488.8	4.4
Total Fixed Capital Exp.	100	100	100	100	100	100	
80/81 $m	1202.4	1464.3	1357.0	1275.1	1419.9	1355.4	3.1
General Government							
%	44.4	41.1	42.6	48.9	48.9	46.0	
80/81 $m	533.3	601.5	577.5	624.1	694.6	623.5	3.6
Public Trading Enterprises							
%	55.6	58.9	57.4	51.1	51.1	54.0	
80/81 $m	669.1	862.8	779.5	651.0	725.3	731.9	3.0

Note: * Includes Fuel and Energy, Agriculture, Forestry, Fishing and Hunting, Mining, Manufacturing and Construction sectors.
Source: ABS 5504.0 and ABS 1303.3; 1307.3.

Queensland is, in fact, distinguished by its very high rate of public capital investment in economic and industry services in comparison with capital commitments to social and welfare services. An enormous 73.3% of public capital expenditure in the State is devoted to the provision of general economic infrastructure: a massive 26.8% is spent on establishing new electrical generation facilities; 18.5% on rail construction and modification; 13.5% on road construction and improvement; and, 9.2% on infrastructural support for the agricultural industries. Despite the slight proportional decline in the share of capital spending going to the economic sector over the period reviewed, most of this contraction has been absorbed by

reduced allocations to the water transport sector. Growth amongst the other above-mentioned purposes has been moderate to low.

This distinctive pattern of traditionally very high economic infrastructural support maintained by moderate growth suggests both the centrality of primary industries to the Queensland economy, the governments' wish to further cultivate that orientation and the severe problems generated by a chronic shortage of capital funds available for the establishment and extension of essential social services: most notably affordable public housing, adequate health care and hospital access and a satisfactory public education system.

Table 14.10

Relative Expenditures from Queensland Budget
(% of Total)

	Education	Health*	Welfare	Primary Ind.	Police**	Transport***
86-87	23.1	19.2	1.1	2.1	4.5	19.3
85-86	22.9	19.2	1.1	2.1	4.5	19.3
84-85	22.8	19.5	1.9	2.1	5.4	20.6
83-84	22.8	19.4	1.9	2.1	5.5	19.6
82-83	23.2	19.5	1.9	2.1	5.5	20.2
81-82	22.6	19.2	1.9	2.2	4.9	20.0
80-81	24.2	14.3	2.2	2.3	5.3	20.5
79-80	24.4	14.3	2.5	2.3	5.3	20.8
78-79	24.7	14.3	2.4	2.1	5.5	20.4
77-78	24.9	14.0	2.3	2.1	5.3	20.4
76-77	25.4	14.1	2.1	2.0	4.6	20.4
75-76	26.1	16.1	2.2	1.9	4.6	22.0
74-75	23.6	16.0	1.9	1.9	4.6	22.5

Notes: * Sudden increase in proportion of State spending on Health in 1981-82 is an effect of change treatment of Federal grants (from specific purpose payments to general revenue). Fall in proportions under other Heads of Expenditure is commensurately overstated (see *Payments to or for the States*, papers accompanying Federal Budget, various issues of *Financial Statement of the Treasurer*, Queensland 1981-82).
** Host department has changed several times
with Mines and Energy 1977-79
with Local Govt and Main Roads 1979-82
with Deputy Premier 1985-87.
***Mainly Railways.

Source: Consolidated Revenue Fund (Queensland Government Budget Papers, various years).

The data in Table 14.10 indicates relative stability in the expenditure allocations over the past 14 years. As this has been a period of economic recession and high unemployment (especially in Queensland) it is surprising that the

State Government's spending priorities have been so inflexible. These data also show that the national propensity for low levels of welfare and social security spending is exacerbated in Queensland. The State spends only $1166 per person on social services compared to the six State average of $1351. This is the lowest per capita of any State. The shortfalls in State spending compared with the Australian averages are: Education 18.2%; Health 22.5%; Welfare 25% and Community Services 40%. Queensland spends commensurately more than average on administrative services (5.2% above) and services to industry (17% above).

Although spending relativities have not altered substantially in recent years, even small percentage changes can have a dramatic impact, as the example of education shows. The decline from 23.1% of the budget in 1986-87 to 22.2% in 1987-88 (following a longer term decline since the mid 1970s) occurred at a time when State school enrollments and school facilities have been increasing (QTU, 1988, p. 4).

Table 14.11

Queensland Government Expenditures 1987-1988
(Major Departmental Allocations)

	$b	% of Total
Education	1.3	22.2
Health	1.2	19.6
Transport	1.1	19.1
Police	0.2	4.3
Welfare		1.1
Primary Industry	0.1	2.0
Other	2.1	31.7
Total	6.0	100%

Source: Consolidated Revenue Fund: Estimates, 1987-1988 (Queensland Government Budget Papers).

Table 14.12

Per Capita Expenditure ($) 1986-1987

	NSW	Vic.	Qld	SA	WA	Tas.	NT	Six States
Education	547.60	636.47	535.87	623.61	599.27	649.38	1115.95	583.75
Culture & Education	26.31	24.46	32.04	53.94	45.96	55.45	183.08	31.90
Health	504.50	525.80	389.75		545.9	588.85	527.96	
Welfare	68.00	74.51	53.92	87.07	93.83	80.09	157.16	71.82
Law, order, public safety	155.86	151.71	147.52	174.95	185.27	173.75	586.45	158.31
Aboriginal Services	0.06	0.06	7.04	5.56	9.58	0.39	338.72	2.63
Sub Total (Total Social Services)	1302.33	1413.01	1166.12	1491.11	1522.76	1487.02	3289.16	1351.49
Administrative Services	106.45	114.44	116.17	111.97	99.13	119.20	316.77	110.38
Community Services	11.45	14.00	7.94	13.48	25.54	16.81	88.99	13.20
Regulatory Services	9.04	13.00	8.00	14.98	17.27	16.45	63.96	11.43
Services to Industry	33.52	44.19	58.86	60.51	86.57	114.00	371.72	50.30
Debit Charges	79.23	102.05	63.29	199.48	85.37	132.05	504.22	95.32
Natural Disasters	2.75	2.28	6.52	0.83	5.34	0.44	5.68	3.27
Business Undertakings (budgetary impact)	230.05	232.60	140.95	125.83	125.22	63.83	160.71	191.90
Total Expenditure	1779.90	1940.81	1577.23	2032.83	1982.63	1979.79	4896.01	1835.41

Source: Commonwealth Grants Commission Report, 1988.

14.5.2 Implications

Table 14.11 shows the current budget disbursements by the Queensland Government; while Table 14.10 (above) reveals the situation for the major categories of expenditure over a longer period. Table 14.12 then allows an interstate comparison of per capita expenditure under different categories for the latest available year (1986/87).

These data show that the national propensity for low levels of welfare and social security spending is exacerbated in Queensland. The State spends only $1166 per person on social services compared to the six State average of $1351. This is the lowest per capita of any State. The shortfalls in State spending compared with the Australian averages are:

Education	8.2%
Health	22.5%
Welfare	25.0%
Community Services	40.0%

Queensland spends commensurately more than average on administrative services (5.2% above) and services to the rural and mining industries (48% and 25%, respectively, above the six-State standard). State spending on industrial development is 43% below the standard level (see Table 14.11).

Expenditure patterns in recent years suggest the government has been confused in its priorities and that its expenditure patterns should be reviewed. It is clear that Queensland has reduced expenditure in certain important policy areas in recent years. However, there seems to be little or no logic to these expenditure reductions. The neglect of industrial development policy seems peculiar for a government eager to sponsor industrial growth.

Whether or not the Queensland Government has a set of policy priorities, it is not possible to examine a government's priorities, or determine any pattern to its expenditure where funds are being moved off-budget and thus are not publicly accountable.

Despite these inadequacies which have serious implications for accountability, in 1987/88 Queensland's performance on Budget outlays won it the 'IPA Review' award for fiscal responsibility yet again. 'The IPA Review' (November/January 1987/88) reported that: 'On a State-by-State basis, Queensland had to be judged the winner of the IPA best budget award both in terms of expenditure restraint and the lowest additional tax take ($26 per capita) of all governments in the period'.

The perception that Queensland is a 'small government' State committed to 'free enterprise' is reinforced in the 'Quality Queensland' (1988) document prepared by the Queensland Government (Queensland Government, 1988). The document stresses the imperative of 'market liberalisation' to harness the 'vitality of market forces' (p. 32), with government services being '. . . made more responsive to market demand' (p. 33) and the State Government acting '. . . as a centre of expertise in strategic public policy and concept development in the State.' (p. 44).

The problem with this strategy however is that even basic infrastructural services such as education, industrial development, law and order and agriculture are well below per capita expenditure in other States. Conversely, expenditure on administrative services is higher in Queensland than in all other States except Tasmania (Northern Territory excluded).

The reality of financial management in Queensland is that expenditure is raised or lowered to divisions on the basis of a 'topping-up or creaming off' basis without any sense of priorities or strategy. The expenditure strategy presented in the 'Quality Queensland' document is devoid of detail on how a strategy incorporating priority setting might be delivered by departments and how the strategy should translate into department and divisional priorities. In other words, 'Quality Queensland' contains no detail on policy delivery systems.

In the 1988/89 Budget, Premier Ahern sought to redress per capita expenditure problems of the past and re-focus expenditure priorities. In Education, Health, Social and Community Welfare and Housing, Law, Order and Public Safety, Rural Industries, Industry Assistance and Development, new initiatives were presented. The problem with these new expenditure measures is that they continue a trend evident for some years in Queensland in moving new expenditure off-budget into Trust Accounts and Special Funds (as shown in Table 14.13).

Table 14.13

Percentage of Departmental Expenditure
Allocated to Trusts and Special Funds

	86/87 (actual) %	87/88 (actual) %	88/89 (estimated) %
Premier	31.4	29.1	23.2
Works	9.5	8.9	9.1
Main Roads	100	100	100
Police	1.8	2.1	1.7
Corrective Services	78.7	78.1	82.5
Prisons	7.3	7.8	10.3
Education	27.1	28.9	30.9
Employment, Vocation	n.a.	12.1	14.3
Industrial Affairs	91.1	91.8	93.8
Environmental			
Conservation Tourism	30.8	27.1	24.7
Forestry	55.9	55.6	65.7
Family Services	3.8	3.2	1.2
Treasury	81.5	69.6	83.5
Health	48.9	48.9	50.3
Industry Development	40.6	39.0	47.0
Justice	39.3	44.1	50.1
Lands	55.2	49.3	55.4
Geographic Information	10.3	13.5	11.8
Local Government	51.6	61.6	63.2
Mines	17.9	25.4	75.7
Community Service			
and Ethnic Affairs	49.6	49.4	55.4
Primary Industries	39.1	28.5	28.9
Transport	17.4	11.2	11.7
Railways	24.8	21.3	15.0
Harbours and Marine	68.0	70.1	93.0

Source: Queensland Government, Estimates of Receipts and Expenditure 1987/88, 1988/89, 1979/80.

This off-budget expenditure of the Queensland Government is to be deplored. Such expenditure is not publicly accountable. It is not possible to examine a government's priorities, or indeed determine if it has any, in a situation where off-budget expenditure is not accountable. Rather than move new expenditure off-budget, expenditure should be justified in terms of strategic priorities. Hence, increases should be delivered only in programs which satisfy such priorities.

As in the case of revenue raising, the Queensland Government should alter the existing stability in expenditure outlays. It should move funds back from Trusts and Special Funds into recurrent programs administered by departments and divisions according to strategic priorities and plans.

14.5.3 The 1988/89 State Budget: New Priorities?

In the 1988/89 Budget speech Premier Ahern sought to redress low expenditure in some areas and refocus expenditure priorities. He promised an increase in the teaching force of 522 teachers. He also promised spending of $15m over the next three years to fund places in higher education, $15m over three years to improve teacher amenities in schools throughout the State, $6m over three years for the Queensland Education Foundation and so on.

In Health, Premier Ahern promised Hospital

staff numbers would rise by 1,300 over the next two years. An extra $2m p.a. would be made available for cancer research and $30m over three years to replace and upgrade the Queensland Institute of Medical Research facility at Herston. In the areas of Social and Community Welfare and Housing, a major $25m program would be implemented in 1988/89 for help and support for housing and accommodation for the aged, handicapped and other disadvantaged people. In the area of law and order, six hundred additional police over three years would be employed to boost the morale of the police force in Queensland which has been dealt a severe blow by the Fitz-gerald Inquiry.

In the areas of productive activity such as Rural Industries and Industry Assistance and Development, Premier Ahern promised a new three year $50m Primary Industry Productivity Enhancement Scheme complemented by a commitment of $104.2m for expenditure on water resource capital works throughout the State.

Industry Assistance and Development was largely restricted to payroll tax concessions and the promise that there would be no increase in electricity tariffs in 1989. Some $15m was made available immediately to seed realistic entre-preneurial activities.

This new expenditure in both welfare and productive areas suggest Premier Ahern is altering the priorities of the Queensland Government in recent years. Yet the real in-crease in expenditure for the Department of Education, the Department of Health, Police , and Primary Industry was either zero or nega-tive, as Table 14.14 shows.

Table 14.14

Changes in Queensland Budget Allocations 1987/88

	Increase $ million	% change from 1986/87 in real terms
Executive and Legislature	+0.95	-1.3
The Premier	+2.5	-0.4
The Treasurer	+96.8	+8.4
The Deputy Premier, Minister Assisting the Treasurer and Minister for Police	+4.5	+5.2
Corrective Services	+3.8	-2.9
Administrative Services and Valuation Education	+26.7	-5.0
Employment, Small Business and Industrial Affairs	+0.9	-3.7
Family Services, Youth and Ethnic Affairs	+6.1	+2.4
Health and Environment	+92.8	+1.6
Industry and Technology	+0.5	-5.3
Justice and Attorney-General	+1.3	-5.4
Lands, Forestry, Mapping and Surveying	+4.9	+0.8
Local Government, Main Roads and Racing	+1.2	+2.2
Mines and Energy and Minister for the Arts	+2.9	-2.8
Northern Development and Community Services	-1.1	-10.2
Primary Industries	-2.4	-8.9
Tourism, National Parks and Sports	+0.7	-5.1
Transport	+71.5	-0.3
Water Resources and Maritime Services	+12.2	+7.9
Works and Housing	+5.7	-3.6
Payments Authorised by Special Acts	+22.7	-0.9
Total	ᴉ 355.5	-1.1

Source: The Professional Officer September/October 1987, p. 463.

Thus increases in the 1988/89 budget do no more than redress expenditure cuts in previous budgets. The Queensland State Government does not have in place a set of strategic priorities or a service delivery system for allocating State Government expenditure.

For most departments, their expenditure is 'topped up or creamed off' by a standard percentage determined by the governments revenue performance. This is the case for the large service departments which do not receive significant Commonwealth specific purpose payments.

Other departments, such as Premiers and Treasury are favoured with large increases regardless of government revenue performance. These departments are favoured not because they are service delivery departments, or even because of the importance of their co-ordinating function but because they hold out the promise of windfall gains to revenue through investment and speculative activity.

The tendency of the Queensland Government to move more and more funds off budget is likely to further enhance the power of the revenue earning departments at the expense of the large service departments which do not receive Commonwealth payments. There is no evidence in existing or future expenditure strategies that revenue earned through Trust and Special Funds activity will ever be made available to enhance services.

14.4.8 Conclusion

The strategy of the Queensland Government in recent years to base its revenue collection on the resource-based activities and delivering tax concessions to business on its main sources of State revenue is collapsing as a result of a growing revenue shortfall in the budget.

The 1988/89 Budget strategy did not adopt a satisfactory revenue collection strategy to deal with the existing situation or with the problem in the near future. Assets sales are not an adequate solution and charging for government services across departments will undermine long and short term revenue collection strategies.

In the short term, the Queensland Government must through an appropriate means broaden its indirect taxation base. The most rational policy option for Queensland would be to become a partner in the SGSL proposals put forward in Part Four. Nevertheless, in the long-term and given the tax raising strategies adopted by the Queensland government in the past (which stand in marked contrast to those of other States), it may be that a special formula would need to be developed for Queensland which would not leave it relatively disadvantaged.

14.5 Privatisation Versus Reforming and Developing State Public Services
14.5.1 Introduction

In contrast with some other States there has been no coherent or co-ordinated dismantling of the public sector in Queensland. This does not mean that the public sector has not been subject to attack, criticism and change, but the changes have proceeded on the basis of starts and stops and political opportunism. There are, however, examples of privatisation and contracting out and these examples may spread in the 1990s (depending on political outcomes in other States), but there is, as yet, no systematic and planned program of privatisation and commercialisation (though the 1988/89 Budget did foreshadow proposals for asset sales).

The following Table provides a summary of what has occurred in Queensland.

14.5.2 Selected Case Studies

The lack of a coherent government policies on reform of the public sector has resulted in the absence of debate in Queensland over the nature and role of the public sector. Those debates which have occurred have not focussed on the problems of dismantling the public sector, but on issues of employment conditions within the public sector (to be discussed below); on 'glamour projects' (such as the proposed commercial space port, and the Multi-Function Polis); on the Ahern regime's initiation of a long term strategy for industrial development; and on the relations between politicians and public sector operations (the Fitzgerald Inquiry).

The case studies which follow focus on three separate areas of recent State Government activity concerned with the public sector. The first paints a general picture of the uneven

Table 14.15

Examples of Privatisation in Queensland

Contracting Out

Mines Department: contracting out of stratigraphic drilling services. Twenty-three positions in the section were made redundant and the work now takes place by contracting. Private mining companies have the opportunity to conduct such work 'in house'. Minimum redundancy packages were offered to workers, some of whom had rendered 30 years service.

Technical and Further Education: contracting out of course delivery. Many of these 'private providers' lack facilities and rely on TAFE to supply space, equipment, etc.

Logan City Hospital: contracting out of pathology services (proposed).

Main Roads Department: contracting out of construction of the Logan Freeway; toll charges for other new sections of highway eg. a Sunshine Coast by-pass.

Franchising

Operation of Brisbane Gateway Bridge.

Load Shedding

Warilda Child Protection Facility: provision of the services and premises of Warilda, a centre responsible for the care and protection of neglected and/or abused children, has been transferred from government responsibility to the Uniting Church. More than 40 workers were made redundant as a result of this transfer of responsibility.

Privatisation

Port of Brisbane Authority: privatisation of pilotage services (1.1.89). The operation was purchased by existing employees who had established a company.

Elements of the Prison Service: it is proposed to lease to private enterprise the new prison under construction at Borallon, a proposed women's prison at Wacol, and the Home Detention Service. This follows recommendations from the Kennedy Commission of Review into Corrective Services. It is not yet clear if these proposals will go ahead, though the State Government passed legislation in 1988 which allows for privatisation of part of the prisons system.

There are no significant Queensland examples of the sale of public assets. During 1988, there was a proposal to sell CITEC (the Government Computer Bureau) to private enterprise, but this idea was abandoned.

Commercialisation

Technical and Further Education: new funding arrangements requiring approximately 20% of monies to be raised privately by each institution (proposed). The most likely method to raise funds will be the charging of fees for services/access.

Government Garage: provision of cross subsidy has stopped and full cost recovery now required. However, the Garage is restricted by order to the public sector and competes with a number of other public service departmental in-house garage services. Other departments can now seek the services from the private sector.

Government Printer (Goprint): full cost recovery now required. While Goprint's marketing strategy is limited to the public sector, there is no proviso that the public sector contract with Goprint.

Department of Education: commercialisation of supply and stores. Schools now purchase from 'Edmart' and can also purchase non-contract items from the private sector.

Conversion to Statutory Authority (Corporatisation)

State Government Insurance Office now Suncorp. The question of privatisation of Suncorp was raised in 1988. No decision taken.

Other

Department of Primary Industries: a widespread phenomenon of DPI professionals leaving to establish their own business with intimate knowledge and access to DPI resources and facilities.

development and application of the government's policy initiatives; the second shows a more consistent approach by the State Government to creating 'flexibility' in State labour markets and the consequent erosion of employment conditions within both the public and private sector; and the third study demonstrates the contradictions faced by Queensland's Conservative Government in planning strategies of economic reform in the absence of a commitment to public sector development.

Application of Policy Initiatives
The Ahern Government commissioned a State strategy study from the Stanford Research Institute in the United States in late 1987. The report was handed to the government in November 1988. The actual report was not made public because it was critical of the Queensland Government in various areas, but a public relations version, entitled 'Quality Queensland' was released with attendant publicity in December 1988.

This document, like the Curran Report in New South Wales, is biased towards privatisation and inappropriate commercialisation. Under the heading 'Key Initiatives – Physical Infrastructure', for example, it suggests inviting expressions of interest from the private sector for provision of new facilities and the expansion and development of existing facilities such as prisons, roads, hospitals, airports and schools. 'Quality Queensland' is discussed more fully in section 14.6.2 below.

Independently of the government's long term development strategy, it has also proposed that Borallon Correctional Centre be leased to private enterprise and has suggested a private sector role in the financing and running of a new international airport to be built in Brisbane. However, these proposals are not backed by even a basic knowledge of the processes needed to be gone through to make such activity appear 'successful'. The example of the Government Garage well illustrates this 'ad hocery'.

In March 1988, a Queensland Treasury Expenditure Review Committee recommended that the Government Garage at Zillmere (with a workforce of 110) be phased out as soon as possible. The Ahern Government announced its intention to privatise the Garage and raised the possibility of an employee/management buy-out. This was expected to be the first of a series of privatisations of government workshop and repair garages: others included the police garage, railway workshops and the Brisbane Metropolitan fire brigade garage. A working party, which included union representatives, was set up to examine the feasibility of the proposed buy-out. It called in a firm of chartered accountants and examined the proposals. The investigation clearly showed that the consequences of the decision to privatise the Government Garage had not been thought through and that with $4.5m loan commitments it would not be commercially viable. Once again the Queensland Government had rushed into an ad hoc decision, putting pronouncement before policy.

The outcome of this process was, for the government, an embarrassing policy reversal. The Queensland Government decided to adopt commercialisation of the Garage from 1 July 1988. Under this scheme, the Garage would not be sold, the workers would remain government employees and the Garage would operate on a user-pays basis. This arrangement is intended to operate on a one year trial basis (ie. until July 1989). Meanwhile, privatisation of government garages in other areas has not proceeded.

The Queensland story in other instances has been very similar to that of the Government Garage – indecision concerning the future status of Suncorp; and a plan to privatise the Centre for Information, Technology and Communications (CITEC) through sale to a US company. In the event, the scheme was scrapped.

Attacks on employment conditions: the public sector as spearhead
The one relatively consistent thread in the Queensland experience are attacks on the terms, conditions and employment status of public sector workers, and attempts to use these as precedents for similar moves in the private sector. The most notorious case is the 1984 South East Queensland Electricity Board (SEQEB) dispute.

The issue of contract labour had surfaced on

a number of occasions between SEQEB and the Electrical Trades Union(ETU), but the immediate flashpoint occurred in January 1984. At this time, SEQEB advised the ETU that the remaining work on the Grantham Estate would be completed by contract labour. The ETU considered that the employment of contract labour undermined the job security of its members and the Gatton SEQEB depot imposed a ban on all work at the Grantham site.

The dispute escalated until, in February 1985, SEQEB linesmen were sacked. Many of these workers have never regained their jobs, and the levels of contract labour in the electrical supply industry have significantly increased. In addition, under new legislation, particularly the Electricity (Industrial Supply) Act 1985, all employment in the electricity industry was removed from the jurisdiction of the State Industrial Commission and placed under a new single person tribunal.

Despite national opposition to the Queensland Government's actions, the victory of the government in the SEQEB dispute of 1985 fostered an expectation that general changes in employment conditions and industrial relations would follow. However, the Minister for Employment did not produce a Green Paper on Voluntary Employer/Employee Agreements until March 1987. This paper proposed the virtual by-passing of the State Arbitration machinery and the setting up of Voluntary Employment Agreements (VEAs). As the Green Paper puts it:

The government has formulated a position that while certain State award and Queensland Industrial Commission standards should be protected for the benefit of employees, other restrictive industrial conditions should be completely negotiable between an employer and the relevant union(s), or between an employer and his/her employees without union interference if the employees wish (Green paper, 1987, p. 3).

The Green Paper encouraged decentralized wage bargaining, individual bargaining in certain instances and the development of company-based unions. Initially the legislation was intended to apply to the public sector as well as the private sector. The similarity between this approach and that enforced in SEQEB two years before is clear, particularly the removal of certain conditions from the Industrial Commission.

After much public and legal criticism the Queensland Government was forced to back down and the industrial relations legislation introduced into Parliament in September 1987 excluded the public sector. Nonetheless, there have been significant shifts towards contract labour within the white-collar areas of the public sector.

As early as 1983, 40% of the most senior Queensland Public Service positions were term appointments, usually for five years. Early in 1987, contracts of employment were offered to all permanent heads of departments. The rush with which this was done attracted critical comment from the Public Sector Review Committee Report (Savage Committee) in August 1987, attacking the hasty introduction of the contracts without working out a systematic basis for remuneration and responsibilities.

The 1987 Voluntary Employment Agreements (Contracts) proposals attempted to:

(i) introduce contracts of employment which could be negotiated at an individual or group level,
(ii) allow for the lowering of award conditions,
(iii) limit the jurisdiction of State Industrial Commission, and
(iv) allow for numerous workplace-based unions to come into existence.

Also in 1987, the Savage Committee Report was presented to Cabinet. It contained a number of recommendations affecting the employment conditions of public servants and most of these recommendations have been built into the 1988 Public Service Management and Employment Act.

There are five major effects of the Act:

(i) it abolishes the 1922 Public Service Act. This Act has formed the basis of the Queensland public Service to 1988;

(ii) it recommended that the role of the Public Service Board be greatly reduced and limited and that on this basis there was no justification for retaining a full time board. This has led to its abolition and the creation of a new central Office of Public Service Personnel management with only limited functions.

(iii) most personnel functions have devolved to departmental level, giving chief executives recruitment and dismissal powers. This pushes the public sector employment framework closer to the private sector model.

(iv) it creates an appeals procedure and a Commissioner for Public Service Appeals. However, appointment on a contract basis precludes appeals (S.32[2][b]), for many job appointments.

(v) the Savage Committee recommendation that departmental heads be given the authority to appoint casual, part-time or contract staff is built into the Act without clear safeguards. S.19(3) states: 'the Governor in Council may, by Order in Council, declare any office or class of office, other than that of chief executive, to be an office or class of office to which appointment shall be made upon a contract basis'. Further appointment on a contract basis 'shall not be subject to any industrial award or industrial agreement or any determination or rule of an industrial tribunal' (S.20[1][c]).

The new Act deals with retrenchments (S.28) in a very brief manner. The Savage Committee recommended that a redeployment/retrenchment scheme be introduced in the Public Service. No such scheme is spelt out in the Act. Instead it is the subject of 'Redundancy Arrangements' set out by the office of Public Service Personnel Management in June 1988. The retrenchment package, approved by the Governor-in-Council, has the force of Public Service regulations. However, the procedures for determining who is to be made redundant and what constitutes a retrenchment situation have the status only of 'guidelines'. Consequently the latter will be more susceptible to varied interpretation, change or disregard.

It is clear that the 1988 Public Service Management and Employment Act plus other changes in the public service constitute a serious and long term complex of changes in the employment conditions of Queensland public servants. There is a clear trend towards the demise of the permanency of employment with widespread contracts down to lower levels of the hierarchy. The speed of change and the extent of this practice are hard to predict and will depend on union responses plus the broader situation in the labour market. At present it is rumoured that the government intends to introduce contract employment below the middle management public service 1-15 classifications. Clearly, the contracts offered to senior public servants were on generous terms; the system was, so to speak, bought in. This will not happen with all levels of staff.

The relationship between such moves in the public sector and government encouragement of similar moves in the private sector illustrates the status accorded to the public sector by the government. The public sector is being used as a virtual spearhead in an offensive aimed at the industrial relations system. The attack encompasses a change to the whole industrial relations system by removing the centralised Industrial Commission from the theatre, and the rejection of the trade unions as the legitimate representatives of the workforce. Such a process ignores a central theme of Award restructuring currently proceeding throughout Australia, which recognises both the central role that trade unions are playing in the process and the need for centralised co-ordinating body to ensure economy-wide consistency.

'Quality Queensland'

This case study examines the implications for the public sector in Queensland of the Ahern Government initiated strategy for economic reform and development published as ' "Quality Queensland": Building on Strength'. As indicated earlier in this chapter, the subtitle is a misnomer. Economic conditions in Queensland are not strong. The State's economy is more volatile and its living standards more precarious and discriminatory than the other States, especially the more densely populated manufacturing States of Victoria and New South Wales.

The peculiar industrial structure with the unusual demographic conditions that pertain in Queensland have not produced a stable economy well adapted to the changes likely to be forced upon the State; and they have been accompanied by a political and institutional system (including public authorities) which are unable to develop the strategies needed for the future. These deficiencies are, indeed, acknowledged even in the politically sanitised 'Quality Queensland' document. It proposes a series of strategic goals to overcome these deficiencies including economic planning based on research and government implementation of initiatives to change the current pattern of economic development.

These are doubtless commendable intentions, especially insofar as they recognize that primary production will not alone 'provide the growth the State desires'. The government does seem prepared to commit its public sector to facilitating or even initiating changes in industrial structure in response to changing technological and global conditions. The question which this case study poses is whether or not the government's strategic emphases are sophisticated enough to deal with the problems identified, that is to generate more manufacturing and value added activity.

'Quality Queensland' poses the challenge to the public sector in the following terms: 'To complement this broadening of the State's infrastructure development, major efforts to improve the decision making processes of government itself will need to be made so that the government has the capacity it needs to effectively introduce new approaches to economic development' (1988, p. 2).

The government's envisaged means include capital investment in infrastructure (although this will have a greater orientation towards technology, skill-development and financial innovation than analogous governments provisions in the past), and public support for the expansion of markets.

'Quality Queensland' goes some way towards specifying the precise activities it expects will provide growth opportunities in the future; and to this extent it is more inter-

ventionist and selectivist than the term 'market facilitation' (used in the document) would imply. It is known from the experience of industry policies overseas where the public sector has a major role to play that specific and detailed targeting, rather than generalized attempts to simply create an appropriate entrepreneurial environment, are necessary for there to be any surety in economic restructuring.

However, the industry policy task is not really one of renewal or regeneration of manufacturing activity, but of creating 'value-added' industries for the first time. Past patterns of development in Queensland did not require a public sector that planned ahead or anticipated changes in the local or international environment, but merely a series of support mechanisms for the agricultural and mining enterprises that emerged almost spontaneously from the natural resource advantages present in the State. Government activity in the past was understandably oriented towards 'facilitation' of market-led activity which was not, itself, a product of public policy.

These are the conditions the current government is seeking to change. They are conditions which any alternative Labor Party Government would also wish to transform. Such transformation of the Queensland economy, utilising the public sector in the way outlined above, cannot occur without appropriate reform of the public sector itself. Most importantly, they necessitate the creation of productive capacity and productive activities for which neither resources nor markets presently exist. The objective itself is laudable. However, the government has thus far shown itself to be incapable of making the policy changes necessary to implement such a strategy.

The risk embodied in the strategic proposals of 'Quality Queensland' is that there is at present insufficient commitment to the reforms necessary to implement such a strategy. The government's record on reform and industrial development indicate that there could well occur a reversion to the ad hoc embracing of any and every project that chanced to be suggested by entrepreneurs with little time or facility for sober evaluation. As noted above, the Queensland Government's record of flirtations with such ultimately untenable glamour projects has marred Queensland's attempts to develop industry policy for the past decade or more.

The actual requirements of success seem not to sit easily with either current explanations of the State's precarious position or with the suggestions for high quality, integrated manufacturing expansion. A significant aspect of the 'emerging conditions in the global environment' cited in the document is the implication that the only viable alternative strategy for Queensland is the path of export enhancement. The industrial development proposed in response is to seek 'niche markets' and to develop more 'downstream processing' (value-added) activities prior to export.

However, 'Quality Queensland' has neglected to fill in the other side of an industrial policy for the State that would make it consistent with the direction of industrial policy in Australia. That is, it does not examine in any detail the opportunities inherent in an import replacement program. The most compelling structural change taking place in Queensland itself is population increase relative to the rest of Australia. Presumably therefore, manufacturing activity which was previously not viable in Queensland may become more so in the future. As technological change is making the economics of scale from large production runs less significant than in the past, there do seem to be opportunities unfolding which the 'Quality Queensland' proposals fail to pursue.

An export enhancement strategy alone may still, of course, deliver considerable rewards. However, it would lock the economy into continuing volatility; and it would perpetuate the past patterns of a narrow industrial base, comparatively restricted skills development and dependence upon foreign trade. If export industries can be successfully developed, this is obviously a good thing; but to devise an entire strategy based upon the quest for new markets for new products would not be to eliminate the fundamental vulnerability of the local economy to changes beyond our control.

The necessary complement, which is to develop manufacturing in a range of import-replacement activities, would have the effect of promoting skills in the workforce, competence in management and relationships with the public sector. This would provide a higher threshold of sectoral integration and inter-industry linkages and hence make future prospects of coping with unexpected changes in the total environment more promising. It would also involve a more serious commitment to industry policy and public sector involvement than envisaged by the 'export-first' proposals of 'Quality Queensland'.

Sophisticated engineering provides interesting possibilities because of the potential for significant multiplier effects within Australia and because they can develop from the relatively high base of education that already exists. Heavy and sophisticated engineering oriented to niche markets offers chances for domestic diversity that could reasonably be expected to produce export spin-offs. If these activities were to be sponsored whole-heartedly, government would need to undertake much of the co-ordination needed to integrate technical training, workforce education, infrastructure support (finance, transport) and marketing. As long as the processes are inaugurated on a high plateau of technical efficiency, they will be flexible enough to adjust to provision of a large range of local requirements as demand conditions change in the future. Such a proposal does of course imply that managerial skills will need to be buttressed by specific manufacturing skills. 'Bottom-line' managerial rationalizations which are as anxious to close down or sell off productive capacity as to extend it, may well be inimical to such a project.

In the most general terms, manufacturing is characterised by complex and often large scale conversion processes based on expensive plant and equipment with determinate performance characteristics. These features in turn impose inflexible time frames as well as physical and technical givens, which considerably complicate both the financing of manufacturing operations and the commercial considerations of matching the products' prices and characteristics to a very complex demand structure. These aspects of manufacturing enterprises force them to make and implement a large number of decisions which are more or less irreversible; and to do so coherently, they must integrate their approaches to these factors in a sequence of steps that express their manufacturing strategies (Ewer, Higgins & Stevens, 1987, p. 58).

Insofar as the public sector infrastructure is structured and expected to provide support for industries thrown up by the market, it will not be adequate to the task envisaged by the government's strategy. The appropriate public sector role is one which will involve the development of a range of specific competences not just to facilitate market tendencies but, where necessary, to undertake policy initiatives which reflect the realities of economic difficulties, especially those relating to the underdevelopment of certain strategic industries. The national co-ordination between the States with Industrial Supplies Offices and, with the Commonwealth, the development of a National Preference Agreement covering government purchasing (which replaced the previous State preferences) provide a model of the sorts of initiatives that will be required in the future.

The current incapacity of the State's public agencies to intervene in undesirable industrial restructuring processes and forge others, explicitly suited to the political and demographic demands of its population, is not, of course a failing unique to Queensland. It is one shared by other States and the nation generally. Nor is it an inevitable deficiency. Industry policy is an underdeveloped aspect of the public sector's responsibilities in many countries. In Australia democratic involvement in policy development for viable manufacturing has been especially neglected:

'. . . no public body has ever been charged with a duty to monitor, still less ensure, the regional integration, modernization and adequate performance of the sector: public sector bodies concerned with its management have instead formed round laissez-faire doctrine which denies any such responsibility . . . Institutional reform constitutes then, an indispensable prelude to industry policy and industrial regeneration' (Ewer, Higgins & Stevens, 1987, p. 119).

The public sector, to facilitate the proposals envisaged by 'Quality Queensland', will need to develop its acumen in areas not foreshadowed in the documents. Entirely new agencies, with distinct skills and capabilities will need to be created. These will require the input of engineers, scientists, demographers, industrial relations specialists and researchers with experience at evaluating successful and unsuccessful industrial regeneration strategies. In essence this amounts to a much more deliberate, institutionalized, and democratic, process of public involvement in decisions concerning investment. The public sector which developed in such directions would also, necessarily, work closely with other bodies with commensurate or complementary knowledge, especially trade unions which have been nationwide pacesetters in policy formulation in this area.

The 'Quality Queensland' Strategy signals its immature appreciation of the difficulty of the task of forging a clearly defined public sector role in industrial development (from a low base) in its list of remaining potentially competitive, emerging manufacturing activities. These are 'related to information technologies, including specialized computing and data processing systems, laser technology, biotechnology . . .' ('Quality Queensland', unabridged report, p. 16; 'Overview' p. 10). In addition the strategy is hopeful that services can be exported, notably in the areas of education, finance, telecommunications. Public sector services would also be commercialized for export (mapping and agricultural extension are the possibilities cited). Where this aspect of the strategy breaks down is in its unexamined preference to enter international markets which are also being contested also by many other hopeful countries. None of the proposed traded services builds on any particular resource advantage or demonstrated success in Queensland. In short, the strategy, despite its genuflection to the need for new infrastructure, does nothing to specify the role that public sector and other organizations would need to accept if the requisite technical, technological, financial and other infrastructural preconditions for the envisaged economic expansion were to be provided. The 'market facilitation' stance, similar in essence to what has elsewhere been called 'supply side economics' is not up to the task.

'Quality Queensland', then, looks more to entrepreneurship than to government, to private rather than public management, for its change of direction. Despite the admission of past errors (which produced low wages and under-developed workforce skills), future diversification and 'quality' are expected to result from an improved 'business culture'; the encouragement to expansion is to be a function of private sector provisions.

Even the six-point 'infrastructure improvement program' and the four-point program for a 'comprehensive management capability' are essentially pleas for smaller government, market liberalization and removal of 'public sector' impediments to efficiency. Queensland's low taxation, is to be retained as a part of the 'new' infrastructure:

> Queensland's position as the lowest taxed State in Australia provides an important incentive to economic growth. A prime concern of the government will be to retain and indeed enhance this position ('Quality Queensland', p. 41).

Not only is the public sector to be denied the opportunity to expand its industry policy acumen, but the proposals for changes are oriented to a strategy likely to exacerbate rather than ameliorate existing dependence on volatile foreign markets.

The contrast with successful macroeconomic policy developments elsewhere, both in Australia and overseas, is quite stark. Whereas an emphatic transition from purely market modes of regulation to institutional forms that allow for research, planning and the development of public priorities characterise industry re-structuring in successful economies, the Queensland Strategy proposes that 'expressions of interest' be invited for private provision of existing and expected facilities. Repeatedly throughout the 'Overview' the intention to seek 'expressions of interest' from the private sector is signalled, rather than any concern to develop extant and potential public sector competences in areas traditionally associated with

non-profit orientations (pp. 15, 17, 23, 26, 27).

The 'Quality Queensland' Strategy therefore sets out a series of activities wherein private sector operators might usurp public sector functions in the near future. These include:

— new or expanded roads, prisons, hospitals, airports and schools;
— transport to tourist areas, transit centres and rapid urban transport systems;
— a science centre;
— 'independent' regional research centres, resource auditing;
— education (especially distance education).

The seriousness of the government's proposals in these directions is as yet untested; however the Strategy also calls for the establishment of a large number of quasi-academic centres of excellence or research centres. The rationale for such centres is that private sector involvement in planning and anticipating and facilitating the restructuring of the Queensland economy could thereby be assured. The centres anticipated in the Strategy are

— Advanced Manufacturing Centres (to provide information, advice, training and evaluation of ancillary service needs for new manufacturers);
— a Centre of Excellence in Mine Productivity and Safety;
— Centres of Tourism Management;
— a Centre in Coal Resource Utilization;
— Centres for the Development of Regional Opportunities;
— a Centre for Commercial Dispute Settlement;
— a Queensland Strategic Management Centre and
— a World Trade Centre.

In some instances these are expected to work in conjunction with existing (or revamped) public institutions (for example, CSIRO, the University of Queensland, the Queensland Science and Technology Council, the Private Sector Economic Advisory Committee, the Queensland Tourist and Travel Corporation and the Premier's Department).

These proposals are all a part of the market facilitation strategy developed in 'Quality Queensland'. Its focus is on the more efficient exploitation of existing advantages (especially natural resource development, see p. 28) and on the attempt to create 'a more advanced economy' (p. 33) by organizing conventional management techniques in a more concerted manner. This is the basis of our criticism of 'Quality Queensland': it ultimately avoids any commitment to a broad ranging, interventionist, public sector led, industrial restructuring. It falls back on precisely the policy preferences that created the State's current malaise. By opting for changes which seek to ensure 'the right climate' (p. 25) for entrepreneurial success; and by orienting its proposed agencies to 'tactical policy and opportunity development instead of actually carrying out operational activity', the strategy abrogates responsibility in favour of grand hopes for autonomous change. This is not how the industrial structure in a peripheral, resource and commodity-dependent part of a small nation can be progressively transformed. By adopting a strategy which is not equal to the task, existing institutional resources in the State's public sector will be squandered.

Housing Policy: Public Versus Private
The relative underdevelopment of public sector provided components of the social wage is not a new phenomenon. An important example of the long-term effects of low levels of public service provision (as opposed to recent cutbacks) exists in the case of public housing in Queensland. Many of these issues have been documented by Withers (1987; 1988a).

The significant economic restructuring occurring in Australia coupled with the decline in the role of government has severely shaken the housing system. Queensland has fared badly in this process experiencing strong economic stagnation and falls in living standards. The heavy slant towards private housing provision that prevails has made Queensland consumers particularly vulnerable to rising costs in all tenures. The political sponsorship of home ownership remains and a public housing system that operates in a traditional 'welfare mode' acts as a deterrent to any moves away from private sector dominance.

Perhaps more than anywhere else in Australia, government policy in Queensland has been slanted towards private home ownership. Compounding the Federal Governments long term subsidies such as interest rate regulation and taxation exemptions and write offs, the State Government has allowed the sale of public stock so that only 2.5% of households are public tenants. Further, and more significantly, the government allocates most of its housing monies to home ownership in the form of low interest loans, second loans (bridging) and interest subsidies. This amount was approximately 55% in 1985/86.

The pressure from a poor public housing sector, and an insecure and low quality private rental sector combined with a high proportion of households living outside the three main tenure forms means that private home ownership is able to retain its dominant position. The absence of any real alternative drives people into owner occupation.

Twenty-two percent of households in Queensland consume their housing as private rental. This figure is around the national average but is somewhat understated as a reasonable proportion of the 8% of households living outside the three main tenure forms can be assumed to be paying rent or payment in kind to the owner of their accommodation.

Private rental is higher in urban areas and drops significantly in rural areas where the 'other' category more than doubles the State average.

The Residential Tenancies Act of 1975 offers only minimal rights for tenants and does not regulate at all the tenancy of camping, caravan dwellers, holiday rental or situations of lodging and boarding. In combination this means that over 30% of households are at the mercy of a completely deregulated housing market.

The steps taken across Australia in recent years to develop a stronger and better quality public housing system, after years of post-war neglect, have not been mirrored in Queensland. Whereas public housing accounts for approximately 5% of stock nationally, in Queensland this figure is 2.5%. Outside Brisbane the situation is even more extreme with only 0.5% of households as public housing tenants.

Table 14.16

Tenure Distribution: Queensland and non-Brisbane

	Queensland 1981	Queensland 1986	Non Brisbane
Home Owners	67.3	65.5	61.3
Private Renters	22.1	21.5	23.0
Public Renters	2.5	2.8	1.8
Caravans	3.2	4.7	
Others	8.0	7.0	9.2

Source: ABS 1986.

At 30 June 1986 total public stock in Queensland was 27,834 dwellings of which 4,203 were Aboriginal housing.

Public expenditure on housing in Queensland leans heavily towards home ownership. Public funds for expenditure on housing are administered by the Queensland Housing Commission. Of the dwellings provided since its inception, to 30 June 1985, 74.9% of dwellings were provided under home ownership schemes and only 25.1% under the rental program.

At 30 June 1986, 9828 households were on QHC waiting lists. This represents a rise of 131% since 1979, given the restricted eligibility criteria (ie. no singles) and the very poor State of the sector in general, this figure can be seen as largely understated. Assessments of housing need are heavily hierarchised with applicants being sifted through five gradations of priority.

Low income earners are least able to compete in mainly private and deregulated housing markets. The political and economic environment in Queensland produces, maintains and sanctions a privatised and anarchic regime of housing provision which denies secure and affordable housing to the most in need. Whereas other States are attempting new strategies and policies, Queensland continues to drift in a situation of discriminatory private sector support and public sector neglect.

14.6 Reforming and Developing Queensland's State Public Services

This section considers the present contribution of the State public sector to social and economic justice in Queensland in terms of the sector's contribution to the social wage and to

social equity more generally. Some areas of underdevelopment and underprovision in this dimension of public service are noted with specific reference to employment, housing, and social welfare responsibilities. A strategy for developing improved community service provision is then suggested by the identification of certain new institutions which must be considered if public sector renewal is to make an enhanced contribution to social justice in Queensland.

14.6.1 Social Welfare Policy

Although many of the responsibilities for social welfare services in Queensland remain with the Commonwealth, the importance of State public sector contributions cannot be overestimated. Welfare services are provided principally by two departments in Queensland: the Department of Community Services and Ethnic Affairs and the Department of Family Services. The former is small size and concentrates on 'ethnic affairs'.

Reference has already been made to the decline in funding (in real terms) of the Department of Family Services throughout the 1980s and to the severe decline in staffing of the department between 1984 and 1987. Data collection conducted by the Queensland Council of Social Services (QCOSS) indicates that this trend resulted in enormous extra pressure on the government and non-government sectors concerned with welfare provision. The situation has further deteriorated with the partial privatisation of the youth and adolescent welfare area failing to result in the savings expected (Lindeberg, 1987, p. 438).

Excessive pressure on welfare services is normally evidenced in the area of emergency relief. In contemporary Queensland, therefore, emergency relief is critical not only because it is a direct, immediate and essential social service but because it carries much of the burden left by a drastically 'run down' department unable to provide an adequate level of income security or maintain adequate permanent assistance programs.

Inevitably, much of the work has fallen to non-government agencies which often exist without adequate funding, expertise or coordination. According to the most recent QCOSS report:

> Queensland organizations confirmed that a significant majority are continuing to experience a heavy strain on their resources which cannot be survived indefinitely. In the last financial year Queensland non-government organizations have experienced a 40% increase in the number of people seeking emergency relief (QCOSS, 1988, p. 26).

The intentions of the present government are clear. In the words of the then Minister, 'there is a much greater realisation these days that those so-called government programs are, in fact, the responsibility of families, community and government' (Chapman, 1987, p. 6). Despite these claims, the need for emergency relief continues to grow and non-government agencies remain pessimistic and unenthusiastic.

In June 1986 consultation between the government and non-government organisations resulted in over 80% of those organisations stating that they wished the public sector to continue distributing services from their offices. Without further consultation the government began off-loading these responsibilities in November 1987. The situation is now critical with over 50 000 income units in Queensland needing emergency relief in the last financial year (QCOSS, 1988, p. 28).

The material presented above suggests that in Queensland the principle of a permanent and increasing social wage has not been achieved. The government's conception of the role of the public sector remains significantly underdeveloped compared with that of other States.

14.6.2 New Institutions

This section outlines some wholly new public sector priorities which need to be placed on the economic policy agenda in order to redress the situation which has been allowed to develop in Queensland. The control of investment is the most important component of economic policy. Market signals are simply too capricious (especially in Queensland) to provide reliable, long term stability. Appropriate institutional settings for public sector sponsored policies to influence investment would probably require the development of a State Bank. Access to finance, on conditions which are sympathetic to macroeconomic outcomes, is an essential part of a sound development strategy for any region or nation. Despite the existence of the Queensland Industry Development Corporation and the Queensland Treasury Corporation, such an institutional commitment does not exist in this State.

The Queensland Government needs a body capable of providing high level research on macroeconomic conditions and trends; capable of ongoing liaison with the private sector; and capable of arranging finance, marketing, supply and processing information for all levels of industry. As modes of manufacturing activity change (by becoming less dependent on economies of scale and needing to respond to 'flexible production' requirements), Queensland's economy will decreasingly resemble its past rural-orientation and will increasingly assume the profile of the more traditional manufacturing States. This will be possible only to the extent that appropriate investment strategies are anticipated, organised and implemented by an activist government.

Paradoxically, the Queensland Government does have a record of involvement in projects which are (unintentionally) suggestive of the innovative role a public sector can play in social and economic development. Queensland's populist Governments have long been interventionist even when the specific investments seem politically unattractive, speculative or nepotistic. Some recent examples of less-than-orthodox public-private relations but which imply public influence over investment decisions are:

– the 'barter' arrangements between Queensland and Turkey regarding power station development and coal supplies.

– the Queensland Government infrastructural support for a film studio complex at Cades County.

– QTTC's investment in a Port Douglas tourist development.

– the government's willingness to override town planning objections to retail, commercial and tourist developments at Toowong, Roma St Station, and Sanctuary Cove.

– the Japanese tourist development at Yeppoon.

– the substantial government investment in troubled engineering and cement manufacturing firms.

– Suncorp's involvement as a property developer, hotel owner and rural landlord.

– the government's hopes for a commercial rocket launching capacity on Cape York Peninsula.

Much of this activity may be defensible to the extent that it involves State influence over infrastructural investments which would not otherwise have occurred. They do therefore, show that public enterprise and the private sector, even in Queensland, are not (and do not need to be) separate and antagonistic. Because of their very quirkiness they also suggest how much better it would be if there were a permanent institutional location for long term research and decision making as well as for genuine democratic involvement in the decisions concerning the State's economic and social development.

The second type of new institution concerns income distribution. If the trend in Australia is towards more public sector involvement of this kind, rather than less (that is towards more State-provided services, more State-initiated production, or a higher 'social wage'), the public sector will need to develop new skills, new knowledge, new ways of dealing with social conflicts and new criteria for understanding what policy provisions are most effective.

In Queensland, too, the industrial relations system's integrity has recently suffered as a

result of interventions of a conflictual and non-conciliatory nature (see Guille, 1985). It is therefore, important that a substantial institutional commitment by the government to appropriate, non regressive means of controlling wage and non-wage incomes be forged in the near future.

The third area which appears to warrant more attention by government (and which therefore requires alteration in the pattern of government spending priorities) is the labour market. Few of the basic conditions of employment (wage levels, wage relativities, employment levels, relocation and retraining opportunities, redundancy or restructuring) are best handled by market mechanisms. In the advanced democracies, these issues have progressively become matters of political decision. Such trends indicate the need for increasingly conscientious political institutions to control (or over-ride) the 'labour market'. People's conditions of employment and remuneration are too important to be left to market forces; they are best decided explicitly, subject to publicly known criteria. As people need in the future to be periodically retrained (to keep up with technological change in employment, for example), the need for new institutions in the public sector will become increasingly recognised.

14.7 Summary and Conclusions

This chapter has shown a State virtually directionless in its attempts to meet the real challenges facing it. Even seemingly positive developments such as the commissioning of an economic development plan have been sabotaged by a government unable to appreciate the very real problems inherent in an unbalanced economy, preferring to push the criticisms of its activity out of the limelight and release instead a glossy public relations booklet.

It has also shown that the Queensland Government's reliance on low levels of taxation and its engagement in tax competition have led to two contradictory developments: the attraction of those population cohorts most reliant on public sector support (particularly the aged); and a financial inability to meet existing and emerging social and economic needs. The Queensland Government must desist from reliance on such policies.

Only be adopting policies designed to overcome this imbalance between demands and the resources available to it can the Queensland Government – of whatever persuasion – establish itself as a competent manager. It will no longer be sufficient (if it ever has been) for the government to rely on low-tax, small government rhetoric and trade union assault.

The first step in such a strategy should be a new strategy for State revenue raising based on the introduction of the State Goods and services Levy. Queensland is one of the States that stands to gain a great deal from a more stable revenue base. First, its increasing reliance on regressive revenue sources – such as the blatant use of fees and fines as a de facto tax collection agency – could be wound back. Second, a more stable source of funds might encourage the Queensland State Government to replace its current industry policy, based as it is on the dubious virtues of tax competition, with an active state development strategy. This alternative approach would be better placed to address the fundamental vulnerability of the State economy, and thereby lay the foundations for a thorough-going attack on the social inequalities endured by many Queenslanders.

Chapter 15

TASMANIA

15.1 Introduction

Tasmania experiences all the problems associated with small island economies elsewhere: in this case the small population (449,000 in June, 1988) proscribes domestic consumption and production possibilities because the domestic market for local products is thin. Consequently, scale economies in production cannot be fully exploited, nor is there anything like an adequate supply of products and services in consumption. Thus the region's economy is dependent on external markets as outlets for its production and on imports to satisfy consumer demand. In other words, the Tasmanian region is relatively open in comparison with the more populous States, and the prices of traded commodities are set elsewhere. This follows because 90% of Tasmania's exports are primary products — the output of mines and farms — and the prices of these are generally determined on world commodity markets. This trade profile has not been brought into better balance, despite sustained attempts to do so. The region's development between Federation and the early seventies rested heavily on a policy of 'hydroindustrialisation', the central feature of which was the incentive offered to manufacturing industries of cheap, clean hydro power. A dozen medium sized energy intensive plants were established in this period of hydro based development, manufacturing alumina, steel plate, paper and pulp, woodchips, frozen foods, zinc and iron-ore pellets.

However, the halcyon days of hydro development gradually faded as the region lost its comparative energy cost advantage and the options for further dam construction diminished. This era was thrust into final oblivion by the High Court decision upholding Federal legislation which effectively blocked the Franklin below Gordon Dam. The legacies are obvious: 12 major industries absorb 70% of Tasmania's narrowly based energy grid and few alternative sources of energy supply have been developed. Hydro power is no longer relatively cheap or abundant. A new direction for economic development remains unclear.

A further distinguishing economic characteristic of the Tasmanian economy is its 'branch' nature: there is little if any regional ownership and control in the private sector and no head offices of major Australian industries are domiciled in the region. The regional economy does not possess a top executive class and local educational institutions tend to export a major proportion of their graduates leaving the region bereft of managerial expertise and also with a relatively slow population growth. This lack of managerial expertise is a major impediment to the development of the region and in addition helps explain the relatively low level of average incomes.

Locational constraints are on balance severe and binding. A major issue is Bass Strait, which separates Tasmanian industries from their interstate markets. The Freight Equalisation Scheme provides subsidies for North bound traffic in particular and is designed to offset the transport cost disadvantages imposed by the restricted transport modal choice.

Environmental considerations have a heightened sensitivity in Tasmania's pristine environment. The Franklin Dam decision, the 'forestry accord' between the Commonwealth and State Governments, Noranda's decision to withdraw from the Wesley Vale Pulp Mill project and the recent State election all indicate the importance of conservation.

Here we have an image of an Australian

region in relative decline. Per capita incomes have not risen with the same rapidity in Tasmania as they have in the rest of the country implying a slower rate of output growth and it is not surprising that Tasmania has Australia's highest unemployment problem.

Inevitably, the role of Tasmanian State and Local Government is a positive one: they must attempt to fill many gaps in the provision of goods and services left by the smaller private sector, and provide a relatively high degree of total capital expenditures, given the relatively low levels of direct investment by business. There are few options for privatisation and an unconvincing case for the application of laissez-faire doctrines. This Chapter explores these issues in depth.

15.2 Demography and Economy
15.2.1 Demography

Tasmania's percentage share of the Australian population has fallen from 4.75% at Federation to 2.79% (1988), which is a reduction of more than 40%. No other region has experienced such a reduction in its population share.

Tasmania's slow population growth is influenced strongly by emigration. Callaghan (1977) estimated Tasmania's population loss from interstate emigration as 70,000 in total for the period 1901 to 1977 and in Table 15.1 we can observe that the net loss from interstate emigration since 1977, amounts to 11,910, bringing a total population loss of 82,000 through interstate emigration since Federation.

Table 15.1

Rate of Population Growth and Net Interstate Emigration: Tasmania 1978-1988

Year	Total Population Growth		Net Interstate Migration Growth	Interstate Migration No
	Tas.	Aust.	%	
1978	0.63	1.18	-0.24	-1002
1979	0.75	1.09	-0.12	-504
1980	0.67	1.24	-0.24	-1016
1981	0.86	1.55	-0.24	-1025
1982	0.59	1.71	-0.51	-2192
1983	0.69	1.38	-0.28	-1211
1984	1.14	1.21	0.16	700
1985	1.16	1.34	0.18	797
1986	0.82	1.46	-0.03	-134
1987	0.33	1.53	-0.64	-2867
1988	0.11	1.56	-0.77	-3456

Source: ABS 3101: Australian Demographic Statistics — Quarterly.

Thus, net interstate emigration explains most of the differential between average Tasmanian and average Australian population growth once the cumulative effects of outmigration on the subsequent birth rate is taken into account. The slow growth of Tasmania's population is evident in Table 15.1, where in each of the last eleven years Tasmania's population growth is well below the national average: it is only in the years 1984 and 1985 when the gap closes appreciably and these are years in which Tasmania experiences a net interstate migration gain, following State Government initiatives in Sydney and Melbourne to sell Tasmania as a retirement destination.

Tasmania's slow population growth warrants considerable emphasis because it is at the centre of Tasmania's economic problems: a small and slow growing population provides limited regional markets and restricts potential investment opportunities. A further important demographic characteristic is population dispersion and the degree of urbanisation; a State by State comparison is provided in Table 15.2.

South Australia and Western Australia have almost three quarters of their total populations residing in their capital cities; while almost 70% of Victorians and 62% of the New South Wales population reside in Melbourne and Sydney respectively. However, only 40% of

Tasmanians dwell in the capital, Hobart. The regional breakdown is revealing: 27.5% of Tasmanians reside along the North West coastal plain with major centres of population at Burnie (24,000) and Devonport (25,000) and a further 25.4% live in the Tamar Valley and on the North East Coast where the major regional town is Launceston (88,000); the capital Hobart (180,000) is the central location in the Southern region which in total accounts for the balance of Tasmania's population

(47.1%). This relatively even dispersion of Tasmania's population between the Northern and Southern regions creates extra demands on the State Government: services must be duplicated in the various centres and much of this is unavoidable. However, some of the duplication cannot be justified on equity grounds; it is due simply to the working of the political parish pump, which on occasions frustrates the efficient delivery of State services.

Table 15.2

Population Dispersion and Degree of Urbanisation:
Australian States 30 June, 1988

State	Population (000s)	% of Aust. Population	% of Tas.	% of State in Capital City
NSW	5657.3	34.5		62.8
Vic.	4234.2	25.8		70.4
Qld	2708.0	16.5		46.3
WA	1521.3	9.3		72.7
SA	1401.2	8.5		72.9
Tas.	447.9	2.7		40.2
NW Tas.	123.1		27.5	
NE Tas.	113.8		25.4	
SE Tas.	210.9		47.1	

Source: The Cuthbertson Report (1985) Tasmanian Government Printer.

15.2.2 Economy

Tasmania's declining population percentage, which is a major concern to regional planners, is also indicative of a further problem: the rate of economic growth must be lower in Tasmania otherwise Tasmanian per capita income (defined as the ratio of State GDP to the population) must have increased faster than Australia's ratio of GDP to population.

The evidence available confirms this view: it was necessary in 1933 to bring into existence the Commonwealth Grants Commission in order to achieve fiscal equalisation among the Australian States. The poorer States such as Tasmania were supported by the standard States (New South Wales and Victoria), according to a specific Grants Commission formula and Tasmania, for example, received a share of CRF tax shares disproportionate to population. Thus, in 1981, the 2.8% of Australians resident in Tasmania received 4.4% of the CRF tax pool and the inimical effects of reducing this to 3.8%

in 1987-1988, are evident in the following paragraphs.

The Commonwealth Grants Commission was established in 1933 to prevent living standards in the mendicant States falling relative to those in the standard States; this reform would not be required if the smaller States such as Tasmania displayed relatively rapid economic growth. This general proposition may be tested by reference to some recent experience of output growth. Table 15.3 provides a breakdown of the growth of Tasmanian GDP by industry and compares the cumulative growth rate of GDP for Tasmania with the overall Australian growth rate from 1959-60 to 1983-84, the latest year for which State GDP estimates were available.

If we compare the overall compound growth rate in Tasmania and Australia over the 24 years from 1959-60 to 1983-84, we find Tasmania's average growth (3.3%) below the compound

Australian rate of (4.0%) and in none of the major industry groups is Tasmania's growth rate above the Australian rate: mining industry output has grown very slowly in Tasmania (2.4% for Tasmania and 7.3% for Australia).

Table 15.3

Growth Rates in Real Gross Product by Industry Tasmania [i]

Year Ending June	Agriculture	Mining	% Manufacturing	Tertiary	Gross State Product
1961	-6.9	7.5	5.8	1.2	1.8
1962	31.5	11.4	1.1	2.1	4.6
1963	-7.3	20.3	12.0	1.7	4.1
1964	-5.0	4.7	2.3	6.2	4.2
1965	2.1	6.9	9.4	4.8	5.8
1966	26.5	19.0	-0.4	-3.2	1.1
1967	-6.8	6.3	13.4	11.0	9.5
1968	-26.0	11.3	-0.2	2.0	-0.1
1969	39.1	47.6	-2.1	8.5	10.8
1970	6.6	15.8	12.9	4.9	7.9
1971	3.4	-1.4	-4.6	3.6	1.2
1972	-4.7	-7.1	-1.5	7.4	2.9
1973	-14.8	-4.9	3.5	8.6	4.5
1974	-3.7	29.3	14.0	-5.0	2.0
1975	-32.7	-23.8	1.4	7.0	0.9
1976	16.7	-27.2	-1.3	3.3	0.1
1977	76.7	36.4	3.1	3.7	8.7
1978	29.6	23.4	-13.0	2.5	2.7
1979	-4.4	-9.9	9.1	6.0	4.1
1980	-30.2	-3.1	11.1	3.4	1.7
1981	-3.8	-33.3	-3.2	6.7	0.8
1982	25.2	-15.8	-9.5	0.1	-1.2
1983	93.0	7.3	-13.6	-3.6	1.4
1984	-36.4	-18.1	7.9	7.8	1.0

Average Growth Rates
Tasmania and Australia Compared
1959-60 to 1983-84

	Agriculture	Mining	Manufacturing	Tertiary	Total
Tasmania	3.0	2.4	2.1	3.7	3.3
Australia	3.6	7.3	2.7	4.2	4.0

Note: (i) Growth rates based on GDP estimates in 1979-80 prices.
Source: National Institute of Economic and Industry Research (NIEIR).
'State working Party' − Supplementary Material: South Australia, Western Australia & Tasmania, Melbourne 25th Feb., 1986, p. 37.

This relatively sluggish mineral sector is exposed in the body of Table 15.3 where since 1971 growth is negative more often than not with a very large negative growth outcome in 1984. The declining contribution of manufacturing and agriculture to overall growth rates is an issue which affects many less developed countries and it is true that Tasmania has several characteristics in common with them. However, the general point emerging from Table 15.3 is that Tasmania's growth rate lags behind the Australian rate in the period 1959-

60 to 1983-84. The significance of this sluggish growth rate is sharpened by the fact that Tasmanians do not experience the same living standards as other Australians; Tasmania's Gross Product per capita remains approximately 90% of Australia's averaged over all States and Territories.

Exports and Openness
The growth of the Tasmanian economy is severely affected in years of recession, as it was, for example, in 1981-82 and 1982-83. One explanation for this may be found in the dependence of the regional economy on exports, 90% of which are agricultural products including timber and minerals, which renders the Tasmanian growth rate vulnerable to any decline of international commodity prices. The export performance of the Tasmanian economy is often advanced as the strongest feature of Tasmania's regional economy. There is some evidence supporting this argument in Table 15.4 where Tasmania's exports per capita exceed comparable Australian figures in each of the years 1979-80 to 1983-84 inclusive.

Table 15.4

Exports per Capita: Australia and Tasmania 1979-80 to 1983-84					
	1979-80	*1980-81*	*1981-82*	*1982-83*	*1983-84*
Australia $	1292.6	1295.0	1301.0	1443.6	1601.9
Tasmania $	1536.0	1547.2	1511.4	1794.2	1781.1
% difference Tasmania — Australia	18.8	19.5	16.2	24.3	11.2

Source: ABS 1302.6 Tasmanian Year Book, 1985, p. 405.

Tasmania's exports per capita exceed the Australian average by approximately 18% over this five year period, but this percentage difference is hardly adequate to justify the claim that Tasmania's export performance is vastly superior to the Australian economy as a whole. This finding is of some significance, as we have claimed that Tasmania is a relatively open region in the opening paragraph of this chapter. The Tasmanian region is exposed to foreign competition, but the evidence for it being more or less open than other Australian regions is not strongly supported by these export statistics.

Incomes
The absence of an executive class earning high incomes depresses Tasmania's average weekly earnings both in constant and current prices. This is evident in Graph 15.1, where Australian and Tasmanian average weekly earnings are compared.

In general, Tasmania's average weekly earnings fall below those prevailing in Australia and in Graph 15.1 we observe the effects of policies designed to reduce the real unit cost of labour. Real earnings have fallen throughout 1986 and 1987, and the drop in Tasmania's real average weekly earnings is more severe.

The smaller size of Tasmania's incomes is also indicated by a more general measure — average household income. The average household incomes and average expenditure for each State are recorded in Table 15.5.

Hobart's average weekly household income ($443.34) at 30th June 1984 is the second lowest among Australia's capital cities; approximately 70% of Canberra's and approximately 9% below Australia's average household income.

The Cost of the Tariff
There is another international aspect of Tasmania's potential for development. This relates to the income redistribution induced by tariff-protection. Tasmanian authorities along with those in Western Australia and

Queensland claim they are disadvantaged by tariff protection provided for industries predominantly 'domiciled' in Victoria, South Australia and New South Wales. In a most important analysis of this issue by Clements and Sjaastad (1984) the role of the tariff as a tax on exporters and a subsidy transferred to the import competing industries is explained. Tariffs are borne as a tax by exporters who import raw materials and capital items not subject to tariff concessions and in the form of additional labour costs given that the level of effective protection and the escalation of unit labour costs are positively correlated. The costs of tariff protection to the Tasmanian region are indicated in the Cuthbertson inquiry (1985) into the impacts of the Commonwealth Grants Commission 1985 recommendations on the Tasmanian region.

Graph 15.1

Real Average Weekly Earnings: Tasmania & Australia

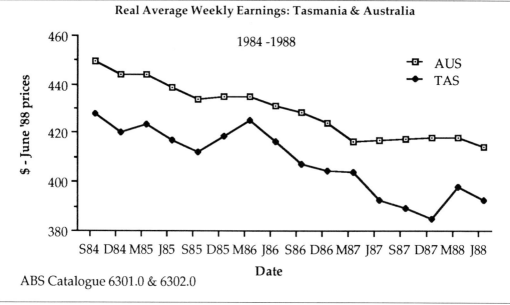

ABS Catalogue 6301.0 & 6302.0

Table 15.5

Average Household Income and Expenditure for Australian Capital Cities

City	Average Household Income $ (Weekly)	Expenditure $	Expenditure/
Sydney	499.23	396.37	0.79
Melbourne	492.49	383.23	0.78
Brisbane	448.41	349.01	0.78
Adelaide	427.94	332.01	0.80
Perth	452.08	363.70	0.79
Hobart	443.34	349.46	0.78
Darwin	597.28	468.33	0.78
Canberra	631.09	474.85	0.75
Australian Average	481.65	378.38	0.79

Source: ABS Cat. No. 6533.0, Household Expenditure Survey.

Consider the distortions created by tariff protection. Table 15.6 presents calculations based on the 1977/78 estimates of Net Subsidy Equivalents (NSE) by State, made by the Industries' Assistance Commission (IAC). These show the amount of money that would have to be paid by an annual subsidy to provide the same amount of assistance as is provided by the average effective rate of tariff. If these IAC estimates are updated to March 1985 prices and if they are divided by the population of each State, we obtain estimates of tariff assistance per capita for each State:

Table 15.6

Estimates of Tariff Assistance per Capita by State
($ March 1985 Prices)

	NSW	Vic.	Qld	WA	SA	Tas.	Aus
Assistance Per Capita	494	731	193	233	505	361	469

Source: Committee to review the Impact of the Commonwealth Growth Commission. Recommendations on Tasmania Tasmanian Government Printers, May 1985, p. 78.

New South Wales, Victoria and South Australia receive effective tariff protection above the Australian average of $469 per capita, and assistance to Victorians in particular, is 56% above. Queensland, Western Australia and Tasmania are well below the national assistance per capita. The export orientated States are not compensated in Commonwealth Grants Commission formula for these tariff induced imposts.

Labour Market

The percentage contributions of particular resource and industry groups to Gross State Product and employment is provided in Graph 15.2.

The major employers of Tasmanian labour are the resource based industries. This is indicated clearly in Table 15.7.

Graph 15.2

Industry Contributions to GSP & Employment %

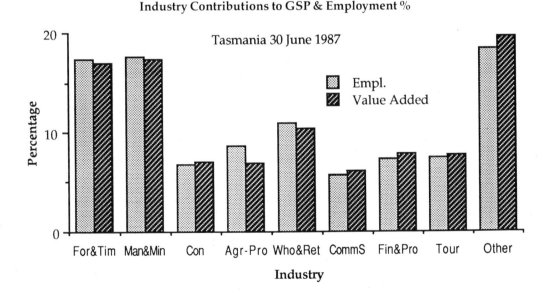

Table 15.7

Employed Persons 15 Years and Over by Industry
Classification: Census Data

Industry	1976		1981		1986		% Change
	No.	%	No.	%	No.	%	1976-86
Agriculture, Forestry & Fishing	12716	7.8	12995	7.6	13066	7.5	2.75
Mining	4213	2.6	4311	2.5	3299	1.9	-21.72
Manufacturing	27670	16.9	26124	15.3	24718	14.2	-10.67
Electricity, Gas & Water	3182	1.9	4641	2.7	5052	2.9	58.77
Construction	12592	7.7	10963	6.4	11325	6.5	-10.06
Wholesale Retail Trade	29144	17.8	29078	17.1	31318	18.0	7.46
Transport & Storage	8266	5.0	8156	4.8	8252	4.7	-0.17
Communication	3136	1.9	3401	2.0	3860	2.2	23.09
Finance, Property	9861	6.0	10959	6.3	12208	7.0	23.80
Public, Defence	7765	4.7	8846	5.2	9002	5.2	15.93
Community Services	24511	15.0	29618	17.4	35036	2.01	42.94
Recreation	9490	5.8	10209	6.0	11911	6.8	25.51
Unclassified	11400	7.0	11301	6.6	5652	3.2	-50.42
Total	163945		170402		174398		

Source: ABS Census Data 1976; 1981; 1986.

The breakdown according to ASIC classification provided in Table 15.7 provides a similar distribution of employment as that portrayed in Graph 15.2: the majority of Tasmanians are employed in resource and service industries and, following the international and Australian pattern, employment is falling in manufacturing, mining and construction.

The growth statistics based on State GDP figures in Table 15.3 present a pessimistic view. The growth of employment is another general indicator of economic growth, but on this criterion, Tasmania's relative performance is no better, as Table 15.8 reveals.

Table 15.8

Employment and Labour Force Growth 1976-1981 and 1981-1986
Tasmania and Australia

	Employment Growth %		Labour Force Growth %		Labour Force/ Employment	
	Tas.	Aus.	Tas.	Aus.	Tas.	Aus.
1976-81	7.00	8.72	7.53	9.50	1.09	1.04
1981-86	5.32	7.62	4.79	6.77	1.10	1.05

Source: ABS Census Data 1976; 1981; 1986.

The important feature of Table 15.8 is the growth of Tasmanian employment, which rose by 7% compared with overall Australian employment growth of 8.72% over the five years, 1976-1981. The gap between Tasmanian and Australian employment growth closed between 1981 and 1986, but Tasmania's employment growth is still less than Australia's. This

does not matter provided the growth of employment is sufficient to accommodate the growth of the labour force. But Tasmania also fails to match Australia on this criterion; the ratio of labour force to employment growth in Tasmania is 1.09 and 1.10 for the periods 1976-81 and 1981-86 respectively. The comparable Australian figures are 1.04 and 1.05. These discrepancies suggest that the Tasmanian unemployment rate will rise in comparison to the Australian rate, as Tasmania's employment growth is less capable of accommodating the growth of the labour force.

The noteworthy feature of Tasmania's unemployment rate since 1980 is that it is consistently above the Australian rate. This is a result not confined to recent experience. In Table 15.9 below, unemployment rates for the Tasmanian region and Australia averaged across all regions are compared at 30th June over the period 1978 to 1988:

Tasmania's unemployment rate is higher than average Australian experience and the gap between them appears to be widening through time. For example in 1978 Tasmania's mid year unemployment rate (6.5%) is only 3% above the Australian rate (6.3%) but the disparity had increased to almost 25% by June 1988. By the end of January 1989 the official unemployment statistics indicate a Tasmanian unemployment rate of 10.5% as opposed to an Australian average of 7.5% of the workforce.

Table 15.9

Mid-Year Unemployment Ratios
Tasmania & Australia 1978-1988[i]

Year	Tasmanian % of Labour Force	Australian % of Labour Force
1978	6.5	6.3
1979	5.9	6.3
1980	6.2	6.2
1981	6.7	5.6
1982	9.5	6.7
1983	10.8	10.3
1984	11.0	9.0
1985	9.1	8.4
1986	8.5	7.9
1987	9.8	8.1
1988	9.1	7.3

Note: [i] At 30th June each year.
Source: ABS Cat. No. 6203.0: Labor Force Australia.

Hardwick (1985) reaches a similar conclusion and also distinguishes between cyclical unemployment (AC) and Frictional-Structural (FS) unemployment from Tasmanian data. The point of this distinction is that aggregate cyclical unemployment depends on the *national* level of unemployment and the *frictional-structural* (FS) is explained by regional factors exclusively. The distinction is developed and applied to UK studies of regional unemployment and in general they show that the more prosperous low unemployment areas of the UK are more sensitive to national unemployment than the poorer high unemployment areas. Tasmania fits the latter pattern in an Australian context and it is clear that approximately 50% of Tasmanian unemployment is explained by national factors and regional influences explain the balance.

The public sector in Tasmania is certainly the major Tasmanian employer of labor, although it is difficult to assess its precise contribution, because no single central organisation had supervised all public sector employment until the office of the Commissioner for Public Employment was established. Some notion of the contribution made by the public sector to total employment in 1977, 1984 and 1988 (each at 30th June) is provided in Table 15.10.

Public sector employment has fallen by 3,574 since 1977, a 9.17% absolute reduction. While the Liberal Government elected in 1982 moved in its first budget to limit staff ceilings in the public service, there can be no doubt that the major effects have been due to cutbacks in Commonwealth funding discussed below. Tasmania has had to cope with a smaller share of a diminishing cake. Further, the introduction of global borrowing limits restricted the capacity of all States to fund discretionary public works; 1984, as a result of these effects, was a watershed for the public sector's contribution. In the last few years real public sector outlays have fallen significantly and public sector employment is down 9.43%. Superficially Table 15.10 suggests that, with an overall increase of total employment of 15.2% since 1984, the reduction of public sector employment has been more than offset by private sector employment growth. Unfortunately, this is misleading as the figures do not distinguish full time, part time or casual employment. Full time employment has not grown since 1984 and the number of males working full time has fallen. The private sector job growth largely reflects increasing participation in the part time labour force by married women. The decline in public sector employment represents a serious blow to the formation of career oriented work for both men and women which has not been compensated by the growth of private sector employment.

Table 15.10

Public Sector and Total Tasmanian Employment
1977, 1984 and 1988 (30 June)

Year	Tas. Public Sector[i] No. of Persons	Total Tasmanian[ii] Employment	% Public Sector %
1977	38,946	168,700	23.09
1984	38,707	169,400	22.90
1988	35,372	195,100	18.13

Notes: [i] Figures for 1977 and 1984 drawn from Chapman (1985, p 80) and for 1988 from the annual report of the Commissioner for Public Employment (1988).
[ii] ABS 1303.6 monthly summary of Statistics.

The Branch Nature of The Tasmanian Region
The Tasmanian export sector suffers a further disadvantage: few if any of the major exporters of minerals and processed metals are locally owned. These industries contribute more than 50% of the value of Tasmanian export earnings, but many major production and employment decisions are made in boardrooms at a distance from the region: such decisions are not influenced by local factors and pressures to the same extent. All the disadvantages of 'foreign' ownership apply, as do the benefits. One firm, North Broken Hill owns more than one half of the Tasmanian timber and mineral resource stock which provides the company with significant bargaining power on sensitive issues such as the setting of royalty rates. Tasmania is, in other words, a branch economy directed by senior management domiciled elsewhere. Some evidence of the lack of domestic sovereignty is indicated in Table 15.11.

The mining, manufacturing, transport and finance sectors are subject to significant external control. Decisions about output, employment, investment, and the mix of products and services are made in national head offices usually in Sydney and Melbourne. Several of these national companies are subsidiaries of transnational organisations and in this sense output — employment decisions in their Tasmanian branches must bear the imprimatur of a 'foreign' parent.

The economic implications of non-local control are profound. Management and administrative functions are centralised in the companies' head offices leaving only a small operative staff in the branches. This has two effects on the Tasmanian economy: firstly, the variety of branch jobs on offer is limited to sub-managerial and non-executive functions. Further, firms specialising in the provision of business services are located near the head offices in Melbourne and Sydney. Tasmanian owned firms do not have access to these specialised services which hampers the establishment and growth of small enterprises in this State.

Non-local ownership of the State's basic industries dampens the multiplier effects of private sector spending. Firstly non-locally owned producers must buy inputs, but the input mix is decided by the head office concerned and primary inputs are often purchased outside Tasmania. Further, a high proportion of profits from Tasmanian branch activities are repatriated to mainland or foreign shareholders and as a consequence much of the income generated by Tasmania's enterprises leaks out of the State and does not do a 'second round'.

Table 15.11

Location of Head Offices Controlling Tasmanian Employment: All Economic Activity: 1975
Location of Controlling Head Office of Enterprise Group

Industrial Sector	Tasmania %[a]	Mainland %	Vic. %	NSW %
Mining	13	87	25	62
Manufacturing	44	56	45	10
Transport, Communication[b]	47	53	49	3
Finance[b]	52	48	19	28
Wholesale Retail Trade	78	22	14	8
Construction[b]	82	18	16	2
Entertainment	88	12	n.p.	n.p
Community Services[b]	99	1	n.p.	n.p
All Industries[c]	68	32	22	9

Notes: [a] Industries employers and self employed persons.
[b] Less reliable data: see comments in source.
[c] Includes agriculture, forestry, fishing, electricity, gas, water, public administration and defence.
Source: ABS,Tasmanian Year Book No. 10, 1976, (ref. 1301.6), p. 405.

Importantly, the decision to expand, contract or even shut down Tasmanian branch operations is taken in distant boardrooms and is more often than not damaging to Tasmania's interests. Several Tasmanian branch operations were established because cheap and reliable energy sources were available at the time and provided a comparative advantage. But this has been lost as the cost disadvantages of Bass Strait eventually came to outweigh the benefits provided by a Tasmanian location.

The Scarcity of Investment and the Export of Human Capital
One of the consequences of the 'branch' nature of the Tasmanian region is the lack of job opportunities for Tasmanian graduates within the State. This same problem may apply to the graduate output from tertiary institutions in other States but Tasmania's export of human capital is disproportionate: for example, only 10% of University of Tasmania graduates of some faculties are employed in Tasmania five years after gradu-

ation, an export ratio which is in excess of any comparable institution in other Australian States.

Tasmania also suffers from a shortage of investment in physical capital, at least in the small scale private sector of the region's economy, and is evident in Table 15.12 where per capita private investment in physical capital is invariably lower than comparable capital expenditure figures in all other States. However, there are signs of improvement: in 1982-83 per capita capital expenditure in Tasmania was only 52% of Australia's $1,028 per capita, but by 1985-86 and 1986-87 Tasmanian per capita private investment had risen to 83% of the Australian average. There are signs in local surveys of expenditure plans that the region is on the verge of a capital expenditure expansion which may push per capita capital expenditure closer to the national average. For the time being we note that investment by firms in the Tasmanian region is relatively low which partly explains why comparative growth rates remain low in Tasmania.

Table 15.12

Private Fixed Capital Expenditure Per Capita by State: 1982-83 to 1986-87
($ Constant Prices)

Year/State	1982-83	1983-84	1984-85	1985-86	1986-87
	$	$	$	$	$
NSW	974	891	1014	1124	1024
Vic.	862	874	998	1214	1134
Qld	1347	065	1041	1127	889
SA	927	880	911	948	887
WA	1592	1173	1351	1912	1912
Tas.	529	592	675	818	909
Aus.	1028	927	1023	1208	1093

Source: ABS Cat. No. 5646.0 (various issues) Estimates of Private Fixed Capital Expenditure: States and Territories.

15.2.7 Summary

It follows from the above analysis of the Tasmanian economy that a larger public sector is almost inevitable, and that there are few options for privatisation, commercialisation or corporatisation. The demise of hydroindustrialisation, noted in the opening paragraph of this chapter, created pressures for restructuring of the island's economy and a new direction for its development, the bare bones of which are now being exposed. There is some distance to go before we have a clear view of the new strategy. Some parameters are already clearly articulated, for example, the political pressures from the conservation – environmental lobby which will change the face of social planning in the island for years to come. It follows that the demands on Tasmania's public services are changing and with it the public service structure; but the case for further reform is a strong one.

15.3 Functions and Structure of the Tasmanian Public Sector

The following discussion attempts to identify the contribution of the current Public Sector structure to the State's economy, and sets out a functional analysis of the State's agencies so that the economic themes outlined above are further developed. This analysis is preceded by a brief historical note centred on the first major reform of Tasmanian Public Services in seventy years and a description of the State's unusual legislature and electoral system which influence the modus operandi of the State public sector.

15.3.1 The State's Legislature

Introduction – State Government
The Tasmanian Upper-House, the Legislative Council, is traditionally a non-party House of 19 members and operates in a quite independent manner. It is by modern standards a powerful Upper House with a capacity to reject any bill including money bills. The Lower House, the Legislative Assembly is a 35 member party house representing 5 electorates. The ALP has governed Tasmania in 44 of the 54 years since 1934. Angus Bethune's coalition government which held the Treasury benches for 3 years (1969-72) and Robin Gray's Liberal premiership from 1982 are the only periods of non-Labour Government.

As the 1989 election indicates, however, the Hare-Clarke Electoral System works in favour of independent candidates and the conservation based independents. Any future government will have to come to some arrangement with the new 'green' lobby.

15.3.2 The Cartland Reforms

Sir George Cartland (1981) conducted Tasmania's first major review of the State Public Sector for seventy years in 1981. He found an organisational structure suited more to the needs of the late nineteenth century than to the dynamics of the present age. In 1976, the affairs of government were conducted by no fewer than 207 agencies: 15 Ministerial Departments, 15 Departmental Offices, 11 Departmental Corporations, 13 Public Corporations, 13 regulatory bodies and 126 others (which might be loosely described as quangos). The consequences for the equitable and efficient delivery of Public Services were obvious. The organisational structure was fragmented, there were many examples of overlapping functions, duplication of services and demarcation disputes between agencies. 'Departmentalism' predominated. This was a legacy of a past age where agencies developed and expanded in an ad hoc fashion as the solutions to specific problems or the demand for services. Policy formulation received little emphasis. Agencies tended to be inward looking, to preserve their own fiefdoms and to develop decision-making processes which took inadequate account of the general economic and social environment. Those problems were exacerbated by the vested interest of individual Ministers who, in a small State, have a considerable capacity to influence the day to day administration of agencies under their control (particularly by restricting the delegated authorities afforded senior agency staff). The Minister's capacity to control day to day operations was offset by the broad range of their responsibilities, as all Ministers took responsibility for more than one major agency and in individual cases, they were (and remain) responsible for four or five major functions. In summary, the Tasmanian Public Sector in November 1981 was neither efficient, economic or effective.

Cartland's objectives were to create a government administration orientated towards the quality of policy advice and to improve the managerial competence of the Service.

Cartland's approach to these problems took the form of two recommendations: The first required the creation of a single Crown Service to ensure the proper co-ordination and cohesion of public service activities. If adopted, the coverage of the Public Service Act would extend to more than 75% of the Public Sector's employees. The recommendation required the dismantling of the Public Service Board and its functions split between a Commissioner of Public Employment, a Department of Public Administration and a Commissioner of Review for review of administrative decisions and an office of Industrial Relations. This recommendation was adopted by the Liberal Government in the enactment of the State Services Act on 30th May 1984. The new institutional structure has operated since this date. The reforms have gone quite some distance towards the achievement of Cartland's vision. The merit principle is firmly entrenched and the centralisation of functions has proceeded, possibly not with the speed the reformers wished to see. For example, the Cartland report envisaged some correspondence between the number of major agencies and the number of Cabinet Ministers (currently 10). This would require the amalgamation of several major agencies, and although some notable amalgamations have taken place (for example, the combination of the National Parks and Wildlife Service with the Department of Lands), the process has been slow.

The second of Cartland's major recommendations was to allow the 'Managers to Manage'. The State Services Act delegated organisational and managerial decision functions to Heads of Agencies giving them pre-eminence in the management of resources in particular, staff. It is this latter provision which carries with it the more significant problems in the implementation of Cartland's report. The Head of an Agency now possesses the power to declare employees 'surplus to requirements'. Those declared surplus may go on an 'unattached list'. The Head of Agency may also declare a person unfit for duty and call on the Commissioner for Public Employment to inquire into the potential suspension of an employee. However many of the Heads of Agency have not reacted to their greater responsibilities in the way expected, displaying reluctance to exercise their increased power fully or to freely accept them. The changed circumstances surrounding employment have undermined the security of employees and the turnover of staff has accelerated. Preliminary research conducted by the Tasmanian Public Service Association (TPSA) indicates low morale among Public Sector employees. The human responses to the restructuring of the State Service may inhibit the general efficiency gains accumulated from the reforms.

15.3.3 Economic Functions

Reflecting the nature of the Tasmanian economy and the consequent large public sector role, the range of State public sector agencies which have an economic function is large.

Many of them also illustrate the problem noted in previous chapters in defining agencies as economic or social: many of them fulfill both types of functions. The following paragraphs outline those State agencies which have a predominantly economic function.

The Metropolitan Transport Trust operates passenger bus services in Hobart, Launceston and Burnie and currently operates at a loss of $12m p.a. State planners do not plan to extend current services and in the most recent initiative the licence to extend Hobart's metropolitan services into the growing Southern Suburbs of Hobart was granted to a private operator. There are no passenger rail services of any kind in Tasmania following the transfer of the State rail to the Commonwealth in 1975.

Transport Tasmania has ventured into shipping services on Bass Strait in direct competition for freight with Brambles and ANL. The Department took a bold step when it acquired the car ferry, the 'Abel Tasman' to replace the ANL service operating through the 'Empress of Australia'. State transport authorities report profitable operations for the TT line, although it is not clear if the accounting standards applied would stand close scrutiny. However, the State Government's initiatives on Bass Strait indicate that it has no compunction about government involvement in the market place provided this can be rationalised in terms of Tasmanian welfare. The rationalisation in this case is the desire to overcome the natural barrier of Bass Strait viewed by State planners as a major restriction on regional growth.

The State Department of Housing is classified as a 'Community business' agency as it recovers rentals from tenants and is in a competitive situation of sorts with private housing interests. Rentals and the rebate system are closely related to household incomes following the May 1988 Economic Statement. The provision of welfare housing was hived off from the separate Department of Construction in 1984. The latter organisation is the fully subsidised provider of public buildings and is correctly classified as a 'Public Service' agency. The Department of Main Roads is another major community business agency as it must tender competitively with private road building organisations for road construction con-

tracts. These arrangements are discussed as one of our case studies. The final example of community business organisations is the Agricultural Extension Service offered primary producers by the Department of Agriculture.

The Hydro-Electric Commission (HEC) occupies a special, well-known place in the history of Tasmanian industrial development as the fulcrum of hydroindustrialisation, a policy which dominated development for the first seven decades of the 20th century. The HEC constructed the dams which provided a cheap, clean source of energy intensive industries such as aluminium, steelplate, lead and zinc ingots, and copper production. Twelve industries currently absorb 70% of the total grid with one (Comalco) absorbing 29%. The HEC enjoyed a substantial degree of financial and political autonomy during its halcyon days as the flag carrier for development. However, hydroindustrialisation could not continue to be the major thrust of a development strategy and as the potential expansion options diminished so did the importance of the HEC. It remains the major Public Trading Enterprise (PTE) in Tasmania, but its role as the development flag carrier was challenged in the seventies and eighties. The HEC was to lose much of its own 'Treasury' function and its accountability tightened. The problem for Tasmania's future industrial development is the absence of a broadly based, diversified and relatively cheap energy grid and Tasmania's apparent competitive advantage has been eroded. The Rivers and Water Supply Commission oversees the provision of regional water supplies while there is a separate Board for each regional supply and charges are fully recovered through Local Government rates and charges.

The major innovation of the Liberal Government was the establishment of the Tasmanian Development Authority (TDA) which almost defies classification; it is a virtual monopoly supplier of business services; a source of agricultural and welfare housing finance and the State's major development agency in the post hydroindustrial era. It is classified as Commercial Service because this best captures the motives for establishing the authority. The TDA absorbed the functions of 3 pre-existing agencies: the Agricultural Bank, the

Department of Industrial Development and the Office of Special Adviser (Development Finance). The TDA was established with a Board and Secretariat drawn entirely from private enterprise. This created problems with the assimilation of public sector staff from the three agencies which spawned the TDA. However, the state services legislation enabled management to replace staff with new appointments. Staff turnover was and remains rapid and the morale of organisation may have suffered as a consequence.

The TDA's charter couches objectives in general terms: to maintain maximum employment in Tasmania; to reinforce the stability of local private business and to improve prosperity and welfare. The TDA in practice set social planning in Tasmania on an apparently new course aimed at the encouragement of employment growth through the development of small business and the successive annual reports of the organisation suggest the organisation has enjoyed considerable success, creating more than 3,500 new jobs in the first 4 years of operation. However, some of the TDA's initiatives later difficulties indicate the hazards of high risk, small business development in the absence of any major industrial expansion, which create small business opportunities. The TDA is distinguished from similar organisations interstate by the limited volume of loanable funds available to it and the financial dilemmas of the VEDC, for example, are not likely in these circumstances.

The State Forestry Commission is or could be a self financing agency managing the State's forests and offering services to the Forest industry. A key issue here is the implementation of a Forest Management Plan designed to maintain the exploration of timber resources at sustainable yields so that demands for sawlogs, pulp and paper mills and the export woodchip are met. The Forestry Commission's management of the State's forests and the conservation demands on the resource have been the subject of several national inquiries and at times intense local debate and a memorandum of understanding between State and Federal Governments about the management of the resource. The Commission has operated at a deficit in previous years raising doubts about

royalty rates and charges, but in the 1988 State budget steps were taken to place the Commission on a proper accounting basis which will go some way towards satisfying critics. The two issues of relevance to discussion of public sector renewal and reform are the question of the accounting standards applied to public sector agencies and the flexibility of public sector agency structures in relation to competing needs such as exploitation and conservation.

Tourism Tasmania is a Ministerial Department with a marketing and promotion arm, but in addition it provides development capital, oversees accommodation standards and undertakes market research. Recent downturns in Tasmania's traditional tourist demand created a groundswell of dissatisfaction with the Department's performance, particularly in the are of marketing and promotion. This led to a number of inquiries and consultants reports where all the options have been canvassed; from full privatisation to contracting out the selling agencies. However, none of these privatisation options have been effected. Structural changes have a cosmetic appearance and, although the staff of Tourism Tasmania are employed now under a separate award; the structure is the same in principle.

The Tasmanian Government Insurance Office provides liability and property insurance, in addition to the insurance provisions of the State's Workers Compensation. The TGIO accumulates substantial reserves from its operations and it is doubtful if any State Government is prepared to lose these by selling the TGIO to private interest. The Motor Accident Insurance Board (MAIB) holds a monopoly over third party insurance claims.

One development which is not consistent with the tenor of the Campbell Inquiry is Tasmania Bank, the State's bank which performs the full range of retail, wholesale, corporate and international banking functions, the last two on a small scale. The original perception of Tasmania Bank was that it would be formed by combining the two Trustee Savings Banks; the Launceston Bank for Savings and the Savings Bank of Tasmania. This proposal foundered on the rock of parochialism and the SBT remained a separate entity and Tasmania Bank was formed by combining the assets of the LBS with the Tasmanian Permanent Building Society. The Bank earns growing profits which will be available to the State Treasury in future.

The Contribution of the State Public Sector to the Economy

The institutional contribution of Tasmania's public sector to the State's regional economy is discussed in Section 15.2. The State public sector clearly makes a major contribution to the Tasmanian economy.

Knowledge of trends in the share of Gross State Product (GSP) are reliable and important to an understanding of changes in the economic role of the State public sector during the 1980s. Total public sector outlays rose significantly as a share of GSP in the early 1980s and

have slumped to such an extent in the second half of the 1980s that the State public sector's contribution to economic activity currently is below that recorded in 1980/81 and is some 5 percentage points below that recorded in 1984/85. This in itself explains a significant part of the current economic malaise alluded to earlier. Table 15.13 demonstrates trends in total public sector outlays in real terms since 1981/82 and as a share of real GSP. While the figures for GSP are estimates based on a model for recent years, it is possible to conclude that for most of the 1980s more than one quarter of Tasmanian economic activity was generated by the State public sector. This is very high in comparison with the larger States. In New South Wales the State public sector accounts for only 18-19% of GSP.

Table 15.13

Trends in the Tasmanian Government's Contribution to Gross State Product
1981/82 — 1988/89
(Constant 1980/81 Prices)

Year	Current Outlays	Capital Outlays	Total Outlays	Gross State Product (GSP)	Total Outlays as Share of GSP
1981/82	716	215	931	3471	26.8
1982/83	717	261	978	3454	28.3
1983/84	771	259	1030	3550	29.0
1984/85	812	309	1121	3736	30.0
1985/86	817	297	1114	3942	28.3
1986/87	816	228	1044	4065	25.7
1987/88P	812	228	1040	4186	24.8

Note: P — Preliminary Data.
Sources: ABS 'Government Financial Estimates, Australia 1988-89' Cat. No. 5501.0 (Table 33); ABS 'Consumer Price Index' for Hobart, Cat. No. 6401.0; National Institute of Economic and Industry Research (NIEIR) October 1988 and estimate for CPI in 1988/89 based on Commonwealth Budget estimate for CPI increase of 4.5%.

The real level of State public sector outlays has fallen 6.6% since 1984/85. While current outlays over this period have been remarkably stable in real terms the level of capital outlays have fallen more than 26% in real terms. This is of vital importance given the low level of private fixed capital expenditure and Tasmania's relatively high unemployment level as outlined earlier in Table 15.9, Tasmania's unemployment rate in June 1988 (9.1%) was 25% above the Australian average (7.2%) in the same period and by the end of January 1989, the official unemployment

statistics provide a Tasmanian unemployment rate of 10.5% as opposed to an Australian average of 7.5% of the workforce.

Social Functions

The Departments of Education, Health Services and Community Welfare deliver important components of the social wage. The State's educational administration is organised on a regional basis reflecting the dispersion of the State's population. The school system is 'neighbourhood' based with schooling compulsory for the age group 6 to 16, the secondary system culminating in the award of the Schools Certificate. It is in the organisation of the matriculation system that Tasmania deviates from the Australian model. There are separate State matriculation colleges preparing secondary students in a fifth and sixth year for the Higher Schools Certificate which is the basis of University entry. Tasmania and the Australian Capital Territory are the only regions to adopt the matriculation college system. The TAFE division of the Education Department administers the para-professional, trade and apprenticeship training and adult education through its four colleges. The State's single University located in Hobart has an enrollment of approximately 5,800 EFTS across the broad spectrum of academic disciplines: the Humanities, Business Studies, Science, Medicine, Engineering, Law and Education. A separate School of Art and Conservatorium of Music are attached to the University. The State's Institute of Technology based in Launceston provides courses in Education, business studies, social work, engineering, air traffic control and nursing. The Australian Maritime College is also located in Launceston. Negotiations about the amalgamation of these three institutions continue within the terms of reference provided by the Commonwealth Governments' white papers on Higher Education.

The State's Department of Health Services was restructured in 1984 and a further review of its functions is current. The provision of public hospital services has foundered on the rock of parochialism, which has led to the over provision of public hospital beds and the duplication of services in particular regions of the State. This has detracted from the efficient delivery of hospital services and is a prime area for reform. A first step was taken by the current Minister when he appointed a single North West Regional Hospitals' Board to replace several independent Boards in March 1989. The Department also delivers Home Nursing, Child, Mental Health, Alcohol and Drug Dependency Services.

The Department of Community Welfare provides Child Welfare, the guardianship program, Foster and family group homes, the adoption program, residential and community youth services, assistance for handicapped persons and for migrant integration. State grants support women's shelters and crisis intervention while grants to voluntary agencies account for 20% of the State's welfare budget. The Tasmanian experience may differ in this regard, because there is no overt privatisation of welfare services through voluntarism. However, our analysis of State expenditure will reveal a reduction of State welfare spending in real terms due to the withdrawal of Federal funding and despite the growth in the need for services.

The State Library Board administers a public library system in which some would claim there is room for further rationalisation: 5 central libraries, 72 branch libraries, 10 depots and 7 bookmobiles service Tasmania's population of 450,000. The system is organised on the customary regional basis. A further example of Community Service organisation is the State Fire Commission which administers fire services. The Service is comprised of 39 urban and 367 country fire brigades. Brigades in the 4 major centres are permanently manned with some volunteers but the remaining services are manned by volunteers. Local Government rates and insurance levies provide a proportion of total funding. The Department of Sport and Recreation is a Community Service organisation established in 1985 and derives some funding from non State sources. The provision of sporting infrastructure in cycling, rowing, basketball, hockey, cricket, the Tasmanian Institute of Sport and the first Australian Masters games are coordinated initiatives of the Department.

Administrative Functions
One aspect of the reforms effected in the State Services legislation is the reformation of the State's internal administration, which broke up the long standing triumvirate of Premier's Department, Treasury and Public Service Board. The Board was replaced by three separate agencies: A Commissioner of Public Employment who determines the size and structure of the staff establishment and determines certain terms and conditions in relation to their employment; a Commissioner for Review who has an overview of the Service and provides an independent appeals procedure,

while the Department of Public Administration performs the administrative functions of the old Board. The dissolution of the old Board's control of Staff follows logically from Cartland's vision to transfer the main authority for staff control to the Heads of Agencies. The second component of the triumvirate, the Premier's Department, was the subject of a separate, earlier review by Cartland and the Department's operations have been altered from an agency which dealt with protocol and routine to one in which policy co-ordination and advice to Cabinet was pre-eminent. A Cabinet Office was established to assess proposals about key policy initiatives and to provide a research and public relations arm. Contract appointments and the use of consultants are the order of the day. The operations of the reformed Premier's Department may have created some friction especially in relation to the activities of contracted advisers and their relationships with other Ministers in the policy process. The State Treasury remains a traditional Treasury Department, but appears to be on the threshold of a new era, one in which financial administration and economy policy and development are separated. This new direction is the result of economic pressures: the need to find solutions to the State's long term unemployment problem; the dearth of private capital expenditure and the presence of tight environmental constraints on development.

The Department of Labour and Industry regulates safety and related standards in industry, administers Workers' Compensation legislation and the State's employment policies. This latter function has assumed a higher profile in a State with Australia's highest unemployment rate and in general the State Governments policy initiatives in job creation involve the subsidisation of wages and oncosts as an incentive for firms to increase employment. The State's Licensing Board regulates the Tasmanian liquor industry. It is ironic to find among this long list of regulatory agencies, a Deregulation Board given the responsibility for advising the State Government about the feasibility of eliminating red tape through deregulation or the achievement of greater uniformity of existing regulations, particularly, at the Local Government level.

A number of agencies regulate particular local industries, and included in this category are the Departments of Agriculture Sea Fisheries and Mines. The functions of these public monopolies also extend to the development of industries falling within their aegis, for example, Sea Fisheries has a stake in the development of off shore fisheries and aquaculture and the Agriculture and Mines Departments possess a significant research capacity available to the industries concerned. The Department of the Environment administers environmental protection legislation, the Department is the final arbiter of the local EIS process and enforces penalties for pollution. The intensity of recent environmental battles, in particular, the debate about the Franklin Dam, the renewal of export woodchip licences and the Wesley Vale pulp mill development, has brought into sharp focus problems about public participation in the EIS process, an apparent questioning of the virtues of fast track legislation. The process surrounding the administration of environmental legislation is one area warranting emphasis in any discussion about public sector renewal and reform. The Department of Lands, Parks and Wildlife is another State agency with a stake in the debate about resource regulation and use. The Department, which recently absorbed the National Parks and Wildlife Service, regulates the use of Crown lands and administers the State Reserve system.

An important reform of the Cartland era was the establishment of the Tasmania Industrial Commission in 1985 replacing a plethora of Industrial Boards. This independent body includes functions previously undertaken by the disbanded Public Service Board and Arbitrator. The Board is comprised of a President, his deputy and three commissioners and makes or amends Awards in relation to permanent, temporary, full time, part time and casual wage rates, allowances and conditions of work. The Tasmanian legislation allows for private arbitration between parties before an individual Commissioner. The TIC is the major arbiter of labour and industrial disputes, while the new Department of Consumer Affairs determines consumer grievances; this Department will perform a broader consumer protection role than the Consumer Affairs Council it has replaced. The Egg Marketing Board and Tasmanian Dairy and Herd Industry Authority perform regulatory functions of the egg and dairy and cattle industries partly subsidised by taxpayers. The latter organisation now embraces the Tasmanian Herd Industry Organisation following the failure to privatise this organisation. THIO's history is discussed as one of our case studies.

The Tasmanian Government Printing Office is a further 'commercial business' agency the subject of several inquiries about its management and structure culminating in the Kearney report (1980) and the subsequent restructuring of the organisation in 1981. The full gamut of privatisation options were canvassed in this report, and all were rejected. The sale of the office and the contracting out of Parliamentary and ministerial administrative printing was rejected because of the need for a fail-safe, quality printing service. However the option of allowing the Government Printer to compete on a fully commercial basis in the local market was also rejected because the Printers entry into the small local market may threaten the viability of small, local printing businesses. Any foray by the Government Printer into commercial markets will occur interstate.

The Tasmanian Public Finance Corporation (TASCORP) was established in 1985 as the central borrowing agency for all State agencies outside the Treasury including the HEC Funds borrowed by TASCORP on behalf of the various agencies are channelled into State and local authorities for development purposes. TASCORP is a profitable organisation whose establishment is consistent with the findings of the Campbell Inquiry (1981) into the Australian financial system.

15.4 The Finances of the Tasmanian Public Sector
15.4.1 Introduction
In order to assess the importance of the financial operations of the State public sector in Tasmania, the information presented to parliament in the form of the budget papers might seem the obvious place to start. However, the legal structure under which the budget information is presented means that a consolidated and comprehensive picture of the public sector

is not available from this source. Given the implications of this for the effectiveness of the parliamentary process a brief description of the deficiencies involved is warranted.

The structure of the financial system and its day to day operations is prescribed by the Public Account Act 1986 and the provisions of the Audit Act 1918. The former provides for both the Consolidated Fund and the Special Deposits and Trust Fund. The split of the Consolidated Fund between Recurrent and Works and Services only broadly follows the separation of current from capital items. Significant elements of capital expenditure occur under Recurrent Services. The difficulties are much more serious with the Special Deposits and Trust Fund which currently comprises a total of 218 individual special deposit and trust accounts for government agencies with receipts of $1.15b and expenditure of $1.17b for 1987-88. The only information parliament is given is a financial statement detailing opening balance receipts, expenditure and closing balance for each account. Thus many important operations of government agencies and departments are not documented for parliament. In addition there are a wide range of State Government activities conducted through 'non-budget' organisations which are entitled to hold their accounts with financial institutions. While these must present annual reports to parliament, there is no requirement for a consistent format that would permit consolidation and allow an analytic overview.

These deficiencies both call into question whether the executive is fully accountable to the parliament and militate against any outside economic analysis such as the one presented here. The analysis which follows is largely based on ABS publications which while consistent and categorised on a sound economic basis, are in a more aggregated form than is desirable.

15.4.2 Public Sector Financing in Tasmania
The resources available to the State public sector have been severely constrained during the 1980s both because of Commonwealth funding cutbacks and the weakness of the Tasmanian revenue base. Table 15.14 shows the financial operations of the State public sector. Some of

the pressures are immediately obvious. Total nominal outlays have increased from $1,023m in 1981/82 to $1,813m in 1987/88. Total revenue collections have risen as a proportion of outlays from 84% to 88% over this period. However, Commonwealth grants as part of revenue were alone 54% of outlays in 1981/82

but had fallen to 49% by 1987/88 revealing much greater stress on local revenue raising. On the other hand borrowings (and changes in the level of financial assets) have declined from about 16% of total outlays ($166m) in 1981/82 to about 12% ($222m) in 1987/88 (line 3).

Table 15.14

Tasmanian State Public Sector Financial Operations 1981/82 − 1988/89
$ Millions[1]

	1981/82	82/83	83/84	84/85	85/86	86/87	87/88[2]
1. Total Outlays	1023	1191	1338	1526	1647	1698	1813
current	787	873	1001	1105	1208	1326	1416
capital	236	318	337	421	439	372	397
2. Revenue	857	990	1175	1297	1356	1472	1591
Taxes, fees & fines	162	172	188	227	254	296	349
NOS[3] PTEs	96	117	148	174	196	234	260
Prop. In./Other Rev	51	66	74	77	85	90	100
Comwlth Grants	548	636	765	819	820	852	882
3. Financing Transactions[1-2]	166	201	163	229	291	226	222
less increase in provisions	21	-5	23	21	32	36	39
4. Deficit	145	206	140	209	260	189	183
less Comwlth advances	52	55	54	55	53	36	19
5. Net Financing Requirement	92	151	86	154	207	153	164
NDB[4]	41	187	128	119	95	226	185
NOB[5]	49	15	4	41	-1	-3	-43
other internal financing transactions[6]	3	-51	-47	-7	14	-71	23

Notes: [1] Errors in addition due to rounding.
    [2] preliminary figures.
    [3] Net Operating Surplus.
    [4] Net Domestic Borrowing.
    [5] Net Overseas Borrowing.
    [4] calculated as a residual.
Source: ABS 'Government Financial Estimates' 1988/89 Cat. No. 5501.0 Table 33.

The best overall measure of the fiscal outcome of the operations of the State public sector is given by the deficit as measured in Table 15.14. The nominal level of the deficit has fluctuated over the 1980s. The outcome of the last financial year influenced by a Labor Government (1981/82) saw the deficit at $145m or just over 14% of total outlays. The incoming Liberal Government ran a deficit of $206m in 1982/83, and attempted to dramatically decrease it in 1983/84 to $140m or 10.5% of total outlays. This

decline, however, could not be sustained, and the Government was subsequently forced to expand the size of the deficit to $260m or 15.8% of total outlays by 1985/86 as a result of the need to finance government expenditure programs in the light of revenue shortfalls. However, the contribution of the State to Gross Public Sector borrowing, shown by the Net Financing Requirement, is heavily constrained by the Commonwealth's imposition of global borrowing limits.

The fact that the public sector has had very little room to move in its fiscal operations during the 1980s is more clearly seen from examinations of Table 15.15 which presents public sector outlays and their financing in constant prices. Total outlays rose significantly during the first three financial years of the Liberal Government (1982/83 − 1984/85) at an average rate of 6.3%. Subsequently, however, total outlays have declined in real terms in every single year. In 1986/87 total outlays fell a staggering 6.2% and by 1987/88 outlays were at about the same real level as that achieved in 1983/84. This means that in per capita terms

public sector outlays have been falling sharply in Tasmania over the second half of the 1980s. In order to better understand what has been driving these trends it is appropriate to look at:

(i) changes taking place in the financing of public sector outlays;

(ii) changes taking place in both the public trading enterprise and general government sectors; and,

(iii) important changes in the financial relationships between these two sectors over the 1980s.

Table 15.15

Tasmanian State Government Financial Operations
1981/82 − 1987/88
$ Million[1] (Constant 1980/81 Prices)[2]

	81/82	82/83	83/84	84/85	85/86	86/87	87/88[3]
1. Total Outlays	931	978	1030	1121	1114	1045	1040
current	716	717	771	812	817	816	812
capital	215	261	259	309	297	229	228
2. Revenue	779	813	904	953	917	906	912
Taxes, Fees & Fines	147	141	144	167	172	182	200
NOS[4] PTEs	87	96	114	128	133	144	149
Prop. income, & other revenue	46	54	57	57	57	56	57
Comwlth Grants	498	522	589	602	555	524	506
3. Financing Transactions[1-2]	152	165	126	168	197	139	127
less increase in provisions	19	-4	18	15	22	22	22
4. Deficit	132	169	108	153	176	116	105
less advances from the Commonwealth	47	45	42	40	36	22	11
5. Net Financing Requirement	85	124	66	113	140	94	94
NDB[5]	37	154	99	87	132	139	106
NOB[6]	45	12	3	30	-1	-2	-25
other internal financing transactions[7]	3	-42	-36	-5	9	-44	13

Notes: [1] Errors in addition due to rounding.
[2] nominal figures adjusted using Hobart consumer price index.
[3] preliminary figures.
[4] Net Operating Surplus.
[5] Net Domestic Borrowing.
[6] Net Overseas Borrowing.
[7] calculated as a residual.

Source: ABS 'Government Financial Estimates' 1988/89 Cat. No. 5501.0 and ABS 'Consumer Price Index' for Hobart Cat. No. 6401.0.

The aggregate figures for the State public sector disguise a number of important structural changes in the fiscal operations of the Tasmanian Government and its management of the public sector.

As Table 15.15 shows total State revenue grew in real terms at an average rate of almost 7% between 1982/83 and 1984/85. This enabled the Liberal Government to both maintain a healthy expansion of outlays (and its attendant contribution to Gross State Product) and reduce slightly the share of outlays being financed by borrowings or other internal financing transactions. The subsequent sharp reduction in real revenue could not be made up by borrowings because of the Commonwealth constraints and hence total outlays had to be reduced.

15.4.4 Public Trading Enterprise Financing

The capital programs of public trading enterprises during the 1980s show a pattern of rapid increase at an average rate of 15% per year in real terms between 1980/81 and 1984/85 and then an equally rapid decline so that real capital outlays had fallen to their 1980/81 level again by 1987/88. On the demand side for capital, this was largely driven by the end of major hydro-electric development in the mid-eighties. On the supply side the global borrowing limits acted as a serious constraint. These changes can be seen in Table 15.16. Current outlays follow the same broad pattern except that they have fallen less in the late eighties as a consequence of the need to service the debt incurred through financing capital outlays.

Table 15.16

Outlays, Revenues and Financing of State Public Trading Enterprises Sector 1981/82 $ Million[1] (Constant 1980/81 Prices)[2]

	1981/82	82/83	83/84	84/85	85/86	86/87	87/88[3]
Current Outlays	97	120	130	135	135	133	130
Capital Outlays	118	145	138	180	166	117	117
1. Total Outlays	215	265	268	315	301	250	247
2. Revenue and grants received	103	120	140	209	183	192	197
Share operating surplus %	85	80	81	61	73	75	75
Share property income & other revenue %	11	15	12	8	9	9	7
Share grants received %	4	4	7	31	18	17	17
3. Financing Transactions[1-2]	113	147	128	105	118	58	51
Deficit	95	153	112	91	97	35	28
Net financing Requirement	75	152	97	90	100	24	15

Notes: [1] Errors in addition due to rounding.

[2] Nominal figures adjusted using Hobart consumer price index.

[3] Preliminary figures.

Source: ABS 'Government Financial Estimates' 1988/89 Cat. No. 5501.0 and ABS 'Consumer Price Index' Cat. No. 6401.0.

The operating surplus of public trading enterprises increased at over 9% in real terms over the period 1981/82 to 1987/88. However, this growth was not enough to finance the capital programs of the sector in the 1980s. As indicated in Table 15.16 the share of outlays financed by operating surpluses declined from 85% in 1981/82 to 61% in 1984/85. This has improved to 75% in the past two years. Increased grants from the budget were an important mechanism in offsetting this. The share of grants rose from 4% in 1981/82 to a peak of 31% in 1984/85 falling back to 17% in 1987/88. Compensation for the cancelled Gordon below Franklin dam has clearly been important in this regard. Despite this most of the additional financing has been through borrowing. The net financing requirement of the PTE sector in real terms over the period 1982/83 to 1985/86 averaged $110m or some 46% above that of 1981/82. This pressure has eased since because of reduced capital expenditures and growth in operating surpluses. The real level of borrowing in 1987/88 was in historic terms a paltry $15m.

One might have expected this to provide greater freedom for the general government sector to expand its capital programs. However, the imposition of borrowing limits previously adverted to and changes in the revenue position of the general government sector have constrained this option.

15.4.5 The General Government Sector

Table 15.17 allows us to analyse trends in real general government outlays and the methods by which they have been financed. The new Liberal Government elected in May 1982 initially aimed to reduce real total outlays by cutting current outlays. While this accorded with their commitment from Opposition to smaller government, in office they quickly learnt that the policy directly affected both the welfare of business and the wider community. This led to a policy reversal and growth in current outlays in the early eighties. For the three years to 1986/87 the real level was maintained and has only recently fallen. Capital outlays also increased in the early eighties to reach a peak of $201m in real terms and, while there has been a subsequent decline, the 1987/88 figure is still 34% above that of 1981/82. This is persuasive evidence that the importance of capital expenditure by general government, given declining capital expenditure by public trading enterprises, was clearly understood. As we will discuss later it is also evident in the government's attitude to debt financing.

Table 15.17

Financing of General Government Outlays 1981/82 — 1988/89
$ Million[1] (Constant 1980/81 Prices)[2]

	1981/82	82/83	83/84	84/85	85/86	86/87	87/88[3]
Outlays							
Current	667	658	701	737	740	737	730
Capital	123	124	153	201	170	165	165
1. Total	800	782	854	938	910	902	895
Financed By							
2. Revenue of which:	743	764	841	874	834	808	806
(a) Taxes, fees, fines	147	141	144	167	172	182	200
(b) PTE Income	4	4	5	5	6	6	5
(c) Interest received from:	74	80	80	77	76	68	65
PTEs	55	60	57	56	55	49	45
Other sectors	19	20	23	21	21	19	20
(d) Other property income/revenue	20	18	23	24	26	28	30
(e) Grants from Commonwealth	498	522	589	602	555	524	506
3. Financing Transactions [1-2]	57	18	13	64	76	94	89
Non Cwealth advances	47	45	42	40	36	22	11
4. Net Financing Requirements	7	-30	-31	22	40	70	79

Notes: [1] Errors in addition due to rounding.
[2] Nominal figures adjusted using Hobart consumer price index.
[3] Preliminary figures.
Source: ABS 'Government Financial Estimates' 1987/88 Cat. No. 5501.0 and ABS 'Consumer Price Index' Cat. No. 6401.0.

Table 15.17 also indicates an expansion of general government revenues in the early 1980s and subsequent decline. However, within this there have been important structural changes in the pattern of revenue, largely the result of a combination of Commonwealth fiscal policies taken in the 'national interest' to curb public expenditure by the Hawke Labor Government and changes in the basis of distributing Commonwealth (tax sharing) grants between the States initiated by the Fraser Liberal Government but which were continued by the Hawke Government. Thus there has been a significant decline in level of Commonwealth grants available to the general government sector since 1984/85. Concession funds or advances from the Commonwealth have declined from a real level of $47m in 1981/82 to only $11m in 1987/88 and there has been a dramatic rise in the real level of Tasmanian taxes and fines since 1982/83. Somewhat surprisingly the government has resisted the pressures to shift some of the fiscal burden by increasing the level of cost recovery significantly. This probably reflects an implicit acknowledgement of the special importance of the public sector in the Tasmanian context. These structural issues are examined in more depth below.

15.4.6 Federal Payments to Tasmania

Table 15.17 provides the recent history of the real level of Federal support to Tasmania. Initially, Commonwealth grants grew from $498m in real terms in 1981/82 to $602m only to decline rapidly to a level of $506m 1987/88. This is a quite massive decline, representing around 11% of outlays and is exacerbated by the significant reduction in advances. For the period 1981/82 to 1984/85 net real advances averaged $43.5m to be reduced to $11m by 1987/88. This trend is confirmed by the projection in Tasmanian budget papers that 47.5% of Consolidated Fund revenue will be from the Commonwealth compared to 61.2% in 1983/84.

Two sets of forces have produced this severe pressure in Tasmania:
— a slowing down in the rate of expansion of total nominal Commonwealth payments to the States culminating in a fall in the real level of payments since 1984/85. In real

terms estimated payments to the States in 1988-89 are about the same as the 1980-81 levels.

— a significant fall in general purpose payments (excluding 'identified Health Grants') to the States coupled with major adjustments to Tasmania's share of general purpose recurrent grants resulting from the implementation of Commonwealth Grants Commission relativities review recommendations since 1981.

While all States have suffered cutbacks, Tasmania has had to face a particularly difficult adjustment especially since 1985/86 when the full impact of the changed relativities began to take effect. Table 15.18 shows Tasmania's declining share of payments to the States. The decline in the share of General Revenue Funds since 1984/85 is particularly significant.

Tasmania's particular problems stem from the fact that the decision to change relativities was made in very different macro-economic circumstances. The Commonwealth's reaction to more difficult circumstances was to renege on commitments which would have led to much smoother adjustment. The May 1985 Premiers' Conference had a profound impact on Tasmania's fiscal position in deciding to implement the relativities assessed by the Commonwealth Grants commission in its 'Report on State Tax Sharing and Health Grants 1985' which was initiated at the June 1983 Premiers' Conference. This report concluded that Tasmania should receive a substantially reduced share of General Purpose Revenue Grants. Similar reports and subsequent Premiers' conferences in the early 1980s had also drawn this conclusion. However, a combination of expansion of total funds to be distributed and 'real term' guarantees of one sort or another were put in place which meant total grants to Tasmania (as distinct from share) did not decline dramatically. In addition General Purpose Capital funds were (more or less) maintained and Specific Purpose Payments (Capital and Recurrent) rose significantly. While the early 1980s had seen a falling share it was a growing cake. Table 15.19 shows what happened to the real level of payments to Tasmania which continued to rise until 1984/85.

Table 15.18

Tasmania's Share of Commonwealth Payments to the Six States
1980-81 – 1988-89
(% of Total)

Year	General Revenue Funds[i]	General Purpose Capital Funds	Specific Purpose Payments[i]	Total Payments
1980-81	4.96	7.01	3.55	4.58
1981-82	4.77	7.01	3.66	4.53
1982-83	4.66	7.01	3.66	4.43
1983-84	4.64	7.01	4.14	4.61
1984-85	4.58	7.01	4.01	4.51
1985-86	4.36	7.01	3.63	4.22
1986-87	4.10	7.01	3.64	4.05
1987-88	3.85	10.37	3.60	3.89
1988-89 (est)	4.09	10.37	3.27	3.85

Note: (i) 'Identified Health Grants' which were paid to the States between 1981-82 and 1987-88, and were classified as general purpose payments have been included in specific purpose payments for the purpose of this table. Prior to 1981-82 and from 1988-89 hospital funding was/is to be provided to the States by means of specific purpose payments. Despite this adjustment there is a break in continuity between 1987-88 and 1988-89 figures since the new hospital funding arrangements, introduced in 1988-89, have the effect of increasing Tasmania's share of general revenue funds while decreasing its share of (specific purpose) hospital funding.
Source: 'Commonwealth Payments to Tasmania 1988-89'; Table 2; Budget Paper No. 3, Government Printer, Tasmania.

Table 15.19

Commonwealth Payments to Tasmania 1980-81 – 1988-89
(Constant 1980-81 prices)

Year	General Revenue Funds[i] $m	General Purpose Capital Funds $m	SpecificPurpose Payments[i] $m	Total Payments $m
1980-81	298.6	91.6	189.6	579.8
1981-82	292.7	83.3	188.6	564.6
1982-83	297.9	79.0	204.9	644.1
1983-84	311.2	79.3	257.9	648.3
1984-85	306.5	80.5	269.7	656.7
1985-86	290.7	74.1	237.3	602.2
1986-87	275.8	51.9	229.7	557.4
1987-88	260.5	31.7	223.2	515.4
1988-89 (est)	257.9	29.6	194.1	481.6

Note: [i] Nominal figures adjusted by the Hobart Consumer Price Index, ABS Cat. No. 6401.0.
Source: Derived from 'Commonwealth Payments to Tasmania 1988-89', Budget Paper No. 3, Table 2, p. 12, Government Printer, Tasmania.

The 1985 Premiers' Conference had a similar process in view in providing for the new relativities to be phased in buffered by special payments over three years. In addition the Commonwealth undertook to increase total funding to the States by 2 % p.a. in real terms for the next five years. In the event the cuts to Tasmania were savage, an 8.3% reduction in real terms in 1985/86 followed by a further 7.5%.

The 1987 Premiers' Conference saw the Commonwealth go back on its commitment to a real expansion of General Purpose Grants to the States on the basis of an unforeseen change in macro-economic circumstances. The axe was felt across the board. General Purpose Payments by the Commonwealth to the States and the Northern Territory for 1987-88 were set at the same real level as 1986-87 based on the forecast of the CPI at the time of the Conference. For Tasmania this meant real reductions of: 5.6% in General Revenue Recurrent Funds; 39% in General Purpose Payments. Total grants fell 7.5% in real terms. A significant side effect was the large increase in the share of Specific Purpose Payments of total payments simply because of the smaller cutback.

In March 1986 the Commonwealth Grants Commission was asked to report on the per capita relativities to be used for the distribution of general revenue grants. The recommen-

dations presented in March 1988 formed the basis for the Premiers' Conference decisions for the 1988-89 budget. The new relativities suggested Tasmania should receive a $11.3m drop in its 1987-88 allocation. The Premiers' Conference agreed to implement the new relativities subject to a guarantee with respect to the level of total Commonwealth funding in 1988-89. Each State and the Northern Territory would be guaranteed to receive the same nominal level of payments in 1988-89 as it received in 1987-88 with the 'top-ups' being financed by the States which were 'winning' under the Grants Commissions recommendations. For Tasmania, as reflected in Table 15.20 this entailed a further decline in Commonwealth payments.

The full impact of the changes in Commonwealth funding, including those made to Loan Council programs, is shown in Table 15.20 which compares 1983/84 with 1988/89, the latest information available.

Table 15.20

Programs for Tasmania 1983-84 and 1988-89
($m Constant 1980-81 Prices)[1]

Category	1983-84	1988-89	% Change
1. *General Purpose Payments*	311.2	264.0	-15.2
2. *Specific Purpose Payments*	258.0	198.6	-23.0
Health[2]	50.0	47.2	-5.6
Higher/Tech Education	41.5	39.4	-5.1
School Programs	24.9	24.5	-1.6
Housing Agreement Funds	18.7	13.5	-27.8
Roads Programs	36.0	24.5	-31.9
South-West Tasmania Comp.	48.4	19.2	-60.3
Employment Programs	7.9	0.1	-98.7
Other[3]	30.6	30.2	-1.3
3. *Loan Council Programs*	217.9	124.2	-43.0
Advances	52.8	15.2	-71.2
Grants	26.4	15.2	-42.4
Borrowing by Authorities	137.8	93.8	-32.4
Total[1+2+3]	787.1	586.8	-25.5

Notes: [1] Nominal expenditure adjusted by Hobart CPI 1988-89 estimate based on Commonwealth Budget Forecast.

[2] Identified Health Grants which were classed as general purpose payments prior to 1988-89 have been included as a Specific Purpose Grant.

[3] Other includes funds for cost escalation for schools programs and Local Government Financial Assistance as well as a large number of important but quantitatively small programs.

Source: Parliament of Tasmania, 'Supporting Budget Information 1984-85 and 1988-89' (Budget Paper No. 1).

Tasmania has experienced a dramatic fall in the resources provided by the Commonwealth, of a magnitude no other State has had to face. Grants and borrowings approved have fallen by almost 26% in real terms over the past five years. The implications for taxation if expenditure and the provision of basic public services were to be maintained are profound and they affect the life of every Tasmanian. We do not believe that the fault for this State of affairs should – as is often the case in Tasmania – be blamed on the Commonwealth Grants Commission. We support the equitable principles by which the Commission distributes funds and while we have quibbles with some technical aspects of the Commissions decisions, which in some cases have significant implications for the final outcome, the central problem is that not enough funds are available for distribution from the Commonwealth. Further, as is clearly demonstrated in the next section, there is very little scope for Tasmania to further exploit its narrow tax base without having crucial detrimental impacts on the level of economic activity, employment and provision of public services, crucial to welfare and the social wage.

15.4.7 State Taxation

All States are subject to the fundamental imbalance between their expenditure responsibilities and their capacity to raise revenue. Under the Commonwealth's fiscal austerity, implemented by funding cuts, all States have been severely squeezed. However, Tasmania has suffered most and furthermore we will argue that its capacity for adjustment is more limited on the revenue side.

The major problem faced by all States is that of a very narrow and largely regressive tax base. The income base, while in principle open to the States since the new federalism of the early seventies, is still in fact exclusively the province of the Commonwealth Government. There is little prospect of any State Government entering this field in a world-wide climate of opinion in favour of income tax reductions. This leaves the other three bases of employers' payrolls, wealth (or property), and goods and services discussed in depth in Part Four. Payroll taxes and taxes on wealth largely through

stamp duties are of enormous importance to the States. Fiscal competition has narrowed the wealth base by effectively ruling out substantial forms of estate or inheritance taxes. The goods and services base is taxed by a variety of instruments. There are levies on statutory corporations providing services, taxes on gambling and insurance. The use of goods and services is taxed using several expedients which get round the constitutional obstacles to indirect taxes. These are mainly motor vehicle taxation on registration and transfer and business franchise taxes. While problems exist in all States in attempting to expand revenue on these bases, it is argued that they are particularly acute in Tasmania. In sum the greater relative severity of Commonwealth cutbacks has produced greater pressure to increase taxation but the regional 'branch' nature of the economy means that capacity to do so is even more restricted than in the other States. The difficulties involved in attempting to widen the tax base and the adverse effects of increases in existing taxes have meant that there has been significant pressure towards privatisation by stealth.

The analysis of taxation which follows is largely based on ABS figures using definitions by type of tax in order to facilitate comparison with other States. Care needs to exercised in moving from these to the information presented in Tasmanian State Budget Papers where tax information is presented following the structure of the Acts under which taxes are administered. Thus, for instance, stamp duties under the ABS definition are much more narrowly defined than they are under the Tasmanian Stamp Duties Act which covers motor vehicle registration charges considered by the ABS to be a tax on the use of goods. However, it is possible to make general linkages between the two sets of information in the discussion of trends in taxation.

Total Taxation Receipts

There is a widespread perception in Tasmania that taxation has increased massively since the first full year of the Liberal Government. Nominal receipts have risen, on budget figures, from $175m in 1983-84 to a projected $359m in 1988-89 (Budget Paper No. 4, 1987-88). The increase is well in excess of inflation and both budget figures and ABS figures show a real rise in taxation of 39%. This compares with a rise of only 13.6% in total State taxation for Australia as a whole over the same period. There are some interesting features in this comparison best seen by taking a longer perspective and looking at sub-periods. Tables 15.21 and 15.22 enable us to examine the trend in real taxation.

Over the period 1981-82 to 1986-87 Tasmanian State taxes rose by 22.6%, that is by the same percent as all State taxation. The finding in the CREA Report on the Tasmanian Economy that Tasmania had a lower than

average rate of increase in real tax collections is due to the data only being available to 1985-86 and is consistent with our remarks on sub-periods. However, the pattern of revenue increase is very different for Tasmania in 1982-83 compared with a substantial increase in the all State's figure. In 1984-85 by contrast Tasmanian real taxes rose by more than twice as much as the all States figure. The estimates for 1987-88 show another large divergence with real overall State taxation almost static (0.9%) and Tasmanian revenues estimated at a real growth of over 10%.

Table 15.21

Real Total Taxes (1980-81 prices) Level and Percentage Annual Change, Tasmania

1981-82	1982-83	1983-84	1984-85	1985-86	1986-87	1987-88
* 138.7	131.9	134.7	155.2	160.4	170.3	187.2
%7.4 **	-4.9	2.1	15.2	3.3	6.2	9.9
147.4	140.9	144.4	166.5	172.0	180.7	200.0
%	-4.4	2.5	15.3	3.3	5.1	10.7

Notes: *Source: Budget Paper No.4 1987-88, Parliament of Tasmania.
   **Source: ABS Taxation Revenue Australia 1986/87 Cat. No. 5506 and ABS Government Financial Estimates, Australia 1987-88 (Cat. No. 5501.0).

Table 15.22

Real Total Taxes (1980-81 prices) Level and Percentage Annual Change All States

1981-82	1982-83	1983-84	1984-85	1985-86	1986-87	1987-88
6567	6860	7149	7662	7774	8049	8120*
—	4.5	4.2	7.2	1.5	3.5	0.9

Source: ABS Government Financial Estimates, Australia 1987-88 (Cat. No. 5501.0).

Taxation Policy and Taxable Capacity

When looking at trends in taxation it is difficult to distinguish between the constraints imposed on a government's ability to tax, through the taxable capacity of the bases open to it, and differences in the policy desire to tax. It is certainly an avowed object of the current Tasmanian Liberal Government to be a low tax government, though, given that no government has ever avowed the opposite, too much weight should not be put on this. The Centre for Regional Economic Analysis presents data aimed at resolving the problem using the Commonwealth Grants Commission's meth-

odology of standardised per capita revenues. These are calculated to indicate what a State could have raised per capita after adjustment for differences in the base. The percentage that actual per capita revenue is of standardised per capita revenue purports to indicate a measure of the desire to tax. On this basis the CREA report concluded that 'overall, Tasmania has the lowest propensity to tax of any State apart from Queensland' (CREA, 1987, p. 278). This evidence needs to be interpreted with care for two reasons. Firstly the period of analysis ranges from 1981-2 to 1983-4. This both includes the oddity of 1982-83 when real tax collections fell by 4.9% in Tasmania when they were rising in other States and pre-dates the large rise in real tax collections which took place in 1984-5 of 15.3% (See Table 15.21). In addition there are well-known problems with the Grants Commission methodology in assessing taxable capacity which probably means that Tasmania's ability to exploit a given base is more limited than the standardised per capita revenue figures indicate. This issue is developed below with reference to specific taxes.

The Tax Mix

In examining changes in the pattern of taxation in Tasmania we must be aware of the interplay of forces such as fluctuations in the level of economic activity with policy decisions. However, the following features of the Tasmanian economy are obviously crucial: the higher than average rate of unemployment, depressed prices of property assets which form the basis of wealth taxation (stamp duties), the 'branch' nature of the economy which means that financial and capital transactions which pertain to the State often take place in mainland centres. All of these have put upward pressure on tax rates on the payroll tax and

property bases to try to maintain real revenue levels. Growth in revenue has occurred substantially through increasing taxes on goods and services. These trends are illustrated in Table 15.23. Payroll tax, while still the most important tax has fallen steadily in percentage terms, taxes on property have remained fairly steady over the period at around 16 to 17%. It should be noted that this is the lowest percentage of all States. On 1986-87 figures, the next lowest is South Australia with 22.1% while the highest was Victoria with 27.2%. The property base used to be much more important to Tasmania before the abolition of death duties which ceased to apply after 1982, though obligations incurred prior to this continued to show up in collections. Indeed given the previous importance of this tax, the most definite trend has been a move away from property taxation, which was progressive in principle, towards a reliance on regressive taxes on goods and services which is driven by a quite massive increase in franchises. This is discussed in detail below. These trends are also obvious in tables using the State Government's budget classification of taxes, a summary table of which is presented in the CREA report, *The Tasmanian Economy: A Survey* (Ch. 12, p. 299).

Table 15.23

Percentage Contribution of Individual Taxes to Total Revenue — Tasmania

	1981-82	1982-83	1983-84	1984-85	1985-86	1986-87
Payroll Taxes	33.5	31.6	29.7	29.3	30.5	27.7
Property Taxes	17.4	15.4	16.1	16.4	16.3	17.9
Immov. Property	4.0	4.7	4.6	4.4	4.2	4.3
Fin. and Capital	13.4	10.7	11.5	12.0	12.1	13.6
Taxes on Provision						
of Goods & Serv.	16.9	17.8	16.3	18.8	16.2	14.5
Stat. Corps Levies	2.8	3.0	3.1	3.0	2.8	2.9
Gambling	9.9	10.7	8.9	11.7	9.6	7.7
Insurance	4.2	4.1	4.3	4.1	3.8	3.9
Taxes on Use of						
Goods and Services	32.1	35.1	37.8	35.6	37.1	39.9
Motor Vehicles	18.9	17.9	17.6	16.5	15.6	13.4
Franchises	8.9	12.9	15.6	15.2	17.3	22.4
Fees and Fines	4.3	4.3	4.6	3.9	4.2	4.1

Source: ABS Taxation Revenue Australia 1986/87 (Cat. No. 5506.0).

Payroll Tax

Payroll tax is the most important own revenue source for all States. Both Tasmanian budget

data and ABS figures are presented in Table 15.24.

Table 15.24

Real Payroll Tax (1980-81 Prices)
Level and Percentage Annual Change Tasmania

1981-82	1982-83	1983-84	1984-85	1985-86	1986-87	1987-88
*{51.1	45.9	44.1	50.3	54.0	51.5	51.9
%	-10.2	-3.3	14.1	7.4	-4.6	0.8
**{49.4	44.6	42.9	48.7	52.5	50.0	–
%	-9.7	-3.8	13.5	7.8	-4.8	–

Notes: *Source: Budget Paper No.4 1987-88, Parliament of Tasmania.
     **Source: ABS Taxation Revenue Australia 1986/87 (Cat. No. 5506.0).

On the budget figures, payroll tax at $90.5m represented 27.8% of Tasmanian Government taxation in 1987-88. This bears out ABS data for 1986-87 which show Tasmania relying on payroll tax for 27.7% of taxes, fees and fines. The corresponding figure for all State Governments being slightly higher at 28.2%.

Table 15.25

Real Payroll Tax Level and Annual Change All States
(1980-81 prices)

1981-82	1982-83	1983-84	1984-85	1985-86	1986-87
2212.7	2211.0	2142.9	2253.8	2283.4	2266.4
	-0.1	-3.1	5.2	1.3	-0.7

In common with other States there has been a slight decline in payroll tax in proportionate terms. Thus in 1981-82 payroll tax accounted for 33.5% of Tasmanian State taxation and 33.7% of all State taxation. However, given the shift in the overall tax burden in Tasmania, this is somewhat surprising and reflects the revenue difficulties of the Tasmanian economy. *With such a narrow tax base the State Government is under pressure to raise revenue from payroll tax but this option has serious implications for Tasmania's higher unemployment rate. Moreover, there is reason to suspect that payroll tax plays a causal role. Many of Tasmania's employers are in a price taking environment. As a result it seems reasonable to conclude that the burden of adjustment is then taken by output and employment.* The implications of this distinction between nominal and effective incidence appear not to be taken into account in the Grants Commission's methodology of assessing taxable capacity briefly discussed earlier. The restoration of the real level of payroll tax collection to its 1981-82 figure may well have been at a high cost in economic welfare. The table also makes clear the greater variation in collections. Under the Liberal Government from 1983-84 to 1986-87 there has been a rise in real terms of 16.6%. This compares with the all States increase of 5.8%. Yet over the whole period 1981-2 to 1986-7 real payroll taxes have not risen in Tasmania and have risen slightly for all States. There is certainly nothing in the present rate structure to suggest a lack of comparative exploitation of this tax base. Tasmania has the same basic rate as most of the other States, at 5%, and surcharges firms with payrolls in excess of $5m at 1% and in excess of $7.5m at 2%.

Taxes on Property or Wealth

Tasmania's revenue base has never recovered from the fiscal competition between the States which led to the demise of estate duties. In 1977-78 estate and gift duties accounted for 5.3% of State taxation putting it in the high group with New South Wales at 5.4% and Victoria at 6.8%. With any sort of inheritance tax or estate duty being effectively ruled out without some sort of agreement between the States, this part of the revenue base has proved a particularly intractable problem for Tasmania because of the lack of suitable alternatives.

Taxes on property consist of taxes on immovable property (ABS category 31) and taxes on financial and capital transactions. In Tasmania, as in other States, land taxes are the most important component of the former, indeed the only significant component. Stamp duties are the most important component in the latter. As was noted earlier Tasmania has the lowest percentage reliance on the property base. The reasons can be seen in an examination of these taxes.

Land Tax
Land Tax is the only significant immovable property tax. Its relative contribution is shown in Table 15.23 as having risen from 4.0% in 1981-82 to 4.3% of total State taxation. This has been achieved, as Table 15.26 makes clear, by a real increase in its level of 34.5%. This is substantially greater than the overall increase in taxation despite the obstacle of relatively lower land values in Tasmania. It is hard to envisage the State Government exploiting this base much further given the constraints faced.

Stamp Duties
Stamp duties under the definition of the Tasmanian Stamp Duties Act accounted for 21.8% of State taxation in 1987-88. Over the period of the Liberal Government, from 1983-84 to 1987-88 there has been a nominal rise of 80.98%, which translates into a real rise of 34.73%, somewhat less than the real rise in total taxation. This does not appear to reflect in any sense a growing perception of the regressive

nature of these taxes but rather the relative difficulty of raising taxation in this area. However, much of this problem pertains to motor vehicle stamp duty on registration and therefore the Tasmanian budget figure is misleading for comparative purposes. This issue is therefore taken up in our discussion of motor vehicle taxation. The problems with stamp duties proper, under the ABS definition, (Table 15.27), appear to be much more severe, the real rise in stamp duties from 1981-82 to 1986-87 being 9% and their share in total taxation falling from 11.4% to 10.0%. The corresponding figure for the total for all States is a real rise in stamp duties of 33% from 1981-82 to 1986-87 and a rising share of State taxation from 15.6% to 16.9%. Given the ad valorem nature of stamp duties and their consequent regressive impact it might seem that Tasmania has fared better than most States. However, it is rather the difficulty of the revenue base, given the branch nature of the regional economy, which is highlighted. Tasmania has been forced to look at other tax bases. Stamp duties vividly illustrate the difficulties of the Tasmanian tax base as this has been a major growth area both at Commonwealth level and for the other States. Tasmania's higher rate of stamp duty does not offset the narrowness of the tax base. Using the Grants Commission methodology, stamp duties per capita 1981-82 to 1983-84 were 115.2% of standardised per capita stamp duties. This indication of willingness to exploit the tax base should be contrasted with its falling share because of the narrowness of the base.

Table 15.26

Taxes on Immovable Property
Real Land Tax $m (1980-81 prices) Level and
Percentage Annual Change, Tasmania

	1981-82	1982-83	1983-84	1984-85	1985-86	1986-87
Level	5.8	6.6	6.6	7.3	7.2	7.8
% Change	–	13.8	0.0	10.6	-1.4	8.3

A disaggregated examination of stamp duties also reveals a disturbing trend towards increasing dependence on conveyances Table 15.28 presents the components of stamp duty drawn from Tasmanian budget papers which pertain

to ABS definition (that is, in particular motor vehicle registration duty is not included). Note that conveyances accounted for only 41.2% of stamp duty in 1981-82 but had risen to 73% by 1986-87 and 81.7% by 1987-88.

Table 15.27

Stamp Duties $m (1980-81) Level and Percentage Annual Change, Tasmania

	1981-82	1982-83	1983-84	1984-85	1985-86	1986-87
Level	16.7	13.0	16.1	18.1	17.9	18.2
% Change	–	-22.2	23.8	12.4	-1.1	1.7

Table 15.28

Components of Stamp Duties $000 Nominal — Tasmania

	1981-82	1982-83	1983-84	1984-85	1985-86	1986-87	1987-88
Adhesive Revenue							
Stamps	483	453	450	428	438	626	643
Cheques	2435	2538	2352	987	7	2	-2
Conveyances	7537	7454	12127	16466	18183	21560	29092
Hire Purchase	1259	909	1075	1429	1234	593	510
Leases	197	175	205	176	247	330	394
Loan Duty	2954	684	15	–	–	–	–
Marketable Securities	416	268	519	848	713	902	2394
Mortgages	992	1392	1793	1854	2277	3303	4389
Rental	1781	1905	1994	2413	2750	1125	165
Sundry	242	341	372	180	652	1265	2122
Refunds	–	–	–	-47	-117	-165	-110
Total	18,296	16,119	20,902	24,734	26,384	29,541	35,597

Source: Budget Papers, Parliament of Tasmania.

Taxes on Goods and Services

Taxes on goods and services fall into two groupings, those on provision, consisting of levies on statutory corporations, gambling taxes and insurance taxes, and those on use of goods and services consisting of motor vehicle taxes and franchise taxes. This distinction is very important in the Tasmanian situation because the biggest changes have occurred in terms of taxes on use of goods and services with a quite massive increase in franchise taxation on petroleum products and tobacco. It is therefore to this group of taxes that we address our specific remarks.

As was shown in Table 15.23 business franchises have risen as a percentage of Tasmanian State taxes from 8.9% in 1981-82 to 22.4% in 1986-87. Given the overall increase in the real level of State taxation, this implies a massive real rise in the level of franchise taxation which has gone from $13.2m to $40.5m in 1980-81 prices. This increase of 206.8% compares with a figure for all States of 94% over this period. Thus, while this has been of importance for all States, the shift in Tasmania is truly dramatic.

While all components have risen in real terms, the table also shows that petroleum has borne the brunt of the change. In 1981-82 petroleum products were 30% of all franchise taxes; they are now 56%. This tax alone has gone from 2.7% of total State taxation to 12.5%. Given the highly regressive nature of this tax, this is a desperate situation but one from which there appears little escape given the State Government's lack of alternatives. It undoubtedly has a negative impact on business activity and tourism, though the magnitude of these effects is difficult to assess.

Problems in Taxation Initiatives

Throughout our discussion of taxation we have emphasised the difficulties with the narrow tax base. It must be also stressed that successive State Governments have attempted to expand the range of taxes. Thus as the CREA report on the Tasmanian economy points out:

'new taxes introduced since 1970 include the

casino tax and licence fees, payroll tax (transferred from the Commonwealth), the Hydro-Electric Commission statutory levy, soccer football pools tax, financial institutions duty, electrical consumption levy and the business franchise taxes on tobacco and petroleum products' (1987, p. 298).

Table 15.29

Real Business Franchise Taxes (1980-81 prices) — Tasmania

	1981-82	1982-83	1983-84	1984-85	1985-86	1986-87
Total Franchise Taxes:	13.2	18.2	22.6	25.3	29.8	40.5
Comprised of:						
Gas Franchise Taxes	—	—	—	—	—	—
Petroleum Products	3.9	8.9	10.2	10.0	11.7	22.6
Tobacco	4.1	4.3	7.4	10.4	12.9	11.9
Liquor	5.3	5.0	5.1	4.9	5.2	6.0
Total Franchise Taxes: Percentage Change Over Previous Year						
	—	37.9	24.2	11.9	17.8	35.9
Petroleum	—	128.2	14.6	-2.0	17.0	93.2
Tobacco	—	4.9	72.1	40.5	24.0	-7.8
Liquor	—	-5.7	2.0	-3.9	6.1	15.4

Source: ABS Cat. No. 5506.0.

However, as we have seen the real growth area has been in business franchise taxes.

The difficulties facing the State Government are well illustrated by the problems encountered with the newly introduced Ambulance levy outlined in the 1987 Budget to come into effect from 1st July 1987. There was widespread opposition to this tax with the result that it has been announced that the basis of the tax is to be altered. The tax is payable by land owners with the rate varying with the category of land. Owners of principal residence and rural land were required to pay $40 while the liability in respect of general land was dependent on its value, rising from $40 for land worth $25,000 or less to $320 for land worth more than $75,000. There was a concession of $20 for principal residences with a sole occupant. While this was no doubt designed to alleviate the otherwise regressive effect on the sole pensioner owner-occupiers, the overall effect of the tax appears to have been regressive. While in the short run it might impinge on the better off who own their own homes, even this does not cater for the large differences in income involved. Moreover, there seems little doubt that in a competitive rental market the levy would be passed on in higher rents in the long term.

The total assessed for 1987-88 was $5,184,400 or some 1.6% of total State taxation. The very adverse reaction to the tax appears in part to stem from the government's attempt to sell a tax increase by 'earmarking' which seems to have backfired. The link to a service in the sense of a crude user pays principle led to complaints by owners of multiple land holdings that they were charged twice. Thus an element of progression was lost in a debate over horizontal equity in a user pays sense.

These difficulties illustrate the fundamental problem for Tasmania. The Commonwealth cutbacks, justified or not from a national standpoint, can not be absorbed by the revenue base constitutionally available to Tasmania without, what appears to be, very regressive impacts. The only other alternative is to cut public expenditure in areas vital to the maintenance of the social wage.

15.4.8 Tasmanian State Government Debt

The Tasmanian public sector, as we have seen, is responsible for a major proportion of capital formation in the State. This capital formation is, broadly speaking of two types:

(a) that which results in income producing

assets (eg. hydro-electric schemes); and
(b) those which produce services to the community (eg. schools and hospitals).

The costs of borrowing for the first type of asset can be covered by the income generated and to this extent does not put a direct charge on the tax base of the government. The costs of borrowing for the second type of asset needs to be serviced from the government budget. As noted in Chapter Eight it is appropriate for the beneficiaries (the community in general) to contribute to debt servicing in this way because of the need to ensure inter-generational equity. It is not appropriate that assets which produce a flow of services over a large number of years are financed by taxpayers at the time of construction.

Public discussion of 'State Debt' is usually confined to Financial Agreement Debt, information on which is available from Budget papers. This debt, incurred on behalf of the government by either the Commonwealth or the Tasmanian Public Finance Corporation (TASCORP) must be repaid from the Public Account. However, it does not include borrowing by State Government Statutory Authorities which is not available in a consolidated form. The annual report of the Auditor-General includes an estimate of the aggregate net debt position of these authorities. These, together with 'State Debt' figures give a reasonable picture of Public Sector Debt and are presented converted into constant 1980-81 prices in Table 15.30.

Table 15.30

Tasmanian Public Sector Debt 1981-1988
(Constant 1980-81 Prices)[1]

Year[2]	State Debt[3]	Other Statutory Authority Debt[4]	Total Debt
	$m	$m	$m
1981	1,020.8	535	1,555.8
1982	974.2	559	1,533.2
1983	914.9	679	1,593.9
1984	888.8	758	1,631.8
1985	882.2	911	1,793.2
1986	859.8	1,082	1,941.8
1987	823.7	1,089	1,912.7
1988	799.8	1,061	1,860.8

Notes: [1] Nominal Debt as at 30th June valued at current exchange rates adjusted by the Hobart Consumer Price index ABS Cat. No. 6401.0.
[2] Year ending 30th June.
[3] Borrowings on behalf of the State for the Public Account.
[4] Auditor General's estimate of debt incurred as a result of borrowings by Statutory Authorities (overseas and domestic) not within the Public Account (State Debt) net of any sinking fund balance.
Source: Parliament of Tasmania 'Report of the Auditor-General', various years.

It is of note that despite public concern at the level of public sector debt in Tasmania (and Australia) these figures indicate that debt has only grown at 2.6% in real terms over the 1980s with most of the growth taking place in the mid 1980s when economic activity was particularly depressed. In the last two years total debt has contracted. Unfortunately we were unable to separate out debt which was for general public infrastructure. However, most of the additional debt incurred as 'Other Statutory Authority Debt' was for the Hydro-Electric Commission and a significant proportion of 'State Debt' in the 1980s has been used to finance general government infrastructure expenditure. In fact in 1985-86 and in the current budget the government has (or plans) to shift resources from the loan (capital) account to finance current services. This — to the extent it has been commented upon — has been justified as a way of preventing sharp reductions in recurrent expenditure as a result of other revenue shortfalls. Short-run smoothing in this way is obviously sensible. However, a key issue is the extent to which this imposes a long term debt burden of future taxpayers.

An interesting feature of Table 15.30, in this light, is the declining proportion 'State Debt' bears to total debt. It is tempting to conclude that this means a higher proportion of debt will be financed by income generated by public trading enterprise authorities. However, 'State Debt' is a burden on the government's revenue base only to the extent that the debt was not incurred ultimately by public trading enterprises which generate income which can be used to cover (or defray) debt servicing costs. Much of

the accumulated 'State Debt' has been used to finance public trading enterprise activities and has been on-lent-by the government. We therefore need a picture of net State debt which accounts for the debt servicing payments to the budget from these activities. This is given in Table 15.31. This shows that the real decline in 'State Debt' shown in Table 15.30 from $1020.8m in 1981 to $799.8m in 1988 in real terms at 1980/81 prices is largely of cosmetic interest. In fact the 'Net Burden' of this debt, that is 'State Debt' repayments as a proportion of Consolidated Fund recurrent receipts has risen over a period to reach an unparalleled 6.2%. It is difficult to disentangle the forces which explain this important trend. One component is that current revenues have been constrained in the 1980s. Other factors are rising interest rates and a higher proportion of debt used to finance general government infrastructure as well as changes in the debt management mechanism.

Table 15.31

Net 'State Debt' Burden on the Tasmanian State Budget 1975/76 — 1988/89
$m

Year	Net Debt Related Payments from Consolidated Fund[1] (1)	Total Consolidated Fund Current Receipts (2)	State Debt Burden[2] (1/2)
1975/76	15.4	322.1	4.78
1976/77	16.3	396.6	4.11
1977/78	21.4	444.3	4.82
1978/79	22.2	495.8	4.48
1979/80	24.8	560.2	4.43
1980/81	35.8	620.3	5.77
1981/82	40.1	683.2	5.87
1982/83	39.9	765.0	5.22
1983/84	45.7	853.1	5.36
1984/85	50.6	953.2	5.31
1985/86	59.9	1024.7	5.85
1986/87	67.8	1107.9	6.12
1987/88	72.7	1201.4	6.05
1988/89 (est.)	77.1	1245.3	6.19

Notes: [1] This column consists of inescapable net expenditure from the Consolidated fund on State Debt. It includes interest payments by the Tasmanian Government to the Commonwealth plus contributions to the Debt Sinking fundless interest payments reserved from statutory authorities in respect of debt and sinking fund contributions.

[2] [1] as percentage of total consolidated fund current receipts.

Source: Report of the Auditor-General and the Statement of Public Accounts (various issues; Government Printer, Tasmania: Budget Paper No.1 Supporting Budget Information (various issues) Government Printer, Tasmania.

The 'State Rate of Interest' or average rate of interest on debt owed to the Commonwealth, has certainly increased from 7.49% in 1978/79 to 11.62% in 1988/89. This understates the true position because borrowings by TASCORP are excluded and they currently constitute about 11% of total State debt. The average rate of interest on this debt was 13.3% in June 1988.

While it is very difficult to break down 'State Debt' by purpose, there seems to have been a rise in the proportion financing general government infrastructure which would increase the burden on the budget.

TASCORP established in 1985 was a major change in the debt management mechanism in line with changes in the operations of the Loan Council. However TASCORP debt for the Consolidated Fund does not have an associated debt Sinking fund. Thus no moneys are set aside to provide for the repayment of the State's debt to TASCORP. It is planned that, upon maturity, existing loans are to be refinanced through further loans from TASCORP. The expansion of the amount of debt without an associated debt sinking fund will defer the burden of the debt on the budget. It is noted that in three years TASCORP debt has risen from nil to 11% of State Debt.

There is also reason to believe that the net burden in Table 15.31 is an underestimate. The Auditor-General has pointed out in his annual reports on the Public Account that several Statutory Authorities run at a loss and receive grants from the Consolidated Fund to service their debts. Thus the real net burden should include these grants. As noted in 15.4.1 grants to public trading enterprises have risen in the 1980s which may mean some cosmetic reduction in the net burden, but it has not proved possible to assess the importance of this effect.

15.4.9 Tasmanian Government Expenditure

General Government Consumption Expenditure
The public sector plays a vital role in a modern economy in providing a wide array of goods and services of direct consumption benefit to citizens. Some of these are accepted even by those who believe in a minimal public sector, or what was termed model 2 in an earlier chapter. At State level this would embrace at least public order and safety and some expenditure on transport and communications. However, much of the consumption expenditure by State Governments is under threat from those who claim that public activity is inherently inefficient because they claim there are no obstacles to efficient private provision. Much expenditure on health and education clearly falls into this category and many of the activities embraced under the general provision of housing and community amenities could also be included.

The Pattern of Expenditure
It is not surprising that the pattern of expenditure varies between the States. This reflects what is perhaps the most important benefit of a federal structure; lower levels of government are better placed to fit the provision of goods and services to local needs. It is also an established feature of our system that the level of expenditure varies between the States reflecting local policy changes; differing needs and differing costs of providing equivalent services. Thus as pointed out in the CREA survey of the Tasmanian Economy:

> 'the broad pattern revealed by the historical record is that the State Governments of Tasmania and Western Australia have consistently spent at above-average levels while those of New South Wales, Queensland and to a lesser extent Victoria have consistently spent at below average levels' (1987, p. 275).

The relative expenditure levels of the States are the complex result of different policy decisions, different demographic degrees of efficiency in provision, to name only the most obvious factors. Given that Commonwealth funding is linked to the notion of enabling the States to provide services of equal quality, these factors form the basis of much dispute. The Grants Commission calculates standardised per capita expenditures adjusted for the non-policy obstacles to service delivery such as population dispersion. There is of course much disagreement as to whether the methodology employed adequately caters for a State's particular disabilities. However, it does permit an indication of the relative importance attached to the different areas of expenditure across the States.

Table 15.32

**Actual Per Capita Expenditure as Percentage of Standardized Per Capita
Expenditure By State and Type of Service, 1981-82
to 1983-84 Service**

State	Education	Health	Law, Order and Public Safety	Other Expenditure	Business Undertakings	Total Expend.
NSW	99.9	96.1	97.4	102.4	110.9	100.6
Vic.	113.9	101.0	94.0	104.8	101.3	106.2
Qld	78.5	92.6	90.1	94.9	81.3	85.2
SA	102.2	103.5	122.9	91.0	99.7	103.2
WA	89.8	121.5	106.8	90.8	79.2	97.5
Tas.	109.5	104.0	158.0	89.7	63.6	104.2
Six States	100.0	100.0	100.0	100.0	100.0	100.0

Source: Business Council of Australia, State Finances: The Forgotten Element of Fiscal Policy (May 1987) Reproduced from, The Tasmanian Economy: a Survey, CREA Dec., 1987.

The table indicates that the Tasmanian Government, as matter of policy, spent more on Law and Order and Public Safety, and to a lesser extent Education and Health than the other States but less than the other States on Business Undertakings and Other Expenditure. These figures are averaged over the three financial years 1981-82 to 1983-84. This difference in pattern appears to have been long-standing. This makes the changes that have occurred in more recent years under the pressure of Commonwealth funding cutbacks even more interesting. Table 15.33 compares the Tasmanian expenditure pattern in percentage shares with that of all States for the years 1981-82 and 1986-87.

Table 15.33

**General Government Final Consumption Expenditure by Purpose as a Share of
Total General Government Final Consumption Expenditure: Tasmania and All
States 1981-82 and 1986-87**

Purpose	1981-82 Tas.	1981-82 All States	1986-87 Tas.	1986-87 All States
General Public Services	8.0	7.4	9.0	8.0
Public Order and Safety	9.9	10.5	7.7	10.3
Education	41.5	42.9	38.5	39.3
Health	24.0	26.2	27.5	28.8
Social Security & Welfare	1.7	1.9	1.5	2.5
Housing & Community Amenities	0.6	0.7	0.7	0.7
Recreation & Culture	2.4	1.3	2.6	1.5
Agriculture, Forestry and Fishing	5.4	3.5	4.7	3.0
Mining, Manufacturing & construction	2.1	0.6	1.9	0.6
Transport and Communication	2.3	3.4	2.2	3.4
Other Economic Affairs[1]	2.3	1.7	3.6	1.9

Note: [1] includes Fuel and energy, and Other as defined in Major GPC Groups.
Source: ABS Cat. No. 5504.0 'State and Local Government Finance Australia 1986-87'.

Most noteworthy is that the expenditure on public order and safety has fallen relatively in Tasmania. This raises the important question of whether the cutbacks imposed on the State have had the effect of reducing the degree of policy independence. We have already adverted to the rising share of specific purpose payments in total grants in this regard.

One vitally important feature of the table lies in the absence of any substantial onslaught on the expenditure components of the social wage. It might have been expected, given the pressure of the financial constraint and the 'user pays' rhetoric of the Tasmanian Liberal Government, that these areas would have been those to bear the brunt of adjustment. However, movements are broadly in line with other States. The only real exception to this is the falling percentage of expenditure on social security and welfare, at a time when it was rising in other States. In terms of the stress faced by disadvantaged groups, this is more

significant than it first appears because it needs to be seen in context. Apart from the obvious fact that it has occurred at a time when Tasmania has the nation's highest unemployment, we have also seen in a previous section that there has been a regressive shift in the pattern of taxation. It should also be noted that, on the usually accepted welfare indicators over this period, Tasmania was worse off than the other States. Average weekly earnings were lower, there was a greater proportion of the population on pensions and on family income supplement. In terms of level rather than percentage share, real net consumption expenditure on Social Security and Welfare has fallen by 22% (ABS 6401.0).

Table 15.34

Private and Public Sector Capital Formation in Tasmania 1981/82 − 1987/88

($m)

Year	Private Fixed Capital Expenditure	Public Sector Capital Outlays	Gross Fixed Capital Expend.
1981/82	221	236	222
1982/83	170	318	291
1983/84	213	337	309
1984/85	263	421	385
1985/86	336	436	393
1986/87	407	372	324
1987/88	463	397[a]	338[a]

Note: [a] preliminary figures.
Source: ABS Cat. No. 5646.0 (various issues) 'Estimates of Private Fixed Capital Expenditure: States and Territories'; ABS Cat. No. 5501.0 'Government Financial Estimates 1987/88'.

General Government Capital Expenditure
As mentioned in section 15.4.2, one of Tasmania's structural problems is the relatively low level of private fixed capital expenditure. Table 15.34 shows the relative importance of the public sector in this regard. This was particularly true in the first half of the 1980s with the leading role of hydro-electric development. Much of this was, as discussed earlier in 15.4.8, financed by public sector borrowing. In our discussion of public sector debt we pointed out that while the same evidence of a shift to financing general government infrastructure, there were serious constraints which prevented the general government sector from taking up the slack from the decline in the leading role of public trading enterprises.

The small nature of the Tasmanian economy means that private sector capital expenditure and public sector capital expenditure are highly interdependent. While Tasmania has shared in the improved national private investment climate, under the Federal Labor Government, as Table 15.34 attests, it is from the lowest base in the Commonwealth. Per capita private fixed capital expenditure remains below the Australian average (see Table 15.12). Hopes for increased private sector investment are based on developments in partnership with the provision of public sector infrastructure. The now abandoned Wesley Vale Pulp Mill was only commercially viable in tandem with significant complementary public sector capital expenditure.

The Wesley Vale project also brings out another important role of the public sector. The benefits of the project were to the Balance of Payments through improved value added in forestry. Much of the discussion on employment was off beam as the net effect on employment growth would almost certainly have been very small. One important reason for this is the lack of appropriate skills in the Tasmanian workforce. One vital role of the public sector historically in Tasmania, for which the HEC, in particular, is justifiably renowned, has been skill formation. The winding back of public enterprise capital formation in Tasmania carries with it this important negative spillover effect. The reduction in the process of skill creation in the workforce renders the economy a less attractive base for private sector investment. This structural problem needs to be seriously addressed.

15.5 Case Studies
As previously outlined, Tasmania has suffered a severe financial squeeze because of cutbacks in Commonwealth funding which it has not been possible to offset totally from the State's own narrow revenue base. In addition, there is no evidence of a widespread assault on expenditure elements of the social wage. Nevertheless, this financial strategy means that the array of measures, which have been termed 'privatisation by stealth', have appeared attractive institutional solutions to the funding problems experienced. However, if we judge the Liberal Government by its actions rather than its rhetoric, there is no strong ideological commitment to the notion that private ownership *per se* is more efficient. In fact, what we see are examples of forced asset sales on an *ad hoc* basis for budgetary reasons (Precision Tool Annex, Tasmanian Film Corporation) coupled with attempts to use market incentives within the public sector through the introduction of commercialisation (Port Arthur Authority), competitive bidding and contracting out (Department of Main Roads) and changes in wages and conditions (Housing day labor force). In addition, we have an attempt at privatising the Tasmanian Herd Improvement Organisation which shows how the process of privatisation can be misguided,

mispecified and finally a farce.

Our case studies aim at examining the processes involved, illustrating the effects of the changes and analysing the constraints. They clearly indicate that there are serious limits to any attempt to harness market incentives in the public sector but also draw lessons for their appropriate use within the context of an integrated program of public sector renewal and reform.

Commercialisation — Potential Advantages
The principle advantage of commercialisation is that the introduction of market signals into the public sector can better direct resources and improve efficiency in the allocative sense. In essence it offers a strategy of reform for the public sector because it is an explicit rejection of the view that ownership per se affects the degree of efficiency, while recognising that price incentives can play a useful social role. Advocates of free market provision reject commercialisation on the grounds that anything which can be commercialised should be privatised. This involves a lack of clarity in thought over the rationale for an activity being in the public domain in the first place and a failure to acknowledge the multi-dimensional nature of such activities. It is as if there are goods and services accidently provided currently by government that could be hived off and more efficiently provided under private ownership. Our case study of the commercialisation of the operation of the Port Arthur historic site illustrates this multi-dimensional issue because there are a host of external factors that would not be captured by private market operations. Commercialisation is, in its nature, a strategy of limited applicability, best suited to those areas where there is a strong degree of jointness in the provision of private and social benefits and where equity in provision is not a central objective. It is thus not recommended for those components of public sector activity which are part of the social wage such as health and education. Nevertheless, it clearly has a part to play in public sector renewal and reform.

There are also issues concerning the process of commercialisation. The forward looking case for improving public sector allocative efficiency with sensible use of the user pays system is easily confused with actual change based on an *ad hoc* response to financial stringency. It is vitally important to examine whether the claimed advantages are realised and at what cost.

15.5.1 Tasmanian Herd Improvement Organisation
Background
The attempt to privatise the Tasmanian Herd Improvement Organisation is an object lesson the folly of privatisation. One can certainly characterise what has emerged as a 'U' turn from the initial full privatisation proposal but such was the comedy of errors in the process that the final act looks like the twist at the end of a French farce. The final act in this case was the Herd Improvement Amendment Act 1988 which effectively amalgamated THIO with the Tasmanian Dairy Industry Authority (TDIA) by putting its functions under the control of that body. However, behind this is a tale of a failed attempt at full privatisation which in the end result has left many costly functions such as laboratory work in the public domain while the profitable services have been franchised out to the private sector. In addition, the new amalgamated organisation suffered from having to start without the services of specialist staff who had left the organisation in anticipation of privatisation as the Minister for Primary Industry himself pointed out in the second reading speech to the Herd Improvement Amendment Bill, 1988. Even more remarkably and apparently indifferent to the irony involved, the Minister also identified, as one of the important immediate tasks that the new Board would face, that of 'reversing much of the change in direction already in place.' This can only mean the preparatory work that was done to prepare THIO for full privatisation.

To understand this turnaround we must look to the process of privatisation which turned up many problems which could have been foreseen, if the case for government involvement had been properly addressed in the first place and proper objectives for improvement and reform devised. It is not argued here that there was no case for privatisation or that commercialisation was not an appropriate strategy. Indeed, there was a strong case for the introduction of market signals in some form. However, the actual process was not driven by clear efficiency objectives related to the dairy industry and the Tasmanian economy but rather by fiscal expediency and the rhetoric of privatisation. The fiscal expediency came from the perception that THIO had been running in recent years at an annual loss of around $750,000. There appears to have been no discussion of what an optimal level of support would have been.

Government Involvement in Dairy Herd Improvement
The operation of THIO was essentially aimed at dairy herd improvement. This is vital to the case for government involvement because of the peculiar features of the dairy industry and its local importance to the Tasmanian economy. There is a case for government support of genetic improvement in many farming industries based on market failure considerations but the case in dairying is strengthened because it is a highly regulated industry all over the world and the force of competitive market signals is already attenuated. However, it is reasonable to ask why the government should undertake and or subsidise herd improvement. In a free market producers aiming to maximise profit should respond to market signals and be willing to pay for better genetic stock as they capture the benefits in higher yields. Indeed it could be argued that subsidy would mean too high a rate of investment in herd improvement and the resources used would have a higher value elsewhere. In this light there is a clear argument for commercialisation (user-pays) and possible privatisation to achieve this. In fact, the Tasmanian Government was in possession of an excellent report to THIO by the Animal Genetics and Breeding Unit, jointly based on the University of New England and the New South Wales Department of Agriculture, which clearly analysed the case for government involvement. The report 'Evaluation of the Breeding Program for the Tasmanian Dairy Industry', (December, 1986) had as its first recommendation the retaining of the genetic improvement program as an entity (p. 5) and presented a clear philosophy of separation of those functions

which needed and deserved government funding from those which could be profitably merchandised such as Herd Recording and Artificial Breeding services. The key arguments are based on spillover or externality effects and the public good nature of some services. It was further recognised that there were efficiency gains from synergy that resulted from the integrated nature of THIO. Thus:

> 'a major strength of THIO is its integrated structure, encompassing all major components of DHI (Dairy Herd Improvement) with the exception of a research and extension capability. This would be the envy of many other DHI operations' (AGBU Dec. 1986, p. 26).

This refers mainly to the linking of artificial breeding functions with herd recording functions. This report recognised that changing world conditions with respect to both the technology of, and trading situation in, genetic material were altering the case for and scope of government involvement. It therefore advocated a number of reforms, many of which were aimed at putting THIO on a more commercial footing. However, the case for considerable public sector involvement still appeared strong to ensure an effective local herd improvement program. This was deemed essential to keep Tasmanian dairying competitive on productivity terms in the world market.

In addition to the many points made in the report, it also needs to be noted that the dairy industry in Tasmania, and throughout Australia is highly regulated and protected. The link between the market price signals and the farm gate is weakened by the operation of a system of price discrimination between the town milk supply and the manufacturing sector. Policies of pooling and averaging are in place to maintain dairy farm incomes. Under such a structure an individual producer does not operate under the competitive assumption of being able to sell as much milk at the given price as he can produce. The result is that the incentive to invest in productivity improvement is weakened. This could, in a technical economic sense, be regarded as a rationale for public sector involvement on second best allocative efficiency grounds (ie. the best alternative in the absence of world-wide deregulation of and free trade in the dairying industry) and also as part of an equitable income distribution policy to farmers.

If the approach of following the report's recommendations had been followed we might have had a sensible program of commercialisation and improvement of an historically very successful program. However, instead we went down the privatisation road, a process which was a debacle.

The Privatisation Process

The privatisation process for THIO reveals a number of interesting features. Firstly, it is obvious that the THIO Board and management were encouraged to think of the process as being an exciting development for them. It would free them from the difficulties of fiscal stringency and the uncertainties associated with annual budgeting for planning. They would no longer be held back by red tape from grasping opportunities in new 'venture' activities opening up as a result of the changed nature of the genetic industry. These concerns were directly addressed in the AGBU report of December 1986 but the rhetoric of private sector efficiency had now taken hold. Even at the time of the report, privatisation was being talked up. As early as March 1987 some employees had voiced concern to the Tasmanian Public Service Association over possible privatisation. There were inevitably great uncertainties over employment but also concern that moves were being made to run down certain programs to prepare the organisation for privatisation. This was the beginning of a long period of uncertainty, initially based on rumour, to be punctuated by general announcements over the next few months which were left without detail. There can be no doubt that the uncertainty caused by failure to communicate intention caused real economic costs.

The THIO Board, with the apparent encouragement of the government, engaged private consultants to develop a corporate strategic plan. There appears to have been discussion of the inability of the then current structure to cope with both the level and uncertainty of its budgetary support, of the well-known problems of the run down state of the operation and then a ritual incantation of the litany on the leanness and entrepreneurial nature of the private sector and the inflexibility of public sector. It was then recommended that THIO change from being a government owned and operated entity to a structure based on a holding company and two private sector businesses operating with the blessing and encouragement of government. The first company was to specialise in what had been the mainstream business of THIO and the second in the venture area scanning the world for opportunities! A key recommendation was that all major parties involved in THIO were to be given the ability to obtain priority shares in both. A timetable to get approval from cabinet by June of 1987 and be ready to changeover in June 1988 was posited. We can immediately see the difficulties posed for the privatisation process. Apart from the lack of any serious attempt to look at any real alternative under public ownership, the notion of proceeding by a sort of management buy-out raises all sorts of issues with respect to the invidious potential conflicts of interest within which the directors and management of THIO could find themselves during the period leading up to the changeover. These problems have been well discussed with respect to management buy-out in the private sector of which there have been $182b worth in the US in the last four years. As it was succinctly put recently in The Economist of 8-14 April 1989, 'in a management buy-out, the managers are in a unique insiders' position.' The simple point of course is that the managers have information no one else has over the prospects and hence value of the assets and are in a position to gain at the expense of shareholders. It is perhaps surprising that a government so imbued with the private sector ethic, and full of praise for the market, could have been so apparently unaware of its occasional failings.

The Tasmanian cabinet gave approval to the privatisation process and went to the very brink before becoming concerned over reports of financial dealings of the organisation in the lead up to sale. In May 1988 it asked for an urgent investigation by the Auditor-General. The Minister, on the basis of the Auditor

General's report, dismissed the Manager of THIO, obtained the resignation of the Board and terminated negotiations with Nationwide Genetics. In a release to the media on June 10th, 1988 he bravely talked of recovery of expenditure when THIO was sold and of being approached by other dairy industry interests.

Outcomes and Lessons
There will no doubt be other twists as this process continues to unfold. At the moment the TDIA is saddled with the totally unprofitable areas of milk testing and herd recording. The profitable area of artificial breeding has been hived off to the private sector and discussions are in hand to have a private firm handle semen collection from licensed bulls and distribute imported genetic material. The real problem in all of this is that it is by no means clear that the final arrangement will be the best available balance of cost and benefit. It may well be that a degree of commercialisation was and is highly desirable. However, the net result has not been achieved as the result of a thought through strategic plan for the industry, but rather by a sequence of events with its own momentum, driven by the slogans of private sector efficiency espoused by the government. The lesson to be drawn from the THIO story is that privatisation is not a political or economic cure-all because the process itself involves undervaluing public assets. The subsequent transfer of these assets to the private sector offers only the appearance of productivity or efficiency gains.

15.5.2 Precision Tool Annexe
Background
The Precision Tool Annexe (PTA) was constructed by the Commonwealth Government during the Second World War to supply precision tools and gauges towards the war effort. The annexe building, located in the grounds of the Launceston railway workshops, was passed over to the State Government in 1945 and was operated by the Transport Commission as a commercial enterprise until sold to the Tasmanian firm Delta Hydraulics in 1988.

The problems in recent times grew out of the May 1975 agreement to transfer the State railway system to Australian National Rail. While the PTA continued to operate, it was no longer part of an integrated railway network and the demand for the PTA's output from Australian National rail diminished from 1975. Losses eventuated, partly because the existing building and some plant were obsolete and required replacement if the PTA was to become commercially viable. Further, the Railway Transfer Agreement of May 1975 only guaranteed the State Government the use of the original PTA building until the end of 1985. The initial approach of the State authorities was to relocate the PTA in a new building in the Launceston region and to upgrade the workforce to 100 about half of whom would be engaged on the production of precision tools and gauges and the remainder on supply of volume engineering components to close tolerances. This project would have involved considerable public capital expenditure at a time when the supply of funds for these purposes from the Commonwealth was drying up. The diversion of scarce funds could only be justified if some alternative market outlets could be developed. Clearly, the State Government hoped that the PTA could successfully tender for contracts under the proposed Commonwealth submarine project; however these aspirations were nipped in the bud when the submarine project was sited in South Australia. Thus the Tasmanian Government was left with the ownership of an unprofitable enterprise requiring large injections of public expenditure.

The main case against the sale of the enterprise was the need to preserve a substantial 'reservoir of skill' in a regional economy where skills are extremely scarce. The PTA was the most significant source of tool makers in the State and the PTA's demand for apprentices was the only reason for the continuation of certain specialised training courses in the State's TAFE colleges. If following the sale of the asset these skills were dissipated, they may be lost to the regional economy altogether. For this reason, the State Government negotiated a contract for sale which attempted to ensure the preservation of the skill base and the apprenticeship supporting it. Three firms indicated an interest in the contract, before Delta Hydraulics, a locally based firm, agreed to the terms and conditions.

The agreement for the sale included certain clauses which guaranteed the following:

- the Purchaser was required to indicate which of the present employees it wished to re-employ and to guarantee the re-employment of all current apprentices.
- the Purchaser agreed to re-employ at least 50 of the present employees and to maintain employment levels for a minimum of 2 years following the sale.
- the Purchaser agreed to employ no less than 4 new apprentices in each year, commencing one year from the date of completion of the contract.

Outcomes and Lessons

The long term future of the PTA was under a cloud from the moment of its separation from the railway base. It is usually difficult to justify, on market failure grounds, the operation of a manufacturing engineering enterprise in the public sector. In the absence of external effects, there was undoubtedly a case for privatisation. However, in the special circumstances of a small economy with a much lower than average level of private sector investment in both physical capital and, most importantly, workforce skills, there is a cost to the region in terms of loss of this leading role in skill incubation. One could still justify sale if alternative public expenditure counterbalanced this in increasing workforce skills. However, there is little evidence of this. The government's attempt at contractual commitment does not extend beyond two years and a private firm will face its own constraints which militate against it serving educational functions beyond its own immediate needs. An important lesson here is the context or environment in which privatisation occurs. Generally, that which is reasonable in a large competitive economy can have serious disadvantages in a small regional economy. For instance a private firm in a competitive environment has an incentive to train for specialised skills and to retain skilled workers during downturns since, if it did not, it might find the skills hard to come by in the upturn. In an uncompetitive regional market the skills can be 'parked' in the social security system in temporary unemployment and picked up at need later. Many other problems of a similar nature exist with the simple minded application of free market dogma, drawn from the ideal competitive system, in the context of small uncompetitive regional niches. It should further be noted that the overall level of skill of the workforce, to which PTA was an important contributor, is an important determinant of private sector investment and we abandon this leading role to the peril of the entire economy. Every economy must maintain these reservoirs of skill.

15.5.3 The Tasmanian Film Corporation
Background

The Tasmanian Film Corporation was sold to private interests in September 1982 during the early days of the Liberal Government and in this case there are stronger indications of an ideological motive, although ostensibly the sale was made in the interests of meeting a State budget deficit of large proportions inherited from the preceding Labor administration.

The history of Tasmanian Government involvement in film production extends back to 1946 with the establishment of the Government Film Unit. The initial organisation had a limited brief confined to the production of service films of educational and development kind; the Unit became the Department of Film Production and was converted into the Tasmanian Film Corporation by legislation enacted in 1977. This act of corporatisation was prompted by the apparent success of its South Australian counterpart in the development of a regional film industry. The relevant Minister in the Liberal Government (Mr Neil Robson) laid the blame for the Corporation's woes on a previous Labor Government's approach (Examiner Newspaper 2/7/82) to the establishment phase when the State Government had not delivered on its promises to establish facilities for the Corporation, adequate access to Loan Funds or sufficient working capital. The Corporation produced some successful feature films including 'Manganini' which accumulated 3 Australian and 4 Overseas awards and it earned further awards for children's films such as 'Fatty and George' and 'Save the Lady'

which was sold in Norway. The Corporation employed 36 persons on a full time basis and provided opportunities for 540 actors, writers and others with technical skills. The Liberal Government officials and advisers acknowledged the success of the organisation, but pointed to the annual impost of $700,000 p.a. on consolidated revenue required to support production costs and to the accumulated losses incurred by the organisation. This latter argument bears closer examination. For example, in the financial year ended 30th June 1982 the loss amounted $204,036. However, this accounting loss is calculated after allowing for the payment of interest on funds borrowed to establish the corporation ($167,041), rent paid to the State Government ($52,000) and payroll tax ($33,913): these three items total $252,954 more than the loss for the year. This analysis emphasises the problems arising from the application of commercial accounting principles to public corporations when they are not structured as private corporations with an equity capital on which dividends are paid out of profits : in the establishment phase of many private corporations the dividend liability is non existent in the absence of profits. Further, it is doubtful if bodies such as the TFC should be expected to return a profit. Their function is 'development stimulation' or 'cultural contribution'. In the case of government owned film bodies, the State Government is normally a major customer but successive Tasmanian Governments had reduced their participation. The Tasmanian Government contributed 78.6% of the TFC's total income in 1977-78, but this contribution had fallen to 47.3% in 1980-81 (Mercury 13/6/82).

The sale of the TFC in September 1982 for $1.2m was based on estimated asset values, but this selling price fell far short of the $3.4m invested by the TFC during its short life span. Further, the State Government paid out the private loans raised by the TFC at a cost of $1.8m. These short term costs were borne to remove continued government subsidisation of the TFC in the future. The private purchaser was guaranteed $600,000 of government film contracts for 3 years following the sale of the Corporation (Australian 21/12/82).

This example brings to light all of the issues

which surround the privatisation debate: the financial motives for selling a government owned asset in the face of tighter budget constraints; the inappropriate and inconsistent accounting principles which are applied to the PTEs making them appear less profitable than they are in a commercial context and the capital shortage issue.

Outcomes and Lessons

Disposal of the TFC amounted to a 'fire-sale' of cosmetic benefit to the State budget at a price which undervalued the enterprise. It highlights both the temptation to sell assets for cosmetic reasons but also the real pressure from fiscal restraint. It clearly illustrates how a blind faith in market mechanisms can obscure perception of non-pecuniary external benefits. In this the inappropriate commercial accounting principles which are applied in the public sector result in inconsistencies which may have played an important role by understating the profit position.

15.5.4 Contracting Out

The contracting out option has been applied to some minor works of the Departments of Main Roads and Housing and to some audit functions of the Auditor General. The pressures on Day Labor employment in the Department of Main Roads began with the decision by a previous Federal Liberal Government in 1981 to contract out all National Highway construction projects, which in Tasmania meant that the Main Roads Day Labor force would not construct the National Highway network in Tasmania. The effects of this Federal Government initiative would be to reduce day labor employment through the retrenchment of 260 men reducing the Day Labor Construction Force from 800 to 540 men if the DMR was unable to compete in the competitive tendering process. The State Liberal opposition's view at that time was articulated by the Opposition Leader (Geoff Pearsall) who expressed a clear view that contract labor was always preferred to day labor on the grounds of efficiency. In normal circumstances, one may argue that the open tender system is bound to increase efficiency and if there is a loss of Day Labor jobs in the public sector workforce, the slack may be

picked up by the expansion of work awarded private contractors. Pressures on Day Labor employed intensified once the State Government decided it would apply the open tendering system to the State's own road works program. The DMR was put in a competitive tendering position with two major private contractors; one operating predominantly in the North/North West region of the State and the other in the South. Considerations of geography and local market structure clearly militate against effective competition in the market leaving in most cases one private bid in competition with the DMR. However, the capacity of the DMR to enter a competitive bid appears to be hampered by the age of its road making equipment, for example, the DMR emoleum plant is 25 years old and although a replacement item has been promised by a succession of State Ministers the situation is unchanged. It is not clear if these consequences represent increased efficiency or not.

The Liberal Government declared preference for contracted labor was extended in the early days of the government to the phasing out of the southern day labor force in the Department of Housing. All maintenance work on Departmental properties was contracted out in the southern region from February, 1983 as a cost cutting measure. The TPSA has on many occasions expressed its concerns to agency heads about the employment of Day Labor Staff on clerical/administrative duties previously performed by members of the State Service. The implication is that Day Labor employment offers a cheaper way for State agencies to complete routine administrative functions.

Our final example of the application of the Contracting out principle is the amendment of the State Audit Act to allow for the employment of private accountancy practices to perform some of the functions required by State Parliament of the State Auditor General, particularly in relation to his review of Statutory authorities and public corporations. Several of the State A-G's recent annual reports express dissatisfaction with the reduction in the size of his professional establishment which he advances as the reason for delays and difficulties in meeting statutory requirements. The contracting out of State Audit practice does not sit happily with long established Parliamentary traditions. The need to preserve the impartial status of the State's audit functions must remain the paramount consideration.

Outcomes and Lessons
The main lesson of contracting out is similar to that of privatisation in the Tasmanian context. Competitive tendering requires a competitive environment, if any of the claimed advantages are to be successfully achieved. With respect to the Audit function there would appear to be dangers to the parliamentary process.

15.5.5 Port Arthur Historic Site
Background

'But however important Port Arthur is, Tasman Peninsula has far more to offer. There is the strongest reason for treating the peninsula as a whole, for regarding its totality as more than the sum of its parts, for naming the Peninsula and not just Port Arthur as part of the National estate. For much of its existence, Port Arthur was only a focal point for a complex of convict stations which survive in satisfying measure and reflect more fully than Port Arthur the changes in penal policy in the age of transportation and beyond.'

R. Ian Jack, Professor of History, University of Sydney (from the Heritage of Australia, quoted in Port Arthur Conservation and Development Project).

The Port Arthur historic site is of obvious importance, as the major convict settlement of the Australian penal system, to the nation's cultural heritage. The economic implications of this are often missed, that is, even in the absence of its role as a tourist attraction, it would still justify public funding because of the public good nature of 'heritage'. This market failure issue needs to be taken up below in our discussion of funding arrangements. In fact, Port Arthur is Tasmania's most important tourist attraction. Helped by its convenient relative proximity to Hobart, a drive of some 100 km south east to the Tasman peninsula, it attracts over half of all visitors to Tasmania.

There is, therefore, a clear external benefit in terms of a spillover effect on the tourism industry which is not captured by any market. Given the depressed nature of the Tasmanian economy, Port Arthur is also significant in terms of the regional economy. Among other things it enables some degree of economies of scale to be achieved in the provision of local infrastructure, such as roads and sewerage, and has an important impact on local levels of economic activity and employment.

Previous Funding and Management Arrangements
The commercialisation of Port Arthur can be seen as an institutional response to the withdrawal of Commonwealth funding which had been generous. Under a joint program with the State a two for one funding arrangement was set up in 1980 for the conservation and development of the site. Over the period to 1985-86 the Commonwealth provided $6,000,000 and the State $3,000,000. It is noteworthy that Port Arthur received more than 25% of all Commonwealth heritage funding over this period which was more than three times that received by any other State. After 1986 the Commonwealth did not renew the arrangement and, while the promise was made of specific project monies, none has been forthcoming.

Over the period of joint funding much effort went into the development of a management plan under the auspices of the National Parks and Wildlife Service. This was based on the Australian interpretation of the International Charter for the Conservation and Restoration of Monuments and Sites known as the Burra Charter. This management plan is very sensitive to the appropriate degree of conservation and restoration and aims to provide visitor and management requirements with minimal impact. It has the very clear thrust that the prime aim is to preserve the site's cultural and heritage value and that encouraging tourism is a secondary aim which must be compatible with this. This is of great importance because the principles of the management plan were explicitly adopted as the philosophy of the commercialised authority. What remains at issue is the capacity of the Authority to live up to this within the constraints in which it operates.

The Commercialisation of Port Arthur — Objectives
The Tasmanian Liberal Government commercialised Port Arthur by presenting a bill to set up the Port Arthur Historic Site Management Authority in July 1987. The essence of the process was to impose site entrance fees since 'one of the functions of the authority is to conduct its affairs with a view of becoming a viable commercial enterprise' as the relevant minister (Mr Bennett) put it. (Parliament of Tasmania [Hansard] 40th Parliament, Second Session 1987 Vol 13, p. 2712, 28th July 1987). It was clearly expected that in the long run at least a surplus would be generated for other public sector purposes. Mr Bennett stated:

'. . . it is anticipated that revenue from a site entrance fee, together with funds generated from concessionaires at the site will result in minimal deficit funding by the government to the management authority in the early stages. When the authority is able to achieve financial viability, provision is made for the authority to pay the Consolidated Fund such amount as the Treasurer may determine, having regard to the financial viability of the authority' (Parliament of Tasmania, [Hansard] 40th Parliament, Second Session, 1987, Vol. 13, p. 2714, 28th July, 1987).

This financial objective was reinforced by a requirement that the authority 'use its best endeavours to secure financial assistance by way of grants, sponsorship and other means' (Parliament of Tasmania, [Hansard] 40th Parliament, Second Session, 1987, Vol. 13, p. 2713, 28th July, 1987). The government sought to protect the heritage value of the site by a provision that the Authority 'must act in accordance with the principles of the previously developed management plan which included adherence to the guidelines for the proper care and maintenance of historic structures as contained within the Australian Chapter of the International Council on Monuments and Sites' Burra Charter and it was emphasised that the Authority's function of promoting the site as a tourist destination had to be consistent with the management plan. There were in addition preservation, maintenance and educational functions and a coordinating role for archaeo-

logical activity. Clearly the government recognised the multi-dimensional value of the site and the potential conflicts. However, one aim of the Bill which appears to conflict with the overall commercialisation thrust was to 'maximise the involvement of the private sector in the development operation and promotion of facilities at the site' (Parliament of Tasmania, [Hansard] 40th Parliament, Second Session, 1987, Vol. 13, p. 2712, 28th July, 1987). While this was qualified with respect to heritage values, the potential conflict with commercial success of the Authority per se was not acknowledged.

Outcomes and Lessons
The current fee structure for entrance to the Port Arthur historic site is set at $5 per adult and $12 per family. These charges do not appear to have been reached with reference to any explicit criteria, except a judgement that the market would bear them without damage to tourism. Given the growth in numbers it would seem desirable to relate pricing to the costs imposed upon the site by extra visitors but there is no information base for this. Nevertheless, clearly some charge will cut maintenance costs. The introduction of user charges, therefore, is a beneficial step, though finding the optimum level more problematic. The expected revenue for the 1988-89 financial year is considerably less than the expected total expenditure. Total own revenue runs at some $839,000 consisting of $640,000 from entrance charges with the balance made up from the operation of the caravan park, publications and fees from concessionaires. Given an estimated total expenditure, both current and capital, of $1.47m, the budget allocation of $200,000 for capital and $380,000 will be needed to bring the two into approximate balance. The figures cast doubt on whether the Authority will ever run at a surplus as the government clearly hoped. On balance this is to be expected because of the public good and externality arguments adverted to previously which imply for allocative efficiency that a degree of subsidy is desirable. Unfortunately, it is not clear that the requisite degree of subsidy is being provided and, while the private alternative of sponsorship is open to the Authority, no such arrangements have as

yet been arrived at. It is clear also that current
funding is adequate only for maintenance and
minor works and not for any major restoration
or conservation work. Given the Tasmanian
Government's budgetary situation any such
funds would have to come from the Commonwealth and proposals for a project on the
model prison have been put forward.

One important feature of commercialisation
is the implications for work and conditions.
The proponents of privatisation often claim
that private commercial practice leads to the
reduction in costs because the cost-padding of
wages and salaries in the public sector is eliminated. This position is rejected here but there is
always the danger that the process of commercialisation when undertaken by a conservative
government will lead to a decline in wages and
conditions. Indeed this may well have been
part of the Liberal Government's thinking as
reference was made in the second reading
speech to new appointees not being subject to
the Tasmanian State Services Act. However,
the actual outcome has been a State Industrial
Award that essentially preserves all the pertinent terms and conditions of the State Service
Act.

15.6 Potential Reforms of the Tasmanian Public Sector

The agenda for the reform of Tasmania's public
sector is partly laid out in the opening chapters
of this book. These include the financial reforms outlined in chapter four; the quest for
appropriate commercial structures designed to
increase the managerial efficiency and accountability of State PTEs; the 'people' problems associated with public sector renewal
which include morale questions amenable
partly to solution by more democratic decision
procedures, award restructuring and associated with this, training and retraining. In
addition to these issues discussed in earlier
chapters, we have noted some further ones
which are of particular relevance in a Tasmanian context, for example, the moral hazards of cutting back the public sector and the
growing demand on services. Further any reform package which adopts as a central
premise, the commercialisation of certain public sector agencies must be viewed in the con-

text of reforms already in process and in
Tasmania they are the implementation of the
Cartland recommendations. These issues are
dealt with in the following paragraphs.

15.6.1 Financial Reforms

The two major benchmarks in Tasmania's
recent economic history are the tightening of
the budget constraint facing the State Government as the Commonwealth Government has
withdrawn real funds at a relatively high rate in
comparison with other States and the increasing electoral support for the environmental
lobby which has tightened environmental constraints to such an extent that the establishment of a major pulp mill at Wesley Vale did not
proceed. The major reform issue of Chapter
Seven is related to the first of these issues: the
funds constraint. The proposal involves the introduction of a *State Goods and Services Levy*
which is a tax on final consumption, to raise
the funds needed to eliminate or severely
reduce a plethora of regressive, unpopular
taxes levied on an ad hoc basis. In order to
assess the feasibility of this tax option in a Tasmanian context, we need first to examine the
task required of such a tax initiative. This requires the assessment of the revenues lost if
certain existing forms of Tasmanian taxation are
removed. This will provide some notion of the
dollar revenues which must be provided by the
State Services Tax. For this purpose, we employ the annual report of the State Commissioner of Taxes for the year ended 1987-88,
which is different from the sources employed
in section 15.5 when we were analysing the
State tax mix. Table 15.35 provides a taxonomy
of State taxation collections.

The proposed SGSL is in essence a tax on
final consumption; thus as a minimum requirement it should replace those taxes of a
similar kind and included in this group are the
Electricity consumption levy; business franchises including those on tobacco, alcohol and
petroleum. However, we are of the view that
the removal of franchises on alcohol and
tobacco will prove counter productive given
the demerit nature of these commodities. A
more efficient way of addressing current Tasmanian problems is to use the revenues raised
by the SGSL to remove the franchise on petrol

and to direct the balance of the revenues raised to alleviate some of the problems confronting the State, in particular, Tasmania has the highest unemployment rate among the Australian States and as we have observed in 15.4.7, one of the heavier incidences of payroll tax which is in effect a tax on the volume of employment.

Table 15.35

State Taxation Collections
1986-87 and 1987-88 (Current Prices)

Tax Source	1986-87 $	%	1987-88 $	%
Estate Duties	30681	0.01	107650	0.03
Stamp Duties	58842191	21.26	71156473	21.78
Lottery Tax	10591260	3.83	19451876	5.95
Land Tax	12635046	4.56	12035970	3.69
Motor Tax	18631617	6.73	19345995	5.92
Fees & Licences (Liquor)	9685314	3.50	12492981	3.82
Racing & Gaming Tax	4713516	1.70	5433441	1.66
Casino Tax	4540168	1.64	4952384	1.52
Payroll Tax	83706523	30.24	90508075	27.70
HEC Levy	8441256	3.05	8945296	2.74
Soccer Pools Tax	1086059	0.39	882951	0.27
Business Franchises				
— Tobacco	19307601	6.98	25835688	7.91
— Petrol	36800780	13.29	37280247	11.41
Electricity Consumption				
Levy	1771630	0.64	3885386	1.19
F.I.D	6003210	2.17	10375129	3.18
Ambulance Levy			3987687	1.22
Sundry Licences	27856	0.01	37784	0.01
Total	276814708	100.00	326715013	100.00

Source: Commissioner of Taxes, Report 1987-88 Table 1, Government Printer,Tasmania.

The revenue raising potential of the States Goods and Services Levy is substantial given that Tasmania's final personal consumption expenditures in 1986/87 were $3,782m and of this some $284m was composed of expenditures on tobacco and alcohol products; thus, for example, if the 5% rate of tax proposed in chapter six were to be introduced it would provide potential revenue of 0.05 (3478) = $174m, or including expenditures on tobacco and alcohol of (0.05) (3782) = $189m. These calculations can never exceed the status of broad estimates given that price increase induced by the tax may reduce final expenditures and given that government(s) may allow exemptions from the tax by commodity, or according to the income of households. On this point, it is the view of the researchers of this chapter that it is more efficient to raise the income tax free threshold

to compensate lower income earners for the effects of the consumption tax and not to provide exemptions from the consumption tax itself.

The imposition of the SGSL would raise revenues, conservatively estimated, to fall within the range $120 to $190m p.a. in 1986/87 prices and would allow the State to remove certain regressive and inefficient taxes from its revenue portfolios. Two prime candidates are the petroleum franchise levy (7.2 cents/litre) which is a major cause of the price differential between petrol sold in Tasmania and other Australian States. This raised $36.8m in 1986/87. A second, highly regressive tax is the ambulance levy which was introduced in 1987/88 and raised almost $4m. This can be removed along with the electricity consumption levy ($1.8m in 86/87). The elimination of these taxes would absorb $40m leaving a further $90 to $150m available for the elimination of the Payroll tax, which in a Tasmanian context is an inefficient form of taxation; Tasmania's unemployment problems are relatively severe, and the payroll tax is a tax related directly to employment.

15.6.2 Award Restructuring

The current pattern of reform in Australia's industrial relations system requires flatter award structures and the provision of training so that workers will have access to the new award structures. These reforms should produce productivity gains which underpin future wage fixing schemes. The current Tasmanian public sector structure does not accommodate these requirements at present. There are 57 separate awards governing public sector employment in Tasmania and many of these awards have very small progressive steps, for example, the Administrative and Clerical Officers Guide contains 21 steps separated by increments as low as $200 p.a. Reforms are necessary and some preliminary discussions between unions and employers are proceeding. The reform of public service grades may be organised around three generic groups: Professional, Technical and General and Clerical-Administrative. The number of levels within each broad grouping can be reduced: the TPSA suggestion is for 5 Professional, 11 Technical and General and 8 Clerical Administrative levels. An individual's progression through these grades needs to be geared to training and skill levels. These reforms are capable of achieving substantial productivity gains and are consistent with the Cartland reforms which envisage a policy orientated and flexible structure.

Some of the potential cost savings produced by the flatter award structure must be devoted to the training of staff because promotion through the new structure is merit based and dependent on the acquisition of suitable skills. This principle of relating training to progression through the award structure is a feature of all union proposals for the reform of Tasmania's public sector award structures. For example, the proposed structure of the Administrative and Clerical grades contains 8 levels to replace the exiting 21. In the proposed new structure

the base grade is an unskilled trainee who proceeds to the next grade by acquiring basic keyboard and/or book-keeping skills. Further progression depends on the individual's capacity to acquire formal qualifications, for example, professional accounting where appropriate. Eleven levels may replace the existing 19 in the proposed General and Technical division. Progression through these will depend on job experience and the achievement of technical qualifications, for example, trade certificates.

The case for reform of Tasmania's public sector award structure is strong and the authors of this chapter support the nexus between flatter structures and the training of the work force as a central aspect of reform. Funds should be appropriated to support better internal service training functions and to improve the access of employees to Professional and TAFE courses.

15.6.3 The Moral Hazards of Smaller State Government

The point is made earlier that there are significant moral hazards in further funding cutbacks of the States by the Commonwealth while the demands on State services grow. This is especially so in situations such as the current Tasmanian one, where unemployment remains at unacceptable levels, increasing unemployment adds to welfare needs automatically, and fund restrictions on the State's capacity to provide for a growing welfare need inhibits the State's capacity to deliver significant aspects of the Social Wage to welfare recipients. In addition the moral hazards of smaller government are also evident in the diversification of the demand for State services. The leading Tasmanian example is the growing demand for the control of industrial pollution of the State's major river estuaries. There is a growing public demand for the control of the output of industrial pollution at a time when financial restrictions prevent the expansion of the Department of Environment surveillance of this issue.

The reform of the State's institutions centrally concerned with environmental issues is a logical response to the heightened perceptions of them. Those institutions with a stake in striking an appropriate balance between development and preservation are not structured to accommodate the competing views of industry and the environmental lobby. They suit neither industry or the environmental lobby, both seeing a bias in the environmental process in favour of the other. A vexatious point from the industry viewpoint is the involvement of Local Government and a plethora of State agencies in the approval of proposed developments. The State Government response has been to create fast tracks in particular to avoid the intervention of Local Government. From an environmental viewpoint, fast tracks for major projects are unacceptable and the EIS process is unsatisfactory. Any proposal with an environmental consequence and which falls within the ambit of State or Federal environmental legislation requires the preparation by industry of an environmental impact statement. However, the environmental lobby argue the EIS process allows inadequate time and funding for the preparation of appropriate responses. The consequence is a political debate which in recent times has expanded into confrontation. Industry's argument is that the absence of fast track legislation will lead to interminable and uneconomic delays which threaten the viability of proposed development. This state of affairs is exacerbated by the presence of Commonwealth Government authority in relation to proposed developments which impinge on the national interest. The Commonwealth's treatment of each case is ad hoc dominated by political considerations, which does nothing to resolve a confused and confusing treatment of development proposals. Some may argue that it is appropriate for the balance of financial benefit and environmental cost to be struck on a political basis given the intensity of conflict, not least of all between regional and national interests. However, it is our opinion that improved public sector structures are required to limit the degree of political involvement. Reforms of this institutional kind must be approached from a national perspective in consultation with regional interests. The agreed structure should guarantee the following: earlier consultation between government and industry and the environmental groups; adequate time and a proper basis for hearing grievances about environmental guidelines and reasonable time

limits on the decision to proceed or reject developments. It is beyond the scope of this chapter to outline the details of these reforms.

15.6.4 Autonomy and Accountability of State Agencies

The State Services Act (1984) implemented the Cartland reforms and considerable progress has been made towards the creation of a more responsive public sector structure with increasing degrees of independence for the management of individual agencies. This has been achieved at some cost in the area of personal relations at least on the basis of evidence gathered by the TPSA The morale problems created by the reforms may be obviated by the reformation of the public sector award structure suggested above and provided the new structure goes along with the extension of training of public sector employees within the service and in educational institutions. However, a major question may be asked of the Cartland reforms: Is increased autonomy reconcilable with the doctrine of accountability? The answer to this question hinges on the achievement of the reforms suggested in chapter five in relation to the commercialisation of some public enterprises and associated accounting issues. None of these appear inconsistent with the thrust of the Cartland report.

Some important financial reforms have been implemented. The establishment of the Tasmanian Finance Corporation (TASCORP) established a central borrowing authority for all non-treasury debt. TASCORP has operated at a substantial profit in each full year of its operation and these have been retained to establish a Reserve base, however, the legislation establishing the agency allows for the payment of dividends to the State's Consolidated Revenues or to clients in future. The State Treasury is the last branch of the central public service core of Premier's Dept, Public Service board and Treasury to move into the new Cartland era. It remained a traditional, conservative Treasury four years after the implementation of the State Services legislation in 1984 even though the operations of the Premier's Department were reshaped at an earlier date following a separate review and the Public Service Board was disbanded and replaced by 3 separate agencies in 1984. The process of reforming the State Treasury to make it more accountable is proceeding at the time of writing with separate policy and development functions defined quite distinctly from the more traditional aspects of financial, budgetary and debt management functions. The Treasury departmental accounting and budgetary arrangements are of traditional form and the only major alteration to these occurred in 1986, when the Public Account Act was effected. Tasmania followed some other Australian States by amalgamating Revenue and Capital transactions as a single Public Account offering greater flexibility in Treasury accounting arrangements, although parliamentary critics of the legislation claimed this reduced the accountability of the Treasurer to the parliament.

The merits of the commercialisation of government or Public trading Enterprise (PTEs) is argued at length in Chapter Five. In essence, the commercialisation of PTEs requires the setting of financial targets such as targeted rates of return on assets (4% p.a. in the case of some Victorian PTEs) and prescribed rates of dividend payable to Consolidated Revenue. The user of PTE services then pays prices set to enable the PTE to meet its financial targets. Commercialisation in this form has the advantage of putting government enterprises on a similar financial basis to private enterprise and financial targeting ensures accountability. There are several hurdles to the implementation of commercialisation and these are outlined in chapter five. It demands appropriate accounting methods in the PTEs created by accrual accounting methods, for example, although the financial gearing of several PTEs is bound to show an excessive indebtedness and in the Tasmanian case very few Public Enterprises are structured with an adequate capital equity base.

The full commercialisation option may apply in time to the following Tasmanian State enterprises: the Tasmania Bank, TASCORP, Tasmanian Government Insurance Office and the TAB. Each of these operates on a fully commercial accrual accounting basis and each is profitable. The TGIO is required to return ⅓ of its surplus to Consolidated Revenue by way of

dividend. Similar arrangements apply to the TAB. The new financial institutions TASCORP and Tasmania Bank are established on a full accrual accounting basis and earn substantial profits. The enabling legislation for TASCORP provides three avenues for the distribution of its profits: they may be retained in reserves, directed as dividends towards Consolidated Revenue, or returned to clients in the same way. Similar options are accommodated in the legislation establishing Tasmania Bank. These organisations have absorbed the majority of profits in the initial years of their operations to establish their reserve base.

The prospects of applying the full commercialisation option to the electricity generating authority, the *HEC*, depend on the final implementation of a full accrual accounting system; an acceptable basis for the valuation of enterprise assets and the capacity of the organisation to meet the government's directed financial targets while preserving or extending cross subsidies, in particular, to disadvantaged groups with a genuine welfare need. For this reason there may be need to recover revenues above marginal cost. Then the marginal cost pricing basis of charging for electricity is superseded by a form of Ramsey pricing as described in chapter five and in which case at least some power charges will be set at the rate the market will bear. In any event, the practical difficulties of measuring the marginal cost of power supply in an organisation as complex as the HEC makes marginal cost a doubtful basis for determining user charges. Many of the cross subsidies transferred to basic industry users, as an incentive for the establishment of those industries at the height of the hydroindustrialisation era, have been removed as bulk power contracts have been renegotiated. The reform of the HEC is proceeding and the organisation is moving towards a full accrual accounting system. Thus innovation and a revaluation of assets is a preliminary to the full commercialisation of its operations. However, the problems posed by cross subsidies and the welfare demand for electricity remain as major obstacles. The HEC currently returns a levy to Consolidated Revenue worth $9m in 1987/88. Changes in the State Forestry Commission's accounting methods were signalled in the

1988/89 State budget. These changes amount to a full commercial valuation of the Commission's assets. The Commission derives much of its revenue from services to the State's forest industries and critics have argued that past deficits are subsidies paid to the industry. Further commercial reforms are appropriate and financial targets for the Commission should be considered once the accounting framework is in place. The prospects of applying the commercialisation option in other areas of Tasmanian public enterprise require closer examination. The Government Printer may compete successfully in the national market, although this participation in the local market is a recently rejected option. The printing office is one of the organisations which may suit the financial targeting option inherent in the commercialisation. The marketing operations of Tourism Tasmania and the continuing losses of the Metropolitan Transport Trust should be examined in the commercialisation framework.

This review of Tasmania's public enterprises finds few opportunities, for the privatisation option in the form of asset Sales. The full commercialisation option is the preferred one and our review reveals that the process has commenced, particularly in the adoption of commercial accounting practices, but that financial targeting and the adoption of the user pays principle are rarely applied in circumstances where they may be appropriate.

BIBLIOGRAPHY

Abelson, P. (1987) 'Privatisation: A Survey of the Issues', paper presented to the Sixteenth Conference of Australian and New Zealand Economists, Surfers Paradise, August.

Abrahami, J. (1985) 'Cutting the Size of Government – the Great Challenge', *Policy Issues*, No. 2, Institute of Policy Studies.

ACTU. (May 1987) *Future Strategies for the Trade Union Movement*, Mimeo, Melbourne.

ACTU/TDC. (1987) *Australia Reconstructed*, AGPS.

Advisory Council for Inter-Governmental Relations. (1982) *The Australian Loan Council and Inter-Governmental Relations*, Report 5, October.

Albon, R. & Kirby, M.G. (1983) 'Cost-Padding in Profit-Regulated Firms', *Economic Record*, 59, 16-27.

Albon, R. (1985) 'The Effects of Financial Targets on the Behaviour of Monopoly Public Enterprises', *Australian Economic Papers*, June, 54-65.

Albon, R. (1986a) 'The Telecom Monopoly – Natural or Artificial?', *Australian Institute for Public Policy*, Policy Paper No. 5, Perth.

Albon, R. (1986b) 'The Scope for Privatisation in Australia', *Information Paper No. IP20*, Committee for Economic Development of Australia, May.

Albon, R. (1987) 'Privatisation or Politicisation of Australian Communications?', in Abelson (ed.), *Privatisation: An Australian Perspective*, Australian Professional Publications, Sydney.

Allan, P. (1988) 'Accrual Accounting To Be Or Not To Be' in Public Accounts Committee of the New South Wales Parliament *Report of Proceedings of the Accrual Accounting Seminar 5 February 1988*, May, pp.33-41.

Argy, V. (1979) 'Some Notes on Crowding Out', *Australian Economic Review*.

Armstrong, H. & Taylor, J. (1978) *Regional Economic Policy and its Analysis*, First Edition, Phillip Allan, Oxford.

Arrow, K.J. (1985) 'The Potentials and Limits of the Market in Resource Allocation', in Feiwel, G. (ed.), *Issues in Contemporary Micro-Economics and Welfare*, Macmillan, London.

Ascher, K. (1987) *The Politics of Privatisation: Contracting out Public Services*, Macmillan, London.

Asquith, P. & Mullins, D.W. (1983) 'Equity Issues and Stock Price Dilution', *Harvard Business School Working Paper*, May.

Atkinson, S.E. & Halvorsen, R. (1986) 'The Relative Efficiency of Public and Private Firms in a Regulated Environment: The Case of US Electric Utilities', *Journal of Public Economics*, 29, 281-294.

Auditor-General of New South Wales. (1988) *Annual Report*, 4 Vols. (NSW Government Printer).

Auditor-General of Victoria. (1989) *Financial Assistance to Industry*, Special Report 11, March.

Auerbach, S. (ed.) (1975) *Rationale for Child Care Services: Programs Versus Politics* Human Science Press Inc., New York.

Australian Bureau of Statistics. *Australian Demographic Statistics*, Cat. No. 1301.0, Various Issues.

Australian Bureau of Statistics. *Victorian Year Book*, Cat. No. 1301.2, Various Issues.

Australian Bureau of Statistics. *Monthly Summary of Statistics, Victoria*, Cat. No. 1303.2, Various Issues.

Australian Bureau of Statistics. *Monthly Summary of Statistics, Australia*, Cat. No. 1303.0, Various Issues.

Australian Bureau of Statistics. *Monthly Summary of Statistics, New South Wales*, Cat. No. 1305.1, Various Issues.

Australian Bureau of Statistics. *Births, Australia*, Cat. No. 5504.0, Various Issues.

Australian Bureau of Statistics. *Foreign Ownership and Control of the Manufacturing Industry*, Cat. No. 5322.0, Various Issues.

Australian Bureau of Statistics. *State and Local Government Finance*, Cat. No. 5504.0, Various Issues.

Australian Bureau of Statistics. *Labour Statistics, Victoria*, Cat. No. 6102.2, Various Issues.

Australian Bureau of Statistics. *The Labour Force Australia, Preliminary*, Cat. No. 6201.0, Various Issues.

Australian Bureau of Statistics. *The Labour Force, Victoria*, Cat. No. 6201.2, Various Issues.

Australian Bureau of Statistics. *Employed Wage and Salary Earners, Australia*, Cat. No. 6248.0, Various Issues.

Australian Bureau of Statistics. (1986a) *Queensland Yearbook*, Canberra, AGPS.

Australian Bureau of Statistics. (1986) *Australian Demographic Trends*, AGPS, Canberra, Cat. No. 3102.0.

Australian Bureau of Statistics. (1986) *Queensland Yearbook*, Canberra Bureau of Statistics, AGPS.

Australian Bureau of Statistics. (1986-87) *Government Financial Estimates, Australia*, Cat. No. 5501.0.

Australian Bureau of Statistics. (1987) *Labour Statistics Australia*, Cat. No. 6101.0.

Australian Bureau of Statistics. (1988) *Australian*

Standard Industrial Classifications, Vol. 1 – The Classification, Cat. No. 1201.0, June.

Australian Bureau of Statistics. (1988) *Queensland at a Glance,* AGPS, Canberra, Cat. No. 1312.3.

Australian Bureau of Statistics. (1988) *The South Australian Year Book,* Cat. No. 6248.0.

Australian Bureau of Statistics. *Australian National Accounts State Accounts,* Cat. No. 5220.0, Various Issues.

Australian Bureau of Statistics. (1988) *Queensland Yearbook,* AGPS, Canberra.

Australian Bureau of Statistics. (1988a) *The Labour Force, Queensland, November 1987,* AGPS, Brisbane, Cat. No. 6201.3.

Australian Bureau of Statistics. (1988b) *The Labour Force, Australia, December 1987,* AGPS, Canberra, Cat. No. 6203.0.

Australian Bureau of Statistics. (1988c) *Employed Wage and Salary Earners Australia,* AGPS, Canberra, Cat. No. 6348.0.

Australian Bureau of Statistics. (1988d) *Queensland Yearbook,* Canberra, AGPS.

Australian Conservation Foundation and National Farmers' Federation, (ACF/NFF). (1989) *A National Land Management Program: A Joint Submission by the Australian Conservation Foundation and the National Farmers' Federation to the Federal Government of Australia,* Canberra.

Australian Consumers' Association. (1988) *Consuming Interest,* No. 37, September.

Australian Council of Trade Unions, Trade Development Secretariat, (ACTU/TDC). (1987) *Australia Reconstructed,* AGPS, Canberra.

Australian Labor Party, (WA Branch). (1986) *State Platform,* Labour Centre, Perth.

Australian Labor Party. (1988) *Labor's Regional Economic Development Plan,* ALP, Brisbane.

Australian Law Journal. (1987) 'Some General Legal Aspects of "Privatisation" ', Vol. 61, No. 6, June.

Australian Law Journal. (1987) 'The Constitution and Control of the Australian Economy: Current Topics', Vol. 61, No. 1, January.

Australian Public Service Federation, (APSF). (1987) *Submission to House of Representatives' Standing Committee on Transport, Communications and Infrastructure.*

Australian Railways Union, (ARU). (1988) 'Investment in Rail 1981-1988: Criteria and Assessment', May.

Australian Railways Union, (ARU). (1989) 'Capital Funding Issues for Railways', unpublished.

Australian Science and Technology Council, (ASTEC). (1987) *Wealth from Skills – Measures to Raise the Skill of the Workforce,* Canberra, AGPS.

Australian Telecommunications Employees Association, (ATEA). (1983) Policy Issues and Public Sector Costs – A Study into an Australian Domestic Communications Satellite System – *'AUSSAT',* June.

Australian Telecommunications Employees Association, (ATEA). (1987) *Submission to the Department of Transport and Communications Policy Review of Telecommunications Services in Australia – Structural and Regulatory Issues,* November.

Ayub, M.A. & Hegstad, S.O. (1987) 'Determinants of Public Enterprise Performance', *Finance and Development,* December, pp. 26-29.

Baldock, C.V. (1983) 'Volunteer Work as Work: Some Theoretical Considerations', in Baldock, C.V. & Cass, B. (eds.) *Women, Social Welfare and the State in Australia,* George Allen & Unwin, Sydney.

Baldock, C.V. & May, C. (1985) 'The Unpaid Worker in Social Welfare', Report Number 1, Preliminary Interview Data, *Working Paper,* Murdoch University, Perth.

Baldock, C.V. & Mulligan, D. (1987) 'Working Without Wages', Unpublished paper prepared for the ANZAAS Congress in Palmerston North, New Zealand, Murdoch University, Perth.

Ball, M. (1985) 'Coming to Terms With Owner Occupation', *Capital and Class,* No. 2, Vol. 24, Winter.

Ball, R. & Davis, J.G. (1984) 'Appropriate Financing and Investment Policies for Telecom Australia', *Report Prepared for the Centre for Management Research and Development for Telecom,* March.

Bannon, J.C. (1987) 'Overcoming the Unintended Consequences of Federation', *Australian Journal of Public Administration,* Vol. 46(1), March, pp. 1-9.

Barker, R.A. (1982) *Review of Recent Population Trends in Queensland,* Brisbane, Co-ordinator General's Department.

Barker, R.A. (1984) *Population Projections for Queensland 1981-2006,* Brisbane, Premier's Department.

Barker, R.A. & Reinders, J. (1983) *Analysis of the 1981 Census,* Brisbane, Premier's Department.

Barnes, R.D. & Else-Mitchell, R. (1977) *Aspects of the New Federalism Policy,* Canberra: Centre for Research on Federal Financial Relations, ANU, (Occasional Paper No. 7).

Barwise, G. *et. al.* (1987) 'In Government – Managerial and Business Expertise', *Practising Manager,* Vol. 7(2), April, pp. 45 – 48.

Bassett, P. (1987) 'Co-ordination Between Power and Telecommunications Networks in Australia', *Telecommunications Journal of Australia,* Vol. 37 No. 2, pp. 71 – 73.

Baumol, W.J. (1982) 'Contestable Markets: An Uprising in the Theory of Industrial Structure', *American Economic Review,* 72, 1-15.

Baumol, W.J. (ed.) (1980) *Public and Private Enterprises in a Mixed Economy: Proceedings of a Conference Held* by the International Economics Association in Mexico City, MacMillian, London.

Beasley, M. (1988) *The Sweat of Their Brows: 100 Years of the Sydney Water Board 1888-1988*, Water Board, Sydney.

Beed, C., & Moriarty, P. (1988) 'Urban Transport Policy' in *The Journal of Australian Political Economy* No. 22, February.

Beesley, M.E. (1981) Liberalisation of the Use of British Telecommunications Network, *Report to the Secretary of State, Department of Industry, Her Majesty's Stationery Office*, London.

Benson, T. (1989) *Limited Access and Shrinking Supply: Housing for People with a Psychotic Disability*, Council of Social Services of New South Wales, (Project funded by the New South Wales Department of Housing).

Bernard, J.T. & Cairns, R.D. (1987) 'On Public Utility Pricing and Foregone Economic Benefits', *Canadian Journal of Economics*, XX(1), February, 152-163. [A comment on Jenkins (1985)].

Berry, M. (1984) 'Urbanisation and Social Change: Australian in the Twentieth Century', in Encel, S. & Bryson, L. (eds.) *Australian Society*, Fourth Edition, Longman Cheshire, Sydney.

Berry, M. (1988) 'To Buy or Rent? The Demise of Dual Tenure Policy in Australia, 1945-60', in Howe, R. (ed.) *New Houses For Old*, Victorian Ministry of Housing and Construction, Melbourne.

Bhaduri, A. (1986) *Macro-Economics: The Dynamics of Commodity Production*, Macmillan, Hong Kong.

Bird, R.M. (1971) 'Wagner's Law of Expanding State Activity', *Public Finance*, Vol. 26, p. 1-26.

Bird, R.M. (1986) *Federal Finance in Comparative Perspective*, Canadian Tax Foundation, Toronto (Canada). ●

Black, D. (1988) 'WA Inc. in a Revolution', *Sunday Times*, August 21.

Block, R. (1986) 'Privatisation of Public Enterprises', *Forecasting the Australian Economy*, AISEC, UNSW.

Bluestone, B. & Harrison, B. (1982) *The Deindustrialisation of America*, New York, Basic Books.

Boddy, M. & Fudge, C. (1984) *Local Socialism? Labour Councils and New Left Alternatives*, Macmillan, Chapters 1, 3, 7 and 8.

Borchadt, D.H. (1980) Checklist of Royal Commissions, *Select Committees of Parliament and Boards of Inquiry: Commonwealth/NSW/Qld/Tas. and Vic. 1960 – 1980 and South Australia 1970-80*, Library Publication (La Trobe University) No. 30.

Bos, D. (1986) *Public Enterprise Economics – Theory and Application*, North-Holland, Amsterdam. ●

Botsman, C. & Rawlinson, P. (1986) *Negotiating Change: New Technology and Trade Unions, An Interview with Pelle Ehn*, Occasional Paper No. 10,

Local Consumption Publications, Sydney, August.

Botsman, P. (1988a) 'Australia Reconstructed: What's in it for the Community Services Industry?', Council of Social Services, New South Wales, March.

Botsman, P. (1988b) 'Australia Reconstructed, Rudolf Meidner and the Politics of the Public Sector', *Canberra Bulletin of Public Administration*, Vol. XV, No. 55.

Botsman, P. (1988c) 'The Capital Funding of Public Enterprises: A Summary of the H.V. Evatt Research Centre Report', *Canberra Bulletin of Public Administration*, Vol. XV, No. 55.

Botsman, P. (1988d) 'Industrial Democracy and the Politics of Production', *Arbetslivcentrum* (The Swedish Centre for Working Life), Stockholm.

Botsman. P. & Mitchell, W. (1988) 'Reforming and Developing Public Enterprises: The Alternative to Privatisation', *Australian Society*, June.

Botsman, P. (1989) 'Rethinking the Class Struggle: Industrial democracy and the Politics of Production', *Economic and Industrial Democracy, an International Journal*, Vol. 10, pp. 123-142.

Bradley, P.G. (1986) *Report of the Mineral Revenues Inquiry in Regard to the Study into Mineral (including Petroleum) Revenues in Western Australia*, Western Australian Government Print, Perth.

Brain, P. & Manning, I. (1987) 'Australia's Economic Predicament' in *National Institute for Economics and Industrial Research Review*, No. 7, Melbourne.

Brain, P.J. (1987) 'Is There an Optimum Capital Structure for Public Enterprise?' *National Economic Review*, pp. 59-84.

Brennan, G. (ed.) (1987) *Constitutional Reform and Fiscal Federalism*, Occasional Paper No. 42, Centre for Research on Federal Financial Relations, The Australian National University.

Brimson, S. (1984) *Flying the Royal Mail: The History of Australia's Airlines*, Breamweaver, Sydney.

Bryson, L. (1986) 'A New Iron Cage? A View from Within', *Canberra Bulletin of Public Administration*, Vol. VIII, 4., pp. 362-369.

Bryson, L. (1987) 'Women and Management in the Public Sector', *Australian Journal of Public Administration*, XLVI.

Buchanan, J. (1987) 'Overcoming the Unintended Consequences of Federation', *Australian Journal of Public Administration*, Vol. 46 No. 1 March, pp. 1-9. ●

Buck, T.W. (1970) *State Platform*, Labour Centre, Perth.

Buck, T.W. (1970) Shift and Share Analysis – A Guide to Regional Policy?, *Regional Studies*.

Buckland, R. (1987) 'The Costs and Returns of the Privatisation of Nationalised Industries', *Public Administration*, 65, Autumn, pp. 242-257. ●

Budget Paper No. 4. (1987) *Commonwealth Financial Relations with Other Levels of Government 1987-88*, (Circulated by the Treasurer on the occasion of the 1987-88 Budget), AGPS, Canberra.

Building Industry Inquiry Implementation Committee, Victoria. (1985) *First Report to the Premier, Minister of Public Works and Cabinet*, Parliament of Victoria, Melbourne.

Building Industry Investigation Committee. (1983) *Parliamentary Investigation into Cash in Hand Payments and Pyramid Sub-Contracting in the Victorian Building and Construction Industry*, Report to the Premier and Cabinet, December.

Buiter, W. (1985) 'The Macroeconomic Effects of Public Investment', *Economic Policy: A European Forum*, Vol. 1, No. 1, pp. 13-79.

Burke, T., Campbell, D., Hayward, D., & Nisbet, P. (1985) *Melbourne Housing Indicators*, Estate Agents Board, Melbourne.

Burke, T., Hancock, L. & Newton, P. (1983) *A Roof Over Their Heads*, Institute of Family Studies, Melbourne.

Burke, T., Leigh, P. & Hayward, D. (1989) 'Private Renting: The Untenable Tenure', Paper presented to the 1989 Conference of Australian Geographers, Adelaide University, Adelaide, February.

Burke, T., Dalton, T. & Paris, P. (1989) *Housing Education and Training*, Australian Housing Research Centre.

Burke, T., Dalton. T. & Paris, P. (1989) *Needs Analysis for Human Resource Delivery*, North Eastern Region Consultative Council.

Burke, T., Pidgeon, J., Mulvaney, J. & Betts, K. (1989) *Needs Analysis for Human Resource Delivery*, North Eastern Region Consultative Council.

Burns, R.M. (1977) *Intergovernmental Fiscal Transfers: Canadian and Australian Experiences*, Centre for Research on Federal Financial Relations, ANU, Canberra, (Monograph No. 22).

Burt Commission. (1989) *Commission on Accountability: Report to Premier*, Western Australian State Government, Perth.

Burton, J. (1983) *Picking Losers — the Political Economy of Industrial Policy*, Institute for Economic Officers, (London).

Business and Consumer Affairs, (BACA). (1988) *Annual Report 1988: Industrial Development; Cooperative Societies*.

Business Research Centre. (1987) *Queensland Economic Forecasts*, Brisbane CAE, Brisbane.

Butlin, N.G. (1959) 'Colonial Socialism in Australia, 1860-1900' in Aitken, H. (ed.) *The State and Economic Growth*, New York.

Butlin, N.G. (1978) 'The Growth of Big Government in Australia 1901-1970', *Australia 1938-1988 Bi-*

centennial History Project: Bulletin, No. 2, Canberra, ANU.

Butlin, N.G. (1983) 'Trends in Public/Private Relations, 1901-75' in Head, B.W. (ed.) *State and Economy in Australia*, Oxford University Press, Melbourne, pp. 79-97.

Butlin, N.G., Barnard, A.& Pincus, J.J. (1982) *Government and Capitalism: Public and Private Choice in Twentieth Century Australia*, George Allen & Unwin, Sydney.

Butt, H. & Palmer, B. (1985) *Value for Money in the Public Sector: The Decision-Makers Guide*. Basil Blackwell, Chapter 10.

Cain, J. (1987) 'Towards a Federal Reformation: the Renaissance of the Australian States' in Birrell, M. (ed.) *The Australian States: Towards a Renaissance*, Longman Cherrie, Sydney, pp. 1-18.

Cain, J. (1989) 'Ministerial Statement on Industry Assistance', March 15.

Callaghan, B. (1977) *Inquiry into the Structure of Industry and the Employment Situation in Tasmania*, AGPS, Canberra.

Campbell, K.O. *et. al.* (1981) *Australian Financial System Inquiry, Interim Report*, AGPS, Canberra.

Carter, G.E. (1980) *New Directions in Financing Australian Federation*, Centre for Research on Federal Financial Relations, ANU, Canberra.

Cartland, Sir G. (1981) *Report of Review of Tasmanian Government Administration I*, (Sept) II (Nov), Tas. Govt. Printer, Hobart.

Cass, B. (1989) 'Targeting and Beyond: Equity in Redistribution', paper presented at a Conference on the issue of Managing with Social Justice: the prospects for access and equity in the 1990s, (Royal Australian Institute of Public Administration), Canberra, April.

Castles, F.G. (ed.) (1982) *The Impact of Parties: Politics and Policies in Democratic Capitalist States*, Sage, London.

Castles, F.G. (1985) *The Working Class and Welfare: Reflection on the Political Development of the Welfare State in Australia and New Zealand, 1890-1980*, Allen & Unwin, Sydney.

Cave, M. & Hare, P. (1981) *Alternative Approaches to Economic Planning*. Macmillan, Chapter 9.

CCH Australia Ltd. (1987) *Planning Occupational Safety and Health*, (2nd Edition), CCH Australia.

Centre for Continuing Education, (CCE). (1988) *Proceedings of Making Public Enterprise More Enterprising Conference*, ANU, Canberra.

Centre for Regional Economic Analysis, (CREA). (1988) *The Tasmanian Economy: A Survey*, Tasmanian Government Printer, Hobart.

Cerexhe, P. (1988) 'The First Swallows of Summer', *Consuming Interest*, Australian Consumers' Association, No. 37, September, pp. 8-12.

Chapman, R.J.K. (1985) 'From Quill to Keyboard: Tasmanian Government Administration in Transition', *Tasmanian Year Book*, (19), ABS Cat. No. 1301.6.

Chapman, Y. (1987) 'Opening Address to the Community Services Conference', in Saunders, P. & Jamrozik, A. *Social Welfare Research Centre, Reports and Proceedings No. 70*, SWRC, Sydney.

Ciccolo, J.J. (1981) 'Changing Balance Sheet Relationships in the US Manufacturing Sector, 1926-1977', *NBER Working Paper No. 702*.

Civil Service Association. (1988) *Staffing Review*, Report to the Ministry of Education, Appendix A.

Clegg, S., Boreham, P. & Dow, G. (1986) *Class, Politics and the Economy*, Routledge & Kegan Paul, London.

Clements K.W. & Sjaastad L.J. (1984) *How Protection Taxes Exporters*, Thames Essays, Trade Policy Roseneath Centre, London.

Cline, K., Cline, G., Rowthorn, W. R. & Ward, T.S. (1986) 'The British Economy: Recent History and Medium Term Prospects', *A Cambridge Bulletin on the Thatcher Experiment*, Faculty of Economics, Cambridge University.

Cline, T. (1987) 'Action Speaks Louder than Words (Need for Good Public Sector Management)', *Local Government Management*, Vol. 21, No. 7, August/September 1987.

Collins, D.J. (1988) 'Partial and Global Measure of State's Taxable Capacities', Australian Tax Research Foundation, Sydney.

Collins, D.J. *et. al.* (1988) *Tax Reform and NSW Economic Development: (NSW Tax Task Force) Review of the State Tax System* (NSW Government Printer).

Committee for Economic Development of Australia, (CEDA). (1975) *Fiscal Federalism: Some Problems and Options*, (P Series No. 16).

Committee of Inquiry into Revenue Raising in Victoria, (CIRRV). (1983) *Report*, Melbourne, Victorian Government Printer.

Committee of Inquiry into the Australian Financial System. (1981) *Final Report*, AGPS, Canberra.

Commonwealth Grants Commission. (1983) *Equality in Diversity Fifty Years of the Commonwealth Grants Commission*, AGPS, Canberra.

Commonwealth Grants Commission. (1987) *Fifty-fourth Report*, AGPS, Canberra.

Commonwealth Grants Commission. (1988) *Report on Revenue Grant Relativities 1988, Volume 1 — Main Report*, AGPS, Canberra.

Commonwealth Grants Commission. (1985) *Report on Tax Sharing*, 1985 AGPS, Canberra.

Commonwealth of Australia. (1986) *Payments to or for the States, the Northern Territory and Local Government Authorities 1986-87 (Budget Paper No. 7)*, AGPS, Canberra.

Commonwealth of Australia. (1987a) *Commonwealth Financial Relations with other Levels of Government 1987-88 (Budget Paper No. 4)*, AGPS, Canberra.

Commonwealth of Australia. (1987b) *Skills for Australia*, (Minister for Employment, Education and Training and Minister for Employment Services and Youth Affairs), AGPS, Canberra.

Confederation of Western Australian Industry. (1983) *Western Australian Economic Review*, June.

Considine, M. (1988) 'The Corporate Management Framework as Administrative Science: A Critique', *Australian Journal of Public Administration*, Vol. XLVII, No. 1.

Cook, Senator P. (1988) 'Speech by Minister for Resources in Opening the 1988 National Soils Conference', Copeland Theatre, Australian National University, (9 May).

Corbett, D.C. (1983) 'Canberra Revisited: Some Questions About National Administration', Text of an Address to the Australian Institute of Public Administration, ACT Group, 27 July, 1983, *Canberra Bulletin of Public Administration*, Vol. 10, No. 4, pp. 13-21.

Corbett, D.C. (1986) *Housing in Darwin: Policies and Their Results*, National Australia Research Unit, Darwin.

Corbett, D.C. (1987) 'Government Illegality and Public Service Boards', *Government Illegality: Proceedings: 1-2 October 1986*, pp. 25 – 35.

Corbett, D.C. (1987) 'The Administrative Organisation and Performance of the States on How Well Do the States Discharge their Functions', in Birwell, M. (ed.) *The Australian States: Towards a Renaissance*, Langman Cheshire.

Corbett, D.C. (1988) 'Public Personnel Administration', *Australian Journal of Public Administration*, Vol. 39, Sept. – December, pp. 398-405.

Corbett, D. (1988) 'Applications of the Commercial Analogy to Public Sector Management: Theory and Practice', unpublished paper for the *ACTU Public Sector Seminar*, (December).

Crabb, P. (1988) 'The Murray-Darling Basin Agreement', *CRES Working Paper*, 1988/6, Centre for Resource and Environment Studies, Australian National University.

Creamer, D. (1943) *Shifts of Manufacturing Industries, Industrial Location and National Resources*, US National Resources Planning Board, Washington DC.

Cribbin, B. (ed.) (1988) *National Guide to Government 1988-89*, Melbourne, Information Australia.

Cullis, J.G. & Jones, P.R. (1987) *Micro-Economics and the Public Economy. A Defence of Leviathan*. Chapters 1-4; Chapters 6-8, Basil Blackwell.

Curran, C.P. *et. al.* (1988). *Focus on Reform: (NSW*

Commission of Audit) Report on the State's Finances (NSW Government Printer).

Curwen, P. (1986) *Public Enterprise. A Modern Approach*, Chapters 6, 7 and 8, Wheatsheaf Books.

Cuthbertson, Sir H. *et. al.* (1985) *Cuthbertson Report of the Committee to Review the Impacts of the Commonwealth Grants Recommendations on Tasmania*, TGPS, May.

Cutler, T., Williams, K. & Williams, J. (1986) *Keynes, Beveridge and Beyond*, Routledge and Kegan Paul, London.

Daes, E.I.A. (1988) *Confidential Report on Visit to Australia 12 December 1987 − 2 January 1988 and 7 − 22 January 1988*, United Nations Working Group on Indigenous Populations.

Dargavel, J. (1987) 'Problems in Australia's Mixed Forest Economy', *Journal of Australian Political Economy*, No. 21, May.

Davidson, K. (1988) 'Moody's Gets it Wrong in its Assessment of Victorian Public Debt Level', *The Age Newspaper*, 23rd September, p. 34.

Davis, B. (1986) 'Public Sector Debt: the True Figures', *Australian Business*, Vol. 6, No. 21, 27, August, pp. 30-31.

Davis, B. (1987) 'Privatisation: The Case for', *Canberra Survey*, Vol. 40., No. 20.

De Angelo, H.L. & Rice, E.M. (1982) 'Minority Freezeouts and Stockholder Wealth', *University of Washington Graduate School of Business Administration Working Paper*.

De Ridder, J. (1986) 'How Efficient is Telecom', Paper presented to the 15th *Conference of Economists*, Monash University, Melbourne.

De Ridder, J. (1987) 'From Mater and Pater to Business and Data', talk to the *Bureau of Industry Economics*, Canberra, 5 November.

De Ridder, J. (1989) 'Community Service Obligations − The ABC of CSOs for Telecom', paper presented at the International Telecommunications Society Asian Region Forum, Merrijog, Australia, March.

De Villiers Commission. (1985) *Report of the Commission of Inquiry into the Supply of Electricity in the Republic of South Africa*.

Department of Employment, Education and Training. (1987) *Completing Secondary School in Australia: A Socio Economic and Regional Analysis*, Department of Employment, Education and Training, Research and Statistics Branch, Canberra, August.

Department of Finance. (1987) *Policy Guidelines for Commonwealth Statutory Authorities and Government Business Enterprises*, AGPS, Canberra.

Department of Immigration, Local Government and Ethnic Affairs. (1987) *Australia's Population Trends and Prospects*, AGPS, Canberra.

Department of Industrial Affairs. (1987) *Green Paper on Proposals for Voluntary Employer/Employee Agreements*, Government Printer, Brisbane.

Department of Industrial Relations, Metal Trades Federation of Unions, Metal Trades Industry Association, (DIR, MTFU, MTIA). (1988) *Towards a New Metal and Engineering Industry Award*, Sydney, (September).

Department of Industry, Technology and Commerce, (DITAC). (1988) 'State Industry Policies: An Information Paper Prepared for Economic Planning Advisory Council', *EPAC*, (January).

Department of Industry, Technology and Resources, (DITR). (1986) 'Improving Australia's Competitiveness: A Discussion Paper, DITR, Melbourne.

Department of Management and Budget, (DMB), (Victoria). (1984) *Draft Requirements for Operation and financial Statements Required to be Prepared by Large Trading/Rating Public Bodies Under the Annual Reporting Act (Sections 10 and 11)*, Melbourne.

Department of Management and Budget, (DMB), (Victoria). (1986) *Victorian Public Sector Debt*, Information Paper No. 2, December.

Department of Management and Budget, (DMB), (Victoria). (1986) *Corporate Planning in Victorian Government: Concepts and Techniques*, DMB, Melbourne.

Department of Management and Budget, (DMB), (Victoria). (1986) *Public Authority Policy and Rate of Return Reporting*, Information Paper No. 1, October.

Department of Management and Budget (DMB) (Victoria) (1987) 'Role of Performance Indicators in Central Resource Allocation Processes', Canberra Workshop 6-7 April 1987, Presentation by Barry Nicholls.

Department of State Development, (NSW). (1988) *Private Sector Participation in the Provision of Infrastructure*.

Department of State Development, (NSW). (1989) *Disposal of Strategic Government Assets*.

Directorate of Industrial Relations Development, (DIRD). (1989) 'Workplace Resource Centres', Department of Industrial Relations.

Directorate of Industry, Technology and Resources, (DITR). (1986) *Improving Australia's Competitiveness*, A Discussion Paper, DITR, VGPS, Melbourne.

Disney, J. (1989) 'What Low Income Groups Expect From Any New Tax System', paper delivered to the Institute of Chartered Accountants in Australia 'Tax − Future Alternatives' Seminar, Sydney, 3 April.

Dixon, J. (1972) 'Federal-State Fiscal Relations' in Dixon, J. (ed.) *The Public Sector: Selected Readings*, Penguin, Melbourne, pp. 263-284.

Donaldson, G. (1961) 'Corporate Debt Capacity: A Study of Corporate Debt Policy and the Determination of Corporate Debt Capacity', *Harvard Graduate Business School Working Paper*.

Domberger, S. (1988) 'Competitive Tendering and Contracting Out: Some Lessons From the UK Experience', Paper delivered at a Conference on Competitive Tendering and Contracting Out, at Graduate School of Management and Public Policy, The University of Sydney, October.

Dow, G. (1984) 'The Case for Corporatism', *Australian Society*, Vol. 3, (5), November.

Due, J.F. & Friedlaender, A.F. (1973) *Government Finance: Economics of the Public Sector*, Richard Irwin, Inc.

Dunstan, D. (1981) Felicia, *The Political Memoirs of Don Dunstan*, Macmillan.

Dunstan, D. (1988) 'The Public Sector and Social Justice', Paper given at the *National Conference on Privatisation*, Sydney.

Dwyer, Q. (1985) 'Do Governments Produce High Interest Rates?', *Journal of Money, Credit and Banking*.

Economic and Budget Review Committee. (1986) *Fifteenth Report to the Victorian Parliament Inquiry into Aspects of State-Federal Financial Relations*, October.

Economic and Budget Review Committee. (1988) *Twenty-fourth Report to the Victorian Parliament, Controls Over Commercial Authority Debt Levels*, May.

Economic Planning Advisory Council (Office of the), (EPAC). (1985) *The Size of Government and Economic Performance*, Council Paper No. 4, October, Canberra.

Economic Planning & Advisory Council, (EPAC). (1986) *Regional Impact of Industry Assistance*, Council Paper No. 20, June.

Economic Planning & Advisory Council, (EPAC). (1986) *Flexibility in Government Spending: Issues in Efficiency and Control*, Council Paper No. 23, Canberra, November.

Economic Planning & Advisory Council, (EPAC). (1986) *Issues in Medium Term Budgetary Policy*, Council Paper No. 16, Canberra, March.

Economic Planning & Advisory Council, (EPAC). (1986) *The Medium Term Outlook for the Rural Sector*, Council Paper No. 7, Canberra.

Economic Planning Advisory Council (Office of the), (EPAC). (1987) *Efficiency in Public Trading Enterprises*, Council Paper No. 24, January, Canberra.

Economic Planning & Advisory Council, (EPAC). (1988) *Income Support Policies, Taxation and Incentives*, Council Paper No. 35, Canberra, November.

Econsult. (1988) *Regional Strategic Assessment Study:*

Draft Final Report, Westernport Regional Planning and Co-ordination Committee.

Econsult. (1989) 'Housing Allowances in the Australian Context', *National Housing Policy Review*. Background Paper No. 1, Department of Community Services and Health, Canberra.

Edwards, J. (1987) 'Great Tax Sale Sets an Agenda for Leaner Government', *Bulletin*, Vol. 109 (5560) 10 March, pp. 18-20.

Eisen, H. (1987) 'Project Management in a Service Organisation', *Australian Journal of Public Administration*, Vol. 46, No. 2, June, pp. 155-159.

Electrical Power Engineers' Association, (EPEA). (1986) 'Public or Private Electricity? – The American Experience', A Report from the Fact-Finding Team from the Electrical Power Engineers' Association, (July).

Electricity Commission of New South Wales, (Elcom). (1988) *Annual Report*.

Electricity Commission of New South Wales, (Elcom). (1989) 'Facing the Future: The Electricity Commission's TEAM. Plan – Training, Efficiency and Multi-skilling Position Paper', mimeo.

Elliffe, P. (1987) 'Boosting the Local Economy', *Local Government Bulletin*, Vol. 42, (4), May, pp. 2.

Elliott, G. & Kearney, C. (1988) 'The Intertemporal Government Budget Constraint and Tests for Bubbles', *Reserve Bank of Australia Research Discussion Paper*, No. 8809.

Else-Mitchell, R. (1978) *The Rise and Demise of Coercive Federalism*, Centre for Research on Federal Financial Relations, ANU, Canberra, (Reprint Series No. 20) pp. 109-121.

Else-Mitchell, R. (1983) 'Unity or Uniformity?' in Aldred, J. & Wilkes, J. (eds.) *A Fractured Federation? Australia in the 1980's*, Allen & Unwin, Sydney (and AIPS), pp. 1-18.

Else-Mitchell, R. (1987) 'Commentary' (on a paper by Cliff Walsh) in Brennan, G. (ed.) *Constitutional Reform and Fiscal Federalism*, Centre for Research on Federal Fiscal Relations, ANU, Canberra, pp. 31-34.

Else-Mitchell, R. & Robson, K.J. (1987) *Achieving Financial Accountability in a Federal System*, Centre for Research on Federal Financial Relations, ANU, Canberra, (Occasional Paper No. 43).

Eltis, W.A. (1975) 'Adam Smith's Theory of Economic Growth', in A.S. Skinner & T. Wilson, (eds.) *Essays on Adam Smith*, Oxford.

Emy, H.V. & Hughes, O.E. (1988) *Australian Politics: Realities in Conflict*, Macmillan, Melbourne.

Encel, S. (1960) 'Public Corporations in Australia: Some Recent Developments', *Public Administration*, Vol. 38, Autumn, pp. 235-252.

Ergas, H. (1986) *Telecommunications and the Australian*

Economy, Report to the Department of Communications, AGPS, Canberra.

Ernst and Whinney Services. (1989) *Corporatisation Review of Systems and Organisation Structure: Grain Handling Authority*, March.

Esping-Anderson, C. (1984) 'Social Policy as Class Politics in Post War Capitalism: Scandinavia, Austria, and Germany' in Goldthorpe, John H. (ed.) *Order and Conflict in Contemporary Capitalism*, Clarendon Press, Oxford, pp. 179-208.

Esping-Anderson, G. (1985a) *Politics Against Markets: The Social Democratic Road to Power*, Princeton University Press, Princeton.

Esping-Anderson, G. (1985b) 'Power and Distributional Regimes', *Politics and Society*, Vol. 14(2), November, pp. 223-256.

Esprie Committee. (1983) *Developing high Technology Enterprises for Australia*, Parkville, Victoria.

Ethnic Affairs Commission of New South Wales. (1987) *Review of the Ethnic Affairs Policy Statements (EAPs) Program in NSW*, October.

Evatt Research Centre. (1988) *The Capital Funding of Public Enterprise in Australia*, H.V. Evatt Foundation, Sydney, March.

Evatt, H.V. (1979) *William Holman, Australian Labour Leader*, (Angus & Robertson, Sydney), 1st Ed., 1942.

Ewer, P., Higgins, W. & Stevens A. (1987) *Unions and the Future of Manufacturing in Australia*, Allen & Unwin, Sydney.

Federated Engine Drivers' and Firemens' Association, (FEDFA). (1988) 'Response to Curran Report (The Electricity Commission of New South Wales)', mimeo.

Farrar, A. (1989) Shifting the Balance: Public Expenditure and Privatisation in the Community Services Industry, NCOSS.

Faulhaber, G. (1975) 'Cross-Subsidisation: Pricing in Public Enterprises', *American Economic Review*, 65(5), 966-77.

Featherston, M., Moore, M. & Rhodes, J. (1977) 'Manufacturing Export Shares and Cost Competitiveness of Advanced Industrial Countries', *Economic Policy Review*, No. 3, March.

Felmingham, B.S. (1983) 'The Role of the Public Sector', Report prepared for the Tasmanian Public Service Association, (TPSA), Hobart.

Fels, A. (1987) '*The Size and Effects of Government*', Graduate School of Management, Monash University.

Fernandez, P. (1986) *Managing Relations Between Government and Public Enterprises: a Handbook for Administrators and Managers*, ILO, Geneva.

Financial Agreement between the Commonwealth and the States. (1987) AGPS, Canberra.

Fitzgerald, T. (1987) in 'Economics: the Dissenting

Voices', *Australian Society*, August, 1987, p. 16-18.

Fitzpatrick, B. (1949) *The British Empire in Australia: An Economic History, 1834-1939*, 2nd Edition, (Melbourne University Press, Melbourne).

Ford, G.W. (1982) 'Human Resource Development in Australia and the Balance of Skills' in *The Journal of Industrial Relations*, September 1982 pp. 443-453.

Ford, G.W., (1984), 'Australia at Risk: An Underskilled and Vulnerable Society' in Eastwood, J., Reeves, J. & Ryan, J. Labor Essays 1984, Drummond, Melbourne, pp.54-65.

Forrest, R. & Murie, A. (1986) 'Marginalization and Subsidized Individualism: The Sale of Council Houses in the Restructuring of the British Welfare State', *International Journal of Urban and Regional Research*, 10, 10.

Forsyth, P J., Porter, M. & Walsh, C. (1987) *Spending and Taxing: Australian Reform Options*. Chapters 5-10. Allen & Unwin.

Forsyth, P.J. (1986) 'Selling Government Monopolies', *Australian Accountant*, Vol. 56, No. 11, Dec., pp. 34-36.

Forsyth, P.J., (1988), 'Altering the Balance Between the Public and the Private Sectors', Paper delivered to University of Sydney, Graduate School of Management and Public Policy Conference, 14 October.

Fox, W.F. W.F. (1986) 'Tax Structure and the Location of Economic Activity Along State Borders', *National Tax Journal*, 39(4), December, pp. 387-402.

Fraser, L. (1986) *Park Access: A Guide for Park Managers and Disabled Peoples' Organisations About Facilities for Disabled People in National Parks*, Report Series No. 5.

Freebairn, J., Porter, M. & Walsh, C. (1987) Spending and Taxing. *Australian Reform Options*, Allen & Unwin, Sydney.

Freebairn, J., Porter, M. & Walsh, C. (eds.) (1988) *Spending and Taxing: Taking Stock (National Priorities Project 1988)*, Allen & Unwin, Sydney.

Freebairn, J., Porter, M. & Walsh, C. (1988) *Spending and Taxing II: Taking Stock*. Chapters 7-9 and 11. Allen & Unwin, Sydney.

Fudge, C. (1984) 'Decentralisation: Socialism Goes Local?', in Boddy, M. & Fudge, C. (eds.), *Local Socialism?*, Macmillan, London.

Galligan, B. (1986) 'Victoria: The Political Economy of a Liberal State', in Head, B. (ed.) *The Politics of Development in Australia*, Allen & Unwin, Sydney.

Galligan, B. (1987) 'Queensland Railways and Export Coal', *Australian Journal of Public Administration*, Vol. 46 (1), March, pp. 77-101.

Galligan, B. (1988) 'State Policies and State Polities', in Galligan, B. (ed.) *Comparative State Policies*, Allen & Unwin, Sydney, pp. 270-293.

Garlick, P.M. (1986) *Electric Energy Systems: Today and Tomorrow: Blueprints of Papers*, pp. 120-125.

Garlick, P.M. (1986) 'The Application of Performance Indicators in Electricity Supply Industry Comparisons in *Electric Energy Conference*, Brisbane.

Garlick, P.M. (1987) 'Asset Replacement in the Public Sector', *South Australian Builder*, Vol. 64, No. 4, May, pp. 12 – 15.

Genberg, H. (1988) *'The Fiscal Deficit and the Current Account: Twins or Distant Relations?'*, Research Discussion Paper, RBA, December.

Gerlach, K., Peters, W. & Sengenberger, W. (eds.) (1984) *Public Policies to Combat Unemployment in a Period of Economic Stagnation: An International Comparison*, Campus Verlag, Frankfurt.

Gibson, M. (1987) 'Rates – What Went Wrong?' *Truckin' Life Magazine*, Vol. 10(9), June, pp. 42-46.

Gleeson, F. (1987) 'Liability of Public Authorities', *Australian Construction Law Reporter*, Vol. 6, No. 2, pp. 5-15.

Glover, R. (1986) 'How Labor Looks After its Own (NSW Appointments)', *Sydney Morning Herald*, 30 August, p. 40.

Glynn, A. (1987) *'Privatisation and the Definition of Public Sector Deficits'*, Unpublished manuscript.

Goldthorpe, J.H.,(ed.). (1984) *Order and Conflict in Contemporary Capitalism: Studies in the Political Economy of Western European Nations*, Clarendon Press, Oxford.

Gordon, R.H. & Malkiel, G.D. (1981) 'Corporation Finance' in Aaron, H.J. & Pechman, J.A. (eds.) *How Taxes Affect Economic Behaviour*, Brookings Institute, Washington, D.C.

Gorman, A. *et. al.* (1987) Consultants to Government: Special Report, *Government Officers Magazine of Administration and Purchasing* Vol. 4, No. 3, March, p. 50-51+.

Government Money Manual (The). (1985) Information Australia – Margaret Gee Media Group Pty. Ltd., Melbourne, semi-annual.

Government (The) of Western Australia. (1986) Managing Change in the Public Sector. A Statement of the Government's Position. *Parliamentary White Paper*, Government of Western Australia, Perth, WA.

Grain Handling Authority of New South Wales. (1989) *Staff Bulletin*, (20 March and 9 June).

Grauvogl, M.V. (1989) 'Privatisation and Prisons in the USA', unpublished paper presented at ACTU/Evatt Research Centre Seminar.

Gravelle, H.S.E. & Katz, E. (1976) 'Financial Targets and X-Efficiency in Public Enterprises', *Public Finance*, Vol. 31, pp. 218-233.

Gray , B. & Brain, P. (1987) 'Don't Rely on the J Curve', *Australian Society*, August, 1987, p. 18.

Groenewegen, P.D. (1982) *Problems and Prospects for Public Sector Growth in Australia*, Centre for Research on Federal Financial Relations, ANU (Canberra).

Groenewegen, P.D. (1983) 'The Political Economy of Federalism, 1901-81', in Head, B. (ed.) *State and Economy in Australia*, Oxford University Press, Melbourne, pp. 169-195.

Groenewegen, P.D. (1984) *Public Finance in Australia*, Second Edition, Prentice Hall, Sydney.

Groenewegen, P.D. (1988) 'Taxation and Decentralisation: A Reconsideration of the Costs and Benefits of a Decentralised Tax System', *Working Papers in Economics*, No. 104, University of Sydney, March.

Groenewegen, P.D. (1988) *A Focus on Reform: Report on the State's Finances: A Critical Review Prepared for the NSW Trades and Labor Council*, NSWTLC.

Groenewegen, P.D. (1988) 'NSW Commission of Audit: A Critical Review Prepared for the NSW Trades and Labor Council', mimeo, August.

Groenewegen, P.D. (1988) 'Innovation Possibilities in State Business Taxation', in Volume 2 of New South Wales Task Force, (1988), *Review of the State Tax System*, August.

Groenewegen, P.D. (1989) 'Federalism' in Head, B.W. & Patience, A. (eds.) *From Fraser to Hawke*, Longman Cheshire, Melbourne, pp. 240-271.

Grossman, P.J. (1987a) 'Federalism and the Size of Government', *Working Paper 87-7*, Department of Economics, University of Adelaide.

Grossman, P.J. (1987b) 'Government and Growth: Cross-Sectional Evidence', *Working Paper 87-10*, Department of Economics, University of Adelaide.

Guille, H. (1985) 'Industrial Relations in Queensland', *Journal of Industrial Relations*, Vol. 27(3), September, pp. 383-396.

Guille, H. (1988) 'The Economic State of Queensland', *The Professional Officer*, 75, 1.

Gustavsen, B. (1985) 'Workplace Reform and Democratic Dialogue', in *Economic and Industrial Democracy*, Vol. 6, No. 4.

Gustavsen, B. (1986) 'Evoloving Patterns of Enterprise Organisation: The Move Towards Greater Flexibility' in *International Labour Review*, Vol. 125, No.4, July-August.

Hall, P. & O'Donnell, C. (1988) *Getting Equal: Labour Market Regulation and Women's Work*, Allen & Unwin, (Australia).

Hall, P. (1986) *Governing the Economy: The Politics of State Intervention in Britain and France*, Polity Press.

Hall-Bentick, F. (1988) 'Advocacy: To Be Or Not To Be', *Our Voice Magazine*, Vol. 4. No. 6 September, Disabled Peoples' International, (Australia).

Harcourt, G. (1977) 'On Theories and Policies', in

Drake, P.J. & Nieuwenhuysen, J. (eds.) *Australian Economic Policy*, Melbourne University Press, Melbourne.

Hardwick, P. (1985) 'The Determinants of Unemployment in Tasmania', *Economic Papers, 4* (2).

Hare, P. (1985) Planning the British Economy, Macmillan, London, Chapters 4-8.

Harman, E.J. (1986) 'Government and Business in Western Australia', *Australian Journal of Public Administration*, Vol. XLV, No. 3, p. 247-262.

Harris, C.P. (1987) *The Structure of Public Sector Borrowing by the Australian States: Some Economic Effects of Interstate Variations in Public Sector Borrowing in the 1970s.*

Hart, I. (1987) 'Cost Recovery in Road Transport: Does it Exist?', *Australian Transport Research Forum Papers*, No. 12, Vol. 1, pp. 1-15.

Hatry, J.P. (1983) *A Review of Private Approaches for Delivery of Public Services*, The Urban Institute Press, Washington D.C.

Hawke, R.J.L. (1988) 'Speech by the Prime Minister to CEDA Luncheon', Melbourne, May 27.

Hawker, P. (1987) (State Film Bodies Series of parts), Part 1 'Going South: The Adelaide Connection', *Cinema Papers*, No. 61, Jan, pp. 20-23.

Hayek, F.A. (1944) *The Road to Serfdom*, Routledge and Kegan Paul, London.

Hayward, D. (1987) 'Origins of the Australian System of Housing Provision', draft Chapter of the Incomplete PhD Thesis *Home Ownership in Australia: Theory, Method and Policy*, Monash University, Melbourne.

Hayward, D. (1989) 'Housing Boom, Housing Bust', *Australian Society*, March.

Head, B. (ed.) (1983) *State and Economy in Australia*, Oxford University Press, Melbourne.

Head, B.W. (1984) 'Australian Resource Development and the National Fragmentation Thesis', *Australian and New Zealand Journal of Sociology, 20,3*, 306-331.

Head, B. (1986) 'Economic Development in State and Federal Politics', in Head, B. (ed.) *The Politics of Development in Australia*, Allen & Unwin, Sydney.

Headford, G.G. (1954) 'The Australian Loan Council – Its Origins, Operations and Significance in the Federal Structure', in Prest, W. & Mathews, R.L. (eds.) *The Development of Australian Fiscal Federalism*, ANU Press, Canberra, pp. 163-176.

Heald, D. (1983) *Public Expenditure, Its Defence and Reform*, Chapters 4-7, Chapters 10-11 & Chapter 13, Martin Robertson, UK.

Heald, D. (1986) 'Interview with David Heald', *ATF Research Notes*, No. 16, Nov., pp. 1-11.

Heald, D. & Thomas, D. (1986) 'Privatisation as Theology' in *Public Policy and Administration*, 1, pp. 49-66).

Hensher, D.A. (1986) 'Privatisation: an Interpretive Essay', *Australian Economic Papers*, Vol. 25, No. 47, Dec., pp. 147-174.

Hewett, J. & Loxley, S. (1988) 'WA Money Magic Fuels Petro Project', *Australian Financial Review*, October 10.

Hewett, J. Loxley, S. & Smith, M. (1988) 'Flawed Stones in a Tarnished Crown', *Australian Financial Review*, October 21.

Hielscher, Sir L., (1987) 'Address, Townsville 1987', *QIMA*, 27 p. 10, December 1987 – January 1988.

Hielscher, Sir L. (1988) 'The Future Direction of the Queensland Economy', Keynote Address at the Committee for the Economic Development of Australia Annual Political and Economic Overview, Brisbane, January.

Hill, D. (1987) 'Improving Efficiency in the Public Sector', *Local Government Management*, Vol. 21, No 1, March, p. 29-31.

Hodgson, G. ( ) *The Democratic Economy. A New Look at Planning, Markets and Power*, Penguin, Chapters 9-13.

Hoe, R. (1987) 'Rolling Back the Deficits, (Government Owned Railways)', *Railway Gazette International*, Vol. 143, No. 8, August, pp. 515 – 518.

Hogan, B. (1988a) 'The Future of Privatisation and Commercialisation in the Australian Public Sector', *Economic Papers*, Vol. 7, No. 4.

Hogan, B. (1988b) 'The Potential for Privatisation in New South Wales', *Economic Papers*, Vol. 7, No. 3, p. 1-10.

Hogarth, M. *et. al.* (1987) 'The Four Men Who Really Manage Australia: Behind the Public Service Masks', *Times on Sunday*, 17 May.

Houston, D.B. (1967) The Shift and Share Analysis of Regional Growth: a Critique, *Southern Economic Journal*.

Howard, C. (1978) *Australia's Constitution*, Penguin Books, Melbourne.

Howlett, D. (1986) 'Public Service Salaries Agreement: Broadbanding', unpublished paper.

Human Rights and Equal Opportunity Commission. (1989) *Our Homeless Children: Report of the National Inquiry into Homeless Children*, AGPS.

Indicative Planning Council. (1988) *Short Term Prospects Report*, March.

Indicative Planning Council. (1989) *Resources Report*, AGPS, Canberra.

Industrial Supplies Office. (ISO). (1988) *National Network Report*, June and November.

Industries Assistance Commission, (IAC). (1988) 'Government (Non-Tax) Charges: NSW Government Submission, IAC Inquiry', unpublished (available on request from the IAC).

Industries Assistance Commission, (IAC). (1988) 'Pricing and Production of Government Provided

Goods and Services', Inquiry into Government (Non-Tax) Charges, Information Paper No. 3, September.

Industries Assistance Commission, (IAC). (1988) 'The Extent of Government (Non-Tax) Charges on Industry', Inquiry into Government (Non-Tax) Charges Information Paper No. 2.

Industries Assistance Commission, (IAC). (1988) 'Pricing and Production of Government-Provided Goods and Services', Inquiry into Government (Non-Tax) Charges, Information Paper No. 3, September.

Industries Assistance Commission, (IAC). (1989) 'The Electricity Supply Industry in Australia', Inquiry into Government (Non-Tax) Charges Information Paper No. 6.

Industries Assistance Commission, (IAC). (1989b) 'Draft Report on Government Non-Tax Charges', AGPS, Canberra.

ICSAI. (1986) General Statement on Performance Audit, Audit of Public Enterprises and Audit Quality, AGPS, (Canberra).

Indicative Planning Council. (1988) Resources Report, AGPS, Canberra.

Indicative Planning Council. (1989) Resources Report, AGPS, Canberra.

Inquiry into the Victorian Economic Development Corporation, (1988) Report, (Ryan Report) December.

Institute of Applied Economic and Social Research. (1981) The Economic Impact of Public Bodies in Victoria, A Report to the Public Bodies Review Committee, Parliament of Victoria, VGP, Melbourne.

Institute of Public Affairs, (IPA). (1987-88) IPA Review, November/January.

International Monetary Fund, (IMF). (1988) 'Commodity Prices Rise Sharply in 1987: Modest Increase Forecast for 1988', IMF Survey, Vol. 17, No. 11.

Inter-State Commission (1988) Waterfront Investigation: Preliminary Findings and Discussion Papers, AGPS, Canberra, August.

Jaensch, D. (1977) The Government of South Australia, University of Queensland Press, St. Lucia.

Jenkins, G.P. (1985) 'Public Utility Finance and Economic Waste', Canadian Journal of Economics, XVIII(3), August, 484-498.

Jenkins, G.P. (1987) 'Public Utility Finance and Pricing: a Reply', Canadian Journal of Economics, XX(1), February, 172-176.

Jensen, M.C. & Meckling, W. (1976) 'Theory of the Firm: Managerial Behaviour, Agency Costs and Capital Structure', Journal of Financial Economics, Vol. 3, pp. 11-25.

Jesson, B. (1987) Behind the Mirror Glass, Penguin.

Johnston, B. (1987) 'Lending to Victorian Statutory Authorities', Law Institute Journal, Vol. 61, No. 10, October, pp. 1028-1030.

Joint Union Advisory Council on Industrial Democracy in the State Energy Commission of Western Australia, (1988) Working Party Report on Skill Development, February.

Jolly, R. (1986) 'Privatisation: Issues Arguments and Implications', Canberra Journal of Public Administration, Vol. 13, No. 3 Spring.

Kairn, V., Kemeny, J. & Williams, P. (1985) Home Ownership in the Inner City. Salvation or Despair? Studies in Urban and Regional Planning, 3, Gower, Aldershot.

Kantor, B. (1988) 'The Pricing of Electricity in South Africa: A Critical Assessment of the De Villiers Commission of Inquiry', Managerial and Decision Economics, 9(4), December, pp. 301-310.

Kasper, W. (1986) 'Privatisation: Market Forces and Distribution of Wealth', Melbourne Chamber of Commerce Journal, No. 14, Sept., pp. 15-17 & 19.

Kay, J.A. (1987) 'The State and the Market: The UK Experience of Privatisation', London.

Kay, J.A. (1987) 'Tax Reform in Context: A Strategy for the 1990s', Fiscal Studies.

Kay, J.A. & Thompson, D.J. (1986) 'Privatisation: A Policy in Search of a Rationale', in The Economic Journal, No. 96, pp. 18-32.

Kay, J.A., Mayer, C. & Thompson, D. (1986) Privatisation and Regulation: The UK Experience, Clarendon, Oxford.

Kearney, C. (1988) 'Fiscal Policy and the Balance of Payments: A Review', Journal of Australian Political Economy, February, No. 22, pp. 27-38.

Kearney, C. & Fallick, L. (1987) 'Macro-Economic Policy and the Balance of Payments in Australia', Economic Analysis & Policy, Vol. 17, No. 2, pp. 131-148.

Kearney, D.A. (1981) Report of the Review of Activities and Functions of the Tasmanian Government Printing Office, Vols. (1), (2), (3), South Australian Government Printer.

Keating, P.J. (1988) 'Address by the Treasurer to the National Press Club', Canberra, May 26.

Kelly, P. (1988) 'Burke: Tarnished Hero', The Weekend Australian, November 5/6.

Kemeny, J. (1981) The Myth of Home Ownership, RKP, London.

Kemeny, J. (1983) The Great Australian Nightmare, Georgian House, Sydney.

Kendig, H. & Paris, C. (1987) Towards Fair Shares in Australian Housing, National Committee of Non-Government Organisations, International Year of Shelter for the Homeless, AGPS, Canberra.

Kerin, P.D. (1987) 'Why Subsidise State Transport Authorities?', Australian Quarterly, Vol. 59(1), Autumn, pp. 60-72.

Kim, E.H. (1976) 'A Mean Variance Theory of Optimal Capital Structure and Corporate Debt Capacity', *Journal of Finance*, Vol. 33, pp. 455-63.

Kiss, F. & Lefebvre, B. (1987) 'Econometric Models of Telecommunications Firms', *Revue Economique*, March.

Kjellberg, A. (1983) *Fackliq Organisering i Tolv Lander*, (Trade Union Organisation in Twelve Countries), Lund, Arkiv Forlag.

Klein, R. (1984) 'Privatisation and the Welfare State', *Lloyd's Bank Review*, January.

Knight, N. & Kaplan, R. (1987) 'Brisbane Conference on Delegated Legislation', *Canadian Parliamentary Review*, Vol. 9(4), Winter, pp. 15-18.

Korpi, W. (1985) 'Economic Growth and the Welfare State: Leaky Bucket or Irrigation System?', *European Sociological Review*, Vol. 1 (2), September, pp. 97-118.

Kowar, A.W. (1981) *The Effect of New Issues of Equity: An Empirical Examination*, Working Paper, University of California, Los Angeles.

Kraus, A. & Litzenberger, R.H. (1973) 'A State Preference Model of Optimal Financial Leverage', *Journal of Finance*, Vol. 28, pp. 911-922.

Kuttner, R. (1984) *The Economic Illusion: False Choices Between Prosperity and Social Justice*, Houghton Mifflin, Boston.

Kwang, NG Yew-. (1987) 'Equity, Efficiency and Financial Viability: Public Utility Pricing with Special Reference to Water Supply', *Australian Economic Review*, No. 3, pp. 21-35.

Labour and Industry Research Unit, (LIRU). (1988) *Society and Economy in Queensland: The Strategic Role of the Public Sector*, LIRU, Brisbane.

Labour Resources Centre, (LRC). (1988) *The Role of the Public Sector in Australia's Economy and Society*, Labor Resources Centre, Melbourne.

Labor Council of New South Wales. (LCNSW) (1988) *A Fair Deal at Work: The Union Movement's Agenda for Industrial Relations Change in NSW*.

Landsdown, R.B. (1989) 'Balancing Community Service Obligations With Commercialisation', paper presented to Royal Australian Institute of Public Administration (ACT Division) Inc. Conference: Managing With Social Justice: The Prospects for Access and Equity in the 1980s.

Langmore, J. (1986) 'Privatisation: The Abandonment of Public Responsibility', in P. Abelson, (ed.), *Privatisation: An Australian Perspective*.

Leibenstein, H. (1966) 'Allocative Efficiency and X-Efficiency', *American Economic Review*, Vol. 56.

Leisch, P. (1986) 'The Australian Government Offset Programme', *Prometheus*, Vol. 4(2), December, pp. 306-323.

Leslie, A.J. (1986) 'Returns to the State as a Forest Grower', *Australian Forestry*, Vol. 49, No. 2, pp. 122-127.

Levy, V.M. (1987) *Public Financial Administration: a Study of the Financial and Accounting Practices of Public Authorities*, Law Bank Company, Sydney.

Lewis, G. (1978) 'Queensland Nationalism and Australian Capitalism', in Wheelwright, E.L. & Buckley, K. (eds.) *Essays in the Political Economy of Australian Capitalism*, Vol. 2, Australian & New Zealand Book Company, Sydney, pp. 110-147.

Lindeberg, K. (1987) 'The Review of the Department of Family and Youth Services', *The Professional Officer*, Vol. 72(4), July, pp. 437-438.

Lindsay, A. (1987) 'The Next Wave: From Accountability to Efficiency', *Herdsa News*, Vol. 9(1), April, pp. 3-5.

Linklater, J. (1987) 'Public Works Private Money', *Triple A*, Vol. 2, No. 11, September, pp. 59, 61, 63.

Loveday, P. (1975) 'New South Wales', in Murphy, D.J. (ed.) *Labor in Politics: the State Labor Parties in Australia, 1880-1920*, University of Queensland Press, St. Lucia.

Lovelock, C.H. (1984) *Public and Non-Profit Marketing Cases and Readings*, Scientific Press, New York.

Lucato, F. (1986) 'Stemming the Privatisation Flow: Water Board Unions Suspect Efficiency Program Hides Other Intentions', *G.O.*, Vol. 4, No. 3, March, pp. 76-77.

McCarrey, L. (1987) 'How the Money Comes and Goes', *IPA Review*, Vol. 42, No. 2, August/October, p. 59.

McDonald, G. (1984) 'Employment, Change and Democratic Response: Intra-State Migration in Queensland', *Migration in Australia: Proceedings of Symposium*, Brisbane, Royal Geographical Society of Australasia, p. 145-168.

McFarlane, B.J. (1982) 'Neoclassical and Radical Economists on Public Sector Undertakings: An Historical Survey', *ANZAAS Congress Paper*.

McGavin, P.A. & Kain, P. (1985) 'The Australian Labour Market', *Australian Bulletin of Labour*, 11, 4.

McHarg, M. (1987) 'Privatisation not for the Faint Hearted', *Health Action: The Magazine for Decision Makers in the Health Service Field*, April/May, pp. 6-7.

McHarg, M. (1987) *Survey of Rehabilitation Services in NSW*, NSW Government Printer.

McMartin, A. (1983) *Public Servants and Patronage: the Foundation and Rise of the NSW Public Service, 1786-1859*, Sydney University Press, Sydney.

McQueen, H. (1979) 'Queensland: A State of Mind', *Meanjin*, Vol. 38(1), April, pp. 41-51.

Mac Farlane, B.J. (1982) 'Neoclassical and Radical Economists on Public Sector Undertakings: An Historical Survey', *Anzaas Congress Papers*, p. 52.

Macintyre, S. (1986) 'The Short History of Social

Democracy in Australia', *Thesis Eleven*, No. 15, pp. 3-15.

Mackay. (1968) 'Industrial Structure and Regional Growth: A Methodological Problem', *Scottish Journal of Political Economy*.

Management Review of Regional Residential Associations. (1988) *Review of Regional Residential Associations*, Office of Intellectual Disability, Melbourne.

Management Review: New South Wales Education Portfolio. (1989) *Schools Renewal: A Strategy to Revitalise Schools Within the New South Wales State Education System*, June.

Marsh, P.R. (1982) 'The Choice Between Equity and Debt: An Empirical Study', *Journal of Finance*, Vol. 33, pp. 121-144.

Martin Committee Report. (1983) *Australian Financial System: Report of the Review Group*, December.

Maskell, C.A. (1982) *Changing Perceptions of the Australian Inter-State Commission*, Center for Research on Federal Financial Relations, ANU, Canberra, (Occasional Paper, No. 26).

Massey, D. (1986) *Spatial Division of Labour*, Macmillan, London.

Masterman, G.G. (1985) *Report of the Ombudsman Under S.31 of the Ombudsman Act, 1974*, Concerning the New South Wales, 26.9.84, Government Printer, NSW.

Mathews, J.E. (1980) *The Commonwealth Banking Corporation: Its Background, History and Present Operation*, Commonwealth Banking Corporation, Sydney.

Mathews, R.L. (1967) *Public Investment in Australia*, F.W. Cheshire, Melbourne.

Mathews, R.L. (1976) *The Changing Pattern of Australian Federalism*, Centre for Research on Federal Financial Relations, ANU, Canberra, (Reprint Series, No. 17).

Mathews, R.L. (1977) *Philosophical, Political and Economic Conflicts in Australian Federalism*, Centre for Research on Federal Financial Relations, ANU, Canberra, (Reprint Series, No. 23).

Mathews, R.L. (1979) *Regional Disparities and Fiscal Equalisation in Australia*, Centre for Research on Federal Fiscal Relations, ANU, Canberra, (Reprint Series, No. 30).

Mathews, R.L. (1982) *Public Sector Borrowing in Australia*. (ed.) Centre for Research on Federal Financial Relations, ANU (Canberra), 1982.

Mathews, R.L. (1983) 'The Commonwealth-State Financial Contract' in Aldred, J. & Wilkes, J. (eds.) *A Fractured Federation: Australia in the 1980s*, Allen & Unwin, Sydney, (and AIPS), pp. 1-18.

Mathews, R.L. (1984) *The Australian Loan Council: Coordination of Public Debt Policies in a Federation*, The Australian National University, Centre for

Research on Federal Financial Relations, Reprint Series No. 62, August.

Mathews, R.L. (1985) 'Changing the Tax Mix: Federalism Aspects', *Centre for Research on Federal Financial Relations: Reprint Series*, No. 63, Canberra, ANU.

Mathews, R.L. (1985) 'Federal-State Fiscal Arrangements in Australia' in Drysdale, P. & Shibata, H. *Federalism and Resource Development*, Allen & Unwin, Sydney, pp. 43-66.

Mathews, R.L. (1986) 'Fiscal Federalism in Australia: Past and Future Tense', *Centre for Research on Federal Financial Relations: Reprint Series*, No. 74, ANU, Canberra.

Mathews, R.L. (1987) 'Summary and Overview' in Brennan, G. (ed.) *Constitutional Reform and Fiscal Federalism*, Centre for Research on Federal Financial Relations, ANU, Canberra, pp. 87-96.

Mathews, R.L. (1988) 'The Development of Commonwealth-State Financial Arrangements in Australia', in *Year Book Australia 1988*, Australian Bureau of Statistics, Canberra, pp. 859-865.

Mathews, R.L. & Jay, W.R.C. (1972) *Federal Finance*, Nelson, Melbourne.

Mathews, R.L. *et. al.* (1985) *Australian Federalism*, Centre for Research on Federal Relations, ANU, Canberra.

Mathews, R.L. (1989) 'Is Business Income Measurable?', unpublished paper.

May, R.J. (1971) *Financing the Small States in Australian Federalism*, Oxford University Press, Melbourne.

Meidner, R. (1981) 'The Expansion of the Public Sector: Some Reflections Considering the Swedish Development', *Arbetslivscentrum*.

Metal Industry Mission. (1988) *Report of Mission to United Kingdom, Sweden and West Germany*, AGPS.

Miller, J R. & Tufts, C.R. (1988) 'Privatization Is a Means to More With Less', *National Civic Review*.

Miller, M.H. (1977) 'Debt and Taxes', *Journal of Finance*, Vol. 32, pp. 261-275.

Millward, R. & Parker, D.M. (1983) 'Public and Private Enterprise: Comparative Behaviour and Relative Efficiency', Chapter 5 in Millward, R., Parker, D. & Rosenthal, L.

Millward, R., Miller, M. & Parker, F. (1958) 'The Cost of Capital, Corporation Finance and the Theory of Investment', *American Economic Review*, Vol. 53, pp. 261-297.

Minister for Finance. (1987) *Policy Guidelines for Commonwealth Statutory Authorities and Government Business Enterprises: A Policy Information Paper*, AGPS, Canberra.

Ministry of Education, WA. (1988) Staffing Formulae Review and Report of the Reference Group, 'Phase One: A Review of Current Levels of Staffing in Government Schools', Compiled by the Human Resources Policy Branch.

Ministry of Housing, Victoria, (VMOH). (1987/88) *Annual Reports*.

Ministry of Planning and Environment, Victoria. (1988) *A Population and Household Forecast for Metropolitan Melbourne*, Information Bulletin No. 2, September.

Ministry of Planning and Environment, Victoria. (1987) *Shaping Melbourne's Future*, VGPS, Melbourne.

Minsie, V. (1988) 'No End in Sight for Plight of School Assistants', *Civil Service Journal*, Vol. 68, No. 8 September 23.

Mintzberg, H. (1983) *Structure in Fives: Designing Effective Organisation*, Prentice Hall, New Jersey.

Moore, D. (1988) 'Drawing the Line Between Public and Private', Address to *Institute of Chartered Accountants Conference on Restructuring Australia's Economy*, Sydney.

Moore, M. (1989) 'Greiner Takes His Case to the Electorate', *Sydney Morning Herald*, 18 February, p. 34.

Morgan, H. (1987) 'Public or Private: Monopolies and the Quiet Life' (Address to the Securities Institute of Australia Victorian Division 1987), *JASSA*, No. 2, July, pp. 2-5.

Mueller, D.C. (1979) *Public Choice*. Chapter 7 and 8, Cambridge University Press.

Mullins, P. (1980) 'Australian Urbanisation and Queensland's Underdevelopment', *International Journal of Urban and Regional Research*, 4, 2, p. 212-238.

Mumford, K. (1986) 'Participation Rates of Women in the Australian Labour Market', *Macquarie University Research Paper*, No. 310, School of Economic and Financial Studies, October.

Murphy, D.J. (ed.). (1975) *Labor in Politics 1880-1920*, University of Queensland.

Murphy, W.T. (1928) 'Australian State Income Tax Schemes' in Prest, W. & Mathews, R.L. (eds.) *The Development of Australian Fiscal Federalism*, ANU Press, Canberra, pp. 275-281.

Musgrave, R.A. & Musgrave, P.B. (1976) *Public Finance in Theory and Practice*, McGraw-Hill, Second Edition.

Musgrave, R. (1985) 'A Brief History of Fiscal Doctrine', in Auerback, A. J. & Feldstein, M. (eds.) *Handbook of Public Economics: Volume 1*, Elswier Science Publishers, Amsterdam, North Holland, pp. 1-59.

Myers, S. & Majluf, N. (1985) 'Corporate Financing and Investment Decisions When Firms have Information Investors Do Not Have', *Journal of Financial Economics*, Vol. 13.

Myers, S. (1977) 'Determinants of Corporate Borrowing', *Journal of Financial Economics*, Vol. 5 pp. 147-176.

Myers, S. (1984) 'The Capital Structure Puzzle', *Journal of Finance*, Vol. 39, pp. 575-592.

National Institute of Economic and Industry Research, (NIEIR). (1986) *The State Working Party Report*, Melbourne.

Neilson Associates. (1988) *Housing Impacts of De-institutionalisation Policies*, Australian Housing Research Council, Canberra.

Nevile, J. (1984) 'Budget Deficit and Fiscal Policy in Australia', Centre for Applied Economic Research UNSW, Working Paper, No. 68.

Nevile, J. (1987) 'The Macro-Economic Effects of Public Investment', A Paper Prepared for the House of Representatives Standing Committee on Transport, Communications and Infrastructure, Canberra.

New South Wales Council Of Social Services, (NCOSS). (1989) *'Privatisation in the Community Services Industry'*, unpublished.

New South Wales Department of Industrial Development and Decentralisation. (1986) *NSW Government Purchasing Policy: An Overview*.

New South Wales Government. (1988) *'Government (Non-Tax) Charges: NSW Government Submission, IAC Inquiry'*, unpublished (available on request from IAC).

New South Wales State Compensation Board. (1988) 'Working Paper for Work-Cover Review or Cross-Subsidisation', October, unpublished.

New South Wales Steering Committee on Government Trading Enterprises. (1988) *A Policy Framework for Improving the Performance of Government Trading Enterprises*, (September).

New South Wales Treasury. (1988a) *Budget Information 1988-89: Budget Paper No. 2*, (September).

New South Wales Treasury. (1988b) *Budget Paper No. 3: Consolidated Fund Estimates: 1988-89*, Volume 1.

New South Wales Treasury Corporation. (1984) *Report of Year Ending* (1983) New South Wales Treasury Corporation 1983 (Sydney). The Corporation 1984 Annual Report.

New Zealand Royal Commission on Social Policy, (NZ RCSP). (1988) *The April Report*, Vol. II, 'Future Directions', Royal Commission on Social Policy (Wellington).

Nicklin, L. (1987) 'Up Hill and Down Scale (ports)', *Bulletin* (Sydney), 1 Sept., pp. 41-42.

North West 2000 Stage II. (1986) *Survey of Firms*, Draft Report, Department of Industry, Trade and Resources.

O'Connor, P. (1989) *Good Deeds Into Good Practice*, New South Wales Council of Social Services, Sydney.

O'Neill, S. & Waters, B. (1989) *Land Transport in Crisis*, Unpublished Paper.

O'Reilly, D. & Sandilands, B. (1986) *Bulletin*, (Sydney), 1 September.

OECD. (1986a) *Economic Outlook*, No. 40, December.

OECD. (1986b) *OECD Economic Outlook: Historical Statistics 1960-1984*, Paris.

OECD. (1986c) *Employment Outlook*, Paris, OECD (September).

OECD. (1987a) *Economic Outlook*, No. 42, December.

OECD. (1987b) *Managing and Financing Urban Services*, OECD Publications, Paris.

OECD. (1988) *Economic Outlook*, No. 44, December.

OECD. (1988) *Human Resources and Corporate Strategy: Technological Change in Banks and Insurance Companies*.

Office of Intellectual Disability. (1988) *Review of Regional Residential Associations*, Melbourne.

Officer, R.R. (1985) 'Financial Target for Public Enterprises: the Criterion for Rate of Return on Capital', *Australian Journal of Management*, Vol. 10, No. 2, December, pp. 83-97.

Opeskin, B. (1986) 'Section 90 of the Constitution and the Problem of Precedent', *Federal Law Review*, Vol. 16(2), June, pp. 170-211.

Painter, M. *et. al*. (1986) 'Public Management Reform: Guidelines for Government Business Enterprises', *Australian Journal of Public Administration*, Vol. 45(4), December, pp. 281-343.

Palmer, R.C. (1986) 'New Local Government Funding Arrangements', *Local Government Digest*, Vol. 12(4), Sept./Oct., pp. 29-33.

Papke, J.A. & Papke, L.E. (1986) 'Measuring Differential State-Local Tax Liabilities and Their Implication for Business Investment Location', *National Tax Journal*, 39(3), September, pp. 356-366.

Paris, C., Williams, P. & Stimson, B. (1985) 'From Public Housing to Welfare Housing, *Australian Journal of Social Issues*, 20, 2.

Parker, R.S. (1978) *The Government of New South Wales*, University of Queensland Press, St. Lucia.

Parliament of Tasmania, (Hansard). (1987) *40th Parliament, Second Session*, 28 January, 1987, Vol. 13, p. 2714.

Paterson, J. (1987) 'The Privatisation Issue: Water Utilities' in Abelson, P. (ed) *Privatisation: An Australian Perspective*, Australian Professional Publications, Sydney.

Pattison, A. (1987) 'Current Issues in TAFE: the Economic and Industrial Context', *Australian TAFE Teacher*, Vol. 19(1), p. 36+.

Peacock, A. (1984) 'Privatisation in Perspective', *Three Banks Review*, pp. 3-24.

Peacock, A.T. & Wiseman, J. (1967) *The Growth of Public Expenditure in the United Kingdom*, GAU, London.

Perkin, I. (1987) 'The Pressure's Rising in Canberrra', *Australian Accountant*, Vol. 57(2), March, pp. 10-15.

Petridis, R. (1984) 'The Western Australian Economy: Retrospect and Prospect', *The Western Australian Yearbook*, 1984.

Petridis, R. (1987) 'The Western Australian Economy: Retrospect and Prospect', *The Western Australian Yearbook*.

Pierson, C.G. (1963) 'Financing of Australian Government Business Undertakings, Capital Formation 1956/7 to 1959/60', *Economic Record*, Vol. 39, pp. 214-221.

Pincus, J. (1985) 'Aspects of Australian Public Finances and Public Enterprises, 1920-1939', *Working Papers in Economic History*, Dept of Economic History, ANU.

Pincus, J. (1987) 'Government' in Maddock, R. & McLean (eds.) *The Australian Economy in the Long Run*, CUP, Cambridge, pp. 291-318.

Pensions Investment Resource Centre, (PIRC). (1989) 'Water Privatisation and Shareholder Action', Proceedings of Conference, 23.3.89.

Petersson, O. (1987) *The Study of Power and Democracy in Sweden: Prgress Report 1987*, Riegeinngskanliets, Offscentral, Stockholm.

Pirie, M. (1985) 'Privatisation: The Facts and the Fallacies', *Challenging and Changing the Role of Government*, Centre 2000.

Plater, I. (1988) 'The United States Experience' in Public Accounts Committee of the New South Wales Parliament *Report of Proceedings of the Accrual Accounting Seminar 5 February 1988*, May, pp. 42-51.

Powell, V. (1987) *Improving Public Enterprise Performance: Concepts and Methods*, ILO, Geneva.

Prest, W. & Matthews, R.L. (eds.). (1980) *The Development of Australian Fiscal Federation Selected Readings*, ANU Press, Canberra.

Public Accounts Committee of the New South Wales Parliament (1988) *Report of Proceedings of the Accrual Accounting Semibar 5 February 1988*, May.

Public Accounts Management Committee, New South Wales. (1988) *Report of Proceedings of the Accrual Accounting Seminar*, 5 February 1988, Report No. 38, Sydney.

Public Bodies Review Committee. (1980) *First Report to Parliament on the Activities of the Public Bodies Review Committee*, Government Private, Melbourne.

Public Sector Review Committee, (Savage Committee). (1987) *Report*, Brisbane.

Public Service Association of New South Wales. (1986) *Submission to the House of Representatives'*

Standing Committee of Transport, Communications and Infrastructure, October.

Public Service Association of New South Wales, (PSA of NSW). (1987) *Privatisation of Computerised Government Information*, NSW.

Public Service Board of New South Wales, (PSB of NSW). (1985) *Operations Manual* (Sydney New South Wales Operations Manual), Efficiency Audit Division 1985 – Annual.

Public Service Board of New South Wales, *Program Evaluation Unit (1986a) Program Evaluation and the Development of Performance Indicators*, March.

Public Service Board of New South Wales, Program Evaluation Unit (1986b) *Development and Use of Performance Indicators – A Case Study: NSW Government Courier Service*, April.

Public Service Board of Victoria (PSB of Vic.) (1988), *Annual Report*.

Pusey, M. (1988) 'Our Top Canberra Public Servants Under Hawke', *The Australian Quarterly*, Vol. 60(1), Autumn, pp. 109-122.

Queensland Council of Social Services, (QCOSS). (1988) *Annual General Report 1988*, Brisbane.

Queensland Government. (1979/80, 1987/88, 1989/89) *Estimates of Receipts and Expenditure*, Government Printer, Brisbane.

Queensland Government. (1986a) *The Queensland Economy* (Accompanying 1986-7 Budget Speech), Brisbane, Government Printer.

Queensland Government. (1986b) *Summary Tables Relating to the Public Accounts 1986-1987*, Government Printer, Brisbane.

Queensland Government. (1987a) *The Queensland Economy* (Accompanying 1987-88 Budget Speech) Government Printer, Brisbane.

Queensland Government. (1987b) *The State Capital Works Programs 1987-88*, Government Printer, Brisbane.

Queensland Government. (1987c) *Departmental Services and Programs: A Budget Perspective 1987-88*, Government Printer, Brisbane.

Queensland Government. (1987d) *Budget Speech 1987-88 Including Policy Statement on Public Sector Reform*, Government Printer, Brisbane.

Queensland Government. (1988) *Quality Queensland*, Government Printer, Brisbane.

Queensland Government. (1988a) *The Queensland Economy* (accompanying 1988-89 Budget Speech), Government Printer, Brisbane.

Queensland Government. (1988b) *Budget Speech 1988-89*, Government Printer, Brisbane.

Queensland Government. (1988c) *Directory*, Brisbane, Government Printer.

Queensland Railways. (1987) *Report of the Commission for Railways* (for the Year ended 30th June 1987), Government Printer, Brisbane.

Queensland Teacher's Union (QTU). (1988) *1988 Budget Submission to the Queensland Government on Matters Relating to the Funding of State Education*, QTU, Brisbane.

Raine, M. (1989) *Report of Inquiry Into Homelessness in Sydney*, Sydney.

Ralph, E.K. (1986) 'Multiproduct Natural Monopoly and Cross-Subsidy', *Telecom Economic Paper* No. 1, November.

Ralph, E.K. (1987) 'Cross-Subsidisation-An Information Paper', File Note, Telecom, June.

Ram Reddy, E.G. (1983) *Government and Public Enterprise: Essays in Honour of Professor V.V. Rananadhar*, Cass., Totowa NJF.

Ramanadhar, V.V. (1986) *Public Enterprises: Studies in Organisational Structure*, (ed.), Cass, London.

Ramanadhar, V.V. (1987) *Studies in Public Enterprise, from Evaluation to Privatisation*, Cass, Totowa NJF.

Redclift, N. & Mingione, E. (eds.) (1985) *Beyond Employment*, Basil Blackwell, Oxford.

Rees, R. (1986) 'Is There an Economic Case for Privatisation?', *Public Money*, March, p. 19-26.

Reform of the Australian Tax System. (1985) *Draft White Paper*, June, Canberra, AGPS.

Report of the Ombudsman under S.27 of the Ombudsman Act 1974 Concerning the Inadequate Offers of Compensation for the Acquisition of Land in Open Spaces, Corridor and Similar Zones. (Ombudsman's Report) (1983) Government Printer, NSW.

Review Committee. (1985) *Report of the Committee to Review the Impact of the Commonwealth Grants Commission Recommendations on Tasmania*, (Cuthbertson Report), Tasmanian Government Printer, Hobart.

Reynolds, J. (1988a) 'Bjelke-Peterson's Economic Legacy for Queensland', Unpublished Paper, Office of the Minister for Foreign Affairs and Trade, Brisbane.

Reynolds, J. (1988b) 'Economic Outlook for Queensland 1988', Unpublished Paper, Office of the Minister for Foreign Affairs and Trade, Brisbane.

Rix, S. (1988) 'Privatisation Lessons Learnt From International Experience' in *FAUSA News* 4 November.

Rix, S. (1989) 'Critique of "Schools Renewal: A Strategy to Revitalise Schools Within the New South Wales Education System"', unpublished.

Roberts, P. (1988) Report on 'From Charity to Industry', a conference held at the Phillip Institute of Technology, October, for the *Productivity Policy Unit, Trades and Labor Council, Perth*, Australia.

Robinson, A.J. (1980) *Federation and Efficiency: a Proposal to Improve the Economic Efficiency of the Canadian and Australian Federal Systems*, Centre for Research on Federal Financial Relations, ANU, (Canberra).

Robson, K. (1988) 'Views on Accrual Accounting' in Public Accounts Committee of the New South Wales *Parliament Report of Proceedings of the Accrual Accounting Seminar 5 February 1988*, May, pp.1-19.

Ronalds, C. (1989) 'I'm Still an Individual: A Blueprint for the Rights of Residents in Nursing Homes and Hostels', Department of Community Services and Health, Canberra, Issues Paper.

Ross, S.A. (1977) 'The Determination of Financial Structure: The Incentive-Signalling Approach', *Bell Journal of Economics*, Vol. 8, pp. 23-40.

Rowe, B. (1988) 'Fiscal Relations Between the Commonwelath and States in Australia', unpublished paper presented to Public Sector Working Party, ACTU, Melbourne.

Royal Australian Nursing Federation, Victorian Branch (1988) *Industrial Democracy for Nurses*.

Royal Commission into Certain Housing Commission Land Purchases and Other Matters, (RCHCLP). (1981) Government Printer, Victoria.

Royal Ministry of Finance (Norway). (1985) *Norwegian Long-Term Program 1986-89 Report Number 83 to the Parliament*, Oslo.

Russell, J.S. & Isbell, R.F. (eds.). (1986) *Australian Soils: The Human Impact*, University of Queensland Press.

Ryan, F. (1989) *Report of Inquiry: Victorian Economic Development Corporation*, Melbourne.

Sallis, E. (1982) *The Machinery of Government: An Introduction to Public Administration*, Holt, Rinehart & Winston, (London).

Salvaris, M. (1988) 'Planning for a Fair Community: Consultant's Report to the ACT Administration on ACT Social Justice Strategy', Public Affairs Branch, ACT Administration, December.

Saunders, C. (1987) 'Commonwealth Power Over Grants' in Brennan, G. (ed.), *Constitutional Reform and Fiscal Federalism, Centre for Research on Federal Fiscal Relations*, ANU, Canberra, pp. 35-49.

Saunders, P. (1985) 'Public Expenditure and Economic Performance in OECD Countries', *Journal of Public Policy*, No. 5, pp. 1-21.

Saunders, P. (1986) 'What Can we Learn from International Comparisons of Public Sector Size and Economic Performance?', *European Sociological Review*, Vol. 2, No. 1.

Schmidt, M. (1982) 'The Role of the Parties in Shaping Macroeconomic Policy', In Castles, F.G. (ed.) *The Impact of Parties: Politics and Policies in Democratic Capitalist States*, Sage, London, pp. 97-176.

Schmidt, M. (1983) 'The Growth of the Tax State: The Industrial Democracies 1950-1978', in Taylor, C.L. (ed.) *Why Governments Grow: Measuring Public Sector Size*, Sage, London, pp. 261-285.

Schott, K. (1984) *Policy, Power & Order: The Persistence of Economic Problems in Capitalist States*, Yale University Press, London & New Haven.

Schott, K. (1987) 'Restructuring Public Enterprise', *Labor Forum*, Vol. 9, No. 4, December.

Schott, K. (1988) 'Debts and Deficits: Is Australia Solving Its Economic Problems?', *Current Affairs Bulletin*, December, pp. 17-25.

Scott, R.H. (1983) *The Australian Loan Council and Public Investment*, Centre for Research on Federal Financial Relations, ANU, Canberra, (Occasional Paper, No. 31).

Scull, P. (1980) 'A Convenient Place to Get Rid of Inconvenient People: The Victorian Lunatic Asylum', in King, A. (ed.) Building and Society, RKP, London.

Seabrooke, J. (1982) *Body Hire Pyramid Sub-Contracting and Cash in Hand Payments*, Public Works Department, Victoria.

Seligman, E.R.A. (1985) *Essays in Taxation*, Macmillan.

Shand, D.A. (1982) 'The Financial Structure and Objectives of Commonwealth Trading Undertakings; A Review', *Australian Journal of Public Administration*, Vol. XLI, No. 1.

Sharkansky, I. (1978) 'National Settings and Public Enterprise: Australia & Israel', *Australian Journal of Public Administration*, Vol. XXXVII.

Sharkansky, I. (1979) *Wither the State? Politics and Public Enterprises in Three Countries*. Chatham House Publishers, N.J.

Shepherd, Richard. (1986) 'Financial Aspects of Privatisation in Australia', *Canberra Bulletin of Public Administration*, Vol. 13, No. 3, Spring, pp. 80-83.

Sheridan, R. (1986) *The State as Developer: Public Enterprises in South Australia*. (ed.) Wakefield Press, Adelaide.

Siddons, J. (1986) 'A Submission on the Future of the State Engineering Works', Metal Trades Federation of Unions, WA Branch, Perth.

Singleton, J. (1977) *Rip Van Australia*, Cassell, Melbourne.

Simms, M. (1986) 'The Dilemmas and Paradoxes of Public Bodies Performing Commercial Tasks', *Politics*, Vol. 21 No. 2, November, pp. 32-40.

Skeel, S. (1987) 'Power Politics;' The SECV is a Prime Example of How State Utilities are in Many Cases Running Dangerous Debt Ratios Often to Satisfy Political Objectives', *Australian Business*, Vol. 7, No. 7, 4 Feb., pp. 34-35, 37.

Sloan, J. & Tulsi, N. (1987) 'The Australian Labour Market, September, 1987', *Australian Bulletin of Labour*, 13, p. 4.

Smith, A. & Fedderson, C. (1989) 'Productivity Measurement and Performance Targets for Telecom Australia', Telecom Economic Papers No. 4, Economics Branch, Telecom, Melbourne.

Smith, C. & Warner, J. (1979) 'On Financial Contracting: An Analysis of Bond Covenants', *Journal of Financial Economics*, Vol. 7, pp. 117-161.

Smith, P. & Marcus, D. (1988) *How Adequately Do Statutory Authorities Meet the Needs of Their Consumers?*, Australian Consumers' Association Paper presented to AISEC (Australia), March.

Smith, R.R. (1986) 'Manufacturing Matters', *Australian Left Review*.

Social Justice Unit, (1987) *People and Opportunities: Victoria's Social Justice Strategy*, August, Melbourne.

Social Structure of Australia Project. (1988) *Workforce Questionnaire*, Brisbane, Department of Anthropology and Sociology.

South Australian Department of Agriculture. (1988) *Annual Report 1987/88*.

South Australian Government. (1987) *The Social Justice Strategy*, (August).

South Australian Government. (1987) *Report of the Asset Management and Replacement Task Force*, South Australian Government Printer, Adelaide, December.

South Australian Government. (1988) *Report of the Asset Management and Replacement Task Force*, South Australian Government Printer, Adelaide, September.

South Australian Government, (1988) *Report of the Auditor-General for the Year Ended 30 June 1989*, South Australian Government Printer, Adelaide, September.

South Australian Government. (1989) *The Budget and the Social Justice Strategy 1988/89*.

South Australian Occupational Health and Safety Commission. (1988) *Inaugural Annual Report 1987-88*.

South Australian Public Service Association Inc. (1989) correspondence.

South Australian Treasury. (1985) *Trends in the Indebtedness of the South Australian Public Sector 1950-1985*, September.

South Australian Treasury. (1988a) *The South Australian Economy*, An Information Paper, August.

South Australian Treasury. (1988b) *The Finances of South Australia*, An Information Paper, August.

Stanbury, W.T. & Thompson, F. (1982) *Managing Public Enterprises*. (eds.) Praeger N.Y.

Standing Committee on Transport, Communications and Infrastructure, House of Representatives, Parliament House, Australia, (SCTCI). (1987) *Constructing and Restructuring Australia's Public Infrastructure*, 1987 Budget Papers of the State Governments, AGPS, Canberra.

State Electricity Commission of Victoria, (SEC). (1987) *Submission to Economic and Budget Review Committee Inquiry into Controls Over Commercial Authority Debt Levels*.

State Engineering Works. (1986-9) *Annual Reports*, Perth.

State Government Task Force. (1986) 'Report and Recommendations on the State Engineering Works Restructure', May.

State Library of New South Wales Research Service. (1983) *Entrepreneurial Activity in Local Government: a Bibliography*.

State Library of New South Wales Research Service. (1984) *Government Involvement in Private Sector: a Bibliography*.

State School Teacher's Union, WA. (1988) 'Staffing Formulae Submission Primary and Secondary Schools', June.

Statutory Authority Manual. (1986) Brisbane, Government Printer.

Steering Committee on Government Trading Enterprises. (1988) *A Policy Framework for Improving the Performance of Government Trading Enterprises* (NSW Government Printer).

Stewart, D. (1987) 'A Fine Line into the Future', *Australian Construction and Mining*, Vol. 20(6), June, pp. 3-4.

Stewart, J. (1988) *Maritime Administration in NSW: Report to the Minister for Transport*, Mimeo, 31 October.

Stiglitz, J.E. (1969) 'A Re-examination of the Modigliani-Miller Theorem', *American Economic Review*, Vol. 59, pp. 784-793.

Stiglitz, J.E. (1973) 'Taxation, Corporate Financial Policy and the Cost of Capital', *Journal of Public Economics*, Vol. 2, pp. 1-34.

Stilwell, F. (1980) *Economic Crisis, Cities and Regions*, Pergamon, Sydney.

Stone, J. (1985) 'Government Expenditure Can be Cut', *Institute of Pubic Affairs Review*, Vol. 39, No. 1, Winter, pp. 8-10.

Stretton, H. (1980) 'Future Patterns for Taxation and Public Expenditure in Australia', in Wilkes, J. (ed.) *The Politics of Taxation*, Hodder & Stougton, Sydney, pp. 43-60.

Stretton, H. (1986) 'Private or Public: a False Choice', *Australian Society*, Vol. 5, No. 11, Nov., pp. 3-4.

Stretton, H. (1987) *Political Essays*, Georgian House, Melbourne.

'Behind the Big Collapse', (1988), *Sunday Times*, November 6.

Sydney Water Board. (1986) *Interim Corporate Plan 1986-1990*, (July).

Tapp, B. (1986) 'A Look into the Past Part 5: The Board and its Thankless Task (SA)', *Highway*, Vol. 25 No. 2 October, p. 8-9.

Taylor, C.L. (1983) *Why Governments Grow: Measuring*

Public Sector Size. (ed.) Sage Publications, Beverly Hills.

Taylor, J. (1988) 'Accounting and Audit Contributions to Public Sector Change', address to the Institute of Chartered Accountants in Australia (Victorian Branch) seminar- Restructuring Australia's Economy: The Public Sector Role (October).

Tegle, S. 'Productivety in Public Services is a Political Issue', paper presented at New Sweden '88 Seminars on Equality and Efficiency, September/October.

Telecom Australia. (1986a) *Telecom — The Facts*, June.

Telecom Australia. (1986b) *Service and Business Outlook*, August.

Telecom Australia. (1986c) *Teleconomy — Economic Comment for Senior Management*, 1986c Issue No. 4-86, August.

Telecom Australia. (1986d) 'Managing Government Business Enterprises: Control and Accountability', August.

Telecom Australia. (1987) *Teleconomy — Economic Comment for Senior Management*, Issue No. 8-87, November.

Tenants Action Project Team. (1984) *Is it What it's Cracked Up to Be? A Report on Tenants' Views on Public Housing in Heidelberg*, Heidelberg Tenants' Association and North Eastern Regional Housing Council, Heidelberg.

'The Politics of Performance Auditing'. (1986) Address at UNSW, *Selected Addresses on Public Sector Auditing*, Vol. 2, pp. 56-70.

Therborn, G. (1986) *Why Some Peoples are More Unemployed Than Others: The Strange Paradox of Growth and Unemployment*, Verso, London.

Thirlwell, A.P. (1980) 'Regional Problems are "Balance of Payments" Problems', *Regional Studies*, Vol. 14, pp. 419-424.

Thomas, T. (1987) 'Railway Leave Tough Times Behind', *Business Review Weekly*, Vol. 9 (18), 8 May, p. 74+.

Thompson, G. (1981) 'Public Expenditure and Budgetary Policy', in *Politics and Power Three*, RKP, London.

Thompson, G. (1986) *The Conservatives' Economic Strategy*, Croom Helm, London.

Thompson, G. (1988) *Privatisation and the Thatcher 'Miracle': Any Lessons for Australia?*, H.V. Evatt Research Centre, Sydney.

Tierney, C.E. (1979) *Governmental Auditing*, Commerce Clearing House, Chicago.

Tomlinson, J. (1986) *Monetarism: Is there an Alternative? Non-Monetarist Strategies for the Economy*, Basil Blackwell, Oxford.

Thompson, G. (1988) *Privatisation and the Thatcher Miracle*, H.V. Evatt Research Centre: Sydney.

Trades Union Congress (TUC). (1989) 'The Ultimate Power Failure: Report on the Consequences of Electricity Privatisation', UK, (March).

Treasurer's Directions, Public Finance and Audit Act. (1983) Government Printer (NSW) 1984.

Treasury of Western Australia. (1988) 'Economic Outlook', Supplement accompanying the *Budget Papers (WA)*, Perth, Western Australia.

Treasury of Western Australia. (1989) Statement of Cash Transactions on the *Consolidated Revenue Fund, For the Month Ended 31st April 1989*, Perth, Western Australia.

Tregillis, S. & Shaw, A. (1988) *The Role of the Public Sector in Australia's Economy and Society*, Labor Resources Centre, Melbourne, August.

Trengove, C.D. (1985) *Improving the Performance of State Enterprises*, EPAC No. 85/07.

Turner, H.B. (1970) 'New South Wales', in Rorke, J. (ed.), *Politics at State level — Australia*, Department of Adult Education, University of Sydney.

Turvey, R. (1971) *Economic Analysis and Public Enterprises*, Allen & Unwin (London).

Tzong-biau L. (1987) 'International Competition: A Challenge from the Asian Pacific Rim', *Political Economy: Studies in the Surplus Approach*, Vol. 3, No. 2.

Unemployment, *Report of Joint Select Committee of Both Houses of Parliament* (1983) Tasmanian Government Printer.

United Trades and Labour Council of South Australia. (1988) *Submission to the South Australian Government on the State Budget 1989/90.*

Valentine, T.J. (1984) *Finance for Australian Industry*, MTIA, Sydney.

Vermaelen, T. (1981) 'Common Stock Repurchases and Market Signalling: An Empirical Study', *Journal of Financial Economics*, Vol. 9, pp. 139-183.

Vickers, J. & Yarrow G. (1986) *Privatization and the Natural Monopolies*. Public Policy Centre, London.

Victorian Budget Paper No. 5. (1988) *Budget Summary Program and Budget Expenditure*, 1988/89.

Victorian Government. (The Next Step). (1984) *Victoria — The Next Step. Economic Initiatives and Opportunities for the 1980s*, Government Printer, Melbourne.

Victorian Government. (1987) *Victoria — The Next Decade*, Victorian Government Printer, Melbourne, April.

Victorian Government. (1987) *Shaping Melbourne's Future*, Victorian Government Printer, Melbourne, August.

Victorian Government. (1987) *Background Paper to Victorian Government Policy Statement: Equity Finance for Victoria's Commercial Authorities*, 6 August 1987.

Victorian Government. (1988) *Victoria — The Next Decade*, Victorian Government Printer, Melbourne, April.

Victorian Government. (1988) *Trading on Achievement*, VGPS, Melbourne.

Victorian Government. *Budget Paper No. 4*, Consolidated Fund Receipts, Various Years, and 1988/89.

Victorian Government. (1986) *Information Paper on Energy Pricing 1985-86*.

Victorian Ministry of Employment and Training. (1984) *Industrial Supplies Office*.

Victorian Ministry of Employment and Training. (1984) *Victoria's Industrial Supplies Office*.

Victorian Ministry of Housing and Construction. (1985) *Review of Housing Policies*, VMOHC, Melbourne, June.

Vipond, J. & Rossitor, J. (1985) 'Housing Costs and Incomes: Which Tenure Contains the Most Stress?' *Urban Policy and Research*, 3, 4, December.

Von Otter, C. (ed.) (1983) *Worker Participation in the Public Sector*, Stockholm, Arbetslivscentrum (Swedish Centre for Working Life).

Wagner, A. (1958) 'Three Extracts on Public Finance', in Musgrave, R.A. & Peacock, A.T. (eds.) *Classics in the Theory of Public Finance*, Macmillan, London.

Wainwright, J. (1987) 'Old Engineering Works Forged its Place in WA History', *The West Australian*, August 22.

Walker, F. (1986) 'The Case Against Privatisation', *Canberra Journal of Public Administration*, Vol. 13 No. 3, Spring 1986, pp. 240-245.

Walker, R. (1987) 'The Public Service Super Menace (the Unfunded Liabilities of Statutory Authorities in NSW)', *Australian Business*, Vol. 7, No. 28, October 1987, p. 105.

Walker, R.G. (1988) 'Accrual Accounting: Necessary But Not Sufficient' in Public Accounts Committee of the New South Wales Parliament *Report of Proceedings of the Accrual Accounting Seminar 5 February 1988*, May, pp. 20-32.

Walsh, C. (1987) 'The Distribution of Taxing Powers Between Levels of Government: the Possibility of State Income Tax Reconsidered: in Brennan, G. (ed.) *Constitutional Reform and Fiscal Federalism*, Centre for Research on Federal Fiscal Relations (ANU), Canberra, pp. 1-30.

Walsh, P. (1985) 'Overseas Experience with Privatisation'. Information Paper, Canberra.

Walsh, P. (1988) 'Address by the Minister for Finance to "The Arthur Young Mini-Budget Breakfast"', Brisbane, May 27.

Walter, J. (1987) 'Political Advisers: the Minister's Minders', *Current Affairs Bulletin*, Vol. 63(9), February 1987, pp. 10-15.

Walton, R.E. (1985) 'From Control to Commitment in the Workplace', in *Harvard Business Review*, 85/2, March-April, pp.76-84.

Warhurst, J. (1986) 'Industry Assistance Issues: State and Federal Governments' in Head, B. (ed.) *The Politics of Development in Australia*, Allen & Unwin, Sydney.

Warren, N.A. (1987) *The Distributional Impact of a Change in the Tax Mix in Australia*, Australian Tax Research Foundation, Research Study No. 6, Sydney.

Warren, N.A. (1988) 'Spatial Incidence of Selected NSW Taxes', in Volume 2 of New South Wales Tax Task Force, (1988), *Review of State Tax System*.

Warry, R.S. & Butler, G.J. (1984) 'Population Movement and the Implications for Education Planning in Queensland', *Migration in Australia: Proceedings of Symposium*, Royal Geographical Society of Australasia, Brisbane, p. 307-360.

Waterson, M. (1988) *Regulation of the Firm and Natural Monopoly*, Chapter 6 and 7, Basil Blackwell.

Watson, N. (1988) 'Summary of Progress On the Program to Develop Consultative Management Arrangements in the State Insurance Office', unpublished paper, Melbourne.

Waverman, L. (1988) *Rate Rebalancing, the Demand for Access and Distributional Equity*, University of Toronto, Research Paper, unpublished.

Webb, M.G. (1976) *Pricing Policies for Public Enterprises*, MacMillan (London).

Webb, S. & B. (1898) *Industrial Democracy*, Privately published.

Wesemann, H.E. (1981) *Contracting for City Services*, Innovations Press, Pittsburg.

Wettenhall, R.L. (1977) 'Commonwealth Statutory Authorities: Patterns of Growth', *Australian Journal of Public Administration*, Vol. XXXVI.

Wettenhall, R.L. (1986) 'Privatisation: a Shifting Frontier Between Private and Public Sectors', *Current Affairs Bulletin*, Vol. 60, No. 3, Nov. 1986.

Wettenhall, R.L. (1986) 'Public Enterprises in Australia', In: *Public Enterprises in the World* (1986) (1), p. 29.

Wheeler, M. (1986) 'Boards of Directors of NSW Public Hospitals: Structure Role and Composition', *Australian Health Review*, Vol. 9 No. 2 1986 pp. 124-12.

Whiteman, J.L. (1987) 'Technological Change and Regulation in Telecommunications', Paper presented at the ANZAAS Congress, James Cook University of North Queensland, Townsville, August 24-28.

Widdows, R. (1974) *Economic Reasons for Population Movement in Queensland 1961-71*, Brisbane, Economics Department of the University of Queensland.

Wilenski, P. (1983) 'Six States or Two Nations', in Aldred, J. & Wilkes, J. (eds.) *A Fractured Federation: Australia in the 1980's*, Allen & Unwin (and AIPS), Sydney, pp. 37-62.

Wilenski, P. (1986a) *Public Power and Public Administration*, Hale & Iremonger.

Wilenski, P. (1986b) 'Public Sector Performance', Paper delivered at the the Lendlease Viewpoint Conference 'Is Growth in Government Healthy?'.

Wilenski, P.(1988) 'Social Change as a Source of Competing Values' in *Australian Journal of Public Administration*, Vol. XLVII, No.3.

Williamson, O.E. (1986) *Economic Organisation*. Chapter 13. New York University Press.

Williamson, O.E. (1975) *Markets and Hierarchies: Analysis and Antitrust Implications*, The Free Press, New York, As cited in Ascher, K. (1987).

Wilson, H. (1971) *The Labour Government 1964-70*, Weidenfeld & Nicolson, London.

Wiltshire, K. (1985), 'The Public Service' in Patience, A. (ed.) *The Bjelke-Peterson Premiership 1968-83*, Longman Cheshire, Melbourne.

Wiltshire, K. (1987) Privatisation: *The British Experience; An Australian Perspective*, Longman Cheshire, Melbourne.

Wiltshire, K. (1988) 'The Australian Flirtation with Privatisation', Paper presented to the International Symposium on Australian Public Sector Management and Organisation, Brisbane, July.

Windschuttle, K. (1987) 'New Jobs in Sydney, Perth and Melbourne', *Australian Society*, April 1987, pp. 18-20.

Withers, G. (1987) 'The State of Housing in Queensland', (unpublished paper), Queensland Professional Officers' Association, Brisbane.

Withers, G. (1988) 'Public Sector Cuts, the Premiers' Conference and the Queensland Walkout', *The Professional Officer*, Vol. 75(3), May-June, pp. 68-73.

Withers, G. (1988a) 'Housing in Queensland: A Profile', Housing Towards 2000 Seminar 24 March 1988, Brisbane.

Wood, G.A. & Bushe-Jones, S. (1988) 'Employment Growth in Western Australia: A Shift Share Analysis', Mimeo.

Woods, L.E. (1984) *Land Degradation in Australia*, AGPS, Canberra.

Worker' Rehabilitation and Compensation Corporation. (1988) *Annual Report 1988*.

Worksafe Australia (1989) *Unpublished Information*.

Wran, N. (1987) 'Address to the Australian Society of Labor Lawyers', Ninth Annual Conference, Perth, 18 Sept.

Xavier, P. & Graham, B. (1987) 'Financial Targets and Dividend Requirements for Commonwealth Government Business Enterprises — Are They Appropriate and How Should They Be Determined and Measured?' Paper presented to the 16th Conference of Economists, Surfers Paradise, Queensland, 23-27 August, 1987.

Xavier, P. (1988) 'Performance Indicators for Telecommunications and Price-Cap Regulation, Paper presented to The Australian Economics Congress, Canberra, August.

Xavier, P. (1989) 'Minding Everybody's Business: Performance Indicators for Australia's Postal Services', Paper presented to The Conference of Economists, Adelaide, July.

Yarrow, G. (1986) 'Privatisation In Theory and Practice' in Public Policy: *A European Forum*, Vol. 2, No. 2, pp. 324-377.

Yeatman, A. (1986) 'Administrative Reform ands Management Improvement — A New "Iron Cage"', *Canberra Bulletin of Public Administration*, Vol. XIII, 4, pp. 357-361.

Zines, L. (1970) 'Federal Public Corporations in Australia' in *Government Enterprise: A Comparative Study*, Friedman, W. & Garner, J.F. (eds.) Stevens & Son, London.

INDEX